CLINT EASTWOOD

CLINT EASTWOOD

a biography

RICHARD SCHICKEL

JONATHAN CAPE
LONDON

First published in the United Kingdom in 1996

1 3 5 7 9 10 8 6 4 2

© Richard Schickel 1996

Richard Schickel has asserted his right
under the Copyright, Designs and Patents Act 1988
to be identified as the author of this work

First published in the United Kingdom in 1996 by Jonathan Cape.
Random House, 20 Vauxhall Bridge Road, London SW1V 2SA

Random House Australia (Pty) Limited
20 Alfred Street, Milsons Point, Sydney,
New South Wales 2061, Australia

Random House New Zealand Limited
18 Poland Road, Glenfield,
Auckland 10, New Zealand

Random House South Africa (Pty) Limited
Endulini, 5A Jubilee Road, Parktown 2193, South Africa

Random House UK Limited Reg. No. 954009

A CIP catalogue record for this book is available from the British Library

Papers used by Random House UK Limited are natural,
recyclable products made from wood grown in sustainable forests.
The manufacturing processes conform to the environmental
regulations of the country of origin.

ISBN 0-224-03811-7

Printed and bound in Great Britain
by Mackays of Chatham PLC

For

Helen Schickel

and

Frances Grace Freeman

CONTENTS

Photographic Inserts follow pages 22, 150 and 278.

CLINT EASTWOOD

PROLOGUE

STRAIGHT STRANDS

One day in December 1982, when he was in New York on business, Clint Eastwood called and invited me to join him for lunch at his hotel. We had met some five years earlier, at the home of mutual friends, and had since kept in touch in just this casual way—the random meal, the casual note or phone call—our agreeable but scarcely intimate relationship surviving even an unfortunate *Time* cover story I had written about him and Burt Reynolds.

As we entered the restaurant this noon we were observed by another acquaintance of mine, a television executive, who was seated at a table with three other men. Putting it mildly, the greeting he waved in my direction was more enthusiastic than I might otherwise have expected. As our meal proceeded I became aware, as well, that he was keeping an eye on Clint and me.

As it happened, both parties rose to leave at the same moment and intersected on the way to the exit. Introductions were now inescapable, and it turned out that one of the men dining with my friend was Abba Eban, the Israeli statesman. As Clint extended his hand to him, Eban, instead of grasping it, dropped into a slight crouch, drew his hand up from an imaginary holster, pointed a finger at Clint and gave a very passable imitation of a six-shooter being fired.

Clint did not catch Eban's name or recognize him (foreign affairs are not his strongest suit), thus did not see this gesture for what it was in part—an invitation to bonding between the two most celebrated figures present. To him, this stranger was just another in a long line of temporarily unhinged fans to be gently turned aside. True to his image, he remained cool under fire, smiling bemusedly until Eban shook off his fit of boyish regression and, at last, shook hands.

I record this anecdote not to embarrass a man whose ebullience is, I imagine, quite unembarrassable, but to suggest that even sophisticated people have a tendency to understand Clint too quickly, too easily. In those days, of course, it was convenient to see him simply as a cowboy or a cop. Now, having won his Oscars for *Unforgiven* and his Irving Thalberg Award two years later, having in 1996 received his Life Achievement Awards from the American Film Institute and the Film Society of Lincoln Center, having simply been before us, on the screens of our theaters, on the screens of memory, for so many years, there is a tendency to think of him as "an American Legend" or "an American Icon," empty phrases that help us to evade his singularity in another way.

★   ★   ★

The truth about Clint Eastwood obviously lies somewhere between the old simplicities and the new pieties. But it is not easily arrived at. For he likes to think of himself as a simple man, operating mainly out of straightforward instincts, sharing with the rest of us the habit of avoiding his own complexities. Whatever the ambiguities of his screen presence, off the screen, in interviews and public appearances, he has presented himself primarily as a nice guy—casual in manner, tolerant of other people's lifestyles and opinions, sensible in the management of his career, unassertive in the conduct of a celebrity's life.

Certainly the man I met for the first time in the summer of 1977 wished to be apprehended that way, which proved to be not at all difficult. The appraising taciturnity of Clint's screen character, not without its occasional menacing undertones, gave way in our friends' living room to a more agreeable kind of reserve. He spoke quietly and listened attentively. He was curious; he had opinions; he expressed them with a certain irony—and a certain surprising volubility. But he did not have the star's typical need to dominate the occasion. More important, he was without that anxious pretense, that desperate desire to be understood as a serious—even an intellectual—fellow, that so many major Hollywood players manifest around journalists.

These qualities, the intervening two decades of friendship have taught me, are authentic. But if they were his sum and substance he would have made no large claim on our attention; in America, nice guys finish anonymously. But our attention he surely had. For his rise to movie stardom out of television, whence in those days few stars arose, by the circuitous route of spaghetti westerns, where stars were not born, but rather went to die, intrigued with its novelty. And the largely fatuous controversy over *Dirty Harry*'s alleged "fascism" had made him seem a dangerous character, a subject for much cheap moralizing in what were then regarded as the better critical circles.

As a reviewer I had been as wary of him initially as any of my colleagues (though not as hostile as some of them), but by the time we met I had started to come around. I had not written about *Dirty Harry,* but I had liked the movie and liked his work in it—that arresting combination of coolness, ferocity and isolation. *Thunderbolt and Lightfoot* reinforced the conviction that he was a more supple and humorous actor than he was generally credited with being; *The Outlaw Josey Wales* demonstrated that he was a director of more power, range and ambition than most people had so far noticed. You could sense in these movies an intelligence and a restlessness, a desire to test the limits of star expectations and genre conventions that suggested he was not going to be trapped forever within the limits other people set for him.

A decade later, Richard T. Jameson, the editor and critic, caught some of Clint's qualities in words of a kind I couldn't quite find earlier: the nice guy, he wrote, was not "an uncomplicatedly nice guy, nor a warm and cuddly one. No movie star of his magnitude has ever been so private at the center of celebrity, or played so openly and artfully with the mysteriousness, the essential unknowability, of his personality."

But I no more than Abba Eban or virtually anyone else wanted to embrace such complexities just then. So during the next few years, I settled comfortably for the knowable Clint. That was particularly easy for me, since we are of the same generation and we come from similar backgrounds—Wasp and the striving edge of the middle class. Growing up, we had gone to the same movies, listened to the same radio shows, devoted more of our reveries than we ideally should have to the likes of Linda Darnell and, of course, to those masculine exemplars with whom they shared screen time in our inner lives.

David Thomson, the film historian, has specifically linked Clint's screen character to those boyhood paradigms of masculinity—his "ease and authority" now "the last demonstration of what star glamor used to mean." And, one must add, what star silence used to mean, too. For as another Wasp, middle-class contemporary, John Updike, observes in his novel *In the Beauty of the Lilies,* where he tries to link America's loss of traditional religious faith with its rising worship of images graven on celluloid, Gary Cooper, Clark Gable and their ilk were also "beasts of burden, all but a few of them . . . unable to explain themselves and unapologetic about the lack; sons of an America where the Bible still ruled, they were justified in all their limitations by the Protestant blessing bestowed upon hardship and hardness." Or, to put it another way, what we knew—Clint and I and others of our kind and time—about that most vexed of topics, being male, had been shaped by forces always cautioning us that real men don't talk about real manhood.

Clint, however, was doing just that—in his way, in his movies. It was almost two decades later that Janet Maslin, *The New York Times* critic, caught him out, suggesting that "America's daunting ideas about manhood" were the prime topics of his movies. I think she's right, and, for that matter, so does Clint. His manner of representing maleness—with a sort of conscious unself-consciousness—is the largest source of his strength. A connection is made with our movie past and its traditional male modelings, but with a certain ironic distance maintained, no descent into nostalgia permitted. At the same time, certain connections with contemporary reality are established. He says he can't play a role unless he finds something in it that mirrors some feelings he has experienced in life, and though he has certainly done movies where it is hard to imagine what those might be, that is true of all the work that has best defined our feelings for him.

But in this early period of our acquaintanceship, when he was making *The Gauntlet, Every Which Way but Loose, Escape from Alcatraz, Bronco Billy* and the movie that he was in New York promoting the day we had lunch, *Honkytonk Man,* I didn't get, or perhaps chose not to get, that point. I liked all these movies to one degree or another, but it did not occur to me at the time that each in its way offered a portrait of—yes— a nice (or at least not bad) guy arrested for a moment on his fall toward the bottom of the standings and offered a last stark choice between two scary alternatives, redemption and annihilation.

When we met in Los Angeles in those days we did not automatically (or ever) head for Ma Maison. That was for Orson Welles. One time we ended up at a near-deserted lunch counter deep in the San Fernando Valley, where a friend of ours had told us the chili was extraordinary. It was, and so was the response of the proprietor as we settled on our stools. He recognized Clint, of course—with a silent nod. And got one in return. And that was it. We were served our food like any other customers and eventually took our leave in the same way: "Thanks." "Come again."

Another time, Clint had heard of a superior hamburger joint (in those days he could still occasionally be lured from his lean and leafy dietary path) somewhere near Western Avenue in one of the city's less prepossessing districts. We piled into an old heap of a Cadillac that had escaped demolition in some movie car chase and that Clint occasionally used as a kind of vehicular alias and headed for what turned out to be an eatery heavily patronized by working-class blacks and Hispanics. Their response to Clint's presence was the same as it had been in the Valley— nods, smiles, no exchange of words after we had placed our orders.

There was in these expeditions an assertion of his right if not to good-guy status then to ordinary-guy status. He has never wanted his stardom to interfere with his ability to go where he wants to go, when he wants to, on his own recognizance. In this age of violently gaga fandom, there is something attractive and refreshing in Clint's determination to go it alone, though it surely helps that he is so tall, in such obviously good shape (so many movie stars are disappointingly short, fragile and vulnerable looking when you encounter them). It helps, too, that people confuse his screen character and his actual one; they vaguely suspect that he might carry a .44 Magnum in real life.

But pleasing as it is when we witness a celebrity claiming common humanity in commonplace venues, these encounters offer something more curious to consider. They put a witness in touch with the salient quality of Clint's screen character, which we might identify, oxymoronically, as a kind of infectious self-containment; that is to say, with the kind of self-possession that encourages its observers to answer in kind.

There's an edge of humorous self-awareness in this posture, a sense that it is something a man is supposed to master, because—well—our fathers and grandfathers, the whole endlessly instructing masculine world, for some reason seemed to value it. To be ironically (but not cynically) aware of the traditions you represent—and this awareness marks not just the way Clint plays his screen character, but the deadpan playfulness with which he toys with the hoary conventions of genre movies—is, of course, to slightly destabilize them. The impulse to subversion in the postmodern world almost always begins in self-consciousness.

Which, of course, must stop well short of self-mockery, avoiding the perils of the obvious put-on, the campy send-up and, worst of all, that hint of self-contempt that makes us want to avert our eyes. Clint's gift is to let us see the dark comedy in the American male's contorting, distorting attempts to achieve his masteries of the moment while at the same time not entirely discrediting the tradition that bids him make this effort.

This is, indeed, more than a gift. It is a saving grace. It redeems from meanness the anger that is also very much a part of his screen character. It redeems his realism, a value he stresses, too, from hopelessness. Perhaps most important of all it is the secret of his stardom's longevity, for this quality also humanizes heroism, draining it of its tiresome and threatening elements. Put simply, irony is both the source of that cool that he has personified for our time and the heart of that unknowability that causes men and women alike to draw in as close as they can to him, trying to catch his message.

★　★　★

All of this is easy for me to say now, impossible for me to have said then. And that is not entirely because of my occasional physical proximity to my subject, or my growing sense of psychological proximity to him. It has obviously required some time for Clint's message to come through clearly, largely because of the critical-cultural static that surrounded him in the first decade and a half of his stardom. In those days, as Thomson said, "critics looked down on Eastwood. Thinking people shunned his films." Which brings me to that failed *Time* cover story of mine. It was written in 1978, and into it went all the incapacities and blindnesses I've just discussed. But also into it went the dubieties of this moment. When my colleague Jay Cocks and I proposed—and reproposed—that piece, we did not include Burt Reynolds in our memos. We thought that more than a decade of unalloyed box-office success, the quality of Clint's work, not to mention the controversy—however spurious we judged it—it had engendered, more than justified his solo appearance on our cover.

But that made our editors squeamish. They knew what "thinking people" thought of Clint. Besides, in those days a *Time* cover, particularly one about a cultural figure, was widely understood as an implicit endorsement of his or her career. And management did not want to seem to be doing that. On the other hand, were we to do a pair of "Hollywood Honchos" (as the cover line eventually identified them), plus a box on Charles Bronson, our editors felt we would be avoiding the hint of false idolatry and embracing a hint of redeeming sociology.

As I reread this effort now, I see that about half of it is devoted not to analysis, but to anxious self-justification: Honestly folks, we're not pandering to the crowd; we have serious sociocultural issues on our minds. Nor was this its only defect. For a correspondent had been dispatched to conduct the main interview with Clint, who, in his shrewdness, judged him to be a good ole boy manqué, easily seduced from the paths of rigorous investigation. They had knocked back some brews together, kicked back in their chairs and talked about girls, golf, God knows what, but certainly very little that was usefully quotable.

Finally, the balance of the piece slid inevitably toward Burt Reynolds. He and Clint were friends at the time, and one could see why. Reynolds was the kind of guy Clint loved hanging out with— bright, funny, articulate and, for precisely those reasons, a great interview, too. That he was an actor who would soon blight his career by making all the mistakes Clint avoided—he began parodying himself and in his efforts to get chummy with the public let them in on too many of his mysteries—was not yet clear. In any case, the piece managed to take Reynolds more seriously than it did Clint, especially in the respect it accorded his directorial ambitions, although by that time Clint had directed more pictures (six) than his pal would in his entire career (four).

No harm, perhaps, was done; at least a respectable publication had tentatively suggested that there might be something more here than met the supercilious eye. Characteristically, Clint's true feelings about the story were not revealed for some fifteen years, when he told me Reynolds had called him after the piece appeared, told him he was going to try to order a blowup of the cover photo for his office and asked if he should get one for Clint, too. "No thanks" was the reply.

Clint is not without a sense of his own stature, and though he would never say it, I'm sure he saw himself as a more substantial figure than his friendly rival, and therefore could not quite understand why they were obliged to share cover and coverage. Beyond that, he might have expected something more decisive and incisive of me. He was right on both counts.

★   ★   ★

And now—long, slow dissolve—it is 1987. I have moved to Los Angeles. I am producing a television documentary about Gary Cooper. I ask Clint if he will be its host and narrator. He thinks it over. He says yes. We agree that his fee will take the form of substantial donations to two charities he names. But financing for the program falls apart, and almost two years pass before it comes together again. Clint registers no impatience. "I'll be around," he says casually. And that is the extent of our understanding. It is unprecedented in my experience of these matters—no agent, no lawyer, not even a letter of agreement; just two people trusting their handshake. One day in the spring of 1989 we are finally ready to shoot his on-camera spots. That morning he doesn't happen to notice when he grabbed a sports jacket out of the closet that the lining had come unstitched. Since he is without a makeup person ("what you see is what you get"), personal assistant or any other attendant, one of our production assistants safety pins the lining back into place. "The trouble with Clint," Burt Reynolds used to say, "is that he doesn't know he's a movie star."

Certainly he never wants to be accused of acting like one. So when he starts in on his first piece, Clint rushes, stumbling and mumbling, even as you or I might. We try a second take, with similar results. I've done a few shoots of this kind, and know this is a common problem. Some actors—maybe most of them—are uncomfortable before the camera, before an audience, when they are unable to wrap a fictional role around themselves and are obliged to play themselves or, more properly, seem to be playing themselves.

This is a role Clint knows how to do in public in only one way, with extreme shyness and casualness. Authority, for him, is not something you assert; it is something you imply, but it is something someone fronting a nonfiction program—laying out facts and interpreting them—must offer.

I call a break. With some trepidation I suggest that he slow down. "Aw," he says, "they don't want to see all that much of me." "Will you let me be the judge of that?" I reply. I know that if he were not here, none of us would be, for it is Clint Eastwood the network really wants on its air, not some old clips of Gary Cooper. This, however, is not the moment to discuss that fine point. I am favored briefly by the Eastwood glare. We go back to work. He slows down. He's terrific.

And he is conscientious in a particular, surprising way. There are always certain combinations of syllables that give an actor trouble. These vary from case to case in unpredictable ways, and one is always prepared to adjust speeches to ease the tongue's passage through an unfamiliar thicket of words. Clint would have none of that. He would do retakes until he had said exactly, to the word, what I had written. The same held true later when he came in to record his voice-overs. It was, in his mind, I'm sure, a measure of professionalism.

But it was a measure of something else as well: intelligence. If his director would not let him play himself in his usual way, well then, all right, by speaking this foreign language punctiliously, getting the accent just right, he would embrace the formalities of the occasion and, literally "play host"—a thin role, just barely enough of one to cover one's nakedness. But a role of sorts.

★   ★   ★

It is one in which he is quite comfortable in other contexts, as I would discover a couple of years later, when I was working on a documentary about the making of *Unforgiven*. It was the first time I had been on one of his sets, and if I was pressed for a one-word description of his directorial manner it would be—well—"hostly": a genial eye ever alert to the comfort of his guests, an air of confidence in his plans for the affair, the abilities of his staff, the balance of his guest list. As a man used to managing complex occasions—*Unforgiven* was his eighteenth film as a director—he had mastered the art of gracefully dividing his time, making sure that no one felt neglected, but playing no favorites either. His judgment of distance—how close he needed to attend this person or problem, how far he could stray from others—struck me as unerring.

"I feel a director's job, besides picking a script, the material you want, is casting the right people," he says. "But then after that the real responsibility is to make those people feel at home. Make them feel comfortable. Set an atmosphere where everybody is extremely relaxed and there's no tension.

"I've been on every kind of set that exists. I've been on sets where everybody was very hyper. But if you start yelling and becoming obtrusive and beboppin' around you give the [impression] of insecurity. Then that insecurity becomes infectious. It bleeds down into the actors and they become nervous, then it bleeds down into the crew and they become nervous, and you don't get much accomplished that way. You have to set a tone and just demand a certain amount of tranquillity. And if I'm not in that mood, if I don't set that tone, then I can't expect anyone else to follow suit."

What he's striving for as a director are, of course, the working conditions he responds to as an actor. "It's tough to walk on a set," he continues. "You don't know anybody. There's fifty, sixty people standing around—one's fixing your hair, another's talking about your wardrobe, and they're all pulling at you, pushing at you, and you think, God, now I've gotta step before a camera, and I've gotta be some character."

In practice, Clint's directorial style is, as these reflections suggest, largely indirectional. "Sometimes"—actually a lot of the time—"I'll let the actors play it a little bit—just, 'Why don't you guys just walk around and talk,' and they'll instinctively do something interesting. Or they'll do something not so good, but you have an alternative for it. You say, 'Instead of going to this window, go to that window' because it's prettier or it's more dramatic or what have you. And pretty soon it unravels itself. That's an expression I use a lot of times, 'unraveling.' Because that's exactly what it is—it's a bunch of things and you sort of unravel them all and there it is, all straight strands."

"He says very little to you," Gene Hackman observed one day, "which I appreciate. Much of what's said to you by a lot of directors is all ego. They say it for the people around the camera, to make everybody aware that they are in charge. And that's not necessary." What is necessary for him, for most actors, is a certain supportive tolerance. "To do the job really well you have to allow yourself to be vulnerable. And when you're vulnerable in front of ninety people, or in case you're on stage, a thousand people, there is a part of you that wants to protect yourself and not make mistakes. But you have to give yourself that freedom to make mistakes. And if you had somebody strong on a set like this, who understands that, that's a real treat."

Morgan Freeman put it even more succinctly: "By and large, he leaves you alone," at most "sidling up" with a gentle comment about the work. "When you make it look easy, that's when you're doing it the best."

But there was more than hostliness in Clint's directorial manner on the *Unforgiven* set. This was by no means an easy shoot. Big Whiskey, the mean and muddy western town where most of the film's action takes place, was constructed on a remote hilltop deep in the ranch country of Alberta, Canada, where neither the living nor the working conditions were easy. One day, contemplating its difficulties and the exigencies of his own double duty as star and director ("You get brain tired—it's an assault on the central nervous system"), a more militaristic term occurred to Clint: "You're just a platoon leader with a backpack on your back the same as everyone else. You just get to point the direction we're going, whether it's east or west." There was modesty even in this metaphor; most directors assign themselves a general's rank when they talk about what they do.

Tom Stern, who had by that time worked as Clint's gaffer for over a decade, summarized his style more simply: "Zen and the art of control." Saul Rubinek, the actor who played W. W. Beauchamp, the movie's mythomanic journalist, observed him passing by one day and said: "He's not an exclamation point, he's a question mark."

There was a note of surprise in the actor's tone. Clint, of course, established himself in the movies as an exclamation point—a tall, lean punctuation mark towering over films that were, in effect, short, sharp declarative sentences. But now, Clint only occasionally satisfies this need. These moments occur, as Meryl Streep observed three years later, on *The Bridges of Madison County* set, when "someone's violated his world—when people talk outside or trucks don't stop or time doesn't stop for the moment he wants to get." Then the outrage blows up out of nowhere, attaining full volume instantly. "My God," says Streep, summarizing the universal response to these outbursts, "where did that come from? Because all day we haven't seen anything, not even a whisper. Then everybody kind of flattens into the walls and furniture."

Unforgiven provided the best—or worst—example that I've ever witnessed of Clint in a rage. It occurred when an assistant director tried to make haste too obviously, during a tense night shoot, when the wind was up, causing torches to flare and spook the horses. The man loudly summoned two absent actors to the set, shattering the decorum everyone was nervously trying to maintain. Worse, the players ran to oblige the call, also disrupting the tenuous calm. This brought a roar from the director: "That's not the way we work, you know that"—along with more hot words to that effect. It was just the kind of thing Meryl Streep would later describe—an offense against the mood he was trying to capture. And, yes, everyone who could find a wall flattened into it, including, one thinks, some part of Clint Eastwood's soul. For when you touch on his anger you touch both the core of his talent and the core of his nature, some knotted place that puzzles and sometimes frightens him as much as it does anyone else.

★   ★   ★

Up to a point, Clint is forthright on this subject. "I've always felt there has to be something burning inside you. I've always felt that an actor has to be in touch with his own anger about something." All the actors he admires, who in some sense formed him, share this quality, beginning with his favorite, James Cagney, and including, among others, John Garfield, Humphrey Bogart and Robert Mitchum.

It is a surprising list, in that it is weighted toward urban types and excludes the great western figures, the ones Clint has most often been compared to, Gary Cooper and John Wayne. Only James Stewart, who did some of his best work in westerns, but came to them relatively late in his career, after he had established a rather different image, is mentioned—again, somewhat surprisingly, but also very shrewdly—in this context: "I think he was more in touch with his anger than any actor of his generation." He's referring to the affronted innocence boiling under the surface of the youthful charm Stewart delivered for Frank Capra as well as to the hard-pressed, hard-bitten westerner he played in the movies he made with Anthony Mann.

Clint also thinks it's fine if this kind of anger spills beyond the character an actor is playing and washes over the audience, too. "I've always had the theory that actors who beg their audience to like them . . . are much worse off than actors who just say, 'Fuck you, if you don't like this don't let the door hit you in the ass.'"

Or as David Thomson has put it, somewhat more politely: "Eastwood has an uncanny urge to make heroic figures into anti-heroes. In other words, the actor refused to be ingratiating, to seek our love and sympathy. He wondered, instead, just how far he could stretch the audience's support."

Having acknowledged anger's shaping force in his screen presence, Clint suggests its source. "I guess it's just we become sensitive to certain subjects—certain subjects piss you off and then you can play being pissed off." This he sometimes oversimplifies, as when Norman Mailer touched on this topic in an interview: "Oh, yeah, it's easy. . . . All you have to do is have a good memory"—in his case, for slights of his early acting days—"[of] knocking on doors and going through auditions and having people blow cigar smoke in your face and not getting the job over and over again."

I think that his anger actually comes from a slightly more mysterious and ambiguous place. It is 1996 as I write this. Since beginning this book more than three years ago, I have been obliged to think obsessively about Clint Eastwood. The best part of that time has been spent in his company, asking him precisely the kinds of questions I could not have asked him in the early years of our acquaintance. Our conversations have frequently circled back on this subject, and out of them a theory of sorts has evolved.

I think his is a rage for order, and also a rage against order. The first of these observations is supported by simple resort to the public record. This is an actor who, as soon as he was able to, formed his own company—Malpaso—and quickly converted it into something much more than the conventional loan-out operation. In the fullest sense of the word he has been his own producer for more than two decades and, of-tener than not, his own director. He has, as well, arranged his relation-ship with the studio with which he has been allied for twenty years so that he functions with virtual autonomy. Once Warner Bros. has agreed to one of Clint's projects, there is no interference from its executives. Of this relationship, unique in Hollywood both for its longevity and its lack of acrimony, Clint says simply: "I watched their money as carefully as they watched it, probably more carefully in some instances. Conse-quently, they don't meddle with me." As important, the studio is also "very supportive about reaching out and letting me try projects that are provocative." If, as I believe, Clint is, in his essence, a subversive charac-ter, we can discern a kind of benign subversion in his working meth-ods—a subversion of those careless, spendthrift and often-hysterical ways in which most movies are made, and which most movie people be-lieve to be inevitable.

Be that as it may, a visitor to his sets quickly sees that, having blunted the possibility of disorder descending on him from above, his director-ial manner assures that it will not arise from below. An Eastwood set is a patriarchy. There is nothing remarkable in this. All shooting companies aspire to this condition, and few do so more self-consciously than "the Malpaso family," as its members often—quite without irony—refer to themselves. Clint's crews are largely composed of people who have worked with him for years, often enough decades, and many of them have been promoted through the ranks over time. Similarly, he tends to cast supporting players who have worked with him previously. He be-lieves this is simply common sense, a way of guaranteeing efficiency and pleasant working conditions for all concerned: "It's better if people can anticipate. You don't have to sit there and explain every detail. You can say, 'I'd like a shot that gives me this effect,' and the camera department

will go, 'Well, gee, what about this?' or 'What about that?' and all of a
sudden they're making suggestions that are right in line with what you're
thinking about. It's really not an auteur thing."

No, it isn't—not in the strictest definition of the term, which, of
course, simply means "author." He's very conscious that movies are a
collaborative medium, which is why when he directs he does not take a
proprietary credit ("A Clint Eastwood film"). But the word "author"
has obvious derivatives, and the issue for Clint the director is akin to the
one he confronted playing Clint the host: how to assert "authority,"
"authoritativeness," without embracing "authoritarianism."

This is obviously a tricky realm, and mostly, as we have seen, he tra-
verses it with a tactful regard for what we might call its psychic ecology.
But it would be pointless to deny that some of Clint's authority derives
from the nuclear capability of his anger. For no one mistakes that explosive potential as merely curmudgeonly or as a colorful working ploy—
akin, say, to those largely idle displays of ego and temperament that
typically accompany what Ethan Mordden, the film historian, has neatly
labeled the "high maestro" manner of filmmaking.

What feeds Clint's temper is a profound sense of the world's unreliability. As we will shortly see in more detail, he was a child of hard
times. Born in the first year of the depression, his first memories are of
dislocation, as for several years he and his family moved from place to
place annually, trying to stabilize their economic lot. His parents were
good people, he loved them, he vaguely understood the pressures they
were under, but he hated the loneliness their travels imposed on him—
always the new kid on the block and in the school, wondering how he
got there. When he recalls these years, the angry note in his voice is unmistakable.

In late adolescence and early manhood he endured what he would
later refer to as his "lost years," in which he wandered about, condemned to hard hourly labor, trying to find—imagine—a place for
himself in a world still as unyielding and enigmatic as he had first experienced it. This added to his store of outrage. For the institutions he encountered in those years—educational, economic, governmental—were
unresponsive, insensitive, clumsy in their impositions.

He has never claimed trauma or even unbearable hardship for these
experiences—but it is clear that they taught him two basic lessons: Do
everything in your power to lessen the impact of mischance, whether it
be cosmic or mundane; do not trust institutions to do this job. Or, to put
the point more positively, turn yourself into an institution and set your
own rules of work and conduct, your own boundaries against intrusion.
Then insist that this institution, this lengthened shadow of yourself, de-

vote itself to the celebration of characters variously subversive, antisocial, rebellious. In a phrase, place the rage for one kind of order in the service of a rage against a different sort of order.

★　★　★

This irony is central to his career. In purely movie terms, Clint has taken the presentation of the heroic male into country he had not previously ridden. Since Howard Hawks placed it at the center of his adventure films, male bonding has been a great recurring motif in American movies, but it is a rarity in Clint's. His great theme has been the opposite: the difficulty men have in making connections with any sort of community. Nor is an Eastwood hero usually granted the kind of relationship with a woman, bantering and antic, that Hawks permitted his protagonists. In most of Clint's movies the male-female relationship is, at best, romantically perfunctory and without much in the way of even an implied future.

Almost without exception his characters are deeply disaffected men, much more profoundly isolated than the kind of classic loners Hawks (and those who have followed him) contrived through his consoling conventions to redeem. When we speak of Clint's films we are speaking of a loneliness more radical, of a protagonist more rebelliously withdrawn, than anyone has ever offered us as the hero of movies intended for, and embraced by, a popular audience. We are also speaking of—to use a phrase that will recur in this book—a kind of brutal frankness, a sense, always present in his work, of the role that chance and human unreliability play in anyone's destiny, a sense that the distance between heroism and victimization is paper-thin. He once told Carrie Rickey, the film critic, that the body of his work adds up not to a politics but a morality, and this honesty of his is its source.

Clint has also said in a quotation that has been much requoted: "There's a rebel lying deep in my soul." But not so deeply that it cannot be summoned forth to animate just about every film he has ever directed, every character he has ever played—fiercely, goofily, guiltily, stubbornly, arrogantly, dreamily, regretfully, romantically, even as a ghostly shade.

What is in his soul is in all of our souls—that rage that we spend so much of our time suppressing and denying, allowing it at most to slip forth in subversive jokes and gossip about the rich, the powerful, the celebrated, in flashes of anger and equally quick descents into gloom about our jobs, our debts, our governments at once so intrusive and so impotent—and, yes, about our fundamental loneliness and isolation.

Acting out for himself, he acts out for all of us, and the irony that by doing so he has himself become rich, powerful and celebrated—in charge of his life in ways denied both to his character and his audience—is not lost on him. It is why, off-screen, he considers himself a good and ordinary and lucky guy; a guy who doesn't want to attribute too much consciousness or calculation to his achievement, a guy who senses that some of his luck consists of being the right man at the right time, capable of crystallizing and personifying a mood a lot of us are in, a mood that has, since the social and political upheavals of the sixties, when Clint first made his mark, deeply colored the life of our times.

You can call what this man does an advance or a retreat from tradition, depending on your taste. But in a time when public figures are forever trying to ingratiate themselves with us, you can see something exemplary in his on-screen refusal to be easily liked, and in his off-screen refusal to be easily understood. In a time when that sometime cock of the walk, the Wasp male, has been obliged to change metaphors in midstream and now often sees himself as a stag at bay, you can find in this screen character, as it has developed over the years, some of the pain and puzzlement of transition.

There are, naturally, people who have fallen out with him—most notably a woman who spent many years in a relationship with him that ultimately failed, but also professional colleagues whose associations with him soured—who see in him a deeper darkness than I perceive. There are also strangers who continue to resent and reject his message. This distrust, so widespread and so full of outrage in the early days of Clint's career, is now greatly diminished, but it is there, especially in some of the odder corners of academia, and it is not without its murmuring influence.

I, however, trust the many tales told on the screen over this long career, and I trust the honesty of their teller. I trust the authenticity of his conflicting rages, and even as I have tried to penetrate them, I trust the enigmatic silences of the man caught between those emotions. I see them as signs of honest, inarticulable puzzlement by a man acting cool and ironic, feeling much of the time otherwise.

ONE

NOTHING FOR NOTHING

W hat an American was Clint Eastwood," Norman Mailer wrote as he worked his way toward the peroration of a 1983 Sunday supplement article on him—as usual for Mailer on these occasions, a blend of interview and meditation on his own and his subject's celebrity. "Maybe there was no one more American than he." Maybe that is true, defining the term traditionally, as it was still possible to do in those days, before multiculturalism became one of our reigning pieties.

Talking to the writer, Clint stressed the lack of grandeur in his background. "My dad was Scots-English; my mother's Dutch-Irish. Strange combination. All the pirates and people who were kicked out of every place else." In other words, there are no Eastwoods in the Society of Mayflower Descendants. It is sometimes Clint's pleasure to slightly overemphasize his lack of early promise, not so much to stress the pluck that underlay his rise in the world, but the luck involved. For example, at the Cinémathèque in Paris in 1985 this exchange between Clint and a questioner from the floor occurred:

"Did you once describe yourself as a bum and a drifter?"

"No."

"Then what are you?"

"A bum and a drifter."

Actually, he had once been so quoted, and there is at least a half-truth in the wisecrack. He was never a bum, but there was a time, during his late adolescence, when he was definitely a drifter. And before that, when Clint was a child, the entire Eastwood family could perhaps have been described as drifters—though scarcely purposeless ones—as Clint's father, Clinton Eastwood Sr., pursued job opportunities up and down the West Coast during the depths of the depression. His son's most basic characteristics—his physical restlessness and his low tolerance for boring routine, his loyalty to the people he works with, his pleasure in, and loyalty to, the little filmmaking community he created around him—can probably be traced to these years. The former qualities he learned by experience; the latter ones he understood as ideals to be strived for.

Still, Clint's heritage is far from piratical. It is essentially middle class, marked by the kind of modest strivings, setbacks and successes common to that class. His father and mother, Clinton Sr. and Margaret Ruth Runner—always known by her middle name—were sweethearts from a very tender age. He was fifteen, she thirteen, when they met in Piedmont, California, not long after her family moved from San Francisco to this prosperous Bay Area suburb, which lies due east of Oakland, due south of Berkeley. His father, Burr, built a house there soon after Clinton Sr. was born and worked as a manager in a wholesale hardware concern. Ruth's father, Waldo, had been a railroad executive—she moved back and forth across the country several times as a child because of his work—and then founded, with a partner, the Graybar Company, which manufactured automobile bumpers and luggage racks.

Clinton was tall and good-looking, star and ultimately captain of the high-school football team, a mainstay of the swimming team and an outgoing, popular young man—then as always, "the first one at a party and the last one to leave," in Ruth's fond description. Their son remembers his mother saying, more than once, "It's a shame he wasn't born rich, because he could have had so much fun."

Ruth was herself tall and attractive—too tall, as it happened, to realize her girlhood dream, which was to become a ballet dancer. She enrolled in a ballet class, taught by one of her grammar-school teachers, when she was eight or nine and from then until she was sixteen dance "was my main purpose," she says. Like her father, who was a talented amateur clarinetist, she had a natural gift for musical expression; when her older sister, Bernice, started taking piano lessons, Ruth would study the exercise book she brought home, teaching herself to play without benefit of formal instruction.

Both Clinton and Ruth endured tragedies in midadolescence, his by far the more poignant. Jesse, his pretty and spirited mother, was stricken with cancer when she was in her forties and struggled against the disease for several years. A graduate of the University of California, where she had been active in dramatics, she, too, had a natural gift for music. Her mother had taught voice and piano in San Francisco, supporting four daughters through this work, after her husband had deserted them.

When his mother fell ill Clinton was obliged to rush home after athletic practices to tend to her until his father arrived home from work. She died when the boy was sixteen. Ruth says her husband almost never discussed Jesse's illness or death and that she cannot remember ever meeting her. Jesse Eastwood did, however, pass on an important legacy, her mother's German-made upright piano—always referred to as "Grandma Andy's piano" (for Anderson, her maiden name)—which would follow Clinton and Ruth on their many travels through depression America and remains in the family, in excellent working condition, to this day.

Ruth's world was sundered when she was sixteen and her parents separated, though apparently with very little bitterness (they never formally divorced). Indeed, if Clint Eastwood is any judge, his maternal grandmother, Virginia McLanahan Runner, preferred the single life. She was a strong-minded, independent woman, who, after her children were grown, lived in a succession of rural retreats, each of them a little more distant from the Bay Area—Hayward, Sunol and finally Arnold, a sometime-goldmining community in Calaveras County.

Clinton Eastwood tried college for a short time—at the University of California—but received virtually no support from his father and did not like school well enough to work his way through it. He was not yet what he would become, a hardworking man successfully struggling against his basic aversion to hard work. It was easier for him, now, at the height of 1920s prosperity, to rely on his charm. He became a bond salesman.

He married pretty, sensible Ruth Runner in 1928. He was twenty-one; she was nineteen. They took an apartment near Lake Merritt in Oakland and were managing well enough until October 1929, when the stock market crashed. Ruth was pregnant at the time, but her account of what must have been for her an anxious period is remarkably calm—"Well, everyone was in the same boat on that one; none of us had anything and we hadn't had time enough to save very much"—perhaps because her husband had not immediately lost his job and perhaps because she was so happily preoccupied with the impending birth.

It occurred on May 31, 1930, at St. Francis Hospital in San Francisco. "I always said he was famous from the day he was born," she says, "because he weighed eleven pounds, six ounces, and he was the biggest baby in St. Francis . . . so the nurses carried him all around and showed him to everyone." One of the local newspapers even ran an item about the birth of this strapping lad. As for Ruth, "I fell in love with him immediately, and stayed that way ever since. He was a dear, charming boy."

He was also a daring toddler. His mother remembers that when she took him for walks along the shore of Lake Merritt he always insisted on going as close to the edge as possible. One day he fell into the lake, "and I had to jump in, pink dress and all," to save him. It was the first of several misadventures, at least one of which surely had a shaping effect on his character, in which Clint encountered large bodies of water to dangerous effect.

The elder Eastwoods were by this time walking along a different sort of edge. Clint Sr.'s brokerage commissions had dropped to almost nothing, and he began looking for some other kind of work. As it happened, Ruth's brother, Melvin, had a refrigeration business in Spokane, and he proposed that her husband come to work with him. This was the first of the many moves the family made during the thirties, though Clint has no memories of it or of their life in Washington. His mother, however, has one vivid recollection of him in this period. It seems they acquired a deer's head and hung it over their mantel. When Clint saw it for the first time "he ran outside and around the house to find the rest of the deer." They stayed in Spokane for just over a year, not very happily. "Working for one's wife's brother is not the most wonderful thing in the world" is the way Ruth puts it.

At that point they began the odyssey that would consume the rest of the decade. As recorded by various interviewers, the Eastwood family's wanderings have taken on the cast of a Steinbeck novel, but that over-dramatizes the case, suggesting a desperation that Ruth never felt. "We didn't even know we were poor . . . we just knew we didn't have quite enough money."

Her casual gallantry matches Clint's recollections of the spirit in which his parents confronted adversity. "I don't recall them ever complaining a lot. She's a strong lady. She wasn't a griper, and they always kind of made do—positive attitude." That was Clinton Sr.'s way as much as it was his wife's. He was, as Clint puts it, "a very personable guy. People liked him a lot and he liked people a lot—a lot more than I do, I think. I mean, he seemed like he was very much at home in the world."

That held true no matter what unpromising corner of it he found himself occupying. After Spokane, the family returned briefly to Oakland, but Clinton Sr. found no work there. Some friends prevailed on an acquaintance of theirs, who worked for Standard Oil, to give him a post, and he was told there was something for him in Los Angeles—pumping gas, as it turned out, generally on the night shift, at the Standard station on Sunset Boulevard where it joins the Pacific Coast Highway north of Santa Monica.

If Clinton Sr. thought this a comedown, he said nothing about it, and the Eastwoods, who now had a second child, Jeanne, settled into half of a double house in Pacific Palisades, then no more than a sketch of a suburb that would not begin to be fully filled in until after World War II. There were only a few other houses on the street.

Clint's memories begin here. He recalls his first encounter with an

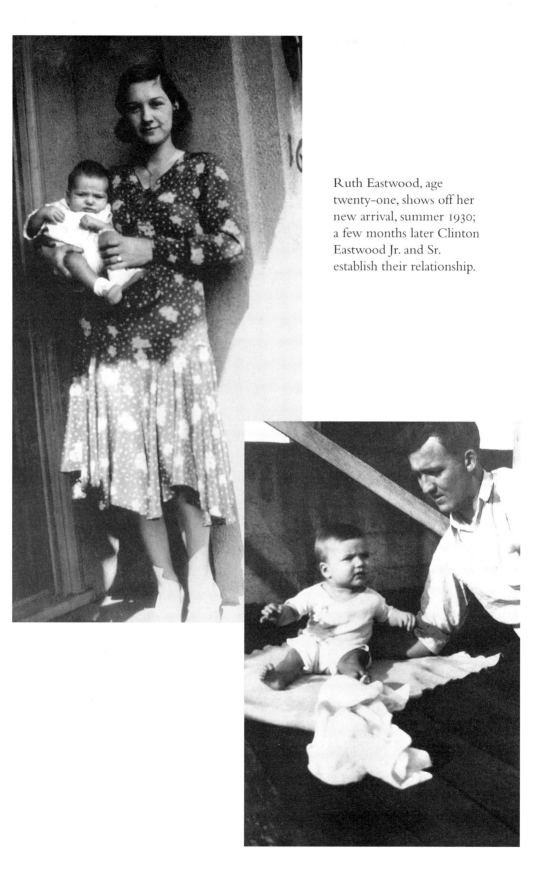

Ruth Eastwood, age twenty-one, shows off her new arrival, summer 1930; a few months later Clinton Eastwood Jr. and Sr. establish their relationship.

The young gun gets the drop on an imaginary bad guy, the young sportsman casts a wary eye at the camera and the Eastwood family basks at the beach, their favorite recreation spot. OPPOSITE: Clint as a young man.

A beefcake day in the Universal talent program, circa 1955, and a rug-cutting night with his wife, Maggie.

ABOVE: Clint and Gia Scala lead talent-school students through a dance class.
RIGHT: Clint got his first main-title billing in *Francis in the Navy* (1955), supporting Donald O'Connor and a talking mule. The other actors are Richard Erdmon and Martin Milner.

On the set of *Rawhide*, which ran for seven profitable years on CBS.

A plain in Spain—no rain in sight. Director Sergio Leone is at his star's right hand in this rare production still from *A Fistful of Dollars*. BELOW: Eli Wallach costarred with Clint in the last of his spaghetti westerns, *The Good, the Bad, and the Ugly*.

A star is born: The Man with No Name sits for his portrait.

angry dog, his fascination with an ostrich egg owned by one of their neighbors, seeing Catalina from the beach and imagining it was China. His mother recalls a little boy with more courage than sense. She remembers one day when he slipped out of sight and she found him pedaling his tricycle on a nearby boulevard, narrowly avoiding oncoming cars. On another occasion she looked up to see her five-year-old son clinging to the rear bumper of a neighbor's car as it took off down the street. Older kids had put him up to this stunt, and by the time Ruth rushed out and flagged down the driver (who couldn't see the little fellow who had attached himself to his vehicle) smoke was rising from Clint's ruined shoes.

One day the family decided to go bodysurfing at Santa Monica beach. "I had Jeannie in the basket," Ruth says, "she was just born, so I was sitting with her . . . and his father had Clint on his shoulder and he went out and this huge wave came in and washed over both of them, and the next thing I saw Clint was not there at all—little Clint. But I saw this foot coming up, and then it turned and went back again and then everybody that was there started to run toward him, including me, and I caught this foot. He was underwater long enough to be frightened."

"It was kind of a big surf, pounding," Clint recalls, "and I can still remember the greenness of the water, and coming up I remember seeing my mother running into the water. And so it made a big imprint on me at an early age."

Once everyone calmed down, his mother sat with Clint at the water's edge "and played in the small waves for a while, because I was afraid he'd never get over it." He did, of course; he spent much of his young manhood around the water, as a lifeguard, a swimming instructor and a devoted surfer.

This was a family determined to put the best possible face on bad times. In this period Clint remembers his father and some friends organizing a garage band—Clinton Sr. played the guitar and also crooned a bit—which performed, usually unpaid, at weddings and other social events. "I don't know how good he was," Clint recalls, "but he would have loved to have been an entertainer of sorts." His mother, who sometimes joined the group, playing a mandolin, agrees; her husband, she says, was an enthusiastic, if untutored, Bing Crosby imitator. "It could have been a good voice," she says, "but he didn't sit still long enough to have it trained."

There was, undeniably, an impatience in the man, a restlessness about him. It was always there, beneath the genial sociability and the professional adaptability. Some of that eagerness to move on, not to dither unduly over details, is in his son; so is the determination to hide

ambition under an easygoing and affable manner. The difference between them would seem to be very largely one of self-presentation,
with the father much the heartier and more apparently open. Both, not
to put too fine a point on it, are Californians, not given to the darker
forms of introspection, loyal to friends and family, yet also resistant to
rootedness, perhaps because historically their native landscape always
seemed so spacious and there was so much of it to explore. Doubtless
hard times impelled Clinton Sr. to range freely in search of suitable
work. But one can't escape the feeling that, no matter what his circumstances, it would have suited him, still a young man in his twenties, his
wanderlust not entirely quenched, to keep moving on.

★   ★   ★

The Eastwoods stayed in the Palisades for roughly a year, then moved
briefly to a bungalow in Hollywood (where Clint remembers a stray kit-
ten appearing on their doorstep and becoming a permanent member of
the household). Thereafter they moved on virtually an annual basis, first
to Redding in northern California (where Clinton Sr. was "the bond
man" at a Bank of America branch), then to Sacramento (more bond
selling, for a brokerage firm), then to the Glenview section of the East
Bay (now he was working in a San Francisco jewelry store), finally back
to Piedmont (where they rode out the war with Clinton Sr. working in
a shipyard).

There was never any panic or desperation in these moves. The elder
Eastwood always had a job lined up before his family began packing.
And Clint never felt unloved or abandoned at any time during this period; his parents were obviously caring and conscientious. Moreover, little as he may have appreciated it at the time, he sees now that they
provided him with valuable life lessons unobtainable by the more settled
children of his generation, or by the children of later, more prosperous
generations.

When they moved, the Eastwoods would load their belongings into
a little two-wheeled cart, which would bounce along behind their car.
From the backseat the kids would sometimes see shantytowns sheltered
under highway overpasses, where less fortunate itinerants found refuge.
The shacks, Clint would later recall, were "made out of Prince Albert
cans [tobacco tins and the like]—they'd take and mash all these cans and
nail them up in some sort of way." He still sometimes refers to the
hoboes they occasionally encountered at rest stops as "knights of the
road," using the old phrase not entirely ironically.

There were always surprises along the way, sometimes pleasant, sometimes not. On their way to Sacramento, for example, they encountered a stray dog—"half cocker spaniel, half whatever, but it was a terrific dog"—along the road and took it in. Like their cat it would attain great age in the Eastwood household. On the other hand, when they moved into their new home there (it was half of a duplex), they found it "was loaded with mice," and Clint still remembers, with a slight shudder, "mousetraps going off all night" until the pests were disposed of. (His mother, it should be noted, has no such memory, insisting on the niceness of this little house a few miles out of town, and is a little cross with her son for implying that their digs were ever, even for a moment, *infra*.) Clint also remembers a sizable chicken coop out back and his father and their neighbor remodeling it into a rentable apartment, though they kept one of its former inhabitants, "Hennypen," as a pet.

A boy could learn a certain kind of realism from this kind of life, a cool ability to accept things and people, success and failure, as they came, and this lesson, especially valuable to actors in their up-and-down lives, Clint Eastwood, steady in adversity and in fame, thoroughly absorbed.

In its way this acceptance of life's changeability supports his habit of restlessness, and his latter-day glamorization of it. How many of his screen characters come from nowhere, heading nowhere? How many of them are men on the loose, questing along open American roads, open American *back* roads? He has homes in Los Angeles and Carmel, a ranch in northern California, a ski lodge in Sun Valley, and when he is not working he is constantly on the move among them. Or he is traveling to promote one of his movies or, in recent years, to accept some award for, or tribute to, his life's achievements. Or he is trying some golf course he has not played, testing some powder he has not skied.

In years past, before he settled more confidently into his celebrity, he would often put on a false mustache and glasses, pull a hat down low on his forehead, in order to attend some faraway sneak preview of one of his pictures or enjoy some other public occasion in anonymity. Disguise freed him from the encumbrance of an entourage, and as he told an interviewer in the early seventies, "I come and go like The Whistler on the old radio program," that is to say, quickly, quietly, anonymously.

Now that he has his own helicopter and his pilot's license, it's even easier to keep moving, and he sometimes feels something like the old pleasures of the road when he's flying: "You get in and just declare your freedom. . . . All of a sudden you're just a number in the sky. Nobody knows who you are unless you happen to be flying by an airport that's familiar with you and they recognize your call number. But by and large you're out there, going where you want to go, and landing where you want to land."

At the time, though, his family's wayfaring made him miserable. Children are natural conservatives. There is comfort in a circumscribed life—it narrows the wide, strange world down to manageable proportions—and that comfort was denied him. He was always the new kid in class, the new kid in the neighborhood, and it made him angry: "I kept wondering why we were moving all the time. But [my parents would] say, 'Well, you know, not for you to question why,' and all that. Or just mostly, 'Well, your dad's got a job, so we've got to go there.' And you always hated it, because, you know, you just get to know a few kids on the block and get accepted a little bit and then, all of a sudden, boom, you're gone."

Always tall for his age (he was more than six feet tall when he was thirteen), he was more than usually self-conscious about his appearance, about his family nicknames ("Sonny" and "Junior," both of which he hated), about his indifferent performance in school. Perhaps because he attended so many schools and was constantly befuddled by new environments and changed expectations, he frequently withdrew into dreaminess. "If I was sitting near the window and the leaves [were] blowing out there, my mind could be a thousand miles away. You sit there, you know, you feel the air . . . and boy I could go off on a trip."

Clint envied the students for whom things came easily. "I had a buddy in school [who] could dump all his books in a locker and go home and the only reason he got a B was through misconduct of some sort. I'd have to go in there and drill my brains to get a passing, decent grade." From grade school through high school, this remained difficult for him. "I didn't have a real go-home-and-study-for-two-hours-so-I'll-get-an-A attitude. It's like the physicist Edward Teller: He always said a genius is someone who does well with a subject he doesn't like, and that would certainly eliminate me."

He was bad at math, liked history and "could have been all right drawing if I'd pursued it." Somewhere along the line his natural left-handedness was trained out of him. He read the usual kid stuff—comics and Big Little Books—joined the family around the radio to listen to shows like *Inner Sanctum* and *I Love a Mystery,* saw *Snow White and the Seven Dwarfs*—probably his first movie—when he was seven and spent a lot of time by himself, often in conversation with "Bill," a toy soldier, if his mother's recollection is right. Clint supplied voices for many of his playthings and made up adventures as he sprawled on the floor with them.

Not close with his sister in those days, he seems to have kept his loneliness to himself. His mother, indeed, was unaware of it. "I didn't realize how shy he was," she says. "I'm not, and neither was his father. I don't know where on earth he got it. But anyway, I guess it was harder on him than I knew." Her recollection is that wherever they went he always found one or two companions; one of them, Robert Baker, whom he met in Redding, remained a lifelong friend.

In her eyes, then, he was all right. And perhaps precisely because she saw him so, that's the way he turned out. Ruth, in Clint's description, was "with all due prejudice a fabulous woman. She adored her children." Above all, "she was very flexible. She was a very understanding mother." Though his father was usually the family disciplinarian, she could be firm if need be. "They weren't overly strict parents, but if you got out of line they'd swipe you on the behind."

And that would then be that; the elder Eastwoods didn't hold grudges or nurse wounds. Clint describes them as extremely tolerant, entirely free of the bigotry and paranoia that so often afflict the temporarily declassed. "My parents never looked down on anybody. They were always fairly open-minded—conservative in handling their own lives, but liberal in their approach to other people's existence," including that of their children.

They were uninsistent religiously and politically. Ruth and the children quietly attended whatever Protestant church was near at hand wherever they settled. Politically, she and her husband apparently supported Roosevelt for two terms, then broke away to vote for Wendell Willkie in 1940. But there is no defining passion to be found in these commonplace religious and political convictions. It was common sense and common decency that ruled their lives, and it was those qualities that they passed on to their children. There were, one gathers, no hidden agendas in the Eastwood family, no dark, twisting pressures, just simple, straightforward expectations and affections, clearly expressed.

Whatever insecurities their restless passage through the world in these years imposed upon their children, there was always, in the Eastwood home, a bed of feelings in which they could securely root themselves. And that, too, would become one source of Clint's strength within his profession. There are no childish emotional needs for which he requires belated compensation from audiences, colleagues, studios. He long ago gathered all of that to him, and not alone from his mother and father. He has fond memories of visits to Grandpa Burr, who also upped stakes during the depression, surprising everyone by selling his Piedmont house and, with his second wife, buying a little farm devoted to apple trees and chicken raising near Sebastopol. It is, however, his maternal grandmother, Virginia Runner, who figures most powerfully in Clint's reminiscences of these years. During their unsettled period it seems that the Eastwoods frequently circled back on her little house in Hayward, sixty years ago a semirural community where Mrs. Runner, then working as a bookkeeper for a food-processing company, could live in solitary contentment, a largehearted, sweetly eccentric woman, warm in her affections, setting for Clint a memorable, often-cited example of the independent life. Clint and his sister lived with her once for an entire school year during a particularly unsettled period, Clint happily sleeping in a tent he had pitched in the backyard. Afterward, he visited her as often as he could.

Clint attributes his lifelong affection for animals to his grandmother, for there was always a shifting population of pets in and around her house. It may be that her move, a little later in Clint's childhood, to seven acres of land, mostly given over to olive trees, near Sunol, was motivated by her desire to support a more extensive menagerie. There she kept chickens (a well-worn family story has Clint lying on the ground in the chicken yard and sprinkling corn across his body so the chickens would clamber up on him) and sold their eggs from a roadside stand. She had a swaybacked horse, raised a few pigs, even, for a time, kept a Nubian goat that was always trying to scale the walls of the garage. Her other daughter, Bernice, who was married to a dentist, lived in nearby Niles, and they, too, had a horse, a somewhat more spirited creature, the first one Clint remembers riding at a pace more exciting than a shamble. One time he spent a few days with them earning pocket money picking apricots on a nearby farm. He also remembers that on his visits to his grandmother he was able to range the nearby hills on long solitary walks, on which he acted out all kinds of imaginary adventures.

Finally, though, the most important thing he took away from his visits with his grandmother was her uncomplicated faith that there was something special about him. He was, his mother says, her favorite grandchild—"anything he did was perfect"—and he knew it. She thought "I was terrific," he told Barbara Walters in one of their television interviews. "I think she thought I was better than I really was." Be that as it may, it was she, alone among this extended family, who predicted a future in some creative field for this seemingly unexceptional boy. He had, she firmly noted, "long hands," which to her, in her grandmotherly wisdom, bespoke a natural gift for the arts. It is an interesting observation, because Clint's use of his hands—graceful, precise and sometimes rather startling in the context of some of his roles—is one of the hallmarks of his acting manner. She did not live to see him become a movie star, but she did see him become a television star on *Rawhide*. "And she never let anybody forget it."

★ ★ ★

As the decade turned, so did the Eastwood family's fortunes. In 1940 Clinton Sr. found a job—"the happiest thing he ever did," says his wife—with Shreve, Crump and Lowe, the well-known San Francisco jewelers, then controlled by the family of a young man with whom he had once played football. They were now back on native ground, living in a pleasant little house in Glenview in the East Bay, where Clint's interest in nature focused briefly on herpetology; one day he came home from a nearby park with no less than thirteen small snakes in his lunch pail. They shared his room peaceably enough—until his mother found one curled up in one of her towels and she ordered them returned to their natural habitat.

Around this time the family was favored by another stroke of good luck. Perusing the newspaper real estate section, the elder Eastwoods observed that one of Ruth's aunts had placed her home in Piedmont on the market. "We knew the house very well," Ruth recalls, "and so we went ripping up the next day and sure enough it was for sale and they would sell it to us for what we would give them. Houses weren't selling in Piedmont at all, so we bought it for very little down and very little a month." Ruth Eastwood was working, too, at this time, for IBM, and, at last, the family was able to settle down; the Eastwoods would remain in Piedmont for eight years, until Clint was in his last months of high school.

It was a middle- and upper-class enclave. Some of California's oldest money (the Crockers of the bank, the Hills of the coffee company, the Witters of the Dean Witter stock brokerage) was settled here. The Eastwoods did not travel in those circles. Indeed, their modest shingled house was close to the Oakland line, and it was that blue-collar port and industrial city, always invidiously compared to glamorous San Francisco across the bay, not conservative Piedmont, that would eventually claim his loyalty. In interviews he gives it, not the suburb, as his hometown.

He attended Havens Elementary School, then Piedmont Junior High School. He made lifelong friends during his first years in Piedmont, among them a good-natured boy named Harry Pendleton, who spent much of his adult life on the fringe of lawlessness and died early; Jack McKnight, who in late adolescence would live with the Eastwoods for almost a year; Fritz Manes, who would eventually work for Clint as a line producer in his production company; Don Kincade, through whom Clint met his first wife, Maggie, and with whom he remains close. Indeed, as a youngster, Kincade was to Clint an exemplary figure, because he was the first in his crowd to articulate an ambition—he wanted to be a dentist—and the only one to follow through on it. Thinking back, Clint shakes his head at the miracle of coherence, confidently knowing what you want and going out and getting it. It was beyond him at the time.

He was still dreaming away most of the school day, and staying pretty much aloof from its official extracurricular life. Sports, for example, were heavily emphasized, and most of his pals went out for them. But though he "teased around" with football and basketball in junior high, team sports didn't really interest him. It was the same with school band. He loved music and, as we will see, was beginning to demonstrate his natural—and, given the musical gifts on both sides of his family, doubtless inherited—talent for it. Issued a flügelhorn, which is similar to a trumpet, but with a softer, warmer tone (some of his jazz idols, like Chuck Mangione and Red Rodney, often played it), Clint easily mastered its rudiments, practiced some with the band, but apparently never played it publicly—"you know, everybody looked down on the band when we were kids, and I was a big cat," meaning he would be painfully visible marching along with his slightly exotic instrument.

His largest interest, very simply, lay in not calling attention to himself, not easy for a boy of his height to manage. There were well-intended attempts to "bring him out of his shell," such as an infamous school play, often recounted in Clint Eastwood profiles and biographies. Their writers have enjoyed the irony of a man who has since become one of the world's most famous actors forced by a teacher to perform in a skit in an all-school assembly, being deeply embarrassed by the experience and vowing never to repeat it. The story is true, but there is more to it than is usually reported. For anxious though the occasion made him in anticipation, Clint turned the event itself to reasonably good account, achieving a rare moment of recognition in his generally anonymous school career. And also learning, as he would later recognize, another little life lesson.

He was in the eighth grade when his English teacher, Gertrude Falk ("I remember her name very well," he says grimly), announced that the class would be doing a one-act play for public consumption and, without auditions, ordered Clint to play the lead. "It was the part of a backward youth, and I think my teacher thought I was perfect casting," Clint once said. His friend Harry Pendleton and a girl named Shuggie Vincent were assigned to play his father and mother, and a couple of other classmates had walk-ons.

He went to Miss Falk and tried to get out of the assignment, but she said, "Oh, you'll be perfect for this," adding that he and the others would be graded on their work. The small consolation she offered was that there would be a prompter off stage in case he forget his lines.

Rehearsals were not reassuring to Clint, and the night before the performance he and Pendleton seriously discussed the possibility of feigning illness. But "I was too chicken to play sick," and, besides, "by this time I'd memorized enough of the play so I thought, Well, we'll go try it and it won't be that bad." Miss Falk, however, had one last surprise for her cast. She informed them, just before they reported to the auditorium, that this was to be a joint assembly with the high school; older kids, their contempt at the ready, would be looking on.

"Jesus, we just about crapped. But there we were, and it was too late; we couldn't cut or run or go home or whatever. We had to go on with it. So we got out there and started in on the play, and everything started going wrong, of course. Harry was reading a newspaper and he had his script inside, and it dropped out on the floor, and I was tripping over things. But it started getting laughs. Even some of the lines started getting laughs. And all of a sudden, I don't know what came over me, I felt I'm into this thing and we're rolling. So we finished it with a minimum amount of screwup." Indeed, in retrospect, he admits "there were moments that I actually felt that spark for a second." He also recalls "guys from the senior high school walking up later in the day, and saying, 'Hey, that was good,' and I was like, 'It was?'" Miss Falk, too, professed herself satisfied. "That's fine," he replied, but "I don't ever want to do that again, ever in my life."

That possibility seemed to him comfortingly remote. Acting was an unimaginably exotic profession, not to be spared another thought, though he liked going to the movies and remembers seeing such signature movies of the time as *Gone with the Wind* and *The Grapes of Wrath*. He has a particularly vivid memory of *Sergeant York*. The legend of the World War I hero, a simple mountaineer who set aside pacifist principles to join the army, and then, at the front, rescued his trapped unit, killing and capturing a vast number of German soldiers in the process, had an understandable appeal for Clint's father. Here was a man who understood duty and loyalty—and making the best of a bad job—in the same way that Clinton Eastwood Sr. did. "He read everything that there was about *Sergeant York*," says Clint, and when the movie (for which Gary Cooper won his first Academy Award) came along in 1941, he eagerly took his son to see it.

A year later, *Yankee Doodle Dandy* had a greater impact, as did James Cagney. Superficially, it's an odd coupling—the lanky, laconic westerner and the short, voluble New Yorker. But, of course, the simplicity of

Cagney's attack, the straightforward way he mobilized his emotions on-screen, would resonate for Clint when he entered the profession. "Plant your feet and tell the truth," was Cagney's oft-repeated advice to young players, and that no-nonsense approach had an obvious appeal to him. He was also, visibly, a working-class guy (which is how Clint sometimes refers to himself) and a private and emotionally reticent man, which, possibly, Clint sensed in some way.

Double Indemnity also made a strong impression on him, and so did Preston Sturges's comedies, particularly *Sullivan's Travels* (of Joel McCrea, he would say, "Maybe he didn't have the stature of Gary Cooper, but he always gave the impression that more was going on inside him than he was revealing"). Treasured along with these films and stars is one slightly more exotic title, *Forty Thousand Horsemen.* The story of an Australian cavalry brigade that fought in Palestine in World War I, it starred Chips Rafferty, was made in 1940 and entered the world market a couple of years later. Its dialogue contained a few mild, but in those days shocking, cuss words. Clint remembers going to it with his family and, when the first "hell" or "damn" was heard, being aware of respectable citizens leaving the theater. The Eastwoods soon followed, but "I snuck back later, because I wanted to see the whole movie; it had a lot of action—horses, and lancers and what have you."

"Snuck" is how Clint and his pals usually went to the movies. "About five or six of us would go, and one guy would go in and he'd leave the door ajar behind the exit curtains. Everybody'd come in and they'd crawl through all the gum and popcorn and spilled colas and stuff and crawl to the middle and pop up. Meantime, as you're crawling by you'd try to pick up a thrown-away ticket stub, so you could say, 'Oh, yeah, here's my stub.'"

They were a lively, occasionally comically troublesome, group. Clint's mother recalls, for instance, the case of stuffy Major Overton, a retired army officer, who, during the war, proudly raised a large American flag over his swimming pool every morning. One day he arrived to find a Japanese flag flying from his flagpole. Clint and his crowd had fashioned it from one of Ruth Eastwood's bedsheets and run it up during the night. The boys were found out and forced to apologize in person to the major, who, in turn, wrote a letter to Clint, praising him for his honesty.

There is a certain typicality in these recollections. One can't help but reflect that this is how American boys of a certain time, a certain class, grew up—mild mischief, scholarly inattentiveness, lack of focused ambition, bits and pieces of popular culture lodging in memory. The virtue of being seen but not heard, much stressed in those days, seemed to be good advice, considering one's shyness and inability to imagine what one might have to say that would make sense to a stranger anyway.

★   ★   ★

But the young Clint Eastwood cannot be portrayed in purely typical terms. He may at times have yearned for typicality—what kid does not?—but by the time he reached early adolescence, unusual self-sufficiency had become a trait of character. By this time, his interest in music had become something like an obsession, and that, too, set him apart.

In the long run it probably shaped his sensibility (and his laid-back manner) as much as anything. But in that time and place, experiments with the flügelhorn aside, musical talent was not widely encouraged or appreciated, especially in a quiet, gawky boy who had difficulty publicly discussing this curious interest. Then, too, music seems to have come easily for him, which is perhaps another reason he maintained a certain secretiveness about it; in those days everyone was taught that the triumphs we had to strive hardest for were the most valuable ones. Finally, as he grew more sophisticated in his tastes, Clint tended to contrast his talent to that of the jazz greats he was now beginning to idolize, and in that company, of course, his modesty was appropriate.

Still, undeniably, his was an authentic and precocious gift. Wherever the Eastwoods settled during their wandering years, Grandma Andy's piano would be sent for, and Clint would fool around with it. Like his mother before him, he taught himself to play at an early age, picking out the tunes he was hearing on the jazz records she collected.

He recalls listening intently to her Art Tatum records and trying to emulate him. He remembers, too, that when Fats Waller died, his mother bought a number of his recordings and told her thirteen-year-old son: "This guy was brilliant and these are classics." The humor of Waller's lyrics—"Ain't Misbehavin'," "Your Feet's Too Big"—hooked him immediately. "Then I started listening to the way he played—he played that stride kind of piano—and I thought, Now that'd be fun to be able to play that." So he tried, and accomplished a reasonable facsimile. Around the same time, he also started listening to the Bob Crosby Orchestra, which was one of the jazzier big bands of the time. Crosby and some of the band's players also formed a band within the band, a smaller Dixieland group called the Bobcats, which cut a number of records, and these, too, caught Clint's ear. His mother encouraged him.

"You ought to keep doing that, keep after this," Clint remembers Ruth Eastwood saying. At some point in their Piedmont years she even paid for some piano lessons with a teacher in Berkeley.

One Crosby record that particularly caught Clint's ear was "Honky Tonk Train"; he liked it so much that he found the original record by Meade Lux Lewis, the pianist who wrote the song, and taught himself to imitate it. Then, "One time I was at a party and was standing around and nothing was happening, so I played 'Honky Tonk Train' and everybody went, 'Wow, hey,' and all of a sudden the chicks started looking at me like I wasn't just this gawky kid sitting in the back." All of a sudden, in fact, he was—pleasingly—the center of attention, "sitting there with the tuna oil in your hair, you know, and the gals around in bobby sox rolled down. It was kind of like that."

One probably should not make too much of the incident, which seems not to have been repeated. Indeed, Fritz Manes has no memory of Clint confessing, or demonstrating, his musical gifts quite so early. In his recollection, Clint tended to avoid parties most of the time, and it was not until two or three years later that his friends became aware of his musical passion.

One might trace the beginnings of a new, less awkward relationship to the opposite sex to this moment, but, again, a certain caution seems to be in order. Clint says he lost his virginity when he was fourteen ("I had nice neighbors"), but that's all he will say about that momentous occasion. He was then, as he was to remain, terribly discreet—not to say secretive—about his sexual adventures. And, besides, he was not that far removed from the tongue-tied grammar-school boy who pined for a pretty red-haired classmate, but could never find the nerve to speak to her.

If music and romance were matters for reserve, his obsession with cars was not, for it was widely shared. Oakland, Clint recalls, was "a town where people were nuts about automobiles. There was a whole society of hot rods and car building," and though he couldn't afford "the real flashy ones," he learned to love beautiful automobiles, and it is a passion, like music, that he has never forsworn. His friend John Calley, who was head of production in Clint's early days at Warner Bros., and who was a California teenager in the same era, understands what cars meant to him. "He went to the drive-in theater and he wanted a chopped-top, lowered and frenched and all that stuff. We all did."

It's a standard form of California dreaming. Even when he was a near-penniless young actor, Clint managed to have a smart little sports car, and since achieving success, he has, it seems, owned at least briefly every known make of glamour vehicle—though most of the time these days he gets around in trucks or truck-based recreational vehicles. The Mercedes, which comes out of the garage when the occasion seems to demand it, is over twenty years old; Calley remembers him driving it when they first worked together: "He likes it and that's enough for him. He keeps it really sharp."

He does that perhaps in tribute to all the unsharp heaps he desperately kept rolling as a teenager. His father bought Clint the first of them—a 1932 Chevy touring car the family referred to as "the bathtub" because it had no top—before it was legal for him to obtain a driver's license. The rationale was that he needed it for his newspaper route, but according to Manes, lots of Piedmont kids had cars before they passed their driver's tests; it was something of a local tradition. In Clint's case, the gift was conditional; he was obliged to take full financial responsibility for the vehicle's upkeep.

The bathtub soon gave way to a '34 Ford, then to subsequent jalopies, even, for a time, a motorcycle. To support those ramshackle wheels Clint took on jobs in addition to his newspaper route: He bagged groceries at the Peabody Market, caddied at the Claremont Country Club. All his vehicles were "running on chewing gum and spit and wire. And brake rods'd be falling off and batteries wouldn't start." One time after one of his repair jobs, his mother remembers, he failed to reconnect the wheel to the steering column correctly, and the car rolled uncontrolled down a hill, with Clint in it, eventually coming to a violent halt against a tree, its driver unhurt, but with the vehicle totaled. It was, as Clint would later characterize it, an *American Graffiti* kind of adolescence.

An automobile was essential to Clint. Very simply, it was "your only form of independence," and, once he entered high school, a vital dating tool: "Oakland's a fairly sprawling city—you couldn't date somebody on the other side of town unless you had a car, so you had to have something." Thinking back, he grins. "Fast cars and easy women—in that order, I guess."

As Clinton Sr. had doubtless hoped, the demands cars placed on his son's wallet taught Clint the value of uncomplaining toil. "You get nothing for nothing," his father would tell him. Or "Don't think the world owes you a living, because it doesn't." When Clint would apply for his after-school jobs, his father would always tell him: "Forget about the dough. Go in there and show them what you can do. Make yourself so valuable that they just gotta have you." It puzzled Clint sometimes—they were talking about bagging groceries and delivering newspapers, after all—but in some measure these exchanges left their mark on his character. Many years later, discussing his moderately troubled passage through later adolescence, Clint would tell an interviewer, "although I rebelled, I never rebelled against that."

He did, however, rebel against conventional piety—very early and, in part, because of his hardworking life and his dad's. During the war, Clinton Sr. was obliged to give up his agreeable life as a jewelry salesman. He was classified 1-A in the draft, and knew that if he was called up his family, with no savings to fall back upon, would be devastated. His only choice was to get a job in a vital defense industry. So he applied for work in a shipyard—not knowing "one end of a boat from the other," Ruth laughs—and somehow got taken on as a pipe fitter.

The pay was excellent, but the hours were long and exhausting, as he pointed out to his son one day when Clint asked him why he did not join the rest of the family when they trekked off to church on Sunday. "It's my only day off," the elder Eastwood said simply. Clint thought that over and replied, "Well, it's my only day off, too." As a matter of fact, he didn't even have that day entirely to himself, since he had to be up at dawn working his paper route. "Well, then don't go," said his dad. "There's all kinds of ways to get a feeling of God, however [He] exists for you."

This squared with Clint's instincts. The Bible stories he had listened to in various Sunday schools had never appealed to him. They seemed terribly remote, and they struck him as distressingly violent, too—"the whole idea of religion based upon impaling somebody, the whole center, torture and torment." Critics of Eastwood's subsequent screen career, marked by so many bloody confrontations, may make what irony they care to out of this, but he says these views had begun to take shape even before this conversation, when he found himself contrasting the discomfort Christian myth stirred in him with the experience of visiting Yosemite National Park with his family.

"You looked down into that valley, without too many people around," he says, "and, boy, that was to me a religious experience." And not an uncommon one for a person of his birthright. "Born again," the naturalist John Muir wrote in his diary upon seeing the same sight for the first time. This Pacific Rim Transcendentalism, a belief that nature in the several majestic aspects that California presents it, is the ultimate source of spiritual renewal widely shared by its citizens and has remained a major force in determining the way Clint has lived his adult life.

★   ★   ★

Clint remained as indifferent to formal education as he was to formal religion. "What he did, he did very well," his mother says, thinking about the time he lavished on his cars and his music, "but he was no scholar." As he entered high school this became a serious issue. There is some dispute as to whether he voluntarily left Piedmont High or was asked to leave. It seems likely that, for a variety of reasons, not all of them having to do with his indifference to his studies, he contrived to get himself removed from a place where he was not comfortable. His pals, of course, were happy to set a bad example for him. Naturally, the report cards with their observations about a kid not working to capacity flowed in. Naturally Clinton Eastwood Sr. sternly lectured his son on the need to apply himself.

Clint's problems, however, were not entirely academic. They were social, too. He fit in happily enough with his own small crowd, and the guys loved hanging out at the Eastwood house, for as Manes puts it, "If a kid could ask to have dream parents it would have been Clint Sr. and Ruth." She was always cooking meals for them, and Clinton Sr., boyish and expansive, was someone to whom they could express themselves freely, a nonjudgmental father figure who, in Manes's account, at times seemed more like an older brother. When they were a little older beer was permitted, and so was smoking (though Clint, even then, avoided cigarettes). But he could not or would not try to expand beyond this circle. "He was off rebuilding a transmission in the afternoon, while we were at football practice, or tearing down an engine," Manes would recall. He didn't even like hanging out at Bud's Bar, where the Piedmont jocks and those from the University of California often met. There was no live music there, only a jukebox stocked with mainstream pop.

He was beginning to gather a sense of Piedmont's contempt for people who didn't match its norm, a contempt that included Clint. "The kids were driving better cars than my parents were," he recalls, "and I learned very early on that I was at the low end of the social structure." His mother confirms this assessment. "Particularly in his class there were an awful lot of wealthy kids, and I could see where Clint would have a funny-looking car and they would have Cadillacs or something."

The prejudices he encountered extended beyond the automotive. He vividly remembers some junior-high schoolmates asking him what his father did, and putting him down when he told them that he worked in a shipyard. Their dads, they proudly told him, were merchants and executives, and his argument that his father was at least engaged in vital war work made no impression on them. He was, as well, acutely conscious that there were no blacks in Piedmont, no Asians, only one or two Jewish families. And precisely because it was so "white bread" (Manes's description) the place was rife with a kind of heedless bias.

"That's where I was first introduced to bigotry," Clint recalls, and though he says he doesn't know how or when the conviction came to him, "I never could stand intolerance. In my soul, I couldn't buy into it."

His response was, as he gently puts it, "Fuck you and move on." Which was quite all right with Piedmont High and, as it happened, with his mother. "That didn't worry me at all, because I knew he was going to be different than the rest of the group." She can't say why, exactly. "Something told me. I never worried about what he was going to do."

When the inevitable call came to meet with an assistant principal to discuss other academic alternatives, she was serene. When she talked these over with her husband, Oakland Technical High School seemed to make the most sense. It offered a course in aircraft maintenance, and that interested Clint more than any of the shop courses at Piedmont. Wartime aviation movies had stirred in him a romantic feeling for flight, and he had even journeyed out a couple of times to Walnut Creek, where there was an airfield and five dollars would buy you a half-hour trip across the Bay Area skies in a light plane.

The youngster (and helicopter-pilot-to-be) who loved tinkering with engines found aircraft maintenance a thoroughly satisfactory subject. But he was not encouraged to see it as his life's work. The instructor constantly reminded his students that this was a poorly paid occupation. "The guy used to joke about it, the teacher: 'Well, there's no real dough in it. You make as much being an auto mechanic, and you don't have the responsibility.'"

In other respects, though, Tech worked out pretty much as Eastwood—and his parents—had hoped. "He was more relaxed at Tech," his mother says simply. He was never a big man on campus. His high-school yearbook records only very few officially sanctioned extracurricular activities. But he liked its ethnic diversity—"it just seemed like it was more real"—and he continues to believe that if he had gone to school in Piedmont, "I would have been stuck in a groove."

There was no danger of that at Tech. To Fritz Manes, the Tech guys looked like tough guys. And there certainly were gangs in the school, though Clint avoided them. By his own (and Manes's) account he bopped all over the Oakland area, drinking beer illegally, looking just a little bit delinquent (a photo from the period shows him wearing a duck's-ass haircut and a leather jacket). He kept up his friendships with his Piedmont pals, but made no attempt to meld this group with the others he knew—it was part of the slightly mysterious air that he began cultivating then, and which he has never abandoned. It is based on nothing more than a natural disinclination to explain himself to anybody.

He continued to work in his after-school hours, and during his high-school summers he worked strenuously. One year during school vacation he baled hay on a farm belonging to one of Jack McKnight's relatives near Yreka, in northern California. The next summer he worked for the state forestry service in Butte County, also in the northern part of the state. It was often extremely hard labor. Butte ranked second among the state's counties in number of fires, and "it was a very hot summer up there, in the hundreds every day, and very dry—lots of brush fires would start. And when there wasn't a fire you'd go out and cut trails and cut timber."

Sometimes in those years he would cut himself a little slack by joining his parents at a vacation cabin they had on a lake near Fresno, and he remembers a couple of summer romances from those days. But his relationships with young women, numerous though they were, do not define Clint in these years any more than his schoolwork or his part-time jobs or his fascination with the internal-combustion engine does. It was, finally, jazz that did so.

He was becoming more and more sophisticated in his understanding of it, in part because of his environment. Oakland at that time had the largest black population of any city west of Detroit, and rhythm and blues was in the air, on the air, constantly. One of the local radio stations, KWDR, devoted a three-hour afternoon slot exclusively to this music, and Clint was addicted to the program. He began playing, as best he could, the tunes he heard on it.

Not that it was the only influence on him. He recalls the Frisco Jazz Band and Lu Watters's Yerba Buena Jazz Band, both Dixieland groups. Clint and friends would drive out to a place called Hambone and Kelly's in El Cerrito, which was basically a black jazz club (and was casual about checking IDs), to listen to music.

There was also a small club on Lake Shore Avenue where Dave Brubeck's trio (it included Cal Tjader and Ron Crotty) "drew like crazy" as he established his style. Clint became a devoted fan, following Brubeck to San Francisco when he began playing there. He also remembers hearing Gerry Mulligan and Chet Baker when they came through town.

Despite the presence of Brubeck and Paul Desmond, the Bay Area in the forties was not yet the avatar of the new jazz sound that it would soon become. In his definitive history, *West Coast Jazz,* Ted Gioia describes it, in these days, as "the last bastion of the mouldy figs." He argues that New Orleans jazz made its way along the railway tracks to San Francisco at about the same time it made its way up the Mississippi to Chicago, but that most of the jazzmen who got their start on the West Coast developed their mature styles (and their reputations) only after they moved east. The San Francisco jazz scene, generally less venture-some than the one in Los Angeles, remained essentially committed to the past. Gioia observes that the San Francisco musicians' union remained divided into a black local and a white one as late as 1960.

Clint ventures no opinion about the Bay Area's degree of hipness in those days. His tastes were eclectic. He was buying Charlie Ventura's records, and listening to Woody Herman's various herds, soaking up a hipper big-band sound than was generally available locally. And he was aware that bebop "was coming in real big," and so he found himself "going around trying to understand bop and what it was about and not being sure I understood it, but wanting to learn more about it." To this end, he went to hear Dizzy Gillespie, the figure who would provide the moral contrast to Charlie Parker in Clint's *Bird* some four decades later, when he appeared with a seventeen-piece band at a club in San Francisco.

But the aesthetic turning point for him was a Jazz at the Philhar-monic concert at the Shrine Auditorium in Oakland in 1946: Coleman Hawkins, Flip Phillips, Lester Young—"I mean, he was like the cat's ass, you know, for tenor saxophone"—and, yes, Charlie Parker, all on the same program.

Bird was, for Clint, "a whole shock to the system. It was just amaz-ing to see somebody do anything with that kind of confidence. He wasn't arrogant or anything, he was just a guy standing there in a pin-stripe suit, and when he started playing it was like, I guess, some sort of free painter, who'd just jump right in there and start slapping paint up there, a totally unplanned deal." It was, perhaps, the sheer cool of Bird's manner that got to him. "I'd never seen a musician play with such con-fidence. There was no show business to it in those days, and this guy just stood and played, and I thought, God, what an amazing, expressive thing." More important, he went away thinking, It would be wonderful to have that kind of confidence doing something—anything—in life.

In his superb essay on Charlie Parker, Ralph Ellison makes a couple of apposite points. One is that when he was creating his legend, Parker meant more to young white jazz aficionados than he did to blacks. "They never heard of him," Art Blakey, the drummer, said of the black audience. Ellison writes: "Parker operated in the underworld of Amer-ican culture . . . where contemporary civilized values and hypocrisies are challenged by the Dionysian urges of a between-wars youth born to prosperity, conditioned by the threat of world destruction, and in-spired—when not seeking total anarchy—by a need to bring social re-ality and our social pretensions into a more meaningful balance."

"Dionysian" is obviously too large a term to apply to the activities and interests of the young Clint Eastwood, and it is difficult to see him as prosperous or much concerned about the threat of the atomic bomb, either. But his interest in modern jazz generally, Parker specifically, does coincide with his parents' return to middle-class status and with his rejection of a middle-class high school in favor of a working-class institution, certainly an attempt on his part to rebalance "social reality" and "social pretensions" as he experienced them. One can read into his passionate interest in the new music a kind of rebellion—or at least a determination to go his own way—that, though masked and politely stated, was quite determined, if narrowly focused. There is no evidence that the other interests that would soon define the fifties hipster—action painting, for example, or coffeehouse poetry—ever caught his eye. Even Stanislavskian acting, though he would eventually embrace some of its techniques, does not seem to have excited the kind of enthusiasm in him that it did in others of his generation. When he talks about actors he admired, figures like Brando and Clift do not figure heavily in his conversation.

Whether or not the modern jazzmen he idolized—instinctive postmodernists that they were—helped shape his own comparable instincts is hard to say. But they certainly had something to do with the way he would eventually present himself as an actor. Ellison observes that this younger generation of musicians consciously and angrily rejected the jubilant showmanship of Louis Armstrong and the other "hot" jazzmen. To them, this was Uncle Tomming, and it also led them to reject—wrongly, as Ellison says—the genius of Armstrong's playing, and downgrade his historical significance. On the bandstands, the result was, as he puts it, "a grim comedy of racial manners; with the musicians employing a calculated surliness and rudeness, treating the audience very much as many white merchants in poor Negro neighborhoods treat their customers and the white audiences were shocked at first, but learned quickly to accept such treatment as evidence of 'artistic' temperament. . . . Today [Ellison was writing in 1962] the white audience expects the rudeness as part of the entertainment." Or, if not that, then certainly an air of effortlessness, a feeling that the players are just casually knocking off their sometimes-astonishing effects.

Clint is not surly or rude as an actor, but his cool, by far the most obvious quality of his work, his powerful desire—amounting almost to a morality—not to woo the audience, his apparent indifference to their rejections, must be traced to the modern-jazz manner. So must his profound desire not to make what he does look costly to him, emotionally or intellectually. He says: "Good acting, like good anything, doesn't look like there's a lot of effort with it, you know. If a person believes, 'Hey, I could do that, 'cause I've felt that emotion,' then that's good. I'm sure a lot of people sat there years ago and watched Nat King Cole [and] said, 'Hey, I can sing like that—he's not really doing anything.' Or great musicians, you say, 'What the hell, they're not really doing anything.'" One could argue, as well, that some of his hallmarks as a director—his preference for letting actors riff on a theme, for example, or his characteristic lighting, which is often like that of a jazz club, general darkness with a few pinpricks of light illuminating the scene's principals—have their roots in jazz.

All of that, of course, was far ahead in a future entirely unimaginable to him in 1946. What he did know without doubt, as he listened to Parker for the first time, was that this music spoke to him with an intensity that nothing else ever had: "I left there thinking, I gotta know more about that. So I started buying records, and listening to them and following him. I caught him at a couple of clubs in later years and we even drove down and saw him when he was playing in southern California."

The richer and more various Los Angeles jazz scene was something Clint and his crowd regularly sampled in their high-school years, and after graduation, too. Typically, a bunch of kids would pile into a car and make the long drive south for weekends of music. They might catch Kid Ory one night at the Beverly Cavern, just to get in touch with the classic New Orleans manner, then hit the Oasis to hear something newer, or the Haig, near the Ambassador Hotel downtown, or the string of clubs lining Central Avenue, in those days the principal thoroughfare of Los Angeles's principal black neighborhood. It was the heart of a jazz scene that began flourishing during World War II when the booming defense industry, working around the clock, had turned L.A. into an all-night town, with workers—a larger percentage than ever before being blacks—looking for off-hour entertainment.

By the time Clint and his buddies were hitting Los Angeles, you might have heard the new music all over town, though not without difficulties. The Los Angeles police, many of its officers unregenerate rednecks from the South, would often stop cars bearing racially mixed groups heading for a jazz club in Hollywood, and it is said that their hatred of the integrated audiences for music in the Central Avenue clubs played a key role in the avenue's precipitate decline in the 1950s. It simply became too inaccessible for a significant segment of the audience.

Still, if you were lucky, there were great musicians to be heard here, and on one of these trips south Clint had his first direct contact with haute Hollywood. He and some of his pals were tooling along Sepulveda Boulevard, skirting the western boundary of Bel-Air, when they were confronted by a small herd of horses, "right on the street, bopping all over the place." The kids stopped, jumped out of the car and shooed them up a little canyon where they found an open gate. They got the animals into the corral and secured it, by which time their owner appeared—"very appreciative, very friendly." They chatted awhile, and then the kids took off. One of them was excited—"You know who that was? That was Howard Hawks, the famous moviemaker!" Clint was impressed: "I was no cineast, but I knew who Howard Hawks was"—the director of *Sergeant York* and countless other action movies treasured by young men of his generation because they were about fractious but good-natured males bonding and working together toward some common goal.

The incident took on significance for Clint in the light of his subsequent career. Aside from a few weeks' work in William A. Wellman's last movie, it would remain his only direct early contact with a legendary figure from Hollywood's Classic Age, a fact he would often publicly regret.

Movies, of course, were then a dream too absurd to countenance. What's odd, all things considered, was that music was too. "I felt that I'd never be able to work doing that. To be a professional musician was awesome." He was, of course, measuring himself against geniuses—Bird and Dizzy and the rest—and it did not occur to him that there might be another level of musical life where, possibly, he could find a comfortable niche. Nevertheless, around the time he first heard Charlie Parker, he began to play in public on a more or less regular basis.

The Omar Club was a long, narrow bar and restaurant on Broadway in downtown Oakland, across from the Paramount Theater. "It was a kinda crazy place," as Clint recalls it, with "a bunch of nice guys that ran it." He and his pals took to hanging out there because management had no objection to minors drinking beer "as long as you had the money to put on the bar. That's the way it was in Oakland in those days—it wasn't too strict." One day Clint started fooling around at the piano, and the owners, liking what they heard, proposed that he play for whatever tips he could make. "So I kinda came down there and played, and then all of a sudden somebody was bringing me in pizzas, and all the guys, all my buddies, we'd be sitting around eating and drinking."

He makes it sound cool and casual, just a bunch of kids kicking back, goofing off. And it may have been no more than that for his pals, but not for Clint. For he also admits that "you could channel yourself into an instrument," let it say for you all the things you couldn't bring yourself to say out loud. "It was almost like a wall you could hide behind." Manes, perhaps exaggerating, remembers him playing eight, ten, twelve hours at a stretch, sometimes until three or four in the morning.

Music became a defining element in his relationships with young women: "I don't think I was ever attracted to a girl who didn't like music, who didn't have some interest in it. We'd spend a lot of time talking about it, listening to the radio and stuff." Some of them, he admits, may have been faking their passion for jazz. And why not? He was a good-looking kid, combining his slightly dangerous air with an agreeably uninsistent manner. "He's always been catnip to the women," his mother says equably, adding that he was never secretive about his relationships; he always brought his serious girlfriends home to meet his parents. Manes, who is a talkative man (Clint used to call him "the Long Goodbye"), says, "The not joining—what it did was create a suction, people wanting to know what made this guy work, what made him tick, what is he all about?"

It worked for him then, as it would later work for him on-screen. And as it generally is in his movies, so it was with his high-school romances—not many heavy commitments. According to Manes, "There were a bunch of romances, until they got to the point of getting really serious and then he'd be off and running."

It is a reasonably accurate description. But Clint was possibly in a little more conflict than he permitted himself to show. Wartime Oakland, with its transient population, had been barraged with propaganda about the dangers of casual sex, and he had absorbed all the official strictures. On the other hand, he was beginning to have some idea of how attractive he was, and an even more urgent sense of how attractive certain members of the opposite sex were to him. In the end, he resolved the issue straightforwardly: "You could sit there and ponder it, and say, 'Well, it's because I feel in control of myself,' or 'I feel flattered,' but really what it boils down to is, 'I don't care. I want you.'"

About the particulars of most of these encounters, memory does not serve him particularly well. Or so he says. He does fondly recall dating a beauty who would a little later be named Miss Oakland, losing her to a "gorilla," then briefly rekindling the relationship many years later, when they were grown-ups. He remembers still more affectionately his first steady relationship, when he was seventeen, with "a cute little Irish girl" named Mary Ellen McElvaney. "I was nuts about her," he says simply, and they were together, to the exclusion of all others, for six or eight months.

But as he edged toward high-school graduation, other concerns began to press in on him. Sometime after the war, Clinton Eastwood Sr. improved his lot substantially. He got a job in sales at the California

Container Company, which would soon be absorbed by the Container Corporation of America, in whose ranks he would subsequently rise to executive positions, eventually, according to his wife, becoming manager of the northwest territory. A few months before Clint was due to graduate from Oakland Tech his father was transferred to Seattle. It was decided that Clint would move in with Harry Pendleton (whose family owned a small apartment complex) so that he could graduate with his class, then rejoin his own family in Seattle.

But the question of what he would do with himself after that remained totally unsettled. He spent the summer after commencement with his parents in Seattle, working as a lifeguard at Renton Beach, then decided to return to Oakland, where he settled back into his little apartment and got a job at the Continental Can factory. But that was too confining, so he returned to Seattle, bringing Jack McKnight with him. They hung out for a while, doing some odd jobs until his father got jobs for them with Weyerhauser timber in the Willamette Valley.

"For some reason, I was really adrift in those years," Clint says. "I was sort of on a sea somewhere, not knowing where I wanted to go, but wanting to go somewhere, wanting to be on my own." He says he even abandoned his interest in music during this time, ceasing to play, not even listening to jazz with his former attentiveness.

Considering what music had meant to him, this is a good measure of his confusion—and, possibly, of his anger at his inability to find himself. He lumberjacked for a while in Oregon, and was injured, not as seriously as he might have been, but with minor lasting effect. He was on a conveyor belt, armed with a sort of grappling hook, the job being to straighten logs so that they slid smoothly into a large circular saw at the far end of the belt. The timber was being dropped onto it by a crane whose operator at some point loosed a load before Clint was ready for it. It crashed down on his legs, pinning him briefly, possibly giving him an undiagnosed hairline fracture, leaving his legs and lower body black and blue, and one of his knees "screwed up" for life.

After this incident he went to work in a pulp mill in Springfield, Oregon—the low point of this period. The smell in the mill was overpoweringly "putrid" and the air outside, trapped in this valley in the Cascade Mountains, was almost equally foul. Clint and Jack lived in a tiny apartment, and in the winter, when the rains came, the damp seeped in everywhere.

About the only thing he got out of this experience was the beginning of an interest in country music. Being lonely, he asked some of the guys he worked with where one went to meet chicks. They named a roadhouse near the Fernridge Dam. That it featured country music didn't sound too promising, but he relented, and found Bob Wills and His Texas Playboys—"more of a western swing band, and I liked him, he was really good, nice musicians, and there *were* some gals out there. I didn't know how to do a western two-step or whatever. But you'll try anything when you get desperate."

It might be argued that at this time he was claiming his manhood in the only way he knew how, emulating his father's peripatetic course as Clint had seen it when he was a child. It might also be argued that he was paying the price for his trade-school education. Whatever its virtues, Oakland Tech was not oriented toward college prep. It did not offer much in the way of literature or the arts, certainly nothing that might have encouraged a bright, unfocused young man to think seriously about further formal education.

This lack of intellectual grounding remains a source of some insecurity for him. He is very self-effacing about his lack of formal learning and abstract knowledge. In one of their television interviews Barbara Walters asked him how, when he was directing himself, he knew if a performance was not working. He made a drilling gesture with his finger at the back of his head and replied: "There's a little guy right inside the back there, and he says, 'Don't do that.' I don't have a lot of brains, but I have a good gut feeling." She followed up: "Do you really feel you don't have a lot of brains, or is that just a kind of 'Aw, shucks'?" "Well, I'm reasonably intelligent," he said, "but I'm not a person who is of high scholastic learning, and I feel that where I've gone today [has] been mostly based on instinct, animal instinct."

Ultimately overbalancing this defect is what he gained from the "lost years," from virtually all of his upbringing. Attending school with people whose chance of escape from relentlessly unrewarding labor was nearly nonexistent, then laboring beside them in thankless tasks, made him, as he puts it, "very sensitive toward people who work at jobs like that. You learn to kind of feel for them and understand how lucky you are to have moved beyond all that."

In other words, he was forging a link with the people who would one day form his core audience. They tutored his "instinct," permitting him to understand their favorite routes of escape. This empathy would ultimately inform Dirty Harry Callahan in one way, Philo Beddoe of the *Which Way* movies in another, Bronco Billy McCoy in still another. Whatever ambitions he later developed for the good regard of critics and more sophisticated moviegoers, he never turned against these early loyalists or talked down to them or behaved cynically toward them. To have done so would have been a betrayal—of himself as well as them.

Still, he did not want to lead a working-class life. If he had not certainly known that before, winter in the Willamette Valley taught him.
One day he went to get his only suit out of the closet, found it "just
soaking wet and all mildewy" and found himself saying, "OK, that's
enough of this crap."

But there was a little more to it than that. He was beginning to hear
the music again, specifically a swing band sponsored by Seattle University that he would catch on his visits home. It was good—Quincy Jones
was playing in it—and its sounds kept echoing in his mind. When he
asked around he discovered that this small Catholic institution harbored
a first-rate music department that took the pop forms as seriously as it
did the classics. Here was a chance, he thought, to get a formal grounding in the music he loved and buttress his confidence in his self-taught
abilities. He decided to return to Seattle and see what it would take to
qualify for admission.

He had to work, of course—first at Bethlehem Steel, where he
joined the night shift tending the blast furnaces, then at Boeing Aircraft,
where he found a job in the parts department. In the meantime, though,
he applied for admission to the college and believed he had a good
chance of acceptance. If not, he was determined to find a junior college
where he could bring himself up to speed academically and then enter
the school. It seemed to him that he had, at last, found his direction.

But now it was 1951. The Korean War had begun the previous year,
and suddenly he was confronted with a draft notice. It had been forwarded on from one of his previous addresses, and he found he had only
seven days before he was required to report for induction. He called the
board, said he was about to enter college and asked for an exemption.
But with a war in progress, draft boards were in no mood to indulge
young men who had wasted years finding themselves while their more
prudent contemporaries had been busy securing their college exemp-
tions. Besides, "I wasn't tricky enough or smart enough to dance
around, or figure out how to dance around." Clint's tone is uncharacteristically bitter about this passage, and Fritz Manes remembers him
turning up in Oakland a few days before induction and spending most
of the time drinking regretfully. Lost, he had been on the verge of finding himself. Now it appeared he must lose himself again in a newly
massing army. He was sent to Fort Ord, on the Monterey Peninsula, for
basic training.

TWO

KIND OF A MAGIC LIFE

It would be agreeable to report irony in full twist at this point in Clint Eastwood's life, to observe this lost young man finding himself, despite his reluctance, trepidation and gloomy anger, in the United States Army. But when you loathe something as profoundly as Clint Eastwood did the military, and its exactions are imposed on you involuntarily, its instructive possibilities are likely to be modest.

Two years in the army, though, unquestionably helped him to develop certain significant aspects of himself. These included the discovery of a previously unsuspected ability to manipulate an institution and a situation not of his choosing to his own advantage, an embrace of a region, a landscape, that would claim his loyalty for the rest of his life and, finally, an encounter with mortality that would help both to focus his ambitions and to imbue him with that mild but palpable fatalism that marks his attitude toward his profession and his fame, armoring him against both disappointment and starry hubris.

In 1951, at Fort Ord, his attitude toward the army and toward the Korean conflict was typical of many young men pressed into service for a war in which America's interests were difficult to apprehend. The army was something to be endured with the least imaginable effort. Early in basic training, for example, one of Clint's top sergeants several times proposed that he apply for Officer's Candidate School—"I evidently depicted what an officer should look like"—and he repeatedly rejected the idea, on the grounds that it would increase his obligation to the army. "Two years is the maximum I want to be here," he remembers saying to the sergeant.

As for the war itself, it was the trip to it rather than service at the front that scared him. "The boat trip over there would have killed me," he says. "You'd hear all the horror stories of World War Two, when they shipped the guys across, and they were all sick on the high seas, and packed in there like sardines." He shudders at the thought of such confinement, the inability to get out and walk. "That's the part you wouldn't have any control over, because you can't go in and volunteer, and say, 'Hey put me in a plane and fly me in there, get me to Seoul real quick.'"

In these circumstances he did something totally out of character—at least as it had shown itself up to now. He worked a con, and his face still beams with pleasure as he recalls it. Having quickly observed that military life is "a constant game of trying to put yourself in a position to do less work," Clint was eager to play. So was a new friend he had made at Fort Ord, a former schoolteacher named Dick Scott. One day, having endured many a dismal indoctrination class, Scott said to Clint, "Let's go over to Division Faculty. I can teach these classes we're all falling asleep in."

"You can," said Clint, "but I can't. I don't have any experience teaching."

"Aw, what the hell. You oughta come over. We'll fake it."

So they did, and found themselves being interviewed by a dubious captain, when a lieutenant wandered by and said, "We need a couple of guys over at the pool." That sounded just right to Clint. "I just casually leaned over and said, 'They got some jobs in the motor pool?' and the guy says, 'No, no, the swimming pool.'"

Better and better. He had a lifesaving certificate from the Red Cross and had worked as a lifeguard, and so was qualified to administer swimming tests and haul floundering recruits out of the water. In those days, as Clint recalls, "I never pushed myself, I was not very assertive," and his temptation was, as usual, to put himself forward very quietly—"I was always the kind of guy who would say, 'Gee, if you ever need anybody. . . .'" But to his own astonishment, having just watched his friend do a wonderful pitch, he found himself "up and selling. 'Have I got a deal for you . . . ,' starting to make it sound like I'd swum with Weissmuller in the Olympics." He says it was as if he could see his whole life flashing before him: his past—full of self-effacement, hanging back—and his future—more basic training, shipping out to Korea, combat—and recognized that this was the brass ring "and I had to grab it."

The captain was reasonably impressed with Privates Scott and Eastwood, but he was not terribly encouraging. The need for warm bodies overseas was pressing. They left his office not daring to hope for much more than "four or five weeks of goofing around and swimming or something." But in a couple of days word came down: They were being transferred to Division Faculty and assigned to duty at the pool.

A master sergeant was in charge of this facility, and he was off partying much of the time, while Clint and Dick Scott did most of the work, which, besides administering swimming tests and teaching the basic strokes, also included cleaning out the latrines.

Still, this was about as good as it got in that man's army. Scott and the rest of the pool staff were soon shipped out, and Clint became the senior man poolside, where he would finagle living quarters. Eventually, he received permission to work out of uniform—in a sweatshirt and a pair of khakis. So it would remain for the rest of Clint's hitch.

The pool became a kind of informal social center. Among those dropping by to improve their tans were a number of actors who had been drafted, including three who would ultimately gain fame as television series leads: Richard Long (77 Sunset Strip, The Big Valley), Martin Milner (Route 66) and David Janssen (The Fugitive). The oft-repeated story is that they encouraged the handsome young swimming instructor to think about an acting career when he got out of the service, but Clint doesn't recall that. It's possible, though, that their talk about their civilian careers piqued his interest. "They all seemed to enjoy themselves" was his dry comment to a later interviewer.

If anyone directly encouraged him to think about acting it was Norman Barthold, who gained a measure of local fame at Fort Ord when a picture he appeared in before being drafted, She's Working Her Way Through College, starring Virginia Mayo and Ronald Reagan, played the post theater. It was a dismal remake of the James Thurber–Elliott Nugent play and film The Male Animal, but the guys were impressed that their buddy had worked in such close proximity to its luscious leading lady, if not the future leader of the free world. Barthold's army job was in classification and assignment, so he was the source of valuable information about who was and was not about to be shipped out. Since his office was nearby, Clint encouraged him to hang out at the pool as much as he liked. "The more I talked to him, the more I thought I wouldn't mind studying acting," he recalls. But he still insists the idea was idle and passing, not a turning point.

Indeed, it may be that the Fort Ord experience that most affected his future work occurred not at the pool, but in various Division Faculty classrooms, where he was expected to take over the occasional teaching assignment and to run the movie projector when visual aids were part of the curriculum. He prepared his material carefully—military history and recognizing military insignia were two of the subjects—and gained a little confidence about making public appearances. But it was a film he was frequently called upon to run that made the most lasting impression on him. This was the documentary John Huston had made for the signal corps during World War II, The Battle of San Pietro. It is, of course, a superbly intimate account of a battle, narrated understat-

edly in the Hemingway manner by Huston himself. Running it over
and over Eastwood became interested in Huston's work and absorbed
the cadences of his unique voice. Almost four decades later, these memories contributed to his decision to make the screen adaptation of *White
Hunter, Black Heart,* Peter Viertel's roman à clef about the director, and
to Clint's ability to mimic Huston accurately when he played him.

★   ★   ★

Not long after he settled into his pleasant routine at the swimming pool,
Clint got a weekend pass and decided to return to Seattle to visit his parents and see a young woman he was interested in. A friend told him that
if you wore a uniform you could hitch a ride on a military aircraft, and
so one Friday afternoon they both turned up at a naval air station on the
Monterey Peninsula. Sure enough, a twin-engine Beechcraft was heading for Seattle, and they jumped in for a bumpy, but otherwise unevent-
ful, trip north. On Sunday afternoon, he and his friend reported to the
Sands Point Naval Air Station in Seattle, not at all certain about getting
a return flight.

They discovered, however, that a couple of Douglas ADs, dive-
bombers under the command of naval reservists, were about to take off
for the Alameda Naval Air Station near Oakland, close enough to Fort
Ord for them to make it back to the post before their passes expired.
These were not, perhaps, ideal aircraft for a person of claustrophobic
temperament. The pilot's compartment contained just one seat. There
was another tiny compartment in the tail of the plane for a radar operator, with a small window, some mysterious instruments, an oxygen
mask and an intercom, with which one could talk to the pilot. Clint
somehow folded his large frame into this tight space.

Somebody showed him how to activate the oxygen and the intercom, and helped him buckle on a parachute and strap himself into the
seat. He was dubious—"I notice it's kind of trashy in there, pieces of
cable laying around"—but with no other options available, he made
himself as comfortable as he could, thus beginning a journey into hell.
It is not a trip that Clint has discussed in much detail in the past. He has
usually skimmed rather quickly over it in interviews, lest it be mistaken
for a heroic adventure. It was not—but it was suspenseful and shaping.

The weather was overcast as they took off—not uncommon in Seattle—but Clint imagined that once they left the area it might improve.
Visibility, however, remained low for the rest of the flight. Worse, about
the time they reached cruising altitude, his door popped open. Air pressure would sometimes close it, but then it would fly open again. He re-

ported this distressing news to the pilot, a Lieutenant Anderson, who told him just to twist the latch shut. He struggled with it for about fifteen minutes, with no success; it was broken beyond in-flight repair. "It was rather chilly in there," Clint recalls mildly. "This is not a heated plane, or pressurized." Once again he reported his difficulties to Anderson, who responded, "Look, I'm busy right now. I've got to get back to you."

Anderson began to take Clint's plight a little more seriously when his colleague, flying the plane in which Clint's friend was riding, radioed: "By the way, your rear door's open." Clint, by this time, was trying to hold it shut with brute force, fighting tremendous pressure. "You've got to get that rear door," Anderson ordered, some urgency now in his voice. Holding it with one hand, Clint groped around for some of the loose cable he had noticed and managed to wire the door shut—precariously. He was still afraid it was going to be pulled off its hinges.

Their troubles were just beginning. Somewhere near Medford, Oregon, the pilot of their companion plane discovered, as Clint later found out, that his oxygen system wasn't working, and radioed that he was going to set down for repairs. So they flew on alone, higher, too, as Anderson tried to get above the bad weather. Clint, finding himself getting woozy in the thinner air, grabbed the oxygen mask—and discovered that it, too, was inoperative.

He reported this new problem to Anderson, and in the midst of their conversation, the intercom began to fail. Clint could hear Anderson, but the pilot could not hear him. Listening in on Anderson's radio transmissions Clint now learned that he was beginning to have trouble transmitting and receiving. Then the intercom failed completely and all communication between pilot and passenger ceased. Clint had noticed some cables running through his compartment that had moved when Anderson had closed his canopy at the beginning of the flight. If they moved again it would mean, he thought, that Anderson was opening the canopy preparatory to bailing out. He vowed to keep his eye on the cables and to parachute out himself as soon as he saw them move.

By this time the plane had been in the air somewhere between two and a half and three hours, and Clint judged they must be near the end of their fuel. He became aware, as well, that they were losing altitude. He guessed that, having lost the use of his electronic navigational aids along with his radio, Anderson was looking for a hole in the cloud cover, so that he could get a visual fix on his position. He also noticed that Anderson had turned west, out to sea, and for a moment Clint got a glimpse of the Golden Gate Bridge and the San Francisco skyline. "And I thought, Oh, God, phew."

But his relief was short-lived. Anderson now turned north, heading toward Point Reyes along the Marin County Coast. (Clint discovered later that, knowing he was about to run out of fuel, Anderson was determined not to ditch above a populated area.) Clint was opening and closing his seat belt, practicing a quick release when the time came to bail out.

But the cockpit cables remained stationary, and the plane was dropping lower and lower. Then Clint heard an explosion—Anderson had blown off an auxiliary fuel tank that was attached to the belly of the fuselage. It was becoming clear that "he wasn't gonna just bail out and say, 'Adios, kid in the back.'" Anderson was taking them down for a crash landing at sea.

Soon they were skimming along a few feet above the water, and at that height Clint became aware of how fast they were going. "It was like being in a high-speed boat." The thought running through his mind was "Well, some people have made it through these things before. . . . I guess I was scared, but I was more resigned." Anderson dropped the tail, it hit the water, "and we bounced along for I don't know how many yards, pancaked along, and then all of a sudden—pow!—we just nosed right in."

There was a brief struggle with the wire that had been holding Clint's door on, but then Clint was out, clambering along the fuselage. The plane was canted in the water, but he was able to stand high and dry on the trailing edge of one wing. Now Anderson's canopy popped open, and here came the pilot, unhurt, and "pretty cool. He wasn't panicked for a guy who'd lost his plane in the ocean. He wasn't seeing court-martials before his eyes."

They could see the cliffs at Point Reyes, three or four miles away, and they were aware that the plane was going to sink fairly quickly. Both of them knew that sinking ships drew survivors down with them, and though they weren't sure the comparatively light plane would do the same, they weren't in a mood to take the chance.

"I don't know about you, but I'm getting the hell outta here," said Clint, and he jumped into the water and swam off to what seemed a safe distance. Anderson quickly followed. It was late afternoon, still overcast, and the ocean swells were high. They vowed to try to stay together as they struck out for land.

They were trying to swim straight in to shore. But the current kept pushing them northward. "And then it started getting dark, and I lost him. I didn't know whether he was alive or where the hell he was. And I wasn't about to start yelling, because it wastes a lot of energy. I went through jellyfish schools and all kinds of things, and they became fluorescent at night. It was like some science-fiction deal. By this time, you know, your mind is—talk about hallucinating." Occasionally he could see the lights of houses and, as he told one reporter, "All I could think of was there was some guy up there sitting in front of his fireplace, having a beer. I wanted to be doing the same thing."

Luckily, he didn't find out until some years later that this area was a breeding ground for sharks, "or I probably wouldn't have lasted. Just the thought of it, you know."

Once he had cleared the jellyfish Clint found himself in a kelp bed. He employed a shallow breaststroke to avoid entanglement with the seaweed and managed to maintain slow headway. "And then I got in past the kelp and started hearing surf up there. On the one hand, you're excited to go in, on the other, you could just get pounded on the rocks. There was a lot of phosphorus in the water that night, and the phosphorus was making the water really glow—it was strange."

But by this eerie light he could make out a spot on the beach where no spray was being tossed up—perhaps, he hoped, a small beach. "So I kind of worked my way into that—just partly luck, because everywhere the water was very rough. And I got into this spot and had a really rough time climbing out." A strong undertow had carved steeply into the beach at this point, and it also kept pulling the exhausted swimmer back into the water. But he found a boulder to cling to and, after catching his breath, was able at last to make his way onto the beach.

Clint had nothing on but a khaki shirt and pants. He had long since kicked off his shoes. He was freezing cold, and he could see that the boulders surrounding his refuge were huge and difficult to climb. The hallucinations worsened now. By the light of the phosphorescent sea he kept thinking he saw Anderson in the water. "I'd run out and grab this one rock and I'd run back and sit there. And then I could see the rock moving back and forth, and I'd run back and I'd grab the rock."

Finally, he calmed himself, accepted the fact that Anderson was nowhere to be found and pulled himself painfully up through the rocks around the cove and emerged on a broad beach, with a strong steady light beckoning in the distance, closer to him than the Point Reyes lighthouse. The straightest line toward it took him across a lagoon, where he startled a flock of birds, which flew up around him unnervingly, and then to a massive chain-link fence. "Your imagination says, 'Well, it's some sort of concentration camp, or some electrical field, I might be killed in here. . . .'" But he climbed the fence anyway, making his way through a field of small antennae, heading toward a concrete blockhouse with the light that had guided him and a very tall antenna on top of it.

The installation was, in fact, an RCA relay station, transmitting radiograms across the Pacific. Inside, he found "this one lone guy, and he looked up and said, 'What are you doing here?' He said it like it was definitely private property, and I said, 'I've just been in an accident,' and he says, 'You mean in an automobile?' And I'm standing there, I'm just looking like shit, and I said, 'No, we were in a plane crash, we were in a plane out here.' He said, 'Oh, yeah, yeah, I heard that Alameda was reporting somebody was missing.'" The radio operator added that he had seen flares being dropped by a search mission.

So the great adventure came to an end, with stunned banalities on the one hand, strangely incurious ones on the other. The Coast Guard was informed, a pickup truck was dispatched to retrieve Clint, and he was reunited with Anderson, whom the tide had drawn farther north than it had Clint, at the Coast Guard station. They spent the night there, and then Clint was returned to the Presidio, the army base in San Francisco, where he was told that there would be an inquiry and that he would most likely be called upon to testify at it. He thinks it possible that he was never sent to Korea because the army wanted to keep him conveniently available for the investigation into the crash, but he was never required to speak on the record about it.

The crash, as it happened, was almost as frightening for his mother and father as it was for Clint. His mother recalls a Seattle newspaper reporter awakening her the next morning to ask, "'Are you related to the Eastwood who went down in San Francisco Bay last night?' And, of course, I almost fainted, because I had put him on that plane. . . . It was very harrowing."

A day or two later, Clint found himself back at the swimming pool, staring into space "like a person feels when [he's had] a concussion," trying to digest the experience, which had not quite run its full course. Four or five months later, he decided to revisit his folks in Seattle. This time, taking no chances, he booked himself on a commercial flight. There was, though, no getting above the clouds in that plane, either. It plowed right through a storm system, "and, Jesus, trays were hitting the ceiling, people were yelling, and it was just a terrible flight." He got off the plane shaking and ashen, and his mother, meeting the flight, thought he was ill. He dismissed her concern casually, but he did not fly again for several years thereafter. "I figured somebody was trying to tell me something."

The question is, what did he tell himself in the aftermath of these experiences? He agrees with his mother, who, considering his several youthful brushes with disaster, not to mention his subsequent good fortune, says that "he's had kind of a magic life." But that has not made him feel invulnerable. Rather the opposite: Clint's struggle with the sea seems to have granted him an abiding sense of the individual's smallness when it is measured against the forces of nature, the vastness of the universe.

Thinking back on his misadventure, Clint also recalls flying across the country in the days before jet planes, when slower speeds and lower altitudes encouraged reflection on the lives being lived on the ground sliding by below, and thinking: "What would happen if a giant stepped on this town? It would be a massive news thing, but from a perspective up here it would be nothing. I mean, there's galaxies going on out to the Milky Way, and you see there are billions of stars." Personalizing the thought, he adds, "If I get hit by a bus somebody will say, 'Oh, Clint Eastwood was run over by a bus,' but it's not going to change anything on the planet. You've just got to be realistic. You get a break, you're here, you do the best you can with it."

He feels approximately the same way about aging. "If you never take yourself too seriously, you're realistic about what happens. Thirty years from now there's going to be a whole new set of people here, and Tom Cruise will be an old guy, and he'll be sitting around going, 'Well, geez, what's my next project?' It's just the way the world is."

Or, at any rate, one thinks, it's the way Clint Eastwood began to perceive the world one night when he dragged himself out of the Pacific Ocean, shivering and seeing things, and realized that he had been given a break, was still here, spared for some purpose it was now up to him to imagine.

★　★　★

Nothing came to him immediately, except, perhaps, a vision of where he would like to spend most of whatever time he had been granted. Clint had a car on the base, and one night, when he had a pass, but not enough time to travel up to San Francisco or Oakland, he decided to visit Carmel, just twenty minutes away, and see if it matched its reputation. In his eyes, it did: He took to driving over there whenever he could.

"One day I was down there, and it was a real beautiful day, the fog bank was moving back, and I was wandering around and thought, you know, if I ever had a buck I'd sure like to live here." Carmel was then largely a community of second homes for people from the Bay Area, but there was a little group of former servicemen who had discovered it while stationed at Ord and had found jobs in Carmel, and that made it seem a plausible goal for him.

For the moment, despite—or possibly because of—his easy duty he found his contempt for the army growing into what would become a lifelong distrust of bureaucracies, especially government bureaucracies. The ill-kempt navy plane that had almost cost him his life had not improved his view of what he describes as "the biggest, most poorly run corporation in the world—the government." But he doubtless would have come to this view even in less dramatic circumstances. Many did. As the economist Milton Friedman has observed, for millions of young Americans military service "enhanced their appreciation of the value and meaning of individual freedom" by giving them a close-up view of "a collectivist organization in action." Clint Eastwood was certainly one of them: "The only saving grace we have is that the armies of potential enemies are probably just as screwed up."

In a way, he was being ungrateful. The relatively easygoing atmosphere at Fort Ord permitted Clint a life as unsoldierly as a soldier's could be. He supplemented his pay—and supported his car—by working first at a nearby sugar refinery, then as a bartender and "floor manager" (a euphemism for bouncer) at the Non-Commissioned Officers Club.

Despite these exertions, Clint had plenty of spare time, some of which he devoted to following a jazz group headed by Lennie Niehaus to its off-post gigs. A onetime reed player and arranger with Stan Kenton, Niehaus would turn out to be perhaps the most significant friend Clint made at the swimming pool. They met when the musician fell and gashed his foot climbing out of the pool. Clint helped him up and conducted him to the infirmary, then stayed with him while stitches were taken. When a medic ordered him to put his boot back on and report to his unit, Clint spoke up for him—"This man has had a serious injury and can't walk"—gaining Niehaus a day or two of limited duty and his lifelong regard as well. They lost touch when they were mustered out, but met later when Niehaus was orchestrating for composer Jerry Fielding. Clint later called him "out of the blue" to score *Tightrope* and he has done the same for the majority of his films since then.

Not that jazz was Clint's sole nonmilitary interest. He also dropped in fairly frequently at Carmel's Mission Ranch—which he would later buy and renovate—for teachers' night, which attracted single schoolteachers with an offer of half-price drinks. There were no serious romantic encounters, at least on his part, but there was one woman who developed an obsession with him, threatening (with what degree of seriousness he could not tell) self-destruction when he tried to end the affair. He would recall this incident, he says, when he read the script for *Play Misty for Me;* it confirmed its realism for him.

But as his military service drew to a close, he was spending more time thinking about his future than he was about casual romance. He was more determined than ever to go to college, and the GI Bill made that more feasible than before. He considered Monterey Peninsula Junior College and College of the Pacific at Stockton, either of which would do for a semester or two, so he could get his credits in order and reapply to Seattle University and its music course. Then a friend of his named Chuck Hill started talking about Los Angeles City College, making it seem, in some way that Clint can't quite remember, rather appealing. Maybe it was its proximity to the well-remembered L.A. jazz clubs. Maybe it was its proximity to the movie industry, for by this time he had made another acquaintance, an assistant film editor in civilian life, and he, too, began encouraging him to try acting. But as with Norman Barthold, there was no urgency in the advice. "I never had anyone say, 'Yeah, here's what you have to do.'" As with so much else in his life at this time, he simply caught a dispassionate drift, and applied to the Los Angeles institution, where he was accepted.

Clint had a few months to spare between discharge and the beginning of school and spent most of the summer in Seattle with his parents. At the end of the summer Clint went to San Francisco to see Don Kincade, among other pals, and to hitch a ride south from there with Chuck Hill. Before leaving San Francisco, Clint was recruited by Kincade for a blind date. He was going with a sorority girl at Berkeley, and she had this friend, Maggie Johnson.

She was, as Kincade recalls, going pretty steadily with another guy. But she agreed to a casual double date—just a few beers at a college hangout. She would recall: "I came down the stairs of the sorority house, and [Clint] had his back to me. When he turned around, I was amazed at what he looked like. Plus he was understated, and that kind of appealed to me. I'm kind of understated myself."

Maggie was tall and blond with a trim figure and a nice sense of humor. She also loved the outdoors, and as Clint told one interviewer, "We hit it off right away. She was the kind of girl I really liked; there was nothing phoney about her." They dated a few more times, and since she was soon to graduate, and was planning to return to Los Angeles—her parents lived in Alhambra—that encouraged him to think that he had made the right choice of colleges.

★   ★   ★

In Los Angeles, Clint got a job managing a small apartment building on Oakhurst Drive, far south in the Beverly Hills flats. He had been led to believe that the work would be light—minor repairs, showing vacant apartments to potential occupants. But in return for his greatly reduced rent he soon discovered that he was on call twenty-four hours a day for emergency repairs and that he was also expected to paint entire units when they fell vacant. It was difficult for him to manage, given his schedule at school. Moreover, since he needed cash, he had also taken a job at a gas station.

He was enrolled in the business administration program at City College—"You know, what everybody takes when they don't know what they want to do"—which he found generally uninteresting. On the other hand, City College, which is close to downtown Los Angeles and boasts a brick, ivy-colored administration building, which in those days occasionally doubled as an eastern college in the movies, had a strong drama department, and Clint began "looking into" its programs, auditing the odd class now and then. The drift toward an acting career was starting to accelerate. Fritz Manes thinks that Clint was beginning to contrast what he was gathering from his courses about the restrictiveness of business life, bound to a desk from nine to five, subject to all manner of corporate constraints, with what he was beginning to sense about the actor's much freer life. "I mean, can you imagine Eastwood in a bank? Or as a real estate broker—take all those tests and do all that stuff? I don't think he wanted to do something that was too taxing. I don't think he realized how taxing acting was."

Certainly the people encouraging his hesitant ambitions in this direction had no sophisticated understanding of what the work entailed. They included Hill, who around this time obtained a job at Universal, and a law student named Howard Cogan, who was for a while Clint's roommate and ran with a young showbiz crowd (he introduced Clint to Mort Sahl, among other aspiring performers). These men didn't know or care much about acting, but they did recognize a hunk when they saw one. Like Manes, they had observed that Clint was "a tremendous presence. He'd walk into a bar and sit down, and you'd see gals start to look over, and you'd see guys start to wonder."

The town is always full of young studs like that—and their gorgeous female equivalents—waiting on tables, waiting for the big break, which just enough of them obtain, thus keeping an essentially hopeless and sometimes self-destructive dream alive. But however others might have seen him, Clint didn't regard himself as beefcake. He simply thought that if looks might possibly get him past some studio gate, then he'd better be "prepared to take advantage of that chance when it came along." So in the evenings he began auditing more acting classes, which were held at the various studios springing up around town in imitation of the Stanislavsky-based instruction available in New York, then far along in the process of revolutionizing the profession.

He was still hanging back a bit, still not entirely committed to this radical course, and he says now, "I probably shouldn't have been an actor at all. I had no great quest to stand up in front of people, in front of an audience." To this day he thinks "the ideal thing would be to act just by yourself, in a room somewhere," though he concedes that "the next-best thing is doing it in front of a minimal crew [i.e., on a movie set]," and, after that, appearing before small audiences of people "who really enjoy it [i.e., in acting classes]."

Looking back, he says, "You thought if the guy had a Russian name that meant that he knew how to teach acting," and adds, "I'm not sure how much benefit they [the acting classes] had. Really, it was sort of a pseudointellectual thing, a fad that people were going through at the time." He cites Paul Mazursky's movie, *Next Stop, Greenwich Village,* as a reasonably realistic representation of the moment's mood as he experienced it.

Actually, Clint seems to have been more interested than he allowed himself to show then or to admit now. If he did not at first understand how deep the "dream of passion" (to borrow the title of Lee Strasberg's memoir) ran, and knew next to nothing about the long history and high reformist ardor that informed the Stanislavskian tradition, he did see what everyone who cared anything about acting in those days saw: that the success of a rising generation of actors (of whom Marlon Brando was, of course, the most visible), trained in one version or another of Stanislavsky's system (the word he preferred to "method," which was Strasberg's coinage), was increasingly inarguable.

This triumph had been long in coming and owed much to such European theatrical émigrés as the director Richard Boleslavsky, the actress Maria Ouspenskaya (both trained in Stanislavsky's company) and Erwin Piscator (a German director who founded the Dramatic Workshop at New York's New School, which sheltered both Strasberg and his rival, Stella Adler, in their early teaching days). After the sensational visit of Stanislavsky's company to New York during the 1922–23 season, many in the American theater were awakened to the value of a new, more intense psychological realism in performance. Boleslavsky's Laboratory Theater kept the flame alive, the Group Theater fanned it, and Piscator guarded it in the years between the Group's failure and the founding of the Actors Studio in 1947. More directly relevant, around 1940 a

Stanislavskian outpost, the Actors Lab, was established in Los Angeles. Many of the teachers Clint encountered were or had been connected to the lab, which was also the object of intense scrutiny by the House Un-American Activities Committee during its wildly misplaced investigation of communism in Hollywood.

The Stanislavskians were a contentious and schismatic crowd, but they all shared an implicit belief that by turning acting into a teachable discipline with generally acknowledged standards they might impart to this craft the respectability of a profession. In turn, they hoped this new status would aid them and their disciples in rescuing Broadway and Hollywood from their shabby commercialism. In this, they failed, but they did at least radically change the way actors looked at themselves and their work. In effect, they were given permission to take themselves seriously. This was no small gift to, among others, Clint Eastwood, so dubious about this occupation, so unwilling to enter it if it represented no more than another form of drifting.

Luckily, one of the first acting teachers he encountered was George Shdanoff, who was, in turn, a disciple of Michael Chekhov, who was reasonably well known as a character actor—he had won an Academy Award nomination for his portrayal of a psychiatrist in Hitchcock's *Spellbound*—but was, within the business, a legendary teacher and theoretician of acting. Nephew of the playwright and a sometime colleague of Stanislavsky in the Moscow Art Theater, Chekhov was at the height of his influence when Clint attended some of his lectures at Shdanoff's studio, for in 1953 he had published his book, *To the Actor,* which he dedicated to Shdanoff. Much discussed in theatrical circles at the time, it distilled the wisdom of a lifetime (Clint still recommends it to young actors).

Chekhov and his followers did not emphasize sense and emotional memory, cornerstones of Stanislavsky's theories, particularly as the influential Strasberg taught them. The Chekhovians felt it limited the actor and was a detriment to ensemble work. Chekhov, like Stella Adler, believed the actor should not be obliged to reach too deeply into himself to pull up the materials of his performance. Rather, he taught actors to reach out to one another and to the audience as well. "The dramatic art is a collective art," he wrote, "and therefore however talented the actor may be, he will not be able to make full use of his ability to improvise if he isolates himself from the ensemble, his partners."

Chekhov developed a psychology of gestures, offering his students a series of exercises to help them in this study, which he codified in his book. Beatrice Straight, the actress who was one of his earlier students and remained one of his most ardent champions, said this was "a way to help actors get the feeling they needed, without thinking." Straight admitted that Chekhov's fear of the intellect led him away from a concern with the well-spoken phrase. "You could spot any Chekhov student by how he spoke on the stage," Straight told the writer Foster Hirsch, "not in the right way." But, of course, a certain eccentric naturalism often arose out of this.

Typically, a Chekhov class contained many eurhythmic exercises, and when, a little later, Clint began doing scenes in class, he remembers repeating certain sets of gestures before going on stage. "If you were playing a very aggressive person, you would do psychological gestures like punching. Or if you're supposed to do a scene where you're going to break up with this gal, you kind of do [brushing aside] gestures and then when you walk on you automatically have that feeling of wanting to be away from that person." In Clint's summary, Chekhov believed that acting was built out of "certain instincts that you already have and the question is just to channel all that stuff into some sort of visual image for you."

In Clint's early film and television work it is hard to discern much technique of any kind, let alone specifically Chekhovian technique. The parts are small and usually peripheral to the plot's main business. He is, at best, an eager presence, trying (sometimes a little too hard) to be helpful to the work at hand and to establish his presence—very far from the easy naturalism of his mature screen presence. But in the long run, Chekhov's influence on him would prove substantial. Chekhov's distrust of an overintellectual approach to acting confirmed and rationalized a similar antipathy in Clint. And his appreciation as a director for the spontaneous gesture, his preference for the rough, unpolished line reading over the more-carefully-considered one, his overall belief that truth is more likely to be found in nonverbal rather than verbal expression, all surely have roots in Chekhov's schooling.

He is also, as both an actor and a director, someone who believes in ensembles—here his jazz aesthetic also comes into play—the atmosphere he established on his sets when he is directing being quite clearly aimed at reducing his actors' isolation, forging them into a comfortably functioning unit. His willingness to let his actors find their roles in their own ways, not imposing on them, is of a piece with that philosophy. Even Stanislavsky's books, as Clint reads them, are about "teaching you to teach yourself. He never talks about himself as a teacher."

But it was another aspect of Chekhov's teaching that appealed to Clint with particular force, and which he found immediately useful in helping to overcome what we might call his stage shyness. That was Chekhov's belief that the actor must "center" whatever character he is playing in some portion of his own physical being. This might be in the curl of his lips or the set of his hips, but whatever it is, that is the phys-ical residence of the fictive figure's primary emotions—the place he is coming from, as we would say now. For Clint, this was a godsend, be-cause "in placing these centers you can actually take your self-awareness away to the point where you're comfortable in front of an audience." Working this way, he was not exposing his whole shy self, only a finite, objectively chosen part of that self. Again, an analogy to jazz occurs. These centers were to him what his piano had been, a way of objectify-ing emotions, expressing them without exposing himself totally.

There is one more aspect of Chekhov's system that Clint does not mention, but Beatrice Straight and others do. That is what she calls "reaching out to your partner and to the audience . . . beaming an aura, sending out qualities in an almost mystical sense." It was at the develop-ment of this capacity that all the instruction was aimed, and ultimately, perhaps, that's what all star actors do in the movies. However they come by this capacity, whether by training or birthright, it is what sets them apart from other performers who may be technically their superiors. Who can doubt that the vengeful protagonist of the Sergio Leone west-erns, or Dirty Harry Callahan, or for that matter Will Munny, are beam-ing something at us that goes beyond characterization as it is usually defined in films and theater? It is admittedly odd, even vaguely comical, to trace the creation of these figures back to ideas that can, in turn, trace their roots back to turn-of-the-century Moscow. But if that journey seems too long and winding to undertake, it should be obvious that in the minds of most of his audience the screen presence we know as "Clint Eastwood" is more aura than man, created out of a lifetime of gestures, which derive not from a complex whole, but from certain as-pects of that whole—"centers," if you will—that he chose to develop and exploit.

One does not want to make too much of all this. Some of what he saw—and did—when, a little later, he became an active participant in, rather than an observer of, acting classes struck him as ludicrous, and still does. The only time he had a conversation with Marlon Brando it was about their student days, and Clint remembers him saying "he felt like a fool in classes because he was playing chickens and I said, 'Well, shit, I had to do that too.' I mean, we did classes where we were chickens or inanimate objects, even." He seems to recall having impersonated a teapot somewhere along the line.

On the other hand, one should not make too little of his studies, ei-ther. The depth of his interest and the length of his involvement with the study of acting may come as a surprise to some, since he has never spoken at length in public about it. The unsophisticated like to believe that movie stars are untutored; this helps sustain the fantasy that their fame and wealth are accidental, thus democratically available to all. Some sophisticates like to believe the same thing; it helps them to sustain their contempt for popular successes they believe to be unearned. But the fact is that Eastwood took much of what he learned very much to heart, and it is still there, informing his work.

★   ★   ★

Clint was certainly not above trying to advance his career by means cruder than dutiful study. Chuck Hill encouraged him to visit the Universal lot, and Clint took him up on the invitation. As Steven Spielberg did later, he learned how to sneak into the studio. "I just visited their sets and just kind of hung out." Was he hoping to be discovered? Surely by this time he had some idea of the striking first impression he was capable of making.

But acting was still an exotic thought. Besides, there were distractions, most notably, Maggie Johnson. Clint had continued to see her since arriving in Los Angeles, and their relationship was deepening. They particularly loved the beach. Surfing was not then, according to Clint, the teenage fad it was soon to become among young Californians. It was a sport for people in their twenties and thirties, and he and Maggie were often at Huntington Beach or San Onofre with their boards. They also liked to bodysurf on gray days at San Clemente after a storm had stirred the waters.

At the time Maggie was living in Altadena, working for a manufacturer's representative. The long distance separating them, and their busy work schedules, helped to make the idea of marriage more attractive to them. Clint thinks he was more reluctant than she was to take the step. He thought they were too young, not well enough established. But, when it comes to marriage, "Guys never have much say about it." Clint shrugs. After all, Maggie came from a nice middle-class background, and in those days young women like her expected to marry after a courtship had proceeded for a certain length of time. Clint, being the obliging young man that he was, never overtly rebellious against social conventions, was not hard to win over, especially since he had the example of his parents' youthful marriage before him.

Above all, marriage "was doable." Clint was still managing the apartment house on Oakhurst Drive, assuring them an affordable rent. If they combined her salary and his odd-job money he could continue his education at City College and they could get by. So on December 19,

1953, they were married in a respectable church wedding, after which they honeymooned in Carmel for a few days.

In retrospect, it seems so terribly fifties. Prosperity, postwar exhaustion, Cold War anxieties—so many large forces have been cited for creating a culture of small, safe hopes, a culture that was conspiring to push young people into marriage as soon as possible. Whatever their immediate prospects, the idea was to get them snugged up and heading toward suburbia. Indeed, Clint and Maggie were slightly above the median age at which Americans married in this decade of falling divorce rates and rising birthrates. But the broad sociological statistics always reckon without restless young men who, for whatever reasons, decide to swim against dictates of caution and the tides of the moment. And Clint Eastwood, as silent as any member of the Silent Majority could possibly be, was one of them. Whatever his goal, it was not a suburban split-level.

THREE

REFINED, AMBITIOUS AND COOPERATIVE

Reflecting on the difficulties he experienced establishing himself as an actor in the 1950s, Clint Eastwood once said: "I just lacked the look that decade seemed to call for." There's something in that. He did not have the introspective sensitivity, or the self-consciously suppressed violence, of Brando or Dean, nor did he have the passivity, the gentility, if you will, of Rock Hudson and Tab Hunter, young dreamboats whose lack of danger and incisiveness suited the other mood of this erotically confused moment.

Tall, solidly built but slender, sandy haired, with cool, appraising blue-green eyes, Clint seemed, if anything, a throwback to the Gary Cooper–Jimmy Stewart type. Those men were still prospering in the movies, of course, but their appeal was to the older audience. The kids seemed to want something else, or so studio executives believed.

Luckily, this aspect of the current conventional wisdom had not been vouchsafed to a veteran cinematographer named Irving Glassberg. He was one of the people Clint had encountered in his forays on the Universal lot, or, to call it by its then-rightful name (which few did), the Universal-International lot. Glassberg saw in him a good-looking young man of a sort that had traditionally done well in the movies. He didn't predict stardom. Indeed, at first he didn't broach the subject of coming to work at the studio. Glassberg was "a real sports nut," as Clint recalls, for whom swimming was a particular passion, and they talked more about that than they did about moviemaking. Clint and Maggie began seeing Glassberg and his wife socially, and eventually the cameraman mentioned the possibility of Clint auditioning for the studio's talent program.

Most of the studios still had such programs, reminders of their glory days, when heavy schedules of in-house production made it useful to have lots of pretty faces and bodies under inexpensive contract—"starlets and studlets," as Jack Kosslyn, an acting coach who began teaching at Universal around this time, characterized them.

The contract players received basic acting instruction and were, in turn, available for small roles and other chores around the lot—dubbing, posing for publicity photos, attending premieres, working in screen tests with still-newer newcomers. At this time, at Universal, they were often called upon to strike poses for the new 3-D cameras the studio was testing. Along with the wide-screen processes and stereophonic sound, 3-D was supposed to offer technological competition to small-screen, black-and-white television, then terrorizing the industry. The young women—some of whom were winners and high finishers in the Miss Universe contest, which offered contracts with the studio among its prizes—were expected to perform the traditional, distasteful starlet duties, which included serving as hostesses at studio functions and providing companionship for visiting exhibitors. The largest hope, both for the studio and the young contract players, was that one of the youngsters would catch the public's fancy and become a star on the cheap, although that rarely happened. Usually they hung around for a year or two, going nowhere, and then were quietly dropped.

Still, it was a way to get started, and Clint was interested, though he insists his attitude remained "typical southern California," meaning rather cool and laid-back. "It was nothing like this kid with a driving ambition, you know." Nor did Glassberg make his suggestion with great fervor. "'You oughta come out here, you oughta do that,'" Clint recalls him saying. "'You know, guy like you . . . what the hell.' I think maybe he was just being nice to me."

But Glassberg actually harbored a little more conviction than that. He spoke of Clint to Arthur Lubin, a director with whom he sometimes worked, and arranged an introduction. Lubin, a onetime actor, had been directing at Universal since 1935, through the years handling every kind of film the studio made, from big-budget items like the Claude Rains *Phantom of the Opera* and the Maria Montez–Jon Hall Arabian epic *Ali Baba and the Forty Thieves* to the early Abbott and Costello comedies. Kindly, efficient, untroubled and untroubling, he was the kind of craftsman, competent but uninspired, who flourished when studios, functioning along industrial lines, needed to grind out "product" without temperamental fuss or delay for theaters that changed their bills twice a week. He, too, saw something old-fashioned in Clint, who recalls Lubin mentioning Joel McCrea for comparison's sake—and not a bad one, considering Clint's long-standing regard for the actor and his amiable way of presenting himself.

The two men prevailed on the studio to shoot an interview test of

Clint. This was not a screen test in the full sense of the word, in which an actor does a staged dramatic scene with another performer. Clint remembers it as "really weird, because they just turn the camera on and the guy says, 'Now walk up here where the camera is. OK, and turn around . . . and turn to your right, and tell us why you want to be an actor' or some dumb question like that. And you give them some really dumb answer."

When Clint saw the test a few days later, he was appalled. As he once told an interviewer: "I thought I was an absolute clod. It looked pretty good; it was photographed well [by Glassberg], but I thought, 'If that's acting, I'm in trouble.'" Still later, he put the point more vividly: "I went, 'Oh shit. Boy this guy'll never be anything.' You're going, 'straighten up, don't do that, what are you wincing about'—you know, all the self-critical things."

But somebody up there—in the front office—liked him. Or at least didn't hate him. The studio offered him a $75-a-week contract with an option renewable every six months (and a $25 raise each time it was picked up). It covered only forty weeks of the year, meaning that his salary worked out to something less than $60 a week, less taxes, when it was fully prorated. Still, the GI Bill was granting him only $110 a month, and even when he added in his earnings from odd jobs, his current income was less than Universal was offering.

Unfortunately, no one else shared his enthusiasm for this new prospect. "I don't think there was any excitement, particularly on Maggie's part. In fact, as I recall, she didn't really like it." Actually, she was ambiguous about it. "I didn't know what I thought of Clint's becoming an actor," she said later. "It was something I hadn't planned on." It was, she said, "a little spooky at first . . . but I got used to it." There was, however, nothing ambiguous about her parents' response; they were firmly opposed. "Her mother didn't love me that much, anyway, and she thought, My God, my son-in-law being an actor!" When he broached the idea with his father, Clinton Sr.'s response was: "Goddamn. Why?" Even if he was not happy in school, his dad advised him, "Don't do that shit. Don't get into that dream stuff." Clint temporized, saying he just wanted to try it for six months. If it didn't work out, he promised he would resume college, possibly even relocate in Seattle. As he pointed out, he would be able to reclaim his government educational benefits if he went back to school within a year. But his most winning argument was that it should be considered merely as continued schooling, sort of like switching majors.

His father's opposition subsided when a contract was offered and it became clear to him that Clint would be earning a steady, if modest, salary for at least half a year. One could also, perhaps, look upon this as an entry-level position in a large, stable corporation—in the final analysis not so very different from the kind of jobs other young men were being encouraged to take as they began their careers in the era of the Organization Man. Or one could rationalize this as a way for Clint to get something out of his system before embarking on some more conventional career.

For his part, the would-be thespian was more excited than he let on. On May 1, 1954, when he drove his battered Ford convertible, its body half covered in primer paint, its torn canvas top aflap, through the studio gates for the first time, he felt he was embarking on "a big adventure," and it remained so for him "every day." He very quickly came to think, as he puts it: "Shit, people are getting paid for this. This is kind of fun, you know. . . ."

He was aware, though not acutely so, that this was not the most propitious moment to embark on a career in the movies. The early fifties were, as every social history of the period stresses, a troubled time for Hollywood. Its unease is explained by a set of simple statistics: In 1949 approximately 87 million Americans went to the movies every week; in 1950 only 60 million people went, and in the years thereafter the trend continued steadily downward until finally, in the late sixties, weekly ticket sales stabilized in the 20 million range. Another set of figures explains the first ones: In 1949 about 1 million television sets were sold in the United States; thereafter sales rose exponentially to 4 million in 1950, and to 32 million in 1954.

Other factors also contributed to Hollywood's discomfort, most notably the settlement, in 1948, of a long-standing antitrust suit under the terms of which the studios that owned theater chains were obliged eventually to divest themselves of them, thereby cutting off a reliable stream of profits and initiating an anxious competition for bookings in the ever-shrinking number of theaters that remained. With the industry's founding leadership aging and adapting poorly to new conditions, many were predicting that the studios were doomed. Some even suggested that in a few years theatrically shown movies would be a thing of the past. No one clearly foresaw that the outcome of the less-than-dire evolutionary changes then beginning to occur would permit all but one of the major studios to survive and prosper. Certainly the untried actor reporting for his first day of studio work on a spring morning in 1954 had no way of knowing that these changes would eventually benefit him greatly.

Clint's description of his new job as a continuation of schooling by other means had been more apt than he knew. Those in the new talent program had a full schedule of classes, occupying five and a half days a week: acting, diction, singing, dancing, horseback riding. Their immediate supervisor, Joan McTavish, filed reports on their progress, or lack of it, every month to Robert Palmer, the studio executive in charge of the program.

On his very first day Clint was obliged to get up in front of the acting class and do a short scene with Susan Cabot, who had already played leads in a few minor films. Looking around the room he recognized other actors and actresses he had glimpsed in the movies, people he imagined to be far more expert than he. It was not a reassuring moment, and he flashed back on the last time he had been invited to make a fool of himself in public—the junior-high-school play.

But he had resolved that "I was going to stay and grind it out," so he plunged ahead. "It was pretty sad," he recalls. "I had absolutely no idea what I was doing, not one iota." But when he finished, and settled back to watch the others, he had a minor revelation: "They weren't so hot either. Even the people who thought they were hot weren't so hot."

He had observed enough acting classes by this time to recognize that "a couple of people had a little technique." But he also recognized the evasions by which actors try to cover their insecurities, and it heartened him. "I thought, Yeah, if I'm going to do this, I'm really going to do this, I'm not going to just screw around with it. I figured I [had] six months to really get my act in gear."

And that's exactly what he tried to do—not always with the studio's full support, as it turned out. He was not the best actor in the program—looking back, he thinks John Saxon ("very intense," in another student's description) probably was—but he was almost certainly the hardest working. He had to be, for this was, by chance, quite a remarkable group of students.

Brett Halsey, later to be a leading man in a number of minor movies, was among them, and he recalls talking about the program to Robert Palmer when they were both working at Twentieth Century–Fox some years later. The executive told him that the studio would have considered the program a success if, say, one in two hundred of the talent program students had made it to stardom. But of the males in this program, by Halsey's estimate, some 80 percent "made it, in the sense of making a living as actors"—among them John Gavin and Clint's old army buddy David Janssen. Some of the women, too, became reasonably well known, including Mara Corday, Gia Scala and Mamie Van Doren.

Clint seems to have been more focused than he cared to let on to his friends in the program. His lifelong habit is to disguise his more passionate desires with a casual air, as if admitting them might bring bad luck, or humiliation. He says he learned by steady, unspectacular accretion.

He was lucky that in his early months at Universal Katherine Warren was the acting coach. She was, in Halsey's description, "very good and patient and knowing and very, very nice." Practical minded (she had been a working actress for many years), she was, he says, "inspiring in her own way," a very good teacher for an insecure and utterly untutored young actor. Some forty years later, when Clint won his *Unforgiven* Oscars, Halsey wired him, "Congratulations from the Katherine Warren School of Acting."

Practicality and an avoidance of high-flying theory were, as always, the keys to Clint's sensibility. When Jack Kosslyn (who would later teach Clint in his private classes and work for him as a casting director) came aboard, he decided to bring in some well-known figures (they included Marlon Brando, Rod Steiger and Lewis Milestone, the director) to speak to the students. Among them was Dan O'Herlihy, the distinguished Irish actor, who had lately received an Academy Award nomination for the *Robinson Crusoe* he had done under Luis Buñuel's direction, and Clint has never forgotten his advice. "Oh, it's really not so much," he told the students, "just get up and do it." At some point someone asked O'Herlihy what the difference was between acting on the stage and acting on the screen. "They're absolutely the same; there's no difference."

"Everybody's sitting there, waiting for this big lightbulb," says Clint, "and it's 'Oh, you may have to talk a little louder in the theater, because you're not miked up, but other than that, it's the exact same thing.'" Clint loved O'Herlihy's demystification of a topic often enough mystified by its adepts.

There is some documentary evidence to support Clint's growing feeling that he may, at last, have found himself professionally. Some of McTavish's monthly reports on Clint survive, salvaged some years ago from a dumpster on the Universal lot by an acquaintance of his. At the end of his first month, for example, the always sympathetic Warren wrote that he was beginning to gain "authority"; despite problems with projection she predicted he "can become a fine actor." The point she stressed was that "he is natural and easy in what he does and has volunteered in classes to do things he isn't suited for to help or gain experience. Cooperative, prompt, courteous and reliable." The diction coach called him "completely green" to the whole business, but found his spirit and attitude "praiseworthy." Summing up, McTavish wrote: "Our experience with him so far is excellent, as he gives promise of being one of the most conscientious boys we have ever had. . . . He is refined, ambitious and cooperative . . . an **extremely** likable boy who has gained admiration from his associates by his good nature and eagerness to learn."

The extant reports, which cover the first five months of Clint's contract, continue to develop the themes set forth in the first of them. By August, Warren saw "strength beginning to show in his work . . . real progress." Even Dr. Vandraegen, the diction coach, who remained the least enthusiastic of Clint's teachers, began to find "surprising facets to his personality," while noting that because so much of what he was doing was new to him, Clint was "slow to respond." The movement and singing teachers were patiently noncommittal, though the latter eventually conceded that "in time" he might become a singing "prospect."

By September Warren was claiming "Definite progress. He can attack parts he couldn't have touched when he first came. Although a placid person, I have discovered some very definite traces of power." In November she wrote: "Clint has evidently been told that he has the easygoing quality of Gary Cooper. We are striving to incorporate this natural quality into strength, virility, authority and versatility." But, she added, he needed more consistent work. Summing up the month's reports McTavish wrote that "he has both intelligence and understanding, and his feeling for dramatic value is unusual considering he has no experience." But she, too, observed that he needed "more seasoning."

Therein lay the rub, for it was hard to learn by doing at the studio in those days. This was ironic, because Universal was at that moment as busy and prosperous as it had ever been. The previous year it had produced more films and shown a greater profit than it had in a decade. Never having owned theaters, it was unaffected by the traumatic settlement of the antitrust case. Indeed, disadvantage was now turning to advantage, for, over the years Universal had been virtually shut out by its rivals' urban chains, it had developed loyal customers among the independent theater owners of small-town America, whose market was the last to be penetrated and diminished by television. Then, too, with independent companies beginning to acquire the old studio chains in the cities, the studio was gaining easier access to those markets.

The problem for Clint and other low-level studio employees was that they were working for an essentially dysfunctional, but self-perpetuating, bureaucracy. Even when its founder, Carl Laemmle, and his son, known far and wide as Junior, were running the company, which has been doing business on the same piece of San Fernando Valley real estate since 1915, it was not known for strong management. The elder Laemmle was notorious for putting ne'er-do-well friends and relatives from his native Germany on the payroll. His son was famous for producing films too extravagant for the studio's resources. Forced out in

1936, the Laemmles were replaced by characterless managers who year-in, year-out pursued the same policy; they made a handful of big-budget features, mainly for prestige, and counted on a large schedule of low-budget genre pictures (westerns, horror films, mysteries, lowbrow comedies and serials), which played well in the small towns, for profits. When William Goetz (Louis B. Mayer's son-in-law) and Leo Spitz (a former RKO executive) merged their independent International Pictures operation with Universal and took over its management in the late forties, they did not radically change this policy, though they stopped producing serials and decreed that henceforth no U-I picture would ever be less than seventy minutes long.

They also arranged to distribute J. Arthur Rank's prestigious English productions, brought in a few ambitious independent producers and, trying to offer what television could not, made a few more Technicolor spectacles than usual. But basically business remained pretty much as usual on Lankershim Boulevard, and Universal remained throughout this decade the town's least interesting studio—cautious, conservative, without inspiration or aspiration. The strategy by which two other fringe majors, Columbia and United Artists, propelled themselves to the first rank in these days, winning Academy Awards and solid profitability, which was to finance independent producers making sophisticated movies that took up themes television could not touch, was beyond Universal-International's range. Its idea of sophistication was a weepy romance starring a mature actress like Barbara Stanwyck or Jane Wyman or maybe a biopic about Glenn Miller or Benny Goodman.

For the rest, it required no stretch of anyone's imagination to go on making Abbott and Costello movies, or to keep Ma and Pa Kettle and Francis the Talking Mule up to their modest speeds. That's what bureaucracies are good at, and as if to reassure this one, Goetz and Spitz appointed one of its creatures, Edward Muhl, who had been at Universal since 1927, head of production. Careful cost accounting insured them all against nasty surprises. Robert Daley, who would soon become Clint's friend, and later his executive producer, worked in budgeting at the studio then and says that actual production costs never deviated from predicted costs by more than one-quarter of one percent: "That's the kind of control they exercised."

In this environment the principal activity of every department head was defending his own territory against intrusion and making sure that nothing happened in his domain that would call unwanted attention to it from the front office. This defensiveness was the main reason the casting department, which one might have expected to look upon the new talent program as an asset, saw it instead as a threat. If producers used these kids it meant there was less for the casting people to do. Then, too, many of the producers felt it was beneath them to use talent program players; in their minds, according to Halsey, it was tantamount to using nonprofessional actors. "Untouchables" is the word Clint uses to describe the young contractees. As a result, says Jack Kosslyn, the contract players "lacked motivation, because they weren't getting parts in pictures."

★　★　★

Eager and innocent of show business and its ways, Clint did not share his colleagues' cynicism, at least in his first months at the studio. The talent program was housed in a bungalow to which a gym (which Clint used regularly) and a good-sized rehearsal hall had been added. One gets a collegiate, even locker-roomish, impression of life among the male students, who were outnumbered two or three to one by the women. They noticed, according to Halsey, that though many of the female students were not terrifically faithful in their classroom attendance, this didn't seem to prevent them from getting such roles as were to be had. It was clear that some of them had, putting it gently, powerful male executives tending to their interests. On the other hand, some of the young ladies were glad to share private "rehearsals" (as the euphemism went) with male students. "We all had the same key to the boy's dressing room," Halsey recalls, "and we had to stagger our visits." One actress in particular, a woman who would later gain a small measure of fame, was, as he puts it, particularly "free with her favors. I think she seduced every guy under contract the first week he was there."

It seems unlikely that Clint totally avoided these extracurricular activities. Mamie Van Doren, beginning her brief career as a second-rank sex symbol, would say of him, many years later, when he was running for mayor of Carmel, "He was always straight and direct—he always knew the most straight and direct path to my dressing room." Clint, naturally, is much more comfortable talking about the guys. Halsey, for example, has remained his friend these many years, and he speaks with undiminished affection for Floyd Simmons, who was at the time his closest friend among his fellow students. He had won bronze medals in the decathlon in both the 1948 and the 1952 Olympics and, like Clint, he was far from being a natural actor (he became acutely nervous when he had to perform). Clint was also reasonably close with John Papero (who was saddled with an unfortunate nom de screen, Race Gentry), and he and David Janssen (who would eventually marry a student he met in the program, Dani Crane) occasionally sneaked away to play golf—the beginning of Clint's lifelong passion for the game. But generally agreeable as most of the group was, Clint remained true to his vow to "grind it out." He was always up and doing, out and about. "It's amazing how many people never went on sets," he says of talent program colleagues. "I went on sets a lot." He went, at first, to study the actors, but soon "found myself becoming more and more fascinated with the directors and what they were doing, because they were obviously managing the total ensemble."

To be actively in charge of things, compared to the more passive role of the actor, was extremely attractive to him, and some of what he learned in those early days would have a continuing influence on him: "The things that impressed you, you remember and use yourself and the things that didn't impress you, you discard."

He was, in fact, fascinated by the entire moviemaking process. This was, after all, a young man who loved to find out how things worked, and his interest in movie technology analogizes to his earlier fascination with the workings of automobile and aircraft engines. What he observed at a studio obsessed with efficiency and cost control, reinforced by his later experiences in series television, where the same values obtain, are clearly the basis of his own frugal working habits as a producer and director. Similarly, his taste for the camaraderie of the set, his sympathetic ways with crew members and small-part actors, stem from these days.

Not that he was uninterested in the comings and goings of the above-the-title crowd. A film he particularly remembers following through production was *Female on the Beach,* in which Joan Crawford played a wealthy widow who, visiting her late husband's beach house, falls in love with the mysterious gigolo next door. He is played by a miscast Jeff Chandler, whom one doesn't believe invulnerable Joan Crawford would either fall for or fear. Typical of the studio's major efforts of the time, the film was neither stylish in the noir manner to which it aspires nor emotionally relevant in any way. Its sole interest was as Crawford's first picture on a new Universal contract (she was having an affair with one of the executives); she insisted on having a vast bungalow remodeled for her use, so she could live on the lot while the film was being made. Everyone was fascinated by the grandeur with which she carried herself, the habits of self-assertion she had learned at M-G-M in its glory days, the youngster in the talent program no less than anyone else. Clint remembers, too, the excitement in the commissary when Clark Gable, who was being wooed for a major production, ate lunch there one day: "That was a real star; not like those semi-stars we'd been dealing with."

His favorite place was the back lot, one of the most extensive in the industry, with some of its sets dating back to silent-picture days. "You could go out anytime you wanted to and check out the horseback riding. I didn't know how to ride, so I'd go riding with the old wranglers—hung out with them." His report cards show Clint moving into the advanced group of riders quite quickly, and before long he was checking out horses and heading alone into the hills southeast of the studio (where D. W. Griffith had shot his major battle sequences for *The Birth of a Nation* four decades earlier). In the fifties, before the studio tour, and before the hotels and the Universal amphitheater were built on this land, it remained a wilderness: "Deer back in there—I'd run up there on horseback, and coyotes would be running across the road. It was really remote. It was really terrific."

The rest of the time he spent prowling the producers' offices, making himself known, offering himself for any available jobs. This was easy to do in those days, before the studio's executive tower and its rather grand producers' buildings went up. You could just wander into bungalow offices, chat up the secretaries and see what was doing. (Because he was lanky, taciturn and boyish, some of them took to calling him "Coop," doubtless the source of his classroom flirtation with a Gary Cooperish persona.) His shyness did not hold him back. Making these rounds was like applying for odd jobs, and his father's advice about showing employers a willingness to do anything that needed doing continued to guide him.

People did begin to notice him. DeWitt Bodeen, then a contract writer at Universal, recalled that "it was hard to miss him. His rangy height, his intense interest in anything to do with film, his wide-smiled friendliness, made him stand out." Bob Daley, in his accountant's office, saw Clint's photograph with two starlets, all of them in bathing suits, on the cover of the studio house organ: "I took one look at this thing—and I didn't know him then, I'd seen him on the lot a couple of times—but I said to somebody, 'This guy is gonna be big. Because he doesn't have the usual pretty-boy looks.'"

But that was precisely his problem. Universal was committed to pretty boys, the fast-rising Rock Hudson most prominently. He was a good-natured, rather passive actor, a seeming paragon of middle-class virtue, and the studio was using him as the earnest, nonthreatening male lead in its "women's pictures" (idealistic doctors were one of his specialties), many of which were directed with a certain sober-glossy panache by the talented Douglas Sirk. (Hudson's agreeable gift for light comedy was undiscovered in the early fifties.)

Also in favor at the time was the edgier and more urbane Tony Curtis, whose best qualities management often buried by miscasting him in period pieces. Just below them on the roster came the wooden but agreeable Chandler and the rather bland George Nader. The most interesting Universal-International releases of the day were the tough westerns James Stewart was making with director Anthony Mann (Stewart's deal was, it is said, the first in which a star participated in his pictures' profits), but he was in a class by himself at the studio.

For all his winning ways, Clint couldn't get in to see the likes of Sirk and Mann. He recalls well-meaning people around the lot proposing that he darken his hair, try dark contact lenses, get his teeth capped so he might more closely resemble the men on whom Universal had placed its largest bets. He remembers an executive telling him to study the way Rock Hudson entered the commissary, "like he owns the place." Well, Clint thought, he does. He couldn't act like Hudson on- or off-screen and saw no point in trying.

Yet eyeing his none-too-formidable competition he was slowly becoming convinced that he had something to offer, even if no one, including himself, could quite define it. He later told an interviewer that he knew he "wouldn't make any impact until my thirties. I was twenty-four then, looked like I was eighteen, and still had a certain amount of living to do." So he contented himself with being considerate, helpful, good-humored—qualities all of us tend to stress when we're new to a job, giving shrewd Jack Kosslyn a vivid first impression: "Nice guy—zip personality, zip talent." He kept this opinion to himself, since the talent program faculty felt obliged to optimism about its charges.

Basically, the problem that everyone—Clint included—was addressing was the cognitive dissonance he set up in even his more sympathetic observers. From a physical presence this imposing, one expected strong stuff of some kind; what one got instead was a kind of boyish sweetness. The kinds of masculinity that interested the fifties audiences—tortured on the one hand, mature and responsible on the other—were not (as we now know) within his natural range. He wasn't James Dean and he wasn't Gregory Peck. His maleness is of a much more straightforward, unmediated kind. Freely mobilized, it is full of anger and free of guilt, and there was nothing in the reigning conventions of the screen, or for that matter in the culture, that encouraged the open expression of those qualities.

Moreover, his capacity for outrage somewhat frightened him. He had schooled himself to suppress the impatience, the anger, always simmering beneath the surface, and it was hard for him to deploy these qualities in his work at his age, in this buttoned-down moment. Away from the studio, however, his temper could let fly in an instant. Not long after Clint started at Universal, Fritz Manes, who was serving the last of his time in the Marine Corps at Camp Pendleton, came to Los Angeles on a pass. One afternoon he repaired with Clint to a bar. "I had on my khaki uniform with the ribbons," Manes recalls, "and we're sitting in this place drinking beer and about six sailors are in there in their white uniforms and some guy says something to me and so, of course, I've gotta stand up and play macho.

"Five fuck yous and that was the last thing I ever said for the rest of the afternoon, because some guy got me right behind the ear, blind-side." But it appears that the same sailor who bolo-punched Manes pulled Clint's sports jacket up over his head, blinding and constricting him. The sailor then kicked him in the face, chipping a couple of teeth. This deeply offended Clint's sense of fair play. So, freeing himself from his jacket, he proceeded to "just beat the shit out of him," as Manes put it. By the time Manes's head had cleared, the police and the shore patrol were on the scene, sailors were sprawled around the parking lot and an ambulance was wheeling up for the man who had led the attack.

★　★　★

It's obvious that a rage this potent can be as scary to its possessor as it is to those on whom it is turned. It is equally obvious that for a man one cannot imagine trying any sort of psychotherapy—he never has—Clint had, at least in one sense, chosen the right profession: training as an actor teaches one how to control and channel dangerous emotions, make them work for you instead of against you. It also seems clear that at this moment his temper was in particular need of tempering.

Entering upon marriage and a new profession almost simultane-ously, Clint had also entered into conflict. Both of them demanded that he abandon his footloose ways. Wives expect you home on time for din-ner. Employers enforce regular attendance on their needs. Clint may have been essentially happy with both of his new commitments, but there is no question that he continued to heed the call of the wild. He still liked hanging out with the guys, liked heading out on a moment's notice for a brew, some music, a day of surfing. A decade after his mar-riage, Clint told an interviewer: "The first year of marriage was terrible. If I had to go through it again, I think I'd be a bachelor for the rest of my life. I liked doing things when I wanted to do them. I did not want any interference. . . . One thing Mag had to learn about me was that I was going to do as I pleased. She had to accept that, because if she didn't, we wouldn't be married."

There's an unwonted harshness in his tone here, an impatient immediacy that belies the fact that he was discussing what were at the time ten-year-old feelings. Perhaps, more than he has ever admitted, he felt that he had not really chosen marriage, that it was another of those irresistible circumstances that had been imposed on him by life—like his childhood moves, and being drafted and falling out of the sky in an airplane. In any case, it is clear that the constraints of marriage came as a shock to him, a shock he never quite got over, as, perhaps, the fact that he remained at least technically a "bachelor" from the time of his divorce from Maggie until 1996 proves.

This is not meant to imply that she was terribly demanding. On the contrary, she seems to have quickly come to understand that her new husband required a long leash, and that the fewer questions she asked about his comings and goings, the smoother their relationship was likely to be.

Not long after he signed his studio contract, Clint and Maggie found a tiny apartment in a complex of three motel-like structures on Arch Drive, within easy walking distance of the Universal lot. Its appeal, however, was more than convenience. Their neighbors in Beverly Hills had mainly been older people, rather stodgy and patronizing of their young building manager and his bride. The Arch Drive crowd was young and lively, in and out of one another's apartments, one another's lives, for everyone was at roughly the same place professionally, either trying to figure out what they wanted to be when they grew up or trying to establish themselves in recently adopted occupations. Over the years Clint encouraged some of his friends to rent in the complex, among them Fritz Manes and Bill Tompkins, a pal he had met in a gym in Seattle, whom he encouraged to become a stuntman and who worked with Clint later on *Rawhide* and accompanied him to Europe for his first Sergio Leone picture.

The longest-lasting friendship of this period—extending without interruption until her death in a car accident in 1995—was with Jane Agee, a striking woman with a voice like Eve Arden's, with whom the Eastwoods formed a "maternal-paternal relationship." She was a large-hearted woman whose enthusiasms were always getting her into scrapes that required advice and sympathy from Clint and Maggie. Later, she married James Brolin, the actor (their son, Josh, is now a rising movie actor), with Clint giving away the bride (and blowing his lines) at their Carmel wedding. Still later, after their divorces, she became "like a guy buddy, just a real pal," someone to whom he could apply for the woman's slant on life's issues—and vice versa. She was never a threat to Maggie or to any other woman in Clint's life.

Indeed, despite Clint's later comments about the early days of their marriage, it was, so far as their friends could tell, serene. Bob Daley, who moved into the Arch Drive complex at about the same time the East-woods did, remembers Maggie as "very sweet, very nice, very outgoing, so much fun to be around." Brett Halsey characterizes her as "Miss Apple Pie All-American Girl." To add to their income and in addition to her regular job she did some part-time modeling for a swimming-suit company. Daley remembers her regaling the Arch Drive crowd with tales of her misadventures in that trade, especially with the experimen-tal designs. One literally disintegrated on her when she plunged into the water. Another was made of a fabric that lost its elasticity on immersion, sagging in all the wrong places while she desperately tried to preserve her modesty. She was, in his recollection, a good sport about any and all misadventures. But she was also, in Daley's characterization, strong-minded. Clint "used to rely on her for a lot of advice."

The Arch Drive crowd was not particularly showbizzy. Aside from Clint, the only performer of even modest prominence that anyone can remember living there was a young actress name Kathryn Grant, who was at the time dating an older man. "Every once in a while this guy would come in with the hat and the pipe, you know, and everybody'd be glued to the windows," Clint remembers. "Bing Crosby [whom Grant would marry in 1957] would go up and they'd go out some-where."

Clint also recalls a young Swedish woman named Lillie Kardell, who lived in the building next door. She had been discovered working in RKO's Stockholm office and had been encouraged to try her luck in Hollywood. She was also at some point in the Universal talent program, but her chief claim to fame was as one of James Dean's lovers in the last year of his life, and Clint recalls meeting him and seeing him around quite a bit at this time. He also remembers meeting Jayne Mansfield at one of the Arch Drive parties. She was completely unknown at the time, and he tried to help her with her career. "I took her over to the Universal lot with me just to introduce her to a few people in talent, and nobody gave her a chance—though there were a couple of directors who would have loved to jump all over her." That, as he says, not for the first time, was the way it was at Universal: They already had their Mar-ilyn Monroe type in the person of Mamie Van Doren and didn't need another one. (Perhaps, though, they did. Jack Kosslyn remembers Van Doren saying to him one day, "I don't dig this Staniskovski," which is something Monroe, who of course did come to dig the Method, per-haps to her sorrow, would never have said.)

★   ★   ★

Clint got his first role around the time the studio renewed his option, in the fall of 1954 (he got a raise to one hundred dollars a week). The part was given to him by William Alland, who, with another producer, Albert Zugsmith, had joined Lubin as Clint's chief studio supporters. Alland was perhaps overqualified for his job (a longtime associate of Orson Welles, he had served as dialogue director in *Citizen Kane* while playing the inquiring reporter). Now casting the sequel of his very successful *Creature from the Black Lagoon,* he offered Clint a one-scene part in *Revenge of the Creature,* which was shot in 3-D. He was to play Jennings, a lab assistant to John Agar's research scientist (even the B-picture leads at Universal were bland), who is studying the half-man, half-fish creature, which eventually escapes and terrorizes a town.

Basically, Clint had to play dumb. One of the lab's white rats is missing, and Jennings not illogically blames a cat that has been placed in the cage with them: "Doc, there were four rats there in that cage when I changed my lights. Now there are only three. It's my considered opinion that rat number four is sitting inside that cat."

The scientist inquires if Jennings is certain he fed all the rodents earlier. "Here, I always feed them," Clint begins, groping in his lab-coat pocket to show what he's been giving them. But as he feels around, he encounters something soft and furry. "Uh-oh," he says, pulling out the missing rodent. He gives a nonplussed look and delivers a line to cover his embarrassment. End of Clint Eastwood's movie debut.

He almost didn't get that far—not in this picture, anyway. The day before the scene was to be shot, Alland took him down to the set to meet the director, Jack Arnold, another former actor now in the early stages of a directing career that would include some of Universal's better genre films, *The Mouse That Roared* and uncounted television episodes. Director and producer immediately fell to wrangling about the scene Clint was supposed to do. Arnold thought it irrelevant and was refusing to shoot it. Alland liked it for some reason—perhaps it was his own invention; he has story credit on the film—and insisted that it be made.

"They were arguing like crazy," Clint remembers. "It was nothing against me, but meanwhile I'm just standing there, this big, gawky kid getting more kind of anxious about the whole thing. Finally, Arnold says, 'OK, I'll shoot it, but we're not gonna use it in the goddamn picture.' So I just said, 'Well, nice to meet you, Mr. Arnold.' "

But as they were leaving the stage Alland told him, "Don't worry about it, you should be there tomorrow morning." But, of course, he did worry: "My first scene in my first picture, and here I got a director who hates the scene and doesn't want to shoot it. You can imagine how adverse those circumstances were." They did not improve when he set to work: Clint blew his lines on the first two takes. From his position by the camera the crusty Arnold could be heard muttering, "That's great, that's just great." Oh, shit, Clint said to himself, I'm really in this over my head. But John Agar—"bless his heart"—reassured him: Don't worry about it, don't listen to him, just relax.

"So I sucked my gut in and jumped in there and did it. And afterward nobody said goodbye or anything. I left there with my confidence knocked back about three notches, because I felt if in every picture we had to go through that, that's kind of an exhausting process."

In time he would make his peace with Arnold. "I joked with Jack about it years later when he came on and did some *Rawhide*s. "It wasn't a bad deal like Abner Biberman or something." A sometime actor and coach in the Universal talent program, now turning to directing, Clint approached Biberman for a part in *Running Wild,* an exploitation picture about delinquent adolescents that he was casting. He was curtly dismissed. Jesus Christ, that was a short career, Clint remembers thinking. He also remembers thinking that a former actor, who must have known his share of rejections, might have put this turndown more kindly, instead of making Clint feel like "a punk kid, hanging around." Years later, when Biberman was working in episodic television, his name appeared on a list of potential *Rawhide* directors that Clint happened to spy in a producer's office. He took out a pencil and drew a line through it. "I'm not a vindictive person, but I just didn't want to see that face on the set."

Clint also remembers a certain nameless Universal executive: "This guy saw me coming and he'd start throwing rocks." A few years later, when Clint was starring on *Rawhide* and his old nemesis had become an agent, they encountered one another on the M-G-M lot, where Clint's program headquartered for a while, "and you'd have thought I was his long-lost son he had never seen." Where was this guy when I needed him? Clint wondered. He understands that most of the time an actor cannot fit the image a director or a producer has in his mind for a particular role. But that is scarcely the actor's fault, and he doesn't understand why people need to get nasty about it.

He has, however, an equally long memory for kindnesses past. Arthur Lubin, for example, recalled getting a phone call from Clint a couple of nights before he won his Academy Awards for *Unforgiven.* Clint had been remembering the director's lonely staunchness in these early days and wanted him to know that he was still grateful. And, indeed, it was Lubin who cast Clint in his longest role of this period, that of Jonesy in *Francis in the Navy,* sixth in the seven-picture series. Lubin directed all but the last of them, developing his curious specialty in verbalizing fauna; a little later he produced and directed *Mr. Ed,* the long-running television series about a talking horse, as well as *The Incredible Mr. Limpet,* a Don Knotts feature for Disney, in which the star was transformed into a talking fish.

Francis had been the subject of a novel by a writer named David Stern, the rights to which Lubin purchased, hoping to interest Universal in putting the talking mule on film. The studio resisted, largely because of the problem of making the animal's lips move so that dialogue could be persuasively synchronized with them. But the director persisted and prevailed—though he always refused to divulge the secret of the illusion.

The basic joke of the series is that Francis is the grown-up, making variously wry and wise observations (drawling Chill Wills supplies his voice) on the childlike behavior of the humans around him. His straight man (except for the last film in the series) is Donald O'Connor, who plays army lieutenant Peter Sterling, always getting into unlikely scrapes and always frantic to cover up the fact that his best pal (and sometime conscience) is this unlikely creature.

In this eighty-minute film designed for the bottom of double-feature bills, Francis finds himself, for reasons the picture does not make entirely clear, in the navy's charge. Apparently he can read and write, too, for he summons his friend Sterling to rescue him. He, however, looks exactly like Slicker Donevan (also played by O'Connor), a rather mean-spirited bosun's mate, who is a womanizer, slacker and general con artist. Much merriment is supposed to ensue from this confusion of identities.

Jonesy, Clint's character, is one of Slicker's navy buddies, none of whom ever quite grasps the situation. Along with two or three other actors, his function is largely to supply reaction shots when things go amiss. He never has more than two sentences of connected dialogue, though his part does run through most of the picture, and because of his size, the eager alertness he brings to his role—no one's going to accuse him of inattention—and with Lubin favoring him in some group shots, he is noticeable. More so than his two army friends, Martin Milner, who plays one of Slicker's other pals, and David Janssen, who plays a junior officer. Toward the end of the film, Clint climbs from a landing craft to a truck ahead of it in a traffic jam and is last seen handsomely semaphoring farewells from that vehicle when it turns onto a side road.

It was a brief but pleasant experience. As he already knew, Lubin was a "very straight-ahead, professional guy, and very encouraging. All the cast and crew thought he was great." Best of all, Clint had billing in the main titles—fifth position—the only time that happened at Universal. That was not bad for a beginner, even in this distinctly minor context. ("Lubin, who has megged all 'Francis' offerings, fails to insert his usual punch," *Variety* opined, fair-mindedly enough.)

It was, though, Clint's high-water mark at Universal. Lubin cast him as the "First Saxon" in a Technicolor epic, *Lady Godiva,* which starred Maureen O'Hara making the legendary bareback ride in a bodysuit, with "a hair wigwam" (as the *Hollywood Reporter* reviewer called it) artfully arranged to create an illusion of nudity rather than to cover it. Buddy Van Horn, who would become Clint's regular stunt coordinator (and three times his director), worked as a rider in the film and remembers Clint as "a skinny-legged kid in tights, saying 'They went that-away.'" Actually, what he said to George Nader, chief of the Saxon rebels opposing their Norman oppressors, was "A column of soldiers is approaching." It was one of his two lines in a part which consisted mainly of intermittent appearances among the yeomen.

Thereafter, Bill Alland gave him another day's work in Jack Arnold's *Tarantula,* about a deadly spider mutated to gigantic size by misapplied atomic energy (a favorite science-fiction theme in the fifties and a reflection of everyone's anxiety about the newly freed atom). Clint, almost unrecognizable in a flight helmet, plays the pilot leading a group of jets in an attack on the creature and has a couple of lines of radioed cross talk.

But after this little rush, Clint seemed to get less work, and nothing that can be seen as progress in his career. The studio was using its contract people ever more sparingly and was beginning to drop them from the payroll, too. There were also changes in the talent program faculty. Sympathetic Katherine Warren left, and her place as the acting coach was taken by a man named Jess Kimmel, who was less encouraging to Clint. In the spring of 1955, when it came time to renew Clint's option, he was told that it would be picked up again, but that there would be no raise this time.

This did not improve his morale, but he said, "'Yeah, I'll stay,' and I had no regrets. I just kind of figured, I'll know as much as I can when I leave here. But I know my ass is out of here in six months."

Despite this accurate assessment of his immediate prospects, Clint got his best assignment a couple of months later. The studio had cast Steve Allen, the first star of *The Tonight Show,* in *The Benny Goodman Story,* largely because of his physical resemblance to the eponymous figure. To promote the film Universal arranged for a program called "Steve Allen in Hollywood" to be broadcast on *Max Liebman Presents,* a variety hour produced by the man who had gained fame as the producer of *Your Show of Shows,* the now-legendary Sid Caesar program. Various Universal stars did bits of one kind and another in the show, and then, having sung a song (something of a surprise), Jeff Chandler addressed the audience: "We'd like to present now, live, one of the highlights from the film *Bright Victory* [one of the studio's 1951 releases]. The three young men featured in this scene—Rex Reason, Grant Williams and Clint Eastwood—were discovered and developed right here on our lot. We hope you, too, will share the excitement and enthusiasm we feel for their future."

Clint had the least of the three roles in what followed, playing a young noncom in an army hospital escorting a blind soldier (Williams) to visit a psychologist (Reason). The handicapped soldier is understandably bitter about his lot and has been refusing to communicate with his family. The doctor places a call to them on his behalf, but he refuses to speak to them, and Clint is summoned to escort him back to his ward. "Well, how did you and the lieutenant get along?" the latter inquires after they leave the office. "Oh, just great, he had all sorts of solutions to my problem. He's just like all the other people around here. He doesn't know what he's talking about." Clint fixes him with the first recorded example of that hard stare that would become one of his acting signatures and replies: "That's funny. You'd think he'd know something. He's as blind as you are." Sting in the score! Astonishment on Williams's face! Then a manly embrace. And he returns to the doctor's office to make his confessional call.

In context, Clint's underplayed naturalism had a ring of truth about it. It was the only role he got at Universal in which he was able to show, however briefly, a certain mature masculinity, as opposed to youthful gawkiness. And his selection for this showcase appearance—there were, after all, plenty of other contract players who could have done the role—seems to suggest that someone in the studio actually felt some "excitement and enthusiasm" for him. But it was just a television bit, and one you had to look pretty hard to find. In the few months remaining on his studio contract he got nothing as good.

The most visible of his later Universal roles (about thirty seconds of shared screen time) was in *Never Say Goodbye,* a quintessentially inane fifties romance—a remake of the 1945 *This Love of Ours,* which was in turn derived, unlikely as it may seem, from a Pirandello play. Set in equally unpersuasive back-lot versions of postwar Vienna and American suburbia, it starred Rock Hudson as an insanely jealous doctor—an emotion he could not imagine, let alone play.

Cast again as a lab assistant, Clint is required to hand over some X rays to Hudson in an early scene and wish him luck on a speech he is going off to make. When Clint reported to the set for his day's work the director, Jerry Hopper, said: "I'd like to see some kind of character. I'd like to see you wear glasses or something." (Quick fixes of this kind are what directing consists of when the basic job is to keep moving through the schedule on time.) Jesus, Clint said to himself, I got a nice bit and here I've got to wear glasses. But dutifully he went off in search of the propman and tried on a selection of eyewear until he found something that seemed all right; maybe better than all right. Glancing in a mirror, he thought he didn't look bad in glasses. He wore them around on the set while the scene was being set up, and the more he did, the happier he became. Indeed, he began to imagine a whole new image for himself, maybe even a whole new career. This will be great, he thought, because if I start doing more charactery things, then they'll use me in more stuff around the lot, and then they won't can me. He even started to wonder if a new hairstyle might be worth a try.

Finally, they were ready to shoot. Clint was introduced to Hudson, and the director started outlining their business. As he was absorbing these instructions, Clint noticed Hudson looking at him rather curiously. Finally, just as they were ready to go, Hudson said, "Where are *my* glasses?"

"What are you talking about?" Hopper asked.

"Well, you know, I'm playing a physician in this film. Don't you think I ought to have glasses?"

It's possible the star was afraid of being upstaged by a handsome unknown who had found himself some interesting spectacles. In any event, a halt was called, and Hudson and Hopper went through the same twenty pairs of glasses that Clint had examined earlier. None was judged satisfactory. "Finally," says Clint, "they take mine off. He puts them on. Perfect!"

Needless to say, both actors in the scene could not wear glasses, so Clint worked without them. "By that time I *really* wanted to wear them." His consolation was that the little scene went off without further incident. It might be noted, incidentally, that never thereafter in the picture is Hudson to be seen with glasses.

Alas, the rest of Clint's career as a Universal contract player also went off without noticeable incident. By this time Jack Kosslyn had taken over Kimmel's classes, and that represented an improvement for Clint, but he still felt he was just playing out his string. He managed to get two more on-screen jobs in his last months there, but they were the least visible of all.

He was one of a group of sailors down in the hold of a World War II supply ship in *Away All Boats,* a 1956 release starring Jeff Chandler as a Captain Queeg figure. Clint vaguely recalls that his one line consisted of calling for a medic, but it is impossible to pick him out of the crowd in the flooded darkness belowdecks. Still, this was one more line than he had in *Star in the Dust,* in which Al Zugsmith cast him as a ranch hand. Clint is only marginally more visible here than he was in *Away All Boats.*

No one looking at his scattered work could say that he was a rising personality, certainly not as a studio executive might define the term. So on September 22, 1955, this one-sentence memo circulated from in-tray to out-tray in the front office: "Please be advised that we will not exercise our option on Clint Eastwood." A little later a payroll termination notice went out; it specified October 25 as "talent's" last working day at the studio.

★   ★   ★

Clint was not overly discouraged, having seen the dismissal coming. People were always talking about the contract players the studio had let go, then been obliged to rehire at better salaries. Besides, he felt he had probably derived what good there was to be obtained from the program. He had learned something about acting, he knew how to find his way around a set and how to evaluate what was going on there, and he had some credits for his agents to mention to casting people. Most important, his spine was stiffened: "The more you struggle the more you kind of say, 'I'm gonna make those people eat those words.' And though you get depressed many times, and I had many moments of saying, 'Well, this isn't going anywhere,' I think in the back of my mind I always felt I had something to offer somewhere down the line."

It may be that the most important thing he got from this experience was a glimpse of the kind of community show business offers. Sometimes it seems like a large orphanage, harboring a disproportionate number of people damaged by the loss or emotional absence of a parent. Clint, obviously, had been fortunate in that regard. But until he signed on at Universal, he had not found a place where he could happily root himself. The studio, for all its blindness and crassness, suggested interesting possibilities in that regard.

Indeed, when he left Universal he looked for work as a contract player at Warner Bros., Columbia (where he did scenes with Felicia Farr and with his sometime neighbor Kathy Grant), Paramount (where one tried out in a room equipped with a one-way mirror, behind which the executives evaluated the hopefuls) and Twentieth Century–Fox, where for the first time in his memory he actually talked back to somebody in a suit. His audition piece was a scene from Sidney Kingsley's play *Detective Story,* in which the eponymous protagonist must plead with his estranged wife to return to him. Clint had studied the entire work carefully and correctly understood this figure to be a hard and inward man, not used to begging for anything, virtually strangling on the words he was compelled to speak. Clint's auditor, the head of the studio's talent program, disagreed entirely with this interpretation. He told Clint that he and his wife had recently come close to divorce, and that he had gone out and bought her a mink coat, dropped to his knees when he presented it and pleaded for forgiveness.

Clint was astonished. Such behavior was entirely beyond his ken. And so were such confessions from a stranger. "I was thinking, Boy, this guy's pussy-whipped. But I kind of went along with it, because I'd never heard anybody talk like this." When the man finished, Clint stammered objections: "'I just can't—this guy wouldn't . . .' and I went through the whole goddamn play with him," pointing out all the reasons the character had to be played the way Clint had interpreted him. It was to no avail.

Nothing came of any of these encounters, but during this period Clint got a couple of jobs in episodic television, the first of which offered him what he would later claim to be the most memorable of these gigs. This was on *Highway Patrol,* and he got it because he knew how to ride a motorcycle, and the producers were too cheap to hire a stuntman. This was typical of Ziv, which produced inexpensive action shows mainly for the syndication market. Almost every actor of Clint's generation passed through its humble portals, and everyone emerged with some story about the operation's astonishing stinginess. And, if they worked *Highway Patrol,* they usually emerged with a story about the legendary drinking of its star, Broderick Crawford.

Clint is no exception. "I remember thinking it was odd, because I'd never seen a guy come in kind of pale in the morning and in a half hour have a glow on. The prop guy told me later what he did: He'd get a bottle of 7-Up, pour half of it out and put vodka in, so he had a shooter going. And then he could rattle off his lines." To avoid memorization, the canny old actor, who was only a few years past his Academy Award–winning performance in Robert Rossen's *All the King's Men,* would take a scissors to his script, trimming all the margins off. After that, he would cut up his lines and place them strategically around the set—one perhaps on the wall next to where Clint was standing, another atop the papers on his desk, a third in the desk drawer he would open at the appropriate moment. "I was so fascinated I almost dropped out of the shot," Clint says.

When his preparations were complete, the camera was trained on Crawford, and he did all his lines with the natural-seeming movements he could not have accomplished if his eyes were fixed on a stationary cue card. Clint and the other actor cued him as he proceeded. When Crawford finished the director called "Cut" and "Print" and said, "OK, now we're gonna come around on you two guys, and Brod, you're through." Whereupon Crawford headed off for another set, because they were shooting two episodes simultaneously. Clint and his colleague then did their dialogue to camera, with a script supervisor reading the star's part.

Another role, on *TV Reader's Digest,* in an episode entitled "Greatest of the Apaches," materialized soon thereafter, and around this time he even got his first fleeting taste of media attention. One day a fan magazine reporter named Earl Leaf called. He told Clint he had an assignment to write and photograph an "at home" layout for his publication. Startled, Clint invited him over to Arch Drive, greeting him, beer in hand, with a question: "Some of my friends put you up to this, didn't they? We're always playing jokes on each other." The reporter assured him that his assignment was legitimate, that an editor in New York had glimpsed him in a Universal picture, found him adorable and wanted to feature him as a "star of tomorrow." She also—ahem—thought it would be nice to meet him next time she was in L.A. "She didn't know you were married, I guess," said Leaf. The reporter, who later wrote a recollection of the encounter, got most of the facts wrong, but gave an accurate impression of a shy young man bemused by the reporter's mission and thoroughly unimpressed with himself.

It was much more important that his little career roll seemed to be continuing. Early in 1956 the faithful Lubin offered him a part in a feature. The director had moved from Universal to RKO, which had recently been acquired from Howard Hughes by a subsidiary of the General Tire Company. The lunatic billionaire had brought the studio to the edge of extinction, but its new management was promising a renaissance, with Lubin's movie *The First Traveling Saleslady* scheduled as its first release. Clint's role offered him several scenes—more than he had had in a movie since the Francis picture. More important, he was to have an "and introducing" credit and a princely $750 salary. Lubin even talked of getting him a long-term contract with the studio.

Starring Ginger Rogers, Barry Nelson and Carol Channing, the film was one of those ghastly fifties comedies full of sniggery sexual innuendos, trying to take advantage of the slightly liberalized production code, which was now permitting somewhat more obvious, therefore somewhat more witless, double entendres. It is a period piece, set in 1897, with Rogers playing Rose Gilray, a free spirit presiding over a corset business. The irony of a supposedly liberated woman trying to succeed by selling other women painfully constricting undergarments was, of course, entirely lost on the filmmakers. The plot has her working off a debt (for stays) to a steel magnate (David Brian) by using her charms to sell his barbed wire to western ranchers. Nelson is the inventor of a horseless carriage whom she keeps encountering and bickering with (a sure sign of true love in bad movies); Channing is Molly Wade, her model and companion on this expedition; with Clint cast as a soldier, Jack Rice, whom Channing encounters in a Kansas City hotel lobby, where he is recruiting for Teddy Roosevelt's Rough Riders. Molly eyes him with supposedly comic lewdness, and he mimes unconsciousness of her libidinous intent. She assures him that she doesn't want to join his outfit ("I can't even ride smooth") and this dialogue ensues:

"Do you like girls?"

"Yes, I do."

"Well, I'm a girl."

"You sure are."

Later on, when Molly introduces Jack to Rose, she says, "Pleased to meet you," eyes him from toes to top and back again and adds, "all of you."

This is a fair sample of the movie's wit, and the scene where he meets the Channing character was Clint's best. Once the action leaves Kansas City, he leaves the picture for several reels, reappearing again when it settles down for a conclusion in Texas, where he leads a ride to the rescue and ends up, of course, in Channing's arms.

The whole enterprise puzzled Clint: "I read this script and I couldn't make head nor tail of it, yet they were going to make it." He could not even understand the excitement buzzing around the set about James Arness, who had a role in the film, because he and Maggie didn't have a television set and had not seen him in *Gunsmoke,* the "adult western" that had begun its endless CBS run the previous fall.

Still, Clint looked fine in his soldier suit, and his gulpy shyness was inoffensive, if not exactly riveting: "very attractive" was the mild comment of the *Hollywood Reporter*'s critic, in what appears to be the first trade review that did more than simply acknowledge his presence in a movie.

The studio contract (which Lubin remembered actually being drawn up) did not materialize. Perhaps RKO's executives were unimpressed with his work. Perhaps its casting people failed to respond to a scene he did for them—he thinks it was from William Inge's recent Broadway success, *Picnic,* about a hobo stud's sexually galvanizing effect on a group of small-town Kansas women. Perhaps the faltering studio was simply uninterested in making long-term commitments to anyone.

Whatever the case, it was the beginning of a bad time, the worst Clint had known since his winter in the paper mill. He did not get an acting job for almost a year. He thinks, perhaps, that younger actors were victimized when older movie players, their own opportunities limited by dwindling feature-film production, started taking roles in episodic television. He continued to feel, as well, that his looks were against him. The only work he got was in a couple of commercials. One of them was for the American Dairy Association ("Milk is the lift without a let-down"), in which he silently gulps milk and chews a sandwich in a spot that featured more prominently one of the Miss Universe contest win-ners who had been with him in the studio talent program. The other was for Greyhound, and it was not without irony. He played a parking attendant, surveying a crowded lot and saying, "We're all filled up"—the implication being that bus travel permitted one to avoid such inconve-nience. It was shot the same day as another commercial in which a bus driver, gray-haired, exuding trustworthiness and looking as much like an airline pilot as possible, leaned out of his bus window to advise view-ers to "leave the driving to us." His one line became something of a na-tional tag line. Clint's definitely did not. "Mine ran once. The other one ran fifty times a day," the residuals from it and various sequels greatly en-riching the actor who played the driver.

The Eastwoods, by contrast, were living on Maggie's salary and on what Clint could bring in from day labor. He and another Arch Drive resident, Bob Morris (who later changed his name to Bob Donner and, at Clint's urging, became an actor), had a regular weekend job sweeping up at the Mode Furniture factory in South Los Angeles. On weekdays, Clint mainly worked for the United Pool Service, digging swimming pools. He remembers leaving his jobs two or three times a day, a coin damp with sweat in his hand, and running down to the nearest pay phone to call his agent. "But there'd be nothing. And I'd do this month in and month out; after a while you get kind of discouraged."

He was also angry. He had tried to get in to see Raoul Walsh when he was casting *The Naked and the Dead,* tried to get an interview with Sam Fuller when he was doing *Run of the Arrow*—men's men that they were, they might have responded to him—but he didn't have the credits, and his agency didn't have the clout, so meetings could not be arranged. There were dozens of other such failures. And even when Clint got an audition it was equally discouraging. Putting aside paying work for a day in order to go out on a call, he would often enter a casting office and confront twenty other young men of roughly the same age, height and coloring and realize they had not sent for him specifically, but were just looking at types. He also knew that before this group of twenty there had been another group of twenty, and that a similar crowd would be coming in after they left. One time a search for an unknown to play Charles Lindbergh in *The Spirit of St. Louis* was launched with much fanfare, and Clint dutifully attended one of the cattle calls for a role that ultimately went to that great unknown James Stewart. He snorts derisively at the hype and at the innocence of his hopes.

He summed up his general feelings very articulately for Norman Mailer: "Oh, I hated it . . . having to deal with some of the most no-talent people in the world passing judgment on you. They're going to pick out the worst aspects of you or anybody else they cast. . . . I wanted to pull people out of their seats and say, 'Don't talk to me that way.'"

But his frustrations spilled out in other directions. One brutally hot day, for example, he and a friend named George Fargo were working on a pool when the foreman started giving Fargo a hard time. Fargo— "kind of a crazy guy"—answered back and was fired. "So he started heading for the door and I started going with him. And the guy said, 'Wait a minute. Where are you going?' and I said, 'Well, I gotta drive him home, so I guess I'll have to be fired too.'" Clint does not make much of this act of loyalty: "I was kind of fed up with doing this particular work, too."

He and Fargo occasionally passed an empty afternoon in a bar with the latter's friend, Robert Mitchum, with Clint fascinated by that yarn-spinner's sardonic tales. They called him "the Goose" because of a strutting stride. Always, however, Clint kept himself fit for work, establishing the near-vegetarian eating habits he maintains to this day, imbibing curious, but obviously effective, health-food concoctions and gobbling vitamins. He also constantly pumped iron at Vince's Gym, on Ventura Boulevard. "You want to get rid of anger," Donner says, "that's one of the ways you do it." You want to stay a movie star, that's one of the ways you do it, too. Clint's obsession with fitness—he runs or works out (often both) daily—has generally been treated offhandedly by observers of his career as either hobby or eccentricity. But it is, in fact, utterly essential to his well-being, his sense of self—and the longevity of his career.

He studied acting as assiduously as he worked out, eventually becoming a regular at Jack Kosslyn's studio, where he would continue to work through most of his *Rawhide* years. Eventually, he even made a believer of his dubious coach, who remembers the exact moment it happened. It was a couple of years after Clint left Universal, when he was doing the scene in Arthur Miller's *All My Sons* in which a young man confronts his father about his wartime crimes of supplying shoddy matériel to the air force. For the first time Kosslyn saw the power Clint could mobilize.

One of Clint's salient characteristics is his ability to compartmentalize, and it is very evident in this period. However anxious he was about his career his friends of this passage rarely saw it. The anger and frustration he so often talks about in retrospect was not manifested to Bob Daley or Bob Donner. The former remembers Clint in these very early days talking optimistically about someday setting up his own production company, with Daley as the business brains, and producing features without the waste of money and motion that he was seeing around the industry.

A little good fortune finally began to flow in Clint's direction in January 1957, when he was cast in an episode of the TV series *The West Point Story* entitled—appropriately, as it turned out—"White Fury." The series was shot on location at the military academy, and Clint and another actor, Jerome Courtland, were flown in to work on it. The grandeur of the setting impressed Clint. So did the midwinter cold along the banks of the Hudson. There was a scene on a nearby ski slope, and "it was so cold that the AD, everybody, were sitting in the car." Only the actors, the cameraman and the director braved the elements. A little later he was back at RKO, working for Lubin again, though in greatly reduced circumstances, as a day player picking up a $175 paycheck playing a pilot (code-named "Dumbo") searching for survivors of a midocean plane crash in *Escapade in Japan*. It is quite a nice little movie, one of Lubin's better efforts, but Clint's contribution to it was peripheral. So was his part in his next film, William A. Wellman's *Lafayette Escadrille*, though it might have been otherwise, for—frustratingly—he came very close to getting a leading role in the picture.

Wellman, whose *Wings* had won the first Academy Award for best picture, had made Cagney's breakthrough movie, *Public Enemy*, and he had also made *The Ox-Bow Incident*, which remains one of Clint's favorite movies (in 1994, asked to present and comment on a movie at the Cinémathèque in Paris, he chose this film, which is a western about a lynch mob); and Wellman was passionately committed to this new project. He had served in the Lafayette Flying Corps, successor to the Escadrille (which had been composed of American volunteers flying under French colors earlier in the war), and the script, which he had been developing for years, drew on many of the director's experiences.

Clint liked Wellman immediately, for "Wild Bill" was one of Hollywood's legendary straight shooters, a tough-sentimental man's man, intemperate and lovable, and the feeling was returned; Wellman had a particular dislike of vain and egocentric actors, which he could immediately see this young man was not. "It was really fascinating," Clint recalls. "He was going on about all these guys [the members of the Lafayette Flying Corps], and he says, 'This guy's a terrific part, and you would be perfect for it.'" The role was that of Duke Sinclaire, one of the two men with whom Wellman enlisted (the other was Tommy Hitchcock, later to become a legendary polo player).

It was a revelation to Clint, this unguarded enthusiasm. Nonetheless, having lost many a role because of his height, he was slumping against the wall, trying to look smaller than he was. Finally, Wellman eyed him quizzically and asked the big question: "How tall are you?"

Clint shot back: "How tall is the guy?" Wellman looked at him, puzzled, and started laughing.

Clint said: "I've got to qualify this. I've lost so damn many parts because somebody said I was too tall or too this or too that." At which point, setting caution aside, he drew himself up to his full height and said, "I'm this high."

To which Wellman replied that Sinclaire was the tallest man in the outfit, and that for once his size was to Clint's advantage. A little later he called Clint's agent and told him Clint should stand by—and start growing a mustache like the one Sinclaire had affected.

But now Paul Newman, who had signaled interest in playing the film's lead, suddenly developed doubts about the screenplay. While these were being addressed, Clint was placed in a quandary, for he was offered a part on the TV series *Death Valley Days*. His new mustache was wrong for the role, but he was loath to lose it so long as there was any chance of getting *Lafayette Escadrille*. He kept the facial hair, did the TV job and was glad that he did. For when Newman backed out, his part went to Warner's tall, blond contract star, Tab Hunter. Now, suddenly, Clint's height and coloring weighed against him. His part went to David Janssen, who was shorter and darker.

Wellman, upset at betraying an implicit promise, compensated by giving Clint a smaller, more anonymous role—George Moseley, a man who had played baseball against another flyer, Princeton (Tom Laughlin), in civilian life, and continued their rivalry in a game on a French airfield. This deteriorates into a brawl, with Clint chasing McLaughlan and even throwing a bat at him, while French onlookers look on in comic amusement. The sequence was all too typical of a movie in which humorous camaraderie and not very persuasive romance were stressed at the expense of aerial action, which was one of Wellman's strengths. The uncompromising filmmaker had, for once, compromised in order to get a beloved project before the cameras. The picture was poorly received by both critics and the public, not least because Hunter's central role is very square and old-fashioned and because Hunter, a quintessential fifties leading man, is without energy or dangerousness.

It would be Wellman's last film; he always said its failure caused him to retire. As for Clint, he had some location fun, put a few dollars in the bank and developed a lasting relationship with the director and his large, warm family—the last being no small reward. "He had a big influence in encouraging me to be a director," he would later say.

For the moment, though, *Lafayette Escadrille* was yet another big disappointment. But not, as it would happen, as grave as the one he suffered on his next assignment. Shortly after Clint finished the Wellman film his agents sent him on a call to Twentieth Century–Fox, where a director named Jodie Copeland was casting *Ambush at Cimarron Pass.* It was not an entirely promising venture. Copeland was a film editor being given his first chance to direct. The budget was minimal. The shooting schedule was eight days, the running time was just barely feature length—seventy-three minutes. The salary offered Clint was $750, but the producers insisted—somewhat debatably—that he was the picture's second lead.

Clint chose to look at it optimistically. How bad could it be? A few days in the deeper, drier reaches of the San Fernando Valley, working in a marginal, but certainly not disreputable, little western—it would certainly be more fun than digging swimming pools.

Little did he know. Everyone's troubles began when Scott Brady was cast as the lead. He was a crude, distinctly uninviting actor, useful only as a blunt, subsidiary villain in B pictures. He should never have been employed as a leading man. Worse, his price was $25,000, which bit deeply into the film's minuscule budget. According to a story that circulated on the set, Copeland had been saying one day that, thanks to his skill as an editor, he would make the forty Indians he was planning to use in the film as menaces to a mixed band of travelers look like four hundred Indians. At which point someone rushed in with the news that Brady had accepted the role. "Without missing a beat," Clint recalls, "Copeland says, 'I'll make those four Indians look like forty.'"

The director was "a nice guy," Eastwood remembers, "but he didn't know what he was doing." And he certainly wasn't strong enough or experienced enough to deal with the fractiousness that quickly developed on the shoot. Brady was another heavy drinker and reported to work extremely hungover. He was surly in general, but took a particular dislike to the leading lady, Margia Dean, who he believed had got the part because she was the girlfriend of a Fox executive. When she objected one day to his habitually foul language, he simply snarled, "Go call your fucking agent." Clint remembers the director saying to him, shortly thereafter, "'Could you please treat Margia nice, because somebody needs to help her out,' and I'm going, 'How can I help her out, I'm just trying to fend for myself here.'"

So it went on the most disorganized and unpleasant shoot Clint had ever experienced. Under budgetary pressure, the producers couldn't afford to keep livestock and their wranglers on for the whole shoot, so the script called for the "marauding savages" to run the horses off after a day or two's work. A western without horses is, obviously, at something of a disadvantage pictorially and in terms of pace; in the most literal sense of the word, *Ambush at Cimarron Pass* is stumbling.

The story is this: A cavalry patrol under the command of Sergeant Matt Blake (Brady) is bringing in for trial a man who has been running guns to hostile Indians. On the trail they encounter a rancher and some of his riders, among them Clint's character, Keith Williams. Their herd has been driven off by Apache. The cowboys are unreconstructed Southern sympathizers, especially Williams, whose mother and sister, it is explained, were victimized during Sherman's march through Georgia. Indeed, Clint's first line in the film has him begging his boss to "let me have just one Yankee." When Blake tells the cattlemen they are surrounded by Indians, Williams refuses to believe him ("He's a liar; all Yankees are liars"). Once the Apache have claimed their horses, they turn over a captive Hispanic woman, Dean's role, to the soldiers so that she can offer them a deal: The Indians, she says, are willing to return their horses if they will surrender the trader's stock of rifles.

Clint's character is all for accepting the offer. "We were doing OK until you came here," he says to Blake. "Seems wherever you bluebellies go, you cause trouble." But the stalwart sergeant naturally refuses the trade, and the little party meanders on, losing someone here, someone there, to the stalking Indians, the while squabbling among themselves. Eventually, virtually in sight of a frontier fort, it becomes necessary—heavy irony here—to burn the rifles they have carried so far in order to make a final run for safety. "We've lugged these rifles a hundred miles—a hundred miles for nothing," someone cries. "No, not for nothing," the sergeant intones. "Sometimes you've gotta lose before you can win."

The thought does not quite parse. Not much in the picture does. Clint has more than once called it the worst movie ever made, though that's not strictly true. It is simply indistinguishable from a hundred, a thousand, "products" made for a price to fill out the bottom half of double bills (a style of exhibition that was disappearing even as the picture was made). Indeed, the trade reviews, taking into account the film's

limited budget and intent, were quite indulgent, with *Variety* listing
Clint among a group of players giving "fine" performances.

If working conditions had been reasonably professional, and the atmosphere on the set agreeable, it would have been just a minor incident
in what was turning out to be a reasonably promising year for Clint professionally. For while the movie was in postproduction, he was cast in
episodes of *Wagon Train, Navy Log* (in an episode narrated by his idol,
James Cagney) and *Men of Annapolis.* Then, however, *Ambush at Cimarron Pass* was released—ineptly. There was no cast and crew screening, no
advance word of its opening. One morning Clint simply opened his
newspaper and discovered that it was playing all over town as a second
feature. That afternoon he and Maggie headed for a neighborhood
theater, sat through a main feature and prepared themselves for the
worst, which turned out to be more dismaying than anything he had
imagined.

As the picture unreeled, Clint "slumped down so low in [his] seat
it probably looked like Maggie was sitting alone," outraged and shamed
"to sit there in a movie theater and watch this pile of crap run by."
Maggie tried to be supportive, but he was inconsolable: "No, this is
just . . . dog shit. I started thinking, I'm going to go back to school. I'm
going to learn something. I'm going to get some other kind of job. I'm
going to jump out of this."

None of his previous setbacks seem to have shaken his obstinacy and
determination as this one did. However modest this film was, it at least
had offered him his first role with, as they say, an "arc" to it—his character eventually loses his bitterness and makes peace with himself, the
past, his former enemies personified by the sergeant—his first to have
some impact on a film's narrative. At the very least he imagined he could
get "a piece of film" out of it, something his agents could show around
town. But there was nothing even that useful to him here. If anything,
the film seemed likely to harm his cause.

At that point he simply did not yet have the skill and the force—the
experienced actor's powerful sense of himself, or, anyway, his self-
interest—to impose himself on a film, to override its incompetencies
while he was on camera. He was still a little too well mannered for his
own good, exhibiting none of the natural unpredictability, the delinquent dangerousness, the role calls for. A sort of stunned sweetness keeps
shining through his fits of anger, vitiating their force.

But if there is nothing to be particularly proud of in this work, there
is nothing to be deeply ashamed of either. An actor far more experienced than he might have been defeated by these circumstances. More-

over, in his youthful disappointment, Clint couldn't appreciate his own good-looking presence, could not see that he was the film's most attractive figure.

He did not want to get by on looks, of course. He wanted to be an actor in the fullest sense of the term. But what he did not realize, as he endured his little crisis of belief on that spring afternoon in 1958, was that appearances, up to now, in his opinion, a defect, were about to become an asset. For *Gunsmoke* and other shows like it were opening television to a new kind of western, westerns that revolved around what we would now call extended families. These programs had a need for lean, strapping, good-natured lads like Clint Eastwood to assume their man-boy roles. His professional luck was about to turn—definitively.

FOUR

IDIOT OF THE PLAINS

It was the kind of call out-of-work actors often make: A friend in the business suggests dropping by the office sometime in order to meet another friend who might, possibly, introduce him to someone else who might, conceivably, do him some good. Nobody expects much of such encounters, but, still, actors live on hope, and the myth of accidental discovery—the starlet, the talent scout, the soda fountain stool—is undying, precisely because it contains a minuscule element of truth.

Being a practical and realistic young actor, Clint Eastwood would not have been dreaming about one of those casting epiphanies. What he knew was that it was always better to be seen than not seen—especially around the offices of a television network. And, besides, his agent had mentioned that CBS was casting a new western series, though he had also been told that they were looking for a slightly older actor for the lead.

So, having nothing better to do on this afternoon in the early summer of 1958, he decided to take up his friend, Sonia Chernus, on her long-standing invitation to visit her at CBS Television City. She was employed there as a reader; the woman she wanted Clint to meet was an assistant to one of the executives, someone with more influence on her boss than her job title suggested. The introduction was duly made, no special spark was struck, and Clint and Sonia repaired to an indoor-outdoor patio area for talk and refreshments.

They had met through Arthur Lubin, around the time Clint was making *Francis in the Navy,* and she had become one of Clint and Maggie's best friends. After Clint founded Malpaso she would join him as his story editor (and would write the first draft of, and receive cowriting credit for, *The Outlaw Josey Wales*). She would also become something of a surrogate aunt to the Eastwood children when they came along. At this moment she had recently found the short stories (by Walter Brooks) on which Lubin's *Mr. Ed* television series would be based, the pilot of which he was preparing to make. When they finished their coffee Clint decided to walk Sonia back to her office. They were strolling along one of the building's long corridors when a man in a blue suit stepped out of an office, glanced at Clint and said, "Excuse me, are you an actor?"

"Yeah, I am."

"What have you been doing?"

"Well, I've done some television, and I just finished this picture, *Ambush at Cimarron Pass.*"

"Fortunately, he hadn't seen it," Clint recalls. He also recalls doing his best, as they chatted, to exaggerate the importance of his other credits. Sonia, meanwhile, stepped out of the man's eye line and made silent signals to Clint, indicating that his questioner, Robert Sparks, was an important figure at the network. A sometime movie producer, now in charge of filmed programming for CBS, he called Clint into his office and asked his secretary to summon Bill Warren to join him.

Clint, at this point, had never heard of Sparks or Warren, though he might have if Sparks had called the latter by his full name, which was Charles Marquis Warren. Born and educated in Baltimore, he became the protégé of F. Scott Fitzgerald when the writer was living there and Warren was a college student. Fitzgerald even recommended him to M-G-M to adapt *Tender Is the Night,* saying "I haven't believed in anybody so strongly since Ernest Hemingway." Nothing came of that, and Warren instead turned to pulp fiction, later graduating to slicks like *The Saturday Evening Post.* Several of his western serials were published as novels, and one of them, *Only the Valiant,* served as the basis for the Gregory Peck movie, released in 1951.

Warren apparently heard of that sale while he was in the hospital recuperating from wounds suffered filming amphibious landings in the South Pacific during World War II, in which he attained the rank of commander. It emboldened him to try Hollywood, where he was soon working steadily as a writer and a director, first in features, then in television. In 1955 he developed, produced and directed many episodes of *Gunsmoke,* but after one season he left with bad feelings all around. He then coproduced and directed a feature, *Cattle Empire,* which was currently in release. A cattle-drive western starring Joel McCrea, it owed something to Howard Hawks's *Red River,* which had, a decade earlier, set the standard for this subgenre. These two films obviously inspired the new series he was developing for CBS.

A thick-browed, fit-looking man in his midforties, Warren appeared in Sparks's office wearing a battered, writerly sports jacket, his manner not at all prepossessing to Clint, who was leaning back into a sofa, his legs stretched out comfortably before him. "Bill, pleasure," was Clint's casual response to their introduction. He did not know then that Charles Marquis Warren was "Bill" only to friends and close colleagues. At work with strangers it was supposed to be "Mr. Warren," in the same way that John Ford, also a former naval person and a maker of westerns, therefore a figure with whom Warren identified, was always "Mr. Ford" on his sets.

Sparks and Warren started describing *Rawhide* to Clint. Each season a group of cowboys would take a herd of cattle from Texas to a railhead up north. Each week they would encounter and overcome some dramatically arresting threat to their progress. There would be some location work with a rented herd of cattle, and the show would be, by television standards, quite realistic.

This was, indeed, the program Clint had heard about from his agents, and he said that he understood the lead was to be played by a man in his forties, which left him out. That's true, he was told, but there were to be several other running parts in the series, most notably the costarring role of a young ramrod, the older trail boss's second-in-command.

The tenor of the meeting now changed. "All of a sudden, I'm sitting up," says Clint. Warren continued to regard him suspiciously, but Sparks "seemed really wired, really enthusiastic." He vowed that he would pull in *Ambush* to study Clint's work, an idea that filled him with dread. But he left the meeting with Sparks promising that he would hear from them in three or four days. Events moved faster than that. By late afternoon Clint's agent was on the phone telling him that Sparks and Warren were not going to look at the film, but instead wanted to test him. "Great, where are the sides—you got anything for me to look at?" No, came the reply, it's going to be an interview test.

"Well, those aren't so hot," said Clint, understating the matter. They had been the bane of his existence over these years. Never comfortable making small talk with strangers, particularly when he was in the role of supplicant, he felt he had lost several jobs when he was prevented from getting into character. "But I'll do anything," he says, dropping into the present tense as he recalls past tension, "and maybe even at this point in my life I feel a little better than I did a couple of years earlier."

He was back at CBS the next day, slightly dismayed to discover that his champion, Sparks, was not present, and that Bill Warren would be conducting the test. Worse, the rules of play had been changed again. Clint was told to head down to Western Costume and get outfitted in some cowboy clothes—this was going to be a full-scale reading, after all.

"By the way," Warren asked, "how are you at dialogue?"

"Well, I'm OK," Clint replied.

"I've got a monologue."

"A monologue?" said Clint, his heart sinking.

The writer handed him "a full page of solid talk. It's a speech where you had to come in and run up to the camera, and you're supposed to be really pissed off, and deliver this monologue to the camera as if it's a group of people. It's about the hardest thing you could ask a person to do."

As it happened, it was also a portent of things to come. For Bill Warren, though he had, as a writer, a rather good feel for the western form, and especially for measuring the moral weight it could comfortably carry on television, had, as a director, no feel at all for his actors' needs. He was peremptory and insensitive, as this surprise demand for a reading indicated.

Very much the naval officer snapping commands, Warren brooked no discussion from people who were not, after all, enlisted personnel, but creative collaborators with whom, all going well, he would be working year in, year out. It was, indeed, an actors' revolt over his dictatorial ways, led by Milburn Stone, that had driven him off *Gunsmoke* ("The whole unit, everybody, thought he was crazy," Clint remembers hearing). No less a figure than William F. Paley, CBS's founder and chairman, had been obliged to intervene, ordering Warren back to writing and producing, and replacing him on the set with less autocratic directors.

It was now becoming clear to Clint that he was a finalist for the role of Rowdy Yates and that this was a do-or-die audition, for only two other actors of his age, together with the three performers (among them the eventual winner, Eric Fleming) who were up for the role of Gil Favor, the trail boss, joined him rummaging for wardrobe at Western Costume. It was also clear to him that there was no time to memorize perfectly the speech that he had been handed. He observed, however, that there were three transitions in it, and he thought if he got those right and improvised a fiery approximation of the other lines, he might get by. It was the sort of thing he had been doing in some of his acting classes, where, as an exercise, the students were encouraged to get the emotions right and forget about being word perfect with the script.

When they returned to CBS and the small studio where the tests were being filmed, Clint discovered he was going to be up first, took a deep breath and went for it: "I just built up a lot of energy, came running in there [and] blew off steam, tearing those words a whole new rear end."

"That's fine. That'll do it. Thank you," said Warren, but Clint caught a dubious look on his face. "I mean, those words—I've just violated everything." He left the studio in that state of ambivalence so familiar to auditioning actors, pleased with some of his work—in this case the dynamism he had brought to the scene—and anxious about what he had left out, in this case, the boss's writerly nuances.

While Clint was changing back into his street clothes, Fleming did his reading (also a long monologue), and as Clint stepped out of the dressing room he overheard one of his own rivals' test. It was not encouraging: "This guy had it word for word—every single word." And his efforts were appreciated: "That's wonderful, Tom, that is wonderful," he heard Warren say. "I go home and I'm saying, Gee, I blew that one, didn't I? I came so close and I blew it."

Cut now to a screening room at CBS a few days later. Gathered there are Sparks, Warren and a delegation headed by Hubbell Robinson, the network's programming chief, out from New York to make decisions about the fall season. The projectionist in the booth, running footage and listening in on their conversations, was, as it happened, an army acquaintance of Clint's (he can no longer recall his name). The man was somewhat startled to see Clint up on the screen. He was not surprised at the silence that followed the test's running. On these occasions everyone waits for power to speak. After a moment, it did. Said Robinson: "That's the guy. I don't need to see anyone else. I like him." The customary chorus of approval immediately arose.

All of this, of course, was reported to Clint some time later, when he encountered his friend somewhere along the long *Rawhide* trail. According to him, Bill Warren never volunteered any opinion about the tests and was never asked for it, either. Clint speculates, doubtless correctly, that Robinson was completely uninterested in Warren's text and whether or not it was correctly spoken. He was concerned only with the first impressions made by the actors. By showing himself, instead of Warren's words, in the best available light, Clint had made the right choice.

Word that the part was his came from Clint's agent, and it was better than he dared hope. The network, which owned the show outright, was hinting that if the pilot looked good it would immediately commit to thirteen episodes, even if no sponsor was signed on. This, of course, was something Clint desperately needed at this stage of his career— steady work (at a starting salary of $700 an episode) and steady exposure in a part that would establish him in the industry, if not necessarily in the world at large.

The *Rawhide* crew was soon off to Arizona to shoot the first episode as well as stock footage of the cattle herd moving cross-country toward the railhead it never seemed to reach. Joining Clint and Fleming as a costar was Paul Brinegar, in the role of Wishbone, the cook (he had played a similar part for Warren in *Cattle Empire*). Others in the regular cast for much of the show's run included Sheb Wooley (also a song writer, most famously of "Purple People Eaters"), who played Pete Nolan, the scout; James Murdock as Mushy, Wishbone's slow-witted helper; Robert Cabal as Jesus (always pronounced "hey-ZOOS"), the wrangler, and Steve Raines and Rocky Shahan (also out of the *Cattle Empire* cast) as the most prominent of the trail hands.

The pilot was well received at the network, which ordered up twelve more episodes immediately. Ironically, *Rawhide* headquartered at Universal in these early days, and driving on this lot as a series lead just three years after he had been casually dismissed from it pleased Clint inordinately.

CBS was generous with the show in its early days, spending somewhat more than usual on its first episodes. Although Warren directed the pilot and several more in this first batch of shows, others were handled by well-regarded television directors, among them Richard Whorf (who had also done some major features), Andrew V. McLaglen (the actor Victor McLaglen's son, who was beginning to make features) and Ted Post (who had been Warren's principal directorial replacement on *Gunsmoke* and would work regularly on *Rawhide* during much of its run). The well-known guest stars included in these first episodes Dan Duryea, Troy Donahue, Brian Donlevy and Margaret O'Brien—people with solid motion-picture credits and recognition value with the television audience.

Then with only nine episodes shot, it all stopped. Clint and the rest of the company were told that CBS had been unable to interest sponsors in the show and that production was being suspended until some advertising time was sold. They were told to hold themselves available, in anxious limbo.

The advertising community was proving ambiguous about the show. In the medium's earliest years westerns had been strictly kid stuff, and pretty occasional, featuring such childhood favorites as the Lone Ranger, Gene Autry and, of course, that early TV sensation, William Boyd's Hopalong Cassidy, which began by recycling his old B-movie westerns, then continued with a series of fifty-two half hours made specifically for television. *Gunsmoke* and *Cheyenne,* both of which began airing in 1955, changed all that. These were "adult" westerns, and they touched a fifties nerve.

While public discourse of all kinds was at this time straitlaced, not to say prim, the consumer culture was, in contrast, quite self-indulgent. You could see it in the clothes of the New Look, swathing women in extraneous yard goods, in the sculptured voluptuousness of automobile design, in kidney-shaped coffee tables and swimming pools, in the emphasis on ease and convenience in products ranging from frozen foods to power mowers. The TV westerns satisfied both sides of this conflict. Shot in austere black and white, portraying a harsher landscape in which actions could have unambiguous (and often mortal) consequences, they reminded people that they were not that far removed historically from harder times, harder choices. Yet these shows did not render the past in an unbearably realistic light; they tamed the West to suit the mild taste of the time.

In any event, the 1956 and 1957 seasons saw the western cycle gathering power, with such new programs as *The Life and Legend of Wyatt Earp, Broken Arrow, Have Gun, Will Travel, Maverick, Tales of Wells Fargo, The Californians* and *Wagon Train* reaching the air. In 1958, as the first *Rawhide* episodes were being shot, *The Rifleman, Bat Masterson* and *Wanted Dead or Alive* (the vehicle that made Steve McQueen a star) were added to the networks' schedules. And this represented just the top of the line. By 1959, the peak year for the genre, the networks were programming no fewer than twenty-three westerns every week, consuming close to a quarter of the available prime-time hours. In the late fifties and early sixties, westerns, on average, commanded audience shares of about 33 percent. Later in the decade these figures dropped somewhat, but until the early seventies there were typically four westerns listed among the top twenty-five shows in the Nielsen ratings. As Richard Slotkin, the best critic-historian of our western mythology, has commented, "No other type of action/adventure show in this period . . . commanded so consistently high a share of prime time over so many years."

Herein lay the problem for *Rawhide.* There was obviously no pressing need for yet another western, yet given the genre's popularity, it made equally good sense to go ahead with the show. Who knew what this market might bear? As this matter was debated, Clint Eastwood despaired. He remembers this period as psychologically devastating, more difficult to endure than his firing by Universal or his jobless year. He had been able to maintain the illusion that he was doing something about these circumstances simply by going out on auditions. In this case he had no alternative but to stay home and fret, listening to rumors about the show's fate.

Worse, he began to feel he had his "whole career sitting in the basement down there in a bunch of cans at CBS." He could mention *Rawhide* when he was being interviewed for a part, but the network refused to let him show any of its footage to other producers. And he was forbidden to pursue or accept a lengthy role in a feature film because the network kept insisting he might be called back to resume work on the series at any moment. Approached about playing the lead in *Tall Story,* a Broadway comedy about a college basketball player dealing with a bribe offer, which Howard Lindsay and Russell Crouse had adapted from a novel by the poet Howard Nemerov, Clint asked his agents to see if CBS would release him. They were rebuffed, adding to his stress.

The strain eventually told on him physically. One day, for example, he and Maggie were having a drink in a bar with Fritz Manes and his wife, Audrey, when, suddenly, Clint slammed his fist down on the table, yelling a stream of expletives, as dishes and glasses bounced every which way. He had looked down at his hand and seen hives suddenly developing there—"one hundred percent nerves" as Manes puts it. On other occasions Maggie told Audrey Manes he had waked in the night hyperventilating.

While he waited, he did appear on an episode of *Maverick* entitled "Duel at Sundown," and it is probably his best early work. He plays a young gunfighter picking a quarrel with James Garner's ever-charming, eponymous character, and for the first time there is some dangerousness in Clint's portrayal—a touch of generational contempt for Bret Maverick, a bit of youthful insolence and unpredictability in his manner—and Maverick responds to him with a trademark trick, smooth talk not quite hiding cowardice. Even when he was "one of the young guys boppin' around town on television series," Clint likes to insist, "I always thought of myself as a character actor. I never thought of myself as a leading man." This performance offers concrete evidence of that attitude.

But it came and went in a hurry, and Clint sank back into his anxious idleness. "I didn't want to see anybody; I just was feeling kind of sorry for myself," he recalls. With Christmas approaching, Clint and Maggie decided to get out of town and spend the holidays with his parents, who had by this time moved back to Piedmont.

They took a train north, and at one of the stops a telegram was delivered to him. It informed him that *Rawhide* was being slipped into the CBS schedule in a good spot, on Friday night between *Hit Parade* and *The Phil Silvers Show.* Production on new episodes was scheduled to resume in early January. It took Clint a few minutes to digest the news. Then as the train pulled out of the station and began gathering speed, he found himself leaning out the window, yelling crazily, obscenely, at the countryside flowing past. From that point on, he says, "it was a very nice Christmas."

★   ★   ★

Rawhide premiered on January 9, 1959, without anticipatory excitement and without generating any large critical enthusiasm. It was just another western, just another midseason replacement show in the eyes of the press. The first episode, "Incident of the Tumbleweed Wagon" (until the 1964–65 season all titles employed this "Incident of" device) was the last of nine programs shot before the hiatus had been imposed on production, and, in a way, it was a curious introduction to the series precisely because it contained so little introductory material—just a shot of Gil Favor and a brief voice-over monologue by him explaining the function of a cattle drive. Its plot also quickly separated Fleming and Clint from the rest of their outfit, leaving Paul Brinegar and other supporting players in dusty anonymity, their characters unestablished.

The famous tag in which Favor commanded his drovers to "Head 'em up, move 'em out" was also missing. But the still more famous theme song ("Rollin', rollin', rollin', / Keep movin', movin', movin', / Though they're disapprovin' / Keep those dogies movin'"), which was written by Dimitri Tiomkin and Ned Washington, who had also composed the compulsive "High Noon" theme, was very much present, and very helpful in establishing the show, for the catchy, silly tune quickly became a hit, while its linkage to a musical convention then reigning in feature films suggested that *Rawhide* aspired to something like their status.

This may well have been true. Warren was a striver, never modest about stating his belief that good, serious work could be done in a form more often patronized than appreciated. Indeed, Warren liked to tell interviewers that if the network would let him he would expand the show to ninety minutes, approaching feature length. He also liked to insist that in creating his show he had not ripped off old movies. No, he said, its source was a recently discovered diary kept by a Texas cattleman named George Duffield on a nineteenth-century trail drive to Abilene.

He acknowledged, of course, that he was operating within severe limits. Television's small black-and-white screen (which made it an antiepic medium), its low budgets (the typical *Rawhide* episode cost less than forty thousand dollars in the show's early days and was made in six days), its implacable schedules (thirty new programs a year) and the restraints of a censorship more niggling even than that of the movies all worked against the achievement of consistent quality and the creation of a spacious mise-en-scène. But if the format of his show suggested, and Warren was trying to fight, these limits, it also, ironically, doomed him to frustration.

For *Rawhide* was intrinsically more at odds with its medium than the other westerns. Its natural subject matter was obviously to be found in the normal perils of trail herding—bad weather, rough country, the spookiness and recalcitrance of livestock on the move. And from time to time the program took up these topics. But you needed to go on location to do so, and the show traveled to places like Nogales, Sonora and Pasa Robles only once a year, and then the cast and crew were obliged to gather stock footage that could be scattered through many episodes, leaving them time to do portions of only two or three of these more epic stories. The rest of the year the crew was confined to back-lot western streets, sound-stage green sets and the ranches most studios then maintained on the outskirts of Los Angeles for outdoor shooting (there was a small *Rawhide* herd on one of them). These tight spots, more than any other factor, imposed a modest scale on the shows. Something Rita Parks, a scholar of the western, wrote applies with particular aptness to *Rawhide:* "The scaling-down process that takes place in the television western . . . turns the bold colors and vibrance of the epic form into the leisurely pastels of the pastoral mode."

The typical *Rawhide* story involved the cowboys coming upon people along the trail and getting drawn into solving whatever issues they presented or were confronting. As a variant, someone from the trail drive (usually Rowdy) would venture into a town or to a ranch on some errand and encounter some trouble he needed to be extricated from before the herd could move on. The idea, obviously, was to come in from the great outdoors as soon and as often as possible into more easily managed environments.

The episode chosen for the premiere was shot at a studio ranch and differs from the series norm because trouble comes to the drovers without their having to look for it. The tumbleweed wagon referred to in the title is a sort of jail on wheels, used to gather lawbreakers from far-flung prairie locales and transport them (in this case) to a territorial capital for a trial. It pulls up to a streamside campsite where Favor's cowboys are settling down for the night, carrying human cargo mixed in the usual way: a man accused of selling illegal liquor to Indians, an army deserter, a silent Indian who has murdered his wife when he caught her with another brave and, more significantly, an English remittance man also accused of murdering his wife, a member of the Luke Storm bandit gang and a hellcatish woman named Dallas (Terry Moore, the program's top-billed guest star), who is Luke's wife, and a classically bitter good-bad woman (she has turned outlaw because her father was lynched by a vigilante mob for a crime he did not commit).

An escape is attempted, in the course of which the marshal in charge of the wagon is grievously wounded, his deputy killed. Gil and Rowdy are obliged to leave their herd and escort the wagon to the nearest fort. Two more escapes are tried, and eventually Storm and his gang catch up with the wagon as the cowmen are trying to get it across a stream. The outlaw leader, who is a standard-issue psychopath, decides to murder Gil and Rowdy, but Dallas intervenes and is killed by her husband, who, in the subsequent confusion, is shot dead by Favor. The episode ends with a low-angle shot of Gil and Rowdy riding off past the crude cross that marks Dallas's grave.

The failure of this episode to do much with Rowdy Yates was not entirely atypical, particularly in the early seasons. He is seen to be attracted to the captive woman, seen to be quietly rebellious toward Favor (instructed not to try chatting up Dallas, Rowdy tells the trail boss, "After dark, when I'm not on night herd, my time is my own"), and he gets the chance to wrestle with Dallas during the first escape attempt—sexless sexiness of the old-movie, old-TV kind. But for the most part Rowdy takes orders and seems to like them. "Rowdy Yates, trail flunky," is how Clint says he used to describe his character, when he wasn't calling him "Rowdy Yates, idiot of the plains."

You can tell from Clint's modified ducktail haircut and from the fact that he alone among the drovers was allowed the occasional passing romance that Rowdy was intended to have a certain demographic appeal; he was supposed to attract young women to a program that had small intrinsic interest for them. That meant that he should have had a sort of mild, outlaw appeal. But Rowdy was never allowed his rowdiness, sexual or otherwise. One runs into women, now in their late forties and early fifties, for whom the young Clint Eastwood was a teen dream, but that was because he was—obviously—a really cute guy, not because of any overt sexiness on his part. Clint was aware at the time of what he was supposed to be doing ("Rowdy was sort of the bopper, but older gals liked Mr. Favor"), yet he was equally aware that for the producers this was dangerous country, occasionally approached but in the end always skirted.

There were times when Rowdy initiated an episode's central action, and other times when he played a key role in bringing it to a satisfying conclusion. But often as not, his contributions to an "incident" were about what they were in his first appearance—a couple of decent scenes and then a few more appearances in which Clint's acting consisted largely of reacting.

All in all it was the guest stars who got to do the most interesting work. The regulars, to the show's writers and directors, were the givens in the weekly equation they had to solve—no reason to fuss unduly over them—and they were, as Clint recalls, often left to their own devices, making up their own bits of business, their own modest subtexts, doing what they could to stay interested and grab a little screen time they might call their own.

But if the regulars were more or less taken for granted creatively, they were vital to the success of the show, which debuted fairly low in the ratings (forty-second in its first week), but made it to the top twenty within three weeks and remained there for four seasons. They, not the guests, had to win the loyal regular weekly audience that all long-lived television programs must recruit. Here the convention of regarding the regular cast as family aided the writers. The ups and downs of their long-term relationships constituted a sort of tacit running story easily sketched in: Gil Favor, the stern but forgiving father figure; Wishbone, the fussy mom feeding them, dressing their wounds, occasionally interceding for them with the trail boss when he became too authoritarian; Rowdy, the number-one son, a good kid, troublesome (or anyway inconveniencing) because he was idealistic and quick to take up the cause of troubled or ill-used people, especially females; and so on down the cast list.

The TV plains were alive with such patriarchies in those days. *Gunsmoke, Wagon Train, Bonanza, The Virginian* and *The High Chaparral* featured all-wise elders rallying a real or surrogate family against the anarchic threat posed by the outsider, the other. It says something about the popular culture's raging need for a particular kind of order that this pattern was imposed on the television western, thereby creating a spurious historical example to reassure the suburban middle-class family that it had made the right choice, should be wary of intruders, adventurings, passionate emotions. Indeed, this imposition was essentially new to the fictive West—a weak coinage that would eventually drive out the stronger species offered by theatrical westerns.

We had, for instance, occasionally witnessed in movies the creation and defense of cattle empires (besides *Red River* there had been *Duel in the Sun* and *The Furies* among others), but in these films the emperor-patriarch was seen as a dark and driven creature, making life miserable for his children. Even in films that did not focus primarily on such characters, the cruelly patriarchal rancher (often attended by his moronic and sadistic get) driving out homesteaders (representing more benign family values) infringing on his domain was a familiar figure.

Gunslinging loners were, too, especially in the late forties and early fifties, as westerns enjoyed a renaissance and gained a new respectability with critics and the middlebrow audience, films like *The Gunfighter* (1950), *High Noon* (1952) and *Shane* (1953). Rather self-consciously "classical" in form and "serious" in intent, they were, perhaps, westerns for people who didn't really like westerns, but all at least concerned

themselves sympathetically with the fate of their professional killers—
which is what a gunfighter is in essence—very different from the traditional western hero, the small rancher or cowboy who is an amateur
with guns, strapping them on reluctantly and only after insistent provo-
cation.

These films in effect prepared the way for tougher, less culturally aspiring but often more interesting studies of the gunfighter—the hard-
bitten wanderers played by James Stewart in the Mann films, the grave,
courtly, profoundly isolated westerner Randolph Scott portrayed in the
austere, low-budget pictures Budd Boetticher made for the star's Ra-
nown company. These lean, hard movies (which have deservedly grown
in repute over the years) offered us, if you will, David Reisman's "inner
directed man" kitted out in chaps and spurs, living by his own rules and
paying a price for his alienation. Or maybe he was a kind of romantic
outcast, almost a poetic figure, so devoted to his rare and deadly art that
he was unfit for normal society, just as real poets, real artists, seemed to
be in the fifties. One could even see him as Richard Slotkin does in
Gunfighter Nation—an embodiment of America's paradoxical self-image
during the Cold War, "at once supremely powerful and utterly vulnerable, politically dominant yet helpless to shape the course of critical
events."

But however you saw him, this much was certain: You did not see
him for long on television. It may be, as many have suggested, that the
popularity of the movie western initiated the western cycle on television. But its key figures, the ripsnorting patriarchs and the radically
alienated gunmen among others, were deemed too rich for the television audience's blood. These were roles for the guest stars to play, characters who briefly, colorfully, menaced the decorous little world they
invaded only to be overcome within the hour by the collective gumption and good values of its permanent residents.

There is something consensual here, some need for nightly reassurance that the family (which was also metaphorically a small corporation), properly managed and controlled, could be an institution for all
seasons, that its leader, its father figure, was capable of mastering all situations. Daddy always knew best, even in the wide-open spaces. The old
general in the fifties White House, the older doctors and lawyers on the
medical and legal shows, the younger but no less controlling fathers of
the sitcoms—all eventually rounded up their charges and headed 'em
out on a righteous path.

When today's right-wing social critics call for the media to celebrate
"family values," it is something like this that they are nostalgically attempting to summon up. They forget—as people refused to acknowl-

edge at the time—that there was always something abnormal about fifties normalcy. At best, that word refers us in any period to a consensus about what the culturally dominant middle class believes to constitute the good—or, anyway, respectable—life for its members and aspirants. Yet everyone knows that millions are excluded—or exclude themselves—from these consensuses. The Era of Good Feelings that we thought we shared in the fifties was in the largest sense a fraud or, at best, a kind of metafiction. On most important matters—the relationships between races, sexes, classes and generations, for example—it grotesquely, even tragically, misrepresented reality, with the mass media amplifying (and in the process further distorting) this misrepresentation.

★   ★   ★

In these early days, Clint Eastwood would not have stated the issue in quite those terms. It would take a few seasons for him to grow restive with the sterilities of his series and for certain other disappointments to manifest themselves. He definitely would have preferred to play a more forceful western figure—someone more enigmatic, more independent, at the least less callow than Rowdy Yates. But before that thought fully crystallized in his mind, the program's lack of true stylistic grit bothered him. The televised West was a very tidy West. The cry, "Get out the nine iron" (a shovel) would go up whenever a horse made droppings on the set. It would not do if the camera accidentally encountered even this much realism. The stock footage of the cattle on the move presented a similar problem; every once in a while the camera would pick up a bull trying to mount a cow, an occurrence the network's standards and practices department would not countenance. Warren was himself similarly compulsive. He insisted, for instance, that cattle on the move always had to traverse the screen in the same direction.

Clint's contempt for inflexibility of this kind remains lively, even in recollection. As a director, Warren was "heavy, ponderous, slow," as Ted Post, who directed many *Rawhide* episodes, says. "He didn't understand that every scene has its own particular rhythms, and the rhythms give it variety, and the interest and the colors." Worse, he "commanded" the actors. "You've got to give them the feeling that they're in control," as Post puts it, "and utilize whatever sensitivity and temperament they have to extract the values that the scene calls for." Warren, in his opinion, "plugged them up."

As a producer Warren was equally difficult to work with, and his behavior in this role had a still larger effect on the company's morale. Clint thinks, perhaps, he had something of a drinking problem, though he kept it reasonably well hidden. He also tended to keep erratic hours, doing much of his work at night, a habit that particularly irritated Fleming. "I love him," Fleming told a reporter after he left the show, "but I loved fifty other men who were trying to make a living and he'd come in at 6 p.m., ready to work when everybody was ready to quit."

A more serious matter was that, as Clint puts it, "there was never a good honesty" between Warren and his coworkers. When the show first went on the air Clint, Fleming and the rest of the regular cast were dismayed to discover that they did not receive billing at the top of the show, but rather at the end.

Warren, it would seem, was attempting to gain an early, authoritative purchase on another problem endemic to series television. The regular performers, embodying characters that don't develop much over the years, become restless, if not downright mutinous, making ever more outrageous demands on their employers. These they can back up, for as a show runs on, power tends to flow toward its regular stars. Network executives like to pretend that they are not necessarily the source of their show's appeal, that they could make do without them, but it is a hypothesis they are not eager to test.

Because of his experiences on *Gunsmoke,* Warren was particularly alert to this problem. Doubtless he thought that by asserting his will at the outset, he would stave off future challenges. His strategy failed. The producer quickly lost on the billing issue and succeeded only in making himself everyone's agreed-upon enemy. "He'd tell you what you wanted to hear, then behind you he'd go off and do something else," Clint says, "and he was always playing one character off against another" within the company.

At first, he focused especially on Clint and Fleming. It was, for Warren, a promising situation, for if he could turn the costars against one another, they would be unlikely to collaborate against him. And they had almost come to blows on their first location shoot in Arizona, when Fleming openly criticized Clint for being slow with some dialogue. Then when tempers cooled, they patched up their differences. They would never become close friends, but they remained by all accounts comfortable colleagues for much of the show's long run.

This was not always easy to manage, for Fleming was, as Clint describes him, an altogether prickly character. "He loved to shock people [with] radical statements—annoy a lot of people." *Rawhide* was just as big a break for him as it was for Clint—maybe bigger, for he had been scuffling along the fringes of their profession somewhat longer. But unlike his costar, the cranky, self-destructive Fleming could not relax and enjoy it. If this was Clint's first big chance to show what he could do, this was—at least in his own mind—Fleming's last chance of doing so, and he made the worst of it.

Fleming was only five years older than Clint, and their backgrounds were not entirely dissimilar. Also a native Californian, Fleming (who was born Edward Heddy) was the son of an itinerant carpenter and had dropped out of high school to serve in the Seabees during World War II. Thereafter he entered show business as a stagehand, took some acting lessons, got an early job in a touring company of *Happy Birthday* starring Miriam Hopkins, moved on to small roles in the Broadway companies of *My Three Angels* and *Stalag 17,* then drifted to Los Angeles, where he found minor roles in television and movies. This was the first job he had ever had with a future that might be measured in years instead of weeks.

Fleming did not, however, bring to it a sense of gratitude or relief, but rather the bitterness accumulated over many frustrating years in the business. His initial suspicion of Warren quickly turned to active dislike, and he maintained that attitude toward the producer's several successors and toward network executives as well.

He was, to be sure, handicapped by the aftereffects of an accident. Working in a foundry during his Seabees days he had attempted to lift a two-hundred-pound steel counterweight and had dropped it on his face. This led to plastic surgery and doubtless contributed to his perpet- ually frozen expression. This he tried to distract from by overacting vo- cally. He was "a hamola" in Ted Post's characterization, someone "you had to cork a lot."

So this isolated man, alternately withdrawn and blustery, never es- tablished himself, as the other prairie patresfamilias did, as a source of warmth and strength with viewers. On-screen he seemed, somehow, to be pasted into this landscape instead of being an organic part of it. Off- screen he became, in effect, the black hole at the center of this little uni- verse, something everyone—especially the writers—had to navigate around.

Fleming did have his strengths: an air of command (mostly a func- tion of his booming baritone) and—a gift Clint envied—his ability to memorize a page of dialogue at a glance and rattle it off without hesita- tion. "If I had a long speech and it had anything in it, it took a lot out of me. But it didn't with him. He'd just clip through it." And he could sometimes be cheerful about his limitations. "Now these guys," Clint would remember him saying about the rest of the cast, "these guys can act. I'm just a hack." But he had no gift for fun and did not much join in the camaraderie of the show, spending much of his time in his dress- ing room or silently reading magazines on the set while he waited for shots to be readied.

Thinking about his costar, Clint recalls meeting James Arness when they were both surfing at San Onofre, and falling into conversation about series television work. "Don't you get sick of it?" Clint asked.

"Yeah, I've been sick of it lots of times, but I make a hell of a good living doing this." Arness paused and added: "You know, I'm just gonna run it till it falls over."

Clint saw the wisdom in this, especially since Arness had an ownership position in his program. "He just decided that was about as good as it was going to get for him. He wasn't going to be John Wayne."

The problem for Fleming, the one that finally subsumed all his other problems, was that he was not even going to be James Arness, and after two or three years on the series he knew it.

Differences in their personalities and talents aside, Clint was at quite a different position than Fleming on his career curve. He was not about to threaten to quit the series, which was Fleming's usual tactic when he was frustrated. He had observed other actors leaving series prematurely, when they reached the first heights of popularity, thereby "losing a lot of income." On the contrary, "It was nice having a steady job in a business where a steady job seemed like it was absolutely unobtainable. You always dreamed of it, actually working every day and getting paid every week and getting a following of sorts." As Ted Post recalls, "He didn't want to stir things up, which would endanger his making a living." In the early years, "The security factor played a very important role, I think. This was a wonderful break that he wasn't going to turn his back on."

Besides, steady work fed into another of Clint's beliefs. He frequently tells an anecdote about a great classical trumpet player of the 1940s, some of whose friends were startled to find him playing in a band at a Hollywood Stars minor league baseball game one day. "Maestro, what are you doing here?" one of them asked. "You must play every day," the musician replied simply. In the same vein Clint sometimes quotes Dizzy Gillespie to this effect: "When you stop using your lip your brain starts doing funny things."

★   ★   ★

Each year Clint stayed with *Rawhide* his salary improved, reaching the neighborhood of about $100,000 a year toward the end of the run. CBS offered to defer part of his salary, and he took the network up on it. It saved taxes, and the money accrued interest while the network held it for him. But more important, "When the series was over I'd be able to sit back rather than have to take the first job that came along." His idea was to escape the television rut by having the financial wherewithal to wait for good parts in feature films. In those days, he recalls, he and Maggie lived very comfortably on a few hundred dollars a week. And, indeed, in *Rawhide*'s second season they were able to move out of their Arch Drive quarters into a larger Studio City apartment. A Sunday supplement picture story shows them miming bourgeois ordinariness there: He helps her hang a picture she has painted, looks dubiously at a dress she bought, grumpily goes over the month's bills, which are spread out on a card table between them.

A couple of years later, they bought their first home, a comfortable, but by no means overbearing, three-bedroom house located on a cul-de-sac about halfway down the north slope of Beverly Glen, with a pleasant view of the San Fernando Valley from its terrace. Clint and his friends dug the swimming pool (it was the occasion for a memorable party), and he put in a gym above the garage. In this period, too, the Eastwoods began renting a retreat in Carmel, where they eventually purchased land, intending to build what they said would be their principal residence—a project that was held in abeyance for years because of zoning squabbles.

They delayed having children. At some point in this period Maggie contracted hepatitis—as Clint says "almost as badly as you can get it without ceasing to exist"—and the disease lingered for more than a year. Clint subsequently suggested that her illness and their fear of its after-effects was one reason they did not begin a family. He also alluded to his desire not to face the problems his parents had confronted trying to provide for children when they were not solidly established financially. But one has to believe it was the commitment children represented that caused him to hesitate, for his commitment to this marriage was not wholehearted. His need to come and go as he pleased, without offering lengthy explanations to anyone, had not abated. It was the way he had conducted his life since adolescence, and he was incapable of altering a pattern that, indeed, persists to this day. He and he alone controls his calendar, and though he rarely breaks dates, he is also reluctant to make them very far in advance. It is one of the ways he defines freedom.

This does not mean that he was, in these days, constantly out with other women. Sometimes he was out with the guys. Sometimes he was out with guys and gals in an innocently mixed group. Sometimes he was out at Jack Kosslyn's acting classes. Sometimes he was just out at the movies. But, yes, he was sometimes out alone with some woman. He was incapable of remaining completely faithful to his wife. It was the unspoken secret of their relationship, though he once came close to revealing it. In his 1974 *Playboy* interview, which contains his most extensive public comments on the marriage, the subject of "open" relation-ships came up, and he characterized Maggie as "a woman who knows how much room I need." She put it differently some years later: "He had this thing about being a loner, like I kind of didn't exist sometimes. He's a very complex person."

Clint was by all accounts affectionate with "Mags" or "Magoo" as he sometimes calls her, and when he spoke publicly about their mar-riage, he stressed its companionability. "Everybody talks about love in marriage, but I think it's just as important to be friends," he said in 1974. He was careful to consult her about career decisions, and she went so far as to attend a few beginner's classes at Kosslyn's studio, trying to gain a better understanding of his work.

In the *Playboy* interview, he stressed Maggie's freedom to do as she pleased, to take up any job or avocation she liked without consulting him. He also mentioned his own lack of sexual jealousy and authoritar-ianism. "I'm not shooting orders to her on where she's supposed to be every five minutes, and I don't expect her to shoot them at me." He sug-gested that this was one of the reasons the marriage had lasted as long as it had.

But there was more to it than that. Besides being careful not to order her husband around, Maggie was also careful to avoid asking him diffi-cult questions. Possibly she was naive. Perhaps she was, as we would now put it, in denial. But the fact is that she seems not to have inquired into his endless comings and goings very often or very deeply. "She had an incredible eraser," says Fritz Manes.

"I was never very realistic about some things," she said some years later. "I used to always hope for the best. I wanted to protect myself. I wondered about it, but I didn't dwell on it, because it probably would have driven me insane. I'm sure there must have been times, but I just preferred to hang in there and not worry too much about it."

It was well along in the *Rawhide* years when she drew Manes aside at a party and rather diffidently asked him if he thought Clint was "play-ing around." She accepted his reassurances (though he knew otherwise), and he believes that Maggie did not fully admit to herself that Clint was unfaithful to her until the late seventies, some time after his relationship with Sondra Locke was well established and widely rumored. Don Kin-cade, Clint's other old high-school friend, who remained close to both Eastwoods, thinks Clint's unfaithfulness placed a strain on their marriage much earlier.

But whatever the case, promiscuity was not, for Clint, one of the prerogatives of his newfound fame. It had been "habitual" for him be-fore his marriage, and it would remain so after it ended: "It just became . . . I don't know . . . addictive . . . like you have to have another cigarette." It consumed half of his life, some thirty years in his estimation.

But "consumed"—a word that implies obsession—is perhaps not quite the right word. His manner when he makes this admission is neither boastful nor regretful. Certainly it appears to be untouched by guilt. The need to have many women was a fact of his life, his nature if you will, and it remains an undeniable fact of his history.

His opportunities increased as his "following" increased, and when he became, as he puts it, "a motion-picture actor of some renown, traveling to locations around the world all the time by yourself," the temptations were almost daily. (Sometimes these reached comical levels. A friend of his recalls sharing a hotel elevator after a banquet in his honor in Paris, and a grinning Clint pulling three room keys out of his pockets; all had been placed there by women he had met at the dinner.) We are perhaps in the realm of evolutionary psychology here. As its great explicator Robert Wright tells us, prominent males, like dominant primates, are designed to capitalize sexually on their status. Fame, power and riches draw the attention of women, their own neurochemistry urges such men on and all the rest is easy moralizing and/or spiteful envy. Given Clint's cool realism, especially about his own needs, it is a plausible explanation of his sexual behavior.

But if that seems too coldly rational, one might resort to John Updike. The writer, who is of Clint's generation and is perhaps the novelist who has most accurately portrayed the sexuality of its men, wrote of one of his protagonists: "What he wanted was for women to stay put, planted in American plenty, while he ambulated from one to another carrying no more baggage than the suit on his back and the car keys in his pocket." It fits Clint—so amiable, so uninsistent, so lacking in macho poses. It fits many men formed by his times.

A modern feminist may deplore this mind-set (as many have deplored Updike's failure to write judgmentally about it). A male may envy another man who is able to act on it so casually. But such evidence as there is suggests that he made no promises, held out no hopes, that he could not fulfill. And the discretion with which he conducted his romantic transactions is obvious, since no public unpleasantness, certainly no scandal, attached to them until his famous falling-out with Sondra Locke in 1989. "Sex is a small part of life," he was once quoted as saying. "It's a good thing—great—but 99.9 percent of your life is spent doing other things."

★   ★   ★

He was obviously a man who knew how to keep things in perspective. Work included. Work especially. Making a television series, like low-budget moviemaking, is potentially a trap. If its repetitiveness does not turn a series lead into a raging egomaniac it can quickly turn him into a hack if he succumbs to its numbing routines.

This was potentially a threat to Clint. Fleming's querulousness and Warren's manipulations aside, *Rawhide* was a comfortable place to work. It would have been easy to sink into laziness and inattention, and sometimes they did. Everyone, for instance, liked fooling around with their omnipresent six-shooters. "I was fairly adept with it," Clint remembers, "because you'd do it all day. You'd have nothing to do but drawing guns, twirling and stuff. You'd have calluses on your hand." While the show was headquartered at M-G-M this activity drew something of a crowd, because people like Elvis Presley and Sammy Davis Jr. loved fast-draw and would drop over to practice with the guys. The latter, in fact, left a pistol of his, which had once belonged to Gary Cooper, to Clint in his will.

But all the idle hours were not idly occupied. If you are alert and open to its processes, filmmaking on this level can offer a practical education that no film school, no dramatic academy, can duplicate. Clint puts it this way: "It's not like you get to wear a different wardrobe each time, or go to a different location. It is like factory work. So how do you take an assembly line job and make it more exciting for you every day?" His technique was to look at an episode from the director's point of view one week, then the next, see how he could vary his character a little bit—"sort of self-experimentation all the time."

Clint never really liked the character of Rowdy Yates. He concedes that over the run of the show Rowdy "grew a little bit," in that he developed from his original incarnation as "a young guy who was not too swift, not too educated, just drifting along wanting to be in the cattle business." From representing "impetuous youth, going off without thinking it through" he became someone "they started giving more responsibility to." But still—"I never got to really play a character with him that I wanted." By that he means that there was no darkness in him, not even some odd quirks. "I kept thinking," Clint once told an interviewer, "wouldn't it be great to play the hero sort of like the villain is normally portrayed, and give the villain some heroic qualities."

But no matter how they fuss and fume actors are finally powerless to alter television formulas. The best they can hope to do is point up a scene here, a moment there. "That was the big challenge," says Clint, "to take a scene that was really bad and make it a pretty interesting scene—or at least passable. It's like taking an F grade and making it a C-minus."

There were times when such craftsmanlike pleasures were satisfying enough. "We were still young, naive people, and we were going around saying we were looking for a great play to do, a great movie to do. And I said, 'You know, there's something about having to do shit every week and trying to put perfume on it and it still may end up being a hog.'" Or as he once put it somewhat more formally: "Having the security of being in a series week in, week out, gives you great flexibility; you can experiment with yourself, try a different scene different ways. If you make a mistake one week, you can look at it and say, 'Well, I won't do that again,' and you're still on the air next week."

Besides learning by doing, Eastwood could study acting by observing. Over the years, as Clint puts it, "Every kind of person imaginable came through." All ages were represented, every kind of experience, every possible approach to the craft. Older movie stars—Barbara Stanwyck, Mary Astor, Brian Aherne, George Brent, Walter Pidgeon, Cesar Romero—worked the show. So did veteran movie character people—Peter Lorre, Walter Slezak, Agnes Moorehead, Claude Rains, Ralph Bellamy, Victor McLaglen, Burgess Meredith. On the other hand, the "New York actors" (as they were then referred to)—the likes of Julie Harris, Kim Hunter, John Cassavetes, E. G. Marshall, Rip Torn, Pat Hingle, George Grizzard—people out of quite a different acting tradition, often signed on. And then there were the young Hollywood comers, actors like Beau and Jeff Bridges, Charles Bronson, James Coburn, Robert Blake, on the way to star careers of their own. There were also what might be called novelty acts: Frankie Avalon, Shelley Berman, Dean Martin.

"That was a great experience for me," says Clint, "watching other people, seeing them operate, watching the different techniques." What was true of the actors was equally true of the directors. "I just would watch everything," Clint says, "the old-timers and the new-timers and some of the hacks, too." Besides those already mentioned for their work on the early episodes of the series, Clint cites as exemplars Tay Garnett, Stuart Heisler and his old Universal nemesis, Jack Arnold, all of whom had extensive experience in features. Clint also remembers as conscientious craftsmen Christian Nyby and Laslo Benedek, both former editors. These men may not have been "auteurs," but they were repositories of vast amounts of professional lore, craftsmen who knew how to stage action or to extract what values there were in sketchy dramatic scenes efficiently, effectively, unpretentiously, and whose pride in their professionalism—in doing their best within whatever limits were imposed on them—armored them against cynicism. It's impossible to say how consciously Clint took in their underlying—dare one say it?—aesthetic values, since in this crowd it was a point of pride not to speak of these matters openly. But he did assimilate the working attitudes of the best directors: their belief that even in cliché forms respectable work can be accomplished if you are knowledgeable and well prepared, their contempt for time wasted on theoretical chat, for money wasted on making the producer feel important or the star more secure. The point—no, the morality—was simple: Get the work and the money on the screen.

It is, of course, equally useful to learn how not to make a film, and *Rawhide* was richly provided with dull directors dutifully, ineptly grinding their way through whatever pages the day's schedule required. "You do 250 hours of television, you learn what makes one prop man good and another fair and another lousy, and what makes one cameraman better than another one," Clint once said. "You learn about leadership, how one week a crew can move very fast and efficiently and the next week drag. About 90 percent of the time, it's the fault of the director."

Many of these "turkeys," Clint once recalled, "didn't direct much; they'd just come in and set up the shots and not tamper too much. And we were regular characters who ran throughout the show, so pretty much you had to guideline your own performance." That, as it happened, turned out to be the most useful experience of all for a man who would eventually direct himself in so many films; it developed the inner eye he keeps trained on himself.

★   ★   ★

None of this should be taken to imply that Clint Eastwood was every day in every way a nice guy. He could not always guard his temper. He lost it most memorably on location in Arizona in the early days of the show. Clint had twisted his ankle rather severely, making it uncomfortable for him to stand. He had to do a riding shot and asked an assistant director to bring a chair out and hide it behind a tree where some camera gear was stored, safely out of the shot, so he could rest for a minute before going on to the next one. Arriving at his destination, Clint found no chair. He sought out the AD and asked, "Did you think I was kidding when I said I wanted a chair over there?" The man was smoking a cigar, and he took it out of his mouth, started waving it in Clint's face and telling him off. Clint shoved him. The man charged him, and Clint dropped him. This set off a quite satisfying general brawl.

Clint's larger dissatisfactions with the show, though growing steadily, were expressed only in the most guarded terms outside the company. In a 1961 *TV Guide* profile of Clint, Bill Warren chose to understand Clint's complaints as the kind that one learns to expect from actors working in a long-running series. "Like any other actor, he beefs now and again, but they're generally justifiable beefs. If he thinks his part is too small in any given script, I'll hear about it." Possibly so. But Clint's restiveness had other, more compelling sources.

Clint rather diffidently mentioned one of them in this same article, which described him as "an amiable, quiet-spoken giant," and made much of his habit of picking struggling bees and grasshoppers off the water in swimming pools and returning them to their natural habitats. ("I always feel they were put here for some purpose and it's not my business to let them drown," he said.) Buried well down in the anonymously written piece was this quote: "I'm under contract to CBS, and sometimes they won't let me do an outside show because of what they call 'sponsor conflict.'" This, Clint felt, was "farfetched." But he quickly added that "it's really not all that important, so I let it go." The reporter also let it go, having bought Clint's self-description—"dull but happy"—and constructed his lackadaisical profile around it.

Actually it was gnawing at him, this inability to expand beyond *Rawhide*. He and the other actors were encouraged to make personal appearances at rodeos—a pleasant way to earn an extra $1,500 now and then—and with Sheb Wooley Clint worked up a double act, singing and telling jokes. (Sometimes, they'd stop off in Las Vegas on the way to their gigs to steal material from the comedy acts there.) But this scarcely constituted a career move. These audiences already knew and liked Clint. He needed to expand his range, establish himself with a more upscale audience than his show attracted.

Curiously, the one show-business realm that was taking an interest in him was the recording industry. It was, as Clint says, "sort of fashionable to take anybody who had a little warmth going, who made it in a TV series or something," and, if they could carry a tune, make a pop single or two to test their teen appeal. This was especially so after Edd (Kookie) Byrnes of *77 Sunset Strip* had a hit with "Kookie, Kookie (Lend Me Your Comb)." So around the time *TV Guide* profiled him, Clint cut a single called "Unknown Girl of My Dreams," backed by the standard "For All We Know."

The record made no impact. "Unknown Girl" was strictly bubblegum, a plaint about an idealized dream girl for whom the singer yearns—not at all Clint's kind of music. It wasn't that he was bad; it was just that he was not very good or, perhaps one should say, not very singular. The disc sounds like a hundred, a thousand, virtually unheeded, long-since-forgotten pop records of the day. But he cut two more singles in the next two or three years and a full-scale long-playing record, *Rawhide's Clint Eastwood Sings Cowboy Songs.*

On all of these records he demonstrates a nice boyish baritone, and there's a musicianship about his work, which possibly surprised such listeners as he had, that is in keeping with his own seriousness about music. He strains a bit in the upper register and uses a certain amount of vibrato to disguise some insecurities of pitch. One feels about his singing what one feels about his early acting efforts—that he is giving it a good, serious shot, doing the best possible job in the circumstances (which includes arrangements that are utterly banal).

The album of cowboys songs is certainly the most ambitious of these efforts and the most conscientiously produced. The other singles are on the "Unknown Girl" level, with one of them offering a piece obviously written to order. "Rowdy" is—no other word for it—a hoot. And it is also, in its way, quite interesting:

I'm gonna leave some day, go far, far away
And find me a home and a love of my own
When I find that little girl, and I will some day,
I'm gonna treat her kind and good, I'll change my Rowdy way . . .

And so forth. The tactic plea is, of course, to take the lonely, wandering lad to heart, something shrewd Tin Pan Alley judged mooning teenage girls ought to be eager to do. They weren't. The recording went nowhere. What's intriguing about the song is that in its banal and calculated way, it gave Rowdy Yates more of an inner life, more of a romantic spirit than the show's scripts typically did. Imagine a Rowdy Yates who was not job and issue oriented, a man capable of long, sad thoughts as the campfire died. It might have been interesting—especially for the increasingly restless actor playing him.

For six months after the *TV Guide* profile appeared, Clint's mood could no longer be called "amiable." "Calm on the outside and boiling on the inside" is how one trade-paper columnist put it, "livid" because CBS refused to allow him to make features or appear on other television programs as a guest star. The network, Clint said, offered him "excuses you wouldn't believe" to justify a policy Clint claimed violated his contract, and he was no longer going to put up with it. "Maybe they really figure me as the sheepish nice guy I portray in the series, but even a worm has to turn some time." Having thoroughly mixed his metaphors, he said he was prepared to go on suspension until an adjustment was made. If he could not work in the United States he claimed—exaggerating hugely—he had movie offers from London and Rome that he was prepared to take.

This tempest was calmed. In the spring of 1962 Clint was permitted to take an outside assignment—on *Mr. Ed,* which after a year in syndication was now in its first season on CBS. Sonia Chernus cowrote "Clint Eastwood Meets Mr. Ed," which had its obvious uses for the network as cross-promotion and as a means of placating Clint.

It was not exactly what he had been looking for. It was, he recalls dismissively, just something that Sonia talked him into doing—the fifty-first of the 143 episodes (every one of them directed by Lubin) in an entirely inconsequential series that has since become something of a cult favorite (it reran for years in the eighties and early nineties on the Nickelodeon cable channel, and it remains a steady seller in the international market). But in some ways Chernus and her collaborator, Lou Derman (the show's head writer), served Clint rather well. He looks swell in modern mufti (golf sweater and slacks for most of the show, a suit in its last sequence), gets to play outrage, comic befuddlement and, in the end, clever authoritativeness. He even gets to be something more than a straight man for two or three brief moments.

As the title suggests, Clint plays a bachelor version of himself, newly moved into the neighborhood where Wilbur and Carol Post (Alan Young and Connie Hines) live in suburban sterility. They have the standard TV neighbors, Roger and Kay Addison (Larry Keating and Edna Skinner), who drop in to comment dryly on their confusions. This episode opens with Carol angry at Wilbur, thinking perhaps he's been out with another woman, when in fact he's been chasing the errant Ed. The horse has wandered off angry because Clint's horse, Midnight, a larger and more glamorous creature ("next to him I look like a poodle"), has been making out with the neighborhood fillies. (Besides accepting the absurdity of a talking horse, viewers had to accept the idea of a suburb full of horses casually dropping in on one another.) In revenge, Carol has proposed Wilbur as writer and star of an amateur show. Mr. Ed, too, has a dark plan in mind—to drive Clint and his horse out of his territory.

He arranges with the phone company to get on Clint's party line. When a movie producer calls to offer Clint a part in a feature—Chernus providing her pal a little wish fulfillment—Ed sabotages the conversation by speaking for Clint: "But you couldn't afford me, you cheap old windbag," he tells the producer. Needless to say, Clint doesn't get the job. A little later his girlfriend (seen stretched out, femme fatale style, on a chaise longue cuddling a lapdog) gets the same treatment. Ed pretends to be the father of a rival and says, "Listen, little girl, if you're smart you'll cut this con artist off right now. He's been promising to marry my daughter for over a year."

Clint traces the calls to Wilbur's house and threatens to punch him out, but, of course, peace is quickly made. The central conceit of the series is that only Wilbur knows Ed can talk, so he can never fully explain the mischief he causes. But, in the horse's hearing, Clint mentions that Midnight is going to work in a film abroad and that he is replacing him with "a pretty little filly." This causes Ed to relent and nuzzle him affectionately. That relation squared away, Clint supplies Wilbur with a script for the charity show, and in the course of directing it patches up the quarrel between the Posts.

No, it definitely isn't *Seinfeld*. Indeed, looking at something like *Mr. Ed* today, one can't help but reflect on how quick the turnover is in pop culture. Connie Hines's bras turn her breasts into unyielding missiles, the art direction turns her house into an unlived-in, shop-window vision of middle-class life, and the scripts turn her into a child, alternately sulky and hysterical. This is perhaps because her only real function is to make sandwiches for a husband who is a wimp and an incompetent (when Clint at one point slaps him on the shoulder, he nearly falls over; at another moment when he playfully punches the guest star in the stomach, his hand is stung by its hardness). Indeed, the show runs on the irony that its only fully human character—libidinous, cynical, imaginatively unfettered—is, in fact, a horse. In the fifties and early sixties, television dared not give those qualities to any creature who might believably, threateningly, act on them.

It cannot be said that his *Mr. Ed* appearance did much to resolve Clint's career frustrations. If anything, its demographic profile was less elevated than *Rawhide*'s, and he was still trapped in low-key amiability. On the other hand, the show gave him the full star treatment. When Carol and Kay realize that a real TV star is standing in the former's living room, they go all swoony, which gives him a chance to demonstrate that he is just a nice, ordinary guy. This was—for that matter, remains—the standard way of presenting celebrity guest performers on sitcoms. When the show's regular cast gets to know the famous person, he always turns out to be very like the best self he presents in whatever role he plays, but charmingly less impressed with himself than the cast is. It could be said, indeed, that this was a historic occasion: the first public acknowledgment of Clint Eastwood as a celebrity.

On *Rawhide,* such concessions as he obtained remained small and grudging, his attempts to assert himself often frustrated. This was now more than a matter of having his ideas about how his character might be developed taken seriously; a desire to direct, animated in part by his belief that the show needed to be reenergized visually, was growing in him.

When the company was on location in Paso Robles earlier that season shooting a cattle stampede, Clint was in the middle of it thinking, God, there's some great shots here, and I'm in a position to get them. So he went to Warren and pointed out that if he was given a handheld camera he could ride low in the saddle or even dismount and move among the animals, getting close-ups that the stationary cameras, set up on the periphery of the action, could not possibly obtain. "I'll get you some really great shots," he promised Warren. No, came the reply, and an excuse was invented about not being in the camera union.

His disappointment grew when he formally sought permission to direct. While the producers and the network executives mulled it over, one of the performers on *Frontier Circus* went over schedule a day or two in his directorial debut—"something that would have been astronomical for a television show in those days," says Clint—and so the network issued an edict: Henceforth no series actors would be permitted to direct their own shows. Or so Clint was told by his producers. They did let him direct some promos for the show, but they were merely placating him, and he knew it.

"At that point I sort of lost my spirit," Clint says. He realized that they were never going to "change the energy" of the show. "Everything had to be the same format. Why tamper with success?" The network had no motive to do so. *Rawhide* ended that season, the last in Charles Marquis Warren's tenure as producer, sixth in the Nielsen ratings. On the other hand, Clint's instincts were correct, as events were about to prove. The next year, with agreeable Endre Bohem, who had been the program's story editor from the start, taking over as producer, the program began what proved to be an irreversible slide in the ratings. It was thirteenth in 1961–62. The following year it was twenty-second, the year after that forty-fourth, a position from which it never rallied appreciably. Each season from 1961 onward there was a new producer, and each year there were changes in emphasis. Play up the guest stars, play down the guest stars; stick more closely to the cattle drive, get away from the cattle drive; have more comedy, have less comedy. Still later, in *Rawhide*'s last seasons, there would be additions to and subtractions from the regular cast. But nothing seemed to make much difference; the program's popularity just kept dwindling.

This could not be blamed entirely on content. Episode to episode the show's quality varied greatly, but no more than that of any long-running dramatic series under pressure to grind out thirty shows a year on six-day schedules. Sampling the series one sometimes finds quite interesting work: a memorably affecting James Whitmore, for example, as a cavalry officer who has lost his command in a battle with Indians and now wanders the plains seeking (and finally finding) redemptive martyrdom; or a stern James Coburn as another soldier whose unyielding inhumanity to a captive Indian child alienates his wife. On the other hand, the show often strained too hard for serious contemporary relevance, and its attempts at comedy were nearly always disastrous. Worse, as the years wore on, the show became repetitive as Gil, Rowdy and the rest of the drovers reencountered all the standard western clichés.

Doubtless this reliance on thrice-told tales took its toll on the audience. Clint was right when he argued that *Rawhide's* often poky manner of presenting them was unhelpful. But these were problems it shared with all its competitors. Therefore, one probably has to look to Eric Fleming and his failure to establish his character as a figure whom audiences could take to heart as the program's chief defect. He was not doing what a series lead must do; he was not carrying the show.

By the early sixties the network and the producers were completely aware of this issue, and their attempts to deal with it made their prickly star more and more angry. This relationship—essentially a downward spiral—became the production's central, hidden drama. Clint did his best to absent himself from it. When the other actors felt they weren't getting the screen time they deserved, he would sometimes intercede for them. When a script didn't seem quite right he would occasionally retreat to his dressing room and try to improve it. But there is not the slightest evidence that he tried to take advantage of his costar's weakening position. When they started shooting for the 1963–64 season Clint's disaffection from *Rawhide* seemed to have been expressed largely as a kind of polite resignation. But he was looking for distraction.

★   ★   ★

The story of how, in his restlessness, he redeemed his career by taking a chance on what was by any standard the most marginal of opportunities has often been told; it is central to the Clint Eastwood legend. But the events occurring in his personal life at this time, when "Maggie and I weren't doing too well," were for a quarter of a century entirely unremarked in the press. They have since been alluded to only occasionally, and then in understandably distant and puzzled terms. But they, too, would have their long-term effects on his life.

Clint's affair with Roxanne Tunis, which seems to have begun sometime in 1963, was not a great passion—at least on his part. "We were friends more than anything" is the way he describes it now. She was at the time twenty-nine years old, a tall and attractive brunette who worked in film and television as a bit player and stuntwoman and was fairly regularly employed in those capacities on *Rawhide*. She had been married, but was now separated, and Clint found her company easy and comfortable, for she was a woman of independent mind and considerable self-sufficiency—far more so than he was as yet aware.

For in the fall of 1963 she discovered that she was carrying his child—and did not tell him about it. Instead, she simply disappeared from his life for a time. It perhaps says something about the nature of their relationship that he did not inquire too deeply into the reasons for her withdrawal. In his mind at the time this was yet another of his casual affairs, if perhaps a little more affectionate than most. "I didn't know how I fit into the picture" is what he says now.

He would not discover that picture's full dimensions until almost a year later, well after the birth of their child. It is difficult to understand the motives for Roxanne's silence. Perhaps she was afraid of what his response would be. Or perhaps she was utterly confident of it. That is to say, confident that he would, as he did, accept responsibility for the child. "It's sort of an odd story," he says, understating the matter. "I don't know what to say about it, other than what it is." As we will see, however, the long-term consequences of this initial silence would be serious, both for his daughter, Kimber, who was born June 17, 1964, at Cedars Sinai hospital, and for Clint Eastwood.

In everyone's defense it must be said that in the early sixties matters of this kind were not openly admitted and discussed, as they are now. Public figures had a reasonable expectation that their privacy would be respected, and a reasonable fear that if it was not the revelation of an illegitimate child—or even an unconventional living arrangement—would adversely affect their standing with the public. The habit of secrecy was easily embraced, particularly by someone as reticent as Clint was, and is, about personal matters.

Moreover, at the time Roxanne disappeared from his life, he was distracted by professional considerations. For, of all things, he finally had an interesting offer of outside work, not on its face a good one, but somehow an intriguing one. It came to him casually enough. He was now represented by the William Morris Agency, oldest and at the time most powerful of the major agencies, and sometime in the winter of 1963–64 it received an inquiry about Clint from its branch office in Rome. The Italian-German-Spanish coproducers of a low-budget western with the working title of *El Magnifico Stragnero* (*The Magnificent Stranger*), to be directed by one Sergio Leone, had for some time been looking for an American actor to play its leading role—an *inexpensive*

American actor, someone who did not command a major star's salary, but who was well enough known to bolster international sales.

The problem was to get Clint, or any American actor of promise or standing, to commit to such a project. Working in Italian films was not considered to be a shrewd career move for an American actor, even though Rome was then the world's most active center of international coproduction, and American companies had been shooting there since the early fifties, taking advantage of the favorable rate of currency exchange and the facilities at Cinecittà, the large and well-equipped Roman studio that Mussolini had built. Even without coproduction the Italian industry was doing well because its home market was extremely reliable, at this point quite unaffected by competition from television. Something like 20 percent of the films made in Italy eventually got released elsewhere, but if budgets were kept within reason producers could frequently turn a profit in their home territory alone.

The trouble was that many of these producers were given to odd, not to say downright crooked, practices. For example, they scratched together money for a week's shooting, then showed that material to potential backers, hoping to gain enough financing to proceed for another week. If they were lucky, they would go on in this fashion until the movie was finished. If they were not, they simply abandoned the project and moved on to something else. Sometimes, too, they would shoot, say, five weeks of a six-week schedule, then claim poverty and ask their actors to finish the picture for nothing. Players working for them were always advised to collect their salaries on the first day of the week, before doing any work.

The films they made were mostly execrable. Moviegoers outside Italy think of its postwar cinema as one of high ambition and large influence around the world. It is after all the cinema of Rossellini, De Sica, Fellini, Visconti, Antonioni, Bertolucci. But these directors represented only the top of this industry's line. Mostly it was devoted to much more popular—not to say vulgar—entertainments. In the fifties its dominant commercial genres were the *films-fumetto* (romantic weepies) and farcical comedies (often starring Toto), made mainly for domestic consumption. These gave way, in turn, to horror films along the lines of those produced by Hammer in Great Britain (but more grisly) and to the Sword and Sandal cycle, spectacles based—very loosely—on biblical tales and the legends of antiquity. In the early sixties these shaded over into pure muscle-man epics, featuring such figures as Hercules (played by the sometime Mr. Universe, Steve Reeves), Maciste, Ursus and Sampson. These received wider international release, but by the midsixties they, too, were phasing out. Always on the alert for something that could be knocked off profitably, Roman producers began turning out vast numbers of James Bond–like espionage and crime fantasies, and they had themselves invented a curious genre, the "Mondo" pictures, largely faked documentaries of variously decadent "worlds." Now they were beginning to make westerns as well.

Their immediate inspiration was the success of a group of films based on the works of Karl May, the nineteenth-century German author of many improbably romanticized tales of the American frontier. These pictures, some of which starred Lex Barker, the onetime Tarzan of American movies, were financed by a German production company, partially shot on location in Yugoslavia and played profitably all over Europe. It seemed to the hustlers of Cinecittà that there was room for more of the same, and in 1963 they produced something like twenty-five low-budget westerns, none of which was widely or immediately exported. They had done well enough in Italy, however, and the producers judged that the home market was still far from saturated. Among those sharing this thought were the managers of the curiously named Jolly Film, who put together a coproduction deal with Constantin, the Munich-based producer of the May films, and Ocean films of Madrid to finance the Leone project.

They had unsuccessfully offered *The Magnificent Stranger* to a number of actors before turning to Clint. He believes one of them to have been Rory Calhoun, who was one of several minor, fading American stars then working steadily in Italy; it was logical, for he had starred in the only previous film credited to Leone, *The Colossus of Rhodes.* Two men who would work for Leone later, when they were all better known, Charles Bronson and James Coburn, also rejected it. "It was just about the worst script I'd ever seen," said the former, well after the fact. "I didn't know who Sergio Leone was, and I'd heard nothing but bad about Italian filmmakers," said Coburn when subsequently he came to contemplate his error of judgment.

But money was as much an issue with them as quality. In those days the asking price for all these actors was around $25,000, more than the producers could pay them out of a budget somewhere between $200,000 and $250,000, and these actors were not inclined to cut their price in order to participate in so dubious an enterprise. Neither was Steve Reeves, who also wanted $25,000.

It was not until Leone and friends spoke to one of Reeves's competitors in the muscle-men genre, Richard Harrison, that their luck began to change. He was one of a group of lesser-known American performers living permanently in Rome and making a decent, if sometimes chancy, living in this film industry, the while enjoying la dolce vita. (Fellini's famous film of that title, produced in 1960, is, of course, a mordant portrait of this show business demimonde.) Harrison already had a commitment for the spring of 1964, but he had seen *Rawhide*, liked Clint's work in it and recommended him to Leone. The director had not heard of him, but got hold of episode ninety-one of the series, "Incident of the Black Sheep," responded, he later said, to the catlike combination of indolence and menace he read in Clint's movements and decided to approach him with the role.

It was, Clint recalls, Sandy Bressler, then a young agent in William Morris's motion picture department (latterly the well-known head of its TV department, now an independent whose major client is Jack Nicholson), who placed the call reporting the offer to Clint and asking him if he wanted to consider it. "Hell, no, I'm not interested in it," Clint later remembered saying, "especially not a European western. It would probably be a joke." "Well," came the reply, "I promised the Rome office that I'd get you to read the script." Clint casually agreed to do so.

What arrived on his doorstep was a carbon copy, on onion-skin paper, of a document that looked more like the manuscript of a novel than a script, with the dialogue embedded in long descriptive passages. A subtitle, or possibly an alternative title, identified *The Magnificent Stranger* as "Texas Joe." A few pages into this curious text Clint identifed it as a free adaptation—or should one say "knockoff"?—of Akira Kurosawa's *Yojimbo*, which he had recently seen.

This did not much bother Clint. His taste in action runs toward straight-faced, self-satirizing exaggeration, and what he read was very much in that vein. Besides, the Japanese master openly admitted that these movies had been inspired in part by the American westerns he admired (among them almost certainly Budd Boetticher and Randolph Scott's *Buchanan Rides Alone*, which has a theme similar to *Yojimbo*'s), so Clint thought it entirely appropriate to complete the circle by rerooting the story in a western setting.

Indeed, the thought that it could easily be remade as a western had, he says, briefly crossed his mind when he first saw *Yojimbo*, but he had judged it "too rough" for American tastes. Now, suddenly, this unknown, working from a place about as remote from the western's native ground as it is possible to get, was offering him a version of it "rougher" than anything he had imagined. It appealed to Clint's sense of the absurd, and to his gambling impulse. He asked Maggie to read the script, and she confirmed his instinct.

So he decided to go for it. He felt he had nothing to lose. *Rawhide* would soon be on hiatus, and he had no work to fill the empty months.

Better still, the figure he was being asked to play—mature, mysterious, deadly dangerous—was about as far as he could get from Rowdy Yates, and the context in which he was to appear was also deliciously far from the maddening gentilities of his television work.

He recalls thinking: I've never been to Italy. I've never been to Spain. I've never been to Germany. I've never been to any of the countries [coproducing] this film. The worst I can come out of this with is a nice little trip. I'll go over there and learn some stuff. I'll see how other people make films in other countries. He knew that if the picture bombed, it would not be picked up for distribution outside its producers' home territories and become an international embarrassment.

The Morris office, having put him in touch with this possibility, did not share his developing enthusiasm for it. An agency is obliged to submit all offers to its clients, but it is also obliged to a certain caution, particularly in cases of this kind. The money was short—a flat fee of fifteen thousand dollars—and the agency was well aware of the Italian industry's reputation when it came to fulfilling even such modest obligations.

It also may be that some in the agency felt the project was more suitable for another of its clients. Lenny Hirshan, who would soon begin his long run as Clint's agent, recalls that the part was discussed with Henry Silva, the character actor whose moon-faced menace would have been interesting in the role. But he also remembers Silva holding out for $16,000, a minuscule increment the producers nevertheless refused to meet. Careers do sometimes turn—or fail to turn—on such small, sticky points.

Clint was not inclined to haggle over money. He did insist on the right to make changes in the long and awkward dialogue passages he had read. And eventually he would get the producers to hire his pal Bill Tompkins to do stunt work, partly because he was unsure about the Italians' skills in this area, partly because he wanted a friend along to help him cope with the mysteries of fringe filmmaking on locations where he did not know the language, with a director who did not speak English.

Clint has never claimed, or been credited for, the large imaginative leap this project represented for him. But it obviously required a certain critical acuity to recognize the solid source of the material, a certain wit to perceive that it might be turned into something more than yet another cheap remake of a better film and a certain self-confidence in his ability to make something dark, ironic and memorable—the anti-Rowdy he had been looking for—out of the near-blank character sketched in the script. Certainly it required a long leap of faith to commit himself to Sergio Leone. There was no way he could have predicted, from the pages submitted to him, the remarkable, indeed, transforming visual style with which Leone would realize the story they outlined.

It also required a certain professional courage to accept this role. He was an established presence on an established television show, still young, not in need of money, with some kind of conventional future—perhaps a lead in another series, possibly some kind of a career in less marginal features—open to him. He was risking status, perhaps even projecting what could be interpreted as desperation, by engaging in this far-fetched venture.

But careers also turn on daring instinct. And instinct, as Clint insists, is his strength. He signed the contract to make the film without meeting Leone or anyone else involved in the production and boarded a plane for Rome in April 1964.

FIVE

BREAKING ALL THE RULES

Clint arrived in Rome conscientiously prepared for *Il Magnifico Stragnero*. He had a few days' growth of beard, which the script called for, and he brought with him the guns, gun belt, boots and spurs he wore on *Rawhide*. He also carried in his luggage several pairs of black Levi's that he had bleached and roughed up, a flat-crowned western hat he had found in a costume shop on Santa Monica Boulevard and a sleeveless sheepskin jacket that he would wear more often in the film than his more famous poncho, which was Leone's inspiration and was purchased in Spain. The script also called for him to smoke cigars—he is not a smoker—and he had bought several boxes of them, long, thin, foul tasting, with their tobacco wrapped around a central strip of bamboo. These he would cut into thirds and park, both lit and unlit, in the corner of his mouth in many of the film's sequences. They had their uses: "They put you in the right mood—cantankerous." In short, he was ready, willing and eager to play an antiheroic—not to say nihilistic—protagonist, scruffy and enigmatic, who never once explained himself and generally spoke only to make an ironic comment on the action.

Besides carrying wardrobe and props, Clint brought with him his undiminished conviction that his character's "atrocious" dialogue must be cut. In this belief, according to him, he at first encountered directional resistance. In this belief, according to Leone, he found encouragement. In the mild dispute that developed on this point over the years, one is inclined to believe Clint; his case is more logical, and it is Leone—intent on staking an auteur's claim—who had a need to insist later that he had been in complete control of every aspect of the production.

Their first meeting, at Clint's hotel, a few hours after he landed, was not altogether cordial. Leone seemed to him "gruff," making an attempt to assert his authority on their first encounter. Clint guessed this display to be something of a sham, and he was right. Leone could not maintain a stern pose for very long; it was alien to his nature, which was intense and excitable, chaotic and childlike. In any case, Clint was not greatly put off by him.

Nor was he disheartened by the warnings he soon started receiving about *Il Magnifico Stragnero*. The day he arrived he ran into Brett Halsey outside his hotel. His old friend was living in Rome, gaining some modest success in Italian movies. So were some other actors Clint had known in Hollywood. At a party Halsey and his wife invited him to a couple of days later, someone told him he should be wary of the project because it had been around a long time. To which he recalls replying, "It may have been around a long time, but I like it. I think it will be fun to do."

And so it turned out to be. Leone "was a guy who loved to eat and loved to make movies." They had to communicate through a stuntman named Benito Stefanelli, whose English was excellent and who was a Leone favorite (he worked all the westerns Clint did in Europe), and through Constantin's Rome representative, Elena Dressler, a Polish Jew who had learned German in a concentration camp, English after American troops liberated it and Italian when she moved to Rome after the war. Her intelligence, courage and worldliness impressed Clint—he had never known a woman like her—and partly because of her good offices he and Leone were soon getting along famously.

For despite their vast and obvious differences in background, they shared certain attitudes and professional experiences. Leone gave Clint— and many interviewers—the impression that they were about the same age, claiming to have been born in 1929 and leading his star to think that perhaps generational bonding accounted for their good relationship. In fact, though, Leone was born January 23, 1921, nine years earlier than Clint. The child of a movie family, his mother was an actress, his father a pioneering director whose career ultimately ran afoul of the Fascist regime. But like Clint, Leone had once imagined himself working in a more conventional field (he studied law briefly), and he, too, had learned filmmaking in a hard, humble school. He did a little acting (he can be seen in a small role in De Sica's *The Bicycle Thief*) and a lot of gofering before beginning his lengthy career as an assistant and second unit director after World War II, working in these capacities, he claimed, on something like fifty-eight productions of every imaginable kind— some of them directed by such visiting American filmmakers as Mervyn Leroy, William Wyler, Fred Zinnemann and Robert Aldrich.

He might well have exaggerated the length of his filmography somewhat, for he was always a man who liked to improve on reality. Later on, Clint would read and hear things about their experiences together that were "totally not true," but also amusing to him. In any case,

Leone's apprenticeship was certainly long and varied, and it fully qualified him to direct when he finally got his chance. This was when Mario
Bonnard, the director of record of *The Last Days of Pompeii,* fell ill just as
production began, and Leone took over. He received no credit for that
assignment, but he did on *The Colossus of Rhodes* in 1961. At forty-three,
as he set out to make *Il Magnifico Stragnero,* he was exactly the kind of
seasoned professional Clint loved to work with.

He was something else as well—a cineast who had seen and studied
thousands of movies in every genre, from every culture, and a man with
a vast romantic affection for America, derived both from movies and
from literature. Perhaps because of his father's profession he had as a
child seen more American films than many of his European contemporaries, and he also recalled reading James Fenimore Cooper and Louisa
May Alcott in his early years, gathering from them an idealized vision of
the United States. But it was not until the postwar period that, as he put
it, "I became decisively enchanted by . . . Hollywood. . . . I must have
seen three hundred films a month for two or three years straight. Westerns, comedies, gangster films, war stories—everything there was." He
was exaggerating again, of course—no matter how movie mad you are,
it's impossible to see ten movies a day—but perhaps by not too much.
The war had dammed Europe off from American movies, and when
they flooded forth in peacetime, they seemed a revelation. One need
only consult the critical writing of the young men who would eventually constitute the French New Wave to grasp the importance of this experience in shaping their cinematic tastes and theories, and so it was
with Leone. "He would always talk about John Ford," Clint remembers,
"and ask what films you liked, what westerns—he was a big western
fan." As it was with moviegoing, so it was with his reading in those
years. After the war, Leone recalled, "Publishing houses came out with
translations of Hemingway, Faulkner, Hammett and James Cain. It was
a wonderful cultural slap in the face."

By the time they met, Leone was convinced that the American genres in general, the western in particular, were in dire need of revitaliza-
tion, an opinion Clint shared. A decade before Pauline Kael was to
become Clint's most implacable critical enemy, and a year or two before
Clint and Leone started work on their remake of *Yojimbo,* she reviewed
it and wrote: "In recent years John Ford, particularly, has turned the
Western into an almost static pictorial genre, a devitalized, dehydrated
form which is 'enriched' with pastoral beauty and evocative nostalgia
for a simple, heroic way of life. . . . If by now we dread going to see a
'great' Western, it's because 'great' has come to mean slow and pictori-

ally composed. We'll be lulled to sleep in the 'affectionate,' 'pure,' 'authentic' scenery . . . or, for a change, we'll be clobbered by messages in 'mature' Westerns." A few years later (1967) she would observe, again quite acutely, that the form had become a kind of rest home for aging stars, men who could no longer play romantic leads persuasively, but whose cragginess of features and traditional styles of self-presentation matched the standard western landscapes and the conventional morality of the genre in ways that were comforting to the older, but still profitable, audience that continued to love the form.

Writing shortly after the Leone/Eastwood westerns were released in the United States, Andrew Sarris, who was Kael's critical opposite, both agreed and disagreed. "The western hero as a classical archetype possesses a certain nobility," he wrote, "but he is too solemn and simpleminded to deserve the majesty of his milieu." He, however, saw in the postwar development of the genre a healthy expansion of range: "The western, like water, gains flavor from its impurities, and westerns since 1945 have multiplied their options, obsessions and neuroses many times over."

Clint, ironically (and laconically), was more in Kael's camp than Sarris's regarding the current state of the art: "To me, the American western was in a dead space." Leone agreed, saying that "the western had been killed off by those who had maltreated the genre." It had lost touch with what Leone understood to be the harsh historical reality of the Old West, had become at once too mythopoeic in tone, too Freudian in its underpinnings. He would say at some later point, "The West was made by violent, uncomplicated men, and it is that strength and simplicity I want to recapture." He also said that America, as an idea, does not really belong to Americans: "They are only borrowing [it] for a time," and so had no hesitation about undertaking his revisionist task.

Christopher Frayling's thorough and scholarly study *Spaghetti Westerns* offers a longer quotation from Leone that reveals much about how the director fell into the lover's quarrel with America that supplied so much of the tension in his work. In childhood, he said, America had been "like a religion" to him. "I dreamed of the wide open spaces of America. The great expanses of desert. The extraordinary 'melting pot,' the first nation made up of people from all over the world." This idealized vision was darkened, he said, by his encounter with real Americans, the occupying army of World War II, who were not at all like the Yanks he had read about. They had energy, to be sure, but "they were no longer the Americans of the West. They were soldiers like any others. . . . Men who were materialist, possessive, keen on pleasures and earthly goods." Casually mixing up his prewar and postwar reading, he said that "in the GIs who chased after our women and sold their cigarettes on the black market, I could see nothing that I had seen in Hemingway, Dos Passos or [Raymond] Chandler. . . . Nothing—or almost nothing—of the great prairies, or of the demi-gods of my childhood."

The disillusioning disjunction between the reality of the American male as he observed him and the images of that figure that Leone had absorbed from books and films was confirmed by his later readings in western history. In another important quotation offered by Frayling, Leone says: "The man of the West bore no resemblance to the man described by Hollywood directors, screenwriters, cineasts. . . . One could say all the characters they present to us come from the same mold: the incorruptible sheriff, the romantic judge, the brothel keeper, the cruel bandit, the naive girl. . . . All these molds are mixed together, before the happy ending, in a kind of cruel, puritan fairy-story." He added: "The real West was a world of violence, fear and instinct. . . . Life in the West was not pleasant or poetic, at least not in any direct sense . . . the law belonged to the most hard, the most cruel, the most cynical."

Western historians might dispute this vision of frontier America as earnestly as they would dispute Ford's more pastoral portrayal of it. The historical truth—in which no moviemaker has ever been interested for very long—is more complex than either interpretation can possibly comprehend. But at this stage in movie history it is indisputable that Leone's view of the West was much more interesting dramatically and, as it would turn out, visually.

In these early days Leone was not quite so articulate a revisionist as he later made himself out to be. But as far as Clint was concerned, he didn't need to be. It was enough for him that, for whatever reasons, Leone and his several writing collaborators had scraped away the western's romantic, poetic and moral encrustations, leaving only its absurdly violent confrontational essence. It was very close to an act of deconstruction, for it might be said that instead of offering metaphors for moderns, as the "message" westerns did, the Leone films were postmodernist in their very essence. Like grander and more self-conscious works in this new tradition, they were fully, wickedly aware of the conventions they were sometimes rendering as ironic abstractions and sometimes completely subverting. In the end, it is the absence of earnest, overt messages—political, psychological, whatever—that constituted the real message of these films, and their profoundest appeal to a young actor restively working in a TV western, the squarest and most reductive version of the genre yet devised. It is also because of this omis-

sion that Leone's films elicited such contempt and controversy when
they were eventually released in the United States.

Clint and Leone did not discuss *Il Magnifico Stragnero* in these terms.
"Realism" was their concern, and their conversations about Clint's character were about enhancing his believability. (This figure, by the way,
had a name—Joe—as he did in all the Eastwood-Leone collaborations;
the more famous "Man with No Name" sobriquet was supplied well
after the fact by an anonymous United Artists marketing executive looking for a way of selling the pictures in the United States.) They asked
themselves what Joe would "really" do, "really" say—or, more likely,
not say—when he was placed in different situations.

Knowing as we do the film they created, realism seems perhaps the
least useful way of describing it. What's memorable and marvelous
about it is the way it severs all ties both with the real West and the romanticized version of it that the movies and the rest of popular culture
had pretty much convinced audiences was real. As *The New York Times*
critic Vincent Canby would later write, Leone's films always had "the
strange look and displaced sound of an unmistakably Italian director's
dream of what Hollywood movies should be like, but aren't."

Yet Leone and Clint were not wrong to concern themselves with
behavioral authenticity. It is important in all movies, of course—the
grounding that makes us suspend disbelief in essentially fantastic con-
structs. In this film it was even more significant. Clint would be the only
American in a company otherwise peopled entirely by European performers, and they would all be working on Spanish locations that were
to the landscape of the American West what the script was to the conventions of the American western: a spare, quite visibly inauthentic representation of what audiences had been taught to expect. The same
might be said for Joe's almost parodic silence and deadliness, the former
deeper, the latter quicker, than we were used to in even our most enigmatic and skillful gunfighters. Somehow, the actor had to give good,
solid, persuasive weight in this context.

In his way—a way that led most early reviewers to believe that Clint
was doing nothing, was perhaps incapable of doing anything, in the
way of conventional acting—that is what he did. The casual and unin-
flected sobriety with which Joe goes about his deadly business contrasts
vividly—and to subtly humorous effect—with the operatic carnage that
follows in his wake. It was a rather distant danger that didn't occur to
him at the time, but Clint was risking critical contumely—assuming any
critic paid attention to this extremely marginal enterprise—with this
performance. He was also offering a bold contrast with Toshiro Mifune's

manner in *Yojimbo*. His is a marvelous performance, but it is quite different from Clint's, nowhere near as still and affectless. His freelance samurai, selling his services to rival criminal gangs, just as Clint's freelance gunman does in Leone's film, much more openly and comically communicates—through shrugs, twitches, flickers of disdain—his disgust with the warring factions.

Each actor fits, and to some degree sets, the quite divergent tones of his film. In their plotting, as everyone knows, the two films are very (but not entirely) similar, and the point that they are driving at is identical, perhaps because, as Sarris observed, similar national experiences were working on both directors. Japan and Italy, he notes, were both defeated in World War II. Therefore, he argues, their western protagonists "are less transcendental heroes than existential heroes in that they lack faith in history as an orderly process in human affairs. What Kurosawa and Leone share is a sentimental nihilism that ranks survival above honor and revenge above morality. Hence the Kurosawa and Leone hero possesses and requires more guile than his American counterpart. Life is cheaper in the foreign western, and violence more prevalent."

So in copying *Yojimbo*'s basic situation Leone inevitably retains its most basic difference from the traditional western. As Kael observed, it is customary, when the mysterious stranger rides into a situation like the one set forth in these movies, that he be offered a clear-cut choice as to whom he should offer his services and "the remnants of a code of behavior." But as she puts it, here "nobody represents any principle" and "the scattered weak are merely weak." Which leaves existential improvisation—stylishly managed—as the protagonist's only option.

In his nicely judged study of Kurosawa's films, Donald Richie points out, as Kael does not, that the Mifune character's moral superiority to everyone he encounters in the violently riven town he enters quite by chance is marginal. He may eventually tame the place, but that's incidental to the money he thinks he can make in the process. Richie argues that since "no great moral purpose looms in back of him," Kurosawa cannot, will not, "be portentous about an important matter—social action." Therefore, "he refuses first tragedy, then melodrama. He insists upon making a comedy," which was, as Kael put it, "the first great shaggy man movie."

Everything thus far said about *Yojimbo* applies equally to Leone's version of it—except that his sense of humor is entirely different from Kurosawa's and so is his style. Much as he would later protest that his true inspirations were Carlo Goldoni's eighteenth-century farce, *The Servant of Two Masters,* and the comically violent puppet shows of his childhood, easy as it is to cite sequences in his film that bear no resemblance to anything in Kurosawa's, Leone's best defense against the charge of plagiarism lies in the attitude he took to this material.

There is a curiosity here. Kurosawa is himself austere and laconic in manner, not at all the kind of man one would imagine being drawn toward a farcical style. Conversely, Leone's voluble, excitable nature suggests a natural taste for high-energy comedy. Yet the humor in his film—and some of its violence—are much more understated. (He did not, for example, quote what may be the most famous shot in *Yojimbo,* in which a dog trots by the camera carrying a severed arm in its mouth.) Indeed, his staging in general is less compressed and bustling, and far more ritualistic, particularly in the way its confrontations are set up, than Kurosawa's is. It is almost as if each made the other's movie. Or to put it another way, *Yojimbo* in its exuberance sometimes seems more Italianate than Leone's work, while the latter's film sometimes seems almost Oriental in its manner.

Not that there was anything enigmatic or withdrawn in Leone's manner when he was at work. On the set he was aboil with energy, fussy about every detail. As Clint puts it, "He loved the joy of it all. I know he had a good time shooting when he wasn't getting furious." And furious he did get, at delays, at incomprehension, for Leone was also a "very nervous, intense and serious guy." He clearly understood that despite its economic marginality this film represented his best, possibly his last, chance to make his mark as a director, and whatever his budgetary constraints, he was determined to realize all its possibilities.

Clint responded, humorously but admiringly, to Leone's intensity. The self-conscious revisionist and the perhaps unconscious modernist had another likable quality as well: disarming naïveté. "He had this childlike way of looking at the world," Clint says. Unlike directors trying to re-create for modern audiences the conventions of, and through them their emotional responses to, the genres they had adored as kids, Leone, Clint thought, was trying to go a step further. He was trying to re-create the very feelings a child brings to his first experiences of the movies—the enormity of the screen looming over him, the overpowering images of worlds previously only imagined suddenly made manifest, made realer than real in the mysterious darkness of the theater.

Considering this point Clint summons up the familiar experience of reencountering as a grown-up some building or landscape that made a huge impression on you as a child and finding it to be smaller, less imposing than you remembered. In all his films Leone was, he thinks, trying to restore this remembered scale to the screen. Clint sees it in the

CLINT EASTWOOD / 142

low angles Leone favored for the characters he played, angles that offered, to put it simply, a child's-eye view of heroism. He sees it, too, in the vast panoramic views of countryside and town streets that Leone loved, and loved alternating with extraordinarily tight close-ups of faces, of guns being drawn and fired, even of boots carrying their wearers toward their violent destinies, the jingling of their spurs unnaturally loud on the soundtrack, "Everything's enhanced," says Clint. "You're seeing the films as an adult, but you sit and watch them as a child."

The films are also full of references to Leone's childhood religion. As the critic Robert C. Cumbow has observed, "The Catholic dichotomy between the material world of death and the spiritual world of life everlasting is grounded in the notion that the material world is inherently defective." San Miguel, the Mexican border town Joe enters, could not be a more vivid symbol of that defectiveness, "irredeemably condemned to immobility, somnolence, to the lack of all resource and development," as the Italian critic Franco Ferrini described it. Since Joe enters not on a hero's impressive steed, but on a humble mule, which is, of course, the way Jesus traveled, we are encouraged to see him as a redeemer of the irredeemable. Before he leaves he will endure a sort of calvary and a kind of resurrection, and he will certainly assist many of San Miguel's residents to find life everlasting—usually before they are quite ready for it.

In any event, there is no doubting the accuracy of Richard Corliss's confident description of Clint's character as "very much the grizzled Christ." All of Leone's films contain religious references of this kind—mock sermons, mock calvaries, disused churches and bell towers, a Bible used to hide a killer's gun. And always, when he comes to the final shoot-out, it is as ritualized as a mass.

His disappointment with religion is of a piece with Leone's disappointment in the failure of contemporary Americans to be the idealists (and saviors) our movies had promised they might be. It doubtless accounts for his sense of humor, described by Clint as "very ironic, dry and a little bit sardonic," not to say cynical, perhaps, full of the arrested adolescent's dismay at discovering that the world is not as it had been promised to him.

Leone's movies' characters—including Clint's—are moved by base instinct. He ends up more or less doing right not because he acts out of any grand principles, but because power equals morality, and his skill with weapons is thus more potent than anyone else's. In effect, he subverts the customary western formula, which always implies that distinctly higher moral standards have the effect of steadying the beset hero's hand, fixing his eye when, at last, he draws.

Childishness of outlook does not necessarily imply primitiveness of technique. As Corliss notes, Leone was a tutored talent "not only a delirious descendant of *both* John Fords, but a spiritual brother of such 'operatic' Italians as Visconti, Bertolucci (who worked on the screenplay of *Once upon a Time in the West*), Minnelli and Coppola—a natural film-maker whose love of the medium and the genre is joyously evident, and infectious, in every frame he shoots."

They spent about a week in Rome, shooting (at Cinecittà) the sequence where Joe, grievously tortured by the Rojos, the marginally more vicious of the two criminal gangs contending for control of San Miguel, recovers from his wounds by taking refuge in a mine shaft (definitely to be compared to Christ entombed). It was necessary to shoot a minimum amount of the picture on Italian soil in order to be eligible for certain subventions the government was then offering producers. But as soon as possible the company moved on to Spain, first to locations in Manzanias, about an hour outside of Madrid on the way to Segovia, then to Almería, in bleak Andalucia, in the southern part of the country.

The set was a small Tower of Babel, with scripts available in Italian, English, German and Spanish. Everyone was friendly enough, but Clint could not communicate with the other leading players—among them Gian Maria Volonté (playing the psychopathic leader of the Rojo gang, Ramon), a highly regarded stage actor and a committed leftist on his way to a distinguished career in more politically conscientious films. One of the producers, Arrighi Columbo, spoke English well, but he and Clint did not take to one another, and besides Stefanelli the only other member of the cast and crew with whom he could communicate in English (and then only primitively) was Massimo Dallamano, the cinematographer, whom Clint admired—he "worked a little bit differently with light," meaning he refused to cast the standard romantic glow over his landscapes.

He was glad he had insisted on bringing Bill Tompkins along for company, and he was happy, too, that he had arranged for Maggie to join him. She spent only a few days on location, her presence providing his only real break in what amounted to eight weeks of hard labor in a harsh land on a budget that permitted few amenities.

Clint scoffs at the often-repeated rumor that Leone had a print of *Yojimbo* threaded up on a Movieola in his trailer so that he could run its equivalent to whatever sequence he was working on. "We couldn't afford Movieolas. We had no electricity; we didn't have a trailer with a toilet. We just went out behind rocks. That was just people trying to put Sergio down when he was a success."

For the moment, he was very far from that status. He was just another director with no name, coping with troubles a lot more serious than the absence of honey wagons. Absence of cash, for example. The Spanish coproducers would claim that the money for the week's salaries was due from the Germans, and then, says Clint, "the money guy from Constantin Films wouldn't show up and the crew was balking and Sergio would go crazy." The relentless insecurity eventually led to defections. Worse, the dailies were coming back from the lab scratched, and this made Leone "paranoid." Though he came to the set each day with his angles all planned out, and did not improvise much with the camera, he shot multiple takes on each setup and printed all of them—as many as six or eight—hoping at least one or two would survive the technicians' rough handling.

One anecdote perhaps sums up the spirit in which the film was made. One day Leone decided that his set required a tree, something from which you could hang a man. None was conveniently available in this sere landscape, but Leone went out scouting and saw just what he wanted in a farmyard. He returned the next day with a truck and a few crew members and began haranguing the elderly farmer in his most impressive manner. Clint: "He goes barging in there and he says, 'We're from the highway department. This tree is very dangerous, it's going to fall and someone's gonna get hurt. We'll take this tree right out for you.' This old guy's standing out there and before he knows what's happening there are these Italians sawing his tree down."

The director's energy never flagged. He liked to demonstrate actions to his actors, show Clint how he wanted him to light up his cigar or whatever, "and of course I'd be laughing because I'd see this guy with these little tiny glasses and the western hat on trying to do me. He looked like Yosemite Sam."

The first thing that drew Clint to this script was Joe's entrance. Clopping along on his mule, ponchoed and unshaven, he spies a house and turns in for a drink at its well. Almost immediately a gang of desperadoes abusively chases a little boy away, and then the stranger sees a beautiful woman, Marisol (played by Marianne Koch, the German actress who starred in some of Constantin's Karl May adaptations), staring piteously at him from behind barred windows. It is obvious that she has been sequestered against her will for sexual use, and that her husband and child (who is named Jesus) are impotent to save her. It is also obvious that this family is to be read as a version of the Holy Family, which means, if one follows out the film's symbolism to its logical end, that a Christ figure will ultimately be obliged to rescue a Christ figure, or a younger version of himself.

Clint, largely innocent of religious training, and certainly not conversant with Catholic belief, read the situation much more simply. "Our hero's standing there and he doesn't do a thing," he says. "You know, your average western, the hero's got to step forth and grab the guy who's shooting the kid or something like that. But this guy doesn't do anything; he turns and rides away. And I thought, That is perfect, that's something I've always wanted to do in a western."

This essentially wordless sequence establishes Clint's character and the premises from which he will operate for the rest of the movie. The sequences that almost immediately follow it establish with similar deftness the iron and irony of his nature. Proceeding into town on his mule, passing a hanged man, he arouses the contempt of gunfighters loyal to the Baxter clan, the Rojos' deadly rivals. They shoot at him, causing the animal to shy. To avoid falling off, Joe leaps from the saddle and catches himself on an overhanging signboard. Now, of course, he must challenge these subsidiary heavies. On his way to this confrontation he passes the town carpenter and places an order for three coffins.

Moving on to his tormentors, he demands an apology on behalf of his animal: "You see, my mule don't like people laughing. He gets the crazy idea they're laughing at him." The gunmen eye him quizzically. He is perhaps a harmless, certainly a self-destructive, lunatic. It is their last, erroneous thought before he throws back his serape and almost literally blasts them out of their boots. This performance serves as a sort of audition for the Rojos, with whom Joe will forge a false alliance, the better to sow the seeds of the anarchy from which he hopes to profit. More important, the scene establishes his preternatural cool: Walking back past the carpenter, he apologetically murmurs, "My mistake—four."

This attitude was not unprecedented. The gunfighter is traditionally given to understatement, which is intended to cause underestimation on the part of his enemies. But there was, in the staging and the playing of this sequence, a black humor entirely new to the genre. Moreover, as Clint says, "Leone had a great visual sense as well as a sense of humor. He was extremely bold. He was never afraid to try anything new."

The contrast between this picture and *Rawhide*, "where everything was regimented," was naturally vivid to Clint. An example he likes to cite is Leone's staging of gunfights. Television had adopted the rule of the old Motion Picture Production Code: If a gun was fired you were not allowed to show its human target in the same shot. You had to show the shot being squeezed off, then cut to the staggering and falling victim. It was an utterly pointless gentility, of course, but for all his studies of the American western Leone had either failed to observe it or didn't understand that it was a near-sacred convention. "So," says Clint, "I didn't tell him. This was fun, because we were breaking all the rules."

Actor and director had their differences, of course. Clint recalls, for example, that they argued about his performance a little bit at the beginning. Leone "wanted me to do a lot of Mifune's type of deals. He liked Mifune's gestures, and I told him, 'Sergio, I've got to do my own thing here. I mean, Mifune was wonderful in the movie but it's a different view, different times, different cultures.'"

They also continued their argument about the script's lengthy rationalizations of Joe's behavior. This disagreement came to a head when they began to work on the passage where Joe finally rescues the tormented Marisol, who has by this time been abducted from the Rojos by the Baxters, then offered back to them in an exchange of prisoners.

According to Clint, a prologue had been written for the picture in which a young Joe's mother was killed in a similar situation. That was never made, and the exposition Leone had written for this sequence was supposed to convey that history. Clint argued that "it doesn't matter where this guy comes from. We can leave it all in the audience's imagination. We can just hint that there's some little incident, some little parallel, and just kind of let the audience draw in the rest of the picture."

Leone, however, remained dubious until Clint at last won him over with a different argument: "OK, Sergio, look. In a B movie we tell everybody everything. But in a real class-A movie we let the audience think."

This, it might be noted, was not the end of attempts to supply Joe with conventionally moral motivation for his activities. Years later, when the movie was sold to American television, a network executive, in order to placate his standards and practices department, had yet another prologue shot. In this one, a man in a serape (not Clint) was seen from the back as a prison warden commutes his sentence on condition that he go to San Miguel and clean it up, in effect licensing his subsequent killings—and confusing some subsequent critical discussions of the movie, since this corrupted print played widely on TV.

Be that as it may, in the film Leone delivered, when the rescued woman tries to express her gratitude to Joe and asks why he helped her, he simply says: "Because I knew someone like you once and there was no one there to help." It is the only time that he openly acknowledges either past or principle, his only humane moment, really, and it is the more effective because of its terseness and brusqueness.

Clint thinks his other major contribution to the way Leone realized the film may have been stylistic. The middle distance was never territory the director comfortably inhabited, and in *Colossus of Rhodes* he had already demonstrated his predilection for extreme wide shots and extreme long shots. "He really liked panorama, and he knew how to do panorama," is the way Clint puts it, adding that herein lay Leone's largest influence on him as a director. Close-ups, however, were rare in that film, and that concerned Clint. Having determined to play his character as stoically as possible, a distantly placed camera would not be able to read his minimal expressions. So he went to Leone and "told him I thought I could sell this character better in close-up."

Most actors, of course, will tell a director something like that—"in all objectivity and sensitivity," as Clint ironically puts it. But in this case he felt he had a legitimate argument, especially given the Italian custom of recording no more than a guide track on location and postsynchronizing all dialogue later on a dubbing stage, where another actor would do the lines. If he was going to be deprived of his own speaking voice, he was determined that his subverbal expressions be understandable. (When the film was released in the United States, three years later, Clint rerecorded his dialogue, relying on notes he made every night about the day's divergences from the script, glad he had been forewarned by his friends in Rome that the Italians would inevitably lose the guide tracks, which they did.)

Leone was receptive to him on this point. "He believed, as Fellini did, as a lot of Italian directors do, that the face means everything. You'd rather have a great face than a great actor in a lot of cases." Of course, once Leone realized that he was going to be tight on his leading actor so often, he had to accord the same privilege to his other players if he was to achieve some kind of visual balance. Thus did a directorial signature, the alternation of extreme wide shots with extreme close-ups, begin its evolution.

Clint concedes that the director might have come to it anyway, given his Italianate love of gargoylish human expression, the fact that he was, by nature, a man of extremes and perhaps above all because of the luck of this particular shoot. The extras and small-part players Leone recruited on location in Spain were mostly drawn from the Gypsy population of Andalucia, and they lacked the practiced anonymity of professional extras. They offered instead the fierce watchfulness, at once stoic and angry, of disenfranchised people who had been ill used for generations.

With his brutally tight close-ups of them Leone created what might be termed a "landscape of masks" that outlined the unforgiving psychological terrain of San Miguel as no amount of verbiage could have. And from his placement of these figures in his frames he derived much of the famous "operatic" quality of his work. For they are like the chorus and supernumeraries of opera (or a passion play, since there is something so ritualistic about this drama), functioning as living scenic elements, primarily present to lend grandeur to the occasion.

This is particularly true at its conclusion, when San Miguel becomes the unlikely site of nothing less than a resurrection. Joe and the Rojos having fallen out, they torture him almost to death before he makes a painful escape, aided by his only ally, the town's saloon keeper. The sadistic gang, believing he has crawled away to die, greet his reappearance, obviously intent on vengeance, as a return from the dead. And when they fire on him, they cannot kill this unholy ghost. They can knock him down with their pistol fire, but he keeps getting up. And he keeps coming toward them. Joe has fashioned a metal breastplate while recovering from his wounds, making himself literally bulletproof. Only Ramon discovers it—the last thing he learns on this earth. Again, this is not an entirely novel invention. But it is an effective one, and its overtones would, as the film scholar Edward Gallafent observes, echo through Clint's career. The power of Clint's Stranger does not entirely depend on his skill with weaponry; it derives as well from "his unbridgeable distance from the world of San Miguel. A figure with no past or future related to the town, he is envisioned for a moment as a gothic avenger from some other plane of being." Clint would establish a similar distance (and offer reincarnations or pseudoreincarnations) in *Hang 'em High, High Plains Drifter, Pale Rider* and *Unforgiven*.

Clint has always shied away from such interpretations of this seminal work (as well as of the films he went on to make himself). He makes no authorial claims regarding *A Fistful of Dollars*. He believes he was always supportive of his sometimes-hard-pressed director, his suggestions specifically practical, aimed at keeping the film within his most effective range. If he was aware of the many subtexts viewers of the movie have since discovered, he said nothing about them. If Leone was consciously aware of them, he apparently said nothing to Clint about them.

Since Clint's recollections of this and their other collaborations have always been generous to Leone and modest about his own contributions, the director's latter-day attempts to diminish those contributions (and Clint's talent) are puzzling and rather dismaying. But they are spread across the record. He told Iain Johnstone, author of a short biography of Clint, that "I take the real life actor and mold the character from him," implying that Joe might have been a more articulate and principled figure if only he had had an actor who was up to those qualities. In Frayling he is quoted thus: "In real life, Clint is slow, calm, rather like a cat. During shooting he does what he has to do, then sits down in a corner and goes to sleep immediately, until he is needed again. It was seeing him behave like this on the first day that helped me model the character." The language barrier, rendering it impossible for Clint to join in the camaraderie of the set, may have caused him to withdraw somewhat, but he has another catlike quality, curiosity, and one cannot quite imagine him snoozing the days away. It seems likely that he kept a quiet, watchful eye on a filmmaking process unlike any he had ever previously known.

Later, Leone's sly digs would give way to outright contempt. After he had directed Robert De Niro in *Once upon a Time in America,* the journalist Pete Hamill asked Leone for a comparison between his first star and (as it turned out) his last one, and he unloaded at length—unguardedly and rather unpleasantly—on Clint. "In reality, if you think about it, they don't even belong in the same profession. Robert De Niro throws himself into this or that role, putting on a personality the way someone else might put on his coat, naturally and with elegance, while Clint Eastwood throws himself into a suit of armor and lowers the visor with a rusty clang. It's exactly that lowered visor which composes his character. And that creaky clang it makes as it snaps down, dry as a martini in Harry's Bar in Venice. Look at him carefully. Eastwood moves like a sleepwalker between explosions and hails of bullets, and he is always the same—a block of marble. Bobby, first of all, is an actor. Clint, first of all, is a star. Bobby suffers. Clint yawns."

Speculating a little sadly on Leone's comments, Clint recalls: "When we were working together he had great things to say. Then later on, after the picture was a success, he tried to say how he developed the performances. And no director really does. They can give you ideas that might make something work. But they're not acting for you." As for the invidious comparison between himself and De Niro, he says, simply, "It was a crack out of envy. People asked me what I thought, and I said I didn't think anything of it. I couldn't tell them that it was just a guy who hadn't been prolific as I had been." Clint adds: "He [Leone] was having a rough time getting things going," because, he thinks, he had difficulty making decisions and "was more afraid to go to the post." Leone also developed a taste for epic filmmaking. These large-scale productions were time-consuming to set up, and both *Once upon a Time in the West* and *Once upon a Time in America,* each in its way a masterpiece, were brutally reedited by their American distributors with the result—almost inevitable when movies are tainted by this kind of tampering—that they fared badly with reviewers and audiences, which, in turn, further embittered the director.

But as their first picture together wrapped in Spain, the possibility of a future conflict between them was unimaginable to Clint, and doubtless to Leone as well. Indeed, it seemed unlikely to Clint that they would ever work together again, for he was confused about the film at that time: "I'd go through various feelings—this thing could be something, this could be nothing." His confidence was not enhanced by the response of Columbo and the rest of the producers. "Jesus, this is a piece of shit," he recalls them saying as they looked at unedited dailies drifting back from the lab. Flying home after a brief stopover in London Clint concluded that what he had imagined as the worst-case scenario for his project was probably about to be enacted—limited release in a few countries, and limited response from audiences, reviewers and the rest of the industry. It would probably not harm his career, but it certainly would not enhance it.

Back home, when people asked him about his summer job, he remained noncommittal: "I had a good time," he would say, or "The picture was a little discombobulated, but it seemed to work all right." The questions soon died down, but Clint then began wondering why there was no word from Rome—no calls, no cables, no letters, nothing.

★   ★   ★

"'Come over here, I want to show you something.' One of those jobs. 'C'mere, I've got something to show you.' 'Oh, really?' 'C'mon over.' 'Oh, OK.'" Thus does Clint Eastwood recall the first teasing announcement of the last thing he expected to be—a father.

When Roxanne Tunis presented Kimber to him, he was stunned. Groping for a way to express his feelings he refers to an accident he had sustained on the Leone shoot: "I was lying on the ground with the wind knocked out of me." He laughs, ruefully. "It's happened frequently in my life—sometimes some physical impact, sometimes mental."

Arrangements were made. There was never any question of his supporting the child. But as things worked out over the years, there was not much chance of his seeing her very frequently, either. Roxanne for a time reunited with her estranged husband, whom Clint says he never met, and then moved about a good deal. His own career kept him away from Los Angeles for long periods of time, and he and Maggie were spending more and more time in Carmel, too. In any case, Clint says, Roxanne did not press him to spend more time with them. He saw their child when they all happened to coincide in Los Angeles. Basically,

ABOVE: *Kelly's Heroes* took Clint to Yugoslavia in 1969. He brought his Norton 750 (which he still owns) with him, and drew admiring glances.
RIGHT: Long, boring shoots—and films—led Clint to launch his own directorial career with *Play Misty for Me* in 1971.

Shirley MacLaine's faux nun reveals her true nature to Clint in *Two Mules for Sister Sara*, 1970.

The Beguiled: Clint and Geraldine Page, deadly antagonists on-screen, were mutually admiring colleagues on director Don Siegel's set. This was the third of five films Clint made with Siegel, his beloved mentor, who is seen below pointing the way on their most famous collaboration, *Dirty Harry*, made in 1971.

Mountaineer Mike Hoover and cameraman Peter Pilafian signal to a pick-up helicopter after George Kennedy and Clint complete an early, harrowing sequence for *The Eiger Sanction* in 1975. Monument Valley is far, far below.

"A hard-put and desperate man": Clint as *The Outlaw Josey Wales* (1976).

Tyne Daly played the cop who captured Clint's affections in *The Enforcer*, the second *Dirty Harry* sequel. BELOW: Clint with Sondra Locke, his companion for thirteen years, in *The Gauntlet* (1977), perhaps her best role.

The orangutan Clyde was Clint's least temperamental costar, in the knock-about *Which Way* pictures of 1978 and 1980, which were among his most commercially successful films. BELOW: Kyle and Alison Eastwood disarm Clyde's natural shyness.

Clint directs Scatman Crothers in *Bronco Billy* (1980) and costars with his son,
Kyle, in *Honkytonk Man* (1982), films in which the director-star takes great pride.

however, the situation remained what it was from the beginning—
"awkward" and "confusing emotionally," in his words.

Secrets always are, and the fact remains that only a few intimates
knew this one, even though, over the years, Roxanne remained, as Clint
says, "a friend," occasionally visiting him on his sets, calling on him in
his office. (Fritz Manes remembers her bringing picnic lunches to share
with Clint.) It was not until the period immediately after Clint's bitter
and very public breakup with Sondra Locke in 1989, when the gossip
press was for the first time baying at his heels, that someone—probably
a sometime friend of Roxanne's—broke the silence.

This, in turn, encouraged Kimber to grant some interviews, in
which her highly ambiguous feelings about her father surfaced. She insisted to one reporter that Clint "was always there" for her emotionally
and financially when she was growing up, asserting that she saw him
every three or four months, remembering the cuddly animals he brought
her, and her mother preparing his favorite pasta dishes when he stayed
for dinner. At some point in her adolescence he invited Kimber and her
mother to join him on a ski weekend in Vail. And when she was approaching her sixteenth birthday he called to ask her what her favorite
color was; she told him yellow, and a couple of months later a Camaro
of that hue was delivered to her. In 1984 he gave her a job in the production office of *Tightrope* when it was shot on location in New Orleans.

But Kimber told less happy tales to the press as well: "I guess we
never had the greatest relationship," she once admitted. She has also said
that after the press revealed her parentage she and Clint had a dinner at
which she begged him to spend more time with her, that he agreed to
do so, and she felt certain he meant it. She added, however, that "I have
tried to make an appointment to see him and he always has other commitments." At various other times Kimber has criticized Clint for lack
of generosity, for disapproving when she married and had a child while
still in her teens, for failure to support her ambitions as an actress. What
she has said about her father has rather obviously depended upon when
she was asked and what the state of their relationship was at that particular moment.

Clint has preferred not to say anything beyond briefly acknowledging the facts of the matter. It is simply impossible to state what his deepest feelings about Roxanne and Kimber may have been or are now.
Aware of his daughter's fluctuating emotions toward him, and that she
has yet to settle into a coherent career, he enters no plea—guilty, innocent or extenuating circumstances—about the way he has conducted his
relationship with her.

After learning of her birth he returned to the routines of *Rawhide* gratefully, for it appears that he took more than his usually conscientious interest in it as filming for the new season began in the summer of 1964. This was not entirely a matter of escaping from the complications of his private life. Since Charles Marquis Warren had left the show there had been a new producer every season, and this year was no exception. Only this time it was a team of them—Bruce Geller and Bernard Kowalski, who had a company called Unit Productions, which subcontracted to CBS to handle the program. They, in turn, hired Del Reisman, who had been a story editor on *Playhouse 90* and on *The Twilight Zone,* to perform the same function for them.

Reisman says the new producers felt Clint had been underused and, to some degree, misused. "We looked at film and we all had the same opinion: that he was too mature and in his mind too sophisticated to be Rowdy Yates at twenty-two, the pebble-kicking kid [Clint was now thirty-four]." Reisman adds, "We spotted his essential discomfort, and also a real western star, the star we had looked for in Eric but saw in the younger man."

The new producers saw something else in him, too. There was, says Reisman, "a kind of dry line-reading quality that we seized on and went for," giving him as much irony "as he felt comfortable with." None of this was talked out with the network's supervisors, certainly not with the other members of the cast, but it was discussed with Clint. "Don't get shocked," Reisman remembers telling him, "we're trying to mature the character."

It was not long, of course, before Eric Fleming sensed the show's balance tipping away from him, not long before he began complaining, which is perhaps too mild a term for Fleming in full cry. One day he loomed up suddenly in Reisman's broom closet of an office, flung a set of keys on the desk and yelled: "I'm gonna walk out on this. If there's any legal action you go ahead and take my house. I don't give a damn."

In the end, it was Geller, Kowalski and Reisman who took the walk—involuntarily—not because Eric Fleming was unhappy, but because William Paley was. He thought the show had drifted far from its basics. The faithful Endre Bohem was brought back again to produce the show until the end of the season.

By this time, however, Clint really didn't care who was in charge at *Rawhide,* for Rome had at last been heard from. During the long silence of the late summer and early fall, the only word reaching him was unofficial, reports in the trades that all westerns were dead in Italy. One or two of the items did mention a movie that appeared to be bucking this trend. It was called *Per un Pugno di Dollari (A Fistful of Dollars),* but the title meant nothing to Clint, until, a little later, his name was linked with it in some item he read. "And I thought—could this be *Il Magnifico Stragnero?* Could this be?"

It was. What he did not know was that a small miracle had taken place in Italy. When the film was completed, it had not seemed particularly promising to its producers. But since they had taken government money to help finance it they were obliged under its rules to open the picture in at least one theater in Italy for a minimum of one week. After screenings in Rome and Naples, where exhibitors were contemptuous of its chances, they chose a theater in Florence for their run. This flew in the face of conventional wisdom, for almost every study of Italian life and history insists that the largely rural south, its population poorer and less educated, is more primitive in its tastes, the urbanized, industrialized north more sophisticated culturally.

But they went ahead anyway, opening the picture in August, without fanfare or hope, and under false pretenses. They tried to make it seem like an American import by giving all of the Italians who worked on it American-sounding pseudonyms in the credits. Leone chose to call himself Bob Robertson, which was a variation on the name his father sometimes signed to his films, "Roberto Roberti." The cinematographer became Jack Dalmas, and even Gian Maria Volonté, not entirely an unknown, was billed as John Wells. Only Clint and Marianne Koch were credited by their real names.

It is hard to say what effect this ploy had on the film's fate, but what is known is that by the end of the week the theater was playing to capacity, and its manager, as legend would have it, was refusing to surrender the print. The picture was enjoying a word-of-mouth triumph, and he was not going to stop playing it while the crowds were still packing his theater. Maybe it was smart, after all, to have opened the film in sophisticated Florence, where audiences could pick up on the movie's revisionist approach. All one can say for certain is the movie struck a nerve, and the producers hastened to prepare a full-scale Italian release for November.

As they did so, *Variety*'s Rome correspondent saw the picture, and on November 18, 1964, his enthusiastic (and prescient) review, signed "Hawk," appeared. The lead read: "Crackerjack western made in Italy and Spain by a group of Italians and an international cast with James Bondian vigor and tongue-in-cheek approach to capture both sophisticates and average cinema patrons. Early Italo figures indicate it's a major candidate to be sleeper of the year. Also that word-of-mouth, rather than cast strength or ad campaign, is a true selling point. As such it should make okay program fare abroad as well."

Noting the "oater's" lack of "epic sweep, grandeur" and offering a warning about its violence and sadism, the critic nonetheless offered a firm endorsement: "This is a hard-hitting item, ably directed, splendidly lensed, neatly acted, which has all the ingredients wanted by action fans and then some." In other words "Hawk" got it in the same instinctive way that the Florentine audiences had. Clint, he added, "handles himself very well as the stranger, shaping a character strong enough to beg a sequel for admirers of this pic."

Sequel? Did someone say "sequel"? Around the time this piece ran, Clint finally started receiving letters from Arrighi Columbo, full of apologies for his long silence and asking him if he would like to come back and make another western with Leone. A phone call was arranged and, as Clint recalls, "My first question was can we release it over here?" Well, er, um. "We have a question—the question of rights to *Yojimbo,*" said Columbo. Clint flashed back to a conversation he had had with the producer on location, when he was asked not to discuss openly their film's source. At the time he had assured Clint that a deal with the Japanese copyright owners was being worked out. Now it was clear that these negotiations had never taken place. Indeed, he would soon learn that the Japanese had tried and failed to enjoin the picture's release in Italy—Italian law prevented them from so doing—but that they had obtained court orders preventing its distribution elsewhere. Oh, swell, he remembers saying to himself, I get in a picture that's a hit and now nobody's going to get to see it because it'll be tied up in litigation for years.

Columbo, of course, preferred to press on to more pleasant matters, like the new Leone project he was proposing. Clint was not about to commit to that until he saw his first collaboration with the director. The producer agreed to send him a print, but in the meantime the album of Ennio Morricone's score for the film arrived from Rome (his billing on the original prints was Dan Savio). Clint had not met him when he was working on the film and had not even heard of him before (this was only the fourth score the composer had written for movies), and when Clint played the record he was impressed.

If Leone was in the process of reinventing the western, Morricone was in the process of reinventing—or, perhaps more accurately, vastly expanding—the language of film score. His budget had prevented the composer from employing a full orchestra for many sessions, but he responded brilliantly to necessity's constraints. Here, as in his other collaborations with Leone, he made superb use of a new instrument, the Fender electric guitar (then sometimes called a "surf" guitar because it was so regularly employed by beachboy pop groups), which had an eerie capacity for vibrato. This he blended with the folk instruments of the

West, the Jew's harp and the harmonica, to state themes with marvelous economy, the while building percussive sound effects (and, later, wordless choral moans and sighs) into his scores. What emerged, as Richard Jameson wrote, was "memories of the Monogram-Mascot stock libraries [they were American poverty-row companies of the thirties and forties] filtered through a modern and European sensibility." As he said, this work "complemented the bizarre exoticism of the film, the familiar made fresh, new and neurotically contemporary."

Actually, Morricone's work was more than a mere complement to Leone's. Harsh and jarring, the score's opening notes immediately signal that we are not in Kansas (or Texas or Montana or any of the other locales of the classic western) anymore, or, more important, in their psychological territory, either. Morricone is not going to rework "Red River Valley" in symphonic form, the way John Ford's composers were obliged to, any more than Leone is going to rework Ford's visual manner or moral themes. He was as committed to shaking us out of those complacencies as the director was, deftly underlining the film's bitter ironies and its subtextual richness, especially in the way it commented on other westerns. To put the point simply: Morricone pulled the whole thing together.

Clint could not appreciate all that listening to the score. He only knew that he had never heard anything quite like it and that he liked what he heard. And then, with unwonted promptness, the print of *Per un Pugno di Dollari* arrived. Clint booked a screening room at the CBS Production Center and one night after work invited a few friends over to see it. He was careful, he says, not to heighten their anticipation. "You want to watch some little joke?" he remembers saying. "There's this thing, and it's all in Italian. I mean, it's [probably] a real piece of shit."

But then everyone assembled, the lights went down, the picture started unreeling, and "in a while we said, 'Jesus, this isn't too bad.' And the end of the picture came and everybody enjoyed it just as much as if it had been in English."

As soon as possible, Clint called Columbo. "Yeah, I'll work for that director again," he remembers saying. Columbo was a little vague about the nature of the new film, promising nothing more than that it would be a sequel. Clint almost immediately heard from someone representing Leone. He told him that although Constantin would still be involved, the producer this time was to be Alberto Grimaldi, an Italian lawyer who was representing Leone in a lawsuit he had brought against Jolly Film, which was withholding his 30 percent share of *Fistful*'s profits in an attempt to force the director to sign with them for the sequel.

Soon enough Grimaldi—who would go on to produce films by Fellini, Pasolini and Bertolucci—and Leone appeared in Los Angeles, eager to get Clint's commitment to a picture they were calling *Per Qualche Dollari in Più* (*For a Few Dollars More*). By now *Fistful* was well on its way to its Italian gross of $4.6 million, and though they didn't have a finished script or a cast lined up, the cult developing around Clint in Italy made him vital to their hopes.

Clint's mother remembers a meeting at his house at which she, Clint Sr. and Maggie listened astonished as Leone marched up and down the living room telling Clint the new film's story, acting out all the key scenes. He remembers a meeting in a restaurant with Sandy Bressler, Lenny Hirshan and a William Morris lawyer, at which the visitors eagerly urged him to sign on. After dinner, as they stood in the parking lot, waiting for the valets to bring up their cars, Grimaldi reached in his pocket and withdrew an envelope containing at least half of the fifty-thousand-dollar fee he proposed paying Clint and tried to press it on him. Clint politely demurred. He would only assure them that if a satisfactory screenplay and contract were drafted he would undertake the project. But, he added, "There's no hurry on it."

There was, though. The Italians needed to follow as closely as possible on the success of *A Fistful of Dollars,* and so in a matter of months the script was finished and a contract drawn. In the spring of 1965 Clint was once again in Rome, preparing to start *For a Few Dollars More.*

★   ★   ★

It would turn out to be a marvelous film, arguably the best of the Leone-Eastwood collaborations. Balanced and shapely, it is at once more elegant and complex than *A Fistful of Dollars,* more tense and compressed than *The Good, the Bad, and the Ugly.* Unhindered by budgetary restraint (he had $750,000 to work with) on the one hand, unclouded by overweening ambition on the other, this film displays its director's contradictory virtues—his bright satirical gift and his dark fatalism—with an easy confidence he didn't always achieve.

Since, as David Thomson has written, "Leone has been tossed back and forth as camp amusement and spacey visionary," this is the film one most wants both his uncomprehending critics and his sometimes sappy cultists to conjure with. An inimitable director with, ironically, many imitators, a man who redirected the movies' historical mainstream without himself ever fully entering it, he was, as Richard Corliss wrote, a man of "seamless contradictions," which included "labyrinthine plots and elemental themes, nihilistic heroes with romantic obsessions, microcosmic close-ups and macrocosmic vistas, circular camera work and triangular shoot-outs, a sense of Americana and European sensibility, playful parody and profound homage"—all of which he is in succinct command of here.

The production process was similar to that of the first film: a short period in Rome, then to Manzanias and Almería, but this time with a short side trip to shoot sequences that required a railroad line. Conditions were much better than they had been before. The locations, representing both American and Mexican border towns this time, contained more interior sets and were generally more expansive and more richly detailed than anything in *A Fistful of Dollars*.

There were no arguments this time between director and star about the nature or volubility of Clint's character. The success of the previous film had settled all that. Clint probably had a few more lines in this film, or at least more that registered sharply. This is mostly because in *For a Few Dollars More* he enters into an edgy partnership with another killer, and that relationship draws out his character, whose name is Monco (Italian for "monk"), which, again, has religious overtones but is, as Cumbow observes, easily mistaken for the Spanish *manco* (one-handed). Clint reinforced this transliteral pun by using his ambidexterity as a character trait. Monco only uses his right hand to draw and shoot; all his less deadly business is conducted with his left hand.

Prosperity brought Clint another American actor to work with—Lee Van Cleef—and it was a great gift for both of them. Up to then the latter had been, in the critic G. Cabiria Infante's recent, nicely punning phrase, one of the "reservoir gods" of American movies, a small-parts player, mainly in westerns (most memorably, perhaps, *High Noon*), whose name, usually low in the credits, caused a small, pleasurably anticipatory frisson among devotees of the genre. His career had been in decline, partly because of a drinking problem he had only lately overcome, partly because of a near-crippling knee injury, from which he had also just recovered.

His casting represented either admirable daring or possibly last-minute desperation on Leone's part. In the script Leone wrote with Luciano Vincenzoni, Van Cleef's character, Colonel Douglas Mortimer, though second-billed to Clint's, is actually the central figure, even a bit of a father figure, to Monco. For that reason the director had at first approached Henry Fonda, whom he thought, correctly, was a good match for Clint—another slender, light-eyed minimalist. But he couldn't meet Fonda's price, and, happily, Jack Palance, who was perhaps as wrong for the part as Fonda was right for it, also turned him down. It was only then that he recalled, or someone suggested, Van Cleef, whose career was rescued by this role, which led to larger, stronger parts in the years ahead. "My story turned into a rags-to-riches story," he would say, "and not a moment too soon."

Van Cleef had done a *Rawhide* the previous year, and Clint says that when they met in Rome his costar, who had worked for John Ford among several other western classicists, expressed some doubts about *For a Few Dollars More*. Clint told him that if he went into it thinking he was doing something straight and traditional it wouldn't work. He advised him to see *A Fistful of Dollars* to get the spirit of the thing.

That Van Cleef did—to splendid effect. In the new film, the languid elegance of this narrow-eyed, hawk-nosed older man, dressed in black and often smoking a curved pipe, which, together with his considered manner of speaking, gives him a deceptively contemplative air, contrasts vividly, even movingly, with Clint's more rough-hewn character. When we see him we immediately know Mortimer is a man with a past, and that it is not a happy one. This suggestion, however, is very delicately made.

The film begins with a powerfully disorienting sequence. We see first a vast, bleak western panorama, with a rider in its center, so tiny in the frame as to be barely visible. It seems to be a classic western opening, and we sit back awaiting the cuts that will bring us closer and closer to the film's protagonist. Instead, the director holds on the distant rider, and we hear whistling, then the scratch of a match and then the sound of someone inhaling and exhaling. The shootist's identity is never revealed—though based on past experience it is easy to guess his identity.

Soon a rifle rings out, the anonymous rider topples from the horse, and then more shots frighten off the horse. Shooting continues to punctuate the main titles, which float in and out, sometimes at odd angles. When Leone's credit appears, shots wipe out all but the Os in his name—which suggest, perhaps, the all-seeing eyes of the auteur. This brings up the film's epigraph: "Where life had no value, death, sometimes, had its price. That is why the bounty killers appeared."

Significantly, the first of these huntsmen-for-profit to appear recognizably is Van Cleef's Mortimer (whose name, of course, suggests the Italian word for death), wearing preacher's garb, reading a Bible, riding on a train, then forcing it to make an unscheduled stop so he can get off where he wants to—at Tucumcari. He may make his living as a bounty hunter, this one-time Confederate officer, but that's incidental to his main purpose in life, perhaps even a form of disguise, an excuse for traveling about in search of his dark destiny.

But he is never less than courtly. Arriving at the hotel in Tucumcari he learns that the outlaw he seeks is to be found in a room upstairs. Mortimer slips the man's wanted poster under the door, is greeted by shots fired through the door, then bursts in. It happens that his quarry is sharing the room with a woman who is naked in her bath. The miscreant flees through the window, and Mortimer, heading back out the door, politely apologizes for the intrusion: "Pardon me, ma'am." Outside, the man he is pursuing mounts a horse and gallops off. Mortimer, at his own horse, unties a canvas roll, in which are tucked at least a half-dozen different firearms. He studies them thoughtfully—a surgeon selecting just the right instrument for his operation—chooses a heavy pistol to which he carefully fits a rifle stock, then, with an expert's unhurried ease, mows his man down.

What lovely stuff this is—"playful parody and profound homage" indeed, with dry humor of characterization and wild exaggeration of action deliciously, almost wordlessly, blended to establish a figure whose enigmatic contradictions draw you quickly into the film.

Clint's character is, perhaps, a simpler one, and, of course, his serape, his cigar, his manner, suggest that "Monco" is a pseudonym for "Joe." But if identical dress and manner have their obvious commercial uses, they may also be misleading. It is true that here, as previously, the Clint character is simply in the game for the money. But as the precredit sequence—and epigraph—suggest, he is no longer an opportunistic drifter. He is, if you will, a man with a prospering career in legalized murder. He is also a much more self-conscious ironist. Admittedly, at a point late in the picture, Monco does say that he hopes to save enough from the rewards he collects to buy a little ranch and settle down, a comment that has distressed some critics; saving up for the good life gives him too conventional a motivation. But that, too, is probably meant ironically: Movie gunslingers are always talking about the ranch and the quiet life they hope to enjoy someday. They don't mean it. And this one especially doesn't mean it.

Monco's lines are usually sharper than that—shrewdly pointed goads to, and commentaries on, the film's action. Consider *his* introductory sequence, when he enters a poker game with his current quarry, who eventually inquires what the bet was. "Your life," Monco says dryly. After which much shooting ensues, five people are killed and Monco has a nice little exchange with the local sheriff, who has stood by impotently during the carnage. "Isn't a sheriff supposed to be courageous, loyal and above all honest?" Monco inquires. "That he is" comes the reply. At which point the gunman removes the badge from the lawman's vest, takes it outside and tells the gawking townsfolk, "I think you people need a new sheriff." Then he tosses the badge into the street, an action that, of course, parodically refers us to the "classic" *High Noon* and prefigures the famous conclusion of *Dirty Harry*.

Like all the films Leone made with Clint, this one is triadic in structure, with its third side the bandit leader, El Indio, once again played by Gian Maria Volonté, this time giving full vent to an evil the deliriousness of which he only hinted at in *A Fistful of Dollars*. A full-scale psychopath, smoking dope, torturing insects, if anything happier murdering innocent bystanders than he is doing away with those who have actually wronged him, achieving a kind of dreamy peace only after he has killed. In one typically Leonesque passage, he is seen presiding over a parody of the Last Supper, his twelve disciples gathered around him in a ruined church as he speaks in parables. Narratively, however, the most important thing about El Indio is that he is a man haunted by some terrible deed in his distant past and obsessed with a criminal masterstroke (the robbery of a supposedly impregnable bank in El Paso) that he is planning for his immediate future.

We quickly guess that somehow his past and Mortimer's are intertwined. We also guess that it will require more than one man to bring him down, that neither the unflappable experience of Colonel Mortimer nor the youthful reflexes of Monco alone can get the job done. The sequence in which the latter form their alliance is as boldly theatrical as anything Leone ever did. Everyone converges on El Paso, where El Indio's men are casing the bank, and the two bounty hunters watch them—and watch each other watching them. Eventually, Monco orders a hotel bellhop to remove Mortimer's luggage and take it to the station on the grounds that this town isn't big enough for both of them. Mortimer then tells the man to return the bag to his room. Ultimately, the servant simply throws up his hands and scuttles away, leaving the two men alone for their confrontation. Now Leone reverses the strategy he favored in his previous film. There, scenes of this sort tended to begin with the antagonists distantly separated. Here, they are on top of one another, comically invading one another's space. They circle one another like sniffing dogs. Then each steps on the other's boots: Now they are like kids challenging one another.

Eventually, they move apart—far enough apart to start some gunplay, as in those western sequences in which, usually, the town toughs terrify the newly arrived tenderfoot by shooting at his feet to make him dance, or shoot his hat off. Monco and Mortimer do both—to excess—but, of course, neither flinches and neither scares the other. Rather, they are mutually impressed, and their duel turns into a bonding ritual. It is, as well, a terrific deadpan-comedy sequence.

The insertion of this long, very funny piece into a movie that is most basically concerned with anarchical violence and vengefulness is a bold stroke. It far transcends the incidental humor—for instance, jokey exchanges between sidekicks as they proceed to more deadly business—that is traditionally permissible in action films. But Leone and his actors carry the sequence off with sureness and panache, while making a very shrewd observation—that masculine violence has its roots in boyish play, the pushing, shoving, scuffling attempts of children to establish mastery within their group or the neighborhood. This is the first (and probably the only) western sequence to make that point explicitly.

The film's plotting soon becomes extremely intricate. There are betrayals, captures, beatings and finally a shoot-out in which all the bandits, save El Indio, are dispensed with, clearing the way for a final confrontation between him and Mortimer. By this time we know something of the event that haunts both Mortimer and El Indio. They carry identical locket watches that, when opened, chime a wistful little Morricone tune. In the cover of Mortimer's timepiece there is the portrait of a beautiful young woman. El Indio uses his to time shoot-outs; when the tune stops it is the signal for him and his opponent to draw. Flashbacks reveal that in the past El Indio killed the woman's husband and raped her, and we understand, of course, that she had some close relationship to Mortimer. What we don't know until the very end is that she was his sister, and that in the course of El Indio's attack on her she seized his gun and committed suicide with it. This revelation is a very powerful one. The movies have, of course, shown suicide as a consequence of rape before, but few have done so with such unprepared-for—and shocking—immediacy, for we also learn from it that this assault occurred on their wedding night, her innocence defiled at the very moment for which it had been defended. No wonder it haunts even the bestial El Indio.

This sequence immediately precedes El Indio's final, fated confrontation with Mortimer. Thinking he and Monco have dispatched all of his gang, Mortimer calls the bandit out, taking his stand in a circular plaza, its boundaries marked by stones. But El Indio has one last ally, whom he sends out ahead of him. In the confusion this man is killed, and Mortimer's gun is shot from his hand. It lies on the ground, just out of reach as El Indio, a pistol in his holster, and thus holding one of the classic gunfight's familiar advantages, sneeringly challenges him to go for it.

He has not reckoned with Monco, who now appears to referee the duel. He tosses his gunbelt to Mortimer, who straps it on. Then he draws Mortimer's watch, which he has, unknown to the colonel, appropriated earlier. Using El Indio's ploy, he tells them to draw when the tune stops playing, and opens the watch. We have arrived at yet another of Leone's signature moments, and the staging is masterful.

When these pictures eventually reached the United States, there was much agitated discussion of their violence, but in fact Leone's interest in death itself was minimal and almost prudish. The slow-motion exchange of shots, with blood colorfully spattering and oozing in aestheticized patterns—Sam Peckinpah's most lasting or, anyway, most imitated, contribution to the grammar of film—was never part of Leone's style. In the heat of action death is often as casual in his films as it is in most movies. But in the end, as he boldly extends time in stalking confrontations (of which this is the first classic example), he gives his people—and his audience—plenty of time to contemplate the consequences of the action on which they are embarked.

El Indio's end approaches slowly, but then suddenly when the watch stops playing its tune. "Bravo," Monco murmurs from the sidelines, echoing an earlier comment on one of Mortimer's displays of marksmanship. After which, the movie reverts to absurdity. Monco starts loading corpses into a wagon to take them to some lawman and collect the rewards on them. Packing them in, he counts his profits—a thousand for this one, two thousand for that one. One victim, however, is still alive; he draws on him, and is, of course, killed. "Any trouble, boy?" Mortimer inquires from afar. "No," comes the reply, "thought I was having trouble with my adding . . ." The cross-reference is to the exchange with the coffin maker in *Fistful*. This return to the absurdity is balanced by an assertion of principle: Mortimer gives him El Indio's body, the most valuable of their many corpses. He will not have the purity of his revenge tainted by mercenary considerations. Monco makes a polite demurrer: "What about our partnership?" "Maybe next time," says the colonel, and off they go on their separate paths.

This calmly stated grotesquery is the intellectual ground zero of all Leone's work, the rich loam in which the seeds of violence are planted, from which it sprouts with such wild profusion. It is this grounding, and the fact that it is carefully calculated, entirely conscious, that set Leone's westerns apart not only from the rationalist traditions of the genre as it developed in the United States, but also from the blood-soaked tradition

quickly developed in the (literally) hundreds of European westerns produced in the aftermath of his success.

But in the end we do not (and should not) attend *For a Few Dollars
More* for comparison's sake. It represents, after all, one-seventh of
Leone's total directorial output, and by no means its most negligible
part. It is, in fact, part of a coherent continuum, demonstrating that the
tone, style and point of view presented in *A Fistful of Dollars* were not
accidental or opportunistic, and suggesting that the director was capable
of sustaining and developing all of them still further.

What is true of Leone is also true of Clint. The first film sketched,
in bold strokes, a screen character—basically a self-contained ironist,
worldly-wise but not world-weary, determined to pursue his destiny
and equally determined not to define it, or himself, verbally—that was
also capable of enrichment. There is something of his Leone character
in much of everything he has done since. And when there is not, he
(and we) are conscious of him going against its grain, so that this early
work is always in some way part of his self-definition on-screen. The
"Dyin' ain't much of a livin'" Clint, the "Make my day" Clint, have
their beginnings in the brutally frank figure who comically tallies his
profits at the end of *For a Few Dollars More*.

By the time he completed this second film with Leone, Clint was
keenly aware that as an actor he had finally found a comfortable stride.
That he was doing something that gave him pleasure and confidence
carried the promise of freeing him from the sterilities in which he had
been trapped for so many television seasons. He was at last being permitted to act his age. And now here comes a representative of *Rawhide*
eager to extend that privilege.

★   ★   ★

Ben Brady, who had previously produced *Perry Mason* and *Have Gun,
Will Travel,* had now been hired as *Rawhide*'s latest executive producer,
and given what appears to have been virtually a free hand in revamping
the show. His first, and largest, decision was to fire Eric Fleming and to
promote Rowdy Yates to trail boss. He flew to Europe to discuss the
change with Clint, whose immediate response was "You mean fire the
wrong guy? Keep Fleming and get rid of me. You really don't need me.
I would prefer to be out of the show." Working on *For a Few Dollars
More,* which he could see was good, and to which there was no bar to
wide and virtually immediate international release, had emboldened him.

But Brady, "a nice guy," remained adamant. "It was just the old reverse psychology," Clint comments, "the more you ask to get out, the more they want you to be there." Apparently, though, he exacted a good price for his continued presence, a salary guaranteeing him payment for a full season's work, even if the show was canceled before all the episodes were shot (the trades later reported a settlement of Clint's final *Rawhide* contract for $119,000).

There were other changes, too. The veteran John Ireland (who was the gunslinger Cherry Valance in *Red River,* and thus in a sense represented a return to basics) signed on as Rowdy's deputy trail boss—and Fleming's replacement as the wise older hand—Jed Colby. Rowdy's old role as the perpetually impetuous youth was approximated by a young English actor, David Watson, whose pip-pip locutions as a radically displaced person offered some broad comic possibilities. Perhaps the most interesting new casting was that of Raymond St. Jacques as one of the drovers, Simon Blake. He was the first black man to have a regular role on a television western, and doubtless an element of sixties tokenism went into this casting. But he was also an imposing actor, less anonymous than most of the cowboys had been, and offered some potentially interesting dramatic possibilities that the show did not live long enough to exploit.

To make room for these characters, other actors besides Fleming were dispensed with and Paul Brinegar professed "utter shock" at these changes. "They have decimated the cast," he said. Fleming, naturally, took a contrary position. He saw his dismissal purely as a money-saving move. "They were paying me a million dollars a year," he cheerfully lied. Clint expressed no pleasure at his "promotion." He asked a reporter: "Why should I be pleased? I used to carry half the shows. Now I carry them all. For the same money." To another journalist he complained: "In the first show of the season they don't even explain how Rowdy Yates is promoted from ramrod to trail boss." Nor did he much care for his new role. It was fine to play a mature male, but not this one. He is, in his nature, a loner, and even in his fifties and sixties, when father figures are age appropriate, he has not yet chosen to play one.

In the end, though, it was probably not these changes, radical though they were, that undid *Rawhide*. It was primarily victimized in its final season by a catastrophic scheduling error. As Clint would tell a reporter early in 1966, "It had been the network's only show to get a rating on Friday night; so they switched us to Tuesday, opposite a show with the same type of male audience, *Combat*." The redesigned series languished for thirteen episodes in its new slot, then was canceled permanently. No attempt was made to bring Rowdy's or anybody else's story to a formal conclusion. The 217th episode, a rerun, simply aired in its regular spot on January 4, 1966, and then the program vanished as unceremoniously as it had begun.

★   ★   ★

Clint was glad to escape the grind at last, and his future looked more promising than ever. For as *Rawhide* was stumbling to its end, *For a Few Dollars More* opened in Italy as strongly as its predecessor had. By the turn of the year it was on its way to a gross there that would exceed the takings of *A Fistful of Dollars* by some $400,000—a pattern that would obtain throughout the world over the next few years. It proved the success of the first film was not accidental, and it made Clint someone to reckon with, someone on whom an American company could sensibly take a chance. That winter United Artists agreed with Grimaldi to supply substantial backing (somewhere between $1.2 to $1.6 million) for the next Leone-Eastwood collaboration, *The Good, the Bad, and the Ugly*, which would be epic in length (three hours long in its original Italian version, two hours and twenty-eight minutes in the version most of the world saw) as well as cost. (In addition to his $250,000 fee Clint was to receive a percentage of the western hemisphere net.) As negotiations for that film proceeded, UA's head of production, David Picker, was also obtaining rights to *For a Few Dollars More*. Clint remembers running into him at the Beverly Hills Hotel, hearing this news and urging him to acquire the full set by pursuing *A Fistful of Dollars* as well. The conflict with *Yojimbo*'s proprietors was still unresolved, but as a neutral party, whose only interest was making money for all concerned, the American company might be able to settle it, Clint thought. This it eventually did by granting distribution rights to the film in many Asian territories to the Japanese, in return for which they ceased legal actions against it.

In the meantime, Clint received an intriguing—even flattering—offer from Europe. Dino de Laurentiis was putting together a film entitled *Le Streghe* (*The Witches*) as a sort of vanity production for his wife, Silvana Mangano. She had become the first of the postwar Italian sex symbols with her appearance in *Bitter Rice* in 1948, but her international standing had been diminished by the rise of Gina Lollabrigida and Sophia Loren, who was married to Carlo Ponti, de Laurentiis's erstwhile partner and now his rival as a high-rolling international producer. The latter's plan was to make an anthology film—a form popular in Europe in this period—composed of five short stories, which would display several facets of his wife's talent and, perhaps, revive her career. To this

CLINT EASTWOOD / 166

end he recruited some of Italy's leading filmmakers (Luchino Visconti, Pier Paolo Pasolini, Mauro Bolognini, Franco Rossi and Vittorio De Sica) to direct the segments. He also planned to employ first-class players to support Mangano—among them, in the event, Annie Girardot, Francisco Rabal, Alberto Sordi, Toto and Pietro Rossi. Given the huge Italian success of Clint's westerns—by now they were calling him "El Cigarello" there—De Laurentiis believed he belonged among them.

When a scenario (not a full script) of his segment arrived, Clint found it amusing even though it was "never a commercial item—you knew that." Still, in its little way, it presented an interesting opportunity—a chance to get out of period costume and play a contemporary male. It also offered him an opportunity to subvert radically his newly created image by playing a middle-management banker who was in every respect the opposite of El Cigarello—passive, impotent, self-excusing, even a bit of a whiner.

This performance is the best early evidence of Clint's confidence in his own identity, his feeling that even before it was fully established he could toy with his image without endangering his audience's loyalty. The project had other attractions, too. One of them, certainly, was the chance to spend another month on his own in Rome as the era of la dolce vita wound down. More important to him were his costar and his director. Mangano's wonderfully sensual performance in *Bitter Rice*—"in which I fell in love with her"—remained a vivid memory, and the idea that he was being sought after to play opposite a star he had long ago admired from afar pleased him deeply. So did the fact that De Sica would be directing his segment. One of the founders of neorealism (*Shoeshine, The Bicycle Thief, Umberto D.*) he was unquestionably one of the great figures of the postwar renaissance in Italian filmmaking. And so it went, first-class all the way: Cesare Zavattini, De Sica's collaborator on his most memorable films, cowrote Clint's segment; the cinematographer of which was to be the gifted Giuseppe Rotunno. Clint was also flattered to hear that he had been competing for his role with no less a figure than Sean Connery, then at the height of his success in the 007 films.

De Laurentiis flew to New York and paid Clint's expenses to meet him there in order to place an interesting choice before him: a flat fee of $25,000 for a month's work or $20,000 and a Ferrari. Thinking to himself he would never buy a new Ferrari, he told his agents to accept the second alternative, realizing as well "that there's no ten percent on that Ferrari."

So it was back to Rome, sooner than he anticipated, for an experience that was as good, if not better, than he had anticipated, in a movie that was, overall, much less good than it might have been. Clint's segment appeared last in the release print of *The Witches,* a tribute to the fact that, slight as it was, scarcely more than an anecdote, it was more smoothly polished and narratively more comprehensible than the other pieces. It was entitled "A Night Like Any Other," and in it, he and Mangano appear as a husband and wife, their marriage having settled into dull routine, enduring yet another excruciating evening at home. The night is enlivened for her (and the audience) by her distinctly Felliniesque reveries about more exciting times past, and her equally wild sexual fantasies. In the last of these she is seen sashaying down the Via Veneto, followed by a crowd of eager men. She leads them to a stadium where Clint appears in a black cowboy outfit, shooting at her admirers. Later, inside the arena, she does a very discrete striptease to the baying delight of the all-male crowd while her husband is observed perched on a light pole, dressed in mufti, carrying a gun, which he eventually turns on himself.

In the domestic scenes, where Mangano wears a pair of particularly awful glasses, she gets to do dowdiness and exasperation. In the fantasy passages she gets to be glamorous and parodically sexy. (What range! we are supposed to exclaim.) Clint gets to do a real character turn, wearing nerdy horn-rimmed glasses (no Rock Hudson to stop him now) and a three-piece suit, talking in an exhausted monotone, avoiding eye contact with her. An utter blank, totally without intellectual or emotional resources, he obsessively complains about the traffic in Rome and the "honk-honk-honk" of its horns, is obsequious to and resentful of his boss, but unable to do anything to improve his working life. He also vacuously attributes the violence of the world to the failure of its population to get enough sleep, and as if to prove the point he actually nods off as his wife hectors him. When they finally retire to bed and she tries to seduce him, he recommends that she calm herself with chamomile tea as he sinks into oblivious slumber.

Watching *The Witches* now it's hard to say if one's amusement with Clint's performance—broad, almost cartoonish, in keeping with the tone De Sica set—is a response to the intrinsic qualities of his playing or to the broad contrast between what he's doing here and his screen character as it has since developed. But there is a kind of indolent self-regard about Clint's Charlie, an utterly unexamined projection of male superiority, that slyly satirizes the most basic subtexts of conventional movie masculinity and hints at bolder subversions (see *The Beguiled* and *Play Misty for Me*) to come.

If De Sica's work served his producer's wife rather better than his directorial colleagues did—it is sleek, energetic and at least comes to a discernible, if predictable, point—it is like the film's other segments in that it has a rather casual, tossed-off air about it. Nobody is digging very deep into himself or into the material to make these little films. It is all very much, in the blunt language of certain contracts, "work made for hire."

When Clint's role had been discussed via long distance, it had been decided that he would be an Italian from Trieste, where light eyes and hair are not uncommon. "So I get off the plane and I go in to meet De Sica and he takes one look and he goes, 'No Trieste Italian, he's American. We're making an American living in Italy, married to an Italian woman'—without missing a beat."

This was more comfortable for Clint. And work on the film was completely agreeable. He liked Mangano, whose English was fluent and who he says had the most beautiful hands he had ever seen. He also discovered that De Sica, despite his grand reputation—the crew always called him Commandatore—was his kind of director. "He was extremely organized. He only shot exactly what he wanted to use, not a frame more." Indeed, though Clint is an extremely "lean" shooter, and has always said that his most important directorial mentor, Don Siegel, was even leaner, De Sica was the leanest of them all. He cut almost everything in the camera, sometimes not even covering an actor's exit if he planned to pick it up from another angle later—doubtless a skill he had acquired in his early days of shooting in the streets, when film stock was perhaps the most expensive item in his minuscule budgets.

As they proceeded, De Sica gave Clint very little direction: "He just kind of stared. I think he was fascinated by American actors, the American style of acting." But with Mangano, he was extremely detailed, demonstrating movements with great precision for her. "It was interesting because I'd never seen a director do this," Clint said. "He'd say, 'I want you to do this pirouette,' and he'd do these great pirouettes."

De Sica was generous in his public comments about Clint. One weekend they traveled to Paris together, where De Sica introduced him at the French premiere of *For a Few Dollars More,* calling him "a fine, sensitive actor" and predicting that "he will soon be one of the biggest stars in the business," perhaps the "new Gary Cooper."

This was prescient of De Sica, but *The Witches* contributed virtually nothing to that outcome. The picture was eventually released in Italy, but only spottily in the rest of Europe. It was picked up in the United

States by United Artists after it had the Leone pictures in hand, but the company never released it in the full (or even the art house) sense of the word. It was dismissively reviewed in *Variety* in 1969, played in a festival of Italian cinema in Los Angeles in 1971 and in the Public Theater's film program in New York in 1979. On none of these occasions did the reviewers pay much attention to Clint, except to register surprise at finding him in this unlikely context.

★   ★   ★

Clint shipped his new Ferrari to New York during production, then, after the film wrapped, met the car and Maggie there so they could vacation by driving it home to California. It didn't work out quite as comfortably as they hoped; they had more luggage than the sports car could accommodate. "We looked like *The Grapes of Wrath*." He laughs, adding, "Of course the vehicles were different."

Scarcely more than a month later, Clint was back in Rome starting *The Magnificent Rogues,* as *The Good, the Bad, and the Ugly* was originally known. He was beginning to think it would be his last film with Leone, because what had turned out to be the opportunity of a lifetime was now beginning to look like a dead end. In particular he thought that as the budgets (and the lengths) of the pictures grew, Leone was becoming more self-indulgent: "I felt he was trying to be more David Lean than Sergio Leone." Which was "fine for him," but not so fine for Clint. The money was good, the billing top, and an element of openly expressed compassion had been added to his character in this script, which also carried a stronger, more traditional moral weight as well. But even more than in its immediate predecessor, Leone would use Clint iconographically in his grand design rather than as a compelling figure in himself. Or to put it another way, as the landscapes of Leone's films expanded, Clint could see that his place in them was contracting.

The basic facts of the movie are these: The place is Texas; the time is the Civil War. A shipment of gold coins, belonging to the Confederacy, has been stolen and cached. Three men, Blondie (Clint), Angel Eyes (Lee Van Cleef), whose evocatively ironic name was improvised by Leone on the set, and Tuco (Eli Wallach)—respectively the good, the bad and the ugly—learn of the treasure's existence and seek it out, expending much blood and cruelty in their quest. Eventually arriving at a military cemetery where the coins are buried in one of the graves, they face off in another circle of stones, with Clint's character this time an active participant (and ultimate winner) in another three-way confrontation.

The simplicity of this main plotline forms part of the point Leone wants to make. For the attempt to achieve an easily defined goal is constantly beset by dislocating coincidences, vertiginous reversals of fortune and, most significantly, the chance, megahistorical intrusions of the war.

As this sometimes-illogical tale develops, Clint's character turns out to be the least interesting of the title figures. Van Cleef has pure evil to play, which is always compelling, and much of the time the movie runs on the manic energy of Wallach's Tuco. A sort of Till Eulenspiegel (though his pranks are less merry than deadly), he is a small-time Mexican *bandido,* constantly seeing his ill-conceived plans go comically awry, constantly coping frantically with problems that are beyond his impulsive ability to calculate. Representing something new in Leone's work, he is a figure who, for all his depredations, offers us a full range of emotions with which to identify: Clint's Blondie, to be sure, eventually resolves all the film's issues—he is, conventionally speaking, the hero—but much of the time he functions as Tuco's straight man.

This movie traffics more heavily in extended torment than its predecessors did, and even though Leone maintains his usual objectivity in these passages, their sheer number creates a somewhat alienating effect. It is Angel Eyes who most enjoys his spot of cruel sport, endlessly torturing and killing in pursuit of the lost treasure. Which is not to say that the good and the ugly are without their dark humors. They are partners in a scam, in which Blondie brings Tuco (a much wanted criminal) to the nearest sheriff, collects the reward, then, as his partner is about to be hanged, shoots the rope away allowing them to escape. When Tuco quite reasonably suggests that since he is the one taking the larger risks he should take the larger share of their profits, Blondie abruptly severs their partnership and quite unreasonably abandons him in the desert, seventy miles from the nearest settlement. Somehow Tuco survives this ordeal, tracks Blondie down and subjects him to a similar calvary. While Tuco rides a horse and protects himself from the sun with a frilly parasol (a nice touch), Blondie is denied water and forced to stumble across the burning sands until, at last, he collapses. Tuco isn't kidding; we have every reason to believe he will leave Blondie to die. But then a runaway stagecoach thunders by. Tuco stops it, and finds in it three Confederate soldiers, two of them dead, the other dying. The latter turns out to be a man who calls himself both Jackson and Carson, known by all the principals to know where the gold is hidden. In return for the promise of water he tells Tuco it is buried in a military cemetery, Sad Hill. When he actually gets a drink he will, he says, provide the name on the gravestone under which the loot is buried. While Tuco goes for his canteen Blondie makes his painful way to the coach, and it is he who is given the final clue to the mystery just before Jackson/ Carson expires.

This revives the partnership. Tuco takes Blondie to a mission hospital to recover from his ordeal. It is run by Tuco's brother, a priest, and they have a bitter confrontation, the priest chastising Tuco for his wicked ways, the bandit chastising the priest for his useless piety. In this exchange, Tuco observes that priesthood and outlawry represented the only opportunities for escape from the poverty in which they were raised. This is as close as Leone comes, in any of these films, to offering a conventional sociopolitical motivation for anyone's behavior; it is much more old left than new, and more old movie than either. This argument essentially restates the ancient James Cagney–Pat O'Brien conflict—not exactly startling in its originality, but startling enough in this context. (There is another sequence, in which Tuco befuddles, then brutalizes, a shopkeeper in order to obtain a gun, that cross-references to a similar Cagney scene in *Blonde Crazy*.)

The film's second act begins with Blondie and Tuco heading for Sad Hill, dressed in Confederate uniforms, when they encounter a detachment of soldiers also seemingly dressed in Rebel gray. Tuco hails them with comically fraudulent cries, both pro-Southern and anti-Yankee, but when the troop pauses the officer in command starts slapping dust from his uniform, and in one of the film's neatest ironies we see that Tuco has been misled by the dust. The man is actually uniformed in Union blue.

They are taken to a prison camp where Angel Eyes is—quite inexplicably—the Sergeant of the Guard. Torture, a hairbreadth escape by Tuco, a false alliance between Blondie and Angel Eyes, a highly coincidental reunion between Blondie and Tuco and a sprawling gunfight then ensue. This is a very busy picture, and in this middle passage its plotting is at its most desperate. Only the good, the bad and the ugly survive this carnage, and they head for Sad Hill, with Blondie and Tuco pausing on their way for what is surely the most morally pointed passage in all of Leone's work. They come upon a large detachment of Union troops, dug into a system of trenches overlooking a bridge that is the key to this sector of the war. The Confederates are similarly entrenched on the other side of the river, and each army has the same objective: drive the other out without destroying the crucial bridge. To this end they launch daily assaults on one another, fecklessly wasting many lives in the process. The Union commander has taken to drink and cynicism in order to endure this absurdity, and Blondie registers surprising sympathy with him: "I've never seen so many men wasted so badly," he mutters.

When the commanding officer is wounded in another futile assault, Blondie appears at his side with a bottle of whiskey to ease him through surgery: "Take a slug of this, Cap'n, and keep your eyes open." He has resolved to end the stalemate by blowing up the bridge, rendering further hostilities pointless. This he and Tuco do, and the captain dies happily when he hears the explosion. Thereafter the pair come upon a young soldier dying in the remains of a chapel—another of Leone's bare, ruined choirs—and Blondie wraps him in his serape (which he has not yet worn in this film) and gives him drags on his cigar. In effect, he is wrapping the boy in his own death-defying raiment, and though it does not stay the boy's fate, this is a tender moment unprecedented in the Leone-Eastwood collaboration.

While Blondie is thus preoccupied, Tuco rides off toward the cemetery, which is just beyond the former Confederate position. Blondie, smiling ironically, touches his cheroot to the firing hole of a nearby cannon—of the many outsize weapons Clint has fired in his films, this is the largest and most self-satirical—and with a perfectly placed shot stuns Tuco and his mount without harming them.

One might observe that neither in the battle scenes nor in earlier prison-camp sequences is Leone at his best. His ambitions may have been epic, but his sensibility was antiepic. Vast enterprises are to him the precise locus of humankind's most destructive delusions, and he is unable to stage them with the kind of romantic conviction David Lean brought to them. Still, this passage at massed arms makes us fully aware of the moral point Leone has been pursuing: that the bloody deeds individuals do in pursuit of private gain, private obsession, are nothing compared to the slaughter nations do in pursuit of grander, more piously stated goals. A substantial number of people have died as good, bad and ugly sought their gold, but probably not more than one well-placed cannonball took out in this military engagement, and at least they have not disguised their aims with sanctimonious prattle.

This is, of course, essentially the point Chaplin made less vividly with the endless speech that concludes *Monsieur Verdoux,* in which he compares the paltry body count of his Bluebeard character to that which could be attributed to the munitions makers, and at least once in talking about this film Leone specifically compared his intent to Chaplin's. It is scarcely a blinding insight, but it is well put here by a director whose work, to this point, had been reviewed almost entirely in terms of its apparently anarchic violence.

Edward Gallafent, among others, also takes this passage to be a comment on America's growing involvement in Vietnam, and it is certainly possible that Leone, backed by a United States company, and sure of its release in America, was thinking of it. But the concrete visual evidence suggests that he must also have had the madness of World War I trench warfare at least equally in mind.

Indeed, Andrew Sarris argues that Leone's effort in his westerns was always to show that there was a continuum between American and European experience. He observes that the typical American western treated the Civil War "as an interruption to our Manifest Destiny," whereas, for Leone, "the fratricidal fury of the Civil War is one of the keys to the rapacity and violence of the American West," a true turning point for a nation "moving toward that nihilistic nowhere with which Europe has been so familiar for so long."

The film's final sequence is both another reflection on the highly organized "crime" of war vs. disorganized crime as it is perpetrated by individuals, and a final release of nihilism. It is Tuco who arrives first at Sad Hill, scurrying madly about to find the grave of "Arch Stanton," which is where Blondie has told him the loot is buried. His small, scuttling figure is photographed several times against a panorama of neatly ranked military graves stretching virtually to the horizon and offering mute testimony to a far larger, more carefully organized criminal enterprise than the one he is intent on completing. But a military cemetery is also a historical marker, an attempt to grant solemn import to anonymous sacrifice. Already desecrated by the original thieves, it is about to be desecrated again by grave robbers to whom history has been an inconvenience and is now an irrelevance.

Tuco finds Stanton's resting place and is digging furiously at it with his bare hands when Blondie arrives, and for the first time in this film he has donned his serape, his mythic garment. Soon Angel Eyes appears, but the grave, when opened, reveals only a skeleton. Blondie now says he will write the correct name of the grave where the treasure is buried and place it in the cemetery's central plaza. Whoever survives the three-way shoot-out he is inviting will then be able to claim the gold.

Let the ritual game begin! And let it take any amount of time the director requires to complete his concluding tour de force. Tuco turns out not to be a deadly factor in the shoot-out; Blondie (we learn later) emptied his gun of bullets the night before. At its end, only Angel Eyes lies dead. Blondie supplies a brutally just coda by directing a shot into his corpse, which contemptuously knocks him into the newly opened grave; another shot sends his hat in after him. Thereafter he reveals that he wrote no name on the rock. For, as he explains, the gold is actually buried in the grave of an unknown soldier, next to Stanton's. Tuco digs it up and scoops coins out of their bags by the handful. When his greed is sated he looks up to see a rope hanging from a tree branch. Blondie then forces him to mount a rickety cross just beneath it and place his head in the noose while he ties Tuco's hands behind him. Echoing Tuco's misadventures at the end of a rope back in their scamming days, this is also another of Leone's mock crucifixions.

Blondie takes his share of the gold, leaves Tuco's share for him (if he can extricate himself from his precarious perch) and rides off, Tuco's curses ringing in his ears. A very long shot away he severs the rope with a bullet, another reminder of their partnership's beginnings and the signal of its dissolution. A concluding image of Blondie disappearing into an empty wilderness space signals the end of Clint's partnership with Leone.

They had not quarreled, and, as he says, "Eli and I had a good time" making the picture. But it was Wallach who had the best time. He had played a Mexican bandit in the first western remade from a Kurosawa film, *The Magnificent Seven,* and was glad he had overcome his initial reluctance to work in this film. He says he had not heard the term "spaghetti western" until his agent called him one day to say that he had an offer to play in one. "That's like a Hawaiian pizza" the actor responded, not realizing that soon enough someone would concoct that unlikely dish, too. But he met with Leone when they happened to coincide in Los Angeles, where the director overcame Wallach's dubiety by saying, "I will show you one minute of one of my movies." He then took him into a screening room where he rolled the unforgettable main title sequence of *For a Few Dollars More.* "OK, where do you want me to go?" Wallach said when it was over.

On location, Leone was attentive and encouraging to Wallach—"He allowed me to have my romp with this little guy"—and Clint was protective. "Listen," Wallach recalls Clint telling him on their first meeting, "never trust anyone on an Italian movie"; he also advised him to follow his lead in any questionable moments. They flew together from Rome to Madrid, stayed overnight in a friend's apartment—they were obliged to share a bed—then, since Clint did not entirely trust the local airlines, they undertook a twelve-hour trip by car to Burgos, in Basque country (a fresh location for Leone), to start production.

Soon thereafter, Wallach had reason to be glad that he had tucked himself under Clint's wing. For when it came time to blow the bridge at the climax of the battle sequence, he insisted on a position more protected than the one Leone originally assigned the actors. Whereupon, typically, someone misread one of the ever-gesticulating director's arm movements as a signal for action and dynamited the bridge before the cameras were rolling. Wallach thinks that if they had stayed where Leone had at first stationed them they might have been injured by flying debris. A week later, when the span was rebuilt and the shot was finally made, they were, at Clint's insistence, in a shallow trench. On that occasion, Wallach recalls, Clint brought along a golf club to practice his swing during the lengthy setup.

When he is packing a golf club away from a course, it is a sure sign that Clint is bored, restive and out of sorts. There is nothing like the repeated swishing of a five iron to keep the world at bay, and that was the case here. He was tired of the haphazard ways of Italian moviemaking, cross about a production schedule twice the length of that of his first film with Leone and very conscious that in the scheme of this film his role was comparatively diminished. As if to point up his disenchantment, Clint was obliged to stop work on *The Good, the Bad, and the Ugly* and fly to Rome, where he held a press conference and launched a civil action against his sometime employer, Jolly Film. It had licensed a couple of old *Rawhide* episodes and was in the process of splicing them together to make a feature they proposed calling—yes!—*The Magnificent Stranger.*

Unaware of Clint's feelings, Leone was talking to him about yet another western, still larger in scale than this one, the film that would eventually be known as *Once upon a Time in the West.* He also mentioned in passing the project that would, almost two decades later, come to the screen as *Once upon a Time in America.* But Clint remained noncommittal. He repeatedly told Wallach, "No more, I'm not coming back anymore." Wallach, who would make several more Italian films, understood completely. "He knew the route. He knew his character. The only thing he had to do was make adjustments to me. Or to Lee Van Cleef." As Clint would later put it: "I could have gone on doing them for another ten years, but there's only so far to go, then you want a character with a different background or obstacles to overcome." He was quite prepared, and financially able, to wait for such parts.

But when his plane landed in New York on November 1, all such thoughts were brutally driven from his mind. For he casually picked up a newspaper at the airport and discovered, to his horror, that Eric Fleming was dead. He had been in Peru, costarring with the English actress Anne Heywood in a made-for-TV movie called *High Jungle.* With the film about half completed, the company was shooting on the Huanaga River in a remote region some three hundred miles north of Lima, when a canoe in which Fleming was riding with a local actor capsized.

The other man was able to swim to shore, but Fleming was swept into the current and drowned. It would be two days before his body was re-covered far downriver, and it would take Clint more time than that to absorb the shock. In his mind, Fleming's death seems to have put a blunt and indelible period to this phase of his own life.

SIX

WHAT WOULD YOU RATHER BE?

You know, it goes back to the old thing we used to talk about all the time in acting classes when I first came to Universal: They'd say, 'What would you rather be, an actor or a movie star?' Everybody used to say they'd rather be an actor, of course. But after you start thinking about it, you say: 'Wait a second, who gets all the great roles?' Movie stars. You're a great actor and you're sitting there waiting for the phone to ring, and it can be a long time coming. So you kind of have to throw all that out and not worry about what being a movie star is, so you can get the roles with more challenge to them."

Thus does practical Clint Eastwood reflect on the course he chose to pursue in the late sixties. He was not unmindful that movie stars make more money than movie actors do. Clint is never unmindful of money, but it is never his first thought, either. The young actor who prudently deferred part of his *Rawhide* salary has remained willing to forgo instant gratification in return for freedom of choice (and, of course, a very nice back-end participation in the grosses).

Yet, as United Artists prepared to release the first of the Leone films in the United States (in February 1967, with *For a Few Dollars More* following in July and *The Good, the Bad, and the Ugly* coming along in January 1968), he was in limbo. Hollywood was interested. There was talk about the phenomenal grosses his films had recorded overseas and therefore talks among producers, Clint and his representatives. But it was easier for all parties to wait a few months and see how the Leone films fared in the American market.

A sort of class prejudice was operating as well. To American motion-picture executives Clint was less the Man with No Name than the Man from the Wrong Side of the Tracks—from television and B pictures, which these low-budget, lowbrow Italian movies were in Hollywood's eyes. Yes, United Artists had put up a substantial sum to make the last of them, but the combined advance it paid for American distribution rights to the first two—$110,000—is probably a clearer measure of how Hollywood valued them and, by inference, their star.

Clint could not evaluate his prospects on the basis of the success, so far, of the Leone pictures. He wondered: "Does this mean I'm going to be Rod Cameron or John Wayne? Or none of the above? Or does it mean that I'm going to be my own person, whatever that might mean?" It would be at least six months until any option was firmly in place, more than four years before Hollywood would fully acknowledge the power of his stardom.

A Fistful of Dollars opened in February. Reviewers had been primed for "something different" by articles in the trades and by a piece that Bosley Crowther, the chief movie critic for *The New York Times*, had written in November 1966. The success of the Leone pictures in Europe, he said, was showing American producers that even if their home market had been softened by television westerns, the appetite for them overseas remained large. "Don't say you haven't been warned," he wrote, characterizing *A Fistful of Dollars*, which he had seen in Rome as "violent and bloody . . . as gory as any western I've ever seen," and Clint's character as "just this side of a brute, long on sadistic inclinations and short on heroic qualities."

Nevertheless, this aesthetically conservative, socially liberal reviewer (who would soon be eased out of his job for failing to comprehend and support the new manners and morals of sixties filmmaking) seemed to see in Leone's "unconventional" film possibilities for generic renewal. "Anti-heroes will flourish and the earth will shake!" he concluded, equably enough.

He retained this bemused tone when he formally reviewed the movie three months later: "Cowboy camp of an order that no one has dared since, gosh, Gary Cooper's 'The Virginian.'" Trying desperately to get with it, he characterized Clint's Joe as "ruthless without being cruel, fascinating without being realistic . . . a morbid, amusing, campy fraud."

This is nonsense, of course. The camp spirit, moving gays to wicked, useful satire of the essentially bourgeois and heterosexual conventions of popular culture, had nothing in common with the spirit animating Leone's films. His subversions were of quite a different kind. When Crowther returned yet again to *A Fistful of Dollars* for his Sunday piece a few days later, he was still calling it a "deadpanned spoof," but now he was "apprehensive that this most faithful and durable type of film [the western] is in for a kind of modernizing that is vicious and cruel . . . a violation of the happy romantic myth that has kept this type of picture popular through the years . . . a dangerous overturning of the apple-cart." He feared, he said, "a swarm of imitations" and "some lasting harm."

He did not specify what would be harmed. The comfortable conventions of a beloved, if tired, form? The movies in general? The body politic in general? The viscosities of Crowther's prose were often difficult to penetrate. So much so that Clint remembers these pieces as positive notices, perhaps understandably, so outraged were the tirades in other quarters.

Crowther's chief rival for New York's middlebrow readers, Judith Crist of the *World Journal Tribune,* as always combining vulgarity and prudery with hearty self-confidence, made much of the fact that the film carried no screenplay credit (admittedly an inexplicable oddity) and wrote that it lacked "the pleasures of the perfectly awful movie. . . . The cheapjack production, drenched in Technicolor and provided by Sam Savio-Musical Edition RCA (who or whatever that purveyor of pseudo-Tiomkin sound may be) misses both awfulness and mediocrity; it is pure manufacture." She did not even get Morricone's pseudonym right, much less the originality of his work. (Tiomkin, indeed!)

When *she* returned to the film for her Sunday piece she insisted the film had nothing on its mind beyond sadism (Clint's vicious beating at the hands of the Rojos got to almost all the reviewers) and "that handful of silver—nay, trunks and trunks full—that comes to those who cater to the lowest popular taste." Her only valid point, one that in its general terms is still being argued, was that *A Fistful of Dollars,* despite its violence, had been given a Motion Picture Association Seal of Approval (its rating system had not yet been initiated), while *Blowup,* a more obviously artistic film, had been denied one, principally because of a nude romp between its photographer-protagonist and a pair of would-be models.

There was more of the same to come. "Like the villains it was shot in Spain," *Time* snidely observed, "pity it wasn't buried there." Philip K. Scheuer of the Los Angeles *Times* thought Leone had "studied and adopted the most sadistic excesses of Hollywood's western directors . . . and gone them one worse." To be sure, a few critics took a more genially patronizing tone, and several recognized Clint as a promising screen presence. Archer Winsten, in the New York *Post,* for example, thought he "should be good for many a year of hero stints." But not one mainstream review betrayed the slightest awareness of, let alone appreciation of, how consciously and profoundly Leone was challenging genre conventions.

Not that it would have made much difference at the time. This was not, initially, a movie for people who read reviews. They would come to it later, as interest in Clint grew and as nonjournalistic critics began to reevaluate Leone's work. For the moment, the film's success depended on the young male action fans, many of whom were drawn to the film by a clever teaser ad campaign. It consisted of a number of small ads, each of which featured some part of Clint's regalia—the poncho, the hat, the cigar—scattered through all the sections of newspapers for several days preceding the film's opening, when the parts were fitted together in a larger ad to form the whole mysteriously menacing image of the Man with No Name (which is how Joe was officially identified in the cast and credits handed out to reviewers).

But if the film's commercial success in the United States depended on the subcritical audience, its first reviews still had considerable significance, for they reflected, without fully articulating, what Christopher Frayling would eventually, and aptly, identify as "the cultural roots controversy." This, as he implies, derived from the critics' sense that they were fighting a desperate rear-guard action against what might be called the invasion of the genre snatchers, the misappropriation by aliens of mythic territory to which they had no rights, ethically, psychologically, intellectually.

In fairness to the reviewers—and to what was left of the older movie audience—it must be said that they were particularly beleaguered at this moment. From the thirties through the fifties, American movies had come neatly wrapped in genre conventions, toward which one could strike one of two poses—comfortable patronization or mild outrage—on an almost whimsical basis. The "important" films, by common-consent definition literary adaptations and examinations of socially significant themes, announced their intentions well in advance, so there was plenty of time to put on your sober face. Similarly, foreign films had mostly been in the sentimental humanist vein, very easy to digest.

Now all that was changing. One had to deal with Fellini and Antonioni, Bergman and Godard and a swarm of angry Brits, all of whom demanded a new kind of critical alertness. At the same time, American films were beginning to overflow their former boundaries, abandon their former pieties. To take just a few examples: *Psycho* had radically narrowed the distance between horror and everyday life, and made explicit its formerly implicit sexual component; *The Apartment* viciously satirized the pieties of corporate life; *Dr. Strangelove* and *The Manchurian Candidate* questioned the premises of our ruling political metaphor, the Cold War; *Who's Afraid of Virginia Woolf?* rudely, obscenely, overturned the conventions of domestic comedy. It could be argued that in the early sixties the best American movies, the ones that "thinking people" were most interested in, were, for once, ahead of—anyway, abreast of—the social curve, predicting attitudes and conflicts that would dominate our intellectual and political life for decades to come.

Into this confusion these spaghetti westerns—the very term is con-temptuous—intruded themselves, and to many they seemed a final blow. Years later, Ethan Mordden would argue in his passionately intel-ligent study of sixties filmmaking, *Medium Cool,* that they were only "taking the western at its word, filming what America's movies were afraid, really, to show." But until Leone, the western had remained a safe haven for traditionalists. Not only that, it was regarded, along with jazz and the Broadway musical, as one of America's unique contributions to world popular culture. Who were these . . . *Italians* . . . to show us how to make an oater, to put in what we, in our wisdom, had chosen to leave out of our beautiful westering saga—its squalor, brutality and vicious economic determinism.

It was all right, perhaps, for Stanley Kubrick to show the high coun-cils of state populated exclusively by dolts, for Edward Albee and Mike Nichols to show American couplehood—that fifties ideal—as screech-ing entrapment. They were Americans; they had a right to criticize. Worse, Leone's stylistic innovations were not as immediately, cheekily, obvious as, say, a Godardian jump cut. Nor did they signal high artistic intent as, say, the stately emptiness of Antonioni's frames did. His inno-vations could easily be mistaken for "cheapjack" carelessness. So by attacking him one could safely address that uneasiness—that outrage—traditionalists so often felt at the movies in those days, that feeling that one no longer entirely possessed one's native ground. Or for that matter the narrative conventions that had ruled all movies, foreign and domes-tic, for almost a half century.

As for Clint Eastwood, the only American visible in the first of the Leone westerns, and the unquestioned star of them all, patronization was his lot. As we've seen, a few reviewers sensed a new star presence here, but if Leone was to be pitied for his ignorance, Clint was to be censured for participating in this travesty. It was his "cultural roots," after all, that were being dug up and left to rot under the hot Spanish sun. And so the suspicion that this nice boy from television might possibly have sold something out was hinted at, especially since word of the ever-larger fistful of dollars he had received for the sequels was widely mentioned at the time in the press.

Things did not improve for him (or for Leone) with the release in July 1967 of their next collaboration. Crowther, after seeing *For a Few Dollars More,* and observing that it was more overtly humorous than its predecessor in some of its passages, moved now to full moral outrage: "The fact that this film is constructed to endorse the exercise of murder-ers, to emphasize killer bravado and generate glee in frantic manifesta-tions of death is, to my mind, a sharp indictment of it as so-called entertainment in this day. There is nothing wholesome about killing men for bounty; nothing funny about seeing them die, no matter how much the audience may sit there and burble and laugh." Crowther had apparently forgotten that "killer bravado" had been one of the charms of American movies since Cagney was a snarling pup.

The other reviews were equally unpleasant. *Cue* was, like Crowther, worried about the film's social implications: "There is something wrong with a society in which the chief attraction of a movie is vicious violence." *Time* deplored its "lofty disdain for sense and authenticity." *Newsweek* simply proclaimed it "excruciatingly dopey."

The rising outrage one detects in the critics' response to *For a Few Dollars More* derives in part from frustration. Despite the reviewers' contempt for *A Fistful of Dollars,* people had gone to see it. United Artists was reporting an impressive number of bookings, often in the better theaters, with grosses that in some situations rivaled that of its James Bond titles. The company enjoyed domestic theatrical rentals of some $3.5 million on the first Leone western and $4.3 million on the second. Even allowing for the expense of prints and advertising, the return on an initial investment of a little more than $100,000 was staggering, probably as good a deal as David Picker ever made in the course of his long career as a studio production chief. And he had *The Good, the Bad, and the Ugly,* which would return some $6.1 million in rentals, ready to go.

It was released in January 1968 and, in a way, engendered the most curious response of all the Leone films. By this time, Crowther had been replaced at *The New York Times.* His outraged response to *Bonnie and Clyde* the previous summer had finally done him in. The Arthur Penn film, written by Robert Benton and David Newman and starring Warren Beatty and Faye Dunaway, was to become one of the decade's touchstone movies, a period piece that functioned as a brilliant historical metaphor—wildly funny and bleakly tragic—for the social unrest of the sixties.

Its implications were none too difficult to grasp but they were lost on poor Crowther. Led by Pauline Kael, who wrote a brilliant essay in *The New Yorker* defending the film—this was before she became a regular reviewer for the magazine—chic New York rallied to the film. Foolishly, Crowther kept returning to the subject, ineptly defending himself to the point where, at last, the *Times* could no longer defend him. The grumble that had been growing around him for years had now become outright contempt, and in the fall of 1967 he was made critic emeritus and replaced by Renata Adler, an extremely intelligent *New Yorker* writer. The trouble was that Adler knew almost nothing about movies, and in the year that she held the job, she would try unsuccessfully to make a critical stance out of the wondering, occasionally offended, fastidiousness of a literary intellectual bringing her largely inappropriate values to film.

One of the first movies she confronted when she took up her post in January 1968 was *The Good, the Bad, and the Ugly*. Her response to it out-Crowthered Crowther. "The Burn, The Gouge and The Mangle (its screen name is simply inappropriate) must be the most expensive, pious and repellent movie in the history of its peculiar genre," she opined. "If 42nd Street is lined with little pushcarts of sadism, this film . . . is an entire supermarket." The rest of her response remained in this vein. Referring to the scene in which Tuco is beaten in order to reveal the whereabouts of the gold, she wrote "that anyone who would voluntarily stay in the theater beyond this scene . . . is not someone I should care to meet, in any capacity, ever."

So it continued to go. In Los Angeles, Charles Champlin, early in his long run as the *Times*'s film critic, began, like Adler, with some wordplay on the title: "The temptation is hereby proved irresistible to call 'The Good, the Bad, and the Ugly,' now playing citywide, 'The Bad, the Dull, and the Interminable,' if only because it is." He asserted, curiously, that "the intent of the violence, like the intent of the film as a whole, is comical," but that the film's "mannerisms and posturings finally become so obtrusive that their effects are diluted." Kael, settling down at *The New Yorker*, found the film "stupid" and "gruesome," but guessed, probably correctly, that its action-fan audience didn't notice or care that the "western theme was missing." *Time* finally conceded some "good" in *The Good, the Bad, and the Ugly*: "Leone's skillful camera work—expertly combining color and composition, with sharp attention to the details of shape and texture," before passing on to the de rigueur denunciations of "beatings, disembowellings [sic] and mutilations." Its anonymous reviewer also tacked on a two-paragraph profile of Clint, characterizing him as "the real man in the money these days," citing some well-paid roles he had by then accepted. He even supplied a modest quote to the magazine: "The critics are mixed, but the public has gone for me." He then permitted his ambition to broaden his range (the magazine had characterized him as a Gary Cooper type) to surface: "I will play almost anything, except *Henry V* and that sort of stuff."

★   ★   ★

Ha-ha. Journalism had plenty of experience processing dopey—or, at best, innocent—young movie discoveries, having its fun with them, especially when, awkwardly, they expressed their ambitions, something

Clint had no experience doing. But at least the newsmagazine acknowledged what the industry, looking at the success of the first two Leone
films in America, and anticipating the returns on *The Good, the Bad, and
the Ugly*, had also at last observed: that a star of some sort was definitely
coming to term. Indeed, even before the first two Leone films had gone
into release, Picker astonished Clint's agent, Lenny Hirshan, by predicting that sometime soon people would be offering him the then princely
sum of $750,000 for his client's services.

That earning that money might only come by working within the
limits of the action picture was not an entirely pleasing prospect to Hirshan's client, or to the agent himself. Being an "action star" was not in
those days what it has become, and action pictures were not yet the
"tentpoles" they now are, with studios risking huge budgets and building their release schedules around an armed and dangerous Arnold
Schwarzenegger or Sly Stallone. In the late sixties, action movies were
still largely low-prestige, low-budget enterprises, and one had to avoid
permanent entrapment in them. What Hirshan and Clint wanted to do
instead was to make enough straight-ahead, reasonably priced action
films to satisfy what they judged to be Clint's core audience, while at the
same time making some more expensive, presumably more prestigious,
films that would, they hoped, establish him with a larger public and as a
major industry player.

Between the successful release of the first *Dollars* movie and the optimistically awaited release of the second, Clint was presented with at
least two interesting possibilities. Leone turned up in Los Angeles to
pitch *Once upon a Time in the West* to him again, offering him Harmonica, the mysterious gunfighter eventually portrayed by Charles Bronson
in the film. It was to be produced by an American company (Paramount), was to be made entirely on location in the United States and
was budgeted at a substantial figure. But their meeting did not go well.
Leone particularly (correctly) loved the movie's opening sequence, in
which three gunfighters await the arrival of Harmonica at a train station
and engage in much memorable and subtly satirical western business.
Somewhat to Clint's impatience he focused on the entrapment of a fly
in a pistol barrel by the figure who was played in the film by the iconic
Jack Elam. "It took him fifteen minutes to get past that part," he says,
and he remembers asking, "Wait a second, where are we headed with
this?" But Leone was not to be hurried, and continued his synopsis at
his own overly detailed pace.

At its end Clint still felt that however artfully the film was accomplished, it would inevitably be perceived as just another pasta dish. He
could also see that though technically he would be the star, the best parts

once again would go to others, in this case to Henry Fonda and Jason Robards Jr. So he passed, telling Leone that he would love to work with him sometime on something that was not a western. In a sense he was wrong. *Once upon a Time in the West* turned out brilliantly, the dark full-scale epic of western settlement that Leone had always wanted to make, rich in brutal irony and wondrous imagery. Though a commercial disaster when it was released (the studio cut more than twenty minutes out of it a couple of weeks into its run), it has since been widely acknowledged as one of the great westerns of its time.

Large but empty commercial vistas had no appeal, either, for around the same time, writer-producer Carl Foreman approached Clint with *Mackenna's Gold.* It was, on its face, just the sort of upscale enterprise everyone agreed Clint ought to be doing—a western to be sure, but one intended for an all-star cast and being advanced under the toniest auspices. For Foreman was then a prestigious figure in the industry; he had written and produced a number of small, serious, critically appreciated films in the late forties and early fifties (*Champion, Home of the Brave, High Noon*), had endured blacklisting and had come back to make the hugely successful adventure film *The Guns of Navarone,* the director of which, J. Lee Thompson, was attached to this new project.

Clint remembers that Hirshan was enthusiastic about the film, though he was not. "I don't get the script," he recalls saying—something about a treasure map, buried gold and the usual mixed, contentious crowd gathering to pursue it. Nor was there anything very interesting about his character, who was a standard hero. Hirshan remembers Clint leaving a meeting with Foreman, saying, "It's just an extension of *Rawhide,*" and telling him that he was going to pass. It was a wise decision, for despite an all-star cast headed by Gregory Peck in the role that Clint turned down, *Mackenna's Gold* flopped miserably.

At this time Clint had another close adviser, his longtime business manager Irving Leonard, and he, too, was playing an active role in developing his career. A small, fastidious man, Leonard acted, as Clint puts it, "like a second father to me." He had taken Clint on as a client when he was freelancing, managing his modest financial affairs for contingency fees. Clint admired Leonard's skills as a lightning calculator—one time at a play an actor did some complicated mental arithmetic on stage and gave the wrong answer, only to hear Leonard cry out the right one from the audience. More important, he gratefully admired his loyalty and general shrewdness; Leonard's firm continues to be Clint's business managers to this day.

Around this time the accountant passed on to Clint a script entitled *Hang 'em High.* A western on a fairly modest scale, it was the work of

Leonard Freeman (a producer-writer working mainly in television, for which he would eventually create *Hawaii Five-O*) and another TV writer, Mel Goldberg. When he read it Clint found in it a "certain feeling about injustice and capital punishment" that he responded to. He also thought the leading role, that of Jed Cooper, a lawman seeking private vengeance while serving a hanging judge who takes a peculiar pleasure in his work, offered him opportunities as an actor that he had not had in the Leone films. Here he would not be, as he puts it, "a symbol," but rather a troubled figure, questioning both his own motives and those of the system he served. "I felt it was time," he says, "even though it was a smaller film, to go ahead and challenge myself in that way."

Clint's feelings for the film perhaps ran a little more deeply than that. For it took up and extended the main theme of a favorite picture of his, *The Ox-Bow Incident,* which through its story of men wrongly accused of, and hung for, cattle rustling expresses, in its way, one of the main themes of his inner life, his abhorrence of false witness, false accusation (it is why erroneous tabloid reports of his doings constantly evoke his outraged litigiousness). The film would also permit him to explore again the resurrection theme adumbrated in *A Fistful of Dollars,* and returned to in so many later films.

This project he and Leonard took to United Artists. At the same time, Clint, acting on Leonard's advice, established his own company, Malpaso, which means "bad step" in Spanish and is also the name of a creek that ran through the property he owned in Carmel at the time. Clint liked the irony implicit in the phrase, but says that he did not then foresee the company becoming the full-scale production entity that it soon turned into. Rather he and Leonard saw it as a typical loan-out company of the kind the movies' above-the-line talent had begun establishing in the 1950s, partly for their tax advantages, partly because they put their owners in at least nominal charge of their own destinies.

The latter promise was particularly appealing to Clint. As an actor for hire there was little he could do to reshape something like *Mackenna's Gold.* But if his company was supplying his services and coproducing a project, he would have much to say about its outcome. Indeed, as he thought about *Hang 'em High*, he found himself thinking about Ted Post to direct it. And he also thought that Post would be a good person on whom to test his opinion of the script. The director had come out of the New York theater and live television and aside from his twenty-eight *Rawhide* episodes he had by this time directed hundreds of other TV hours. He also taught in some of the same acting schools that had shaped Clint's own ideas about performance.

So Clint made an appointment with him, arriving at Post's Beverly

Hills home carrying with him, besides the *Hang 'em High* script, a novel and a brief treatment for another original film—projects that UA had proposed to him. The fact that Post was a voluble, volatile man from Brooklyn increased his value to Clint. If so different a sensibility responded as he had to *Hang 'em High* it would seem more likely that the film could find a broad audience. Clint briefly described the material he had brought with him, asked Post to study it and then get back to him. He did not offer his own evaluations of the properties.

When they next talked, Post told Clint that he thought *Hang 'em High* was the best of the lot, and it was only then that Clint said he agreed. His judgment confirmed, he and Leonard told UA that Clint would commit to this project if UA would sign Post to direct it. This created an immediate dispute. Post recalls Arnold Picker, David's father, who was operating head of the company at the time, calling from New York to argue against him. He and Clint and Leonard were all in the latter's office, listening as the elder Picker raised his objections: "We have a list of directors we gave you. They're all very experienced and talented people who have tremendous track records. . . . I mean, we know Teddy is very good at what he's doing, but that's television, not features," he said, ignoring the fact that Post actually had two theatrical films to his credit at this point.

Clint, however, remained steadfast. According to Post, he told Picker, "I know most of these directors you recommended, I've worked with most of them. I prefer Ted Post. I did a lot of shows with him. I feel very comfortable with him." Says Post: "He was very patient, very soft-spoken. He was rare in our profession, somebody who could react with a saneness and soberness that you don't see around too often."

So Post was signed. He and Clint then went to work on the script, pointing up the dramatic tension of some scenes, adding bits of dialogue and action that they thought sharpened some of the script's characterizations. Post says they made no large structural changes, but their work led to the first of what would turn out to be many conflicts with Freeman, who was also to have sole producer's credit on the film.

In deference to the writer, Post and Clint backed away from many of their revisions, vowing instead to improvise them on the set, where they imagined that Freeman would not always be present, perhaps because he proved largely indifferent to the picture's casting. According to Post, he had a relatively free hand in this matter, recruiting Pat Hingle, Bruce Dern, Ed Begley Sr., Charles McGraw, all of whom had worked on *Rawhide*, and Inger Stevens, who had not, and who, according to Post, initially resisted working in a western opposite Clint, whose work she did not know.

They all worked together happily enough—Stevens embraced Post on her last day of work, fulsomely thanking him for an altogether excellent experience—but there was further acrimony between Post and Freeman. As Post recalls it, Freeman appeared on the White Sands, New Mexico, set "with the Cecil B. De Mille boots and the riding crop, banging the crop against the leather, going on the set and changing things." Post and Clint watched this performance with some astonishment, and Post said he would speak to Freeman about usurping the director's authority. "No, don't you do it, Ted," said Clint, "I'll do it." Clint drew Freeman out of everyone's earshot and talked earnestly to him. Shortly thereafter, the producer withdrew and was subsequently not much seen. What did you say to him? Post asked Clint, who replied, " 'If you come on the set again, there'll be no set, no crew, no actors, no director. Stay away.' And he stayed away." At least until postproduction began.

Eventually Post and company put on film—for a budget Clint says was less than that of his last Leone film—an intelligent western well within genre traditions, but not without some complexities and originality as well. Most of the latter quality was concentrated in the excellent opening sequence, where Jed Cooper, Clint's character, is discovered driving a small herd of cattle he has recently purchased across a river, in the course of which he has to dismount and rescue a calf from the stream. Cradling it in his arms, and very much resembling Rowdy Yates in costume and innocent attitude, he emerges on the other bank to confront a group of armed riders, who accuse him of rustling the herd and killing the rancher and his wife to whom it belonged. He tells them that he is a former lawman, now trying to start a small ranch of his own, and produces a bill of sale for the cattle.

The riders, all in the employ of a rancher called Captain Wilson (Begley), ignore the document and prepare to string him up. Clint plays his youthful terror very persuasively. Dern's eager villainy as the most vicious of the riders is also effective. His pleas for patience and further investigation ignored, Jed is left swinging from a rope as the posse rides off. It's a nice, dislocating moment—you don't expect the star to be (to all appearances) killed this early in the picture. Indeed, when Clint gave the script to his old pal Bob Donner and told him to choose a small part he thought he could play, Donner read a few pages and called him up excitedly, suggesting he play the guy who gets hung in the first reel. Clint laughed and told him to read on a little further—that character was the hero.

For Jed is saved by the fortuitous appearance of a tumbleweed wagon, under the command of that most authentic of western actors, Ben Johnson. He throws Jed in with the rest of the prisoners he has been collecting and takes him back to Fort Grant, territorial capital of what will one day be Oklahoma. There Jed's innocence is proved to the satisfaction of Judge Fenton (Hingle), a curiously ambiguous character, who earnestly (and frequently) states his belief that law is the basis for civilization, but who also likes his work just a little too much.

Fenton knows Jed will seek vengeance against the men who lynched him, and since he's shorthanded—just fifteen marshals to police seventy thousand square miles—he proposes a deal: He will swear out warrants for Jed's tormentors so that he can track them down legally while also pursuing other miscreants for the judge. It's an offer Jed can't refuse. The young man who was so gentle with his straying calf has overnight become a darkly brooding figure who will dress himself entirely in black (and affect a rather familiar cigar) for a film in which his close-ups often emphasize either the rope scar on his neck or the black scarf he wears to hide it. Unquestionably a large part of this character's appeal for Clint was that he could be read as a transitional figure, blending a little bit of Rowdy Yates with a lot of the Man with No Name.

An advocate of swift, sure punishment for crime, Jed is also, for obvious reasons, aware that the law does make mistakes, usually when it is least sure of itself. The debate over this matter is the central argument of the film, although there is, to be sure, plenty of gunfire as, one by one, Jed captures and/or kills the men whose careless malice almost cost him his life.

Almost always these confrontations place him in interesting moral dilemmas. For example, he tracks down Bruce Dern's character in the desert and must then conduct him, and two young confederates who have joined him in a rustling expedition, back to civilization. "You'll never get me to Fort Grant alive—boy," the outlaw sneers. "Then I'll get you there dead—boy," Jed sneers back.

The bandit is very nearly proved correct, but his two confederates come to Jed's aid. Despite his efforts to place this extenuating act on the record at their trial, Fenton sentences them to hang in a mass execution that is the film's vividly staged centerpiece. Disgusted by the circus atmosphere surrounding the hangings, Jed retreats to bed with Jennifer (Arlene Golonka), a whore whom he has befriended—and finds that he is impotent. (This is not, by the way, a condition many stars have chosen to play, and at one point as the half-naked actors filmed the scene, Clint looked up and inquired in mock innocence, "Is this the way Gene Autry got his start?")

At that juncture, Captain Wilson stages an assassination attempt on him, the shooting timed to the moment when the execution crowd's noise is at its height. Grievously wounded, Jed is nursed back by Rachel, the rather mysterious figure played by Stevens. We have met her earlier, peering into the tumbleweed wagon, studying its haul, visiting the jail to spy on new arrivals. When Jed regains some strength they visit a deserted ranch for a picnic. There she tells him that she seeks three men who surprised her and her husband in this very place, killing him and repeatedly raping her. She turns aside Jed's gentle advances, but then a storm blows up, and they take refuge in the ranch house where, eventually, they consummate their affair.

This passage is Clint's first movie love scene, and even Joan Mellen, in *Big Bad Wolves*, a study of masculinity in American movies, which is highly critical of the unyielding nature of his image, concedes that he shows himself to be a "gentle and tender lover" here. In fact, it is one of the few conventional romantic sequences Clint would play until *The Bridges of Madison County,* almost three decades later. In the films in between there would often be no love interest, or only a very casual one. When more complex and fully drawn female figures are present they sometimes actively threaten Clint's character (*The Beguiled, Play Misty for Me*), or they have powerful agendas of their own (*The Enforcer, Bronco Billy, Sudden Impact, Heartbreak Ridge)*. These make for testy romantic transactions, and on Clint's part, often enough, a certain befuddlement, offering little in the way of soft, mutual enchantment.

In fact, the promising *Hang 'em High* romance goes nowhere. Sometime later, when Jed is fully recovered, and is riding out of town to resume his quest, Rachel stops him, and this dialogue ensues:

"You asked me once if I could ever stop looking. I think now I can. Can you?"

"Well, Rachel, there's a difference. I'm not looking for ghosts. The end of my trail's at Red Creek [Wilson's ranch]."

"Maybe not. What then?"

"I don't know."

The film's final confrontation takes place at night and has the air of a haunted-house sequence. It concludes with Jed killing two men, Wilson committing suicide and Jed finding one old man hiding in a back room. He pleads for his life, reminding Jed that he was the only one in the lynch party who argued against hanging him. When Jed tells him he must escort him back to Fort Grant for trial, he adds, "I just want you to know, I don't hold you to blame—for what that's worth." "It's worth something," his captive says quietly—his manly acceptance of fate impressing his captor.

Now, once again, Jed pleads with Fenton for a life, finally flinging his badge down and telling him he will no longer be party to legalized lynching. At which point, the judge relents—for once. The last we see of Jed he is riding out of town, passing Rachel with no more than a silent nod. Two members of the captain's crew are still at large, and Jed must bring them to justice before he can rest.

What is best about this movie is its unswerving quality; it does not impose improbable changes of heart or mind on its leading figures. Cooper and Fenton remain bound to the destinies their natures impose on them, and the film remains bound in ambivalence toward both of them. Though Jed forces Fenton to his single merciful act, it is clear that this does not signal permanent reformation on his part. Though Jed is capable of other, similar acts, it is also obvious that he will not forget the injustice done him, will permit it to go on driving him even after he has brought down the last of its perpetrators. There are, after all, plenty more like them. (It is interesting to note that a second love scene between Jed and Rachel, one that would have implied a romantic return to her once his final obligations to his past were discharged, did not make it to the film's final cut.)

Against this virtue one must set certain obvious defects. *Hang 'em High* is, by the standards of the genre, a heavily plotted film—and an extraordinarily talkative one. There is also something just a little too tidy about the way it looks. Fort Grant is a familiar, back-lot sort of western town, very finished and built up, lacking the dusty disreputability it needs to support the judge's insistence on the rawness and lawlessness of his domain. In the end, one cannot escape the conclusion that the film's ruling sensibility—no matter whether it was Post's or Freeman's—was a television sensibility. About that we cannot be entirely certain since the two quarreled their way through postproduction, too, with Freeman making his own cut of the film even as the director's cut was being made. Clint tried to arbitrate, though he was mostly on Post's side.

When *Hang 'em High* was released in the summer of 1968, a few of the critics were convinced, against the evidence before their eyes, that it was a spaghetti western in disguise—"Only because I was in it," Clint snorts. *Time,* for example, called it "the year's grisliest movie." Given its release immediately after the Martin Luther King and Robert Kennedy assassinations, and the riots at the Democratic Party convention in Chicago, the magazine's reviewer thought to lead off by quoting, approvingly, a rhetorical question of Lyndon B. Johnson's: "Are the seeds of violence nurtured through the screens of our theaters?" Kevin Thomas in the Los Angeles *Times* agreed that "in these exacerbated times . . . it is increasingly difficult to stomach displays of one man's inhumanity to another even when that is the very thing the filmmaker is supposedly deploring."

One or two critical contrarians actually mourned the demise of the

Man with No Name, preferring his nihilism to the troubled conscience of Jed Cooper. Most reviewers, however, welcomed the moral earnestness of the film. "*Hang 'em High* has its moments," wrote Howard Thompson in *The New York Times*. "It even has a point, unlike those previous sado-masochistic exercises on foreign prairies. . . ." *Life* praised it for saying "some interesting things about the complex nature of justice," and called it the best western of the summer. Implicit in many of the reviews was a sense of relief that the movie did not challenge genre or moral conventions.

In a sense, then, the weaknesses of *Hang 'em High* served Clint as well if not better than its strengths did. By bringing him back to native ground in a role that did not overtax the natives' patience or traditional belief system, it proved to be exactly the right career move for him. And it fared well at the box office, doing slightly better in North American release than *The Good, the Bad, and the Ugly* had done, much better than the earlier Leone films. Indeed, when the year's figures were totaled up, *Hang 'em High* was its twentieth-highest-grossing film, and Clint made the first of his eighteen consecutive appearances on the annual Quigley Publications poll of exhibitors, in which they are asked to name the year's top box-office stars. The serious bets Hollywood had begun placing on him between the making of *Hang 'em High* and its release were now odds-on.

★ ★ ★

In that period Hirshan and Clint were able at last to establish their two-tier policy for the latter's career. The agent made a three-picture deal (later extended) at Universal, where, in effect, Clint would do his basic bread-and-butter movies—some of which turned out to be his most interesting work—over the next seven years. At the same time Hirshan began signing him for the big-budget, star-ensemble projects deemed necessary to establish a larger respectability for him.

It was a phone call to the agent from Jennings Lang that set this train of events in motion. Lang had been a powerful agent at MCA, beginning his career there in 1938, and had become an executive in television production at Universal after the agency merged with Decca records (which by this time owned the studio) in 1959. He had, unfortunately, gained his largest fame for his role in one of Hollywood's more memorable scandals: In 1951 he had been shot (in the groin, appropriately enough) by producer Walter Wanger, who believed (correctly) that Lang was having an affair with his wife, Joan Bennett, who was also Lang's client.

Blunt, hearty and sometimes rather crudely manipulative—with a widely admired skill at mixing the perfect martini—Lang was a tough and ambitious executive. By this time he had grown restive with television, and he came right to the point in a meeting with Hirshan: "I want to be in the picture business, and I would like to be in the Eastwood business." This was fine with the agent. Lang was a major player in Hollywood, and a man who got things done. The agent asked if Lang had anything ready for Clint to do immediately.

Lang opened a desk drawer, pulled out a script and tossed it to Hirshan. It was called *Coogan's Bluff,* and when he read it, Hirshan liked the basic story—about an Arizona sheriff who comes to New York in order to extradite an escaped murderer, James Ringerman, and escort him back to his jurisdiction for trial—and so reported to Lang at their next meeting. "Jeez, it's terrific," he remembers saying. "And Clint I'm sure would like it; I'd like to give it to him." Whereupon Lang excused himself and trotted down the hall to one of his associates' office. Hirshan heard him tell the man to stop thinking of *Coogan's Bluff* as a two-hour television movie: "We're gonna do it as a feature with Clint Eastwood."

This was late summer 1967, and Lang wanted to go into production that fall. For that matter, so did Clint and Hirshan, who by this time had another deal in the works, which would require Clint's services in Europe beginning around the first of the year. There were problems, though. The script Hirshan passed on to Clint was the latest of three versions, each by a different writer, all judged to be in some way wanting by Lang and others at the studio. Clint himself saw only potential in the draft that he read, not a shootable script.

The basic story, he thought, offered an opportunity to expand his screen character, bring his westerner out of the past and off the plains and into the contemporary urban jungle. Just as important to him, Walt Coogan also offered him some comic opportunities. He was a shrewd rube, hiding his smarts under a countrified manner, enduring the patronization of his big-city counterparts until finally, satisfyingly, he proves to be their equal. The film also adumbrated the antibureaucratic theme that would, in time, be addressed much more forcefully in *Dirty Harry.*

Before the script's shortcomings could be rectified, *Coogan's Bluff* lost its director. Alex Segal, well-regarded for his stage and television work, had committed to the project, but either had a falling-out with the studio or encountered unspecified personal problems and withdrew. As a result, *Coogan's Bluff* was granted its largest significance in the Clint Eastwood filmography, for Lang proposed replacing Alex Segal with Don Siegel. This was largely a matter of convenience—Siegel was under contract to the studio and at the moment had no assignment—but he was also right for the job. He was a seasoned action director whom Lang sensed was Clint's kind of guy, a decisive filmmaker who didn't waste time, words or film on the set, mostly because he was about as well grounded in his craft as it is possible to be. Having begun his career at Warner Bros. in 1934 shooting inserts, he had progressed to directing second units and supervising montage sequences, moved on first to the shorts department (where two of the films he oversaw—*Star in the Night* and *Hitler Lives?*—won Academy Awards in 1945), and then to features, most of them low budget, at least two of them, *Riot in Cell Block 11* and *Invasion of the Body Snatchers,* genre classics.

By this time his credentials should have brought him to bigger budgets, more prestigious projects. But, as Clint would later say, "you get into a rut in this town," and the director was now carrying himself with what Andrew Sarris called a certain "jocular fatalism," which sometimes lost its jocularity. Siegel once told an interviewer about his frustration after the success of *Invasion of the Body Snatchers:* "I didn't get a job offer from anybody, nor did I hear anybody in the industry say, 'My God! This kid's really got it.'" Even after he directed Elvis Presley in what was surely his best movie, a tense little western called *Flaming Star,* Hollywood kept him in his unexalted place, though he was beginning to attract some critical attention abroad and in the small American film journals.

What he needed was a rising star to pull him out of his "rut." What the rising star Clint Eastwood needed was a first-rate action director who could also help him find some charm in a screen character who had up to now been an essentially antisocial figure. Before meeting, Siegel and Clint were dubious about one another, mostly because each was unfamiliar with the other's work, and so when someone proposed Mark Rydell, a sometime actor and a prolific television director, to Clint, he sent him *Coogan's Bluff.* The director, who had just finished his first feature, *The Fox,* gave him a mixed response: He liked the script well enough, but felt he needed more than a few weeks to prepare it. Clint then asked him, "What about Don Siegel? The studio keeps talking about Don Siegel."

Somewhat to his surprise, Rydell responded enthusiastically. "He's great. I worked with him as an actor [in *Crime in the Streets* in 1956], and he's the only director I know who'd be ready to go in a month."

Impressed by Rydell's recommendation and appreciative of his generosity, Clint decided to run three of Siegel's pictures, liked what he saw and agreed to meet with him. The director, hearing that Clint had studied some of his work, reciprocated by running Clint's Leone films, which, in turn, impressed him. Clint remembers their first encounter taking place in Siegel's Universal office. Siegel recalls that he flew to Carmel in a private plane piloted by Universal's casting director, had a couple of drinks with Clint in his "surprisingly modest" cabin, "discussed dames, golf, dames, the glorious weather, etc." and was about to repair to a golf course with him, and perhaps stay overnight so they could have a more extensive conversation, when Lang phoned to summon Siegel back to the studio. The director and the actor had not yet exchanged more than a few substantive words about *Coogan's Bluff,* but that was not really the point of the meeting. They had sized each other up, liked what they saw and silently decided that they could probably work together.

At which point, still unhappy with the script, Siegel went to Lang and proposed that a writer named Howard Rodman, who was working with him on another project, be engaged to write an entirely fresh variation on the film's basic theme. Rodman, in his turn, proposed that he and Siegel work on it in New York, where they could scout locations in the process.

It sounded like a boondoggle to Clint—"You don't have to be on location to write a good story"—and it was in part. Cameras, a gold-painted typewriter, a swell suite, were charged to the production. But less than a month after he had begun, Rodman turned in a finished product that both Siegel and Lang liked. Off it went to Clint. And back he came to the studio, requesting a meeting, to which, he said, his agent, his lawyer and his business manager would accompany him. "Sounds ominous," Siegel said to Lang. "Entourages are born to dislike everything," said Lang.

As it happened, Clint's people didn't have to say much. He did most of the talking, and what he said was "I hate the script." He felt that Rodman and Siegel had vitiated the strengths of the draft he had committed to without bringing any new values to it. "I figured you didn't like it, so I steered Rodman in a different direction," said Siegel, "thinking you wanted a change."

According to both men, their argument grew more intense as the meeting wore on, and it began to look as if the project was going to disintegrate then and there. At which point, Lang intervened: "Look, you guys both behave. Why don't you just sit down and talk about it, just the two of you. Get rid of all these other people, myself included. . . ."

This they agreed to do, with Siegel insisting that before they start Clint read all the previous versions of the screenplay. When he had done so, they repaired to his office, unbound all the scripts and spread their pages around on the floor, where for a couple of days they crawled about, scissors in hand, choosing a scene here, a bit of dialogue there, occasionally scribbling bridging material of their own devising. All of this they pasted down on clean sheets of paper. When they left after the first day Siegel lettered a large "Don't Touch" sign and put it on display in the center of the mess so the cleaning lady wouldn't throw anything out.

In the course of this process, they began to rekindle their good first impressions of one another, and Siegel suggested bringing in Dean Riesner, a screenwriter he thought was the best on the lot, to help them. After a day's work all three were getting along famously, and Clint decided he could leave the rest of the work in the writer's hands. He was told not to do any major rewrites until he had finished pulling together the best material from all the previous drafts so they could all see what they had and what they didn't have.

Riesner worked quickly, and by October they had a solid shooting script. The picture was cast, and, with Siegel worrying about the vagaries of November weather in New York, they went into production. It was then that bonding between star and director was completed.

In some ways theirs was the attraction of opposites. A compact, sad-eyed, mustachioed man, Siegel often wore a little tweed hat on the set, and always a dapper cravat, which was a sort of lucky charm for him. Though he had strong opinions and a quick, if laconic, tongue, Siegel knew how to guard both. Much has been made of the fact that he was, politically, a liberal, while his star is well known for what are thought to be conservative views. Indeed, when *Dirty Harry* was attacked for its apparently reactionary subtext, Siegel cited his credentials as a liberal in defense of the film. But he and Clint shared a view of the world that transcended left-right political disagreements.

In an acute review of their next collaboration, *Two Mules for Sister Sara,* critic Joel Doerfler wrote that every Siegel film he had seen had been "centered on the conflict between an old moral universe in which the individual was sovereign, and a new collectivist age in which uniqueness and individual initiative are obliterated by egalitarian and bureaucratic forces." In that sense, he argued, Siegel was a conservative whose films expressed "an overwhelming dread of modern mass society" through their accounts of protagonists who are outsiders and misfits in that brave new world. To put it simply, he had been making Clint Eastwood films long before he began making Clint Eastwood films.

And he was making them in a way that complemented, in a practical way, the values they expressed on-screen. At work Siegel was like his most typical protagonists in that he did not dwell long on anything—a scene, an idea, a technical problem. He intellectualized nothing and regretted nothing, constantly moving ahead without a lot of protective coverage in the can. This, of course, squared with Clint's ideas about filmmaking as neatly as Siegel's inherently individualistic philosophy did with his. Weighed against these affinities, the differences in their bio-rhythms or their opinions about electoral politics meant little.

For it is, finally, good-humored, unpretentious and efficient professionalism that is Clint's most important measure of a man, and that Siegel always provided him. "He knew exactly what was going to be shot, and he would do no more," Clint says. "Some of these guys," Clint wrote in an obituary tribute to his mentor, "print ten takes; they don't know what it looks like, or they're not quite sure what their next set-up is. Often he'd just print the one." It was spontaneity he was after and hesitation that he feared. It's like baseball, as Clint puts it; if you wait for the perfect pitch you often find yourself trudging back to the dugout with your bat on your shoulder. Indeed, Siegel was always "rooting for the shot so badly" that he would automatically cross his fingers the minute he called "Action." "I'd be doing a scene and I'd look down and I'd see Don's fingers crossed right under the camera, and I'd start laughing."

Clint also appreciated the fact that Siegel "worked well under pressure. If something wasn't working, or a set collapsed, or if something wasn't in the same direction he had planned, he could always make adjustments." And, according to Clint, he was always happy to listen to his actors' suggestions for bits of business or staging that hadn't occurred to him. "He always used to joke: 'If the idea works I'll take credit for it; if it doesn't work, it's your idea.'"

In the shorthand that developed between them, a shot or a newly minted piece of dialogue that the actor wanted became a "Clintus," something the director was pushing for became a "Siegelini," and the give-and-take was mostly good-natured and collegial. Siegel believed Clint was "inclined to underestimate himself as an actor," but felt it prudent to keep silent on that topic much of the time. For he had the Hollywood veteran's invaluable skill at judging just when (and how insistently) he could ask a star to reach for something difficult, and when it was prudent to back off.

He was tactful even about this tactfulness: "He doesn't require, and I don't give him, too much direction. A good rule with Clint is that when you give him a direction, be sure you're right about it. If you don't think you're right, don't say it." But he also acknowledged that with this actor discretion was often the better part of valor. "You can't push Clint," he once said. "It's very dangerous. For a guy who's as cool as he is, there are times when he has a very violent temper."

In their first shoot together, they established the terms of their relationship very successfully. The problems they never entirely solved were the contradictions of Coogan's character and the narrative in which it was embedded. A good case in point occurred one day when Susan Clark, the rather cool and reserved actress who played Julie, a social worker and Coogan's chief love interest, was talked into allowing Clint to suddenly pull her into a hot embrace in a scene where she was supposed to just brush past him. "It's too obvious," Siegel remembers her saying. "It's obvious you don't know what you're talking about," he remembers Clint saying. "Let's shoot it, Don."

Like many of the quotations in *A Siegel Film,* his autobiography, this one does not ring entirely true. Throughout that book he seems to be exercising the director's prerogative to improve the script as originally written. It seems unlikely that Clint, given his tenderness about actors' feelings, would have spoken quite so harshly to Clark, especially since he says he enjoyed working with her. But we may also assume that he supported Siegel in some way, because in the finished film the scene is as the director proposed. And it works well; there's a nice spontaneity about it. But the general thought from which Clark's specific objection arose, that the script, the director and perhaps even the star were pushing the Coogan character in a direction that was too improbably (and too unpleasantly) macho, is well taken.

This tone is set early in the picture, when Coogan, having captured a runaway miscreant in the desert, pulls his jeep up to a small ranch house, handcuffs his prisoner to the steering wheel and pops inside for a casual toss in the hay with the married woman who lives there. Later, in New York he uses Clark's character in a similarly offhand way. They meet when a nameless character tries to fondle her breasts, she slugs him, and Coogan admires her spunk. It is not really funny; it is of a piece with the lack of subtlety with which their entire relationship is developed. There follows a mildly patronizing passage when Coogan and Julie go out to dinner and she tries to pick up the tab. "You're a girl, aren't you?" Coogan asks. "There are rumors to that effect," she replies. "Then sit back and act like one."

There's worse to come. Coogan beats a woman while trying to get information—and then for good measure savagely rapes her. Later that night—at 4 a.m.—Julie appears at his hotel to chastise him for an earlier rude departure. However angry she is, this off-hours visit implies that she is more in thrall to him than her strong character should be. Indeed, at the end of the picture, when Coogan has completed his mission, we get our last glimpse of Julie literally jumping up and down and waving frantically at him as his helicopter pulls away from the landing pad. There has been no reconciliation scene, nothing to explain this quite out-of-character behavior—except the sheer irresistibility of this stud.

Set aside, for the moment, questions of taste and morals, set aside, as well, a quarter century of feminist outrage at portrayals of this kind of male-female relationship, set aside, finally, the fact that a still-forming star image was being carelessly handled in these passages, and this fact remains: His sexual behavior was woefully out of character for Walt Coogan, or, at any rate, outside the character the film was elsewhere trying to establish.

This other Walt Coogan was, in fact, a rather engaging figure. When he is not mistreating female characters there is sometimes a sort of shy courtliness about him that puts one a little in mind of Gary Cooper when he played a rube at large in the city. Underneath that manner there is plenty of quiet, comically expressed shrewdness as well, exemplified by a wonderful exchange with the cabdriver (Louis Zorich) who picks him up at the heliport when he first comes to town. Arriving at their destination the cabbie informs him, "That'll be $2.95, including the luggage."

"Tell me—how many stores named Bloomingdale's are there in this town?"

"One. Why?"

"We passed it twice."

"It's still $2.95."

"Well, here's three dollars—including the tip."

A little more of that kind of badinage would have been welcome, and would have helped sustain the film's best tone, which is tough-comic and particularly well put in the relationship that develops between Coogan and Lee J. Cobb's weary, testy New York detective. The former has the frontiersman's contempt for bureaucratic ponderousness, the latter is scornful of Coogan's professional qualifications and increasingly fed up with the outlander's interference in his routines. ("This isn't the OK Corral around here. It's the city of New York. We've got a system. It isn't much, but we like it.") Their relationship develops more logically than the one between Coogan and Julie does.

The contrast between the sureness of these scenes among men and the crudeness of almost all the scenes that involve Coogan with women is jarring. Coogan's adventures in the demimonde where Ringerman's drug dealer allies are to be found and through which Coogan must pass in his search for the escaped criminal are also poorly realized. The hippie characters he encounters there are rather coarsely portrayed in a way that plays into the conservative cliché of the time, which saw long hair and love beads as serious threats to good order. These sequences seem near to silly now, and at the time they had a clueless air about them— Hollywood guys trying to be hip and knowing and not quite making it.

Or was this, as certain gender scholars have recently had it, a truly reactionary movie, despite Siegel's liberalism and Clint's generally amiable tolerance of lifestyles the opposite of his own? It's obvious the film partook of middle- and lower-class America's unease—on the brink of becoming outrage—over the counterculture, over the early stirrings of the feminist revival, over the way authority everywhere was being questioned. But one does not think of Clint eagerly advancing these attitudes, for he was not (and is not) the ideologue liberal strangers sometimes imagine him to be. Preoccupied by his suddenly accelerating career, he responded to the Vietnam War, for example, with a sort of dispassionate disapproval. The conservatism attributed to him never embraced the Cold War anticommunism, and he says that he projected his own former attitude about the Korean War onto the new conflict. Having himself not wanted to fight, he could well understand why this generation of young men didn't want to fight. The idea of anyone's dying in an inconclusive war, in which neither the nation's existence nor a high moral principle is at stake, is anathema to him.

This relaxed attitude is a fairly typical Eastwoodian response to public issues. He may vote Republican most of the time, but his political beliefs were then, as they are now, far from the standard right-wing positions: He is mildly in favor of gun control and strongly in favor of abortion rights (and most of the rest of the feminist agenda), he is close to being a First Amendment absolutist, and his hatred of anything that hints at racism is very close to the surface. The best label for him is probably "libertarian," but of a distinctly live-and-let-live kind.

On none of these matters, obviously, did Walt Coogan express himself. On none of these matters would Clint Eastwood's screen character ever have much to say. The central issue for that figure would remain the same for decades: how to preserve his outraged individualism in an increasingly bureaucratized world while at the same time permitting his best qualities—good humor, even sweetness, certainly a tolerance for individual eccentricity—to come engagingly to the surface. Or to put it another way: how to keep his righteous anger clearly focused on the appropriate targets, not let it overflow into other realms as it does in this movie, where it too often reads as brutal inconsiderateness.

Some of *Coogan's Bluff*'s crudeness can be excused; everyone would do better with more practice. But still, it remains what it apparently was from its first-draft script, a muddled and tone-deaf movie, never finding its true pitch, constantly wandering—lurching, actually—from key to key. This is not something Clint, operating under time pressure, not completely certain of exactly what he wanted to project in this role—how tough did he need to be? how soft could he afford to be?—fully addressed.

In purely commercial terms, such niceties were unnecessary. In the mind of someone like Jennings Lang, the picture was always meant to be what Hollywood likes to call "product," something inexpensively designed to satisfy a certain corner of the market. If it made a pleasant profit (which it did) and cemented his relationship with a new star (which it also did) then, as far as the studio executive was concerned, *Coogan's Bluff* served its purpose. As for Clint, the picture established *his* relationship with an important studio, enhanced his sense of security at a moment when that was welcome and incrementally expanded his screen character's range. Its largest benefit to him—the beginning of his collaboration with Siegel—was, of course, an entirely unintended consequence.

When it was released a year later, audiences and, for the most part, reviewers accepted *Coogan's Bluff* in the spirit with which it was offered, as minor entertainment. To be sure, the increasingly impotent National Catholic Office for Motion Pictures (successor to the Legion of Decency) roused itself to offer a "condemned" rating, calling Coogan "a cynical and sadistic police officer" and the picture "socially irresponsible and exploitative." Some reviewers followed on that tack.

But Vincent Canby in *The New York Times* called it "a joke told by someone with no sense of humor" and compared Clint to actors like Alan Ladd: "He doesn't act in motion pictures; he's framed in them." His predecessors greeted Clint with outrage; Canby offered a cooler form of contempt: "Tranquilized beyond all emotion," Clint was, he said, "an unconscious parody of himself and, for that matter, of all movie superheroes."

Time magazine's review was heavily colored by the writer's enthusiasm for Don Siegel's set-piece action sequences, notably a terrifically energetic fight sequence in a pool hall, where the close confines of the setting greatly intensified the action, and the concluding chase, in Fort Tryon Park, which is also well done. This setting is appropriate for Coogan—outdoor turf where he feels comfortable, as opposed to mean city streets—and he gets to impress the lumbering New York cops with his nervy agility. "Fast, tough and so well made that it seems to have evolved naturally, almost without benefit of cast, crew or rehearsal," *Time*'s critic wrote (somewhat incomprehensibly). "Those who are willing to look beyond this carefully nurtured air of artlessness, however, will see some of the best American moviemaking of the year." The reviewer even had a few kind words for Clint, who, he wrote, "performs with a measure of real feeling in the first role that fits him as comfortably as his tooled boots."

This was catch-up reviewing, a long-delayed tribute to a filmmaker the magazine's previous reviewers had either ignored or patronized. It was also an acknowledgment, like others occurring around this time, that in the matter of Clint Eastwood, the people had spoken; they had found in him something they liked, or feared, or anyway were fascinated by. It was time, at last, for reviewers to begin following the crowd.

This was a well-established pattern. Clint was not the first star (and not the last) to have been at first dismissed by the critics for his lack of obvious theatrical training and credentials, put down as a lunky, hunky Hollywood phenomenon, then reconsidered as his popularity with the people proved irresistible. As such performers refine as well as broaden their screen personae—or in some cases merely persist as audience favorites—their "development" gives aid and comfort (and Sunday pieces) to reviewers as they reevaluate. This would be increasingly true of Clint, though it must be said that it took him longer to win the kind of critical endorsement he now enjoys than it did some other actors, in part because he added variations to his screen character rather patiently, in part because of the controversy that surrounded his Dirty Harry characterization and his persistence in so often returning to it.

Clint was certainly aware of what was being said critically about the Leone films as they came out and was aware of the reviews of his first American productions when they appeared. He has an acute sense of who his critical friends and enemies are. One suspects, indeed, that he is more hurt by bad notices than he lets on. But he has also always been a man with his own agenda, and at this moment it did not revolve around reviews. Nor was the question of establishing the full dimensions of his screen personality uppermost in his mind or in the minds of his advisers. They were all more intent on reinforcing the foundations of a career the full scope and solidity of which was not yet clear.

This means, frankly, that they were, for the moment, more interested in money—which is how Hollywood determines status—than they were in critical prestige. A little more than a month after finishing *Coogan's Bluff* (and months before either it or *Hang 'em High* was released) he was off to Europe to make *Where Eagles Dare* (reported salary, $500,000), after which he was scheduled to start *Paint Your Wagon* (reported salary, $600,000). Sooner than expected he was approaching the $750,000 fee David Picker had predicted for him. More important, these big, mainstream pictures would, whatever their modest intrinsic merits, force people to stop seeing him as a curiosity, begin to see him for what he wanted and needed to be, a major industry player.

SEVEN

LESSNESS IS BESTNESS

The habits of insecurity die hard. "It takes a long time for an actor to get over the thought that whatever he's doing at the moment may be his last job" is the way Clint Eastwood puts it. For some actors it is never completely put to rest, which is one reason anxiety—not to mention desperation—floats so freely through show business. As he approached thirty-eight, Clint thought he might be old for the game, just beginning to establish a star career at a time in life when the careers of other leading men (and certainly leading women) were starting to decline.

Actually age was part of his good luck. He had been spared the premature accretion of fame, money and cosseting that turns actors who receive these boons when they are too young into spoiled brats. The fact that Clint still felt obliged to spare a prudent thought for the dubious future kept him in touch with two significant realities—that of the business he was in and that of his audience's lives.

Grasping, at last, the brass ring, he did not at this moment think his ride on the carousel would necessarily be a long one. Indeed, a couple of years later, with several more successful movies behind him, he was still saying to a reporter, "We are like boxers, one never knows how much longer one has." His thinking, as of 1968, was that if he was lucky, the merry-go-round would keep spinning for him until he made it through his forties. This is one reason why, as he has often said, he was beginning to think about directing; it was something he might do when the public had grown tired of him on-screen.

So he decided that if he took up all the reasonable offers he could handle, and worked very hard, then when the music stopped he would have enough put by to see his family through in comfort, no matter what. And a family, in the full sense of the word, was what the Eastwoods were about to become, for Maggie was now pregnant. They considered therefore whether or not he should accept the offer to costar in

Where Eagles Dare, a World War II adventure story, which was to begin shooting in Austria and in London in January 1968. But she was not due to deliver until the spring, and though the picture had a long schedule, they couldn't see how it could possibly go five months. He should be back in plenty of time for the baby's birth.

In Salzburg, where the company was headquartering for the first portion of the shoot, he got his first glimpse of grand-scale international celebrity, for his costar was Richard Burton, four years into his first marriage to Elizabeth Taylor, an event that had redefined the relationship of public figures and the media and, it might be said, redefined the nature of starry excess.

"I get off the plane in Salzburg in Levi's," Clint recalls, "and I've got this old canvas bag with all kinds of holes in it, and Elizabeth and Richard came in on their own private jet and they've got entourages—she's got a couple of secretaries, and he's got people, and they've got clothes" (not to mention jewels and all the other accoutrements of cheerfully flaunted wealth).

It was no less wondrous to Clint than it was to people gawking from a far greater distance. The couple welcomed him warmly; with friends and coworkers they were generous and convivial. No sooner had Clint checked into the hotel where they were all staying than the phone rang, and he was invited to join them in the bar for drinks—many for Burton, a couple of beers for Clint. It was the first of many such sessions for them, and the beginning of what would turn out to be a congenial working relationship, and, for Clint, a lesson in how not to be a star, for he was about to witness, close-up, an actor in the process of sacrificing self-interest to self-indulgence.

Burton was an intelligent and extremely well-read autodidact who was also a great raconteur, with a vast fund of anecdotes at his command. These he had gathered over the course of a restless life that had taken him from a Welsh coal-mining village to the higher realms of the English theater, thence to Hollywood and Broadway, and finally to the infamous production of *Cleopatra,* where he and Taylor met, fell in love and abandoned their spouses to wed.

Burton's storytelling was like his drinking; there was something grim in its relentlessness. Both were walls he constructed to hide behind—from strangers, of course, but also from friends and, most significantly, himself. It was this veiled quality, the sense he imparted of hiding out behind technique and a glorious voice, that finally precluded greatness on stage and authentic stardom on-screen. Similarly, in private one could spend many an entertaining hour with Burton but never penetrate his essential reserve and what one imagined was some essential

disappointment with himself—possibly for his profession (his loathing
for which filled many pages of his diary), possibly for his compromised
conduct within it, for the poor lad from the large family had an inordi-
nate need for wealth, which had led him to many foolish professional
decisions.

For Clint, he was another in the long line of loquacious men, as
quick with their opinions and wit as he is shy with them, whose company he enjoys. "He was very, very different than I was," he says of Burton, "but yet not in a lot of ways." Which is a way of saying they had
both known the bite of hard times and shared a reluctance to carelessly
expose their deeper feelings. They also discovered, within the first few
days of meeting, that they signed on for *Where Eagles Dare* (or "Where
Doubles Dare," as Clint apparently dubbed it at the time) for similar reasons. Someone asked Burton why he was doing the picture, and he
replied, "Because Clint's doing it." Whereupon Clint said he had committed to it "because Richard's doing it."

If it now made good sense for Clint to associate with prestigious ac-
tors in high-budget projects, Burton, too, needed to make some new as-
sociations. In the years immediately before and after his marriage to
Taylor in 1964 he had enjoyed his largest popular successes (*The V.I.P.s,
The Sandpiper*) and his greatest critical success (*Who's Afraid of Virginia
Woolf?*) working with her. But his Broadway *Hamlet* had, at best, a mixed
reception and was tainted by the media circus that staked its tents nearby.
His other films of this period (*Becket, The Night of the Iguana, The Spy
Who Came In from the Cold*) had not proved that he could carry a picture
commercially without resorting to his jointly held celebrity. His more
recent pictures with Taylor (*The Taming of the Shrew,* a filmed version of
their theatrical production of *Doctor Faustus* and *The Comedians*) had
failed, and they could not have had high hopes for their recently completed *Boom!*—a deeply disastrous adaptation of Tennessee Williams's
The Milk Train Doesn't Stop Here Anymore.

Some sources suggest that Burton initiated *Where Eagles Dare* by
telling his friend Elliot Kastner, an American and a former agent who
was partnered with Jerry Gershwin in a London-based company specializing in expensive international coproduction, that he wanted to do
something that he could take his sons to see. In any event, it made sense
for him to work with a rising action star in a picture that had no artistic
pretense and appealed to the male audience; by so doing he might establish himself in what amounted to a new field for him. And commercially, this pairing of supposed cowboy and supposed intellectual made
sense; it might conceivably bring two normally disparate audiences to
the movie.

Kastner spared no expense to achieve this end. The rest of the cast was first-rate (it included Mary Ure in a costarring role and such worthies as Patrick Wymark, Michael Hordern and Donald Houston in supporting parts), and the director, Brian G. Hutton, a former actor and TV director who had just finished another Kastner-Gershwin thriller, *Sol Madrid*, had all the time and budget he needed to master difficult conditions.

Clint liked him, and they had only one awkward moment, early in the picture, after Clint encountered a friend of his, an actor he had previously worked with, in his hotel lobby. When he asked the man what he was doing in Salzburg, he replied that he had driven in with his girlfriend from Hamburg, where they lived, because she was up for a small part in the picture. Clint, however, knew the role had already been cast and asked Hutton what was going on.

"I'm just going through the motions," he said, "because the girl who has been cast has an in with one of the producers, and we're trying to make it look legit."

This brought back all the anger he had felt at the carelessness and insensitivity he had experienced as a struggling actor. "I just got incensed," he would later recall. "What do you mean, you're 'just going through the motions'?" he said. "How can you do this? You're an ex-actor yourself. You know what it's like."

"Well, I'm getting this pressure to do it."

"Well, just stop it, because I'm not going be part of it."

Clint was establishing one of the patterns by which he would exercise his newfound power; the feelings of actors were—and are—to be treated with elaborate sensitivity. That power, it should be noted, was greatly enhanced by the film's eventual commercial success. As Hirshan would later say, it "became an Eastwood picture, not a Burton picture," despite his client's second billing. By this he means that within the industry Clint was perceived as the star whose presence made it go with the broad, action-oriented audience.

For Burton, alas, the picture turned out to be an end, not a beginning—the end to his brief run as a major movie star. About all he gained from *Where Eagles Dare* was Kastner's long-term loyalty; he employed the actor in something like a half-dozen subsequent movies, all of them box-office failures, like virtually every other movie Burton did in the course of the erratic downward spiral that consumed the rest of his life.

As for the film itself, Quentin Tarantino, one of its comparatively rare fans, accurately described it, in the course of a colloquy with Robert Zemeckis, as a "bunch-of-guys-on-a-mission" movie. "Isn't that the one where Clint Eastwood kills more guys than anybody else in movie history?" Zemeckis asked when Tarantino raised the subject.

Yes, that's the one, another work in what was then a popular sub-genre, owing much of that popularity to the very man who wrote this screenplay—his first—Alistair MacLean. He specialized in what the English like to call "Boy's Own" adventure stories (after the Edwardian children's magazine), and it was the hugely successful adaptation of his novel *The Guns of Navarone* in 1961 that had begun this movie trend. Indeed, it is said that the reason MacLean decided to write an original screenplay was that all his other tales had either been made as movies or were under option for that purpose. Kastner persuaded him to this unfamiliar task by assuring him he could always novelize the screenplay later, which he did.

The soldiers' ostensible mission is rescuing a captured American general, who was supposed to be privy to the plans for D Day, before the Nazis, who are holding him in a remote *Schloss* (reachable only by cable car), can make him talk. But that's just a pretext—the general is really an actor hired to sow confusion in the enemy's ranks. Alone of the group parachuted into the Austrian Alps (and obliged to wear German uniforms in order to penetrate the Nazi lair) Burton's character, John Smith, knows that their operation is really designed to expose a ring of double agents operating within British intelligence. This information is long withheld from the audience. We know only that there is a traitor among the invading group, with suspicion being directed at Smith for some time. It is not until the climax that the chief villain is revealed to be the London spymaster who sent them forth.

It's less a plot than an excuse for a lot of violent, essentially meaningless action, nicely characterized by Tarantino: "Eastwood would just stand at the top of the stairs and wait for the Nazis to congregate, and then mow them down." Yet even though he came to dominate such memories of the film as people retain, Clint's character, Lieutenant Morris Schaffer, can scarcely be said to dominate the film. He does not speak German, which means he has to stand mute in the enemy's presence, and even when it is safe for the agents to talk among themselves, Burton, as the unit's leader, has all the best lines.

One gets the impression that, as the production inched along, Clint was generous to his costar on-screen and protective of him off-screen. This was his kind of picture, not Burton's, and he was doing what he could to ease his colleague's way. It was, Clint quickly observed, booze, more than the rigors of production, from which Burton needed protection. His capacity for it was, to Clint, amazing. As was his ability, most of the time, to carry it without visible ill effects—"just one eye sagging a little, but that's about it."

Nevertheless, there were times when alcohol rendered Burton balky. There was, for example, a sequence in which he and Clint, mounted on a motorcycle with a sidecar, are supposed to speed down an icy, twisting road, pausing now and then to affix dynamite sticks to high-tension towers, the plan being to detonate the explosives later on, when they are making their escape. The sequence was scheduled for early afternoon, and Burton appeared weaving slightly and dubiously eyeing the antique motorcycle he was supposed to pilot.

"You *can* drive this thing, can't you, Richard?" Brian Hutton inquired. Burton replied with an incomprehensible, but not exactly reassuring, mumble. At which point Clint stepped forward. He was a veteran cyclist—at the time he owned two such vehicles—and happily volunteered a role reversal: "I tell you what, Brian, I'll drive it and Richard rides."

Relief all around, Hutton now pressed on to outline the rest of the business. Clint would skid to a stop, and Burton would hop out, attach the dynamite sticks (actually balsa wood and, of course, carrying no charges), hop back in, and they would speed off to the next stop (and the next shot).

"I don't handle explosives, Brian," said Burton, now obviously quite out of things.

"What?"

"I don't handle explosives."

"But it's balsa wood, Richard."

The star, woozily intent on asserting his prerogatives, shook his head adamantly.

"And Brian's looking at me like, 'Damn this guy,'" Clint recalls.

So the director manqué offered another suggestion: "I say, 'Richard, look, why don't we do this? Just you put this one set of balsa-wood things down here and then there's a hostel down the road. We'll go down there and have a shot, you and I.'"

"Good idea," Burton enthused. "Good idea."

"So I go back to Brian and I say, 'OK. You've got one shot on this, so you better get it.'" This, happily, he did.

Eventually they wrapped in Austria and moved on to studio work in London—much of it fussy rear- and front-screen-projection special effects. There, if anything, Burton spent more time drinking; he had a number of favorite pubs to which he introduced Clint, who could be counted on to get him back to the soundstage more or less on time, in more or less functioning condition, for their next call. The indulgences with which Burton was favored are sometimes visible on-screen. There was, for example, a sequence, shot in the studio, in which he and Clint are supposed to be pulling themselves up the castle walls on ropes, hand over hand. Clint is visibly straining as he toils upward, while the older and manifestly less-fit Burton seems to be making the climb effortlessly. But he was positioned on a crane and only had to mime his ascent, while Clint had to pull himself up under his own power.

Clint shrugs ironically at this memory. By this time he was increasingly preoccupied by Maggie's rapidly impending delivery, increasingly impatient with delays in production, which by early May was a month over schedule. Film and nature were now in a race to the finish line, with Clint equally impotent to speed up the former or slow down the latter. While he seethed, his parents came down to Los Angeles to be with Maggie, and his father called Clint to tell him that the birth was no more than a few days off. Two more days, Clint said. Two more days and I'll be out of here. "Just hold tight," he said to his wife.

But that was impossible. Kyle Eastwood was born in St. John's Hospital, in Santa Monica, on Sunday, May 19, 1968. In London, Burton's response was predictable: "Let's go out and celebrate." So was Clint's. "Wait a second," he said. "I don't want to go out drinking in pubs. I want to get the hell out of here." A day or two later, he did.

Despite the fact that Clint's character in *Where Eagles Dare* was the most abstract figure he ever played—a pure killing machine, vouchsafed not a single humanizing moment, romantic or comic—it did not stir the kind of agitated comment his work for Leone had or his work as Dirty Harry soon would. This is the more remarkable when one recalls that it went into release in 1969, when antiwar sentiments were at their height in the United States and such headlong displays of "'traditional" masculinity were at a deep discount in the better cultural circles.

But this was the kind of film that does not bring out the best in critics and no one had anything very interesting to say about it. *Time* dubbed it "Mission Ridiculous," and found it "melancholy" to see Burton in it. *Life* called it "inelegant" while Vincent Canby in *The New York Times* thought it had so many predictable situations that it threatened to become "as numbing as an overdose of novocaine," but somehow didn't. In general, the range of response to the movie was very narrow, from amiable dismissal to amiable indulgence—formulaic responses to formulaic filmmaking. The ironic appeal of *Where Eagles Dare* for a subversive, postmodernist like Quentin Tarantino is much more interesting to consider. In his films, typically, people get killed because they are in the wrong place at the wrong time—that is to say, they die quite whimsically, proving, at best, that we live in a chance universe. Equally typically, his films—like Leone's, like any that actually make us feel the astonishment of sudden, violent death—are criticized because they offer no obvious moral justification for the deaths they deal out; lack of same, in fact, being their basic moral point. Thus in Tarantino's remarks about this movie one may read a sort of seriocomic envy for the ease and simplicity with which moral questions about mass mayhem, at least as absurd as any presented in *Reservoir Dogs* or *Pulp Fiction* (or *The Good, the Bad, and the Ugly*), are elided.

The nameless creatures who die so unceremoniously, without evoking more than a bemused response from the audience, are brothers under the skin to Tarantino's wrong place–wrong time victims. The thought that, in reality, these German soldiers were probably draftees, that some of them must surely have doubted the cause that obliged their service, that most of them must just have been dumb kids like so many of our own soldiers, does not occur to us, especially since they are slaughtered en masse, impersonally, usually at some distance from the camera. Hey, they're Nazis—and dumb Nazis at that. Let's rub out a bunch more.

At the time, the only people to discuss this point were a pair of college journalists. Deliciously innocent yet determined counterculturists, they unaccountably turned up poolside at the Las Vegas junket MGM staged to promote the picture, where their "interview" with Hutton was recorded by a wicked journalist named Bernard Drew. "Why did you pick a glamorous war?" one of them inquired. "Why didn't you do something on Vietnam? Would you have treated the Vietcong as you did the Nazis—all morons?" His female partner chimed in: "Even in the most frivolous of entertainment there has to be one moment of reality. Did *all* of the Nazis have to be such bad shots?" They weren't entirely serious; they were goading the director, trying to get him to admit to selling out (he had earlier made some small, earnest, unprofitable pictures), while proposing that evil Hollywood might better have parceled out this film's large budget to their contemporaries, struggling to make "personal statements." Eventually they got the explosion they wanted ("For fifteen lousy goddamned stinking years I paid my dues . . ."), an outburst that plagued Hutton for years in Hollywood, where such complaints are supposed to be confined to the "community."

Finally it all comes back to generic conventions, doesn't it? We're used to movie heroes doing slaughter within the well-established morality of standard-issue war movies, westerns and crime dramas. It's only when a movie strays outside those lines, asks its audience to think actively about the assumptions that routine action dramas are built on, that its "violence" (or its gender implications) is deplored.

At this time—though it is doubtful that anyone around Clint articulated it in so many words—the effort was clearly to edge Clint away from that morally interesting fringe, position his developing screen character at the center of the movie mainstream, where it could function less controversially, and with this expensive and successful film—so obviously not a B picture—that goal was achieved. Whether a critic mildly liked or mildly disliked the film itself, none of them attacked his work or worried in grand cosmic terms over what his popularity might suggest about the state of the national psyche.

Where Eagles Dare would become MGM's biggest hit of 1969 (it grossed close to $7 million in North America alone) as well as Clint's biggest box-office success to date. This pleased him, of course. But it also displeased him. He could see that films of this kind lacked the singularity and impact of the Leone films, and he hated their long, tedious schedules. He did not want to become just another well-paid Hollywood gun for hire, lacking autonomy and range of choice.

Circumstances would soon crystallize these still-somewhat-inchoate feelings. If he now knew how not to be a movie star, the film he now began would teach him more than he ever wanted to know about how not to make a movie. Insignificant in and of itself—a film with no historical resonance—it would nevertheless have an impact on Clint Eastwood's personal history almost as significant as that of *A Fistful of Dollars* or *Dirty Harry.*

★   ★   ★

It was to be a musical—a lavish, no-expense-spared musical, a form that Hollywood, looking back on the midsixties grosses of *My Fair Lady,* *Mary Poppins* and *The Sound of Music,* had decided represented the high, if risky, road to vast profits. *Camelot, Star!* and *Doctor Dolittle* had thrown doubt on this supposition, but at this moment the game was still on, and Paramount was determined to get in on it.

The creators of *My Fair Lady* and *Camelot,* Alan J. Lerner and Fritz Loewe, had one more property in their trunk, the least successful of their Broadway collaborations, *Paint Your Wagon,* a saga of the California Gold Rush. Lerner, who signed to produce the project, assured Paramount that playwright Paddy Chayefsky could rewrite and update it so that it appealed to the sensibility of the sixties, especially since he would be working under the guidance of director Joshua Logan, who had shared a Pulitzer Prize for his work in adapting *South Pacific* to the stage.

How could anything possibly go wrong? As it happened, almost everything did. It began the first day Clint reported for work on the Paramount lot. Logan had decreed a week or two of rehearsals on a Hollywood soundstage before the company left for location on East Eagle Creek, in Oregon's Wallowa-Whitman National Forest. Clint drove up to the gate in his customary underwhelming vehicle, in this case a tan pickup truck, gave his name to the guard and was told that there was no pass for him. "Well, you know, I'm supposed to be here," Clint replied mildly. "They're kind of expecting me down there."

The guard said he'd have to make a U-turn, find a phone somewhere and call a number he'd be glad to give him. Clint was now afume: "I'll tell you what, buddy. I'm gonna go over to Universal—here's my number there. If anybody calls here asking for Clint, just tell them I'm over there, because I can get on *that* lot."

One imagines a screech of tires, the smell of burning rubber. When he arrived at his Universal office he told his secretary to inform callers that he was out, then withdrew into his office to read some scripts. The phones began jangling, and after a time his assistant appeared: "God, they're going crazy down there."

Clint accepted the next call, playing dumb. "You know, fellas, I couldn't get on, and I thought maybe I'd been replaced."

When he returned to Paramount he found Logan, the rest of the principal cast and key department heads, like William Fraker, the cinematographer, gathered in a corner of a cavernous soundstage, with the actors, scripts in hand, reading their lines as they moved about at Logan's command. He was blocking action as if this were a theatrical production. It was essentially busywork, since the crucial element in movie staging, the camera, was missing.

Elsewhere, other lunacies were occurring. Tom Shaw, a veteran and expert assistant director, who specialized in complex, large-scale productions, had signed on as the film's associate producer, and one day found himself at the center of a perplexed and angry group of horsemen and stuntpeople. They had been called in for auditions, because, even though they would not have speaking parts, they had to look like the citizens of a mining camp. But they found themselves grouped with chorus boys and, like them, being asked to take their pants off so that the casting people could study their legs. This was not something these rough-and-ready types were accustomed to. Worse, Shaw got the distinct impression that someone in the production hierarchy was perhaps thinking of saving a few dollars by having the dancers double as riders and as drivers of the film's many horsedrawn vehicles. It was ridiculous—musical-comedy performers trying to master the arcane (and dangerous) art of driving a six-up or an eight-up, every bit as ridiculous as asking one of the riders to attempt a jeté.

Shaw quickly straightened out this confusion of realms, but not without a sense of foreboding, which elsewhere, for different reasons, Clint was also entertaining. For a man who did not like to overthink a performance, Logan's rehearsals were intolerable, and Clint found himself wondering if he had made a terrible mistake when he signed for this picture.

He had been drawn to the project for two reasons: because it offered him a chance to sing and because he liked the first script he was shown. Musically, he would not encounter serious problems. Lerner had at first thought Clint might have to talk his songs, as Rex Harrison had in *My Fair Lady*, but then he listened to some of his old records and had a session at the piano with him, where Clint handled the *Paint Your Wagon* melodies well enough. He knew, of course, that he didn't have a big musical-comedy tone, but thought, I'll try to sing what the character is, not try to come out with a booming voice, which he feels works better anyway on-screen. It had always worked for Fred Astaire, hadn't it?

The screenplay, on the other hand, turned into a growing issue. Chayefsky, who was struggling with a writer's block at the time, had signed on largely for the money (his fee was $150,000 plus a percentage of net profits that never emerged) and for the opportunity to practice his craft on something that did not involve him emotionally. This strategy worked for the writer; when he finished the job he found that his block had dissolved. Moreover, he produced something that attracted not only Clint, but Lee Marvin, then regarded as an even more bankable star.

Chayefsky's work bore no resemblance to the book Lerner had written for the 1951 Broadway production, which recounted the adventures of a widower and his daughter searching for new lives, new wealth (and in her case a new love) in a California mining camp during the Gold Rush era. The playwright retained the setting of the original show, and found a place for most of its songs (plus some new ones that Lerner wrote with André Previn) but threw out everything else. His was a story about the creation of a frontier menage à trois involving an old miner, Ben Rumson (Lee Marvin); his friend, known only as Pardner (Clint); and a young woman named Elizabeth (in which role, after much dithering, Jean Seberg was cast). No-Name City, the site where this non-action takes place, eventually, literally, collapses as a result of rampant greed (Ben and some friends secretly tunnel under the town searching for gold, weakening its foundations).

"Not an up story at all, kind of a moody piece, very dark," is the way Clint characterized it. Indeed, in the first draft he read, Marvin's character actually died at the end. "I'd never seen a musical with this kind of a story line before," he says, and he remembers thinking, This is very bold—maybe these guys are on to something.

Possibly so, although even in Clint's fond description this early draft sounds, at best, like a Tin Pan Alley version of the Weill-Brecht *Mahagonny*. At worst, it seems to be about what one might expect from some older Broadway types trying desperately to refurbish a decrepit property and use it to bridge the then-notorious generation gap. What he seems to have seen here was something like the *Fistful of Dollars* scenario. If the western had then seemed tired, the movie musical, despite its recent commercial success, now seemed positively moribund, the glory days of the first postwar decade, when Hollywood was making originals like *Singin' in the Rain,* long gone. It was therefore reasonable for him to think, based on what he had read initially, that this project might revitalize this form as the Leone pictures had the western.

This was perhaps naive of him, but not totally so. The deal memo he signed before going off to make *Where Eagles Dare* prudently provided an escape clause; if he did not approve of *Paint Your Wagon*'s final shooting script he could leave the project. As his work in Europe dragged along, Clint spared an occasional thought for this revision, and finally he called Hirshan to inquire after it. In a matter of days it was in his hands—the work of Lerner, who would eventually receive writing credit on the finished film, with Chayefsky, whose services had now been dispensed with, getting an adaptation credit.

"I get this thing, and I start reading it, and it's now totally different. It has no relation to the original, except the names of the characters. They had the threesome deal, but it wasn't a dark story at all. It was all fluffy. Fluffy, and running around talking, and they're having Lee do *Cat Ballou II*." This accords with Chayefsky's recollection that no more than six pages of his work remained in Lerner's version. So Clint called Hirshan immediately and said, "This has really gone haywire. Just get me out of this. Get me totally, completely out this."

That was not easy to do. People had committed to *Paint Your Wagon* because Clint had. "The next thing you know, here come Lerner and Logan," flying into London to argue that musicals have to be upbeat, cheery. That's what audiences expected. "Yeah, but it was so interesting," said Clint, making a hopeless plea for a return to the first draft.

They, of course, misunderstood him. They thought he was signaling disappointment at the size of his role in the new script. They assured him that they were willing to do still more rewriting in order to "make your character more important," which, apparently, they did in the next draft.

But that was not at all the message Clint was trying to send: "I'm trying to explain to everybody that I don't need a big part. Bigness isn't bestness; sometimes lessness is bestness."

The next revision was, he thought, "somewhat better." But it was "still 180 degrees from where we started." His impulse to pass was still large. But his agency and the studio were pressuring him to sign the contract. A green light had been flashed; the vehicle was now moving; people were counting on him. Implicit in this argument was another one: You don't want to become known around town as difficult, and you especially don't want to discommode a major studio. And because there was a romance in his part, it remained a good career move, something that might ingratiate him with an audience that had not yet seen him. So he gave in: "I'm taking it on as sort of a *Rawhide* deal: How can I make this interesting, if at all?"

It is possible that Clint's attempts to rescue what he had originally valued in the Chayefsky script ultimately did both himself and the production a disservice. What the huge company went off to shoot in the summer of 1968 at an eventual cost of some $20 million (more than anyone had ever spent on a musical) was neither the revisionist film he wanted to make nor the lighthearted entertainment everyone else wanted to do. The movie they eventually made veered constantly, hopelessly, from one tack to the other; what humor and romance it offered was dour, and its other aspirations were so vaguely stated as to be indefinable.

In situations of this kind, the hope is always for a miracle, and these are always centered on the director. But Logan was no miracle worker. He was, from the first day to the last, overwhelmed by the task at hand: "He was a terrific guy," Clint says, "I really liked him, but he just knew nothing about film—nothing."

Certainly he knew nothing about making this kind of film. He was, of course, a highly regarded theatrical director, whose shows had been among the signature hits of postwar Broadway, but his relatively few movies had been made in carefully controlled situations and had involved very little complicated action. He was totally out of his element in this wilderness, making what amounted to a quasi-western. One of Shaw's enduring memories of Logan on location is of a man in a hat, topcoat and delicate shoes, all more suitable for a stroll down the Great White Way, picking his way through the mud and horse droppings of the set, trying to line up a shot he could only vaguely imagine.

This situation was not completely of the director's making. In his autobiography he says he had argued strongly against location work, except for exteriors, preferring the more comfortable alternative of back lot and soundstage shooting. But he says production designer John Truscott had argued strenuously for "realism," and had won everyone else over—possibly because it would give the production a unique visual quality, possibly because extensive Austrian location work had contributed much to the success of *The Sound of Music*. So, while Logan was preoccupied with rewrites, Shaw and Truscott crisscrossed the western states in a Paramount jet, looking for a location, finally settling—somewhat dubiously—on this isolated area in Oregon. The nearest accommodations were in Baker, some sixty miles away, and the road between it and the production site was narrow and twisting, which meant that supplying the shoot was a logistical nightmare; above the line people were ferried in and out by helicopter every day.

That, as it turned out, was not the worst of the problems. When Shaw and Truscott had scouted the location in the spring it was still covered with snow, which mantled an extremely rocky terrain. This was crucial information, for to achieve the movie's Sodom and Gomorrah climax Truscott planned an elaborate hydraulic system, which would enable his sets to collapse on cue. But installing it with bedrock so close to the surface proved to be an expensive nightmare. Clint recalls that it cost $300,000 to rig the system on the town saloon alone. "It's a lot of money now," he says mildly, "but it was a lot lotter then."

Such problems might have annoyed a director used to marshaling large, rough forces in remote areas, but it would not have daunted him. Clint remembers thinking, the first time he saw the Eagle Creek site, Boy, this is fabulous. John Ford would go crazy in a place like this.

"The first day was kind of slow," Clint says, "and I figure, well, they're just kind of getting their feet on the ground." But the days that followed were no better. He observed Logan consulting extensively with his immediate staff—an invitation to disaster. A director may ask questions of his cameraman or AD—but only from a position of strength. If his inquiries are too needy or clueless, if they betray a lack of command, others will quickly arrogate his power.

Especially if you are as tensely wired as Alan J. Lerner. To Logan he seemed "pieced together by the great-great-great grandson of Dr. Frankenstein from a lot of disparate spare parts." He openly questioned some of Logan's choices for setups on the first day of shooting, and once simply stepped forward and started lining up a shot, telling the extras where to stand (and move) while Logan was still thinking it over—the movie equivalent of lèse-majesté.

Very early in production Lerner called Clint in to tell him that he was thinking of replacing Logan. Clint was dismayed. "Replace him," he remembers saying. "He's only shot a couple of days' worth of stuff."

"Well, he just doesn't understand the thing."

"Let me ask you something, Alan. You guys worked together, and he's prepared this thing for a year. How come now you're deciding he's not the guy for this picture?"

Lerner's answer was not entirely satisfactory; Clint thinks that, at least in part, the producer was shifting blame for his own failures to the director. He simply was not knowledgeable enough or secure enough in himself to organize this curiously misshapen project or to give Logan the support he desperately needed.

Soon after this conversation a planeload of men in suits arrived from the studio offering Logan reassurances, but also looking grim and worried as they tried to ascertain the extent of the chaos that had been reported to them by Lerner. It is one of the reliable constants of motion-picture life that studio executives never know what to do when a production is in trouble. In fairness, it must be said that their choices are often limited, and firing the director is the most difficult of them. It taints a film, often irreparably, especially in this day of the sacred auteur, and, of course, it makes it appear that they didn't know what they were doing in the first place. They came, they conferred, they departed silently, leaving authority still divided between an indecisive director and an equally insecure producer.

The production was now "a ship, literally, with no captain on the deck," as Clint describes it, a condition particularly upsetting to that very queasy sailor Lee Marvin. An alcoholic exactly the opposite of Richard Burton in that he showed the effects of drink almost immediately, he was, as Clint says, a man who needed to know on a daily, perhaps hourly, basis what course they were on. "The minute you said, 'Well, I'm not sure about this or that,' Lee immediately went, 'Pour me a double.' "

In his autobiography, Logan was still speaking of Marvin as a courtly Southern gentleman, at heart not very different from the director himself, and that, unfortunately, was the way he treated him on the set. Only once did he let his true feelings publicly slip, when he told Marvin's biographer, Donald Zec, "Not since Attila the Hun swept across Europe leaving five hundred years of total blackness has there been a man like Lee Marvin."

What Marvin obviously needed, what he had received from other directors when he did his best work, was stern discipline administered by a man's man. To Lerner and to Tom Shaw that suggested Richard

Brooks, a literate, tough-minded character, as blunt in conversation as Logan was circumspect, who had a reputation for handling complex productions (among them *Elmer Gantry* and *Lord Jim*), and difficult actors (among them Lee Marvin, whom he had directed without incident in *The Professionals*).

Brooks, who had a powerful collegial feeling for others of his profession, refused to take over the picture. Naturally, this whetted everyone's appetite for his saving presence. Everyone except Clint's, that is. When Lerner mentioned Brooks to him, he responded, "I've always liked Richard Brooks. I'd love to work in a picture with him. But I don't think you should write this guy off. I don't really think you're being fair to the guy. Why doesn't everybody who's not being supportive of him right now get together and be supportive of him, and let's try to get this movie on track."

Anxious Alan Lerner (he frequently wore white cotton gloves to prevent himself from picking and gnawing at his cuticles), however, was still determined to hire Brooks, and flew to Los Angeles to plead with him directly. The director told Lerner that if he had not informed Logan of this approach he was acting unethically. He also repeated Clint's argument; it was late in the game to be discovering that he had hired the wrong director. At the end of the meeting Brooks believed that he had heard the last of this matter.

He had not. Marvin now called to support the producer's plea; Brooks responded by urging cooperation on him. Then Joyce Haber, the gossip columnist, printed an item claiming that Logan was on the verge of dismissal and that Brooks was the "likeliest candidate" to replace him. This leak was obviously not accidental. Haber was being used by Lerner to provoke Logan into quitting, which he may have imagined would still Brooks's qualms about replacing him. In this he reckoned without Brooks's most salient qualities—his stubborn rectitude and his almost comically paranoid certainty of everyone else's deviousness. He might consider taking over for a director who had left of his own volition, or had fallen ill. But he would not angle for another man's job. Nor would he be placed in a position where he might seem to be doing so. Now, even if Logan could be forced to leave the production Brooks would never replace him.

There, finally, the matter ended, and everyone went back to work—for five endless months. The snows would be flurrying again before the company quit its location and moved back to the studio (where, as it turned out, they had to rebuild the saloon set that had caused them so much trouble and expense earlier). Disorganization being ever the mother of more disorganization, "all the things that could go wrong did go wrong," as Shaw put it later. The horses drawing a stagecoach that was carrying a group of women extras, who were playing hookers, ran away heading for a ravine, and only a quick response from the horsemen (Buddy Van Horn among them) averted a tragedy. The bright idea of hiring hippies as extras (they lived in a temporary tent commune on site) didn't work out; they were frequently in a near-mutinous state over pay and living conditions. Day in, day out the actors were engaged in shots that struck them as ludicrous. Clint remembers warbling one of his songs—seeking authenticity, playback was not used—in a scene with Seberg so far out in a field that they could barely see the camera, on which was mounted a 1,000-mm lens; this made for a radically fore-shortened shot, supposedly making them appear to be at one with na-ture. Of course, the opposite effect was created; the shots looked jarringly artificial.

In general, however, realism was heavily stressed—Clint remembers much fuss about costumes, the details of which were rigorously authen-tic to the period, but which the camera could not see—and distinctly misplaced: Who needs realism in musical comedy? And that, finally, is what's wrong with Marvin's performance. He was properly grizzled and disheveled looking, this hard-used man, but called upon to play a dirty old man, he stubbornly, charmlessly remained . . . a dirty old man. When rolling his eyes and broadly commenting on his own raffishness, his performance is clumsy, unfunny, distancing. He is, finally, the oppo-site of a star; he is a black hole, swallowing this little universe.

Another metaphor occurs to describe his working behavior. Overt rebelliousness eventually disappeared and Marvin became something like a scary ghost haunting the production's by-ways, spreading chaos whenever he appeared. Clint credits Michelle Triola, Marvin's longtime companion and eventual initiator of the famous "palimony" action against him, for doing her best to restrict his intake of alcohol, but she could not be everywhere with him. Typically, Clint says, "His stand-in would come over to my trailer and say, 'Lee's going to come by here in about ten or fifteen minutes asking for a beer. Tell him you don't have any.' So I hid all the beer and it became this kind of game all the way."

Except that whenever possible Clint chose not to play in it. Logan would later describe Clint as "warm and decent," his words correctly implying that, as much as possible, Clint distanced himself from the on-going hubbub. He did his job and maintained a pleasant, cooperative, but reserved, manner. He had rented a farmhouse and did chores around the place. He found some locals who knew where the good fishing was and often joined them on their expeditions. One of the helicopter pi-lots ferrying him in and out of the set was an instructor, and when Clint showed an interest in learning to fly the contraption he started teaching him to do so, inspiring a stubborn ambition to fly that, almost two decades later, Clint would realize. Some nights, Clint would bunk in his trailer on the set and enjoy the peace of the wilderness.

Eventually, he found himself keeping more and more company with Jean Seberg. "Jean and I were close buddies." Pause. "I really liked her a lot." Another pause. "I was kind of nuts about her." He has had his share of location romances, but this is the one he speaks of most tenderly.

It was her fragility and vulnerability that attracted him, a sense that this was a woman who needed protection, as both her professional and personal histories seem to prove. As a college freshman from a small Iowa town, she had won a nationwide talent search for the title role in Otto Preminger's production of *Saint Joan,* for which she received disastrous reviews. After appearing in another Preminger production, *Bonjour Tristesse*—in this period the producer-director specialized in a kind of wooden sensationalism, adapting popular, slightly scandalous novels in a metronomic manner—she rescued her career as Clint had by appearing in a marginal European film that became a surprise international success, Jean-Luc Godard's *Breathless.* She confirmed her abilities with her complex work as the schizophrenic heroine of Robert Rossen's *Lilith* and continued to divide her time between European and American filmmaking. Married (not entirely happily) to Romain Gary, the French novelist and diplomat, she had involved herself in various radical causes (notably supporting the Black Panther movement), but yet retained the saving air of innocence that had marked her work for Godard.

Clint seems to be correct when he comments, "She just wanted a peaceful life," and they achieved a semblance of it by absenting themselves from the chaos of production whenever they could. Clint had a motorcycle with him, and when they were not required on set they spent many days together. Seberg was sufficiently smitten that in a later interview she dropped an obvious hint about their affair to a gossip columnist, but, given their other commitments, it could only be a thing of the moment. In the years that followed, her unhappiness and confusion deepened, and after a decade of troubled relationships she died of an overdose of sleeping pills in 1979.

Their performances do not so much reflect their affection for one another as their remoteness from the production process. Sometimes it almost seems as if they're working in a different picture. He is more a juvenile than a potent romantic lead; she's more an ingenue than a mature sexual being. But, in a curious way, this worked for them; their romantic passages are little islands of calm and sweetness in a sea of desperation and discontent. And by and large they would escape responsibility for the picture's failure. Critics mostly dismissed their work with a bland sentence or two, while Hollywood blamed Logan, who would never direct another picture.

· But in another way, *Paint Your Wagon* did have a major, and continuing, effect on Clint's career. As the muddle persisted right up to the very last days on location, he firmly resolved never again to place himself in such circumstances. "That's when I came to the conclusion, after the fifth month, that I was going to be really active with Malpaso. I was going to go back to doing just regular movies."

That is to say, relatively small-scale films employing good, but not necessarily big-name, actors, and certainly none that carried with them any explosive personal baggage. By this he also meant that he would direct at least some of these films himself. As he put it on one public occasion, "If I'm going to make mistakes in my career, *I* want to make them, I don't want somebody else making them for me." Or, as he put it a little more colorfully later on, "if these guys can blow this kind of dough and nobody cares about it, why not take a shot at it, and at least if I screw up I can say, well, OK, I screwed up, and take the blame on it." This realization, and this resolution, constituted for Clint "a turning point in my career."

It was the most important decision, in fact, since accepting *A Fistful of Dollars.* For the moment, however, this was a largely negative turning point; knowing now what he *didn't* want to do—further pursuing the stardom-by-association strategy—he still didn't know precisely what he wanted to do, beyond making more manageable films. What their subject matter might be, what developments he might permit his screen character, when, exactly, he would begin to direct, remained unclear to him. And, in fact, he was at the moment committed to two rather routine movies, neither of which would advance him along the path he was beginning to imagine for himself.

But at least he was done with *Paint Your Wagon,* except for recording his songs, attending to the usual looping chores and showing up for the premieres in New York and London. "Gulp," he said when confronted by Nelson Riddle and a full orchestra on the recording stage, but he persevered. When he finally saw the film in completed form he thought it was "cut defensively," meaning that wherever there was a choice the more conventional material was used to make a film that was without energy or sense of movement. It contained very little dancing, and what there was of it was not integrated into the plot. The songs (some of which, like "Wanderin' Star" and "They Call the Wind Maria," were agreeably melodic) were clumsily staged and sometimes simply played over other action, almost as if they were a kind of narration. Its attempts at spectacle were glum and distant, and the big finish, the town collapsing, was unpersuasive. "Fiascoesque" was Clint's neologistic final judgment.

Some reviewers, like Vincent Canby, were surprisingly tolerant of it; "amiable" was his word for it. Here and there Clint got a good notice. The Los Angeles *Times*'s Charles Champlin wrote favorably of him (his "stoic and handsome dignity stands out and he sings in an unscholarly baritone which is fine"). The reviewers who liked his work were responding to Clint's strategy of polite reserve—the old Rowdy Yates manner, come to think of it. "People were so favorable to me," Clint now observes, "because they didn't like anything else about it."

This was essentially true. "Coarse and unattractive" was Champlin's summarizing phrase. "Rarely has a film wasted so much time so wantonly," said *Newsweek*. In this chorus of disapproval Pauline Kael's voice was the most devastating, and her savage, career-long dislike of Clint—not just his work, but, it often seemed, his very being—was enunciated here. She discerned his strategy—"he hardly seems to be in the movie"—but unlike some of her colleagues, viciously chastised him for his withdrawal: "He's controlled in such an uninteresting way; it's not an actor's control, which enables one to release something—it's the kind of control that keeps one from releasing anything. We could stand the deadpan reserve of Nelson Eddy's non-acting because he gave of himself when he sang, but Eastwood doesn't give of himself ever, and a musical with a withdrawn hero is almost a contradiction in terms. . . ."

If her case against Clint's work in this instance is perhaps justifiable, her larger generalizations about him as an actor are wrong, and her endless animus against him remains, like so many of her curious passions, inexplicable. Perhaps no more so, however, than her notion that films like *Paint Your Wagon* evidenced the terminal decadence of the whole Hollywood system.

It, along with the other expensive musicals of the moment had "finally broken the back of the American movie industry," she gleefully crowed. The major studios, part of "a rotting system" she insisted, "are collapsing, but they're not being toppled over by competitors; they're so enervated that they're sinking under their own weight"—rather like No-Name City itself, one might say. This ludicrously overdramatized the situation. All that was coming to an end was a mode of exhibition, road showing, in which overlong, overstuffed movies like *Paint Your Wagon* were made to be shown on a reserved-seat, two-shows-per-day basis at advanced prices—mostly because the public felt it had too often overpaid for too many big, bad movies.

That did not mean, however, that the whole Hollywood system was tottering, only that it was once again in transition. Indeed, *Paint Your Wagon* did not turn out to be the insupportable disaster Kael imagined it would. It was certainly not worth the trouble and anxiety it caused, but eventually it returned $15 million of its $20 million cost in domestic rentals and probably made back much of the rest overseas and in television licensing. Nor did it bring down Paramount's management, which skipped blithely on to the profitable likes of *Love Story* and *The Godfather.* Like all radical critics of capitalistic enterprises, Kael underestimated their adaptability and their capacity for survival.

Her opinions about his work aside, Clint agreed with many of Kael's judgments on *Paint Your Wagon.* In a general way, indeed, he agreed with her view of the Hollywood system; it was slow, cumbersome, often stupid in its decisions. He did not, however, think it was ripe for revolution. What he guessed was that a cooler, more amiable and self-interested kind of subversion might be practiced on it by a man increasingly confident of his own skills, power and judgment, and increasingly wary of other people's opinions about what he should and should not be doing.

EIGHT

I'M AN ACTOR, YOU KNOW

Autonomy was a dream easier to define than to realize. It would take Clint a half decade to attain the kind of control over his professional destiny that he wanted, mostly because of his long-term commitment to Universal. The projects this hierarchical and routinizing studio urged on him were generally unimaginative and often vexed—sometimes by scripts in need of major revision, sometimes by inept producers, most often by indifferent handling when they went to market. On the other hand, when Clint developed projects he thought were more interesting, they were treated as indulgences more to be patronized than enthusiastically supported. It could be argued that all the films he made at Universal were useful to him in that they firmed and settled his relationship with his audience, but the history of this period is, from his point of view, one of increasing fractiousness and restlessness.

The first of the two films Clint made in 1969, *Two Mules for Sister Sara,* would prove to be a case in point. In some measure the movie owed its existence to him. While *Where Eagles Dare* was in production, Elizabeth Taylor showed him an early version of the script, which producer Martin Rackin was set to do at Universal, and they made a handshake agreement to costar in it. When Don Siegel arrived in London to do some looping for *Coogan's Bluff,* Clint gave him the screenplay, and he said he'd like to direct it. Unfortunately, there were already complexities about this project of which they were unaware.

There is certain irony in this, for the story they all liked is very basic and straightforward. It recounts the adventures of a seemingly mismatched man and woman who meet under desperate circumstances—he rescues her from an attempted rape—in the Mexican desert, circa 1865. Hogan, as Clint's character was eventually called—curious how many figures with Irish names this Wasp has played—is an American mercenary who has sold his services to the Juaristas rebelling against the dictatorship of the French puppet government of Emperor Maximilian.

He is supposed to dynamite a fort, abscond with its treasure of gold and receive half of it for his troubles. Sara is, supposedly, a nun (she turns out to be a whore in disguise), idealistically committed to the Juaristas' cause and seeking funds for them, while the French try to apprehend her. Along the trail, this odd couple shares many adventures, some comical, some suspenseful; in the end, of course, the fortress is very satisfactorily blown up, she reveals her true occupation, he turns out to be not quite so hard a case as he had seemed and they ride off into the sunset together.

This story, at least in its broad strokes, was the work of Budd Boetticher, director of those admirably austere Randolph Scott westerns of the fifties, and one imagines from his dismayed comments about the final version of *Sister Sara* that he had something like their tone in mind for this film. Certainly he had it in mind to direct it. Unfortunately—and here is where some of the film's troubles began—he sold his material to Rackin, a sometime screenwriter and studio production chief who had recently had the effrontery to remake *Stagecoach* and the chutzpah to announce that this time they were going to do it right. An almost parodistic version of a Hollywood operator—all gold chains, sunlamp tan and tough talk—he quickly fired Boetticher and turned to Albert Maltz for a rewrite.

Maltz, an occasional playwright and novelist, is best known today as one of the Hollywood Ten, imprisoned and then blacklisted for their refusal to testify to their Communist political convictions before the House Un-American Activities Committee in 1948, and this would be his first credited screenwriting in more than two decades. His draft suited Rackin well enough, but Siegel and Clint thought it still needed work. More than they initially imagined, for Elizabeth Taylor now rather mysteriously disappeared from the project. Siegel believed she might have quit when the studio refused to shoot the picture in Spain when Richard Burton was also scheduled to be working there. Clint thinks the disastrous reception of *Boom!* may have affected her standing at the studio, especially given the scarcely less dismaying prospects Universal must have seen in *Secret Ceremony,* which it was soon to release. Her movie career was spiraling downward as quickly as her husband's.

Besides, Shirley MacLaine was available, and she seemed to be hot. She had just finished *Sweet Charity,* which, for reasons known only to motion-picture executives, they were certain was going to be a huge hit, and they wanted a quick follow-up for her. Or maybe they were just typecasting; the Bob Fosse film was the third in which she had played an adorably indomitable hooker.

The part as originally written had called for a Hispanic woman, and it had been thought that Taylor might just get away with such an impersonation. The red-haired, fair-skinned MacLaine obviously could not, and anyway, there was something about her spirit and manner—so feisty and forthright, so essentially comic—that made her nun's masquerade implausible at first glance. So in the next rewrite, Sara became an American expatriate, and instead of holding back her true identity until the end of the picture, as Boetticher had intended, broad hints that she was not what she seemed to be were almost immediately dropped— Sara puffing on a cigar or swigging liquor when Hogan's back was turned or using bad language to his face. Also lost was a mutual-redemption theme dear to Boetticher, in which "one who you believe is a nun becomes a beautiful person because she falls in love with a bum, who becomes a beautiful person because he is in love with an unobtainable person." From his point of view there was worse to come.

Of this Boetticher was at the time unaware; though he had a story credit on the film, he was not consulted at any stage of the production and did not see it in finished form until its Los Angeles premiere, where he sat fuming directly behind Clint and Siegel, incensed at what he saw as the spaghetti-like direction in which his material had been taken. Boetticher, who had a particular and often-expressed loathing for Leone, had "motivated" his protagonist in a way that he no longer was. "My men have become tough for a *reason*," he would say, and though Hogan is presented as a former idealist soured by the slaughter he had witnessed in the Civil War, very little is made of the point. When Sara asks him, "If money's all you care about, why did you fight in that war?" he replies, "Everyone has the right to be a sucker once." The casual cynicism and brevity of the speech was entirely too Leonesque (perhaps by now we should say Eastwoodian) for Boetticher.

In his study of Clint's films, Christopher Frayling, relying heavily on an interview with Boetticher, adds that Hogan "seemed to be much more concerned about personal style—about cultivating his ironic, detached stance in order to enhance his status as a walking piece of mythology—than about behaving in a remotely credible way." This, too, was Leonesque. Clint's work for him always suggested that when there are no reliable values to resort to, heroes must fall back on personal style; it is what they have instead of personal honor in the modern world.

Nor was that the end of the film's "homages" to Clint's movie past. Ennio Morricone supplied its score, and the visual connection between Hogan and the Man with No Name is stressed. He appears in his first sequence unshaven, wearing a serape-like vest and smoking a cigar. The three men assaulting Sister Sara are also out of the Leone school; third-world second heavies, if you will—dark, dirty, visibly Hispanic and intent on defiling a figure they take to be a holy woman. (Siegel would later write that he intended to cast Americans in these roles, but that Rackin, trying to save a few pesos, insisted on hiring locals for the parts.)

Most significantly, Hogan confronts them with No-Nameish cool. After a minimal exchange of verbiage he shoots two of them, whereupon the survivor grabs the almost-naked Sara to use as a shield. Hogan, however, pulls out a stick of dynamite, lights its fuse with his cigar and tosses it at their feet, confronting the bad man with a cruel choice: If he lets go of Sara and runs, he will be shot; if he holds on to her he will be blown up. He runs, Hogan shoots and then ambles casually down from his position on a rise to cut off the fuse with his knife, his pace being especially irritating to Boetticher, who found it—who would dispute him?—unrealistic.

So is the dialogue that follows: "They said they were going to kill me." "Well, they're not saying much now." It is the harbinger of many similarly brusque exchanges, with Hogan, in general, getting most of the toppers. She's always either blithering idealism or quavering alarm, thus ever in need of a sharp slap with a smart line. These are well enough written, however, and since incident follows incident—they range from a confrontation with a rattlesnake to an Indian attack to the demolition of a railroad trestle to the final, suspensefully managed attack on the fort—at a very satisfactory clip, the movie is, in its entirely unambitious and predictable way, entertaining. A director like Siegel can always provide canny professional crispness in lieu of conviction.

Stanley Kauffmann, when he reviewed the movie, was obviously aware of Boetticher's complaints, but argued that newfangled stylistic tics or no, the film was basically "an attempt to keep the old Hollywood alive—a place where nuns *can* turn out to be disguised whores, where heroes *can* always have a stick of dynamite under their vests, where every story has not one but two cute finishes." Clint too was aware that the movie had a certain lineage. "It's kind of *The African Queen* gone West," he told a journalist at the time. It also owed something to another John Huston film, *Heaven Knows, Mr. Allison,* his desert-island fantasy, set in World War II, in which Robert Mitchum (whom Boetticher said was one of the actors he had in mind as he wrote) played marine roughneck to Deborah Kerr's nun. Clint's attitude toward Boetticher's script and its revisions was—and remains—quite neutral. "I read his script," he says, "and it really wasn't any better. It was a little different interpretation."

That reinterpretation was not easily arrived at. This was a rugged shoot, not made any more comfortable by MacLaine's temperament. She is an actress who tends to question a director rather closely about every shot: Why do you want me to move now instead of then? Do we really need this line? Wouldn't it be better if . . . ? And she drove Siegel crazy. In her defense, it must be said that the location in and around Co-coyoc, thirty miles from Cuernevaca, was particularly difficult for her. She did most of her own stunts, some of which were quite taxing, and she proved to be especially sensitive to sunburn, so it was necessary for someone to trail her around with a parasol whenever they were shoot-ing outside, which was, of course, most of the time. Moreover, she was by nature a nightbird, not entirely happy to arise early in order to catch the morning light—particularly, as Clint recalls, when her lover of the time, Sander Vanocur, the television newsman, visited her. Eventually she became ill and caused the picture to shut down for a few days.

But Clint related to her affably enough. "Shirley was great fun," he recalls. And though she scarcely discusses this film in her memoir of her acting life, she did write, in a picture caption, "I loved Clint even though he was a Republican." All of her troubles were with Siegel, and they came to a head one day when, in order to hold everything he wanted in shot, he asked her to dismount from a mule on its off-side. This offended her sense of realism, a fight ensued, and she stormed off the set, with even Clint losing his customary cool and yelling imprecations after her. Siegel ordered him to stay out of it and then quit the set himself, in-tending, he said later, to quit the picture as well.

But that evening MacLaine knocked at his door to tender an apol-ogy, he invited her in for a session in which they both vented their grievances, and peace of a sort was restored, though even a few years later Siegel was still rankled by her. In 1974 he told his biographer, Stu-art Kaminsky, "It's hard to feel any great warmth for her. She's too . . . unfeminine. She has too much balls. She's very hard." A couple of decades later, when he came to write his autobiography, Siegel's opin-ion of her had softened somewhat. After their peace parley, he reports, "she was a doll. When working, she was most cooperative. My major re-gret was that I never really sat down and found out what made her tick."

Rackin, however, he never did forgive. Their problems had begun in Hollywood when he had inserted a page in the shooting script bear-ing this ominous legend: "There are to be no changes in the script, without exception, unless you obtain the oral or written approval of the Producer, Martin Rackin." He and Siegel were discussing this directive in the latter's office one day when Clint happened by. The director handed the script to him, pointing out the offending sentence. Clint eyed him blankly and said, "I don't see anything wrong with that."

He got the reaction he expected from Siegel—barely suppressed apoplexy—then wandered toward a window, turned slowly back to face the two men and said, "There's one way, Don, to handle situations like this." At which point he ripped the page bearing the producer's order out of the script, crumpled it up and tossed it across the room.

This effectively backed Rackin out of the film's creative process. But it did not prevent him from interfering in the production process. Trying to cut corners, he refused to pay for movie-trained horses, which do not shy around equipment. Riding one of them, Clint was thrown when a camera boom, swinging alongside him, spooked the animal. Later, when it came time to shoot the raid on the fort, Siegel found the set, on which Rackin had supervised construction, flimsy and inadequate. About the only argument he won was for his choice as cinematographer, the great Gabriel Figueroa, who had shot Luis Buñuel's Mexican films and who, on Clint's recommendation, would be employed on his next movie, too.

Clint was loyal to his director in all of his disputes with Rackin, and they worked together companionably, with Clint full of suggestions, usually proposing the more complicated, time-consuming shot, feeling that if his friend had a flaw as a director it was his low-budget habit of opting for the simplest, cheapest setup. "He can dream up absolutely impossible shots," Siegel told a visiting journalist, "but the trouble is that they sound good." Of course, he slyly added, when they didn't work, they were not discussed subsequently.

Overall, the filmmaking process was very similar to the one they had endured on *Coogan's Bluff*—messy, contentious, improvisational. And the results were about the same, too—modest profitability and mixed reviews when the film was released a year later. Clint, in the critics' view, had settled down nicely after his boyish Italian escapades. If some agreed with Kauffmann about the regressiveness of *Two Mules for Sister Sara,* others found in it a certain classic grace. "A movie lover's dream," Roger Greenspun called it in *The New York Times.* "I'm not sure it is a great movie, but it is *very* good, and it stays in the mind the way only movies of exceptional narrative intelligence do."

★   ★   ★

Many of the more serious reviewers tended to see *Sister Sara* as they had *Coogan's Bluff,* more as a Siegel film than as an Eastwood movie, but in their eyes that at least placed Clint in good company. This was useful to him, because on the *Sister Sara* location, for the first time in Clint's experience, the press flocked around, more interested in him than in any other aspect of the production, making their first crude sketches of his off-screen persona. Indeed, it could be argued that over the long run the movie is most interesting as the avatar of his primary celebrity image.

Clint was not very helpful either to the reporters or to himself. He was obviously ill at ease in their presence, and innocent about their needs. Every star eventually has to supply the press with a basic personal narrative to work from, something that can support a simple, attractive image, and Clint did not yet have his story straight. In order to present him to their readers in an easily comprehended form, the journalists were obliged to adapt one of their standard formats to his case.

They settled on a variation on what might be called the starlet-phenomenon yarn. In this tale, an attractive, but not obviously talented, individual—usually a woman—suddenly, mysteriously, seizes the public's imagination, and the press, looking to find shrewd manipulation, either by the new star or by that creature's handlers, seeks explanations. When the press's subject is not forthcoming, or appears to be as puzzled as everyone else by his or her good fortune, much is made of this inarticulateness, and a sort of "lucky stiff" text emerges.

Clint's natural wariness with strangers was deepened by the fact that most of what had been written about him had been contemptuous reviews. He had no reason to think interviewers would be more kindly disposed. "You'll find the conversation pours like glue," one frustrated reporter told another as the latter approached her task in Mexico. To Wayne Warga of the Los Angeles *Times,* who wrote two pieces about him that summer, Clint said, "Actors have their bag, and journalists have theirs. I'm not that talkative, and their job is to get me talking. It may just become chic to blast hell out of me." Then he waited a beat and added, "So permit me to introduce myself"—in a dead-on imitation of Bela Lugosi.

But that moment aside, he didn't really know how to let his playful, self-satirizing side out, and his interrogators, unaware of its existence, didn't know how to bring it out. Some of them talked about his fitness regimen, some about his fondness for cars, and one of them, Aljean Harmetz of *The New York Times,* dug an observant quote out of Irving Leonard, who paired "his fussiness about his cars and his body."

The biggest news out of Cocoyoc was the revelation of his humane relationship with the lower phyla. It had once or twice been hinted at previously, but an English journalist who had not succeeded in getting more than a couple of connected sentences on him was on the set one night when a moth "as big as a bat" suddenly dived into a shot. Many hands grabbed at the creature, which was held captive in a pool of light. One grip, "stamping, swearing, swatting," was particularly eager to kill it, until Clint shouted, "Leave it, leave it, they need killers like you in Vietnam." He moved forward, elbowed the man aside and "then cupping his hands gently he guided the moth into the safety of the dark."

The reporter quoted him thus: "I think violence of that kind is so un-necessary, don't you? It wasn't doing any harm."

Other stories like it emerged from this shoot: Clint insisting that the resident armadillo be released when it refused to eat in captivity; Clint seeing a bunch of iguanas brought to the set "strung on a string like a bunch of bananas" and buying them for five pesos and releasing them in the wild. They presaged a string of such anecdotes that have appeared through the years: Clint rescuing a drowning bee from his swimming pool, Clint feeding rose petals to a pet turtle named Fred in his back-yard, Clint warning his daughter, Alison, not to step on a cockroach on the set of *Tightrope* because it, too, has its place on the planet. In 1969 Harmetz got him to trace his attitude back to his grandmother's farm, where he said he learned to identify with animals "Dr. Doolittle style."

It played well. It was the human-interest touch journalists are always looking for. But it did not vitiate their basic lucky-hunk line. His famous self-appraisal as a bum and a drifter, quoted by Warga, stems from this shoot, and its follow-up—"As it turns out, I'm lucky, because I'm going to end up financially well-off for a drifter"—supported the idea that, purely fortuitously, he was forging a potent link with young working-class males like himself. Playing the kind of autonomous figures they ad-mired, he was himself achieving the kind of autonomy they dreamed of achieving.

Clint did not discourage this take—it seemed to satisfy most in-quiries while leaving his privacy intact—and neither did Maggie. She told Harmetz, "Clint gives the feeling of a man who controls his own destiny," an idea he expanded on slightly: "My appeal is the characters I play. A superhuman character who has all the answers is double cool, ex-ists on his own without society or the help of society's police forces. A guy sits in the audience, he's twenty-five years old, and he's scared stiff about what he's going to do with his life. He wants to have that self-sufficient thing he sees up there on the screen." To this thought he ap-pended somewhat surprisingly, somewhat gratuitously, another, darker one: "But it will never happen that way. Man is always dreaming of being an individual, but man is really a flock animal."

Hardly an optimistic view of human nature, but the writer did not pursue the line of questioning it suggests, except to note that, "Like most western heroes and the men who play them, Eastwood is a politi-cal conservative." The reference here was to John Wayne and Gary Cooper among others, and it represented the other, more halfhearted, but equally unproductive, way the press tried to position him in those days. (In a matter of months he would begin his decades-long attempt to avoid political labeling, recording his first published denial of activism, his first insistence that he voted for candidates from both major parties.)

The journalists couldn't imagine that he just might be an actor acting. This was not, as they all knew, what the movies' lucky stiffs did to get ahead. That was art, or at least artifice, and thus beyond them. Harmetz, for example, catching Clint at home, nursing a cold, "encumbered by a wife, a baby and the rules of civilization," conceded that he was not entirely the character he played, but still insisted he was "not *not* the character either. . . . Sitting uncommitted, holding himself in reserve, even in what should have been the safety of his own living room Eastwood echoed the caverns of the man he portrays on the screen." "Caverns" is, of course, a euphemism for "emptiness" (the amorality of the Leone character was still much on this writer's mind), and it never occurred to her (or to anyone else) to undertake more serious spelunking. You did that with actors out from the East, people who had studied with Lee or Stella, Herbert or Uta. It was not worth the effort in cases like this one.

In fairness, it must be said that Clint in those days did not volunteer information about, say, his training as an actor or his interest in jazz. Presenting himself as a guy who had just "tripped across the movie business" he gave the reporters what they needed and got them out the door. To only one reporter, who asked him if he might feel uncomfortable playing someone other than a westerner, did he state the obvious, "I'm an actor, you know, not a *real* cowboy."

It is, perhaps, a matter of small consequence; a somewhat more resonant portrait of Clint Eastwood would eventually emerge in the media. But it may be a matter of some importance, too; this notion of him as a silent primitive would affect the reception of his work for years to come.

★ ★ ★

Clint moved almost without a break—he would spend nine months of 1969 on location—from Mexico to Yugoslavia to make *The Warriors* (to be referred to hereafter by its final title, *Kelly's Heroes*). Financed by MGM, and featuring an all-star cast, it was a self-contradictory enterprise. A military adventure, to be made on something close to an epic scale, it was also supposed to be an antiwar satire, somewhat along the lines of such contemporary films as *Castle Keep, M*A*S*H, Catch*-22 and *Too Late the Hero,* all of which, one way or another, spoke to public disgust with the war in Vietnam.

It was this aspect of the project that stirred Clint. Around this time he confessed that he had voted for Nixon in 1968 because he regarded Johnson's bombing halt as a cynical electoral ploy on behalf of Hubert Humphrey. But he still had no enthusiasm for the Vietnam adventure or for militarism in general, and Troy Kennedy Martin's original script expressed these feelings—in Clint's opinion, movingly and adroitly. This was the story of some military misfits who take some time out of World War II to do a little free-enterprising. It begins with Clint's character, the Kelly of the title, interrogating a captured German officer—he gets the man drunk—and learning that the enemy has cached $16 million in gold bullion in a bank in the town of Cleremont, some thirty miles behind the front. When their commanding officer goes on leave, he proposes to the topkick left in charge (Telly Savalas) that their unit stage an assault on the bank, strictly for private profit. Their principal coconspirators are a Bilko-like supply sergeant, Crapgame (Don Rickles), and the commander of a tank unit, Oddball (Donald Sutherland, doing a nice turn as a sort of premature hippie). In a subplot, a publicity-crazed general, played by Carroll O'Connor, tries desperately to keep up with their penetration of enemy lines and claim it as a bold tactical stroke of his own.

Running more than two hours, *Kelly's Heroes* is a messily contradictory and never fully resolved movie. Besides being, occasionally, an antiwar satire, it is also from time to time a caper (or bunch-of-guys-rob-a-vault) comedy, an old-fashioned service (or bunch-of-goldbricks-goof-off) comedy and, yes, a straight bunch-of-guys-on-a-mission piece. To put the point simply, it tried to be all things to all audiences and so, naturally, ended up a muddle—although, right up to the end, Clint thought it could be straightened out.

At Clint's behest, Don Siegel was offered the picture, but he was tied up on postproduction with *Sister Sara,* and so, with Clint's approval, the assignment went to the pyrotechnically inclined Brian Hutton. He, not unnaturally, wanted to stress the kind of action that had worked for him in *Where Eagles Dare,* which went into its successful release just before this film went on location. And he had a wondrous range of equipment to play with. Tito's Yugoslavia had developed a profitable sideline renting units of its army to visiting film companies. Along with the troops came some rather interesting matériel, for when Yugoslavia broke with the Soviet Union, it acquired from the United States great mounds of surplus military supplies. Clint remembers taking machine guns, still protected by the grease they had been packed in, out of their original World War II crates and driving vintage jeeps with perhaps two hundred miles on them. Ever the auto collector, he tried to buy a couple of them but was defeated by red tape.

Such diversions were, however, rare. The day Clint arrived at Novi

Sad, close to their first location, offered a fair prediction of things to come. The "suite" he had been promised had been turned into two rooms by the simple expedient of hanging a blanket in the center of a single room; it looked, he says, like the motel scene in *It Happened One Night*. Amused, he retreated to the lobby, where he discovered Don Rickles, his wife and an assistant, all encumbered by steamer trunks, checking in. Rickles had insisted, contractually, on accommodations equivalent to Clint's and eagerly inquired about their quality. Clint was noncommittal, but awaited the comic's response with considerable interest.

Rickles was still talking about it more than two decades later. Remembering Clint for an interviewer, he said, "I didn't realize how easily pleased Eastwood was—living in a kind of motel." He added: "A very down-to-earth guy—give him a bottle of beer, and he's happy . . . A pick-up truck and a dog."

As the months wore on, Rickles provided most of the entertainment for what proved to be yet another endless shoot. He told a reporter the most interesting activity available was his changing clothes. Clint spent considerable time tooling around the countryside on a new motorcycle he had acquired in London on the *Eagles Dare* shoot—a powerful (and classic) Norton 750, which he still owns. Essentially the straight man to the assembled pranksters, and their leader in the action sequences, his was an ungratifying role, and his work is, at best, stern, even grim, and perhaps the least interesting he had done as a star. Off camera he remained a tough interview, if anything less forthcoming than usual. "I can never think of anything clever or witty to say," he informed one visiting writer. "In fact, half the time I can't think of anything to say." "I'm always a little closed in," he said to another, "and I don't go around telling people what I think of this or that."

Hutton offered a more interesting perspective. "We went twenty years . . . from 1947 when Brando hit until 1967 when Clint hit, with actors who, for the most part, played characters who were confused, not sure of themselves, unable to cope, befuddled. Now Clint is a throwback to the strong, silent men of the thirties. Clint's character has always been a guy who knows who he is, knows what he wants and goes out and does it. Regardless if he's good or bad, at least he's certain."

In life, as on-screen, as the director was soon to discover. There came a moment, late in the fall, when everyone had simply had it with this picture. When the director asked some of the players and technicians to stay on a few more days to perfect some sequence or other, Clint (among others) simply deserted him. The shot footage was scheduled for shipment to Paris, and Clint declared that he was going to be on the same train with it; he had given all that he could to this endless enterprise, had a date to celebrate Thanksgiving there with some friends, and that was that.

If, on the whole, *Kelly's Heroes* had been relatively untroubled in production, it was severely troubled in postproduction, much to Clint's disgust. The film was victimized largely by the troubles then afflicting Metro-Goldwyn-Mayer, which was financing and distributing it, and whose history is an object lesson in how modern financial shell games can reduce a great institution to a shell itself. The picture had been green-lighted by a management team headed by Robert O'Brien. But then control of the studio's parent company, Loewe's Inc., was acquired by Edgar Bronfman Sr. and Seagrams, whose new managers tried to turn this into a back-lot picture. They were fought off by its producers, Gabriel Katzka and Sidney Beckerman. By the time they were in active production, controlling interest in the studio had been acquired by Kirk Kirkorian, the corporate raider, who installed James Aubrey as head of production. As Kirkorian prepared to strip MGM of most of its assets (the famous auction of its props, the sale of its back lot and ultimately the sale of its invaluable film library took place during his regime), Aubrey, who had been known as "the Smiling Cobra" in his network days, announced that the studio would cease to take the large gambles (*Mutiny on the Bounty, Doctor Zhivago, 2001: A Space Odyssey*) that had made its corporate life so harum-scarum over the last decade. Impressed by the huge return *Easy Rider* in 1969 had made on a minuscule investment by a rival studio, he said that from now on MGM would concentrate on similarly modest productions in hopes of making a similar killing.

Given this philosophy he was bound to look askance at *Kelly's Heroes.* It was not only not his kind of picture, it was not his picture in any way. It was left over from two previous regimes, and like most executives in this situation, he saw no reason to make his predecessors look good. So he picked at it unenthusiastically. After seeing Hutton's cut he ordered the title changed from *The Warriors,* first to *Kelly's Warriors,* then to *Kelly's Heroes.* He also ordered substantive revisions, possibly because the film's several, contradictory themes discomfited him, perhaps because they did not offer him a clear marketing strategy, perhaps because he felt this must be a "Clint Eastwood" picture as he defined the term, that is to say, a straight-ahead action-adventure movie. Hutton, who did not have final cut, had no choice but to oblige Aubrey, and when Clint saw what had been done to the film, he told the director, "Brian, you can't release this." To which the director, who had been fighting the good fight, replied wearily, "Well, that's the way they want to do it," adding that the studio had a release date "creeping up on them." The implication was that even if the studio liked Clint's ideas there wouldn't be time to execute them.

In general Clint felt that the film's comedy now played too broadly, and specifically he was dismayed at the excision of a transition scene between the picture's second and third acts in which, as he recalls, he and the character played by Telly Savalas "just sort of summed up the philosophy of these loose ends, and what the war had done to them." He goes so far as to say that "its soul was taken out, a little bit of its soul was robbed." Surely it sounds as if his best scene, one in which he got to do something more than bark commands and look determined, was missing.

He had, as well, a purely practical complaint—that "creeping" release date. If it was held to, *Kelly's Heroes* would open in many major markets virtually day and date with *Two Mules for Sister Sara.* "Why should I open across the street from myself?" Clint asked Aubrey. "How much can they tolerate of one actor?" Besides, he said, if they could spend a little more time in the editing room he was certain they could deliver a cut that satisfied everyone's needs. "Let me just come in and show you what I'd do. In one day, I guarantee you—one day—I'll have something to show you."

In retrospect Clint makes this discussion sound more reasonable than it actually was. By the time it took place he was on location with Don Siegel in Louisiana, shooting *The Beguiled,* and Siegel recalls him spending the better part of a day in his trailer on the phone yelling at Aubrey "in a fury." Knowing the force of Clint's anger when one is faced with it in person, he suggests that Clint might have been more successful had he been able to confront Aubrey directly.

Possibly so. Nothing focuses Clint's outrage like an authority figure trying to patronize him. One of the studio chief's main arguments for haste was that he had to get the sixteen-millimeter prints for armed forces distribution out by a certain date or the studio would be "in big trouble." Clint couldn't believe it, nor should he have. These prints represented pennies; he was talking about changes in the picture and its marketing that might have meant millions to the studio. The best Clint could obtain from Aubrey was a promise to think over his arguments, but he never heard back from him, and the movie opened on the production chief's timetable.

Kelly's Heroes returned only about $600,000 more in rentals than the competing *Two Mules for Sister Sara,* which had cost considerably less. Nor was it a critical success. Most reviewers simply noted its mixed means and motives and passed unimpassioned negative judgments on it. Roger Greenspun unconsciously lent belated support to Clint's arguments when he observed that when the bank caper began to result in a substantial amount of killing, "the film has no resources above the conventional antagonistic ironies and comradely pieties of most war movies." He said that because it so easily accepts the idea that its subject is not war but "burglary masquerading as war," the film "becomes a denial of moral perception that depresses the mind and bewilders the imagination."

In a way this was *Paint Your Wagon* all over again, though on a smaller scale, with less extensive personal acrimony. Once again a studio had been trying to have it both ways, making a traditional genre film but at the same time giving it a hip, countercultural spin. The industry seemingly could not grasp the fact that there were now two distinct audiences out there, each of them potentially profitable, but not to be confused, not to be appealed to simultaneously.

There was sometimes advantage to be found in this confusion, for the industry was momentarily willing to take chances on certain marginal enterprises—who knew what the next *Easy Rider* might look like? And Universal had in hand something that was, in its way, just as curious, something out of the Hollywood mainstream and off what everyone assumed was Clint's main line. Though it would not be generally recognized as such, it would become, at least in Clint's mind, the first clear, public signal of his resolve to carve out a career path that could not be confused with that of any other Hollywood star.

★   ★   ★

"I wasn't sure an audience was ready for that, or wanted that, but I knew I wanted it," Clint says of *The Beguiled*. He wanted it because it was a strange and complex story, because it was such a totally unexpected vehicle for him and for the best and simplest of reasons—because it was "something I could act, something besides just gunning people down."

There is some question as to who first presented the project to Clint and in what form it came to him. Don Siegel would remember Clint giving him Thomas Cullinan's novel to read while they were working on *Two Mules for Sister Sara* and recalled it having been sent to Clint by Jennings Lang. Clint remembers getting a first-draft screenplay to read and thinks it was Lenny Hirshan who provided it. It is certain in any case that by this time a script—again by Albert Maltz—existed and that the agent thought well of it.

What's also beyond question is that Clint responded very quickly to whatever material had been sent to him. He read it in a night, found himself disturbed and intrigued by it and passed it on to Siegel for a reality check. The director also loved it. He told Clint he thought it could be their best movie.

Certainly it would turn out to be the oddest item in their filmographies, not at all the sort of thing anyone would naturally associate with either of them. *The Beguiled* is, for want of a better term, Southern Gothic, heavily sexualized and, as one or two critics observed, not without elements of very black comedy. Set in the waning days of the Civil War, it tells of a Union soldier, John McBurney, left wounded on a battlefield in the Deep South. There he is discovered by a preadolescent schoolgirl, who conducts him back to the seminary she attends, where he is nursed back to health. In the course of this sojourn he indeed beguiles—perhaps "temporarily maddens" would be a better description—both students and faculty, with deadly results.

It is a dark and claustrophobic piece and, precisely because the setting is so isolated and so spatially compressed, very intense. After some four years of war and virtually no contact with men, these isolated females are, putting it gently, in a state of high sexual tension. And McBurney, once he starts feeling better, is more than willing to take advantage of as many of them as possible—quite casually, with much misrepresentation of his past and of his true, manipulative nature, for he was a reluctant and distinctly unheroic soldier, as we learn from flashbacks.

This is not at all a Clint Eastwood role—certainly not as people saw his screen personality at the time. It is not, in fact, a role one can imagine interesting many leading men, given its totally unheroic qualities. All unredeemed, unrationalized slyness aside, he is either bedridden or hobbling about on crutches for the entire length of the film. And, in the end, he gets dead.

The largest problem Clint and Siegel had with Maltz's screenplay was its insistence on an upbeat ending permitting McBurney to escape the dark fate for which the story inevitably prepares him (and the audience). It made no sense to them, and it sent them both back to Cullinan's novel, the rereading of which convinced them of the correctness of his much gloomier conclusion. This, in turn, sent Siegel into extensive confabulations with the screenwriter. The latter, as the director later put it, could not give up on his idea of turning the movie into "a romantic love story," while Siegel clung to the belief that it had to remain "strange and fierce." He invoked Ambrose Bierce, Edgar Allan Poe, Tennessee Williams and Truman Capote. He even went so far as to screen *Rosemary's Baby* for the writer, hoping to get him in the right mood. "I said, 'If you'd written this script, Mia Farrow wouldn't have given birth to the devil. She'd have given birth to healthy blond twin sons.'"

But Maltz couldn't deal with that approach. To begin with, he said, "These lovely children, taken in by this beguiler, distress me." But, Siegel argued, that was only what they seemed to be. The whole point of the story—its central irony—was that these females must ultimately prove themselves to be deadlier than the male. "Pull off the mask of these innocent, virginal nymphs and you will reveal the dark, hidden secrets of wily manipulators," he remembers saying.

"I don't agree," he recalls Maltz replying. "I believe in people."

"But not all people. Surely you are aware of evil people you do *not* believe in."

And so it went—around and around, through at least one more full draft and other, lesser rewrites, with pressure building, for star and studio were fully committed to the film; a production designer had been hired and casting discussions were under way. But still Maltz, whose sensibility combined a taste for popular-front uplift with Hollywood hoke in equal parts, couldn't see what the director was driving at. Like many people of his ideological leanings he believed everyone capable of reform, if not total redemption. So he clung to his principles, until, at last, he was fired.

At Lang's suggestion a woman named Irene Kamp was brought in to work on the script, and she did two drafts that were unsatisfactory to all concerned. Finally, the director did what he had done on *Coogan's Bluff:* He gave all the extant material to yet another writer, hoping he could paste their best bits together in a serviceable screenplay. The man given this formidable task was Claude Traverse, the film's associate producer. When he had digested everything, his advice was to return to the book and write a new script that was as faithful as possible to it. This he did in a month, anonymously; the screen credit on the finished film bore Maltz's pseudonym (John B. Sherry) and Kamp's (Grimes Grice).

The shoot was completely agreeable, perhaps the happiest Clint had experienced since returning to American moviemaking. There was, it would seem, virtually no contention in the cast, and he found Geraldine Page, playing the headmistress, particularly enjoyable to work with. She was—or could be—a highly mannered actress and, though right for this role, certainly not the kind of player one imagines Clint falling in with easily. Indeed, before the fact he thought her "out of my league, being a big star on Broadway and all." But, he told an interviewer, "when we started she told me she was a big fan of mine on *Rawhide,*" and that set him at his ease. So did her work, for this is one of her most confident performances, its surface gentility rendered without flutter, her inner demons kept on a short leash.

Clint credits Page with generating much of the good feeling that permeated the production. "She just set an example for all the young players," he says. When a cast is almost entirely female, he observes, it is not unusual for things to "get a little competitive in wardrobe," for "the makeup to become different every day." But not in this case. Page was, as he puts it, "such a ballsy actress"; she just came in without makeup and said, "'This is the way I am, this is the way I want to do it,' and then these other young gals were sort of drawn into it." As for her working methods, Clint compares them to those of another actor with a legendary theatrical reputation, Lee J. Cobb. She was, like him, "ready to go right away, ready to roll, no BS. If there are insecurities, they have them under control; they just step right up to bat."

Exteriors and some interiors were shot on a decayed plantation near Baton Rouge, with most of the interiors made on Universal soundstages. The work of the production designer, Ted Haworth, was superb, and his settings were exquisitely lit by Bruce Surtees, a longtime camera operator promoted to director of photography on this film precisely because Siegel, with whom he had frequently worked, was convinced he could give him a look he wanted, but had never before attempted to realize.

The cameraman, who would soon be known as "the Prince of Darkness" (and become Clint's regular director of photography for a decade and a half), studied the play of candlelight at home, taking stills lit entirely by these flickering sources and figuring out how to duplicate the effect on set. Similarly, "For the daylight scenes I made sure that no light came from on high," Surtees recalled. Both on location and soundstage he used old-fashioned arcs, which provide a very white, bright light, set outside the windows, as the main light source. His great contribution was to ground an exotic story in a kind of unnatural naturalism—his images were shadowed but not oppressively or portentously so. One always feels that someone might just throw open the shutters and let the healing sunlight in, though that never happens.

Carl Pingitore, the editor, was another significant contributor to the film's singular qualities. He would go on to cut Clint's first film as a director, *Play Misty for Me,* as well as the masterfully edited *Dirty Harry,* on which he also served as associate producer and postproduction supervisor. The method by which he was engaged for *The Beguiled* says much about the Siegel-Eastwood working style. The director decided to interview several Universal staff editors for the post. Pingitore was a veteran and expert editor, but because most of his experience had been in television, he did not think he had much of a shot at a feature film. When Siegel asked him for his resume and qualifications, he bristled. "It just hit me wrong," he recalls, so he snapped back, "I've survived for thirty years." Which was, of course, exactly the right response to a man who saw himself in a similar light—a professional persisting against indifference, watching less gifted men get the good jobs.

What Siegel and Clint had put together was a curiously mixed bag—action star, method actress, a sprinkling of what might be called starlets, a director known for his quick-step pace and no-nonsense style, a cameraman shooting his first feature, an editor out of down-and-dirty television. But they all rubbed each other the right way, and the film has a freshness about it, a resistance to cliché, that keeps the viewer unsettled.

The Beguiled announces its singularity with a bold stroke in its very first moments. After the child, Amy (played by Pamelyn Ferdin), finds McBurney, who has a broken leg among other wounds, and is helping him back to her school, a Confederate unit, mopping up after the battle, approaches. The soldier pulls the child down with him into the foliage to hide from them. He ensures her silence not by placing a hand over her mouth but by kissing her—long and hard, almost passionately. It is a totally unexpected moment and even a quarter century later, after we have absorbed so many cinematic shocks, it retains its capacity to startle and discomfit. Indeed, in the entire Eastwood canon (including its many and often discussed violent passages), there is nothing that quite compares to its unexpectedness.

The school to which McBurney is conducted is located in a run-down, moss-enshrouded mansion. It soon becomes clear that something more than compassion compels Miss Farnsworth and her charges to succor this stranger. The women know that if one of the patrols that keep passing the school finds him he will be sent to Andersonville, the infamous prison camp, where, as a wounded man, his chances of survival would be almost nil, and they make much of this. But he is, as well, a little like the crow Amy keeps as a pet—a strange wild thing to be toyed with.

Despite McBurney's condition, and the unfailing politeness and gratitude he manifests in the early days of his recuperation, he is more dangerous than he seems. The first evidence of his true nature appears early, when, as Nellie (Mae Mercer), the black slave of this curious household, tends his wounds, he comes on to her. He stresses that they are both, in effect, prisoners and proposes an alliance that is implicitly sexual, overtly practical—a joint escape.

As Edward Gallafent suggests, one of the richnesses of the film lies in its sharp, but lightly sketched, awareness of class and social biases. The fact that McBurney is a mere corporal, not an officer, adds to his charm for these isolated, marginalized and declassed Southern belles, irrelevantly perusing lessons in French, deportment and Bible studies while a war rages on their doorstep. He is rather like the gentleman caller in Tennessee Williams's *The Glass Menagerie,* "a nice ordinary young man" (in the playwright's words), whose connection with the energetic practicalities of common life carries with it a promise of regeneration—the same promise, one might note, that Stanley Kowalski more dangerously offers in *A Streetcar Named Desire.*

This is a particularly potent lure to Edwina Dabney, who was played by the tragic Elizabeth Hartman. Soon to withdraw from her profession into reclusiveness (she committed suicide in 1987), she is described by Clint as "very, very fragile, a little frail bird"—the Laura–Blanche DuBois figure in this film. Shy, repressed, "nervous," she is awakened by the presence of a male figure, who precisely because he is wounded is less threatening to her than he would have been in a fully healthy state. He, in turn, feels safe around her, perhaps even drawn to her because of her apparent purity. As the film develops, so does a curiously ambiguous courtship. The possibility that he may genuinely care for her cannot be completely dismissed; neither can the possibility that he may merely be using her.

The oldest and prettiest of the school's students, Carol (Jo Ann Harris), sees him in a much less complicated way. She is all libidinal energy, to whom McBurney is simply the convenient, even heaven-sent, instrument of sexual initiation. He sees her as temptation and threat. In her beauty and obvious availability she is a male fantasy incarnate. But if he were to sleep with her and they were found out, his relationship with Edwina would be compromised, and he would have Miss Farnsworth's wrath to contend with. For he has recognized the headmistress as another kind of threat. A mature and, in some mysterious way, experienced woman, capable of recognizing masculine wiles and stratagems, there is beneath her genteel airs and graces a disturbing hint of darkness.

In these early passages there is an odd and dislocating quality in Clint's playing, an almost languid passivity broken by sudden outbursts of aggressiveness. It's as if the membrane of politesse he has drawn over himself is not strong enough to contain his thrusting male impatience. There is, as well, something animalistic in his presence. He is a creature at once compelled forward by instinctual drive and at the same time naturally wary of what may be a baited trap, which at the movie's turning point snaps shut on him.

One night, both Edwina and Miss Farnsworth have reason to anticipate a visit from him, but he is waylaid on the stairs by Carol and, at last, his caution deserts him. He goes with her, is discovered by Edwina, and when they struggle he is pushed down the stairs, rebreaking his leg. Upon examination, Miss Farnsworth declares that gangrene has set in and that the limb must be amputated. The movie remains deliberately ambiguous about the necessity for this operation. It is possible that she is telling the truth. It is more likely that she is having her revenge on him for not coming to her bed.

The operation, shot from an overhead angle, has the quality of a crucifixion (it is not the only Christian iconography Siegel alludes to in the movie). In Pingitore's first cut it ran some seven minutes and was, he recalls, too strong for most stomachs, even Siegel's. It is not easy to take even in its final version. In any case, when McBurney returns to consciousness he, at least, evinces not the ·slightest doubt about Miss Farnsworth's true motive. Now the wary animal becomes a raging beast. He attempts to rape Nellie; he invades Miss Farnsworth's room, discovers letters from her brother that reveal to him their incestuous relationship; he confronts her with her sin in front of the entire school.

She evades his charges, even turns them to her account—far from being corrupt, she makes the girls believe there was something beautiful (and asexual) in this relationship and reduces McBurney to impotent rage. Why, he cries, did she condemn him to the life of a cripple, why didn't she go all the way and castrate him? He announces his intention to "have my fill" of the women before leaving. In the course of this diatribe, he kills another of Amy's pets, a turtle, and though he is instantly remorseful, all—except Edwina—turn against him.

Now that he is completely broken, Edwina feels it is safe to give herself to him. After they make love they make plans to leave together. A false calm now settles over the old mansion, a polite supper is served and a seemingly contrite McBurney reverts to his old soft and mannerly ways. But, of course, Martha Farnsworth cannot rest easily while he is alive and in possession of her secret, and with the complicity of the others she serves him poisoned mushrooms and he dies. The movie ends with the women sewing a shroud for him.

★   ★   ★

The finished film justified both of Clint's initial responses to the material: It was a terrific movie, one of the most powerful and interesting films he ever made; and it was, indeed, a picture for which there was no appreciable audience. *The Beguiled* would be one of the few unambiguous flops of his career. It was impossible to place it in any convenient genre category, and it did not satisfy its star expectations, either. Actors like Clint may suffer endless abuse and indignities as long as they eventually explode in righteous wrath. If, however, at the end of a film they simply subside, their loyal followers feel shocked and cheated.

On the other hand, the film certainly permitted him to do more (or less, depending on your point of view) than merely "gun people down."

Clint has never been good at articulating his larger aspirations for a movie, so that a casual phrase must be understood to encompass more than it immediately implies. Indeed, if we accept the critic J. Hoberman's idea that Clint's most interesting films are bound together by their preoccupation with "the social construction of masculinity as mediated by superstardom," then that preoccupation must be dated from this film, which largely owed its existence to his passion for it.

With the rise of gender scholarship in the universities, *The Beguiled* has lately been read as an exercise in misogyny, an expression of male dread of the devouring female. Two academic writers, Paul Smith and Dennie Bingham, have made much of a remark by Siegel to Stuart Kaminsky, in which he echoed his comments to Maltz: "Women are capable of deceit, larceny, murder, anything. Behind that mask of innocence lurks just as much evil as you'll ever find in members of the Mafia. Any young girl, who looks perfectly harmless, is capable of murder."

It sounds, or can be made to sound, rather shocking. But in this instance one suspects the director should not be taken too literally. When he spoke to Kaminsky he was still smarting from the film's commercial failure, and, in any case, he had a tendency toward direct and uncomplicated statements, which was of a piece with his directorial manner. He was ever the brutally objective observer of the human condition.

Whether he was dealing with a prison riot, an alien invasion or dangerously denied sexuality, Siegel coolly respected the internal logic of his stories. If they brought us, eventually, to some outrageous place, we always had a sense of arriving there, as we often do when life brings us to some irrational corner, through a series of steps that are not in themselves particularly menacing. He didn't like to foreshadow and he didn't like to direct our sympathies one way or another. He was not about to play these women as victims any more than he was about to play McBurney as a poor lost soul.

But manner aside, isn't there something quite unexceptionable at the core of his argument? As modernists, as feminist sympathizers, aren't we obliged to accord women equality in evil as in all things? As realists, aren't we obliged to acknowledge the tension, verging at times on hatred, that exists between the sexes and is, indeed, the crux of much drama and fiction? In the particular case of *The Beguiled,* wouldn't it be more useful (and more accurate) to read it not as a narrowly misogynistic work, but as a broadly misanthropic one?

In fact, it balances its admittedly dark vision of femininity with an equally devastating portrayal of masculine nature. McBurney may have entered this female web through mischance, but he always imagines, in his male egotism, that he can escape full and fatal entrapment in it and, indeed, turn the misfortunes of war into good fortune. "You know," says Clint, "he's totally justifiable. What guy wouldn't try to save his life in a situation like that?" And then, "With seven girls hauling you around on a stretcher say, 'Hey, well, I'll grab a little nookie while I'm here, and who cares?'"

As a man who was himself used to taking his sexual pleasure when and where it presented itself (he had an affair with one of the women in this cast), Clint understood his character as entirely typical of his sex, succumbing "to what we all succumb to through life, which gets us all into trouble"—that is to blind, and in this case fatal, instinct. In that condition, "A man's brain has a way of lowering itself down out of the cranium, down into"—he pauses, searching not entirely successfully for a genteelism—"the lower extremities." Thus, as these women come to represent the male's darkest fantasies about the opposite sex, he comes to represent the female's darkest fantasies about the footloose and feckless male: at best, a casual user of her body and careless abuser of her trust; at worst, a cock of the walk to whom any woman is but the unearned entitlement of unearned status.

For him, then, this is, finally, the story of a fucker fucked, possibly even a projection of retributive fears he may have known. And its conclusion represents for him an ironic, unpleasant, but in no sense tragic, comeuppance, more final than those usually meted out to the sexually restless, but not different in spirit from them. This role, permitting him as an actor to be both more voluble and more overtly sexual than he had ever been before, also encouraged him to subvert not only his own image but the standard leading-man image common to most movies, blending it, if you will, with second-lead caddishness.

Still, without denying that *The Beguiled* presents a particularly vivid portrayal of a particularly deadly engagement in the war between the sexes, Clint offers another reading of it that is, so far as one can tell, unique to him. He suggests that the film is about the mysterious workings of blind faith. Rather surprisingly, he analogizes it to *Unforgiven*. In the later movie it is wildly exaggerated rumors of unspeakable violence visited on a woman that drive and justify Will Munny's mission of vengeance, a series of misapprehensions and mischances, their effects heightened by the violent, near-anarchic context in which they occur, that brings everyone to grief. Something similar, he argues, is going on here.

In normal times, Clint suggests, McBurney might not be a bad guy. He certainly would not be a guy whose goodness or badness, strengths and weaknesses, would ever seriously be tested by circumstances. Imagine him in peacetime as, say, an itinerant peddler taking refuge from a storm at Miss Farnsworth's place. He might or might not in such an instance find himself in bed with one of the ladies. But early the next morning he would move on, having created nothing more consequential than some sort of traveling-salesman joke. Or write the scenario from the women's point of view: In peacetime Miss Farnsworth and her charges would offer the beset traveler gracious, flirtatious "Southern hospitality," and if, perchance, something more than that innocent interchange occurred, it would be resolutely denied and, again, he would be waved off without regret.

But in this case such easy escapes are impossible. Because he is caught behind enemy lines his movements are restricted, and because the military situation is fluid, it is quite rational for the women to want to keep a man around the place and for him to stay put until he is rescued by his fellow Yankees. Having been thrown together by the combined workings of chance and megahistorical forces—by fate, in other words—they are then held together by them, in the process "bringing out the worst of himself and the worst of them, too."

To read this film in these broader terms is to give a fuller and more accurate account of it than the gender specialists, blinkered by narrow ideological concepts, are able to provide. It is also to place it more usefully in the larger context of Clint's career. Fate's workings are a topic that has always greatly interested him. So, obviously, do the tormented conflicts of men and women—it would seem more so at this time in his life than at any other—for his next film would take up and vary many of the themes explored in *The Beguiled.*

★ ★ ★

By now Malpaso was a fully functioning, if minuscule, independent production company. Sonia Chernus had come aboard as Clint's story editor, charged with finding material he could develop on his own, and on February 1, 1970, Robert Daley, his old pal from Arch Drive, came to work for the company as its staff producer. He had by this time gained much valuable experience—at Ziv in its declining days, as head of production at Desilu, the TV-production concern founded by Desi Arnaz and Lucille Ball, then as coproducer of the *Doris Day Show.*

Daley's first task, which he began working on as *The Beguiled* finished shooting, was to prepare *Play Misty for Me,* scheduled to shoot in the late summer and early fall in Carmel. This project had a long history. The original story had been written some years earlier by Jo Heims, a tiny one-time legal secretary whom Clint had known since his apprentice days. They had never had a romantic relationship, but they had shared aspirations; she was as eager to succeed as a screenwriter as he was to succeed as an actor. Clint responded strongly to her sixty-page treatment of a story about a disc jockey who enters into a casual affair with one of his fans, only to discover that she is far from casual about it, turning into a violent stalker when he tries to end their relationship.

He saw in it a more melodramatic version of the woman in his days at Fort Ord who would not let go when he tried to end their affair. In the years since he had heard many similar stories, from both sexes, and he came to believe that obsessions of this kind were more common than most people acknowledged. So he took an option on Heims's story for a couple thousand dollars, and flogged it unsuccessfully around town. "I was still the kid from Europe. I didn't have quite enough juice to pull it off." While he was working on *Where Eagles Dare,* Heims contacted him, reporting an offer from Universal, and he, looking at his heavily booked immediate future, gave her permission to make the deal.

But the script lingered in his mind, and at a meeting with Jennings Lang he brought up *Misty:* "There's this little property you've got, this story I'd like to do. It's an odd little story about a disc jockey." Clint was shown an unsatisfactory script that the studio had developed. He decided to go back to the original, working a little bit with Heims on a new draft, then bringing in the ever-useful Dean Riesner, who did a thorough polish and eventually shared screen credit with Heims. Clint says that his own largest contribution to the writing involved the character he wanted to play. He knew a disc jockey not unlike the Dave Garland of this film—"a big fish in a small pond," a little too casually enjoying the perquisites of local celebrity—and wanted Dave to have something of this man's sleepy egotism.

When the script was more or less to his liking, he went back to Lang and Lew Wasserman, the head of the studio, who remained dubious. "Why would you want to play a disc jockey, and why would anybody want to see Clint Eastwood play a disc jockey?" he remembers them asking. And also: "Why would you want to play in a picture where the woman has the best role?" His reply was "I don't know, why does anybody want to see anything? But it's a good suspense piece."

By this time Clint was fairly certain he wanted to make his directorial debut with this film. It was an ideal piece to break in with, small in scale, technically quite manageable, yet with a suspenseful narrative that would sustain an audience's interest even if the director nodded here and there. Moreover, it occurred to Clint that since the script had always been set in a small city, that city might as well be Monterey and the rest of the extremely photogenic, extremely familiar peninsula he called home. He told the Universal executives that he would shoot every scene on location, sparing them the cost of set construction. His final argument was the simplest, and probably the most telling. He told his studio bosses, "I'm gonna do it for zip."

At the time, Daley says, the International Alliance of Theatrical Stage Employees (IATSE), the union to which most movie craftspeople belong, had a lower pay scale for members working on productions budgeted at less than a million dollars, and Clint knew he could bring the picture in for less than that—if he worked for Screen Actors Guild and Directors Guild minimums. Clint remembers Lenny Hirshan quietly but urgently signaling him to shut up as he started to make this offer to the shrewd and frugal Wasserman.

"I know exactly what they were saying behind my back," Clint later told an interviewer. "We'll let the kid fool around with it. He'll do that and then he'll probably do a couple of westerns for us, or some other adventure-type film that will seem more commercial at the outset." But he didn't care; he was about to make the first movie that he had discovered and nurtured from its beginnings.

Clint began rounding up a crew he was comfortable with, signing Surtees as director of photography and Pingitore as editor. When he talked to the latter he asked the editor if he had any tips for him. "Do you need the money?" asked Pingitore. No, said Clint. "Then go have fun, enjoy yourself. If I see something wrong [in the dailies] I'll let you know." Don Siegel, who along with Clint's old *Rawhide* colleague Christian Nyby, endorsed his Directors Guild of America membership application, advised him simply to be sure he got plenty of sleep, the primary requisite for directing being, in his view, unflagging energy. Clint asked Siegel to take a small part in the picture as a bartender. He wanted him around, Clint said, in case he needed advice, but his presence on the set was primarily talismanic.

Casting appears not to have been difficult. Jessica Walter, who played the psychotic Evelyn so memorably, remembers hearing that the studio was urging him to cast a star, somebody on the level of Lee Remick, in the part, but Clint ran *The Group*, the 1966 adaptation of the Mary McCarthy novel, which featured eight actresses who were then relatively unknown, and noticed Walter as Libby "with the big red scar for a mouth." She wasn't quite certifiable, "but she was on the edge, this woman," as Walter describes her, and seeing something of the quality he was looking for Clint asked Walter to come in for an interview.

She remembers liking the script, spotting a problem with it, but resolving not to say anything about it at their meeting. She had not, at that time, seen a Clint Eastwood movie, and she was, she says, "shaking in her boots" when she met "this big hot star" in his bungalow office at

Universal. But "he was so kind and laid-back," and when it became clear
to her that he was not going to ask her to read (he never does, since he
assumes that if he likes someone's work there is no further need to prove
professionalism), she permitted herself to be "bowled over" by him, the
first in that long, unbroken line of performers who have succumbed to
this director's punctilious regard for their needs and feelings.

He poured her some carrot juice, which she forced herself to drink,
took her for a little stroll around the lot and solicited her opinion about
the script. Thus encouraged, she offered her one criticism, of a prologue
that showed her character in an insane asylum. She thought it robbed the
movie of surprise. The sequence was never shot. They also discussed a
point that worried him: The script never showed where Evelyn lived,
and it never gave her a working life. He wondered if both those matters
should be addressed briefly. Walter thought not; lack of such information would give her character more mystery and menace. Again, ultimately, he agreed with her.

He cast Donna Mills in the other leading female role, that of Tobie,
the girlfriend from whom his Dave Garland is estranged when he meets
Evelyn—fear of commitment, naturally. This was on the recommendation of his pal Burt Reynolds, who knew her and told Clint to watch
her on the soap opera on which she was then working.

Then, taking Siegel's advice about getting plenty of rest, he decided
to take a vacation before starting work, and with Maggie and little Kyle
repaired to a rented house on Lake Tahoe, where his contentment was
brutally interrupted. Earlier in the year Clinton Eastwood Sr. had suffered a mild dizzy spell while he was hiking with Clint's mother during
a vacation in Hawaii. He checked in with his doctor on their return but
was assured that tests showed nothing seriously wrong. There had been
no alarm in the family. But on July 22, 1970, Ruth Eastwood called
Clint to tell him that his father had died suddenly of a heart attack. He
was only sixty-three years old.

His sometime friend Fritz Manes, who with his wife was visiting the
Eastwoods at the time, thinks this was a major turning point for Clint.
"He's had a lot of bad disappointments—we all have—but the major
impact in Clint Eastwood's life was losing his dad." He also suggests that
Clint's emphasis on fitness now intensified.

Clint disagrees. Yes, of course, his father's death "hit me like a load
of bricks," and, yes, he may have felt a degree of anger about it, thinking his father had been careless about diet and exercise, perhaps lulled
into a false sense of security because his own father had lived into his
nineties. And, yes, maybe Clint did devote himself a little more rigorously to his own fitness regimens thereafter (though it is hard to think

there was much more that he could do). But he says that his prevailing emotion at the time was regret over lost opportunities. He wished now that he had found more time for his dad in his later years, had exchanged more thoughts and feelings with him. He also rejects Manes's contention that he went into a particularly long period of seclusion after his dad's passing. Work, as the commonplace holds, being one of grief's best anodynes, Clint returned to preparations for *Misty* after no more than a couple of weeks of mourning.

On the eve of the first day's shooting, indeed, he remembers retiring in a confident mood. The neophyte director could think of nothing he had left undone. A moment later he was bolt upright, groping for the light switch. He was in the first scene, and focusing on his new job, he had entirely forgotten to memorize his lines.

The film was shot in sequence, so the first day's work was in the barroom where Dave Garland and Evelyn Draper pick each other up while Siegel, in his bartender role, watches benignly. Clint immediately demonstrated what would become one of his trademarks as a director, his dislike of lengthy rehearsals. This, as it happened, suited Walter; she doesn't like them either. Siegel, though, found himself unexpectedly uncomfortable in front of the camera. But he got through it all right and afterward he and Clint went out for some beers, with Clint later recounting their conversation this way:

"He said, 'You seem to have it under control.' I said, 'Well, I feel like everything's going all right.' He said, 'So, I'm going to head on out.' And I said, 'Okay. Head on out. I loved having you here.'"

Clint had learned his lessons from Siegel very well. "I didn't know what he was like inside," Walter told a reporter as the picture went into release the following year, "but he had this wonderful calm strength that was very reassuring." His main concern, as it always would be, was establishing an atmosphere in which, without pressure, he and the other actors could find and develop their characters. On his way to work, Walter remembers, Clint would stop by her house in the morning and quietly leave a bottle of dairy-fresh milk on her front porch. More important, he made her feel "like you're the only person who could possibly do the role, and whatever you do, it's gonna be gold."

In her case, it was. In outward manner she thought Evelyn should be "apple pie," neat and well groomed and the kind of woman who, when she appears at Dave's door wearing a fur coat and reveals that she has nothing on underneath, still asks if she can come in for a Coke. Beneath the cool surface was both need and rage. The need, as Walter sees it, was "real simple—she had to have this man or die. I don't think that's so hard to understand." Clint's performance, conversely, went well beyond laid-back. His Dave Garland is, until threatened, like some well-favored high-school jock basking in self-regard, divinely comfortable in his own handsome skin, happy with his local celebrity and its entitlements, which include having the prettiest girl in his class on his arm and the right to hit on her peers as well.

There is unquestionably a kinship between Dave and John McBurney. They are both in their way rather smug male animals. The difference between them is that Dave thinks he has already found an Eden, while McBurney is still looking. This makes for a contrasting development of the two figures. McBurney is wary when we meet him, then disarmed by circumstances he is sure he can master, and never really knows fear—except, perhaps, at the last moment before death. Dave Garland, in contrast, is utterly without wariness at the outset and comes to know fear intimately and extensively.

Clint was unquestionably drawing on something of himself for this role, too. Like Dave, like any man who has known many women, the quality, and especially the staying power, of his feelings for them remain open to question. Something Susan Clark, his *Coogan's Bluff* costar, said about Clint rings true, at least at this time in his life: "Part of his sex appeal is the constant mystery," she said. "How deeply does he feel? How deeply is he involved in life?"

That matter was certainly open for inspection in this performance. His response to Evelyn's escalating possessiveness is slow and dim precisely because that emotion is as unimaginable to him as it is to Clint (recall his repeated public insistence that his own wife was entitled to the same freedom of movement that he enjoyed). Conversely, we understand that his withholding nature, his "mystery," is one of the things driving poor Evelyn crazy. Initially alluring—we are all inclined to believe that our true love is the key that will finally unlock a withdrawn lover's secret heart—it ultimately maddens even people whose sanity is less delicately poised than hers.

No less than in *The Beguiled,* he was offering a significant commentary on two of modern masculinity's driving forces—its fear of entrapment by, and its need for mastery over, the female—acting out, if you will, the very bill of particulars repeatedly read out against men in formal feminist writing, in informal female conversation. Both of these traits are expressions of a larger one, namely self-absorption.

The basic trick of movie stardom consists of denying this (very hard for most actors to do), while conforming to the notion that fulfillment requires transforming romantic involvement with another. But in both these movies Clint dispenses with that fiction. There is no boyish vulnerability waiting to be discovered beneath these self-reflexive surfaces, no subtle plea for sympathy, which is the signal most male movie stars send out. The passages in which Dave tries to show such needs to Tobie are, in comparison to the scenes with Evelyn, perfunctory.

The film has other flaws, notably those longueurs that are fairly typical of a first-time director. There is a long alfresco romantic passage, culminating in skinny-dipping and lovemaking between Dave and Tobie, that is both too lyrical and too languid in its pace. Driving into work one morning Clint happened to hear on the radio a recording of "The First Time Ever I Saw Your Face" by Roberta Flack and fell in love with it. The record was out of print by that time, but he found a copy of it in a cutout bin somewhere, brought it in and insisted that it be used to underscore this sequence. Unfortunately, the piece ran something like four minutes, Pingitore could not find a way to shorten it (and was not much encouraged by the director to do so), and so the sequence was extended beyond its worth. The same thing happened with a sequence Clint shot at the Monterey Jazz Festival; he fell in love with the music and let it run on. Here, at Jennings Lang's insistence, cuts were made, which Clint grudgingly accepted.

According to Pingitore, a certain amount of tension developed between Lang and Clint in postproduction. The picture, he recalls, was owned fifty-fifty by the studio and Malpaso, and "they were like the cattlemen and the sheepmen" disputing turf. "Someone should have had fifty-one percent," he says. These squabbles, relatively minor and apparently creating no permanent rancor between Clint and Lang, nevertheless predicted larger disagreements with the studio.

★　★　★

These problems began early in 1971 as *The Beguiled* was being readied for release. It was obvious to Clint that it required special handling, which Universal had no capacity to provide. "If you had a couple of names and a formula, a middle-of-the-road project," the studio was competent to handle it, he says, but "they didn't know how to do anything with something unusual." This was particularly frustrating to him, because Clint was in contact with two men who had much grander ideas about promoting it, Pierre Rissient and Bertrand Tavernier, French cineasts whose public relations firm in Paris specialized in promoting the work of foreign filmmakers. The former had worked as an assistant to such directors as Jean-Luc Godard; the latter had written extensively for journals like *Cahiers du Cinéma* and *Positif* and had directed some features. Their backgrounds gave them credentials with the critical press that other publicists lacked.

They particularly revered a number of older American directors whose work these influential publications had championed, and their work for them was a significant factor in extending beyond cult circles the critical recognition of auteurs like Howard Hawks, John Ford and Raoul Walsh. They were also enthusiasts for younger directors carrying on this tradition—Sam Fuller, Budd Boetticher, Sam Peckinpah and Don Siegel. It is not too much to say that in the period from 1965 to 1972 Rissient and Tavernier were crucial figures in sending the revisionist word on all these directors out from France to their cinematic co-religionists elsewhere, and from there into general cultural circulation.

Rissient knew Clint's work from the Leone pictures, and sometime in the late sixties they met for the first time at the Universal commissary. Later, when *Two Mules for Sister Sara* opened in Paris, he helped promote it, and he recalls a lunch meeting there with Jennings Lang and Clint where, warmed by Lang's bonhomie, Clint was apparently more outgoing than he had been on their previous meeting. Rissient found himself "very, very surprised by his sense of humor. He could be quite nice, or sarcastic, and also you could make a joke and he would be very fast, you know, to catch it."

Rissient, a large, bald, passionate figure, who seems always to be dressed in a loud, open-necked sport shirt that he does not tuck into his pants (it was his garb at the Academy Awards ceremony at which Clint won his best director and best picture Oscars for *Unforgiven*), took Clint's work, first as an actor, then as a director, to heart, and their relationship has persisted for close to a quarter century. In the time since he and Tavernier closed their office (so the latter could return to directing), Rissient has become a benign, if slightly mysterious, figure, working the international festivals and cinematheques, discovering new filmmakers, promoting his old favorites, Clint among them.

When he saw *The Beguiled* he thought it Siegel's "best film," and proposed a showing at the Cannes Film Festival in the spring of 1971— either in or out of competition, whichever he could manage. This would cost a little money, and it would mean delaying the movie's release date, scheduled for early April, until after the festival, but Clint loved the idea. He craved this kind of recognition, and it was just what he thought the movie needed to establish itself with reviewers.

He took the idea to Lew Wasserman and was turned down. "Absolutely not," he remembers Wasserman saying. "I won't put any money in that. I won't get involved in that." The mogul had something of the old studio arrogance about him; he and his executives always knew best: Their collective wisdom always had to take precedence over the whims of mere "talent." "I didn't know how to overcome that," Clint says, "the infighting and so on." But it surely shadowed his hope of making inexpensive, somewhat offbeat movies requiring hand-tailored marketing and distribution.

The way *The Beguiled* was handled justified this anxiety: "They did no promotion, they just let it escape." Escape, as it were, under false pretenses—such campaign as the studio mounted suggested that the film was some kind of Civil War military drama. In Universal's defense it might be argued that, quirky as the picture was, it is hard to imagine what sort of campaign might have worked for it.

This was a point Vincent Canby stressed in his *New York Times* review. It had, he wrote, no natural audience: It was not for action fans, not for horror cultists, since it lacked any element of the uncanny, not for general audiences, since it was so grisly. Its "very fancy, outrageous fantasizing" (he particularly mentioned a three-way sexual encounter Miss Farnsworth imagines between herself, McBurney and Edwina), he guessed, would "strike horror in the hearts of those Siegel fans who've made a cult of his objectivity," while "people who consider themselves discriminating moviegoers, but who are uncommitted to Mr. Siegel, will be hard put to accept" what he thought were improbable twists of plot and characterization. The upper-crust movie audience tended to tolerate odd blends of terror and erotica only when they carried a certain European cachet, as, for example, *Repulsion* had. (Canby also said Clint "simply by reacting well has become an important actor of movies.")

Some of the other reviewers were more enthusiastic. *Time*'s Jay Cocks offered a brief, sophisticated appreciation of Siegel's style and called it "the most scarifying film since Rosemary birthed her satanic baby." In Los Angeles, Kevin Thomas of the *Times* said that the "fortuitous collaboration" between Siegel and Eastwood "reached fulfillment" in a film that was "a triumph of style, totally engrossing and utterly convincing." These were representative of the best overall set of notices an Eastwood picture had yet received.

It's doubtful that a Cannes showing would have improved *The Beguiled*'s reviews or its box-office takings. But it would have improved Clint's relationship with the studio, which was now, on his part, a wary one, and soon to deteriorate further. For the release of *Play Misty for Me* in the fall of 1971 was also uninspired. "They had a brilliant preview of it in San Jose," he recalls. "People were just screaming out of their seats," but this response meant nothing to the marketing department. They "still didn't handle it—they just kind of let it out." At the time Clint was retaining Warren Cowan, the legendary Hollywood publicist, to help him compensate for the studio's inattention, and he asked Cowan what

he should do. "I said, 'Let me add two words to the title,'" the press
agent later recalled. "He said, 'What words?' and I said, 'Alfred Hitchcock's. . . .'"

"A good little scare show," Jay Cocks called it, and that was about as
good as it got for *Play Misty for Me. Newsweek*'s Paul Zimmerman criticized Clint for an inability to "discriminate between the really good
stuff and the draggy scenes that kill the suspense." Roger Greenspun was
particularly harsh. Clint, he said, had made "too many easy decisions
about events, about the management of atmosphere, about the treatment of performance—including the rather inexpressive one of Clint
Eastwood . . . who is asked to bear more witness to a quality of inwardness than his better directors have yet had the temerity to ask of him."

That he was actually not trying to play inwardness, but rather self-
absorption (quite a different matter), did not occur to this reviewer. Like
his colleagues, the film put him somewhat at a loss. If you could not
fairly compare *Play Misty for Me* to a Hitchcock film—though it certainly did invoke one of Hitchcock's major themes, the intrusion of violently irrational disorder on a serenely untroubled universe—what
could you compare it to? We can now see, to films as yet unmade. For
some of the major elements of future Eastwood movies—their directness of address, their plainspoken psychological realism—are present in
this movie's best passages.

Obviously, no one could see that at the time, any more than they
could see *Fatal Attraction* sixteen years in the future. Yet when that
mighty, trashy hit appeared in 1987, critics eagerly pointed out its debt
to *Misty;* interestingly, it was the *only* source they could cite. This, in
turn, suggests what should have been obvious at the time: that this was
a highly original movie, one that in its central role reversal duplicated no
previous film and proved itself to be unduplicable without risking suggestions of plagiarism.

This the public seemed to acknowledge. For despite Universal's
lackluster distribution and the general critical dimness about it, *Play
Misty for Me* did quite decent business. This was both a vindication and
a disappointment; it did better than the studio brass had predicted, not
nearly as well as its star and director thought it could. Clint remembers
getting a call from the manager of the cavernous Cineramadome in
Hollywood, where the picture was succeeding despite its inappropriate
venue, begging him to intercede with the studio. It was insisting on
pulling the movie in favor of a good, but ill-fated, family movie. "Can
you do something about that?" the man asked. "The audience just keeps
coming." Clint got a similar report from the owner of a large chain of
California theaters. He, too, was under pressure to replace *Misty* with

newer products and wanted to keep the film on his screens. In both cases Clint says his pleas were contemptuously dismissed.

Finally, despite its travails, *Play Misty for Me* returned something over $5 million in domestic rentals, and counting its overseas, television and home video sales, at least doubled that amount eventually, which meant that Malpaso's back-end percentage probably exceeded what Clint's normal salary might have been. In other words, he had won his gamble. And, in a sense, Universal lost it.

In Lenny Hirshan's view, the studio simply did not understand how deep Clint's commitment to his films runs. "Do you have the right theaters? Is your ad campaign right? Are you spending enough on television? Are you supporting the picture—all that kind of stuff" interests him profoundly. He was not yet ready for a full-scale mutiny over these matters, but he was restless. And, at this moment, a project he had been tracking for some time, one that had eluded him twice before, suddenly presented itself again under the auspices of an old and highly trusted friend now working for a rival studio. He accepted it immediately. If it did not completely change his life, it unquestionably altered forever his status in his profession, and in the larger world beyond it.

NINE

SHADY HABITS, ARCHAIC RESPONSES

It was Jennings Lang who first brought *Dirty Harry* to Clint's attention, at least two years before it went into production. At the time Universal controlled the original screenplay by the husband-and-wife writing team of Harry Julian Fink and R. M. Fink and had, Lang said, offered it to Paul Newman, who turned it down on political grounds. "Well, I don't have any political affiliations," Clint said, "so send it over."

He quickly saw what Newman was talking about, which was what everyone would be talking about once the movie was released: the attitude the script took toward the constitutional rights of accused criminals. At this time, a few years after the Supreme Court's rulings in the *Escobedo* and *Miranda* cases, this was one of the issues by which Americans were defining themselves politically. Clint saw problems of narrative and characterization in the script as well. But he also saw in this story of a big-city police detective engaged in a deadly duel with a psychopathic serial killer the potential for a riveting movie. And he saw in that cop, Dirty Harry Callahan, a character who was uncannily right for him. He says he would have wanted to play him if he had been a Fourth Amendment absolutist.

Harry was not, in this early draft, quite the man he would become, but he was cool in crisis, hot in his anger at the vicious criminal he pursues—and in his contempt for the clueless municipal bureaucracy that frequently muddles that pursuit. Clearly a working-class guy, there was much class resentment in the rage Harry directed at his deskbound superiors, interested primarily in covering their asses while preventing him from doing his duty. To put it mildly, these were feelings Clint knew well but had never explored in a role. Moreover, he discerned "a sadness about him, about his personal life," that he had not touched in his work either.

But somehow the script slipped away from Universal—going first to ABC's film unit, then to Warner Bros., which is when Clint heard about it again. That studio, in decline throughout the sixties, was acquired in 1969 by Steve Ross's Kinney National Service Company, a conglomerate soon renamed Warner Communications. This signified Ross's commitment to reviving what was for him the most glamorous of his holdings. So did his appointment of a new management team headed by Ted Ashley, a powerful agent, with able, eccentric John Calley as head of production, and Frank Wells, who had been Clint's close friend and attorney for many years, as head of business affairs (and, ultimately, studio president). It was Wells who called Clint, just as he was beginning work on *Play Misty for Me,* to ask him if he was still interested in *Dirty Harry.*

He was, but could not commit to it until he had finished *Misty.* Wells said he couldn't wait. When it took over the studio, the Ashley regime had written down some $60 million worth of the previous management's projects and even now, two years later, remained desperate for product. Besides, cop pictures—especially ones featuring roguish protagonists—were hot just then, and Warner Bros. was eager to partake of the heat. Siegel's *Madigan* (which has several points of comparison with *Dirty Harry*), *Coogan's Bluff, The Detective* and *Bullitt* had all been successful, and *The French Connection,* destined to be the biggest of them all, was going into production. This interest doubtless had something to do with the "law-and-order" furor of the Nixon years, but it also had to do with filling a gap. For two great traditional (and psychologically related) pop figures, the westerner and the private eye, had all but disappeared from the screen—the former at best the subject of elegies, the latter largely ignored. There was a need to find a contemporary place for hard loners—traditional males, if you will—to live plausibly. And the most readily available wilderness, the concrete wilderness, suddenly seemed more interesting and dangerous than ever—"crime in the streets" being the operative catch phrase in this respect.

Thus it was that the trades announced, in the fall of 1970, that Frank Sinatra, who had been one of Ted Ashley's agency clients and the star of *The Detective,* had been signed for the film. It was now retitled *Dead Right,* and Irvin Kershner was set to produce and direct it. In November, however, Sinatra withdrew from the picture; it was said he had hurt his hand in an accident and could not start the picture on schedule.

By this time, Clint was available. But when Wells called to re-offer him the project, he had to admit that the script had changed several times since his former client had last seen it. Clint asked Wells to send over whatever he had, and shortly thereafter "a whole mess of scripts" arrived at his office, "first drafts of this and that." He didn't like any of them, but sought second opinions from Robert Daley and Don Siegel, who felt the Finks' script offered the only worthwhile possibilities. Clint remembers advising Wells to "just keep those other scripts and do them under other titles," so remote were they from the story he wanted to tell.

Everyone agreed the script still needed revisions. Clint asked Siegel if he would work with a writer on a revision of the Finks' script with an eye to directing the film in the early summer of 1971. Siegel proposed Dean Riesner, but said he was not sure he was himself free to work on the project; his contract with Universal did not permit him to undertake outside assignments. Clint said he would speak to Lew Wasserman, and quickly secured Siegel's release.

The first question director, writer and star addressed was locale. The Finks' story had been set in New York, but Siegel, having done two *policiers* there recently, did not want to return so soon. Seattle seemed a fresh possibility, but one Sunday in December, Clint and Siegel both happened to catch the TV broadcast of the last football game the San Francisco 49ers played in antique Kezar Stadium, and it suggested the same idea to them: An abandoned stadium would be the perfect lair for their killer, an empty, floodlit football field the perfect arena for a violent confrontation between detective and prey. Siegel liked San Francisco; he had used it effectively in *The Lineup,* also a story about murderous stalkings, twelve years earlier. And so they visited San Francisco, where they were assured they would be able to shoot in the stadium before demolition began and convinced themselves they could offer a view of the city different from that of *Bullitt,* which had recently offered a highly picturesque vision of it. They looked no farther.

Riesner and Siegel worked on the script for six or seven weeks, making their largest contributions to its last third, excising an ending in which the psycho attempts to hijack an airplane, replacing it with a simpler and more powerful sequence in which he abducts a school bus full of terrified children. Clint recalls that in the first draft Harry was older and wearier, therefore warier with his tongue because he was closer to retirement. He says that for a time he considered aging himself somewhat for the part, but that idea disappeared as the new draft took shape.

This went smoothly enough, though Siegel (who "always needed an opponent," as Clint later put it, "either the studio or a producer") at one point threatened to quit when John Calley sent him a memo comparing scene by scene the Riesner and Fink scripts, to the advantage of the latter. Siegel claimed that it required Clint's intervention to back the production chief off. It's hard to determine now who is responsible for what in the final screenplay, on which all three writers shared credit, but Clint disputes the claim to authorship that John Milius, then early in his curious career as an unabashed macho-anarchist gun nut (and one of the few truly interesting modern Hollywood characters), has advanced. Milius wrote one of the drafts Kershner worked on (he insisted on part of his pay being a new Purdy shotgun and refused to start work until it was delivered) but Clint says that, at most, "we might have taken a few good items John had in there."

★   ★   ★

Given a seven- or eight-week schedule that, as Clint says "seemed like an eternity" in comparison to the B-picture timetables he was used to, Siegel responded with a craftsmanship and conviction unusual even for him. This powered the film beyond its humble genre origins to blockbuster status, making it the largest and most immediate commercial success its star had so far experienced. That, in turn, had a transformative effect on Clint's career, finally, indelibly incising his image on the moviegoing mind, and also making him instantly, iconographically, identifiable even to people who don't go to the movies much.

For all its clarity, this image was at the time, and for many years thereafter, subject to radically contradictory readings, so much so that the conflict over its meaning became the central issue of Clint Eastwood's public life. That he did not intend this to happen, that much of what was darkly inferred about Dirty Harry Callahan and the actor who played him was based on the shakiest of suppositions, not to mention certain overheated political metaphors of the moment, does not diminish the force of this controversy or the persistence of its afterlife.

In order to understand this phenomenon it is necessary to disentangle the several strands of which it is composed—the movie and the character Clint played in it as both were intended, how they were perceived by the huge audience that responded so hungrily to them and how they were understood by that influential minority of one, Pauline Kael, whose curious review of the film caused a sensation in politically fastidious circles at the time and continued for a long time to condition all subsequent responses to the film and, to a degree, Clint's career.

The movie is not complex structurally; it simply recounts a duel to the death between a psychopathic serial killer, who calls himself Scorpio and chooses his victims at random, and Clint's professionally disaffected yet increasingly obsessive Harry Callahan. Caught between them are the police and municipal hierarchies, who are inclined to pay Scorpio the ransom he demands to cease his depredations and equally inclined to ignore Callahan's instincts, which tell him that this is a criminal who cannot be bought off. Eventually we will see that hunter and prey are virtually doubles, with only the thinnest margin of sanity separating them.

The film's first act is largely devoted to establishing Callahan's character, situating him in his milieu and enlisting our sympathy for him. In this passage Scorpio is seen as no more than an increasingly menacing shadow, albeit a perversely intelligent one. Callahan, on the other hand, is richly drawn as a kind of classic American knothead-hothead, ever at odds with conventional wisdom, for that matter conventional good manners, yet cunning and dedicated and therefore invaluable to the powers he serves. He is very funny in his brutally frank way, and very busy. This opening act, essentially a succession of short, punched-up confrontations, both verbal and physical, intersperses scenes showing Harry in rebellious confrontation with his bosses with action sequences in which he foils an attempted bank robbery and an attempted suicide, engages in a spectacular rooftop gun battle with Scorpio and gets himself comically mistaken for a Peeping Tom. The idea, of course, is to show the hectic pressures of a cop's working life and to establish the fact that in the heat of the action a policeman does not always have the luxury of consulting the rule book.

In the second act the mood darkens, and the tension ratchets up. For now Scorpio announces that he has abducted a fourteen-year-old girl and buried her alive, with an air supply sufficient to sustain her for only five hours. He will provide information about her whereabouts in exchange for $200,000. From his messages it is clear that he has raped and tortured the girl. Harry is charged with delivering the ransom, Scorpio engages him in a long, cruel chase, in the course of which Harry's partner is almost killed, and Harry and Scorpio at last confront—and wound—one another. The latter escapes, but Harry tracks him to his Kezar Stadium hideout and in the center of its floodlit gridiron beats out of him information about where he has hidden his victim. She is, however, dead when the police arrive.

The film's last act begins with Harry being reprimanded for his failure to respect Scorpio's civil rights and learning that the criminal has been released from custody because of this failure. Harry's argument that a girl's life was at stake and that there was no time for legal niceties is contemptuously dismissed. Now, astonishingly, Scorpio hires another criminal to beat him up, painfully manufacturing evidence for the charge of police brutality he brings against Harry.

Thereafter, still seeking a payoff from the city, Scorpio proceeds to the school-bus hijacking, offering to exchange the lives of its passengers for money and safe conduct out of the country. Harry, again against orders, drops off an overpass onto the roof of the careening vehicle, which comes to a crashing halt at a gravel pit. There, at last, he corners and kills Scorpio, and throws away his badge in what turned out to be—considering the four sequels that were to come—not quite the definitive gesture of disgust it seemed to be at the time.

This outline reveals the essence of the film's appeal to its basic, action-oriented audience, with even Kael forced to concede that it was "a stunningly well-made genre piece." As such it could not be said to encourage—putting this point as ironically as possible—a nuanced contemplation of the legal issue it raises.

One must also say that nothing in the movie can fairly be construed as "fascist"—the word Kael so sensationally used to characterize it. On the contrary, it is clear that the filmmakers, knowing they were taking a strong position on a controversial issue, were at pains to limit their argument, to make certain nothing in the film could be read as an endorsement of racism or any other kind of reactionary thuggery. It is not too much to say that *Dirty Harry* is a movie about extenuating circumstances, an exploration of all the factors—political, sociological, psychological— that bring Callahan to the particular, and very possibly defensible, dirtiness that so exercised Kael and those who have followed her.

★   ★   ★

Begin at the beginning, with the brilliantly efficient sequence that establishes Harry's character—the only one, incidentally, that was shot on the back lot. Callahan is discovered at a lunch counter, ordering a hot dog. His dialogue with the counterman makes it clear that he is a regular customer for both lunch and dinner, which also suggests that Harry does not have much of a life outside his job. That he is excellent at that job becomes obvious in a matter of seconds. Something going on at a bank across the street alerts him. He orders the counterman to call a police number and report a suspected robbery in progress, then ambles out into the street, still chewing on his hot dog (an homage, perhaps to the great Cagney scene in *White Heat* in which he continues to gnaw a chicken leg while blasting away a prisoner he has sequestered in the trunk of a car).

Now a getaway car careens up the street, and Harry draws and fires, nailing its driver. Harry also exchanges shots with another criminal, each of them suffering minor wounds. But his opponent, a black man, is knocked to the sidewalk in front of the bank. Harry strolls over to him, his enormous gun—the soon-to-be-immortal .44 Magnum—casually in hand. The criminal's gun is on the sidewalk within lurching reach, if he has the nerve to go for it. There is a silent exchange of glances that also contains an exchange of complete, almost brotherly, understanding between two violent men. Then, in an up-angle, comes the most famous, and probably the most important, speech Clint Eastwood ever uttered on film: "Ah, ah, I know what you're thinkin'—did he fire six shots or only five?" he says, speaking in his softest, most reasonable tone. "Well, to tell you the truth in all this excitement I've kinda lost track myself. But being this is a .44 Magnum, the most powerful handgun in the world, and would blow your head clean off, you gotta ask yourself one question: Do I feel lucky?" He pauses, offering a sweet, almost boyish, smile: "Well do you, punk?"

The criminal, who is not a young man, and has a rather resigned air about him, looks again at his gun, at Harry, then subsides. Harry grins, grabs the other man's weapon and turns away as sirens announce the arrival of more cops. But the criminal, his bond with Harry established, speaks again: "I gots to know." Harry allows himself another understanding half smile, levels his gun at the perp—there is a close-up of a sweating face, alarmed eyes—and we hear a trigger click on an empty chamber.

This was for Clint, and for the picture, *the* transformative moment. His career undoubtedly would have continued successfully enough without it, and the movie would have done well enough without it. But this vivid passage, so rich in telling detail, cleanly, clearly summarized what Clint had been trying to say with his screen character in his previous films. And it summarized this specific character before we were entirely certain of his name. Suddenly, we knew them both—"Clint Eastwood" and "Dirty Harry Callahan"—and liked them both, liked them because however preternatural the cunning and bravery they projected, they seemed to operate out of pissed-off premises we shared, but with a coolness and humor under pressure we could only wish for. In these few moments a star established his superstardom.

Think a little bit more about this sequence. Start with Harry's costume, notably his battered sports jacket with the leather patches on its sleeves. This is not a jacket that has seen better days; it has never *had* any better days. It is just something he picked up off some inexpensive peg. Consider, too, his amble into deadly action. It's not reluctant, but it's not eager, either. He's a man reporting for overtime, which he could do without, but has long since learned is inescapable. Think, too, about his nonstandard weapon. It's like a tool a workman has bought for himself, having learned the equipment supplied by the company (and chosen by bean counters) is not always adequate to the exigencies of fieldwork. He may even know it's kind of silly looking—this hard-on of a gun—but he doesn't give any more of a damn about that than he does about the rest of his attire.

It is also important to take into account Harry's attitude toward his antagonist (Albert Popwell). Yes, he's a black man and a criminal. But Harry accepts that quite neutrally. If blacks compose a significant element of the modern urban underclass, it stands to reason that they must compose a significant element of the criminal class, too. That's just the way things are. He treats the man as a fellow professional—well, all right, a fellow craftsman, since neither cop nor crook (nor, come to think of it, actor) is an occupation calling for board certification. They are jobs you pretty much learn by doing. Finally, consider Harry's feigned confusion about the number of shots he has fired, and his deadpan response to the bank robber's question on that point. It's a guy joke, a reference to hundreds of movies everyone has shared, in which the question of how many bullets may or may not remain in a gun has been cornily crucial to the drama. It is also a kind of test—if you pass it with coolly flying colors, you're a member of the great masculine club, color and job classification transcended.

Think now about Raymond Chandler's famous "Down these mean streets" description of his private eye. Almost every phrase in it applies to Harry Callahan as well as it did to Philip Marlowe: He is "neither tarnished nor afraid. . . . He is a relatively poor man or he would not be a detective at all. He is a common man or he could not go among common people. He has a sense of character or he would not know his job. He will take no man's money dishonestly and no man's insolence without due and dispassionate revenge. He is a lonely man. . . ."

Something Norman Mailer once said of Clint's idol, James Cagney, also applies. He observed that tough as he was, "you always had the feeling this was a very decent guy," which, he added, was not only a sweet and sentimental thought, but a necessity for audience appeal: "There is nothing more depressing than finding a guy as tough as nails and as mean as dirt."

In other words, this lowlife transaction encourages us to connect Dirty Harry with his hard, sardonic forebears in modern crime fiction—the Hammett-Chandler-Burnett-Thompson school. At the same time we can now see a connection with what was to come—the cheekiness of the Elmore Leonard–Carl Hiassen manner, perhaps even a hint of that cheap-seats postmodernism, with its emphasis on the fatal potential of mischance, that the Coen brothers and Quentin Tarantino would one day exploit (much to Clint Eastwood's pleasure, it might be added).

One is free, of course, to take or leave cultural allusions of this kind. But about one thing we can be very clear: This passage entirely absolves Harry of the suspicion of racism—no matter what his opinion of *Miranda* and *Escobedo.* Moreover, and more important in the scheme of the film, it separates Harry's normal mode of operation—his nonchalant manner of handling what he regards as routine police work—from the obsessive passion he will bring to the Scorpio case.

The movie continues to stress these points. Siegel, in his autobiography, says he was not certain audiences would read the first scene correctly, so he and Riesner devised two short sequences that make Harry's racial attitudes utterly unambiguous. In one of them, Harry is in a hospital emergency room having the bank robber's shotgun pellets removed from his leg. The doctor attending him is a black man, and their affectionately barbed dialogue reveals that they grew up in the same neighborhood and are old pals. In another scene his new Hispanic partner, Chico Gonzales (Reni Santoni), asks another detective why Harry is called Dirty Harry. "One thing about Harry, he plays no favorites. Harry hates everybody—Limies, Micks, Hebes, fat Dagos, Niggers, Hunkies, Chinks." "What about Mexicans?" the young cop asks. "Especially Spics," says Harry, who's been listening to this exchange. He then gives a big wink to the other detective. His only expressed prejudice is against "college boys" (which Gonzales also is). But competence is the antidote for that, and Chico soon wins his regard.

Harry, in his way, is like the marines—he needs a few good men, one of whom, in Santoni's reserved, appraising performance, Gonzales quickly proves to be. He can't afford to pass one up for stupid reasons. His motives are not entirely professional. Having no life outside his work—his wife, we later learn, is dead, the victim of a hit-and-run driver; his apartment is glumly functional, a place to sleep, change clothes, knock back a brew—he needs some rough, authentic human contact. So the pair gets into trouble together and helps each other get out of it. They banter a little, exchange guarded confidences, stay well short of intimate revelation. It may be pretty standard action-movie stuff, the old pro and the rookie developing mutual respect through mutual reliance, but it helps to humanize Harry in our eyes.

Their first joint venture is, visually, the film's most stunning passage—the rooftop stakeout that turns into a shoot-out with Scorpio, their exchange of rifle shots shattering and short-circuiting electric signs, creating an explosive, spectacular and dangerous light show, in the noisy, blinding confusion of which their quarry escapes. This was, for the movie's actors and technicians, its most dangerous scene. Siegel and Bruce Surtees pondered it carefully, slowing their usual pace to a point where Clint emerged from his trailer in full grumble. Trying to hurry things along, he yelled at a special-effects man. Surtees, normally also a low-key operative, got snappish at this intervention—it was, he said, the most complicated sequence he'd ever tried to photograph and he didn't need any additional pressure. As politely as possible, Siegel ordered his star back to his trailer and returned to work. He was startled, a moment or two later, to receive a kiss on the back of his head. It was from a chastened Clint, and it was meant as both apology and endorsement of everyone's efforts.

The movie is very shrewd in its alternation of these big-action passages with smaller, comically tinged contentions. For example, we find Harry and Chico a couple of nights later cruising the North Beach strip joints trying to spot their man amid the sexual lowlifes. Sure enough, they see a shadowy figure who looks to them like Scorpio. Harry pursues this figure up an alley while Gonzales circles around to head him off. The suspect enters a building, and as Harry peers through a window, he is mistaken for a Peeping Tom and surrounded by angry, threatening citizens, from whom Chico glibly extricates him.

Whereupon they are plunged into a more perilous situation, the suicide scene, where with cops, firemen and gawking bystanders milling impotently about, Harry is hoisted by a crane to try to talk a jumper out of hurling himself from a sixth-floor balcony. The sequence has nothing to do with the film's main line, everything to do with establishing the thankless peril of the policeman's lot. And like the rooftop firefight, it is a riveting bit of filmmaking.

Clint directed it. Siegel was down with the flu and couldn't work, but he might have ceded the piece to his star anyway. There was no room for him to work with the actors on that narrow balcony and, as important, Clint was in the grip of an inspiration. "I've seen a suicide sequence on the news," he said to Siegel, "the same sequence we want to do, and it was just great. They put up nets and stuff under some guy who was threatening to jump and the guy ended up jumping and the shots were great, it was really exciting." It was also unfancy, raw and realistic. And, he thought, inexpensive to imitate. "If these guys can do it on the news," he said, "if they can catch it in ten minutes or something like that, why the hell does it take a movie company six days?"

He rescheduled the scene for a night shoot, reasoning that it would be more dramatic and that working in the off-hours would reduce crowd and traffic-control problems, described what he had seen on TV to Surtees and asked him to duplicate it. The DP responded happily, throwing a harsh, artless light on the scene. And so, with searchlights darting nervously behind him, Harry is craned up to the balcony where he distracts the jumper first with a comic-sickening description of the mess he is about to make, then with a wry complaint about all the paperwork he's going to create for the detective. The mise-en-scène Clint created, along with the casualness of the dialogue, so at odds with the suspenseful situation, refreshes a familiar situation. And after he intercepts the jumper's lurching leap and brings him safely to earth, it gives Callahan a chance, finally, to explain his nickname to Gonzales; it is because he gets "every dirty job that comes along."

"The studio allowed six nights for this shot," Clint contentedly told *Life* reporter Judy Fayard. "I told them I could shoot it in two. So I'll finish it in one—really stick it in and give it a twist." He was as good as his word. When he wrapped at 5:30 a.m. and flopped into his canvas chair after a night of crawling around on his hands and knees and wrestling with the jumper six stories up, "not a single wrinkle shows in his sharply pressed suit," Fayard wrote.

The analogy is self-evident: If Harry Callahan were a movie star or director this is how he would operate. And vice versa, of course: If Clint Eastwood had been a cop he would have worked his cases Callahan style. No point in denying it—there were some quite unmediated aspects of the actor in Harry Callahan.

You can read something of his nature in his mistrust of the production bureaucrats' projections; in his opinion, they simply lacked the set smarts he and Siegel had gathered shooting miles of film. You can read it in the compulsion to straight-ahead action: Don't futz around; just pipe some light up there and get on with it. Finally, there's the open dislike of the men in suits, sitting around in their big offices, acting grand, playing abstractedly with other people's lives.

All of this you can see yet more clearly in one of the film's early sequences, when Callahan is summoned to the mayor's office to answer questions about the still-developing Scorpio case. The dialogue goes like this:

"All right, let's have it."

"Have what?"

"Your report. What have you been doing?"

"Oh, well, for the past three-quarters of an hour I've been sitting on my ass in your outer office."

Consternation is registered by John Larch, playing the chief of police, and Harry Guardino, playing Harry's immediate superior (both of whom, incidentally, are excellent, as is cold-eyed John Vernon as the mayor). The latter contemptuously ignores the sally. He is too self-important to acknowledge it.

It's highly doubtful that Clint Eastwood and Lew Wasserman ever had an exchange like that; they're both too smart for it. But had Clint ever imagined such a transaction—with Jim Aubrey, perhaps? One had better believe it. Even his good friend Frank Wells, who had been among the executives insisting that the jumper sequence required several days' work, was not immune to Clint's distrust of noncombatants. Wells was visiting the set one day when Siegel was doing a shot in which Scorpio, eluding pursuit, slides down a banister. The first take looked fine to the director, and he moved on. "How come he's only doing it once?" Wells asked Clint. "'Cause he knows what he likes when he sees it" came the brusque reply.

Which is pretty much the way things went on this production. Despite the logistical problems posed by shooting in a big and busy city—certainly the most daunting Siegel and Clint had encountered in the course of their collaboration—they stayed ahead of schedule. It cannot be stressed too firmly: This emphasis on brisk efficiency, on getting the job done without dithering over fine distinctions, is more than a matter of pride; it is a morality. And that morality informs the morality of this movie as surely as any abstract political considerations do.

With Harry memorably established, the business of the film's second act is to put a face on Scorpio as he moves out of shadow into closer—ultimately hand-to-hand—conflict with Dirty Harry. This face belonged to Andy Robinson, a young actor trained at the Royal Academy of Dramatic Art on a Fulbright scholarship and discovered Off Broadway playing the title role in an adaptation of *The Idiot*. Looking younger than his years (Robinson was then in his early thirties) and naturally soft featured, he suggested infantile premortality and proposed evil as a kind of colic, rendering him helplessly restless, implacably angry. Since this was the actor's first movie, he had no image to defend, so there was an astonishing purity in his malice that suited the movie's moral scheme perfectly. Not for a nanosecond does he suggest some mitigating explanation for his behavior.

It was perhaps overclever of the filmmakers to give him the clothes and manner of a hippie dropout. Yes, in the San Francisco of that moment this was a good disguise. And, yes, it would surely have appealed to Scorpio's perverse nature. But this made it look as if the moviemakers agreed with those who perceived in the counterculture a real, possibly bomb-throwing, threat to the status quo: Asked recently, if he had known in advance the liberal hubbub *Dirty Harry* was going to cause, whether he would have permitted Scorpio to use a peace symbol as a belt buckle, Clint sighed deeply and replied, "No, probably not."

But costuming aside, when Scorpio commits the kidnapping that begins this act, and we learn the full extent of its sadism, the moral complexion of the movie alters radically. The stalking sniper is surely a dangerous figure, but he kills quickly and cleanly, with profit and the pleasure of spreading chaos (which forensic psychiatry tells us is the most common motive for serial crime), the driving forces behind his actions. A sicko he may be, but he is not yet beyond the reach of rational understanding. The vile crime against the child places him, in Harry Callahan's eyes, in our eyes, entirely beyond the pale.

He moves farther and farther beyond it as things develop. For when Harry is obliged, against his better judgment, to deliver the ransom to Scorpio, the psychopath leads him from phone booth to phone booth, at each of which the detective gets a call telling him his next destination, the idea being both to madden him and to delay rescue of the victim until it is too late. When, eventually, they confront each other, the ski-masked Scorpio, who is armed with a submachine gun, gets the drop on the detective and brutally beats him. Only an intervention by Chico, who has been trailing Harry, prevents him from being killed, though Chico is himself grievously wounded in the encounter. In the confusion, however, Harry manages to drive a knife into the psychopath's leg. He then traces Scorpio to his Kezar Stadium hideout and in a superbly handled sequence at last lays hands on his foe and brutally beats information about the abducted girl's whereabouts out of him as he whines for mercy.

But it is, as we know, a bad collar. Not only does the victim die, but Scorpio goes free, and Harry is contemptuously chastised for his actions. "You're lucky I'm not indicting you for assault with intent to commit murder," the district attorney informs Harry. "Where the hell does it say that you have the right to kick down doors, torture suspects, deny medical attention and legal counsel? Where have you been? I'm saying the man had rights." To which Callahan replies rather sullenly, "Well, I'm all broken up about that man's rights." To strengthen this point, a law professor from notoriously liberal Berkeley is brought in to reiterate Harry's crimes against civil liberties.

This letter-of-the-law legalism is not entirely persuasive. The Miranda Rule has been interpreted to apply only to formally charged suspects being held in custody. Since Harry was in hot pursuit of a criminal who had, putting it mildly, resisted arrest, a certain leeway on this point probably would have been allowed. Besides, it would have been the suspect's word against that of a police officer as to how he had acquired the wounds that here serve as his passport to instant freedom. No matter how punctilious the authorities were in upholding his Miranda rights, it seems likely that a real-life Scorpio would have been held in jail for some time and would surely have stood trial for his assaults on the policemen if not for the murder of the girl. He might yet have got off on a technicality—but not this quickly and easily. The scene in the DA's office, the scene that would eventually provide the heart of the argument against the movie, is logically tenuous and crudely tendentious—a little too deliberately provocative, in short.

At this point, however, the movie had not yet plumbed the depths of Scorpio's depravity. Now comes the brilliantly perverse sequence in which he pays another criminal—as it happens, a black man—to beat him up. His aim is to display these wounds, claim Harry inflicted them and charge him with police brutality. When his hired assailant does not bring sufficient fervor to his task Scorpio goads him on with racial epithets. This is, as Kael says, a "virtuoso" plot development, so far as one can determine without precedent in any form of crime fiction, its sheer boldness overcoming its whacked-out improbability. Called upon to answer this new charge, Harry is contemptuous:

"Anybody can see I didn't do that to him."

"How?"

"'Cause he looks too damn good."

After that, it is on to the school-bus hijacking and the movie's conclusion. It's a good scary sequence—the terror of the children, Scorpio's escalating frenzy, Harry's grim pursuit and jump onto the bus, all superbly orchestrated by Siegel. Clint felt he had to do the jump himself, since the camera was so close on him he could not be persuasively doubled. It was Clint, too, who suggested the film's final location—the rock quarry where the bus, out of its hysterical driver's control by now, crashes through a chain-link fence to be halted, finally, by a huge gravel pile. He remembered the bleak site from childhood drives with his parents, when they would take the ferry from Oakland for outings in Marin County.

Scorpio, cornered, his back to the water of the quarry's sump, confronting Harry and his .44 Magnum, grabs a boy who has been fishing here as a shield, but Harry is not to be denied. He fires, wounding Scorpio, the boy escaping during the exchange of shots. Now the situation duplicates the one earlier in the picture, a wounded criminal on the ground, his gun just out of reach, wondering whether the policeman looming over him has any rounds left in his gun. It was, Clint says, his idea to reprise his first-reel speech at this point, but, of course, in an entirely different tone—"double pissed" as opposed to "foxy." This time, of course, his opponent goes for his gun. And this time Harry does have a bullet left—more than one in fact.

A full and gratifying circle having been described, Clint was hesitant to gild the sequence more. The script originally called for him to throw his badge away, which added a reprise (once again of Gary Cooper's concluding gesture in *High Noon*) to a reprise, and long before they went on location Clint objected to the action. However angry he was at his superiors, Harry would not quit what he knows is the only possible job for him. Siegel thought he could, given his temper, given the way he had been hampered by authority, but he proposed a compromise: Harry would pull out his badge, study it, make as if to throw it, then put it back in his pocket. It was not quite so strong a closing shot, but it would do. Clint thought it struck just the right ambivalent note.

But on location, preparing to do this scene, Clint suddenly relented. He came to Siegel and offered to throw away his badge after all. He thought now that Siegel was right; it offered the decisive note the picture needed to strike at the end. At the practical level this change of heart nonplussed Siegel. If he had known Clint was going to discard his shield he would have had the prop man order a handful of backup badges for repeated takes. Having none, he ordered a cloth sunk under the water, to aid recovery if needed. But even with Clint throwing left-handed, Siegel got a perfect take on the first try.

★   ★   ★

On July 23, 1971, not long after *Dirty Harry* wrapped, Judy Fayard's piece ran in *Life*—as a cover story, no less, the first major American magazine to accord Clint this distinction. The cover line may have been snide ("The world's favorite movie star is—no kidding—Clint Eastwood") and its rationale may have been dubious—Fayard cited a poll of the Hollywood Foreign Press Association and his number-two standing in the latest Quigley poll of exhibitors (behind Paul Newman, but ahead of John Wayne and Steve McQueen)—but it was the act, not the facts, that was important. By risking that week's all-important newsstand sales on his image, the fading but still-powerful magazine altered perceptions of him. Up to now, given the odd route he had followed to stardom, the media had treated him as a curiosity, very possibly a short-lived one. *Life,* in contrast, was suggesting that an authentic force, perhaps even a new sociocultural icon with whom everyone was now obliged to reckon seriously, had been born.

The solid box-office performance that fall of *Play Misty for Me* tended to confirm that impression, and, in Clint's mind, so did Warner's hopeful attentiveness as *Dirty Harry* moved through postproduction. Its executives drew director and star into their marketing plans, treating them not as wayward "talent," but as intelligent adults with something to contribute to this effort. Says Clint: "They called us over and said, 'We want to show you guys what we got, kind of get your enthusiasm,' and they had this whole layout of stuff, how to release it and promote it, and it seemed so progressive compared to what they were doing at Universal." To this day he keeps on his office wall one of the posters that was eventually rejected. The headline reads: "Dirty Harry and the Homicidal Maniac. Harry's the One with the Badge."

Clint began thinking that perhaps Warners was the place for him. He also began thinking *Dirty Harry* "could be a successful movie." Even so, he was quite unprepared for the public's response to it, let alone the critical controversy it engendered. By the time it was ready for a sneak preview at Graumann's Chinese, Clint was on location near Bishop, California, shooting *Joe Kidd*. He remembers a phone report from someone at the studio telling him "the place just came unglued; people were going crazy," as the audience cheered Harry on.

Similar responses greeted the picture as it went into release during the 1971 Christmas season, where it far outstripped the other holiday releases, eventually returning some $22 million to the studio in domestic theatrical rentals alone. Critical reaction was much more measured. Roger Greenspun in *The New York Times* found it "a sad and perhaps inevitable step downward" from Siegel's previous police dramas, with Harry an "iron-jawed self-parody" of the dutifulness Siegel had previously celebrated. He noted, but brushed off, Harry's carelessness about civil liberties, insisting instead that it was the film's failures of "credibility" that fatally flawed it. Others linked the film to a readily discernible upsurge in violent movies, yet another attempt to test the limits of the rating system that had replaced the Motion Picture Association of America's tattered system of prior restraint, the production code, three years earlier.

The only completely positive review in a major publication came from *Time*'s Jay Cocks. He observed that the film was "bound to upset adherents of liberal criminal-rights legislation," but went on to say that reinforced the movie's theme: "that both cop and killer are renegades outside society, isolated in combat in their own brutal world." Citing the film's "desperate awareness that . . . the only end of movement is pain," Cocks also implied a notion that action films, because of their highly conventionalized nature, create a set of moral imperatives—perhaps even a moral universe—all their own, to which the standards by which we judge other movies only awkwardly apply. He placed *Dirty Harry* on his magazine's ten-best list for 1971.

He was alone not only in his praise for the film, but also in his writing about it as something more than lowlife entertainment, worthy of sustained attention. The movie opened on the same day as Sam Peckinpah's *Straw Dogs*, which, given the director's reputation and the film's particularly vivid rape scene, seemed to require much more sober thumb sucking. Certainly nothing in these early considerations predicted Kael's vicious assault on the picture.

One still gropes for some rational justification for it. All one can say with certainty is that at the moment, she, like many of her colleagues, wanted her readers to stop and think about the increasingly bold portrayal of violent behavior on the screen. Two weeks earlier she had been forced to come to grips with Stanley Kubrick's *A Clockwork Orange,* two weeks later she was obliged to contemplate *Straw Dogs,* and both disturbed her as deeply as *Dirty Harry* did. One needs to consult those pieces to discover the full context of her outrage.

Discussing Kubrick's film she had written that "we are gradually being conditioned to accept violence as a sensual pleasure," that directors like him were "desensitizing us" to its horrors. At the same time she was aware of "an assumption that if you're offended by movie brutality you are somehow playing into the hands of the people who want censorship." Obviously, this placed the responsible reviewer in a difficult position: One did not want to give aid and comfort to forces that had for decades juvenilized American movies; at the same time, one did not want to endorse that which one found distasteful merely because it was chic and challenged the "squares," as Kael called them. Her strategy was to substitute passionate analytical contempt for censoriousness. She concluded her review by asking: "How can people go on talking about the dazzling brilliance of movies and not notice that the directors are sucking up to the thugs in the audience?"

Dirty Harry became her next case in point. In its way it was a more difficult one. Her arguable objections to *A Clockwork Orange* had been based on its chilly eroticizing of violence, but that argument was inapplicable here. We knew there was an erotic element in Scorpio's choice of a kidnapping victim, but aside from a briefly held long shot of her nude corpse being lifted out of her tomb, nothing of the torments he inflicted on her were shown or even discussed in detail. The film was as discreet as anyone could wish when it came to linking sex and violence. But as a serious critic with a reputation for burrowing "deeper into movies" Kael would not simply register her squeamishness about the film and let it go.

She did not charge the film with vigilantism, an issue that has preoccupied its latter-day commentators. She obviously recognized that many, if not most, of the heroes in American popular fiction and film are in some sense vigilantes, obliged eventually to take the law into their own hands because the organizations charged with enforcing it are too dumb, numb or crooked to do so effectively.

But fascism, with its implication of racism—that was hot, strong stuff. And never mind that it misconstrues Harry's character and the movie's intent. The dictionary defines fascism as "a political philosophy, movement or regime . . . that exalts nation and often race above the individual and that stands for a centralized, autocratic government headed by a dictatorial leader, severe economic and social regimentation, and forcible suppression of opposition." There is nothing in that definition that fits Harry Callahan. He has nothing to say, exalting or otherwise, about nation; he is, as we have seen, color-blind when it comes to race, and the only opposition he wants to suppress is the criminal class; if he actually favored "centralized, autocratic government" or regimentation, his relationship with the paramilitary structure he serves would be—shall we say?—somewhat less contentious than it is.

As a scholar named Eric Patterson would argue a few years later, crime is a pretext, not a text, in this movie and its sequels: "The real target . . . is the power structure in which the Eastwood character is enmeshed." His rage is directed against "the mayors and police commissioners who are concerned primarily with protecting and perpetuating their own power, and who perceive Harry Callahan and others like him simply as a means to those ends." If, he says, the films endorse certain "reactionary policies," they also "embody an element of protest against exploitation which is surprisingly radical." Read in this way Harry's indifference to *Miranda* and *Escobedo* becomes logically explicable; they sound to him like more bureaucratic mumbo jumbo, yet another incomprehensible—and uncomprehending—memo from on high.

Kael's case against the rest of the movie is similarly overstated and more deviously argued. By making Scorpio motivelessly malign, a figure beyond the reach of ordinary sociopsychological explanation, the film makes "the basic contest between good and evil . . . as simple as you can get . . . more archetypal than most movies, more primitive and dreamlike," imparting to it the "fairy-tale appeal" of "fascist medievalism." By this she meant that it showed crime to be the product of inexplicable wickedness, "without specific cause or background. . . ."

This, she argues, sends a deliberately perverse message. For if evil is in fact beyond human comprehension, a sport of nature, then by implication we are all licensed to kill without compunction or regret when we encounter it. If, on the other hand, "crime is caused by deprivation, misery, psychopathology, and social injustice"—conditions for which everyone is obliged to bear a burden of guilt—then its artistic representation must engender in us some "sympathy," some "responsibility" for the criminal.

Yes—if this were a remake of *Knock on Any Door* or *Dead End*. Or, possibly, if that black bank robber had turned out to be Harry's chief antagonist. But none of that is true. Nor is this least "dreamlike" of fictions by any means the first to present us with a villain whose monstrousness passed all rational understanding. What psychological explanation can we offer for the doctors Moriarty and Marbuse? Or, for that matter, Iago and Richard III? In certain contexts we have always relished characters who proclaim their wickedness in a large and fiery hand and are relieved when they fail to excuse themselves with tales of "deprivation" or "social injustice." They speak to our instinctive understanding that from time to time figures transcending our customary definitions of good and evil appear in our lives, or, anyway, in our tabloids. In the modern world, they are often serial killers like Scorpio: the Boston Strangler, the Hillside Strangler, Ted Bundy, Son of Sam, Jeffrey Dahmer, to name a few of the many strange creatures who have swum up from the murk of modern life and are not to be explained adequately by poverty or parental abuse.

There is something uncharacteristically prissy, almost social worker-ish, in the language Kael uses to address this issue. It reflects an ambivalence about the movie audience and about the people who make movies that runs unresolved through the entire body of her work. She understood, better than most, that movies affect us "on sensual and primitive levels" and are therefore "a supremely pleasurable—and dangerous—art form." So even though she was a populist, she was ever a nervous one. In 1969 when Lawrence Alloway curated a retrospective exhibition entitled *The American Action Movie: 1946–1964* at the Museum of Modern Art, he observed in the accompanying monograph that action pictures embrace "a pragmatic willingness to kill when that is required by the situation and a highly developed short-term skepticism about moral principles." He identified this attitude as part of the nation's "covert culture," which he rather nicely defined as that generally unspoken collection of "shady habits, archaic responses and conflicting impulses that are sufficiently general to form patterns of related ideas and images." The action movie, Alloway observed, consistently drew on, and catered to, this culture, and he noted—with near-comic mildness—that "there seems to be a greater interest in violence in the mass audience than is tolerable to elite critics of society."

Kael could not accept a vision of the mass audience that acknowledged a certain raw and honest realism in some of its otherwise execrable tastes. She preferred to see it as essentially innocent, unable to defend itself against exploitation by a motion-picture industry, toward which she always took a Manichaean stance. Utterly bereft of moral and aesthetic aspirations this system, as she saw it, corrupted not only its audience, but all whom it employed. Or almost all. For within it there toiled a few people whose artistic integrity was exemplary, lonely rebels pursuing their singular visions, struggling against desperate odds to function as true artists, in the process often rendering themselves unemployable. These few, these brave unhappy few, she always championed.

Donald Siegel, unabashed maker of bluntly, unapologetically violent B pictures, a man who, despite a Cambridge education, seemed never to question the values of the covert culture, was not one of them. Clint Eastwood, up out of television and spaghetti westerns, this new lowbrow favorite who had yet to demonstrate qualms or regrets about doing harm to people on-screen, was not one of them either. By their works Kael knew everything she needed to know about them, which was that they stood for all that she loathed about the hateful system that had corrupted the medium she loved and was forever threatening the masses that she both idolized and patronized.

If this seems an overly schematic representation of Kael's position, one need only study her review of Peckinpah's *Straw Dogs.* He was the only western revisionist to rank with Leone, and it is possible to argue that finally a serious critic had to side with one or the other—the starkly, darkly romantic Italian or the lushly elegiac American. Kael had long since chosen the latter (which may have made Clint guilty by association with the former), for he was her kind of rebel angel, a hugely talented director and often a very sympathetic figure, wearing, especially around his more impressionable admirers, an air of soft-spoken victimization.

He was, as well, a self-destructive alcoholic whose contentious relationships with producers were legendary and, to some, a further earnest of his integrity. He was often out of work, and when he did work he was always having his pictures taken away from him and recut by other hands. Nor was he always careful in his choice of material, which, indeed, became increasingly incomprehensible in the later years of his career.

Be that as it may, Kael's agony as she confronted *Straw Dogs* was clearly visible. On its face, it was everything she despised; the story of a wimpish mathematician living in rural England whose wife is raped and sodomized by village yobbos and who in avenging her reclaims his manhood. It is a thoroughly nasty (and thoroughly riveting) piece of work— talk about eroticizing violence!—expressing at least as many of the covert culture's values as *Dirty Harry* did (the woman, for example, seems to invite the rape, then eventually relaxes and enjoys it, virtually parodying moronic males' suppositions about sex crimes). But there was, Kael argued, a higher purpose at work here. Peckinpah wanted us "to dig into the sexiness of violence," she said, while exhibiting a worked-out "aesthetic of cruelty." His slow-motion representations of bad behavior "fix the images of violence in your imagination," "make them seem already classic and archaic." Thus, in her mind, was "a fascist classic" born—a statement of authentic belief on the part of an authentic artist, as opposed to the "greedy, opportunistic" fascism of those hacks Siegel and Eastwood.

There is a desperately rationalizing note here, a need to maintain consistent support for a director to whom the critic was deeply committed. Moreover, like a lot of people, Kael could tolerate prodigies of violence when it was aestheticized (and somewhat distanced) in the Peckinpah manner. There are slo-mo hails of bullets in such Kael favorites as *Bonnie and Clyde* and *The Godfather* that were not approached in *Dirty Harry*. These scenes are perfectly defensible, but one can also argue that in the intricately interconnected modern world violence is visited on us suddenly, inexplicably, that it is often a matter of finding oneself by chance in a deranged person's line of fire. That being so it is as feckless (and misleading) to salvage the absurd and terrifying moment by prettifying it as it is to look for its sociopsychological explanations. One resists it as best one can, with an assertion of outraged personal morality. It's not much, but it's what Dirty Harry Callahan has.

★   ★   ★

In the end, the argument over this movie centers on two related questions: With what degree of darkness does one view contemporary life? And how does one judge the intent of the filmmakers?

On the first point twenty-five years of history have served *Dirty Harry* well. As Henry Louis Gates Jr. has written, over the last couple of decades a tendency in our culture has developed "which unites our lumpen proles with our post-modern ironists to celebrate transgression for its own sake." This was something no one would have predicted in 1971. One might perhaps more easily have perceived a point David Thomson has since made: "Those saved by the social revolutions of the 1960s were only ever a few. Eastwood guessed, or knew in his bones, that Harry's 'dirtiness' was a refreshing reclaiming of common sense and direct action as far as middle America was concerned." Or the one comedian Dennis Miller later made in one of his monologues: "Somewhere along the line society took the wrong fork in the blame road and decided to give criminals the benefit of the doubt. How did they become the victims? C'mon, everybody knows that's a buncha shit, and that's why *Dirty Harry* made Clint a big star." Both remarks reflect the way we live and think now.

No serious commentator today would advance a description of

criminal motives as naive as Kael's. In fact, serious general discussion of crime's causes and cures has been largely silenced. Few care to think much about the former, and few believe any of the latter, however hopefully they are advanced, are likely to have a large effect on the problem. Whether or not crime has become an epidemic may be statistically debatable, but fear of crime is unquestionably epidemic. We may still retain a residual capacity for outrage over "dirty" cops like Detective Mark Fuhrman, who surfaced in the O. J. Simpson trial, but even liberals no longer wish to "understand" criminals; we simply want them to be punished. This is not entirely because we have all succumbed to reactionary rhetoric. Unrealistic and ineffectual sentimentalism of the kind Kael indulged in played its role in bringing us to this pass. Like it or not, we live in a *Dirty Harry* kind of world, and, if anything, the movie seems more prescient—more "realistic" if you will—than alarming.

This leaves the question of intent. Had this movie been released in a less polarized political climate, this question would never have arisen. But these were not normal times. The war in Vietnam was still on, the college campuses were still rife with protest (the killings at Kent State had occurred only a year previously), and a parallel between taking a hard line on crime and taking a hard line on the war was often drawn in those days. The class issues implicit in the film were similarly potent. Harry's working-class roots and attitudes were the source of his appeal to the mass audience. It is obvious that by subjecting his activities, his moral decisions, if you will, to second-guessing by a temporizing bureaucracy, the film placed him under pressures every working stiff, for that matter every middle-management drone, in America understood. Maybe they couldn't talk back to their superiors or take action on their own recognizance, but when Dirty Harry Callahan did, they knew exactly where he was coming from—a place in their own hearts—which was something they no longer knew about a lot of movie heroes. Elsewhere in those days, in all the better circles, blue-collar males were the objects of scorn and fear. When they were not actually members of the police force, "pigs" like Harry, and their hard-hatted brethren formed the hard core of the hated Silent Majority, often not so silently mounted muscular counterdemonstrations against war protests.

No matter that Harry Callahan never said a word about any of these issues. No matter that the film carefully particularized his anger. It was easy enough to extrapolate from his bluntly expressed attitude about criminal rights a whole range of unspoken opinions, make him into a generalized symbol of much that was hatefully illiberal in American life at that time. The failure to anticipate this response was, frankly, not very smart of the moviemakers. The possibility that they duplicitously in-

Immortality, Hollywood
style: Clint's hands emerge
from the wet concrete of
the Chinese Theater's
forecourt, summer 1984.
BELOW: Eleven years later
he initiated Jim Carrey,
who worked in two of
Clint's films, to the
charmed circle.

A form of immortality: the make-my-day moment from *Sudden Impact* (1983). Burt Reynolds and Clint, friends off-screen, did not click on-screen in *City Heat* (1984).

Alison Eastwood plays Clint's on-screen daughter in *Tightrope* (1984). BELOW: Clint is sworn in as mayor of Carmel, California, at the City Hall (April 15, 1986).

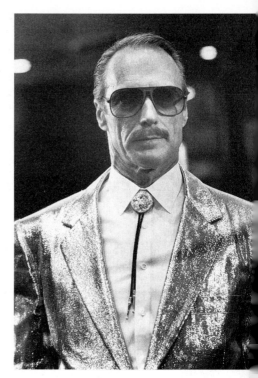

Character actor at work: as a war hero (*Heartbreak Ridge*, 1986), disguised as a casino sharpster (*Pink Cadillac*, 1989) and playing a figure based on John Huston in *White Hunter, Black Heart*, 1990.

Director at work: with Forest Whitaker in *Bird* (1988) and Gene Hackman in *Unforgiven* (1992).

Frances Fisher and Alison Eastwood flank Clint and his *Unforgiven* Oscars, after the Academy Award ceremony, March 29, 1993. BELOW: Clint and his costar Kevin Costner discuss how to achieve *A Perfect World*, somewhere in Texas, 1993.

Shoulder deep in *Madison County*, Clint and cinematographer Jack Green line up a shot. Head over heels emotionally, Clint displays his vulnerability to Meryl Streep.

Clint and Dina Ruiz, a wedding portrait, April 1996.

tended Harry as a metaphoric endorsement of a whole range of reactionary attitudes cannot therefore be definitively disproved—except, perhaps, by resort to the films Clint made after this one, and to the authentic anger this line of criticism elicted from him and from Siegel.

The latter's response was simple: "I don't make political movies," he said truthfully enough (and in one variation or another on the theme, often enough). "I was telling the story of a hard-nosed cop and a dangerous killer." When he claims in his autobiography that "Not once throughout *Dirty Harry* did Clint and I have a political discussion," it is entirely plausible. When he adds, "We were only interested in making the film a successful one, both as entertainment and at the box office," that rings true as well.

Clint, because he has been so frequently questioned on this matter, has offered a wider variety of responses over the years. He has accused his critics of leftist extremism. He has invoked the Nuremberg argument, holding that a man has a duty to oppose laws he feels to be unjust and that failure to do so constitutes a punishable crime. He has likened Harry to the Peter Finch character in *Network*, urging his listeners to declare themselves mad as hell and unwilling to take it anymore.

Most of these statements betray his singular lack of talent for abstract argument. He has been most effective when he has followed a line similar to Siegel's. Discussing Harry's character, he has insisted that "I'm, as an actor, not out to play my political feelings. I mean, that would be boring as hell, to preach some statement I have about where I thought the country was going, what was wrong with it." Conceding on one occasion that Harry was an "authoritarian" figure, he nevertheless insisted the authority he stood for was that of the autonomous individual forced to function "in a world of bureaucratic corruption and ineffectiveness." Or as he has also put it, "Harry is a terribly honest character, and I like that. He's not a political animal, and he doesn't understand political intrigue."

Discussing the film in general he has said: "It's just the story of one frustrated police officer in a frustrating situation on one particular case." As early as 1974 he told his first serious biographer, Stuart Kaminsky: "The general public isn't worried about the rights of the killer, they're just saying get him off the streets, don't let him kidnap my child, don't let him kill my daughter. There's a reason for the rights of the accused, and I think it's very important and one of the things that makes our system great. But there's also the rights of the victim. Most people who talk about the rights of the accused have never been victimized; most of them probably never got accosted in an alley." Twenty years later he put it even more simply: "The real romance of the film [is] the audience is sitting there going, 'Yeah, if I was stuck down there for five hours, I wouldn't want some guy talking about the *Miranda* decision. I'd want somebody out there trying to get my ass out of there.' That's just kind of basic. I didn't see anything political about that."

He is not—and Siegel was not—a literary-political intellectual. He is not accustomed to, is in fact flummoxed by, close ideological examination of his motives and works, because quite literally he can't see anything that grand and abstract in them. Clint obviously had no trouble understanding, believing in, accepting the consequences for, the very limited didactic aim he perceived in this movie. But that was not the only, or even the main, reason he made it.

He did it because of all the roles he had been offered up to this point in his career, this one, in his opinion, stated the frustrations of the typical American male, in relation to his work, in relation to whatever system he served, most accurately, while at the same time portraying his impotent rage, his growing sense of isolation in a rapidly changing world.

Then there were the kinetics of the matter. All movies, as Clint likes to say, are "what-if deals." They take a real guy like Harry, thrust him into an improbably melodramatic situation and then show us what happens, and here the what-ifs, their rush and excitement—their kinetics—were terrific.

Finally, no matter what other claims their creators may make for movies like *Dirty Harry,* or we may make on their behalf, all action movies are finally about—yes—action. As we have occasion to observe almost every week in the theaters, movies of this type routinely subvert their own plausibility, along with such ambitions toward fine moral distinction and high moral instruction as their makers may harbor, on behalf of sustained and exciting movement. In that sense, action movies are like action painting; their primary interest is in (and on) their surfaces. A critic is, naturally, free to regard that as juvenile, as socially and culturally irresponsible, as a self-indulgent affront to cultivated taste. But it is as a rule absurd, and utterly unrealistic, to see ideological motives, let alone ideological malevolence, as their prime cause.

★   ★   ★

The *Dirty Harry* controversy had almost no concrete effect on Clint's career. The film's popular success could not have been stemmed or even slowed by a single review, especially one that appeared somewhat belatedly in a magazine with a limited, upmarket circulation. Indeed, elitist dubiety about Harry never afflicted the mass public—he was their guy, and their pleasure in his kick-ass ways was entirely untinged by guilt. The film, after all, generated four sequels, all of which turned out to be hugely profitable, as did other films that profitably cross-referred to it.

One might even argue, perversely, that Kael's attack had a number of positive short-term consequences for Clint. Aside from granting the film a significance its makers had not expected, it furthered Clint's emergence as an important new cultural figure. The critic's feverish imaginings about a man who was, as we know, being portrayed in the press in those days as a rather opaque figure imparted to him a dark glamour he had not previously enjoyed. She made people wonder: Did this guarded and enigmatic character have a devious political agenda, more threatening than, say, John Wayne's, who had at least always been forthright about his reactionary views? Was he something more than an actor who specialized in playing dangerous characters? Was he, in himself, a dangerous character? Unwittingly, Kael made him into a subject for speculation in circles where scarcely a serious thought had been spared for him previously.

The long-term effects of her piece were slightly more ambivalent. It is true that as the most fashionable voice in her field, Kael had a view of Clint (which never softened) that would exert a continuing influence on younger critics, with this piece setting the basic terms of discussion about him for at least a decade and a half. Interviewers kept asking him about it, and anyone attempting a critical overview of his career was obliged to conjure with it. Even now, when he is the beneficiary of one of the most astonishing reversals of critical fortune in movie history, a minority continues to hold with Kael.

Yet it could be as well argued that this contempt has had a goading effect on Clint. He was surely aware of protesters at the 1971 Academy Award ceremonies (at which, incidentally, *The French Connection* was named the year's best picture) carrying placards reading "Dirty Harry Is a Rotten Pig." He would have seen *The New York Times* article in which a Harvard student identified Harry as a "Nietzschian superman" pursuing "sado-masochistic pleasures." Reports of characterizations like Joan Mellen's in her book *Big Bad Wolves* (in which he is represented as the embodiment of "a virtually fascist endorsement of the tough cop") have drifted his way.

Clint says he doesn't care about any of this. About Kael's relentless distaste for him he says he feels more sorrow than animosity: "When somebody is that dogmatic, I feel like I do about somebody who's prejudiced against Jews or blacks or whatever." Up to a point, one believes him, and believes as well that he would have chosen to toy with and test the limits of his screen personality and pursue his directorial ambitions no matter what anyone said, if only out of pride and restlessness. One of his most often reprinted quotations is "I'd hate to turn around twenty years from now and say, 'Well, I did 900 cop dramas and 800 westerns, and that was it.'"

But still, who would not have wanted to prove the culturati wrong, show oneself to be more complex and accomplished than they imagined one to be? There are moviemakers who can live happily by their grosses alone. Then there are others who require the good opinion of serious people—the cultural arbiters, if you will—to achieve satisfaction. They want film-festival screenings, museum retrospectives, meaningful awards from prestigious critical bodies and from their peers in the industry. Clint is one of this kind, and from the midseventies onward there has been on his part and his studio's part a quiet, conscious effort to respond to—and encourage—interest of this kind. To make his way out of the covert culture without denying his roots in it, to win the respect of, or at the very least acceptance by, a more self-consciously discerning group—these have been the unspoken subtexts of Clint Eastwood's mature career. It has been pursued, one has to think, all the more stubbornly because of the outcry against *Dirty Harry,* and all the more successfully because of the clout its great box-office success bestowed on him.

TEN

AUTHORITATIVE NORMALCY

Movie stars are never a throng, but at any given moment there are several dozens of them jostling for our attention. What *Dirty Harry* did for Clint Eastwood was to set him apart from this crowd, establishing him as a unique, unduplicable screen presence— someone like John Wayne in his way, or James Cagney and Cary Grant in theirs, actors whose key roles it is impossible to imagine anyone else playing.

These names from Hollywood's classic era are deliberately evoked. For even now, granted the wealth and power to play the game any way he wanted, Clint continued to reject stardom's fussy modern manner of making one high-risk, heavily anticipated and promoted movie every couple of years. It was partly a matter of temperament—his dislike of waiting around, taking meetings, suing for the favor of executives whose nervousness expands as the budget does. Partly it was a matter of calculation. The old way of being a star, exerting an inescapable presence through steady production, simply made better sense to him. Joe Hyams, the Warner Bros. executive who has supervised promotion for him for twenty years, once asked Clint why he made this choice and got this reply: "Name all of Clark Gable's pictures, Joe." Of course, he couldn't— no one could. Nor, after a time, could one easily separate the good from the bad and the indifferent among them, either. But taken together they had made an indelible impression.

Moreover, in fecundity Clint saw the hope of a larger freedom. The possibility of more or less sneaking what he would never openly identify as a "personal statement" or a "personal project" into a large filmography was more of a factor for Clint than it was for stars of Gable's generation. "I don't recall that it was such a purposeful step, but it probably was," he says. He would juxtapose movies that pressed only lightly, if at all, on comfortable genre limits and his own abilities, with projects that consciously challenged those limits.

The films Clint made in the three years immediately following *Dirty Harry* are exemplary in this regard: a totally conventional western and a remarkably unconventional one, a modest little urban romance (which he directed but did not appear in), a routine *Dirty Harry* sequel, an utterly unclassifiable male action film and an espionage adventure that was all too classifiable.

The first of these movies, *Joe Kidd,* the film he was making when word of *Dirty Harry*'s sensational sneak preview was relayed to him, is among the least interesting films he ever made as a star. Except for a desperately improvised but rather colorful ending, it is utterly without distinguishing characteristics.

Its beginnings were as inauspicious as its final form was uninspiring. Clint drove from Carmel to Bishop, Nevada, the location for the first few weeks of shooting, in his pickup truck, suffering from a bad case of the flu. As the first days of work on *Sinola* (as the picture was originally called) proceeded, some of the symptoms lingered. They didn't prevent him from working, but he continued to feel awful. An allergy of some sort began to seem a logical explanation for his miseries. Horses came under suspicion, and reports of that theory made one or two gossip columns. It contained a nice, low irony: Mr. Impervious, the man who walked unscathed through hails of bullets, rendered sniffly and puffy like an ordinary mortal by the very creatures on which a portion of his livelihood depended.

Reporting to a local doctor for shots, wandering foggily, unhappily, through the days, Clint refused to accept this notion. He had been hanging around horses unscathed for almost two decades. Yet the mystery continued, until one day he returned early to his motel room and found it infested with cats who had taken to sneaking in after he departed in the mornings. He changed accommodations, and the sniffles abated, but the late-developing allergy continues in mild form. To this day the animal lover is unable to keep furry pets in his home (he makes do with birds).

The incident had another, perhaps more significant, consequence. A woman working on the picture, with whom he began keeping company, thought incorrectly that his illness might be psychosomatic and recommended meditation to Clint. At first the idea struck him as outlandish, but over the weeks, as she talked about its benefits, Clint became more and more intrigued. She recommended a teacher in Los Angeles, and when the production wrapped he began taking instruction, establishing a lifelong habit. Meditation is not, for him, a matter of mantras and the lotus position; it is just a few minutes most days when he clears his mind of distractions, emerging from his silence, he says, focused and energized.

Joe Kidd would have profited from some concentrated contemplation. It was a range-war western, and respectable talent was involved in it: The script was by Elmore Leonard, the director was John Sturges, the action specialist who had made *Bad Day at Black Rock*, *The Magnificent Seven* and *The Great Escape* (but also, alas, *By Love Possessed* and *Ice Station Zebra*), and it included in its cast Robert Duvall giving a rambunctious performance as Frank Harlan, a corrupt tycoon trying to remove Hispanic ranchers from land that he covets.

Though Malpaso has a production credit on the project, it was put together by producer Sidney Beckerman (of *Kelly's Heroes*), who brought it to Clint. "I liked John Sturges and they made a good pitch," he says equably. The screenplay was incomplete when Clint signed on, but this did not particularly bother him; he had, as we know, agreed to other films when they were in similarly sketchy forms. His eponymous character, working first for Harlan, then taking up the cause of the exploited immigrants who are led by Luis Chama, played by the intelligent but not very fiery John Saxon, had the kind of mystery and ambiguity he liked. That in the end Joe's conscience is awakened by the plight of the dispossessed also commended it to him.

But the script remained in a state of flux. Leonard would write some new pages and show them to the producer, who would then scratch them out and substitute dialogue of his own. After which, says Leonard, "I'd take the script back and before our meeting with Eastwood I'd cross out everything he wrote and put my own dialogue back in. The producer never said a thing—I think he just liked to cross things out."

What no one got around to putting in was a dynamic climax, that burst of resolving action that all pictures of this kind require. Its absence worried Clint: "I'd never done this before, start a picture and not have an ending." But he accepted all the veteran professionals' assurances that one would be found before they needed it.

James Fargo, beginning a decade-long involvement with Clint as an assistant director and, ultimately, the director of two of his features, says the relationship between Clint and Sturges was good. "Clint doesn't like indecision," he says, repeating a familiar theme. "He wants people to arrive on the set ready to go. This is what we're gonna do— boom, boom, boom, boom. A-B-C-D." This was Sturges's preferred style, too.

Pressed by the daily demands of production the director was unable to focus for long on the ending, but he did notice that the narrow-gauge

railroad that ran through Old Tucson stopped just yards away from its saloon. What if . . . ? he began to wonder. He had always wanted to do a
train wreck, he confided to Bob Daley. The idea kept gnawing at him,
and one day he proposed that they fire up the engine and, with Clint at
the controls, run it right off the track, through some outbuildings and
into the bar where the subsidiary bad guys were gathered. It would, he
said, make a very photogenic mess. "Jesus," Clint remembers saying,
"anything at this point; let's end it." So it was done, and in its way, it
worked. It made no sense, but it put an exclamation point of sorts on
the picture.

The film was greeted with sleepy indifference when it went into release in June 1972. The reviewers gave the impression of idlers tipped
back in their chairs on the porch of the general store whittling, spitting,
languidly yupping and noping. "Business as usual," said one. "A concise,
solidly crafted western," said another. "Tacky" and "aimless," said a
third. The only interesting comment came from Roger Greenspun,
who found a nice, summarizing phrase for Clint's screen presence; praising his control of his effects and mannerisms, he detected "a kind of authoritative normalcy" in his playing.

Maybe that phrase applies equally to the actor's life in this period.
He says it was only after the success of *Dirty Harry* that he finally felt secure in his career. In 1972 he actually managed a six-month hiatus between films, the longest he had taken since he had begun starring in
American films. Before *Joe Kidd* went into release, he became a father
again—almost missing this birth, too. The Eastwoods were in Carmel in
early May 1972, then decided to return to Los Angeles to await the birth
of the child, due a couple of weeks later. In her delicate condition Maggie decided not to drive down with Clint and Kyle, but to fly in ahead
of them. While they were still on the road, however, labor pains began,
and she called Bob Daley at the Malpaso office, telling him she was
about to check in to Santa Monica hospital. He and Sonia Chernus
rushed to meet her there. Attending to the paperwork, Daley found
himself mistaken for the expectant father. "They kept calling me Mr.
Eastwood, and I kept saying, 'Don't you people ever to go to the
movies?'" Clint arrived before Alison did on May 22.

Maggie, typically, was up and doing, back on the tennis courts by
late June, practicing for the celebrity tournament she and Clint hosted
every summer in those days at Pebble Beach. Then, in August, Richard
Nixon appointed Clint to the National Council on the Arts, the first official acknowledgment of his arrival at star status, and given the controversy over *Dirty Harry,* a typically Nixonian gesture of contempt for
liberal opinion. Clint had not put himself forward for the appointment

and, startled by it, called Charlton Heston, that somewhat unlikely but devoted champion of federal arts funding, who said, "Do it—you'll love it."

He did. He developed a large respect for the late Nancy Hanks, the spirited, charming and very able director of the National Endowment for the Arts, and he became, as he puts it, "a voice for the smaller American arts," especially, of course, jazz. It is not, he says, that he had anything against opera or symphonic music or regional theater, but they had stronger backing from corporations and from their well-connected, well-to-do boards, making it easier for them to win large matching grants from the NEA. Populist that he was, he felt that "man in the street, woman in the street" projects, work that didn't attract much upscale interest, needed encouragement.

Finally, completing a year of domestic tranquillity, in October 1972 Clint's mother remarried. Her new husband was John Belden Wood, whom she had met on a Hawaiian vacation earlier that year. Clint escorted his mother down the aisle and even little Alison attended, cradled in the arms of her nurse.

★ ★ ★

One gets an impression of Clint riding easily, even proprietarily, through high-celebrity country during these days, sure of his own power, confident that he could now pause to investigate whatever byways he encountered along the trail—as, for example, the curiously memorable picture he put into production in the late summer of 1972.

High Plains Drifter was a western from an unexpected source, Ernest Tidyman, who had written the *Shaft* novels and the films based on them—the latter offering the movies' first black private detective—as well as the screenplay for *The French Connection*. It had come to Clint as a very brief treatment—somewhere between three and ten pages, depending on whose memory one consults—and was developed by Tidyman into a full-scale script, then put into final form by the faithful Dean Riesner, who, much to Clint's annoyance, was denied on-screen credit in a Writers Guild arbitration.

The movie partakes of some western conventions—mostly by extending and varying the *High Noon* theme—but it transcends them, largely through the manner of its realization. Its premise, much of it revealed in flashbacks, is that a town called Lago depends for its prosperity on a nearby mine. The mine, unfortunately, is on federal land. In order to prevent that information from leaking out, the leading citizens hire a gang of three bandits to work for them as enforcers; they flog the town's honest sheriff to death when he threatens to reveal the community's secret, most of its citizens impassively watching him die. Thereafter the townspeople betray the criminals to the law. Now, having been released from jail, the bad guys (headed by Geoffrey Lewis, an actor who would become an Eastwood familiar, eventually appearing with him in five more films) are heading to Lago, vengeance very much on their minds.

So, too, is a tall, bearded stranger, wearing a flat hat and frock coat, who emerges out of a shimmering heat haze at the beginning of the picture. It is, of course, Clint, truly a man with no name this time. He quickly establishes his credentials as a gunslinger in Lago, and the townspeople beg him to defend them against the oncoming killers. He agrees to train some of them as a sort of self-defense force. Before their climactic confrontation, however, he obliges them to paint the town (constructed of raw wood) bright red and to rename it—Hell. Whereupon, he deserts them, allowing most of them to be killed by the marauders before he reappears to wipe them out. As he leaves town for the last time, a midget (Billy Curtis), who has been his one trustworthy ally—he has actually appointed him sheriff—asks him what his name is. "You know my name," the drifter says.

But therein lies the rub, and the largest interest of the picture. The midget doesn't know the stranger's name or anything else about him. Neither does anyone else in the film. Or anyone in the audience, for that matter. Some critics wrote confidently that the drifter was the ghost of the martyred sheriff (though in the flashbacks it is clearly Buddy Van Horn playing the part, uncredited). Others insisted that he must be the murdered man's brother. Still others identified him as an avenging angel. Bob Daley remembers Clint telling him not to respond to this speculation, to let the enigma hover unanswered.

Clint now says the script definitely identified the drifter as the murdered sheriff's sibling and that "I always played it like he was the brother." He adds, however, that "I thought about playing it a little bit like he was sort of an avenging angel, too," and surely his performance has a touch of the ghostly about it. Indeed, as he admits, the drifter's detailed knowledge of previous events, expressed in dreams, suggests he possesses information he could not have acquired except through supernatural means.

It is, however, the film's setting and realization, its firm and quite original directorial slant, that give *High Plains Drifter* its distinction and lifts it definitively into the realm of allegory. It is not usual for directors—especially star directors—to act as their own location scouts, but Clint did so in this case. His first thought was Pyramid Lake, Nevada, and he and Bob Daley drove there to look it over. As they headed back to Las Vegas, their car ran out of gas. The producer, who was driving, was beside himself with apologies and offered to get out and thumb a ride to the nearest gas station. That was fine with the fuming Clint, but Daley had no luck; cars kept whizzing heedlessly by them. Time, Clint thought, to exert some star power. Time, he soon discovered, to learn its limits. He was no more successful than Daley. Finally some Hispanic farmhands in a battered pickup recognized and rescued them. He has always found in this story, which he often recounts, a nice ironic lesson about fame and too great a reliance on it.

Pyramid Lake stands on Paiute Indian land, and the tribal council was deeply divided about leasing it as a movie location, so someone suggested Mono Lake in California as an alternative. Clint had visited there in the past and remembered its eerieness. Situated in a desert, it was not quite a dead sea, but the fresh water that once ran into it had in those days been diverted to supply Los Angeles (in recent years the lake has been rescued). Stalagmites could be seen rising above the radically lowered surface of the water. Arriving in the vicinity, Clint drove down a rutted, disused road, came to a point overlooking the lake and said, "Yeah, this is the spot." Within a four-minute drive from it he found all the other locations he required, save one—the bleak desert out of which the drifter rides at the beginning of the picture, and to which he returns at the end; that was shot outside Reno.

The town itself was the work of genial, gifted Henry Bumstead, whose career as a production designer encompasses almost the entire history of sound film. He had designed *Joe Kidd,* and Clint would call on him almost twenty years later to design Big Whiskey for *Unforgiven* as well as several subsequent films. Bumstead built the village in twenty-eight days, complete with interior sets, and in its rawness, its suggestion of impermanence, it is something of a masterpiece. Reminiscent of silent-film western towns (one thinks of *Hell's Hinges,* the William S. Hart film), its primitiveness says something about the heedless greed of its residents, their lack of rootedness and their lack of interest in building for the future. It—and they—parody the western town in most movies, where neat churches and schools bespeak hopes for more civilized times to come.

Clint stoutly denies that this movie—any of his movies—constitutes a critique of middle-class values. "I have great respect for the middle class, because they're the people who are trying to make things happen in the world," he says. But the kid who contrived to get himself expelled from Piedmont High remains alive in him. The only thoroughly bourgeois character he ever played is the banker in *The Witches,* in which, of course, he satirized the type, and excepting his next film, *Breezy,* it is impossible to recall an Eastwood movie in which a middle-class citizen is portrayed sympathetically. *High Plains Drifter* is almost entirely populated by mean-spirited hypocrites, entirely absorbed by economic self-interest.

As always he was a considerate director. Verna Bloom, the female lead, was about to marry Jay Cocks, the critic, and discovered the picture's schedule conflicted with their wedding trip. To oblige her Clint hired a double to do some long shots he needed to make early in the shoot, permitting her to report a few days late. That thoughtfulness continued when they settled in on location. Bloom played Sarah Belding, wife of Lago's hotelkeeper. At first seemingly hostile to the stranger, she alone seems to understand that there is some connection between him and the murdered sheriff. As for the drifter, he knows—just how is never explained—that she alone tried to aid the sheriff when he was undergoing his calvary. Eventually, they come together and share a very discreetly handled night of love. Too discreet, Bloom now thinks. "I would have liked some hot stuff," she says—speaking strictly as an actress, and speaking correctly, too. There has been tension between these two characters from the start, and the sequence begins with Sarah attacking the stranger with a pair of scissors. Some of their edginess should, perhaps, have been reflected in their sexual encounter. But the scene ends with their first embrace, and they are next seen the morning after, happily glowing.

This is typical of Clint's handling of the comparatively few romantic interludes he has directed himself in, up to and including *The Bridges of Madison County.* There is always something gentlemanly about them, as if, as a director, he does not want to seem to be imposing himself, as an actor, on his female colleagues, obliging them to some possibly embarrassing display—even if some dramatic edge is lost as a result.

This is, of course, of a piece with his general manner as a director, his reluctance to enforce his opinions about how a scene should be played unless he is asked or unless the player is in visible trouble. As Bloom puts it, "He doesn't give you a specific direction about how to go about doing this or that, but he has a very clear idea about what the scene is about, and how he wants the scene." She, like other actors who have worked with him when he was directing himself, reports no sense of him disengaging from the scenes he was in so as to keep an eye on himself. "When he was doing a scene he was just as much involved in [it] as anyone else."

He indulges himself no more than he indulges other actors; two or three takes are his typical limit. But he can be as patient as the situation requires, and Bloom was witness to a prodigious effort of that kind. She had a scene with another actor that required her partner to make a fairly long speech. She observed the player poring over the script all morning and thought it just possible that they might be in for trouble when they did the scene after the lunch break. The man did well enough, however, in the master shot. It was when they came around for his close-up that his problems began. He just couldn't get all the way to the end without blowing his lines, and the takes began mounting up. According to Bloom, Clint's pleasant demeanor never wavered. Finally, on the twenty-second take, the actor got far enough along so that a pickup of his final words could be smoothly made. At which point the actor said, "Clint, I know you're gonna hate me, but I just can't help it, I gotta ask—can I have just one more?" This indulgence Clint did not grant him, but Bloom says she still admires the man's nerve.

The movie is worthy of admiration, too. In its bleakness of setting and its view of human nature, in its refusal to present any psychological rationales for its characters' behaviors and in its determination to strip the western to its brutal essence, it owes more to Sergio Leone than any other Eastwood movie. Indeed, to turn that stock western character, the mysterious stranger, into a figure that can be persuasively understood as apparitional is to take revisionism into previously uncharted realms.

Two or three years later, John Wayne wrote Clint protesting the movie. Wayne had always been encouraging and supportive of him. Dropping into the dead-on vocal impersonation of the older actor he sometimes does, Clint recalls Wayne saying to him more than once, "We ought to work together, kid." So when he found a script in which he thought they might costar Clint sent it on to Wayne, noting in his cover letter that the piece, though promising, needed more work. Too much more, in Wayne's estimation. But in rejecting the proposal, he launched into a gratuitous critique of *High Plains Drifter.* Its townspeople, he said, did not represent the true spirit of the American pioneer, the spirit that had made America great.

It was, like all the arguments about Clint's work in those days, most basically an argument between modernism and traditionalism, but the actors didn't acknowledge it any more than the critics did, and "out of respect for his seniority," Clint made no rejoinder. The West has always been a location for Clint, not a passion. He has never identified the region or its people as the font of American virtues, and he has certainly never seen himself as their personification as Wayne did. "I never considered myself a cowboy," he once said, somewhat testily, "because I'm not. I guess when I got into cowboy gear I looked enough like one to convince people that I was." Period. He's an actor, you know. Once, at a press conference in France, a critic rendered woozy by one of his own interpretive flights accused Clint of trying to diminish Wayne by casting Billy Curtis in this film; the midget, he said, bore a powerful facial resemblance to Wayne. It was a startling idea to Clint, who for a brief, panicky moment found himself thinking, "Damn, does he really look like John Wayne?"

That much of a revisionist he was not. Dave Kehr, the critic who is one of Clint's most faithful supporters, makes a more useful observation about the film. At the end, he notes, when the drifter is riding back into the shimmering emptiness of the desert, he just pops off the screen; one frame he's there, the next frame he isn't. It is a device, Kehr observes, that Clint would repeat at the conclusion of several films—*Firefox, Pale Rider, Unforgiven*—and the director acknowledges his fondness for it: "I just like it. . . . Time passes and it's gone, the whole thing. The fable has ended." Is life itself the fable? Or is he talking only about those fables of heroic action that we—moviegoers and moviemakers—conjure up together out of need and nothingness? The point is simply that Clint, more than most of his public, more than most movie stars, more, certainly, than John Wayne, whose identification with the character he played, the values he personified, became almost total, is always aware that the imaginary figures he embodies are fictions. They are created out of thin air and bound to return there. It is akin to his consciousness that his public persona is a megafiction, an abstraction from reality—and also a chimera.

Not that *High Plains Drifter,* deliberately austere and eerie though it is, is compulsively calculated. There is, for example, an early passage in which the town whore, played by Marianna Hill, deliberately bumps into the drifter on the street. There is no particular reason for her rude approach and even less reason for its consequences. He hauls her into a stable and rapes her, with pain turning to pleasure, in accordance with the traditional male fantasy, as the act proceeds. "Isn't forcible rape in broad daylight still a misdemeanor in this town?" she cheerily asks at the end. Well, no, and it probably never has been—which is such point as the scene has to make. But the sequence plays gratuitously, as Clint now admits: "I might do it differently if I were making it now. I might omit that." Even at the time, he knew it was (as he anachronistically puts it) "politically incorrect." He has no good explanation for why he went ahead with the sequence anyway.

Except, possibly, the nihilism that dares not speak its name. Clint, like many of us, sometimes does things just to do them, or to have done them. And isn't that, finally, the most interesting of the unspoken connections he makes with his audience? Seen in this light the rape scene looks less like a clumsy narrative diversion, more like the crux of the matter. Taken together with the sudden heedless coupling of the stranger and Verna Bloom's character, the mad insistence on painting the town red before the final confrontation, it imparts to the unnervingly silent stranger an anarchic unpredictability unique in this genre.

It says much about Clint Eastwood that at the moment when he felt he was finally fully in control of his destiny, he risked this tightly wound and single-minded film, so harsh in its light and its angles, so mannered in its style, so black in its humor, so unforgiving in its view of human nature. Far more than *Dirty Harry,* it tests, redefines, the nature of screen heroism, asking the audience if it can come to terms with the darkest (or anyway the most enigmatic) side of Clint's screen character.

When the film was released in April 1973, the reviewers had no such perspective on it. Their response was perhaps more varied than any that had greeted a previous Eastwood movie. Vincent Canby thought it might be a parody of some sort, characterizing it as "part ghost story, part revenge western, more than a little silly, and often quite entertaining in a way that makes you wonder if you've lost your good sense." Judith Crist, predictably, thought it a "Middle-American, R-rated substitute for *Deep Throat,*" a "male sexual fantasy restricted, in our grand Puritan tradition, to the rape of a whore and the instant seduction of a 'good' woman and then sublimated in all sorts of virility rites." In the *Saturday Review,* Arthur Knight did better than most with it, if only because he stressed the strength of its direction. He praised its "compulsive and surrealistic" imagery and hailed Clint as "a formidable new talent" among directors.

★   ★   ★

By this time Clint had been named the nation's number one box-office star in the annual exhibitors' poll, with Universal using that news, released in January, to herald its spring release of *High Plains Drifter* in full-page trade-paper ads. It was the fifth in Clint's record string of consecutive appearances in the top ten, but the first of four times he headed the list. (He is second to John Wayne in total number of appearances—twenty-five to twenty-one—but Wayne's streak was interrupted in 1958, with no one else approaching these numbers; it is the main thing they have in common.) Clint would lead the list again the following year, 1974, thanks mainly to the success of *High Plains Drifter,* which would open strongly and in its first year return more than $7 million in domestic rentals to Universal.

Before that picture was released, Clint had completed principal photography and most of postproduction on what has turned out to be one of his most obscure films. *Breezy* is the story of a May–December—perhaps one should say a March–December—romance between a divorced, fiftyish real estate salesman, played by William Holden, and a teenage hippie waif played by Kay Lenz in her first substantial movie appearance. Written by Jo Heims, it is itself rather waiflike, thin, somewhat undernourished, occasionally tough-talking, but eager to find a home in someone's heart.

"I think I said to Clint, or maybe he said to me," Bob Daley recalls, "'It won't make a dime and I don't care; let's do it.'" Partly they were operating out of affection for Heims. (Daley remembers that around this time the Writers Guild was on one of its semiannual strikes, that Heims was scheduled to be picketing the main gate at Warner Bros. at noon and that he and Clint bought her a fancy lunch, complete with silver, crystal and fine napery, set up a table and served her as her fellow scriveners milled past them.) Partly they were operating out of Clint's desire to test himself as a director with unlikely material and partly out of knowledge that the film could be done quickly and frugally at virtually no risk to Universal. Clint remembers presenting it to the studio along with the commercially surefire *High Plains Drifter*.

What drew him to *Breezy* was its theme: "the rejuvenation of this cynic through this naive creature." One suspects, as well, that he thought it was time to demonstrate his softer side, though Clint rejected Heims's suggestion that he play the leading role, that of the divorced, somewhat-depressed real estate agent, Frank Harmon. He didn't think he was right for the part—not in comparison to William Holden, who appears to have been his first and only choice for it.

Holden had been something of a Wasp *beau idéal* in the fifties, an actor capable of both cynicism and idealism and, in his best performances, of mixing the two qualities in a way that suggested a certain darkness beneath the veneer of American good nature. This reflected something of his own ambivalent character, for he was one of those stars haunted by the suspicion that acting was not a fit occupation for a grown-up. Pleasant and tractable on the set, Holden was given to making dismissive comments about his own talent and the motion picture business in general, from which he absented himself as frequently as possible. His largest passion was for a game preserve he had established in Kenya, where he spent a great deal of time. He was also an alcoholic, alternating periods of sobriety with days of binge drinking. He was fifty-five at this time, and partly because of his own indifference, partly because of changing times, partly because his hard living was now etched on his face, his career had dimmed.

Breezy, however, seemed to stir something more than dutiful professionalism in the actor. Clint remembers a preproduction meeting at the end of which Holden, having risen to leave, stood in the doorway and said, "You know something? I've been this guy." Clint replied, "I thought so."

Casting the title role was a much trickier proposition. The actress had to be young—*Breezy* was seventeen according to the script—capable of playing hippie waywardness while at the same time suggesting qualities that would make mutual, albeit hesitant, attraction between her and a man more than twice her age plausible. She also had to manage seminude love scenes with aplomb. Clint and Bob Daley interviewed dozens of candidates for the role, among whom was Sondra Locke—the first time she and Clint met. "She sat there in Clint's office on the couch," Daley remembers, "with her legs folded up underneath her, and she was just like a little waif—very strange little girl." Clint knew her work from her debut film, *The Heart Is a Lonely Hunter*—"I thought she was a good actress"—but felt she was too old for this role (Locke was twenty-six at the time) and decided not to test her.

In the end he had something like fifteen candidates he did want to see on film, and Holden spent three days on a stage playing a sample scene with each of them—work above and beyond the call of duty for a star of his rank. Lenz, whose father, Ted, was a well-known West Coast radio broadcaster, was included among them because Joe McKinney, the makeup artist on *High Plains Drifter,* had just done a television program with her and recommended her. Once Clint saw her work with Holden—"There was such chemistry between them," as Daley puts it— he quickly decided she was right for the part.

Clint treasures his memories of Holden. There was, he says, a particular thrill in directing an actor whose work he had enjoyed long before he had himself become an actor. More than that, "He was just a prince to work with; he was always the first guy there, ready to work." At the time, he said, they had agreed "not to intellectualize an unintellectual art," and Holden praised his director on every possible occasion: "I'd forgotten what it is like to make pictures this agreeably. I'll work with Clint any time he asks."

Lenz, rather like the character she was playing, was full of innocent enthusiasm. "I called him Bill," Lenz would recall many years later. "My God. And I was yelling, 'Hey, Clint.' I had so very little experience, I couldn't even hit the marks, but what a kind guy William Holden was, and what a very nice man Clint was." He granted her veto power over her nude scenes; unless she approved a shot, he would not include it in the final print. She also appreciated Holden's gentlemanliness in their love scenes. When she was obliged to disrobe he kept his eyes riveted on hers. "I could have been wearing tinfoil and he wouldn't have known it. I couldn't have done it without him." Holden, who only had to take his shirt off in the scene, quickly draped it around her when the most revealing take was completed.

The film, though, seems willfully deaf to its most discomfiting resonances. For a work exploring a potentially explosive—and, to many minds, scandalous—sexual encounter, it is not a very sexy movie. It has its comic and melodramatic passages, but overall its tone is bemusedly realistic, as if it is just relating a curious, mildly interesting story—not much more than an anecdote, really—in an unforced, even artless, way. "Remember Frank Harmon? Ran into him the other day. Damnedest thing. He was with this kid. . . ."

Frank and Breezy meet when a stray dog is hit by a car. She is beside herself. He takes it to a vet and eventually adopts it. Eventually he adopts Breezy, too, and permits her to charm him out of his shell ("Do you mind very much if I love you?"). Difficulties, of course, ensue. When they run into his ex-wife and friends from his former life, he finds himself embarrassed. They split up, but then Frank's former lover, a woman of his own age, is involved in an accident in which her husband, to whom she has been married only a week, is killed. Visiting her in the hospital, Frank is forcefully reminded of life's brevity, and of the need to grasp what happiness one can, however fleeting it may be. Reunited with Breezy he says, "I don't know, if we're lucky we might have a year," to which she replies, "Just think of it, Frank, a whole year."

Her infallible optimism—"I never wake up in the morning with someone who made me sorry I was there, but I'll bet you have"—reads perhaps more fatuously than it plays in understated context, which is no more than mildly critical of the hippie lifestyle (in its view, that's just another kind of conformity) and portrays its heroine more as a loner than a communard, almost a young female version of the character Clint typically plays, appearing out of nowhere to unsettle the comfortably settled.

Similarly, it is no more than mildly sympathetic with Frank's emotional immobility. It observes his self-pity without particularly indulging it. At one point Breezy tells him that if he were an Indian his name would undoubtedly be Black Cloud. When his former lady friend tells him that she is going to get married, he apologizes: "I feel a terrible sense of loss. I just wish it could have been more." To which she replies: "It was—I just wish you could have been there." Been there emotionally, she means. As for his friends, tsk-tsking over his affair with this child, the film's dismissiveness stops short of satire. It simply argues that age, social status and long-term calculation are not—or should not be—

of much moment in comparison to grasping those few moments of intense happiness life occasionally offers us. It says, gently, that some lovers do flout convention and that our responses to them perhaps ought to be more generous than they usually are.

One may like the film for its refusal to age its hero down or its heroine up, for pushing the movie convention of the much older leading man involved with the much younger leading woman about as far as it can be pushed and doing so less nervously than, say, *Love in the Afternoon* did, for setting its story in quotidian Encino instead of a romantic capital like Paris, where popular fiction has conditioned us to expect and accept all sorts of curious romantic happenings. But finally the film is less challenging than it might be. Aware that it is flirting with absurdity (or, at the least, laughter in the wrong places) on the one hand, erotic danger on the other, it settles for good nature, good taste and a light slathering of sentiment, supplied mainly by a title song that does not represent Michel Legrand and Marilyn and Alan Bergman at their best. Once again, Clint was too polite in his eroticism.

The film, which did no more than recoup its very low cost, was virtually thrown away by the studio—another slight silently stored by its restive director—and treated casually, more often than not jokingly, by the reviewers. Most of them praised Holden's work and welcomed Lenz's freshness, and a minority thought well of the film, but few of them observed its largest significance: that it completed a very enterprising trio of movies by a new director who was signaling a desire to explore an unusually large range of material.

★   ★   ★

By the time he finished work on *Breezy,* which was released in November 1973, Clint had two new scripts nearly ready to go and was committed to a June start date for one of them, *Magnum Force,* the first of the *Dirty Harry* sequels. In the meantime, however, he endured, and survived unscathed (except in his own mind), one of his unhappiest public appearances. He agreed to appear on the Academy Awards broadcast on March 27, 1973. With *High Plains Drifter* scheduled for release three weeks later it couldn't hurt. And besides, this was the first substantial acknowledgment of his rising status by establishment Hollywood.

Clint is never entirely comfortable when he is obliged to disport himself before large audiences on formal occasions, but on the appointed evening he was more or less calmly in his place, down front in the Dorothy Chandler Pavilion, with Maggie beside him, when a harassed Howard Koch, the show's producer, suddenly materialized before him. Charlton Heston, one of the program's four hosts, and the one supposed to open the program, was missing (a flat tire on the freeway), and it was now just minutes from airtime. Would Clint fill in for him? No, no, he demurred, he was not prepared, and besides, "Where's Gregory Peck and all those guys?"—Hollywood's designated dignitaries. Unavailable, said Koch. But what would I say? Clint asked. Just read whatever the TelePrompTer has on it, Koch pleaded. Oh, go ahead, Maggie chimed in. Oh, all right, Clint finally said, and permitted himself to be hustled backstage, seconds before the orchestra struck up the overture. A couple of minutes later he was shoved on stage.

The desperate Koch had forgotten that the opening monologue was full of jokes tailored for Heston, mostly revolving around his screen impersonation of Moses in *The Ten Commandments.* Clint gamely started in on them, but soon found himself squinting unhappily at the prompter, visibly distraught. "It's not good writing to begin with, but at least it has some relevance to Heston. With me it made no sense, and I'm drying up." He was also hearing the hearty guffaws of his pal Burt Reynolds riding over the nervous titters of the audience. He was rescued, rather rudely, by Heston, who practically straight-armed him away from the microphone in order to launch into what was left of his dismal routine. Exiting rather shamefacedly, Clint asked someone backstage for a beer; a six-pack was produced and he recalls chugalugging most of it before slinking back into the auditorium.

Meanwhile, the most memorably disastrous of all Academy Award broadcasts rolled on. Marlon Brando was nominated for best actor for *The Godfather* and favored to win—Hollywood welcoing a prodigal home. The actor, however, left his appearance in doubt, until just before airtime, when a woman calling herself Sasheen Littlefeather (her real name was Maria Cruz, and she had once been named Miss American Vampire) appeared in the lobby, announcing herself as Brando's surrogate. Dressed in tribal regalia, she engaged Koch in a spirited negotiation about the four-hundred-word speech Brando had given her to read in case he won. It was a polemic about the condition and treatment of Native Americans, with particular reference to their portrayal in the movies. The producer said it was too long and informed her that he would cut her off after two minutes. She, of course, protested, and Koch found himself hoping against hope that one of the other nominees would upset Brando.

No such luck. He won as predicted and "Littlefeather" made her way to the stage, where, maintaining considerable dignity amid boos and catcalls, she improvised a shortened version of his speech, concluding on a conciliatory note: "I beg at this time that I have not intruded upon this evening, and that we will, in the future, meet with love and under-standing in our hearts. Thank you for Marlon Brando."

There was no applause, and Michael Caine, who was one of the hosts, came on to say that if a man had a message to impart he ought to have the gumption to deliver it himself. Finally, it was Clint's turn to present the best picture prize—as it happened, to his friend Al Ruddy, producer of *The Godfather*. By this time he was back to himself, and iron-ically suggested that perhaps it might be dedicated to "all the cowboys shot in John Ford westerns over the years."

Still, after the show Clint told Koch, "Howard, I'm never coming back here again." What if you get a nomination sometime? the producer asked. Well, in that case. . . . But Clint thought this a remote possibility. He didn't make that kind of movie. In the years ahead he talked occa-sionally, with a certain asperity, about all the great figures—Howard Hawks, Alfred Hitchcock, Cary Grant, so many others—who never won an Oscar and had to wait into old age to collect the honorary stat-uette traditionally presented the Academy's *refuses*. He also took to imag-ining the time when his turn would come. "I'll be so old they'll have to carry me up there. . . . 'Thank you all for this honorary award' and splat, goodbye Dirty Harry."

Things worked out more happily than that, of course. He won his two Oscars for *Unforgiven* in 1993, returned the following year to present the best picture award to his friend and occasional colleague Steven Spielberg and came back again in 1995 to accept the honorary Irving Thalberg Award, all without geriatric incident. But until 1993 he con-tinued to reject all offers to appear on its award show.

★   ★   ★

Reincarnating Dirty Harry turned out to be less simple than it might have been. Clint remembers John Milius calling him when he was on location doing *High Plains Drifter* to pitch an idea for the sequel. The ac-tivities of the so-called death squads in Brazil had begun to be heavily reported in the American press, and the writer was, as Clint puts it, ob-sessed with the subject. These secret, extralegal bands of right-wing po-licemen functioned as vigilantes, executing political opponents they could not legally apprehend. They had initially regarded themselves as idealists, preposterous as that may seem, but had quickly succumbed to corruption, becoming hit men for hire to anyone with a grievance and money. What if, Milius asked Clint, Harry Callahan's San Francisco po-lice department found itself harboring such an organization? Clint was immediately enthusiastic. The story was novel, and it would give his character a chance to establish unequivocally his antifascist credentials. He and Milius quickly made a deal.

The other script Clint had in hand was Michael Cimino's *Thunderbolt and Lightfoot,* a marvelously eccentric caper-cum-buddy picture set in Montana. It was submitted to him on a Friday—Cimino was also a William Morris client—and he optioned it the following Monday. "I just liked the oddness, the crazy characters," Clint remembers. "Michael must have written it in some hallucinative state." It needed some polishing, Clint thought, and he also had to consider the nonnegotiable condition Cimino had attached to the script's sale—that he be permitted to direct the film, which would be his first feature (a graduate of Michigan State with an MFA in painting from Yale, he had been a successful director of commercials in New York and had cowritten *Silent Running* in 1971).

Now, however, a problem arose. Sixty pages into his screenplay for *Magnum Force,* Milius was offered his first opportunity to direct—his own script for *Dillinger.* He asked Clint to find someone else to finish the *Dirty Harry* project, and Clint, in turn, asked Cimino to do so. The latter set aside rewrites on *Thunderbolt and Lightfoot* and completed Milius's script with no apparent difficulty.

The film's basic situation is straightforward: All over San Francisco distasteful people—drug dealers, mobsters and so on—are being eliminated. No one much mourns their passing, but, well, murder is murder, and something must be done about it. Suspicion briefly falls on Harry Callahan, with his well-known predilection for taking the law into his own hands. But Harry, as we also know, tends to shoot from the hip (and the lip), usually when he's angry and under pressure. These well-planned crimes are more like executions than murders—and do not fit Harry's MO. Eventually he discovers that they are the work of a group of young policemen—neatly turned out, chillingly correct in manner and very competent.

An old partner, Charlie McCoy (Mitchell Ryan), and a new one, a black man named Early Smith (Felton Perry), are both murdered by the death squad, and, needless to say, this rivets Harry's attention, which is more and more focused on Lieutenant Neil Briggs, played by Hal Holbrook (in a nice bit of off-casting) with an American-flag pin in his lapel and a deadly primness in his manner. Harry has initially underestimated him as just another one of his bureaucratic nemeses, but it soon becomes clear that Briggs is more dangerous than he looks, that he is, in fact, the organizer and leader of this Americanized death squad.

The movie's tag line, which Harry keeps muttering in this situation, is "A man's got to know his limitations," but the arrogant and self-righteous Briggs does not. He lures Harry into a car, ostensibly to discuss the case, then draws a gun on him and orders Harry to drive them to what is obviously intended as his execution site. This—as a hundred movies have taught us—is a mistake. It is a good idea, never recognized by villains, to shoot first and talk later.

In this case it provides a moment for what passes in context as a philosophical exchange. It begins with Briggs expressing disappointment that Harry hasn't joined his secret service. "I'm afraid you've misjudged me," Harry says with mild and comical formality—it's the movie's most resonant moment, since the line is obviously addressed as much to *Dirty Harry*'s critics as it is to Briggs. The lieutenant responds with a historical analogy: "A hundred years ago in this city people did the same thing," says Briggs. "History justified the vigilantes. We're no different. Anyone who threatens the security of the people will be executed. Evil for evil, Harry. Retribution."

To which Harry replies: "That's fine. But how does murder fit in? When the police start becoming their own executioners, where's it gonna end? Pretty soon you start executing people for jaywalking, then executing them for traffic violations. Then you end up executing your neighbor because his dog pissed on your lawn."

"There isn't one man we've killed who didn't deserve to die," says Briggs. "Yes there is—Charlie McCoy." Briggs has no answer for that, but he asks Harry what he would have done in the situation. "I'd have upheld the law," Harry replies.

"What the hell do you know about the law?" Briggs snaps. "You're a great cop, Harry. You had a chance to join the team. But you'd rather stick with the system."

"Briggs, I hate the goddamn system. But until someone comes along with changes that make sense, I'll stick with it."

This, of course, elicits contempt from Briggs. Harry's a dinosaur, on the verge of extinction—just moments from it, in Briggs's eager view. But, of course, it is Briggs who is nearing the end. The climactic dockyard chase, quite well staged, involves motorcycles and concludes on the flight decks of two moored aircraft carriers—with Harry dispensing first with Briggs's acolytes, then the lieutenant himself, in a well-timed, quite spectacular, car explosion.

One could argue that *Magnum Force* proves that it makes no difference what the political subtext—if any—of an action film is. If its violence is expertly enough staged, and comes at satisfyingly regular intervals along a fairly suspenseful plotline, people will accept it happily and heedlessly. Certainly it helped establish the value of sequels, those franchise properties, especially in the action genre, which have become such a dominant force in Hollywood's recent economic history. For when it was released in the 1973 holiday season, *Magnum Force* surpassed *Dirty Harry*'s grosses. Cimino recalls being told that it returned more money to the studio in its first weeks than any previous Warner Bros. film.

Curiously, this success did not rub off on the film's director, Ted Post, who to this day remains unhappy, not to say bitter, about that outcome. His troubles began on the set, where, he says, he found Clint to be a changed man since *Hang 'em High*. Formerly he had been treated as a mentor; now he felt he was being treated as a hired hand.

A visiting reporter caught the essence of this revised relationship, without sensing its underlying tension. She observed Clint working out a camera angle with cinematographer Frank Stanley while Post stood by saying, "Whichever way you want it." She then quoted Post: "He hasn't changed since I first knew him. He was just the same in *Rawhide* days, always supplying imaginative ideas. I'm not an auteur director. I'm interested and happy working with someone who collaborates and contributes."

One can almost hear the gnashing of teeth. For there were few equivalents on this picture to the "Clintus-Siegelini" give-and-take, and Post deeply resented it when Clint took over the direction of several scenes or countermanded some of his suggestions to other actors. At one point, Post remembers Clint saying to him, "You have to learn to let go," which particularly outraged him.

Clint expresses puzzlement over Post's unhappiness. He continues to regard him affectionately and respectfully, and looks back on *Magnum Force* as a congenial collaboration. It is difficult to reconcile this disparity, but one suspects that it began with a failure on both sides to address forthrightly the change in their relative status since they had last worked together.

In that interim, Clint's career had clearly flourished while Post's had not. Clint was now an experienced director in his own right. He was also, in a much fuller sense than he had been on *Hang 'em High,* the film's producer, therefore its ultimate source of authority. Most important of all, he was now in full possession of a highly defined screen character, the presentation of which he knew more about than anyone. None of this, it appears, did the headstrong Post take into account.

Thus Clint's "helpfulness" in taking over some scenes—it is always his tendency simply to do what needs doing, rather than discuss it—seemed to Post a challenge to his authority. So did the fact that he ignored Post's proposals that he impart more animation to a performance the director judged "draggy." Having known him best at a very different stage of Clint's career, Post just could not see what Clint's costar, Hal Holbrook, easily perceived, namely that "that silent containment of his is his most powerful instrument."

Holbrook says that he sensed no overt tension between director and star on the set. "They consulted on everything," he says, though he also remembers being "surprised that Clint directed as much as he did." This included his major scene with Clint, the confrontation in the car. There were cameras mounted on both front fenders, and a soundman crouched in the backseat with his equipment, leaving no room for the director. It turned out to be, for Holbrook, a memorable experience, because besides directing and acting, Clint was driving, navigating the vehicle through freeway traffic, rendering him more unfocused on his role than usual. "He'd stop in the middle of a speech, not liking the way he was saying it," Holbrook recalls. Naturally, Clint would apologize for breaking his partner's rhythm, but still it was, Holbrook says, "like getting ready to jump over a gap between cliffs and somebody grabbing you just as you were ready to go." Yet it all worked out in the end. It is by far the best scene in the movie.

If Post's grievances were confined to the not-unusual push-and-shove of star and director on a set, he would probably not be quite so bitter as he is today. But he is convinced that *Magnum Force* harmed his reputation: "Because this kind of phony rumor got around, saying, 'Oh, Clint directed the whole thing.' And that's what hurt my career. I was soaring, ready to bounce into the big time." Then, suddenly, as he tells it, he couldn't get a job in features.

Post somehow blames Clint, though he admits that no one who repeated these bad reports ever attributed them to him. But this is highly unlikely; it is not the way Clint does business. Even in instances where problems on the set were more serious than they were here, Clint has always remained silent—or protectively evasive—about their causes. What seems more likely is that others working on *Magnum Force* exaggerated their differences. It happens; people working within the small, closed world of a movie location tend to improve their stories in retelling them to outsiders; it makes them appear more knowing and important.

The tensions between Post and Clint probably did not diminish the quality of *Magnum Force*. It is what it is—a reasonably efficient, reasonably entertaining, not very ambitious, movie. Its limits are self-evident, and not to be attributed to Ted Post, though adding insults to injured feelings many critics did. They did not recognize the advantage of surprise that Don Siegel had enjoyed on the original *Dirty Harry.* Nor did they see that its script was in almost every way intrinsically superior to that of *Magnum Force.* The sequel's villains, for example, are more chilly than chilling, it fails to provide Harry Callahan with the kind of funny and quirky moments that humanized him in the earlier film and it doesn't put anyone into the kind of suspenseful jeopardy that its predecessor did. To put it ludicrously: The script is too . . . well . . . intellectual, too much in love with the idea it is exploring, insufficiently concerned with developing character and circumstances in which to catch the audience up.

Not that the reviewers cared very deeply about any of that. Most of them wanted simply to prove their superiority to the film. A few wanted to worry anew about the question of Harry Callahan's fascism, though Pauline Kael had moved on from it. She used the movie to repeat her previous animadversions on affectless violence and Clint's supposed failures as an actor. That "containment" which Hal Holbrook had so admired was to her "wooden impassivity," something that "removes the last pretensions to human feelings from the action melodrama."

Nothing new here. Yet Kael did reveal an elitist bias she did not usually admit in her generally populist musings: "While actors who are expressive may have far more appeal to *educated people* [emphasis added], Eastwood's inexpressiveness travels preposterously well. . . . He's utterly unbelievable in his movies—inhumanly tranquil, controlled and assured—and yet he seems to represent something that isn't so unbelievable." Or, perhaps, so unenviable.

It's a scary thought—the notion that it is only in the guise of cool amorality that one can successfully oppose the cool immorality of modern life. It implies that decency's last refuge is to be found in superior style, not superior ethical insight. It is also an acute thought. For despite her contempt for Clint, Kael was picking up on the source of his power as no other critic was. She saw that he was operating in a radically revised movie context: "This is no longer the romantic world in which the hero is, fortunately, the best shot; instead, the best shot is the hero." She also saw that he answered a need felt in an audience "grown derisive about the triumph of good," saw that he was "the hero of a totally nihilistic dream world." Her mistake was her belief that this was a totally cynical construct. She, like most commentators on violence in film (then and now), refused to countenance the possibility that this fantasy had its roots in a revised, if generally inchoate, sense—held, however reluctantly, by many among us—that contemporary reality is . . . yes . . . largely nihilistic. From this there arose, in her case, a failure to understand that the disturbing effect Clint created in her was far more than accidental, that it was . . . yes again . . . a well-calculated one.

That this represents something like a worldview he was about to prove with the choice of his next movie—much lighter in tone than any he had previously attempted, but also much more complex in its probings of our contemporary craziness.

★   ★   ★

Thunderbolt and Lightfoot is full of genre references—among them the plotting and execution of a complex, high-stakes robbery, the unlikely bonding of the title buddies, played respectively by Clint and Jeff Bridges, and the freewheeling encounters with eccentric characters that mark the typical road movie. But Michael Cimino's work is more a commentary on, rather than a redeployment of, genre conventions. It is also a meditation on American maleness in the immediate aftermath of Vietnam, a critique of certain American traditions normally unquestioned in movies of this kind, and at its best, an extended Looney Tunes—loose, shaggy, crammed with whacked-out incidents that arise out of nowhere and send us off on astonishing vectors.

Unexpected and goofy, the script just naturally tickled Clint—the broadness of its characters, the boldness of its incidents. If there is anything Clint loves, it is exaggeration. This is an odd thing to say about an actor famous for his minimalism, but it is demonstrably true. His Leone character exaggerates the deadly silences of the traditional western hero; Harry Callahan's choice of weaponry satirizes the central, speak-softly-big-stick dualism of American heroism; a little later the *Which Way* pictures and *Bronco Billy* would exaggerate the mulishness of heroic single-mindedness to great comic effect.

The picture opens with the discovery of Clint's Thunderbolt in the last place you'd expect to find him—wearing a turned-around collar, preaching from a pulpit to the sparse, dour congregation of a country church. His text is about the leopard lying down with the kid. The kid, in this case, will turn out to be Lightfoot (Jeff Bridges), who is seen stealing a spiffy Firebird in a sequence crosscut with Thunderbolt's sermon. This is soon interrupted by gunfire, and the preacher takes to his heels, cross-country. He is rescued by Lightfoot in his stolen vehicle.

It's a cute meet, all right, and it sets the tone for what follows. It develops that Thunderbolt's pursuers, Red Leary and his dim-witted sidekick, Goody (respectively George Kennedy and Geoffrey Lewis), are former confederates in the successful robbery of a bank depository. They believe he has made off with their share of the loot, when, in fact, Thunderbolt has hidden it behind the blackboard of a one-room school that has now seemingly disappeared from the face of the earth. Eventually Red and Goody catch up with Thunderbolt and Lightfoot, a fight

ensues, and it leads to a surly, snarly peace during which Lightfoot proposes a new alliance aimed at precisely duplicating the former crime. His
theory is that the authorities will not expect lightning to strike twice in
the same place.

The consensus is that the idea may be just lamebrained enough to
work. And it does. But the thieves fall out again, Goody is killed, and
then Red is done in during a police chase that ends when he crashes his
vehicle into a department-store window, where vicious guard dogs tear
him to shreds. Before that, however, he has administered a severe beating to Lightfoot. He and Thunderbolt hit the road to nowhere again.
Along their way, however, they find the old schoolhouse. It has been
moved and set up as a nostalgic roadside attraction. They find the money
from the first robbery exactly where it was hidden, whereupon Lightfoot suddenly dies of the injuries Red inflicted on him.

Aside from its tragic denouement, the film sounds like a fairly routine action piece. But the plotline—stretched between the opening sequence in the near-moribund church and the near-closing one in the
disused school, both symbolizing the decline of traditional institutions—is not the point. The life of this wayward movie is to be found in
its excursions away from its main line, all of which suggest that nothing
in America is what it once was, or, perhaps one should say, what we
once, in deluded confidence, thought it was.

Example: Thunderbolt and Lightfoot stop to buy gas and engage in
conversation with the station owner. "Somewhere in this country there's
a little old lady with seventy-nine dollars and twenty-five cents," he ru-
minates. "The five cents is a buffalo nickel. If she cashes in her investment, the whole thing'll collapse. General Motors, the Pentagon, the
two-party system and the whole shebang." Things, he mutters, are running downhill and if we stop to think about it we'll all fall down.

Example: Our heroes hitch a ride with an old guy in a beat-up car.
The character is played by Bill McKinney in the first of his seven appearances in Malpaso productions, who as an improvisation—encouraged, he said later, by Clint—made the man talk as if he had a cleft
palate. This lunatic keeps a caged raccoon in the front seat next to him
and has rigged the car's exhaust so that it empties carbon monoxide into
the car. No reason is given for this; apparently it's just his way of dicing
with death. He also has a trunkful of rabbits, which, again for no reason,
he starts shooting with a shotgun (most of them blithely hop away as he
begins firing). Is this idle, if hilarious, surrealism? Or is this a symbol of
the impotent rage of a country that has lost its way?

Example: Preparing for the robbery, the criminals take jobs driving
little trucks (complete with loudspeakers that chime a merry tune) from

which they are supposed to sell ice cream door-to-door. The idea is to case their escape route from these ludicrous vehicles. They reckon without their customers, particularly a little boy who persistently asks for a flavor Red doesn't have in stock. Finally, the exasperated criminal fixes him with his most menacing stare and snarls, "Hey, kid, go fuck a duck." No sweets for the sweet in this movie. Cimino recalls having to shoot this scene several times; Kennedy and Clint kept breaking up, and the camera crew laughed so hard they shook the boom on which they were riding. Who can blame them? What joy to travesty everyone's expectations. What joy to travesty American piety in general, to show and keep showing, in the most casual and offhand manner, hypocrisy's descent into irrelevance.

What the movie says in its quick-step, sidelong sort of way is that the American center, if there ever was one, has not held and, perhaps more important, that ordinary people know it—or, rather, in their inarticulate way sense it. Cast loose from their traditional moorings they drift into misdirected rage and paranoia.

But it is in the relationship between its two title characters, and in their relationship to others, that the movie achieves its most striking effects. In his suggestive and sympathetic reading of the film, Robin Wood observes that *Thunderbolt and Lightfoot* owes something to *Bonnie and Clyde* structurally: An outlaw couple meets by chance, makes common, fractious cause with an older couple, constituting themselves as a "gang," perpetrates crimes (in this case a single crime) that, though initially successful, ultimately bring them to chaos and death. A significant difference between the films is that Thunderbolt is quite clearly a representative of the most tolerant American values, in effect mediating between rigid Red and lightsome Lightfoot, who symbolizes something like countercultural values.

Item: Lightfoot, cruising along in a van, spots an attractive woman on a motorcycle, pulls up beside her and starts trying to make time with her. Whereupon she hauls out a hammer and starts beating on the truck. "I think I love you," he cries happily.

Item: When they pick up a pair of young women and take them back to their motel, Thunderbolt casually accepts the fact that the sexual transaction may involve money while Lightfoot is outraged at the thought. In his world, if sex is not free (in every sense of the word) it is immoral; in the older man's world the cash nexus happily grounds all activities in practical reality and encourages a useful emotional detachment. In the course of Thunderbolt's lovemaking his partner (played by June Fairchild) notices some scars he carries. They are the remnants of his service in Korea, he tells her. "I've heard of that war," she responds vaguely. What is history to her—to anyone in this movie—except an ir-relevance?

Item: Lightfoot keeps tweaking the stolid Red, infuriating him with a casual contempt for his repressed and repressive attitudes. At one point he tells him about seeing a naked woman in a window, and that gets the older man's voyeuristic blood running. He keeps asking avid questions about the incident. Lightfoot's response to the last of them is to kiss Red. "I'll kill you for that," Red snarls. And eventually, he will—for it and all of the younger man's other generational transgressions.

Largest item: For purposes of the robbery Lightfoot is obliged to don drag in order to distract a guard at the bank and, in the getaway, to look like Thunderbolt's date at a drive-in movie. Lightfoot is very much at ease cross-dressed, and rather attractive at that. Lightly played, these scenes suggest that here is another line, in the traditional American view the most inviolable of all, that is more easily crossed than most people dream. Or as Wood puts it, "It is the essentially gentle Lightfoot, with his indeterminate sexuality, his freedom from the constraints of normal gender roles, and his air of presocialized child, who constitutes the real threat to the culture."

To put all this simply, there is no end to the cultural confusions with which *Thunderbolt and Lightfoot* toy. And no end to the good nature, the lack of pretense, with which it does so. In that sense, it remains Cimino's most assured work. He does not strain to impose obvious meaning on his material here as he would in his great success, *The Deer Hunter,* or in his great failure, *Heaven's Gate* (an early script of which was optioned by United Artists as part of the *Thunderbolt and Lightfoot* deal). Whatever reputation for grandiosity accrued to Cimino in the wake of *Heaven's Gate*'s astonishing cost overruns and equally astonishing failure at the box office, he was in 1973 a very Eastwoodian filmmaker—prudent, frugal, fast moving.

Because Cimino was a writer-director realizing his own vision, Clint was inclined to grant him considerable leeway. But the director deserves credit for sizing up the situation accurately and handling it intelligently. He resolved that no big deal be made of Clint's first appearance on the set. When he arrived, there was no break in activity, no more than a ca-sual greeting from the director and those crew members who had worked with him previously. Cimino thought that if the star were given a messiah's welcome, power would flow away from the director to him.

Indeed, it was Jeff Bridges, not Clint, who gave Cimino his biggest scare. The night before they were to begin shooting, the actor knocked on the director's door around midnight, looking distraught. As Cimino recalls it, the dialogue went something like this:

"I've got to talk to you," said Bridges.

"Sure, come in."

"I can't do it."

"What?"

"I can't do it."

"You can't do what?"

"I can't play this character."

"What do you mean, Jeff?"

"He's too good. He's too good. I'm afraid I can't be as good as he is, and I'm really worried."

"Well, I'm not worried."

"What do you mean, you're not worried? You've never even made a movie before, how can you not be worried?"

"Well, I'm not worried because I have the best actor in the world to play the role, and if I didn't have you, I don't know who would play it, because I didn't have a second choice."

"He said, 'Really,'" as Cimino remembers, "and his whole face changed, and he said, 'OK,' and he walked out the door. I closed the door, I went into the bathroom and promptly threw up."

Bridges's memory of this scene is slightly different. He would remember Cimino saying, "You *are* that guy. There's nobody else who's going to be that character, so whatever you do is appropriate. You don't have to worry about trying to emulate somebody else, because you're it, you're the prototype." That, said Bridges, "was very liberating."

Throughout, Cimino maintained a similarly sunny relationship with his other star. Sometimes, he recalls, when he was in the midst of making a setup, Clint would "sort of sidle up to me by the camera [and say] 'What do you think about putting the camera here?'" pointing to some other spot, "and I'd say, 'Well, that's interesting, but I think it's better the way we have it,' and he'd sort of smile, you know, almost as if he's saying, 'Just testing.'"

Cimino says that Clint reserved his impatience for himself—when he blew a line or a bit of business. With other actors he would make all the takes necessary for them to settle comfortably into their line readings. The incident the director remembers most vividly occurred one time when they were making the last shot of the day, with the sun sinking behind the mountains as Clint and Bridges completed a scene. It seemed fine to Cimino, and he called a wrap. But as the crew started breaking down the equipment he noticed a troubled look on Bridges's face. "What's the matter, Jeff?"

"You know, Michael, I really don't think I got it on that take."

"What do you mean? I thought it looked pretty good."

"I really think I could do it better."

"OK, we'll do it."

"You're kidding."

"No. We'll do it. Get back in the car and we'll do it."

At this point, however, Clint had disappeared into his trailer and was changing out of wardrobe. Cimino asked an assistant director to summon his star back to the set.

"Tell him yourself, here he comes right now." And indeed, he was wheeling the movie's Firebird down the dirt road where they'd been working, a spume of dust flying up behind the car. Cimino flagged him down, told him that Bridges thought he had a better take in him and got no more than a nod followed by a roar as Clint wheeled the car around, heading back to his trailer. He was back in a moment, dressed for the shot, which they managed to squeeze in just seconds before the light failed completely. "I mean, that's Clint," says Cimino.

That's Clint, perhaps one should say, when he has confidence in a director's or a fellow actor's judgment. He will give anyone twenty takes on a trial basis, but, as Cimino observes, you had better print one of the later ones (the shot just described was the one used in the picture). If you don't, he will not be so patient later.

Cimino says he asked Clint at the end of every day that he worked if he was content with the way things were going, if there was anything he wanted to change. "Every single time he said, 'Nope, I want you to shoot . . . exactly the way you envision this movie.' I mean, he didn't change one period, one comma, one word in the script; the way I wrote it was the way it was made." What he did do, according to Cimino, was step back a bit in performance, so the focus of the picture shifted to Bridges. (Cimino told Bridges his main job was to try to make Clint laugh, "because nobody's ever seen him smile in a movie before," and that he managed several times.)

Clint took "a kind of joy in what Jeff was doing," and that shows in the movie, and in the support he later offered his costar, in the form of trade ads proposing him for an Oscar nomination. When Bridges got the nomination, "Clint was like a proud father," in part because this was the first such recognition anyone involved in any of his pictures had secured.

"Michael, you'd better enjoy this," Cimino remembers his longtime friend and sometime producer, Joann Carelli, telling him, "'cause it's never going to be like this again," which, obviously, it has not been for him. He had only one bad day on the production—the last one. They were working on the robbery sequence, scheduled to take two more days, when Bob Daley came to Cimino, telling him the wrap party was set for the following night. Can't be, said Cimino. Going to be, said Daley, Clint's leaving day after tomorrow.

Cimino guesses this was some kind of final initiation. But whatever it was he says it induced "a state of total shock." He went down to the hotel's kitchen, obtained a roll of brown wrapping paper and spent the night with it rolled out on the floor, making the most detailed shot list of his life. Two decades later he would remember precisely the number of setups—fifty-six. Next morning he unrolled it for cinematographer Frank Stanley, who registered appropriate dismay, and they set to work.

"All day long all you heard was 'Cut. Print. Next setup. Cut. Print. Next setup.' The minute the camera was on the head—on the floor, on the dolly, wherever the hell it was—we would do the shot." And so it went, from 7:30 a.m. to 7:30 p.m. when Cimino made his last take—an insert shot of a clock. At the wrap party he confronted his grinning star and said to him, " 'Well, we made it,' and he just sat there with that smile, you know, 'I didn't think you wouldn't.' "

Later, according to Cimino, Clint offered him a three-picture deal which Cimino, who knew his destiny lay elsewhere, turned down. But Clint has remained a friend and supporter. In recent years they have developed other projects together that, for whatever reasons, have not worked out. Clint has remained loyal to *Thunderbolt and Lightfoot* as well.

He accompanied Cimino and some studio functionaries to Denver for a sneak preview, at which, as was his habit in those days, he appeared in what he fondly believed was a disguise—in this case a Groucho mask (glasses and false nose) with a baseball cap pulled low over his face. "What the hell are you doing?" Cimino asked. "It's so no one will recognize me," Clint said, for this was not supposed to be a celebrity occasion, but a true, working preview, to test audience reactions to the film. "And he walks like two steps and a guy says, 'Hi, Clint.' "

It played well in Denver and played well enough when it went into general release in June 1974. Rex Reed, writing in the New York *Daily News,* called it "a demented exercise in Hollywood hackery," as he identified Cimino as "a no talent . . . about whom you are unlikely to hear more." Others were far more appreciative. Jay Cocks called it "one of the most ebullient and eccentric diversions around," particularly praising Cimino's "sinewy" direction, "his feeling for the almost reflexive defenses of masculine camaraderie and for its excesses." The *Times's* Howard Thompson judged it "a modest, enjoyable winner."

That was pretty much the way it went critically, with many reviewers correctly perceiving in Clint's performance something they had not seen in him before—something relaxed, bemused, unthreatening. This, far more than *Magnum Force,* was the antidote for those who had found *Dirty Harry* poisonous and was the harbinger of the lighter roles he began to assume a little later.

According to Steven Bach, the United Artists executive who could not control Cimino when he came to make *Heaven's Gate* (but wrote a marvelous book about the experience), UA records revealed the picture "returned rentals of a solidly profitable level . . . a respectable, if not spectacular, hit for Eastwood." Not respectable enough, by the star's standards. He thought the studio mishandled the film, in pretty much the same ways Universal had mishandled its releases of his off-beat titles. By pushing it as a standard Eastwood action-adventure, UA slightly disappointed his core audience's expectations while not reaching the middle-class, middlebrow audience he was always seeking in those days. According to Bach, his relationship with the studio became so acrimonious that he vowed never to work there again—which he has not.

★   ★   ★

He had reached virtually the same conclusion regarding his relationship with Universal, and he was close to doing something definitive about that, too, but he owed the studio one more picture and, as he saw it, one more chance to let it do right by him. More important, producers Richard Zanuck and David Brown, then headquartered on the lot, had a project that interested him.

The Eiger Sanction—another Paul Newman reject—was an adaptation of the first in a series of novels about an art-collecting college professor with a profitable second career as a hit man for a CIA-like espionage organization ("sanction" was the series's euphemism for "killing," and was employed in all its titles). Published under the pseudonym "Trevanian," they were popular, particularly vacuous, airplane reads of the period.

Clint didn't think any better of the story than Newman did. In it, the character he would play, Jonathan Hemlock (the name alone suggests something about the writer's inventive capacities), is drawn out of retirement as both a spy and a mountain climber in order to "sanction" two Communist assassins. In return for his services he is to receive, among other rewards, an agreement from the IRS not to tax his largely stolen art collection. The script includes a swishy spy (rather uncomfortably played by Jack Cassidy, the singer), a nubile female of the sort usually found in James Bond adventures and a spymaster who can't stand light, lives always in a temperature-controlled environment and requires an annual change of blood—also a rather Bondian invention.

A send-up of sorts was perhaps intended, but that was not entirely clear, and, anyway, Clint was never particularly interested in espionage as a subject, whether spoofed or not; he had something else in mind at this time, so even though Bob Daley and Jim Fargo urged Clint to get the script, which already had been revised at least three times, and rewritten one more time, he ignored them. What he most deeply cared about was the project's potential to realize his ideal of making movies in isolation with companies as small as feasible, enhancing efficiency by reducing distractions and wasted motion. Nothing could be more to his liking than shooting a film's crucial sequences on a remote mountaintop in Switzerland, which would perforce limit cast and crew to a daring handful.

The idea was that everyone would do double duty. The actors, himself included, would help haul equipment and, whenever possible, do their own climbing. When that would be too dangerous the professional mountaineers guiding them would serve as stunt doubles and, as well, play small roles. Clint would direct the picture himself, eliminating yet another figure he deemed unnecessary from the production's rolls—and, more important, from the mountain's sheer walls. Finally some special equipment, notably lightweight, disposable batteries to power a specially adapted camera and recording gear (devised by Peter Pilafian, the soundman who doubled as occasional stuntman and camera operator), would be employed.

Something more than frugality (or proving a point) was on Clint's mind. He was convinced that the authenticity of the climbing sequences, the lack of the fakery that had attended most Hollywood mountaineering movies, would redeem the narrative's implausibility—which it did in the eyes of some reviewers and many moviegoers. In his postproduction comments one discerns pride in an adventure successfully undertaken, but also a sense that if he had it to do over again he would, at the very least, choose a different venue for his experiment.

Eiger means "ogre" in German, and, at an early meeting with Mike Hoover, the climber-cameraman who was credited as climbing adviser on the film, and Dougal Haston, another alpine veteran, Clint was warned that it ranks with Everest and K-2 as one of the world's most dangerous mountains. It had, at the time, claimed forty-one lives. After the two mountaineers were told what the script was going to require of them, Haston, a taciturn Scotsman, who had remained silent throughout, finally spoke up. "You're out of your fucking minds," he said.

According to Jim Fargo, the AD who was present at that meeting, they were told the Eiger is not technically difficult to climb. Its dangers stem from the fact that it is, as Fargo puts it, basically "a pile of rotting limestone," making rock slides an omnipresent danger, and from its capacity to make its own weather, meaning that one can start out on a morning under a cloudless sky then find oneself, without warning, trapped in thick clouds or even a blizzard.

But Clint was not to be deterred. The book had specified the Eiger, and the Eiger it would be. The book had specified that Jonathan Hemlock was an expert climber, therefore Clint Eastwood would try to become one also. He may have begun to have regrets about the latter decision even before he got to Switzerland, when Hoover took him on a training climb in Yosemite. Clint had done a little rock climbing when he was a kid, but he was not prepared for the levels of difficulty Hoover was introducing him to, and about halfway up a rock face Clint "flamed out" as Hoover later put it. "He looked up at me and said, 'Gee, I don't think I can make it.' I said, 'Well, Clint, you really don't have much choice, do you?' Then he reacted characteristically—he got pissed off. He pulled in his chin and gritted his teeth and with absolutely no technique at all, just blood and guts, he moosed his way up. No skill, no brains, just pure muscle. It was gruesome to watch."

Before going to Switzerland, Hoover, Clint, George Kennedy (whose character is eventually revealed to be the villain) and a small crew shot a sequence, supposed to be a practice exercise for the main characters, in Monument Valley, where they scaled the Totem Pole, a rock spire 640 feet tall and only 18 feet in diameter, which provided one of the film's most striking passages. The Navajo tribe, whose reservation encompasses the valley, had forbidden climbing on this formation, which has religious significance to them. Hoover, however, proposed that his little group would remove pitons and other hardware left by previous expeditions, thus restoring the rock to pristine condition. This gained him permission to make the ascent. When his party attained the top Clint insisted that the others be helicoptered off first, and one of his happiest filmmaking memories is of waiting alone atop the Totem Pole, watching the dying sun paint Monument Valley, John Ford's favorite location, thus almost as revered by filmmakers as it is by the Navajos, in glowing reds and golds.

No such epiphany awaited him on the Eiger. Clint had decided that the hardest and most dangerous work on the mountain should be done first, and it went well the first two days. By midafternoon on August 13, 1974, when the light began to fail, they had virtually completed a sequence in which a rock slide imperiled the film's climbing party. A wrap was called, and helicopters were summoned to begin ferrying everyone back to Kleine Scheidegg, the 129-year-old hotel near the Eiger's base, where the company was housed.

As this operation began, Hoover remembered that they had not got any shots from the climbers' point of view as the boulders rumbled toward them. He thought he could grab these while the airlift continued. Armed with a handheld camera he rappelled down to the ledge where the day's action had been staged, accompanied by a young but experienced climber, a twenty-six-year-old Briton named David Knowles, who had, like Hoover, attained the Eiger's summit on a previous climb. His job was to prevent the rubber rocks being cast down on them by another mountaineer, Martin Boysen, from bouncing into the lens.

They made their shots and were gathering up their gear, Knowles telling an anecdote from a previous climb, when they heard the sound of a huge rock—nothing fake about it—heading toward them.

Hoover: "It sounds real close and I instantly cover and crouch into the wall as close as possible. I hide my hands so as not to lose any fingers. Feel pretty good. It smashes into the small of my back and I almost black out as a smaller shower of rocks continues. I feel a weight on top of me. I can't move my legs, so I pinch them and am so happy to feel the pain. Dave must be okay. But he's on top of me—hanging upside down—dead."

The rock had struck Knowles on the head. Hoover believes it happened so fast that his partner felt neither pain nor fear. Hoover himself suffered a mild pelvic fracture and severely bruised muscles. The remaining crew, Fargo among them, lowered a rope and pulled Hoover up to the point where the helicopter was making pickups. There was no time, however, to recover Knowles's body before the light completely failed, and he was left where he had fallen until the following morning.

A wake was held, and Clint considered canceling the production. The climbers, however, urged him to go on. They knew the risks of their trade, ran them habitually and felt that moviemaking added nothing to them. For his part, Clint came around to the view that aborting the production would render Knowles's death—not to mention all the hard and dangerous work that had preceded it—meaningless.

He soon found himself engaged in what remains for him the most frightening stunt he ever attempted. The situation is, literally, a cliff-hanger. He's dangling on a rope over an abyss, and George Kennedy's character has the drop on him. Clint is supposed to cut himself free and then fall—more properly seem to fall—some four thousand feet through the air, apparently killing himself (he does not, of course). Clint was, naturally, rigged with hidden ropes so that he would fall only a few feet, disappearing under an overhang, out of the camera's view. They did the shot first using a dummy that could be seen free-falling toward the pastures below. But they needed a closer shot of Clint heading in the same direction. It would be a fabulous shot, Clint remembers thinking. But, he adds, "I must say, psychologically it was tough."

Dangling over an abyss, "I could see this pasture way down below, and I could hear the cowbells ringing, and I thought, Why am I not sitting out there with those cows sunbathing?" He thought too about another irony in his situation—he was hanging from a rope that could easily sustain ten thousand pounds of pressure but that, stretched taut by his weight, could be easily slashed with his knife. Despite his safety line ("I must have tested that rope ten times"), he found himself not entirely eager to cut the rope that was visible in the shot and that was indeed supporting his weight. But finally, willing himself to trust the hidden safety line, he cut himself loose and got for his pains a shot every bit as thrilling as he had hoped it would be. He describes himself as "drawn out," for several days thereafter, "always coming and sitting downstairs." Dougal Haston said to Clint, "'I couldn't do that.' I said, 'Why not?' He said, 'It's against a mountain climber's nature to cut your own line.'"

It is the climbing sequences of *The Eiger Sanction* that people remember, precisely because they are so visibly unfaked, and often so beautiful—perhaps the most effective such footage in a fictional film since the silent "mountain films" made by German filmmakers (Leni Riefenstahl among them) in the twenties. When it was released in the spring of 1975, a substantial number of reviewers felt that these passages went a long way toward redeeming a preposterous and totally unfelt narrative.

There were, naturally, some nastier notices. One of these, by Joy Gould Boyum in *The Wall Street Journal,* called it a "brutal fantasy," criticized it for locating its villainy in "homosexuals and physically disabled men" and despised its glorification of what the reviewer called "the All-American warrior hero." In a way, she had come closer to the point of this curious exercise than anyone; its dangerous making had largely been impelled by the director's desire to pose a distinctly masculine challenge to his own courage. In that sense, it is the only time this most reasonable filmmaker flirted with something like unreason.

Clint freely admits this "probably wasn't the best film I ever made," but it was a movie on which one man had lost his life and many others, including himself, had risked theirs, and precisely because that was so he wanted a response from the studio that acknowledged this harrowing effort. But once again, the marketing and promotion people registered puzzlement over his work. This is in itself puzzling. After all, *The Eiger*

Sanction was visibly an uncomplicated action-adventure film, with nothing about it that challenged its star's image or the audience's expectations. Yet at meetings he found people asking him, "How do you think we ought to do this thing?" and heard himself replying, "I'm here asking you. What do you need? I'll do it." He also found himself saying, "not out loud, but to myself, and later to Bob Daley, 'Well, what we do is we don't release any films here for a while.'"

That could not have been easier for him at this point. He had fulfilled his Universal contract. Frank Wells had been "making overtures" for Clint to come to Warner Bros. and, most important, Clint had a project in hand in which he believed passionately and that he was not about to let Universal mishandle.

So early in 1975, some months before *The Eiger Sanction* went into profitable release, Clint put in a call to Wells. He asked him, half jokingly, if he could guarantee that no tour buses—the studio tour being one of the many petty annoyances one puts up with at Universal— would ever come chugging by his door. Wells laughed and assured him that the studio had no tour and no plans for one. All right, then, how would they like it if Clint moved to the Warners lot? They would, Wells told him, like it very much. "By the way," Clint remembers saying, "I have this western I'm interested in. . . ."

ELEVEN

A LABOR OF LOVE

B ased on the work of a thoroughly disreputable author, marred in its making by a disharmony unduplicated by other Eastwood productions, the occasion on which Clint entered a relationship that would radically change his personal life, *The Outlaw Josey Wales* turned out to be, for all of these distractions, the most completely satisfying movie he had yet made—and, as one looks back over his career, one of the best films he ever made. Sweeping in the variety of space and emotion it encompasses, it is explicitly reconciliatory in the message it offered a socially fractured nation and implicitly reconciliatory in the way it blended the manners and morals of the traditional western with those of the revisionist school.

The film's basic story came to Clint's attention in the form of a scrawny, badly printed little novel called *The Rebel Outlaw: Josey Wales,* bearing the imprint of a publishing firm in Gant, Alabama, that no one had ever heard of. Hundreds of such unsolicited offerings—books, scripts, treatments—poured into the Malpaso office every year, and the normal procedure, as it is everywhere in Hollywood, was to return them unread within twenty-four hours, a quick turnaround being the first line of defense against the meritless plagiarism suits that often follow the release of successful movies. But this volume was accompanied by an ingratiating note from the author, whose name was Forrest Carter. It spoke of Clint's "kind eyes" (not a phrase normally applied to them) and prayed that they would look in that spirit on his humble offering.

Something in this plea tweaked Bob Daley's sympathy, and he resolved to give it a glance. A few weeks later, he found himself with nothing to read over dinner (he was a bachelor between marriages at the time), so he took Carter's little volume home with him. He found himself completely hooked; he finished the book in one sitting.

As the movie would later retell the story, Josey Wales is a farmer trying to live peaceably on the Kansas-Missouri border during the Civil

War. But in the pretitle sequence, Northern raiders, Redlegs, burn out his farm and kill his family (his wife is played by Bill Wellman's daughter, Cissie, his son by Kyle Eastwood). He joins Rebel guerrillas and fights through the war with them. When it is over, Fletcher, the Rebel leader (John Vernon), believing an honorable surrender has been arranged, unknowingly leads them into a massacre by the Redlegs. Josey and a young soldier named Jamie (Sam Bottoms) are the only survivors. Though the latter is seriously wounded, they head for Texas where they understand other Southern sympathizers have taken refuge. Wanted men, war criminals as their enemies see them, they are pursued by Terrill, the obsessed Redleg commander (Bill McKinney) and by the guilt-stricken Fletcher, always trying to temper Terrill's passions. The young man soon dies, and Josey proceeds alone. A bitter, silent figure in a forbidding landscape, his sole desire now is to avoid further commitments that might lead to further losses and betrayals.

Fate, however, has a different plan for him. Along his trail waifs and strays keep joining him—among them a sly and funny old Indian (memorably played by Chief Dan George), an Indian woman (Geraldine Keams) who has been cast out by her tribe and rescued by Josey from virtual slavery, an old lady (Paula Trueman) and her granddaughter, Laura Lee (Sondra Locke), whom he saves from the brutal predations of Comancheros, even a snarly but redeemable hound dog. The Locke and Trueman characters are heading for a ranch left to them by their son and brother, and Josey agrees to escort them there. It stands on Indian land and a deadly confrontation with Chief Ten Bears (Will Sampson) and his tribe seems inevitable. But Josey rides out alone to parlay with them. He tells the chief that they are both in their ways outcasts, betrayed by unfeeling government policy, and Ten Bears accepts his proposal of peaceful coexistence. Thereafter, Josey dispatches Terrill, accepts a truce from his former commanding officer and at last settles down to a new life, carving a civilized corner out of the wilderness for himself and his own makeshift tribe.

It was late by the time Daley finished reading the novel that outlined this tale, but he could not resist calling Clint in Carmel to share his discovery. Normally a rather phlegmatic man, Daley had never reacted to anything with such urgency before, and Clint, who would remember him saying, "God, this has so much soul to it," was intrigued by his enthusiasm. The next day Sonia Chernus endorsed Daley's opinion. Now Clint wanted to read it immediately, and it was hand-carried to him by air. The following morning he told Daley to secure the rights for Malpaso.

It took Daley two days to reach Carter at the Alabama phone number he had given in his covering letter. "He was out in the woods some-where," the producer recalls. When they finally connected, Daley found himself wrapped in what seemed to be the toils of folksy innocence, though Forrest Carter was not at all what he appeared to be. That, how-ever, would only be revealed much later. For the moment he was, as Daley informed him, a writer in need of an agent, which he offered to help him find. The writer said that wouldn't be necessary, and called back a day or two later informing the producer that he had engaged someone in the William Morris Agency's New York literary department to represent him. Since Clint was a Morris client Daley told him there might be a conflict of interest. Carter said he didn't care, and, in fact, the agency cut a pretty good deal for him, considering his, and his book's, lack of status—as Daley recalls, a twenty-five-thousand-dollar payment for the screen rights, with ten thousand dollars more due on com-mencement of principal photography and a final fifteen thousand dol-lars to be paid out of net profits if they should accrue. With a firm movie sale in hand, Carter's agent was also able to secure republication of the book, under a new title (*Gone to Texas*) by a mainstream mass-market paperback house.

Chernus asked for, and was granted, a chance to adapt the novel. While she was working on it, Daley got his somewhat-disconcerting first glimpse of Forrest Carter. They had kept in touch as the script pro-ceeded, and one day he told Daley that he was going to be in the neigh-borhood and would like to drop in and meet him and Clint. The latter was out of town, but Daley assured Carter of a warm welcome. Where are you going to be? he inquired. "Dallas," came the reply. Geography apparently was not the writer's strong suit.

He said he'd be arriving the next day, so Daley told Carter to be on the lookout for Art Ramus, who worked for the company as driver, oc-casional security man and general factotum. He was a large man, a for-mer basketball player close to six feet, eight inches, in height, not to be missed. Carter, however, was not on the flight, and as Ramus was call-ing in to report this to Daley the writer rang on the second line saying he'd got drunk with some friends the night before, been thrown in jail and missed his plane. He'd be on the next one, he assured Daley. Carter appeared as announced—staggering drunk. Ramus hustled him into a bar, propped him up at a table and once again made for the phone. He told Daley that the man was in no condition to be brought to the office. The tone of their sotto voce conversation suddenly changed when Ramus burst out, "Oh, God, what's he doing?" "What's going on? What's happening?" an alarmed Daley cried. "He's taking a whiz in the middle of the Satellite Lounge carpet," the driver replied, "and here come the cops."

Ramus hastened to Carter, wrapped his burly arms around him and told the policeman, "Officer, I'll take care of him—he's my father." With that he hustled his charge to his station wagon, made him lie down in the backseat and drove him to a motel, where he administered hot coffee and cold showers until the man sobered up.

The next day Carter appeared in Daley's office, dressed in cowboy regalia and acting as if nothing had happened. His opening words, however, were: "Well, I don't wanna take up any more of your time. I guess I'd better go home now." Daley says he had to physically restrain him so they could discuss *Josey Wales.* This went well enough, and Daley proposed that Carter stay over another night. Though he could not join the party he asked Ramus and two of Malpaso's secretaries to have dinner with the author. Once again he turned up drunk, and in the course of the meal he drew a knife, held it to one of the women's throats and told her he loved her and that he would kill them both if she didn't agree to marry him.

By now it was clear to everyone that they were dealing with sociopathy of some sort, though its full depths would not become known until after the film was released. On the other hand, this strange creature had somehow managed to write this story that they loved, and it fell to Daley to keep him placated. It was not easy. At a certain point Carter was convinced by friends that he was being exploited by a rich and powerful movie star and began demanding more money. Finally, Clint bought a measure of peace by advancing him, out of his own salary, the fifteen thousand dollars due Carter when the picture went into profit.

Prior to its publication in 1976, Carter showed Daley the manuscript of another book, *The Education of Little Tree,* a memoir of what Carter claimed was his orphaned childhood, when he was raised by Native American grandparents. This, too, interested Malpaso, but when he pursued the rights Daley discovered that Carter had optioned them to three other producers. This was fortunate, for they discovered a couple of months after the release of their film that Forrest Carter was, in fact, Asa (Ace) Carter, a virulent segregationist who had organized a particularly vicious subgroup of the Ku Klux Klan and had been an anti-Semitic and red-baiting radio broadcaster as well. Before that he had also been a speechwriter for George Wallace (author, apparently, of his infamous "Segregation now, segregation tomorrow, segregation forever" phrase) though he later broke with the Alabama governor because he became, in Carter's warped view, too liberal on the race issue.

His past history on the further fringes of American lunacy was exposed by an Alabama newspaperman, Wayne Greenhaw, just as *The Outlaw Josey Wales* was released, and though his widely reprinted story did not harm the movie, it tainted *The Education of Little Tree,* which made no great impression on its initial publication. With its failure, one might have imagined this strange tale would conclude, especially since Carter died of a heart attack three years later.

But this is America, where memories are short and reinvention a national pastime. Somehow, *The Education of Little Tree* made its way to the University of New Mexico Press, which reprinted it in paperback in 1986. Its sentimental representation of Native American culture, with particular emphasis on its ecological soundness, struck a chord in the eighties, and it became a word-of-mouth bestseller. Robert Redford and Steven Spielberg, among others, expressed interest in making a movie of it.

Remarkably, nobody recalled the earlier stories about Carter's rancid past until 1991, five years after *Little Tree*'s republication. Then Dan T. Carter, who said he might be a distant relative of Asa and is a scholar specializing in the history of modern racial politics in the South, wrote a piece for the op-ed page of *The New York Times,* reexposing the author. Other commentators expanded on his work, pointing out that though young Asa did have a grandfather of Cherokee descent he never lived with him and that his grandmother had died before he was born. Dan Carter erred factually in his description of Asa Carter as a "friend" of Clint Eastwood, and critically in misreading Clint's work in general, the adaptation of Carter's novel specifically. He suggested that the violence of Clint's movies, among others, besides demeaning popular culture, matched quite naturally with Carter's racism, though the latter was not manifest—rather the opposite—in the movie version of *Josey Wales.*

Clint was on location, making *Unforgiven,* when this article appeared, and he sent a polite letter to the *Times,* pointing out that he had met the man he knew as Forrest Carter only once. He also observed, "If Forrest Carter was a racist and a hatemonger who later converted to being a sensitive, understanding human being, that would be most admirable."

Did Carter's writing, all of which was apparently completed during a silent withdrawal from political life that began in 1971, represent a genuine conversion and atonement? Or was it an elaborate hoax? One thinks of F. Scott Fitzgerald's famous dictum about the test of first-rate intelligence being its ability to hold opposed thoughts simultaneously and still function; here was a third-rate mind—and a very disturbed one at that—managing the same trick. Bob Daley observed some of this schizophrenia firsthand. He saw a decent side to the man, reflected in warm, supportive letters he received from Carter on the death of his father. He also saw vicious anti-Semitism, directed at William Morris agents, when the arguments about money started up. He finally came to the conclusion that Carter was basically an opportunist, willfully burying—but not necessarily abandoning—his racism so that he could rejoin decent society.

One inescapably imagines the adventures of Josey Wales, this Southern sympathizer, this "hard-put and desperate man" (as one character describes him in the screenplay), this outcast redeeming himself, as a wish-fulfilling fantasy on Carter's part. One of his novel's subtexts, a distrust of government, which first brutally betrays and then obsessively harries his hero, would seem to reflect the author's profound suspicion of federal authority. One could speculate as well that the idea, implicit in the book, that ordinary people, left to their own devices, can work out their conflicts peaceably—a metaphoric expression of what had been a typical Southern response to federal enforcement of civil rights laws—reflects, in housebroken form, one of the author's core beliefs.

Knowing nothing of the author's racist past, these notions, in the benign form the book presented them, spoke clearly to Clint—particularly to his wariness about government—though needless to say, they were not for him, as they were for Carter, a coded argument against racial integration. When he discusses this film, Clint rarely fails to mention that it was developed in the aftermath of those two great betrayals of trust by American authority, the Vietnam War and Watergate.

For whatever reason, he was unusually angry—and open—in his contempt for statism at this time. Shortly after *The Outlaw Josey Wales* was released, when he was in England promoting the film, he was quoted as saying: "Today we live in a welfare-oriented society, and people expect more, more from Big Daddy government, more from Big Daddy charity. That philosophy never got you anywhere. I worked for every crust of bread I ever ate." He was also feeling isolated, lacking, as he said "the gift it takes to enjoy fame." When a trade-paper reporter asked him why blacks tended to be such enthusiastic supporters of his work, Clint said: "I suppose they see me as an outcast. I play a lot of outcasts."

Some of those feelings, more ambiguously stated, are certainly to be found in the film. But hard-put and desperate though he may be, Josey Wales retains a dry, wary, saving sense of humor. It is only in his climactic parlay with Ten Bears that his disgust with government is articulated. But the fact that officialdom speaks in "double-tongues" is a conventional, even stylized, trope in such movie encounters. We expect and accept it quite equably.

Looking back on the film now, Clint insists that it was the other aspects of Carter's story that provided its largest attractions. The most obvious of these was "the saga of it"—its movement across vast landscapes, the rich variety of characters and situations it encompassed. None of his other westerns had, or would have, these qualities. Nor had they heretofore offered a "total chronology"—a motivating back story with significant emotional development proceeding from it: "I'd always played the guy who appeared out of nowhere." He also liked the way it portrayed Native Americans neither sentimentally nor as savages. It treated them with "a certain humanness that we hadn't seen in the movies in a long time." In particular in Chief Dan George's marvelous performance as Lone Watie, who often functions as a kind of chorus commenting on the action, the movie grants to at least one Native American a quality almost never attributed to his race by popular culture, a wise and ironic sense of humor.

Finally, however, it was the reconciliatory note struck by the film that constituted its most significant virtue in Clint's eyes. Entirely aware of the parallels the film draws between the Reconstruction era and the post–Vietnam era, Clint insists that he intended, as well, a more generally pacifistic message—"It was just any war, any war you can name in history." In this connection, he raises a familiar irony: Man, the planet's most intelligent creature, is also the one that "can raise the most mayhem." He adds: "At the time I felt that it was a statement that mankind has to find a better solution than just battling themselves into the ground." If not, "there'll be no one left, eventually; we will have gone the way of *T. rex* and the rest of the dinosaurs."

The film presents this theme with considerable indirection. Josey Wales must inflict considerable "mayhem" in pursuit of peace. But in the negotiated settlement with Ten Bears, and in his final exchange with the last of his soldierly pursuers, in which they pretend not to know one another and go their separate ways as if nothing had happened, a "better solution"—a sort of forgiving amnesia—is definitely endorsed.

The theme of reconciliation is presented in similarly indirect fashion. Josey is, on the face of it, one of Clint's classic, wounded loners—"A reticent-type person, he doesn't want relationships." But as Clint also puts it, "The more he doesn't want them, the more they keep imposing themselves upon him." Working on, manipulating, that shred of good nature that is still present in him, until at last, without his ever overtly acknowledging it, "this little commune" heals and restores him to the human family. It was the first time his radically isolated screen character had come to such a comfortable end, the first time a film did not leave him as it found him—alone with his self-sufficiency.

★ ★ ★

All of these ideas, together with a great deal of its dialogue, were transferred more or less intact from book to first-draft adaptation by Sonia Chernus. Dean Riesner then did some work on it, but Clint still felt the screenplay needed more suspense and hired Philip Kaufman for the final polish, thinking he might also be a good choice to direct the film.

Quiet and somewhat intellectual in manner, Kaufman was a graduate of the University of Chicago with a degree in history who had briefly studied law, drifted around Europe and tried writing fiction before becoming enamored of film, particularly postwar European film. After some low-budget apprentice work he had written and directed *The Great Northfield Minnesota Raid,* an antiromantic variant on the Jesse James legend, which Jennings Lang had produced at Universal and Bruce Surtees had photographed. He followed that with *The White Dawn,* a rather glum and claustrophobic tale of nineteenth-century whalers shipwrecked in the Arctic and falling into brutal conflict with their Eskimo rescuers. Clint particularly responded to the film's unblinking realism.

Kaufman discovered what Clint thought was the key to unlocking the full dramatic power of *The Outlaw Josey Wales.* In the book and in the first draft the protagonist's old enemies, the Redlegs, had simply faded out in the last half of the story; in Kaufman's revision they were kept alive, hunting him, haunting him, for the length of the movie, keeping tension alive. Clint thought this invention important enough to earn Kaufman the right to direct the film.

Jim Fargo, however, quickly began to have doubts. Scouting locations with Kaufman, the AD thought he was somewhat indecisive and began to fear trouble with the always impatient Clint. They did, however, finally settle on a variety of sites in Arizona, Nevada and northern California, with the first major sequence on the production schedule the rapacious assault on Laura Lee's wagon by the Comancheros, set for the desolate country outside Page, Arizona. It was there, during the first few days of principal photography, that things began to fall apart for Kaufman. He began the sequence before Clint arrived on location, and he was disappointed in the dailies that were forwarded to him. So was Bob Daley; "milquetoast," he called them; "there was just no power whatever in the thing."

Matters did not improve when Clint began working with Kaufman. As Fargo put it, "Phil was the kind of director who comes out there prepared, but likes to sit there and look and say, 'Now what if we did this? And what if we did that?' And Clint's just going up a tree." This, to him, was self-indulgence.

Kaufman's story is otherwise. Years later, he told a reporter that "the original novel . . . was kind of grim and right-wingish, and I thought it would be a good idea to take a slightly different approach, maybe inject some humor into it. Eastwood didn't think so."

The description of the book is not entirely inaccurate, but it is obvious that Clint raised no objection to the lightening of the movie. The finished film is full of humor; it is one of its salient qualities. Kaufman also put it about that Clint resisted his efforts to probe more profoundly into the material. David Thomson has written: "Philip Kaufman asked for more takes. 'Why?' asked Clint. 'What do you want me to do different?' And Kaufman said he wasn't sure, but he felt repetition would take them deeper. For Clint, repetition sounded like indecision, wasted time and going over budget."

The crisis came with what Clint now refers to as "a Captain Queeg incident." The conclusion of the Comanchero sequence begins with the near-magical appearance of Josey Wales, backlit, riding over the crest of a sand dune, with the sun behind him, partially blinding the superior force he was about to attack. The shot was planned for magic hour, late in the afternoon when the sun is low and glowing, the shadows particularly long and photogenic. One day a small party, consisting of Clint, Kaufman, Fargo, Surtees and Fritz Manes, Clint's high-school buddy who had just joined Malpaso, set out to grab it.

As it happened, Fargo and Kaufman had scouted these dunes, and the director had placed a discarded container of some sort along the road to mark the place where he planned to place his camera. Over the intervening weeks the ever-shifting sands covered his marker, but he was determined to find it, and he ridiculously kept halting the little expedition to search it out.

It was absurd. There were dozens of heights suitable for the shot, and time pressure was mounting; magic hour does not last forever. Finally, at one stop, which appeared entirely appropriate for their purposes, Clint proposed setting up. The director demurred. So Clint told him to take one of the vehicles and a driver to continue his search while the rest of the party waited. As Kaufman prepared to depart, Clint turned to Fargo and asked where he'd put the camera.

Fargo was standing in a declivity with a nice up-angle on a nearby ridge. "Right here," he said, pointing at his feet. "Get the camera." "God, I can't. That's the director over there." "Get the camera," Clint repeated. "Let's shoot it." The minute Kaufman decamped they did, then packed up, leaving Manes with a car to await Kaufman's return. The director, according to Manes, saw that his authority was now fatally compromised, and proposed a confrontation with the star, from which Manes says he dissuaded him.

It would have been too late in any case. That night Clint placed a call to his lawyer to discuss the ramifications of firing the director and taking over himself. "If I kept him," Clint says, "I knew I couldn't keep my promise to the studio as far as schedule and budget went. And since I'd put my own money up to buy the story, I thought I had that right."

There is more to the decision than that, of course. Even if Kaufman suddenly became a model of efficiency, Clint could see that the temperamental differences between them would make a good working relationship impossible. Kaufman continued to shoot for the remainder of the week. But when Daley arrived on location at the end of work on Saturday Clint drew him aside and told him he was going to let Kaufman go. He was, Daley reports, anguished about it, but rejected the producer's offer to accompany him to the final confrontation. What passed between them no one but Clint and Kaufman know. All the former says is, "It's the hardest thing I ever did in my life." For a man whose own memories of the cruelties and insecurities of the movie business are always lively it surely was, and there were consequences for both of them. It was three years before Kaufman directed another movie, and Clint's action caused the Directors Guild to promulgate a rule forbidding one of its members from being replaced by anyone working in any capacity on the picture from which he or she has been removed.

★   ★   ★

Genuine as the issues between him and Clint were, Kaufman was to a degree the victim of Clint's growing confidence in his own abilities. The polite young actor, eager to learn, the aspiring director, acquiring the rudiments of that craft by observation and by relatively modest doing, were—perhaps somewhat to his own surprise—creatures of the past. His power was unquestionable now, and he had all the skills required to handle any kind of picture. There was no longer any need for him to tolerate styles and methods antithetical to his own. From this point onward he would either direct himself or he would employ people he knew would defer to him.

As for *Josey Wales,* Jim Fargo says "it became a labor of love," with even the weather contributing to the sense of well-being that now settled over the production. Clint has spoken most volubly on the pleasures of working with Chief Dan George. "He just had a great charisma. In fact, the first time I saw him he came in in an all-white suit—white tie, white shirt, white coat—and he looked like some Indian god, and he had this great big Swedish gal who was a little bit taller than he was, and she was his 'nurse'—at least that's the way it was presented to me." Once or twice he appeared on set a trifle worn by evenings spent dancing or otherwise partying with his companion, but he was always ready to work. And Clint kept giving him more to do, so effective was his presence in the film. At his age (an estimated seventy-seven) the chief, who had given a similar, and similarly touching, performance in Arthur Penn's *Little Big Man*—a much angrier use of the western form as a Vietnam metaphor—five years earlier, did have some trouble remembering his lines. "When the camera was rolling," Clint remembers, "I'd say to him, 'Chief, just forget about all those lines, just forget all that dialogue and everything you've been rehearsing, and just sit here for a minute.' So we'd sit there and the cameras would roll, and then I'd say, 'Now tell me that story, you know, about the Indian that came over the hill.'" Quickly the chief would find himself taken up by whatever tale he was telling, recounting it in his own words, but coming close enough to the script and, in his immediacy, vastly improving on it. "I'd find myself mesmerized," Clint would later recall. So much so that on one occasion, when Josey and Lone Watie are saying what they both imagine is a final farewell, he brought Clint to tears, and Clint thought for a moment he was going to lose it completely. "I thought, God, how am I going to keep my composure if he's going to tug me like this?"

But tug at him the old man was supposed to do, and Clint's delicate—and generous—relationship with the chief particularly impressed Sondra Locke. She spoke of it several times in subsequent interviews. She also spoke of Clint's insistence on realism, with a special emphasis on deglamorization, in his work with her. In her account, he kept shooing the makeup man away from her and registered dismay when she went to her trailer to make repairs on her own. One time, when her eyebrows were singed by fire and she asked him what to do about it, he replied, "Oh, the stumps look fine."

He had cast her for her vulnerability and because, as he put it, "She didn't look like she came out of some Hollywood casting session." What he discovered working with her was an eccentric intelligence that intrigued him.

Locke is a fragile-looking woman, five feet, four inches, in height, weighing scarcely more than one hundred pounds, with luminous blue eyes. Born and raised in Shelbyville, Tennessee, she was, as she frequently told interviewers, a shy and dreamy child, somewhat disaffected from her parents and drawn early and deeply into the fantasy world of the movies. When she was eleven a young man named Gordon Anderson, four years her elder, and equally detached from mundane reality, moved to Shelbyville. They quickly became inseparable ("the weird two, the town dreamers," as she put it later), memorizing movie scenes and playing them with one another. Sometimes he would hold a mirror up to her face so she could get an idea of what she would look like in a close-up. Eventually, because their school did not have a drama teacher, he directed her in a production of the hoary thriller *The Monkey's Paw*, which they took to a statewide competition and against the odds won—he as best director, she as best actress.

Thereafter, she attended junior college in Nashville, where she also did some acting and continued to think about performing professionally. Anderson, meanwhile, moved to New York to pursue an acting career. There he heard about a talent search concentrated in the Southern states in which an unknown was to be sought for the role of Mick Kelly, a fourteen-year-old tomboy, in the film adaptation of Carson McCullers's *The Heart Is a Lonely Hunter*.

Like most of her work, it was a story about outcasts and their inappropriate affections, here a deaf-mute living in a small southern town. Anderson thought Locke, who was now twenty years old, would be perfect as the adolescent who befriends him. He came home to prepare her for one of the open calls scheduled to take place in several large cities. He had her bind her bosom with an elastic bandage and buy some sack dresses to further disguise her mature figure. He also thinned and braided her hair, painted freckles on her nose and even wrapped another bandage, slightly bloodstained, around her knee, suggesting that she had perhaps skinned it falling out of a tree. In this getup, she later reported, she felt transformed, knowing how her character "would act, feel and think."

Off they went to a tryout in Birmingham, where they found hundreds of young women, most of them sponsored by local theatrical organizations, gathered to compete for the role. Marion Dougherty, the casting agent who later worked on a number of Clint's movies, told him that Locke's audition was the last of the day, and that her associates told her that, since she had no sponsorship, she was not obliged to read her. But knowing how far she had come, Dougherty decided to hear her out. She was electrified by the performance. Locke was asked to come to New Orleans for another audition, repeated her success there and was then flown to New York, where after lightening the deep Southern accent she had been affecting, she was given the role.

She had insisted all along that she was only seventeen, and that fiction was maintained—in fact, heavily stressed—in publicity about the film, though by this time Warner Bros. knew her true age, since she had been free to sign her own contract, without parental approval. But no one could resist the story of the "shy office worker" catapulted to "overnight stardom" at a tender age. As it happened, she was very effective in the film, winning an Academy Award nomination (along with her costar Alan Arkin).

Locke and Anderson soon married, living for a time in his boyhood room in his parents' house, before moving to Los Angeles, where they settled in to what was described as "a Gothic townhouse." She collected fairy tales in rare editions while he took up art, doing portraits and carving balsa-wood figurines to order. He also helped manage Locke's career, which, excepting the 1971 horror hit *Willard,* did not prosper.

Living virtually as brother and sister they remained intensely dependent on one another. Indeed, at no point in her fourteen-year relationship with Clint did Locke ever move in permanently with him or totally abandon Anderson. At some point Clint bought a house where Anderson lived and Locke frequently stayed, and until 1979, when Maggie and Clint legally separated, Locke and Clint tried to maintain—not at all successfully—the fiction that they were, as the saying goes, "just good friends."

They had been more than that, of course, from their idyllic early days on location. It is clear that theirs was an attraction of opposites. She had never known well such a traditional male. He had not known well a woman who combined the fey and the ambitious in quite her manner. To put it simply, he was not Gordon, and she was not Maggie, and each was ready to try a radical otherness. That he could wrap a strong, protective arm about her—a gesture not unknown or displeasing to him—was a given. That he could advance her career in ways previously unavailable to her was another given, and not displeasing to her.

In the years ahead Clint would provide Locke the range of roles the rest of Hollywood refused to grant her. But for the moment, he played her very close to what had become her type. Indeed, in her first scenes in *The Outlaw Josey Wales* there is an almost-addled quality about her. One feels that Laura Lee may possibly be arrested in some childish state, or that she may have been traumatized by some earlier incident, so silent, wide-eyed and ready to bolt does she at first appear. Eventually she's able to shoot a marauding Redleg point-blank, and to lead shy Josey to seduce her, but even in this company of eccentrics she is distinctly an odd little creature.

★　★　★

As for Clint, he knew what his screen character had come to represent, and he had no desire to back away from the realism it embodied. In an interview published shortly after *The Outlaw Josey Wales* was released, he insisted, "I do all the stuff Wayne would never do. I play bigger-than-life characters, but I'll shoot a guy in the back. I go by the expediency of the moment." But he has since remarked that he also knew that for him "it was time to get back to a western that was sort of a traditional kind." What he was trying to make sure people understood was that even though he was playing quite a conventional western figure he was still in his own mind the anti-Wayne, and that even though *Josey Wales* will eventually arrive in something like John Ford country, it will do so via a distinctly non-Fordian route.

Still, the fact remains that there is no "expediency" about Josey Wales; when it comes to gunfighting he is as punctilious as John Wayne or any other western traditionalist ever was. He's quicker than most of them—almost magically so—but not once in this film does he take unfair advantage of an opponent.

By far the most famous of these sequences—a classic western face-off—occurs in a saloon where Josey, Laura Lee and the rest of their party have paused. A pair of bounty hunters observes him, and one of them enters the establishment, where this dialogue ensues:

"I'm looking for Josey Wales," says the gunman.

"That'd be me," says Josey, speaking from a deeply shadowed corner of the room.

"You're wanted, Wales."

"I reckon I'm right popular." Pause. "You a bounty hunter?"

"Man's got to do something to make a living these days."

"Dyin' ain't much of a living, boy," comes the reply that has entered into the canon of Clintisms. "You know," he adds, "this isn't necessary. You can just ride on."

The bounty hunter thinks that over and leaves. But in a moment he returns. "I had to come back," he says simply.

"I know," Josey replies. A sense of resignation and regret flows between the two men. Whereupon Josey Wales blasts his nameless adversary to kingdom come.

It is the movie's key scene. But it is not just the understated power of its dialogue that makes it memorable. Its darkness and claustrophobia constitute a conscious rejection of the plein air conventions typical of such confrontations. So does the palpable air of reluctance with which it is carried out. It's as if both Josey and the bounty hunter are aware that it is mythic tradition—movie tradition, if you will—that compels them forward. They would both prefer to reject it, but they cannot.

Clint might call this realism. We might label it, once again, "brutal frankness." A critic might deplore its "self-consciousness." But the point is the awareness of the traditions from which the film always operates, its determination that we share in its knowingness.

Take, for example, a line of dialogue that occurs after Josey and Jamie have killed their night-stalking assailants early in the film. They do not have time to bury them, which the youngster regrets. "Buzzards gotta eat, same as worms," Josey replies flatly. The boy's death, a few scenes later, is handled with a similar lack of sentiment. He has been in a bad way for some time, but as with Lightfoot before him, there has been no foreshadowing of his demise. The movie suggests that his chances of living and dying are about equal. When he does go, it is without preparation, without speechmaking. One minute he is chatting amiably with Josey; the next he is dead. It is marvelously shocking and marvelously casual at the same time, as real as the representation of death can ever be in a movie. And Josey's response to it is both buried and harried (his enemies are in particularly hot pursuit at the time). In any event, what is there to say except what we already know? That every time he makes a commitment to anyone, the object of his affections will be taken from him by cruel chance. When he says, as he does more than once in the movie, "I don't want no one belongin' to me," he is speaking from an emptied heart and bitter experience.

When, later, Josey is organizing his surrogate family to defend their new home, he instructs Laura Lee in the grim reality experience has taught him: "Now remember, when things look bad and it looks like you're not gonna make it, then you gotta get mean, plumb mad-dog mean. 'Cause if you lose your head and give up then you neither live nor win—that's just the way it is."

He's a hard man, this is hard country, and life is ever a hard thing. Josey never forgets it, and this movie never forgets it either. We achieve release from this knowledge only through the exercise of irony. Deeply withdrawn as he is, Josey has a sense of humor that is his—the movie's— saving grace, maybe its moral imperative. Whenever anyone presents Josey with a plan, a prediction, a hope for the future, the most he will offer is some variation on the dubiously offered phrase that is his leitmotif: "I reckon so." There is always something cautious and cautionary in the way he uses it: Don't understand anything too quickly; don't count on anything too certainly.

Most unheroic. Like his nasty habit of chewing tobacco. At the beginning of any significant action, and sometimes at the end of it, Josey always lets loose a stream of tobacco juice—a running gag (and a mechanical effect) that is also a release of tension and a signal of his humanity. Imagine that! A hero with a nervous habit. In its way, it's as substantial a bit of revisionism as any Clint undertook.

Indeed, the best way of positioning this film is to measure it against some of John Ford's traditional tropes. We may begin with the difference between this film's and Ford's films' attitudes toward the frontier military establishment; in *Josey Wales* it is the source of disorder, not of order, of irrationality, not rationality, as it is in Ford's. Compare, for instance, the meeting of Josey and Ten Bears and the one between John Wayne's cavalry officer and an old Apache chief as their forces ride into battle in *Fort Apache*. Both bring together strong and respectful foes, but Ford's ends in weary acknowledgment of their impotence to halt conflict. *Fort Apache* ends with another cavalry troop riding out to do battle with Indians all over again. Remember, too, that one of its sequels, *Rio Grande,* is, as Richard Slotkin has observed, a full-scale Cold War parable, in which the military is identified as the last best hope for the defense of American decency, its Indian enemies as thoroughly dehumanized, cruelly, deceitfully intent on destroying our way of life.

In *Josey Wales,* however, the Indian and the white man are, from the start, in perfect, contemptuous agreement about the blindness and stupidity of the government power that has marginalized them. Their problem is to find a way of making a separate peace, one that places them beyond the reach of blundering and duplicitous officialdom and its military servants.

It is also instructive to measure *Josey Wales* against what many regard as Ford's masterpiece, *The Searchers.* Both, obviously, concern a man whose domestic tranquillity has been shattered by the sudden depredations of murderous and rapacious raiders. Both trace his long search for redemption. But Ford's film is marred by an irredeemable racism, in which Indians are portrayed either as hopelessly lost in savagery or childishness. Worse, obsession is portrayed in Ford's film as a trait, if not heroic, then, in the circumstances, forgivable. In *Josey Wales,* obsession is portrayed as dehumanizing, the force, whether it be expressed in political or racial terms, that has robbed this hero of everything he holds dear, and from which he desperately runs. (In this connection one thinks of Clint's comment that probably the hardest thing for him to attempt as an actor would be "a religious zealot; it would be fun to play, but I would be playing without an identification.")

These attitudes, too, are very clearly set forth in the long exchange between Josey and Ten Bears. Whether we understand theirs to be metaphorically a discussion of the greatest of American issues, the race issue, or of the need for rapprochement between classes and generations in post-Vietnam America or even of the Cold War, the message is clear: We really have no choice but to knit up the vast American family and live together harmoniously.

This point is underscored by the film's final, and most remarkable, confrontation between Josey and his pursuer, Terrill. Catching him alone, Josey advances on the man who massacred both his family and his comrades in arms, who has pursued him so unjustly and implacably, his face contorted in a terrible rage, both pistols drawn. But when he triggers them, over and over again, their hammers fall on empty chambers.

His rage can be read as a need to wreak his vengeance with his bare hands. But it is also possible to see that this man, too, is being offered a choice between a deed of life and a deed of death. For we understand that Josey will be satisfied by a metaphorical victory and that his opponent need but acknowledge it in order to be freed. We read astonishment in Terrill's face—and finally a desperate assertion of his irredeemable nature. He draws his sword, Josey grasps it, they struggle briefly and then Terrill is run through with his own weapon.

In the film's coda, Josey also achieves mutual forgiveness with the last of the pursuers, his old commander, Fletcher, who pretends to believe that the man he is confronting is a "Mr. Wilson," pretends to believe a story that Josey Wales has gone to Mexico. Fletcher says he thinks he'll follow him there and tell him that the war is over. "What say, Mr. Wilson?" "I reckon so," comes the reply.

This film has one final subtext that should be mentioned: It is palpably a meditation on celebrity. Josey Wales begins his life within this narrative as an anonymous figure. But as he proceeds along his path, making one vivid assertion after another of his prowess, he becomes a public figure, a source of rumor, legend and awe, creating—without entirely meaning to—an image almost like that of a movie star in that it simultaneously distances and entrances his public. In time, and again like a movie star, he becomes aware of his new position and of the effect he has on others; it becomes a factor in the calculation of his actions. To some degree, all gunfighter movies (which, besides being a saga of redemption and resettlement, *Josey Wales* also is) partake of these themes—his reputation always precedes the quick-draw artist, is always a source of his strength in that it has the effect of staying or making tremulous the hands of his adversaries, a source of vulnerability that encourages people who want to make a similar name for themselves to challenge him.

Precisely because this film toys so frequently with this theme, it suggests a final comparison with yet another John Ford film—*The Man Who Shot Liberty Valance*. In that movie a tenderfoot, played by James Stewart, is credited with ridding a terrified town of a particularly hateful badman. As a result, he goes on to a distinguished political career while the man who actually did the deed, played by John Wayne, sinks into destitution and anonymity. When many years later the truth about this occurrence is about to be revealed, those in the know agree to bury it. And a frontier editor speaks what has become perhaps the most famous line in the entire Ford canon: "When the legend becomes fact, print the legend."

In other words, provide the populace with a lie—all right, a myth— that will help people to live their lives more securely, more gracefully. Ford, naturally, believed that. So did Wayne; it was the source of his quarrel with Clint. Both Ford and his star must have known that the entire westering saga, as it has been told and retold through the movies, through all of our popular culture, is a gigantic lie. But that was always all right with them. It was, they thought, a useful lie, something to guide Americans through the troubles and ambiguities of twentieth-century life.

Josey Wales does not want to live within that lie. It is too brutal, too costly, too hard on a man caught in its toils. And *Josey Wales,* the movie, does not want to live within it either. It wants to suggest that a man may escape from the falsehoods that have grown up around him. And find a satisfying life in a modestly defined ordinariness, even if that requires a change in identity.

The Outlaw Josey Wales as it finally emerged on-screen in the bicentennial summer of 1976 offered a middle ground between western revisionism and western traditionalism. In effect, the sometime spaghetti-western star pulls back from the brutal demythologizing of those films (and Peckinpah's as well) but stops well short of embracing Ford's sentimental conservatism. This was a shrewd career move for Clint. The film's careful attention to genre formalities reassured older classicists in the audience who had remained dubious about him; the tough-mindedness of the action satisfied the younger portion, which had been his chief support.

★   ★   ★

As westerns go, as movies go, *The Outlaw Josey Wales* is obviously a very rich text, but also one that is not particularly difficult to read. Yet the critics scanned it with maddening superficiality. To them, it was either just another western or, worse, just another Eastwoodian bucket of blood. By and large they did not review it so much as they used it to confirm their worst expectations of Clint.

Mostly they thought it was too long (135 minutes). And everybody, whether their opinion of the film was favorable or unfavorable, missed all of the movie's most interesting points. There was no comment anywhere about its pacifist subtext, its relationship to genre traditions, the variant Clint was offering on his own screen character. "A prairie *Death Wish*," wrote one. "Simplistic . . . fun and games," said another. In *The New York Times* Richard Eder, a slumming drama and literary critic, claimed Clint's chaw represented the full extent of a characterization in which the actor "seems to be thinking and feeling nothing, and is therefore almost invisible to the camera." Perhaps the oddest of these reflections was offered by Jack Kroll of *Newsweek,* who scarcely reviewed *Josey Wales* at all, so delighted was he by a conceit called "Erb-Man," a neologism he concocted from the initial letters of the last names of Clint, Burt Reynolds and Charles Bronson. He defined this creature as cool in manner, catatonic sexually, indecisive when it comes to action and practicing "an oddly abashed form of machismo," signifying "the confusion in contemporary masculinity." Worse, he said, Erb-Man made B movies disguised as A movies and were not nearly as effective in them as the likes of Chester Morris and Richard Dix.

There are times when the willful failure of reviewers to observe what is actually taking place on a movie screen ceases to be a minor annoyance and becomes something like a minor sin. The personae in question here have virtually nothing in common; *The Outlaw Josey Wales* is visibly not a B picture in design or intent, and the need to keep its director-star trapped in disrespect is inexplicable.

There were, of course, reviewers who responded to *Josey Wales.* Kevin Thomas, who pursued Clint's early career sympathetically and intelligently, in the Los Angeles *Times,* called it "an imaginatively and eloquently devised" epic that was also "a timeless parable on human nature." At the end of the year *The Outlaw Josey Wales* actually found its way onto *Time* magazine's ten-best list. Such views were then still in the minority, however.

Pauline Kael did not review the film, but a couple of months before it opened she made a speech at Filmex, a festival then held in Los Angeles, and called Clint "the reductio ad absurdum of macho today." In his opinion, this constituted gratuitous violence to his reputation, and he made a regrettably naive response to it. He quoted a psychiatrist friend to Mary Murphy, the Los Angeles *Times* gossip columnist, to this effect: "He says Kael actually feels 180 degrees the opposite of what she says and that often a man or woman obsessed with preaching great morality is more interested in amorality."

Oh, dear. Intellectual wrangling—not to mention psychological theory—is not an Eastwoodian strong point. Asked to comment by the columnist, Kael replied, "Eastwood's response is perfect . . . in fact, it's sublime."

Apparently, however, the exchange had a larger effect on the critic.

For a little later she called Clint up. "I hear you're angry with me," he recalls her saying.

"Well, I was just having some fun," he replied, not wanting to admit that a goat had been gotten. "I didn't imagine you really meant it."

"No," she said, "I'm just a dumpy little movie critic, and I have to do that," he quotes her, doubtlessly paraphrasing. She then went on to say that she needed to call attention to herself, "keep her ratings up," as Clint puts it. "I understand completely," he remembers saying. He also remembers her saying that she hoped they could meet sometime, which he continues to think is the most astonishing aspect of their exchange.

In his dogged way Clint continued to pursue the matter. A month later, in a lengthy interview in the *Village Voice,* he was heard to growl: "She was taken by *Last Tango;* it seemed to be romantic to her. But for me, that movie was an affront to women. . . . I mean if buttering up a girl's ass and giving it a probe job is romantic sex, or represents male tenderness, then I'm sorry, but I'm on a different plane from her. Higher or lower, depending on whose opinion. Jesus, how can she not see that as violent?" This was not an entirely unreasonable review of the reviewer, though it was not an entirely fair consideration of the movie, either.

As for *The Outlaw Josey Wales,* Clint is surprisingly equable about its initial dim reception: "I was still persona non grata then," he said recently. But he was then—and remains—utterly confident of its worth. "I suppose if that story were being submitted to me today I'd feel the same way about it, and go after it with the same enthusiasm I did then. I don't know if I can say that about a lot of the things I've done. I do believe that if I'd made that picture in 1992, in place of *Unforgiven,* it might have received the same amount of attention, because I think it's equally as good a film. I think the subject matter of *Josey Wales* is timeless."

So it has proved to be. At the time, Clint was consoled by the fact that European critics received it much more favorably than their American counterparts did. Gradually, over the years, others have come around to his view of it. In retrospective considerations of his career, it now tends to be regarded as a turning point—"his best work to date," according to an admiring 1982 essay in *The New York Review of Books;* "the most ambitious and emotionally rich of the Eastwood-directed westerns," as David Anson put it in 1985; "one of his best pictures," David Thomson conceded.

Six years after its release it received a treasurable accolade—and a brief, smart reading—from an unlikely source. Orson Welles years before had approached Clint in Spain about appearing in one of his many unmade projects. Later he would approach him with his hopeless script *The Big Brass Ring.* Now he was making one of his many latter-day ap-

pearances on Merv Griffin's talk show, and the conversation turned to
that summer's releases with Welles saying something not very enthusiastic about Clint's *Firefox,* to which he quickly appended praise for *The
Outlaw Josey Wales.*

It brought applause from the studio audience, and agreement from
the host, who is a friend of Clint's. "That was a wonderful film," said
Griffin.

"I suppose Clint Eastwood is the most underrated director in the
world today," Welles rumbled on. "I'm not talking about him as a star.

"They don't take him seriously," Welles added, "the way they don't
take beautiful girls seriously. They can't believe they can act if they're
beautiful—they must be a little ugly to be taken seriously by men. And
an actor like Eastwood is such a pure type of mythic hero-star in the
Wayne tradition that no one is going to take him seriously as a director.
But someone ought to say it. And when I saw that picture for the fourth
time, I realized that it belongs with the great westerns. You know, the
great westerns of Ford and Hawks and people like that. And I take my
hat off to him. I'm glad to have had a chance to say that."

Here, in an unexpected context, an appropriately admiring linkage—between Clint's film and the tradition it grew from and commented upon—was made for the first time in public, and an appropriate
irony regarding the overwhelming power of his image and its effect on
critical opinion was observed. These were matters of obvious moment
to Welles, who had endured analagous misunderstandings of himself
and his work, and in the years ahead they would slowly, almost imper-
ceptibly, become commonplaces in the critical (and popular) discourse
surrounding Clint Eastwood and his work.

TWELVE

I'M WHO I WANT TO BE

I n every great star career there comes a time to signal in some completely obvious way that whatever the joke about you is, you're in on it. In this matter, timing is everything; self-satire offered too soon suggests cynicism, too late it proposes cluelessness. Clint, now utterly secure in his stardom and freedom of choice, caught the moment perfectly. Four of the five movies he made between 1976 and 1980 offered broad, mainly comic variations on his screen character, each a little more radical than its predecessor until, finally, he had moved about as far as it was possible for him to get from Dirty Harry Callahan. The other film of this period, *Escape from Alcatraz*, went to the opposite extreme, toward a stark minimalism of characterization like that of the Leone pictures, but, if anything, darker and more enigmatic.

This shift was mirrored by a radical change in his private life. By the time the decade turned, his marriage would be over—though the formalities of its dissolution would not be completed until 1984—and his relationship with Sondra Locke, publicly denied for some years and always somewhat unconventional in its particulars, would become a central fact of his life. It would seem there was a contentment in the first years of this relationship that had been absent in the later years of his marriage and that surely contributed to the ease and good humor that is visible on the screen.

The first film in which the change was apparent was *The Enforcer*, the second sequel to *Dirty Harry*. Jim Fargo was once again serving as associate producer, and beginning to worry because a director had not yet been named. Finally, one spring day, in the midst of an office party, Clint and Bob Daley called him into the latter's office, to press him on what seemed to Fargo an annoyingly minor point. "Who are you going to get for your assistant?" Clint inquired.

The question rendered Fargo, who was planning to double as the production's first assistant director, somewhat snappish. "Clint, I can't be thinking about getting a second at this stage. We gotta get a director in here."

"Look," came the grinning reply, "if you're gonna be the director of this thing, you gotta have a good first."

Thus, slyly, did Fargo learn that a long-standing ambition was about to be satisfied. It was his sangfroid, tested in the contrasting fires of *The Eiger Sanction* and *The Outlaw Josey Wales,* that won him the promotion, as well as his ability to stand up to the star when he had to. On the former picture he had set up the camera and called "Action" and "Cut" for a little talk scene and had been bold enough to propose a second take. Why? "Because it was terrible."

"What do you mean, it was terrible?"

"Listen to it," said Fargo. So they played it back, and heard three flubbed lines, as Clint hurried through some dull exposition.

"All right," he grumbled, and repeated the scene. All right, he probably thought, this guy can withstand pressure.

Not that Fargo, or anyone else directing Clint, or any other actor working in a Malpaso production, is permitted to assert a large authoritarian ego. "Basically, you work with Clint like he works with actors," says Fargo. "And that is give them the chance to do what they can do. Make your suggestions, and make them as suggestions, not as demands. . . . Let's face it, you're not going to be able to tell Clint how to play Harry Callahan."

This script had come to Clint in a way almost as curious as *Josey Wales* had. Its first draft, entitled *Moving Target,* was the work of two young San Francisco film students, Gail Hickman and Scott Shroers, who had handed it to the maître d' at the Hog's Breath, the restaurant Clint and some partners had opened in Carmel, hoping it would be passed on to the proprietor. Somehow it was, and Clint liked it: "Their effort was better than the ideas of several professionals I'd read." Malpaso bought it, turning it over to the veteran Stirling Silliphant and—who else?—Dean Riesner. They received screenplay credit on the film, with the youngsters reduced to a story credit, though they insisted that many of their scenes remained in the finished film.

Once again, San Francisco is being terrorized by a crime wave, perpetrated this time by a self-styled revolutionary cadre, similar to the Symbionese Liberation Army, which kidnapped Patty Hearst in 1974. These fictional revolutionaries are not moved by principle; they're into crime for the money. But like their real-life models they do kidnap a prominent citizen—the mayor no less—and hold him hostage on Alcatraz.

But story is not this movie's main line of business. Humorous self-awareness is. Everyone involved in *The Enforcer* obviously knew what

Harry had come to represent to the audience, and they play to those expectations, entering into a kind of us-against-them conspiracy directed
at the middle-class, middlebrow right-mindedness that was bound to
greet these films. The filmmakers encourage the audience to revel with
them in wretched excess—low humor, outrageous behavior, action
heightened well beyond realistic bounds. In effect, they treat their critics exactly as Harry Callahan treats his superiors, cheekily challenging
them to make prissy fools of themselves, then going on to show how
dumb they are by getting results—in the case of the movies, smashing
box-office results.

Take, for example, a sequence many reviewers would single out as
particularly lacking in both realism and social responsibility but which is,
in fact, one of its best set pieces. Some bandits, foiled in a liquor-store
robbery, are holding clerks and customers hostage while the police, who
have them surrounded, impotently try to negotiate an end to the stalemate. Arriving on the scene, Harry engages in the following dialogue
with the cops' commander, thin-lipped, captious Captain McKay (Bradford Dillman).

"What do they want?"

"They want a car." Pause, as Harry begins edging away. "What are
you gonna do?"

"Give 'em one."

Since we are entirely aware of his impatient nature, we start smiling
to ourselves the minute Harry speaks, our pleasure growing as he settles
himself behind the wheel of a vehicle and revs the motor. He wouldn't,
would he?

Of course he would. He rams the car full tilt through the store's
plate-glass window, its glass and that of the store's stock shattering spectacularly. Naturally, the bad guys' strutting arrogance quickly turns into
sniveling surrender.

Is this improbable, as many reviewers held? Naturally. Is it dubious
police procedure, imperiling the innocent as it does? Doubtless. Is it
funny to see the world's most famous knothead delivering his predictable goods? You bet it is.

Needless to say, Harry's attitude toward authority has not improved,
and we eagerly—and not for long—await his exchanges with it. Hauled
before a board of inquiry, headed by a lady of the perpetually appalled
liberal persuasion, he is informed that "the minority community's just
about had it with this kind of police work."

"By minority community I suppose you mean the hoods."

"They're American citizens, too."

McKay is naturally obliged to second the board's opinion—and, equally naturally, to cover his ass. "I never said to use excessive violence," the captain primly informs him. "What'd you want me to do, yell trick or treat at 'em?" comes the reply. McKay responds by taking Harry off active duty, assigning him to a desk job in personnel. "Personnel? That's for assholes."

"I was in personnel for ten years" comes the completely self-satisfied reply.

And so it goes. Clint's performance is often very funny because like all splendidly splenetic movie figures—from W. C. Fields to Daffy Duck—there is a kind of aplomb in his outrage that derives from an un-apologetic sense of his own nature. Harry's enemies do parody liberal piety—an Episcopalian minister who has been taken in by the self-styled revolutionaries gets particularly rough treatment—and the detective's sallies against them do constitute a harsh, premature critique of what we have since learned to call political correctness.

But his true cause is, as ever, common sense and common decency, a point he makes, with typical obliqueness, in an exchange with a black revivalist preacher who is also a police informer and is played, interest-ingly enough, by Albert Popwell, the "do you feel lucky" bank robber in *Dirty Harry*. The minister tells Harry he's working for the wrong side. "You go out there and put your ass on the line for a bunch of dudes who wouldn't let you in the front door any more than they would me."

"I don't do it for them," Harry responds.

"Who then?"

"You wouldn't believe me if I told you." Meaning, of course, that he does it for all the powerless people who, regardless of race, creed and color, are trying to lead secure and honest lives.

But we know all that; *The Enforcer*'s largest interest lies in its variation on another convention of the series—Harry's relationship with a new partner. As always, it begins in suspicion and ends in affection and re-spect. But there's more to it this time because the tyro is a woman, Kate Moore, appealingly played by Tyne Daly, in a kind of rehearsal for her role on *Cagney and Lacy*. The love that develops between them is only chastely suggested, but it is the more affecting for that quality, and the source of the movie's distinction.

Chunky, square faced, capable of a rather mannish manner, but with a certain vulnerability about her, Daly was Clint's choice for the role—"the kind of girl who might get into this kind of thing." Others were urging a dishier actress on him, but he screened one of Daly's previous, rather small movie roles and said to Fargo, "I don't see how you cannot consider her."

Daly told reporter Todd Coleman she turned the role down three times: "I thought the woman was just there to be made fun of, to be the butt of all the jokes." But she went through her scenes line by line with Clint, humanizing and strengthening her character. "If she's going to be as heroic as she possibly can be," she argued, "then let me kill a bad guy." This she was permitted to do in the film's climactic confrontation. "A lesser or more greedy star" would not have allowed this kind of creative participation in his project, she reflected. Clint, of course, welcomed the improved realism. He told a reporter at the time, "When my lawyer saw her on the set he thought she was the technical advisor."

Their working relationship now happily established, they attempted something unique in an Eastwood movie, a full-scale improvisation of a long and complicated sequence called, with conscious irony, the "romantic" scene, by the filmmakers. By this point in the picture, Kate has proved herself a game girl—she even dares to kid Harry about the size of his .44 Magnum and its obvious sexual overtones—and they settle down for a companionable drink in a bar. Both actors thought they could wing something better than whatever had been written. Fargo decided on a two-camera setup, one close-up on Daly, the other on Clint, which shot for shot looked fine. But over the course of the work—which at one point Daly interrupted in order to make a trip to the ladies' room (it stayed in the release print)—they never repeated their lines in exactly the same way. That meant their singles could not be cut together coherently. And that called for another Malpaso rarity—retakes. This time Fargo backed off and used a dolly to get some wide shots and some over-the-shoulders that provided the editor, Ferris Webster, with the material he needed to make a smooth sequence. The result is one of the best scenes in the film—two loners trying to establish a connection.

The movie was greeted by the usual critical disdain, with Richard Eder reaching new heights of cluelessness with his complaint that the film "lacked ideas." These are never, of course, prerequisites for action films, but what's extraordinary about him and almost all the rest of the critics is their failure to acknowledge the originality of the relationship between Harry and Kate, the quality of Daly's work or the extraordinary conclusion to which that relationship comes. For, of all things, the movie ends in tragedy. In the attempt to rescue the kidnapped mayor Kate is killed. She dies cradled in Harry's arms, wrapped in his anguished love.

It is an entirely unexpected, completely affecting and, one would have thought, totally obvious ending: This moment completes the arc of a plotline that had never been tried on the screen before, a female police officer overcoming gender prejudice and achieving full equality with a male partner.

It was a feminist critic, Marjorie Rosen, writing in *Ms.*, who alone caught the significance of Daly's character and her treatment in the film. "Harry has found . . . an equal, a partner of similar mettle and courage," she said. "The strength of the film is his process of discovery as he turns from belligerent to respectful." This she called "exhilarating," since his "unabashed apprehension . . . parallels that of most men more than most of us would like to believe. Therefore, the film nourishes our hope that contact has—or can be—made." She particularly praised the film's climax, in which, as she approvingly put it, Kate "dies like a man."

That said, one also has to say that there is something rattletrap about the way *The Enforcer* veers from action to comedy to fighting romance. Certainly today, attitudes having radically changed, Clint would retract its casual contempt for homosexuals, admittedly a feature of several of his early action films. It is also possible he might have encouraged its writers and director to a greater consistency of tone. Or perhaps not. He seems to have liked brusque switches of mood—particularly in contemporary urban action pieces—perhaps because they struck him as truer to the city's rhythms. Be that as it may, the film seemed to be taking it too easy on itself, and that encouraged reviewers to be, perhaps, too hard on it. Neatness always counts with them.

★   ★   ★

The motives of his next movie, *The Gauntlet,* are, if anything, more deliriously mixed than those of *The Enforcer.* At a cost of $5 million, the most expensive Eastwood movie up to that point, it, too, offers a leading female character who is something more than the male lead's passive companion. In this case she is, in fact, smarter than he is and in a position to affect the narrative's development more significantly. Moreover, this movie wants to parody, by pushing them to excess, the wild-ride conventions of the action film, to offer a critique of authority different from, but as blunt as, that of the *Dirty Harry* films and, improbably enough, to establish a link between itself and yet another genre, that of romantic comedy. It has a lot on its plate.

The Gauntlet was a script (by Michael Butler and Dennis Shryack) Warner Bros. had in hand, and the studio first proposed it to Clint as a costarring vehicle with Barbra Streisand (whom he dated for a brief period later on); she, typically, hesitated over the project; he, typically, grew impatient, deciding, finally, that he would direct and that he could probably carry the picture commercially without Streisand's help.

To no one's surprise, he cast Locke as Gus Mally, a shrill and foul-mouthed Las Vegas prostitute with a college degree. "I thought," says Clint, "Wouldn't it be interesting to cast somebody who's used to playing a kind of waify type as a hooker, instead of having a come-up-and-see-me-sometime vibe?" He thought it equally interesting to cast himself as a dumb cop, a sort of anti–Dirty Harry, a man who has never questioned authority, never done anything to call attention to himself and is, when we meet him, drinking himself into oblivion.

What we understand from everything the movies have taught us about ill-matched couples thrown together and obliged to take a dangerous journey together—he's supposed to extradite her from a Las Vegas jail and escort her to his home city to testify in a gangland trial—is that she is going to reanimate him ("I love those guys who are learning as the picture goes by," says Clint) and that he is going to tame her by touching the soft center hidden beneath a hard exterior. What we learn as this film proceeds is that the first thing she tells him is correct. Someone wants to murder her and that removing her from what amounts to protective custody is the first step in that process. We also learn eventually that that someone is Blakelock (William Prince), the Phoenix police chief, and that he has chosen Ben Shockley as her escort precisely because he is such a lousy cop.

Because Gus so violently resists removal from jail he has her gagged, strapped to a gurney and conveyed to an ambulance he has ordered to take them to a car he has rented. As they pull up to it, the automobile explodes. Immediately thereafter they find themselves pursued by two other cars. Evading them, they take refuge at her home, a dusty bungalow on a desert lot. Shockley phones Blakelock, requesting a police escort to the airport. Instead he tells the Las Vegas cops that a desperate criminal gang is holed up in the house, and they lay massive siege to it.

There follows one of the most remarkable action sequences in the Eastwood canon. The cops are armed with the latest in assault weapons, which they are eager to try out. When the call to surrender goes unanswered, they saturate the building with bullets (according to a press release, which probably didn't exaggerate by much, 250,000 squibs were set in its walls, their bullet-sized charges set off electronically). The result is a truly terrifying, strangely comic and characteristically Eastwoodian excess. This is a full-scale firestorm, sustained far beyond our expectations. When eventually it subsides, we hear the house start to groan and see it start to tremble, whereupon it shudders comically and collapses in upon itself.

In this sequence the camera picks up a sign reading, "God Makes House Calls," and when it is over a cop offers an inane moral to the episode: "Cap'n, they should have surrendered." Sign and dialogue both signal the director's satiric intent, which was not merely to send up generic convention, but to comment on the observed realities of the moment. Clint says he got the idea for the sequence from television coverage of the Los Angeles Police Department siege of a building where elements of the Symbionese Liberation Army had gone to ground.

This sequence also encapsulates one of the film's main themes, for just as Ben Shockley is Harry Callahan's opposite, *The Gauntlet*'s characterization of authority is the opposite of *Dirty Harry*'s. Ben's superiors are portrayed not as impotent prisoners of political correctness, but as fools of quite another kind, setting themselves arrogantly above the law, indulging in every kind of overkill to assure their ultimate victory. An analogy to Vietnam is inescapable.

At the time, Clint preferred to see *The Gauntlet* as a straightforward chase with some comic-romantic overtones. He drew particular attention to the woman's role: "The girl's part is a terrific role, not just token window dressing like in so many action pictures. Her part is equal to the male part, if not even more so." He suggested comparisons to *It Happened One Night* and *The African Queen,* with the latter perhaps being the more apt if only because it, too, posits a drunken and defeated hero reforming himself under the tutelage of a high-spirited woman.

But rich as it is in references to romantic comedy, the film's dominant tone is bleak; the countryside through which the couple moves is relentlessly harsh, and photographed in hard, flat light by Rexford Metz, a legendary aerial photographer whom Clint had promoted to DP. Moreover, the film is once again full of Clint's brutal frankness.

For example, there is Ben and Gus's escape from Las Vegas. Still trusting Blakelock, Shockley asks for him to send an escort to meet them at the Nevada–Arizona state line, and he commandeers a police car driven by what seems to be a good ole boy (played with his usual relish by Bill McKinney) to take them to this rendezvous. As they proceed, however, this nameless cop launches into an ugly fantasy about Gus's life as a hooker that amounts to nothing less than attempted verbal rape. She resists with a cool catechism of everyday police piggishness and thuggery, as vicious a case against law enforcement as the screen has ever offered. She concludes by saying that the filth she encounters in her life can be soaked off in a long hot bath, while the rot in his brain can never be excised—except by blowing it out with a service revolver. By the way, she sweetly wonders, does his wife know that he masturbates? The man screams, and almost loses control of the car.

She reduces her tormentor to impotent, quivering rage, and Gus finally convinces Ben that caution is the better part of valor. When they near the state line, they send the cop on alone, and, sure enough, he and his car are decimated. It is a repeat, on a slightly smaller scale, of the bungalow shoot-out—excessive force excessively applied. They take refuge in a cave and play their extremely broad equivalent of the Walls of Jericho scene in *It Happened One Night.*

He: "For two cents and a stick of gum I'd beat the shit out of you."

She: "Whatever gets you off, Butch."

He: "After I was through, where would I leave the money?"

She: "I don't want your money, Shockley. I love you for your mind."

Whereupon he slugs her, and she doubles him over with a knee to the groin.

The next morning, he taxes her about why, exactly, everyone is so interested in her. She tells a story about a mobster setting her up with a memorably perverse John, who obliges her to strip and lie facedown on the bed in his hotel room, where he holds a gun between her legs with one hand. What he was doing with his other hand is, as she says, not hard to imagine. We are far beyond a conventional hooker hard-luck story here. More important, Shockley recognizes Blakelock from her description.

As he does, however, the silence of their refuge is shattered by the roar of motorcycles as the usual scruffy gang draws up outside their cave. Trapped, Shockley brazens it out, threatening to arrest the lot of them: "I got this gun, I got this badge, I got the love of Jesus in my pretty green eyes," he shouts. It is, of course, a variant on another classic movie scene—Cary Grant's single-handed threat to arrest the entire Kali cult in *Gunga Din,* except that Clint plays this as a mad scene, a ploy that turns out to be more effective than Grant's brilliant parody of heroic cool. He drives the gang off, all except three of them—one whose cycle he has shot up and a couple whose bike he takes for his and Gus's use.

Soon a police helicopter is chasing them in an expertly managed action sequence that ends with the chopper crashing into a high-tension tower. Now they hop a freight—and find themselves sharing an empty boxcar with the three cyclists they left behind at the cave. They get the jump on Shockley, tie him up and start to beat him insensible. Gus diverts them by pulling open her blouse and offering herself to them. As they assail her—the woman is a full participant—Shockley manages to free himself and throw them off the train.

Recuperating from their ordeal in a motel room, Shockley and Gus confess their variously broken and unfulfilled dreams. By the end of this conversation she is proposing to him in perhaps the only way a woman could propose to such a character—indirectly. She calls her mother in New York and describes this man she's met and the life she says they are going to share—after they take care of some business they have in Phoenix.

Yes, Phoenix. For he has decided he can run no farther. He must confront Blakelock and try to bring him to justice. "At least someone will know I tried." "Who? Blakelock?" asks Gus. "No. Me."

It makes sense on one level. If they continue to run, inevitably they will be caught and dispensed with on some anonymous back road. On the other, more practical, hand, the scheme is ludicrous. He proposes to hijack a bus, armor it with steel plate and then drive it, via a pre-announced route, down the main streets of Phoenix, encouraging Blakelock to assault it with all the forces at his command. Just why Shockley is so certain of Blakelock's response is never made clear, nor is the case persuasively made for his not having the bus quietly apprehended on the open highway before it arrives in town. Hey, we've got a movie to make here, and one in dire need of climactic spectacle.

At least another 250,000 squibs were rigged on the bus, the streets were cleared, the extras—mainly off-duty Phoenix policemen—were uniformed and armed, and the gauntlet was run. Why no sharpshooter ever took aim at the naked rubber tires of the vehicle remains one of those great unsolved movie mysteries—rather like the one about why the Indians didn't shoot the *Stagecoach* horses. In the end, the bus collapses under the weight of the firepower directed at it, just like the bungalow and the police car before it. But it does attain the courthouse steps, where Blakelock goes bonkers when his awed, cowed police force refuses his order to kill Ben and Gus. It is she, indeed, who kills the police commissioner after he has wounded Ben.

Bob Daley thought the whole sequence senseless: "Three hundred thousand bullet holes and not one tire went flat, and nobody got nicked. The audience—we lost them right there." Don Siegel took another tack. After seeing a rough cut and making some complimentary remarks, he said there was just one more shot missing. What was that, Clint asked. "I'd like to have seen a shot with four or five hundred dead cops lying in the street." What he meant was that with officers lining both sides of the narrow streets and firing madly at the bus, they would inevitably create carnage in their own ranks.

Clint was not amused. Whatever strain his concluding sequence placed on credulity, it represented, like the film's other set-piece action sequences, tour de force moviemaking, quick-cut and complex in a manner he had not previously attempted.

Daley remembers Clint confronting him one day for his lack of enthusiasm. "You've been telling people *The Gauntlet* is one of the worst movies you've ever seen," he said to Daley. "No, that's not true. It's one of the ten worst, but not the worst," Daley replied. Recounting the exchange he adds, "I meant it to be humorous, but it didn't sit well with him."

Neither did a series of mishandled sneak previews in the Mid-Atlantic states. One of them was scheduled for the night a local team was playing a championship football game, so that the audience was full of older people volubly offended by the film's violence and bad language. None of the previews was supported by print, television or radio advertising, and John Calley remembers making frantic calls back to the studio, trying to mobilize some last-minute support for the showings. He also remembers hand-lettering cardboard signs and tacking them up in a desperate effort to fill the gap. Fritz Manes called a media-buyer friend in the middle of the night, seeking help in getting a few last-minute commercials on the air.

A Warner Bros. executive lost his job over this incident, and Manes thinks Calley's heroic generalship may have saved the studio's relationship with Clint. For the star was present for the chaos. Ironically, he had in his possession part of the solution to whatever marketing problems the picture presented. This was a spectacular painting, the work of the celebrated fantasy illustrator Frank Frazetta, which he and Sondra had picked up from the artist in Connecticut and were carrying in the back of a new Ferrari Clint also acquired on the trip. The artwork represented a substantial investment on the studio's part (and a substantial worry as it knocked about unguarded in the car), for it was intended as the centerpiece for the film's advertising campaign, a ripsnorting montage featuring the bus looking menacing, an overmuscled Clint looking heroic and a bosomy Sondra looking imperiled. It was hip-regressive, its air of old-fashioned movie ballyhoo proposing old-fashioned thrills.

It worked. *Newsweek*'s David Anson suggested that Frazetta's work caught the "captivatingly lunatic" spirit of a movie that he said was "like a sword-and-sorcery epic recast in tacky Southwestern drag." His tone of bemused indulgence was adopted in many of the reviews. Vincent Canby, for example, wrote that even though the movie did not have "a single thought in its head . . . its action sequences are so ferociously staged that it's impossible not to pay attention most of the time." He even offered a few words of sharply observed (if backhanded) praise for Clint's performance: "Mr. Eastwood's talent is his style, unhurried and self-assured, that of a man who goes through life looking down at other men's bald spots."

Curiously, the improbable invincibility of the bus as it crawls through the concluding gauntlet didn't seem to bother most reviewers; even Pauline Kael's predictable screed omitted mention of it. Like Gus Mally's little house, the critics were beginning to collapse under the weight of Clint's seemingly irresistible firepower. It is odd that so many of them picked this, the most blatantly violent movie Clint had ever made, to abandon their resistance, but such was the case.

The notice that summarized this turnabout was Tom Allen's in the *Village Voice.* Clint's movies, he said, were beginning to contain a certain "sophisticated character interplay within spectacles pitched low to the mass audience." Noting Locke's "full partnership" in the action, and terming her work "the most naturally unaffected" of the year, he also observed the emergence, "slow and crude," of a new Eastwood character, "a vulnerable male who needs a woman to lean on." He called "the plodding weakness" of Shockley "a much more audacious concept than the preening invincibility of Harry Callahan."

Why he and some of his colleagues chose this, the most relentlessly violent of all Clint's movies, instead of the more thoughtful and complex *Josey Wales,* as the occasion for surrender is impossible to say. But this much is certain: A rude beast had been perceived slouching toward the Bethlehem of the New Masculinity, waiting to be reborn in more cuddlesome form. From now on his progress would be watched with slow but steadily increasing sympathy.

★   ★   ★

In the months immediately following *The Gauntlet*'s release Clint did his best to maintain the fiction that all was still right with his marriage, that his relationship with Sondra Locke—about which increasingly serious rumors were beginning to circulate—was simply that of two mutually respectful professionals who enjoyed one another's company at work. He spent a lot of time in Carmel that winter, and he invited journalists from significant publications into his new home, where Maggie submitted to brief interviews with them. There may have been a certain lack of warmth in such comments as they offered about their marriage, but at least it was being placed on display.

Locke, too, did what she could to allay the gossip. In *People,* for example, she said: "Everybody would love for us to say, 'It's all true, we're madly in love.' . . . Even if it were true—which it isn't—I certainly wouldn't talk about it." Asked about her husband's reaction to the rumors, she said, "We don't sit down and talk it out. He figures if there's any truth to it, I'll be the first to tell him; if there's anything to know, he'll know it." The most she would concede was that "when the actor you're developing a rapport with is directing, you feel much more camaraderie about scenes, and you can relate in a much tighter way."

But the very fact that the magazine dared report rumors about them irritated Clint, and he fired off a letter to the editor that read, in full: "I have just finished reading your untalented article on a very talented subject—Sondra Locke. It's sad that you found it necessary to indulge in adolescent titillation."

But he was living a lie, which he now admits. For he knew that his relationship with Sondra was different in character from his previous affairs and that his marriage was, in all but name, over. Indeed, it's likely that it had been, in his mind anyway, for a couple of years.

It was, he says, the splendid Carmel house, the construction of which had consumed seven years of their lives, that created irreconcilable differences between him and Maggie. It was a showcase home, the only hugely impressive one (as opposed to the purely comfortable) he has ever occupied. A redwood-and-Douglas-fir crescent set on twelve acres overlooking the bay, it had four bedrooms, a split-level living room with two fireplaces and all the other accoutrements of success—Jacuzzi, gym, projection room. His mother's old upright piano was built into a specially created niche.

Given Clint's long and frequent absences, the house became very much Maggie's project. That troubled him. He started to feel cut out of her consultations with designers and builders. As he began to see it, he was the one working hard to pay for a lifestyle growing ever more expansive, and he felt his wishes and opinions were being ignored. He says they came to crisis, ludicrously enough, over a detail—the placement of a showerhead. The one in the master bathroom was, he thought, too low for a man of his height.

Needless to say, they patched up this silly quarrel, but the issues it symbolized were not so easily ameliorated. Sondra or no Sondra, they were drifting toward an event not uncommon in the prospering classes—the dream-house divorce. In this scenario, the new home is supposed to compensate for years of hard work, sacrifice and disappointment and at the same time signal arrival at unshakable stability. When it does not, the inevitable question arises: "All that for this?"

Indeed, what matter decor and amenities when the things that were wrong before you moved in remain wrong? By this time, according to Don Kincade, Clint's old friend, who would remain affectionately loyal to both parties in the future, Maggie could no longer deny his infidelities—and, denials or no, this latest one was far more obvious than the others. Fritz Manes was staying in the Eastwoods' Los Angeles home in this period, his own marriage in temporary disarray. When Maggie called there looking for Clint when he was out with Sondra, Manes tried to cover for him—not very plausibly.

Clint, however, maintained his silence about Sondra, merging it into his larger silences, which surely played their part, too, in the sundering of this marriage. In recent years he has become a little more emotionally open, but this has always been hard for him. "Women," Clint says, a sort of sad befuddlement in his tone, "always want to know what you're thinking." It is a mystery to him, this desire to penetrate the deepest reserves of his privacy. It is equally a mystery to him why anyone would think that bringing things up out of this murk and discussing them would profit either party. At our cores, he believes, for whatever reasons, we are what we are, and there is nothing much to be done about that—beyond simply accepting the hard facts of personality. For this realist, that may be the ultimate reality. For a marriage, of course, it is the ultimate peril.

One will never know from them precisely why or when Clint and Maggie finally agreed to abandon their marriage. But in early 1979 the Eastwoods would announce their legal separation. Clint was now routinely referred to in the press as one of the world's richest actors, and the property settlement that followed a year later reflected the truth of those reports. Maggie, it was said, received at least $25 million under this agreement. In the years thereafter, they restored their friendship. Clint has recently said that their relationship after marriage was much better than it was during it, and their son, Kyle, has said: "It wasn't bad as divorces go. There was no weird custody thing. We lived with my mom and saw my dad whenever we wanted to." It seems to have been a little harder on Alison, then only seven years old, her bond with her father not as fully formed as her brother's was (they began sharing a passion for jazz when Kyle was very young). But no one who knows Clint has ever doubted the strength of his affection for his children or his eagerness for them to share in his life, which meant sharing his work. As a little girl Alison was often on his sets, frequently wielding the slate that marks the beginning of a take. Each child would eventually be given a major role in one of his pictures.

★   ★   ★

If early in 1978 Clint was still being circumspect about the state of his marriage, there was nothing cautious about his choice of projects, for this was the year he costarred with an orangutan. *Every Which Way but Loose* had come to him through one of his secretaries, whose husband hoped to produce the Jeremy Joe Kronsberg script. According to Manes no one at first thought of it as a likely prospect for Clint. Its proprietors hoped he might pass the script on to Burt Reynolds. Riding the seventies crossover of country music and cultural style into the mainstream, Reynolds had just had a $100 million grosser with *Smokey and the Bandit.* But Clint, as it turned out, was not uninterested in doing something basic and blue collar.

Feelings about *Every Which Way but Loose* were, however, decidedly mixed among Clint's advisers. Daley read it and loathed it; Manes read it and liked it—"this is us growing up in Oakland," he remembers saying, not entirely inaccurately. Lenny Hirshan thought it was awful, as did Bruce Ramer, Clint's attorney, and most of the studio brass. Sondra, however, confirmed Clint's impression that there was "something hip about it in a strange way." It was "the entertainment piece" he had been looking for, full of action, but all of it comic and more overtly subversive of his macho image than anything he had yet tried.

Clint's character, Philo Beddoe, lives in a tumbledown house with his pal Orville (Geoffrey Lewis), Orville's harridan mom (played with wonderful relish by Ruth Gordon) and his pet ape, Clyde (who was played mostly by an immature male named Manis, though two other orangs were used for special tricks). Philo makes his living as a trucker and as a bare-knuckle boxer, under Orville's dim management. He falls in love with aristocratic-seeming country-western singer Lynn Halsey-Taylor (Locke), who sleeps with hunks who happen to catch her fancy, but is also mysteriously committed to a sexually enigmatic male friend, to whom she returns after her fling with Philo (art imitating life, Clint thought). He decides to pursue her, accompanied by Clyde, Orville and the latter's girlfriend, Echo (Beverly D'Angelo). In the course of this odyssey he fights a few bouts, incurs the enmity of a pair of dim-witted cops and a gang of over-the-hill bikers who call themselves the Black Widows, but doesn't get the girl.

This sounds more coherent than it plays: The construction of *Every Which Way but Loose* was every which way but tight, except in one particular—Philo's hugely comic, strangely touching relationship with Clyde. The orang is gentle, cuddly, somewhat mysterious, occasionally mischievous, completely faithful and, above all, a good listener whose needs are uncomplicated and easily satisfied. Putting sex aside, he offered everything guys dream of finding in gals and rarely do; everything guys hope to find in other guys and sometimes do.

The terms of their endearment are established early on, when Clyde gets in trouble by stealing Oreos from Orville's mother. After placating her, Philo encounters his pal and points a menacing finger at him. The ape throws up his arms in surrender. Philo goes "bang," and Clyde flops down, pretending to be shot. Oh—somebody's sending up his image and, as the movie proceeds, masculine ways in general. When Orville lets Clyde have a few brews in a bar, Philo is outraged: "How many times have I told you—I don't want him drinking beer except on Saturday night." When Philo takes Clyde to meet Lynn he lectures him: "Clyde, Clyde, you're going to meet a lady now. I want you to handle it. No spittin', pissin', fartin' or pickin' your ass."

All that goofiness aside the picture actually has a point to make. At the end, Philo throws a big fight he's in the process of winning, for the best of reasons. He doesn't want to be a marked man, somebody everyone feels obliged to challenge. Maybe, one thinks, he's smarter than he looks. And maybe this movie is smarter than it looks. Its charm lies precisely in its obliviousness to its own "hipness," its refusal to nudge and wink at the audience. It lets them recognize that quality—or not—in their way, in their own good time.

For Clint, the charm was working with Manis. The creature was part of an animal act owned and trained by Bob Berosini, who mostly worked Las Vegas and had been recommended to Clint by the director of a primate lab he consulted, and he turned out to be, for Clint, something of a soulmate.

"The orang is an introvert, and the chimp is an extrovert. Chimps love to perform, roll their lips back and do all that kind of stuff. But orangs are kind of cool. They love to study things, and they're kind of shy. You have to coax them into it. I didn't get overly friendly. I'd always pretend I didn't notice him, then he'd start studying me, because I wasn't looking at him and staring him down. I'd feel him start picking at my ear and looking in my ear, you know, doing little things like they do to you. And always grabbing my Adam's apple. Eventually he got to really like me. In fact, it used to make Berosini jealous, because sometimes he'd be calling him and I'd call him and he'd come running to me." This relationship worked so well, as Clint admits, because Manis was young and innocent. You can't, he says, work this way with a fully mature orangutan, because "they start exercising dominance. They're liable to take your head off when you least expect it."

This, of course, was a trait not unknown to mature actor-filmmakers. Once again, Clint fell into disagreement with his director, Jim Fargo. Mainly this was because Fargo, as Alain Silver, one of his assistants, puts it, "had the notion that he was directing the movie." He perhaps overstates the case slightly, but the point needs stressing: For all the amiability between them, authority on Clint's sets resides in only one place. It can be reasoned with, but it cannot be ignored without predictable consequences. It is, as we have seen from the outset, the first principle in dealing with a man who must assert what control he can over the uncontrollable world.

Director and star fell out in particular over a sequence in which the biker gang menaces Locke's character. Fargo set up its crucial shot, in which a shotgun is suddenly stuck out the window of her truck to drive the Black Widows away, in such a way as to disguise the fact that she is with another man. Clint thought this revelation should be made, and that the gun should not be wielded by Lynn. "It was very clear," says Silver, "that he didn't want any violence attached to her." Unfortunately, he did not discover what Fargo had done until the bikers—whose last day on the production this was—had been released and sent home. They had to be called back, amid a certain amount of producerly fuming. And, ultimately, with a predictable consequence. As Silver says, "Once you're on Clint's bad list, you don't come back." Fargo never did.

This despite the fact that he was the director of record of what is, dollars in, dollars out, the most profitable movie Clint Eastwood ever made, returning more than $51 million—about ten times its cost—in domestic theatrical rentals alone. This was an astonishing figure, especially considering that when it was first screened for the studio's executives one of them firmly pronounced the film unreleasable and that when it was first screened for critics it was considered unspeakable. "Alarming," "blundering," "lumpy," "a junk heap," "a disgrace"—these are a fair representation of the descriptions applied to it. Rona Barrett told her readers that Clint's fans deserved an apology.

But Barry Reardon, newly installed as Warner's head of distribution, had from the start thought otherwise. At that first executive screening he remembers saying, "That picture's going to make us a fortune." Terry Semel, who had just moved up from Reardon's job to become the studio's chief operating officer, agreed. Together they decided to open *Every Which Way but Loose* simultaneously in both small towns and in the big cities. This was then a novel release pattern, as was the size of the national television-ad campaign they mounted for the film. Clint, who had been afraid his movie would be shunted aside in favor of the much more expensive and risky *Superman,* which was opening almost simultaneously, was delighted. "That's where it played, out in mid-America. People would go back. And it would play for weeks and weeks and weeks and weeks."

★   ★   ★

By the time *Every Which Way but Loose* was ready for release, Clint had completed principal photography on the last of his five collaborations with Don Siegel and the first of two collaborations with screenwriter Richard Tuggle, which would have a significant impact on his career.

Escape from Alcatraz was the first script Tuggle ever attempted, and for once the movie gods looked down from their heavenly screening room and decided to reward innocence. Working as an editor for a health magazine in San Francisco in the seventies, Tuggle one day took the tour of abandoned Alcatraz, where he heard the story of a hard-case armed robber, Frank Morris, who in 1962 had masterminded the only escape from the Rock on which the file was not closed; the authorities had neither recaptured Morris and his confederates nor recovered their bodies from the icy waters of San Francisco Bay. It was just barely possible that they had accomplished the impossible.

Intrigued, Tuggle went looking for an out-of-print book about Alcatraz escape attempts by J. Campbell Bruce that recounted the story in more detail. Suddenly fired from his job, Tuggle, a lifelong film buff, decided to use his free time to write a screenplay about the incident. When it was done, he secured movie rights to the book from Bruce (who lived nearby in Berkeley), moved to Los Angeles and endured a succession of rejections from studios and TV networks until Bruce told him that when it was first published he had sent his book to Don Siegel and had received a mildly encouraging response from him. Tuggle, who admired *Riot in Cell Block 11*, ascertained that the director was represented by Lenny Hirshan and sent his work to the agent. He glanced at it and judged it worth passing on to his client, who for the first time in his career invested money of his own—$100,000—to secure the property. Naturally, Siegel showed the script to Clint, who agreed to play Morris—subject to his approval of some rewrites.

At which point what had been a straightforward success story veers into murky territory. Something went wrong between Clint and Siegel. The former says that the problem centered mainly around the rewrite. The latter, in his memoir, hints that his reluctance to set up the project at Warner Bros. was the issue. The director was angry about its failure to mount an Academy Award campaign for *Dirty Harry* and, moreover, had been flatteringly pursued by Paramount.

Lenny Hirshan: "I called up Mike Eisner [then in his early days as Paramount's head of production]. I say, 'Mike, Don found a script and it's terrific and I'd like to send it to you this afternoon and hopefully we can do it.' And he said, 'What's the name of it?' and I said, '*Escape from Alcatraz*,' and he said to me, 'You got a deal.' I said, 'Mike, you've got to read the script first.' He said, 'Don Siegel directing a picture entitled *Es-*

cape from Alcatraz, you got a deal.' I said, 'Please, Mike, take a read. I'm sending you the script.' He called me the next morning. He says, 'I told you, you got a deal.'"

What they very soon did not have was a star, and there is implicit agreement among those close to the scene that what Clint and Siegel were really arguing about, albeit indirectly, was control of the production. To oversimplify the matter, *Dirty Harry* had made Clint a superstar, and it had made Siegel an A-list director. "Their relationship, in the beginning, had been more father-son," says Tuggle, "but as Clint had gotten more successful, as had Don, there got to be a competitive feel. And so, basically, Clint felt to some extent he probably didn't need Don to do this movie, and Don felt to some extent he didn't need Clint." Eisner agrees with this observation, at least as it applies to Siegel. He appreciated Clint's growth as "an artist and director," but "may have been more interested in getting the performer, not the artist."

Other actors were approached, but all of them turned down the project, and the agreed-upon start date, in October 1978, was fast approaching. So Eisner reminded Siegel that whatever their current differences, he and Clint were really still friends and that it was time to make peace. According to Tuggle, Siegel replied that he couldn't, that "it'll look like I'm crawling on my hands and knees." "Don," said Eisner, "in my job I do that every day."

Shrewd Michael Eisner has the engaging habit of cloaking the voice of power in disarming man-to-man vernacular. So Siegel made an appointment to join Clint for a sandwich and a beer in his office—where he was made to wait in the anteroom for forty-five minutes (according to Tuggle). But he emerged from their meeting with a deal, and, more important, a reconciliation.

The film was as physically arduous as any either of them had ever worked on, for the chill is perpetual on Alcatraz, and they were working in the late fall, usually at night in order to avoid the tours that constantly interrupted their day shoots. The cold and the dampness seemed almost to seep into Bruce Surtees's film stock.

As Siegel has said, he made a black-and-white film that happened to be photographed in color. He also made a coolly objective film, with the camera backed off as much as possible, away from the characters, so we are always aware of the walls and bars that confine them. Morris is very often seen in low angles suggesting that this is a man who will not easily be overmastered by this massive construct of stone and steel.

The film's perfectly matched visual and emotional tones are established in a great opening sequence, virtually without dialogue, during which a handcuffed Frank Morris is escorted from a police car to the Alcatraz launch, then into the prison building, where the rough initiatory formalities are conducted. They conclude with him stripped completely naked and being conducted down "Broadway," the wide corridor running between tiered cells in which most of the inmates are housed.

It is a chilling study of dehumanization. The late Don Simpson, working for Eisner before beginning his famous action-movie partnership with Jerry Bruckheimer, called Clint and told him that they could excise his nude scene if he wanted them to. Clint, nearing his fiftieth birthday, replied, "Nah, this may be the last time I'll be able to work bare-assed." (Around this time rumors that Clint had had a face-lift began circulating, to which he responded, "If I lost my squint, I think my whole career would go down the tubes.")

Realism, in short, continued to be something more than an aesthetic with him, even as he approached an age when it is in short supply among actors, even when it was becoming an increasingly scarce commodity, especially in action releases. It is hard to think of a major American film of its moment, intended for a broad audience, that was more austere in design or development than *Escape from Alcatraz*.

Its incidents are archetypal: Morris fending off first a sexual attack in a shower, then a vengeful one in the yard from a brute named Wolf (Bruce M. Fischer); a terrible stay in solitary; a prisoner (Roberts Blossom) cutting off his finger when the sadistic warden (Patrick McGoohan, relishing every mean bone in his body) takes away his painting privileges; another prisoner (Frank Ronzio) tormented by the warden, running amok and succumbing to a heart attack. Frank's developing friendships are based mainly on tersely whispered, emotionally unrevealing exchanges with these men along with Charley Butts (Larry Hankin) and the Anglin brothers (Fred Ward and Jack Thibeau), with whom he will make his escape attempt, and, most notably, English (Paul Benjamin), a black man who runs the prison library and whom he goes out of the way to ally himself with by deliberately invading black "territory" in the prison yard.

This may be, as critic James Bernardoni suggests, the most Hawksian of Eastwood films, but it is at pains to mute the camaraderie that develops, as it does in a Hawks film, as men pursue a large and dangerous enterprise. Bonding here is a thing not spoken of, not even suggested by ribbing and shared jokes as it usually is in Hawks's work. Nor is there much in the way of back story or motivation. Don Simpson had argued for more of both, but all he got was a single word. One day in the prison yard English asks Morris what kind of childhood he had, and receives an unimprovable reply: "Short."

Indeed, what sets this movie apart from most everything else in its genre is its reluctance to curry audience favor for Morris and his coconspirators. Ultimately, we don't care whether they are good guys or bad guys, or what their hard-luck stories may be. It is what they do, not who they are, that we are involved with. Over many months they are required to excavate escape routes from their cells using homemade tools. Tuggle and Siegel understand that the audacity, cunning and patience required by this huge, inching effort is in itself redemptive, that it renders anything else these men have done in life unimportant, that without cuing we will inevitably come to see their accomplishment as inspiring.

Clint had never much liked prison movies—"not enough sprawl to them"—but Morris was a highly intelligent man (Clint was shown prison records reporting an IQ over 140) with very little formal education, and he could identify with someone employing native wit to master an intricate task. Alcatraz also represented authority at its most crushing, the escape from it the ultimate act of rebellion against it, and he could certainly relate to that.

Clint was to the film what his character was to the escape attempt—the man who kept it together. Siegel reported him eagerly clambering over, into and through every nook and cranny of the disused prison on their first scouting trip, relishing every dank possibility they discovered. Once they started work, it was to him that Siegel looked to shush the tourists when they interrupted shooting, buying their silence with the promise of autographs. It was Clint, controlling his temper, who placated the park service rangers, always fussing over potential damage to a national monument (and San Francisco's number one tourist attraction). For example, graffiti left over from the Indian occupation of the island and from various hippie infestations were regarded as historically precious, and the moviemakers were not allowed to paint it out permanently. He could not understand by what leap of the bureaucratic imagination acts of desecration were converted into memorials.

But his good humor and Siegel's were unwavering. An oft-repeated recollection of the shoot involves Patrick McGoohan, who had taken to fortifying himself against the cold with odd nips from the bottle and who was always anxious to leave the location on time. One day, as the clock crept toward quitting time, Siegel asked him to stay for one more shot, an insert of his hand dropping a nail clipper that Clint's character would soon filch as a useful escape tool. McGoohan demurred, saying, "Well, it's just a hand shot, you can get any actor to do it." As Tuggle recalls, "Don looked over at Clint, and looked back at McGoohan and said, 'I don't think we can do that.' And McGoohan said, 'Why not?'

And Don said, 'Because I don't think we can get any actor in Holly-wood whose hand is shaking as much as yours to match the shot.'" Clint was dispatched to soothe the outraged actor.

Ever the realist, Clint did not think that Morris and his confederates actually made good their escape. He consulted his friend Jack LaLanne, the fitness expert (he had advised Maggie on diet and exercise when she was carrying Kyle), who had actually swum the waters around Alcatraz as a stunt, and convinced Clint that no one could survive the cold and the currents without special training, which the prisoners, obvi-ously, could not have managed. Siegel agreed. In his first cut he strongly implied that the escapees had died in the water. But that was too glum even for Clint. He insisted on a restoration of a little sequence in which the warden finds evidence (a chrysanthemum, the film's symbol of re-sistance to authority) that they made it to the dry land of Angel Island. It was the right decision. True to life or not, he (and the audience) wanted this great effort to be rewarded.

Clint did more than the usual amount of work on postproduction. Siegel was pressed by preparations for his next film—Burt Reynolds's *Rough Cut*—which took him out of the country, and there were some problems with the director's cut. Most of it was concentrated on mate-rial shot on a Paramount soundstage, where a cell block had been re-created with flyaway walls so the camera could work in tight spaces. Much insert material was made there—details of the escapees digging their way to freedom—and for once Siegel had more material than he knew what to do with. Clint asked for a dupe of this footage, reworked it with Ferris Webster and showed the results to Siegel a couple of days later. The director liked it and admitted that perhaps he had just got too close to the material. Later on, with Siegel shooting in England, Clint supervised the film's mix.

They were rewarded by some of the best reviews they had ever re-ceived. Vincent Canby insisted that "this is not a great film, or an espe-cially memorable one," then proceeded to write as if it were both, insisting "there is more evident skill and knowledge of moviemaking in any one frame of it than there is in most other American films around at the moment." As for Clint's performance, he still wondered, "Is it act-ing?" confessed he didn't know, but called him "a towering figure" in the movie's landscape. Most of his colleagues were less reserved, with Frank Rich in *Time* pretty much summarizing critical response with his praise of the film's "elegant" cinematography, its "controlled idiosyn-cratic performances" and Siegel's "lean" direction. As for Clint: "At a time when Hollywood entertainments are more overblown than ever, Eastwood proves that less really can be more." One or two reviewers even compared it to austere Robert Bresson's great prison picture *A Man Escaped*—more aptly than they perhaps knew, for the revered French director had acknowledged the influence on that film of Siegel's *Riot in Cell Block 11*.

The film did as well at the box office as it did with the reviewers. It took in only about half of what *Every Which Way but Loose* did and only about a quarter of the year's top grosser, *Superman*. But it was a solid fifteenth on 1979's list of box-office grossers, making Clint the only star with two vehicles represented there. What was particularly pleasing to him was that its grosses were virtually the same as those of *Apocalypse Now*, which he had turned down, and which, in its long agony of production, had cost $10 million more than *Escape from Alcatraz* took in at the domestic box office. "With Francis Coppola's budget, I could have invaded a country," he commented dryly.

★   ★   ★

He also could have made four or five movies like *Bronco Billy,* one of the films of which Clint remains the most proud. It was possibly the most casually acquired of all his projects. He was having dinner one night with Sidney Beckerman at Dan Tana's, an informal Italian restaurant on Santa Monica Boulevard, much favored by movie people of his generation, when a young woman—"a little blond gal"—an acquaintance of the producer, wandered over to speak to them. Clint learned that she worked for Dennis Hackin and Neal Dobrofsky, young writer-producers getting a start in the business. The next day she called and asked if she could drop off a script Hackin had written. "It's a thing called *Bronco Billy,*" she told him. "Oh, is this Bronco Billy Anderson?" he asked. No, she said, obviously never having heard of the actor who was, briefly, the silent movies' first western star.

He said he'd take a look at it, and later in the day found the script sitting on his secretary's desk. He picked it up casually—"I thought I'd give it four or five pages"—but found he couldn't put it down. "I finished the whole thing right there at the desk," thinking, as he recalls, Goddamn, this is wild. It's like Frank Capra—if Frank Capra were directing today, I'll bet he'd want to direct this.

Intrigued, but a trifle hesitant—this was, if anything, farther off his path than *Every Which Way but Loose* had been—"I thought about it for a couple of days, and I gave it to Sondra Locke and I said, 'Let me know what you think of this script.' And she read it and she said, 'I think it's just utterly charming.' So I went ahead and made it."

Just like that—in five and a half weeks, in the country around Boise,

Idaho, on what Clint calls one of the most "affable" shoots of his career. The genial cast and crew obviously took a cue from this sweet tale of one Bronco Billy McCoy, honchoing his game but understaffed Wild West show along the back roads of a contemporary West increasingly indifferent to the very traditions his show celebrates.

"There was something so beautifully naive about it all," Clint says, "a guy who's a shoe salesman in New Jersey goes out and has this dream of becoming a modern-day Tom Mix or something like that." Not to mention a "dream of making this group of losers become something, become an example for young people and teach values that a lot of people think have long been lost in America. He had great virtues—though obviously his brain had snapped, and he had gone into another era."

Among his losers he numbered Lasso Leonard James (Sam Bottoms), who does rope tricks and is a Vietnam draft dodger; Chief Big Eagle (Dan Vadis), a snake handler who refuses to use nonpoisonous snakes in his act or to remove the venom from his rattlers ("He's a proud Indian," Billy says, unperturbed, when he is once again bitten); his wife, Lorraine Running Water (Sierra Pecheur), who does "authentic" tribal dances and whose pregnancy adds to the perils of the little company; Lefty LeBow (Bill McKinney), who has lost a hand in a gun accident ("I told you that shotgun act wouldn't work"), and Doc Lynch (Scatman Crothers), the ringmaster, keeping a bemused but sympathetic eye on this odd lot, none of whom is odder than their leader.

Billy is actually pretty good at what he does—trick riding, fancy shooting and knife throwing, though in the latter activity he's occasionally a bit shaky. His routine consists of placing a large wheel, bedecked with balloons and with a pretty assistant strapped to it, in whirling motion, then, blindfolded, launching his blades at the balloons. Occasionally, he misses them and comes perilously close to his assistant. Loses more girls that way.

Which is where Locke's runaway heiress, Antoinette Lily, comes in. In order to claim her inheritance, she has been obliged to marry, choosing dopily scheming John Arlington (Geoffrey Lewis), who, unable to abide her temper, leaves her penniless, but still snooty, at a gas station. It's there that she meets Bronco Billy, who is looking for a new target and offers her the job. They instantly learn to despise one another—he because she continues in her uppity ways, she because he's such a hopeless square.

Billy's lifestyle is based on three inviolable principles: reverence for children, fanatical loyalty to one's friends and a belief that in America one can be anything one sets one's mind to becoming. Billy's manner as he states, and acts out, these beliefs is grave and courtly, his language formal in the style of bygone dime-novel (and B-movie) western heroes. We soon come to understand that something more than naïveté is operating here. Bronco Billy has achieved an almost-saintly state of grace in his simple faith. It is not his problem that, like a religious fundamentalist, his creed is, to most of us, laughably primitive. It is our problem—or, more specifically, Miss Lily's, who besides being the movie's love interest is also the voice of our skepticism, a voice that exists to be awed into silence by this gently cracked true believer.

Not that the movie makes much of this conversion. It is as objective in its way as *Escape from Alcatraz* is in that it takes no position—indignant or indulgent—about its protagonist. We laugh at Billy and his ways, but there is no superiority or cynicism in our laughter; the movie simply won't countenance it.

Consider a typical encounter between Billy and his "little pardners," as he habitually calls the kids who are his last reliable audience. A bunch of them are standing around admiring his car, an antique Pontiac with a steer-horn hood ornament and revolvers for door handles. He impresses them with a fast draw and then offers a little homily: "I don't take kindly to kids playing hookey from school. I think every kid in America ought to go to school, at least up to the eighth grade." "But we don't go to school today, Bronco Billy. It's Saturday." "Oh. Well, I've been riding late last night. A man and his brain get kind of fuzzy when he's been on the range."

His fanatical sense of loyalty is demonstrated with similar directness. Its most comical expression comes when he confesses to Miss Lily that he did seven years in jail for attempted homicide. Seems he caught his wife in bed with his best friend. "What did you do to him?" she asks. "I shot *her*." A man doesn't turn against a friend—especially a best friend—that easily.

A sterner test arises when a sheriff comes around looking for Lasso Leonard. The only way to prevent him from being arrested for draft evasion is for Bronco Billy to permit himself to be bullied and humiliated by the lawman. It's a nice moral dilemma. Like Clint himself, Billy is highly ambivalent about the war, but he is, of course, a patriot and no fan of radical dissent. Still, this is his friend. He has no choice but to defend him.

He will also, reluctantly, contemplate breaking the law himself. Desperate for money, he decides to lead his troupe in an old-fashioned train robbery. As they wait at a crossing, mounted and armed, he justifies this desperate defense of his dying dream to Miss Lily: "I was raised in a one-room tenement in New Jersey. I was a shoe salesman until I was thirty-one years old. Deep down in my heart I always wanted to be a cowboy. One day I laid down my shoehorn and swore I'd never live in the city again. You only live once. You've got to give it your best shot."

"Are you for real?"

"I'm who I want to be" comes the firm reply. Which is not much of a lawbreaker. This may be an old-fashioned robbery, but this is a new-fangled train—a speeding behemoth that hurtles heedlessly by the little band galloping futilely beside it, pistols impotently waving.

Eventually, Bronco Billy and friends come to crisis. A fire destroys their tent, and Miss Lily deserts them (she discovers her husband is claiming she's dead and as her presumptive widower has launched a wild scheme to abscond with her inheritance). It is Billy's faithfulness to principle that saves the show. Every year on their rounds his troupe has given a free performance at an insane asylum, whose inmates sew American flags for therapy and income. Because of his kindness they stitch together a tent, made entirely of stars and stripes, for them to play under. And Miss Lily, contrasting the empty vanity of the New York life to which she briefly returns with the sweet simplicity of tent-show life, comes back to Bronco Billy in time for the triumphant performance (to a packed house) that concludes the film.

Clint was not immune to the symbolism of this sequence. This was, if you will, the big tent—the big, visibly *American* tent politicians are always wistfully talking about. "I wanted to say something about everybody being able to participate," Clint told reporter John Vinocur. "America is the maddest idea in the world, put together by madmen. So here comes this tent" with its "collage of crazies" gathered happily beneath it. The reconciling message is not so very different, come to think of it, from that of *The Outlaw Josey Wales*. Here, however, a new generation is being recruited for the community, though in his dimness Billy never finds the metaphors appropriate to his great, self-appointed task.

"I've got a special message for you little pardners out there," Billy says in his curtain speech. "I want you to finish your oatmeal at breakfast and do as your ma and pa tell you, because they know best. Don't ever tell a lie and say your prayers at night before you go to bed." The looks on the little pardners' faces are variously rapt, restless and uncomprehending, as Billy presses serenely on to his utterly banal conclusion. "And so, as our friends south of the border say, 'Adios, Amigos.'"

It is sublime—a perfect parody of low-business pieties and clichés, but for once felt and meant as a sober summary of a man's character and philosophy. It is also wonderfully played by Clint—how the man loves playing dumb—and beamishly reacted to by the rest of the cast, with

Scatman Crothers's nods of encouragement and endorsement particularly well timed.

There may be things that are not quite right about this movie. One does wonder how a company this small, this lacking in a capacity for spectacle, attracts any audiences at all. One wonders how a shoe salesman and ex-con ever got together the capital to purchase even an outfit as modest as this. And, yes, as many critics observed at the time, there is something shrill in Locke's performance. She isn't quite to this manner born, doesn't have the saving ironic glint in her eye that, for example, Claudette Colbert flashed as the ur–runaway heiress of *It Happened One Night*.

But these flaws are modest in comparison to what's right with the film. Its light (the cinematographer was a newcomer, David Worth) is warmer, more dreamy and glowing, than it usually is in an Eastwood production, and its people are Capraesque in that economic affliction is not allowed to sour their eccentric kindliness. We also see in it some of Clint's best directorial qualities, his easy pace and the confidence with which he digresses from his main line, his ability to sustain a chosen pitch without strain. He knows the values this movie defends have a quaint air about them—they are funny looking and funny sounding—and that you have to play them very straight. To satirize them is superfluous; it's been done. To celebrate them too enthusiastically is self-defeating; you begin to sound like a right-wing crazy high on his own loopy rhetoric. *Bronco Billy* simply asks us to contemplate certain core values—kindness to the weak and tolerance for the eccentric, loyalty to the jointly striving group, above all a belief in the redemptive and reinventive possibilities of a free country—and after we're done chuckling at the way its protagonist states them, ask ourselves if they are really so quaint, so irrelevant, after all.

One could argue that this movie is, in its way, its director's most self-referential work. For Bronco Billy is Clint, or the Clint who might have been had Malpaso turned out to be a rundown Wild West show. He is the same guy with the same values, but operating out there on the eccentric fringe of things instead of at the center of our admiring attention, living in a place where we (and he) would inevitably perceive him as more quixotic than exemplary. That urge David Thomson has mentioned, to see "just how far he could stretch the audience's support," is operating here as surely as it is elsewhere. He wanted to know if we'd accept goofy righteousness as eagerly as we did the more outraged kind.

As it happened, we did not—at least in our customary numbers. Warner Bros. thought it had, perhaps, another *Every Which Way but Loose* here. The industry, conscious that a trade-paper poll had early in

1980 named Clint the top box-office star of the seventies, aware that he had not had a flop since *The Beguiled*, also expected great things of *Bronco Billy*. The reviews, though mixed, were on the whole encouraging. Richard Corliss in *Time* said it was "as if one of the faces on Mt. Rushmore suddenly cracked a crooked smile. Watching *Bronco Billy* millions of moviegoers are likely to smile back." If some critics insisted on biting their lips, the majority agreed with Janet Maslin's assessment that Clint "never seemed more sweetly accessible."

But it opened, as they say, "soft." It didn't help that Maslin described Billy as an outsize Peter Pan, and that others made the same point less memorably. Soon learned disquisitions were appearing in the trades and elsewhere about the movie's disappointing grosses. It was of a piece, some said, with other failures of the summer—Burt Reynolds in *Rough Cut*, Robert Redford in *Brubaker*, John Travolta in *Urban Cowboy*. All of them, it was said, seemed to promise the audience its favorites in familiar roles, then disappointed by slightly off-casting them in pictures that did not satisfy genre expectations, either. Exhibitors—traditionally whiners—insisted that this "product" was just not going to live up to its advance publicity the way the summer's great hit, *The Empire Strikes Back*, did.

Clint was not amused. This was a child of his heart, and he thought Warner Bros. had not prepared the public for it properly. So studio executives backed one of their jets out of the hangar one Saturday and "wearing sack cloth and ashes," as John Calley put it, flew up to Jackson Hole, where Clint was making *Any Which Way You Can,* the sequel to *Every Which Way but Loose,* to placate him with promises of a revised and enhanced ad campaign (on which, prudently, they delivered). Even so, the movie passed into legend as a rare Eastwood flop.

But that's not so: The film was a disappointment only in relation to expectations. Eventually it did quite a tidy business—returning some $15 million to the studio in domestic rentals and a similar amount from overseas distribution. It also produced a hit single for Warner records, "Barroom Buddies," a duet sung in the film by Clint and Merle Haggard—at long last a musical success. This was not bad for a picture that had cost around $5 million, and not at all bad as a conclusion to a five-year period during which Clint achieved a quality and range of workmanship—and of box-office success—that were unprecedented in his career to date and never quite so seamlessly paralleled in the years that immediately followed.

THIRTEEN

MY FATHER'S DREAM

Clint Eastwood turned fifty a couple of weeks before *Bronco Billy* opened. This fact was duly noted in the press. Here and there writers attributed the sunniness of the film and the sweetness of his performance to the mellowing effects of maturity, and Clint was inclined to agree. The "sexy legend," as *Cosmopolitan* called him in the title of the profile it ran coincidentally with the film's release, suggested to its writer that "serenity" and "tranquility" were qualities he now required in a relationship. Inevitably, he said, "the warrior ego gives way to something higher," and he implied that he had reached that "plateau" now.

This new mood was reflected in real estate as well as in relationships. Making a personal appearance in Shasta County, raising funds for the family of a highway patrol officer killed in the line of duty, Clint had been given a tour of the Bing Crosby ranch. This was something like home country for him, since he passed a boyhood year in nearby Redding. Learning that the Crosby estate—the singer died in 1977—intended to auction the ranch off, he was determined to bid on it and won the property in the fall of 1978, while he was making *Escape from Alcatraz*. Since then, it has become his most closely guarded retreat, the place he often goes to clear his mind and put himself in top condition before shooting a film or to unwind (and often to make the first cut) after he finishes principal photography. The ranch buildings are simple in design and decor, the vast acreage surrounding them a nature preserve, offering him unsurpassed solitude.

His contentment, as he began a new decade, was thus nearly perfect. For after four years he could see that the most significant of his commitments, the one with Warner Bros., tested and proved by its quick and accommodating response in the *Bronco Billy* crisis, was close to ideal. As of 1980, Ted Ashley and John Calley were in the process of departing, with Frank Wells soon to follow. But Steve Ross was still setting the tone of the place, Clint's allies Terry Semel, Barry Reardon and Joe Hyams were still aboard, and Robert Daly, recruited from CBS to be the new CEO, was his kind of guy. To succeed in the movie business, Daly once told Connie Bruck, Ross's gifted biographer, you need three things—"the intelligence and the financing and the guts to stay at the table and play"—and all these he and his associates at the studio had, as their long and successful reign would eventually prove.

These virtues, translating into stability and great steadiness in adversity, have been vital in sustaining a relationship between star and studio unduplicated in the modern American motion-picture industry and crucial to Clint's long-running success. If, like so many stars, he had been obliged to wander from studio to studio, hawking his wares to anxious strangers, enduring the long delays between pictures that this process entails, he clearly would not have made as many films as he has. Nor as an actor-director for hire would he have been able to mount his quirkier projects so quickly and easily; he might, indeed, have found himself bankable only in a much narrower, action-oriented range, which as he aged would have rendered him increasingly implausible and irrelevant to the young male audience for whom those films are made. What happened to Burt Reynolds and Charles Bronson in the eighties, what is happening to Sylvester Stallone in the nineties, could have happened to him.

Consistent success aside, it may be that the most important element in Clint's relationship with Warner Bros. is its lack of long-term contractual ties. Malpaso has headquartered in the same five-room Spanish-style stucco building on the Warners lot—people used to call it the Taco Bell—since *Josey Wales*. Rather dimly lit and until a recent refurbishment decorated more by accretion than design, it stands not more than one hundred yards from the studio's executive building. But nothing other than propinquity and incalculable self-interest link Clint with management. Whenever they agree on a project—and Clint has released all but two of his twenty-five films between 1976 and 1996 through Warner Bros.—Lenny Hirshan and Bruce Ramer negotiate a deal for it alone. He is, in theory, free at any time to work elsewhere; Warner Bros. is, in theory, free at any time to ask him to leave.

To put it simply, where there is no contract, there is nothing to argue about—not among men determined to treat one another honorably. But unspoken trust, a quality that, like good movies, has always been hard to come by in Hollywood, requires further exegesis. In this instance, it begins with the corporate culture Steve Ross established as he put together the Warner Communications conglomerate. Ross may have betrayed a certain slipperiness in some of his dealings, but no entrepreneur of his era inspired greater loyalty among his associates. Famously generous with salaries, bonuses and perquisites, he was yet more generous with freedom. He had a mystical belief in talent and a sort of boyish wonder in its presence. He thought that given patience and un-questioning support, gifted people would over the long run deliver con-sistently profitable work. Conversely, he believed that nagging oversight of their plans, extensive second-guessing of their failures, would only distract their energies and dim their spirits.

A lifelong and knowledgeable movie fan, he loved the studio more than any of his other corporate holdings and indulged its management and its stars more fully than anyone else. Warner Bros. was, like Malpaso, a self-described "family"—albeit a much more extended one—and proba-bly, in the last analysis, no less a patriarchy than its competitors. But in this case, as opposed to Universal, for instance, the patriarch smiled be-nignly down on it from a distance, leaving day-to-day decision making to trusted lieutenants. He sent gifts and extended invitations to glam-orous getaways and events and always left the keys to the family's several airplanes on the mantelpiece where everyone could grab them and take off.

Nothing could have suited Clint Eastwood better. "My father's dream in life was to own a hardware store," he once told a reporter. "I'm his son." Though Malpaso is obviously dependent on the studio for fi-nancing and marketing, more than any comparable operation in Holly-wood, it is run like a small free-standing business, with its sole proprietor enjoying astonishing autonomy. No one can remember a time when Clint was denied a project he wanted to make.

John Calley and the late Frank Wells set the tone of this relationship. The former has, he says, seen every kind of bad and stupid star trip, and though he is not an uncynical man, he remains somewhat awed by Clint's voyage through the heavenly realms. "The messages he got from himself about what he wanted to do were much more significant than most guys got. He never fell into that horrible trap: 'Well, yes, I'm a star and, yes, it's a huge success, and, yes, I can do anything I want, but to make sure I can do that for the rest of my life I'd better do three or four more of the same and then I'm really established.' And then twelve years later they're still doing the same movie and it's not fashionable anymore and they're gone." He adds: "I was very comfortable being passive with him. I mean, I just figured he knows more about it than I do, so why fuck with him."

Calley—smart, volatile, unguarded—amused and delighted Clint, but Wells, besides being Calley's perfect balance wheel, was his old friend and trusted adviser. A former Rhodes scholar, he was as lanky as Clint and, more important, as dry, reserved and commonsensical. If

Clint didn't know he was a movie star, then Wells didn't seem to know he was a movie mogul, so distant was his style from the clichés associated with that breed.

Wells had perfect trust in Clint's skills, instincts and frugality. "Clint's greatest moment of pride," Wells said, "was not when he called you up to say, 'Hey, I made a good one, come on down and see it.' It was when he called you up the last day of shooting and you had to play a guessing game as to how much under budget they were." Clint became, he said, the standard by which the studio's executives judged the work of other independent producers.

By never spending the studio's money foolishly, he always managed to make foolish amounts of the stuff for it—and for himself. A studio executive said recently that 95 percent of Clint's films have made money, and Barry Reardon estimated a few years ago that in worldwide theatrical release alone they had returned something over $1.5 billion to Warner Bros. This figure did not include all the takings from *Unforgiven* and none from *A Perfect World* or *The Bridges of Madison County*. Nor did it include home video sales or television licensing or any of the other ancillary sales the Eastwood library continuously generates (Robert Daly says he often sells the subsequent TV licenses for an Eastwood movie for more than he gets for the first run). All in all his grosses for the company far exceed $2 billion—and do not include the monies generated by the eighteen films he has starred in or directed elsewhere, which surely add another billion to his works' total earnings.

That this is accomplished with few displays of temper and none of temperament is, of course, vastly relieving. Henry Bumstead likes to say, "Clint takes the bullshit out of filmmaking," which is a rare enough gift for people in his line of work, but a benison beyond price for the inhabitants of a studio executive suite.

By now, so far as an outside observer can tell, authentic affection rules Clint's relationship with Daly and Semel. They do business by doing favors for each other. When Warner's high-flying video-games division had crashed without warning in the early eighties, bringing stock prices and profits down with it, Clint went to Daly saying that if it would be helpful, he could have his new *Dirty Harry* film ready for Christmas 1983, when it would have a salutary effect on the company's balance sheet. He delivered *Sudden Impact* as promised, and it turned out to be the most profitable entry in the series.

But this sense of mutual interest extends far beyond the movie of the moment. Through the years Clint has cheerfully joined Warners executives on all kinds of "state" occasions, helping them to open new theme parks, theaters and stores all over the globe. They, in turn, have been alert to every opportunity to advance his standing with those writers and institutions that take films seriously, an effort that began in earnest in the early eighties. He carefully made himself available to writers for small, serious film journals like *Film Comment* for interviews more extensive than he granted the popular press, and much more soberly cinematic in subject matter. These writers spoke his language, and one can sense his comfort with them. Here and there phrases like "one of the most honest, influential and personal filmmakers in the world today" began to be applied to him. Here and there social and cultural commentators began to write seriously and sympathetically about him. This kind of thing made it acceptable, in turn, for an institution like the Museum of Modern Art to mount a one-day retrospective of four of his films in December 1980 with Clint in attendance.

This was a great moment for him. As he told a reporter a few years later, "They don't do that for many actors or actors as young as I am. These things, they usually wait until somebody's coughing badly. It was very nice." So nice that when Joe Hyams sent him a picture of the two of them taken on this occasion and asked him to autograph it, Clint hesitated over it for some weeks, searching for the right words. It finally came back inscribed with thanks for what Clint called one of the happiest nights of his life.

It was just the beginning. Clint has returned to MoMA many times. He has, as well, given the *Guardian* lecture at the British Film Institute twice and been appointed one of its fellows; has been named both a chevalier and a commander of arts and letters by the French; had retrospectives of his work staged at just about all the significant film archives, museums and festivals; contended for the top prize at Cannes and has been chairman of its jury. Of late, of course, the more prestigious of the career achievement prizes—the motion-picture academy's Thalberg Award, the Life Achievement Awards of the American Film Institute and the Film Society of Lincoln Center—have come to him.

He is, to be sure, the kind of American filmmaker foreign cineasts adore—someone with roots in the humble genres they have long respected more than American critics have—so some of the recognition from abroad would doubtless have come to him in the natural course of events. It is also true that with John Wayne's death in 1979 an opening was created in the celebrity pantheon. That they were, as we have seen, essentially antithetical in their ambitions and in the attitudes they brought to their work was less important than the forgiving affection in which they were so widely held, and the opportunity that offered analysts to say something knowing and sympathetic about the popular culture they usually felt obliged to abhor.

That a newer generation of critics, determined not to be seen as middlebrow fuds in the Crowther-Crist vein, had come along helped Clint's cause, as he himself has recognized. That, unlike Wayne, he could be seen as an auteur, seriously involved in the process of creating movies instead of just making rich deals to participate in someone else's enterprise, also recommended him. This fawning, indeed, became so intense that James Wolcott felt obliged in 1985, in a particularly vicious *Vanity Fair* assault, to insist that "the truth is not that Clint Eastwood's films have gotten 'hip,' but that movie critics have gotten so square." This he attributed to the desire among liberals in the Reagan era to prove they had *cojones* as weighty as any neo-con, missing the point that their needs were more cultural than political, and missing, too, the insinuating revisions Clint kept adding to his screen character.

Still, one cannot entirely evade the point: No one gets the kind of acclaim that has accrued to Clint over the last decade and a half without institutional support. If nothing else, the logistics of celebration have to be attended to, and in this respect Warner Bros. has been wonderfully attentive.

In essence, studio and star have achieved a blend of the old Hollywood and the new. Clint's career has been nurtured as such careers were when studios looked upon them as long-term investments to be guarded and guided over many years—the difference here being that the patronization (and resentful dependency) that sullied those arrangements are absent. At the same time Clint and Warners have in their dealings come closer to the mutually beneficent ideal everyone imagined for the era of independent production, eliding that paranoid friction that is more typical of these arrangements.

It's all very reasonable. Aside from taking the nonsense out of moviemaking it sometimes seems that Clint has drained the drama from it as well, and there is a slightly perverse downside to that. For we like to think that making movies is a desperate enterprise, a form of high-stakes gambling in which people risk everything in pursuit of some impossible dream. We want brutal conflict between the visionary artist and the visionless studio boss. We want sudden rises to fame and fortune, equally sudden descents into ignominy and poverty. These make good copy. Ultimately, they make undying legends. Griffith, von Stroheim, Welles—these are the figures that command such historical imagination as is generally brought to bear on Hollywood's past; they are the dark exemplars of its propensity first to flatter genius, then to abuse it, then to crush it. Along with such victim-performers as Garland and Monroe they are the source of its black glamour, engines of the tragic celebrity drama that keeps the world attuned to its doings.

Two things are usually omitted from our consideration of these scenarios. One is that there is a powerful self-destructive element in them; Hollywood's victims are usually first the victims of their own needs and weaknesses. The other is that most of the more treasurable older movies were created by moviemakers who learned to bend the system to their own ends. Vernacularists working their own variations on genre conventions, they conceived themselves more as artisans than as artists, their art being something that was generally recognized long after their craft was rather dismissively acknowledged. This does not mean that such now-famous auteurs as Hitchcock, Ford, Hawks and Lubitsch were without egocentricity or eccentricity. It does mean, however, that they were most basically men who got on with their business, building their huge filmographies while manipulating to their own advantage essentially benign relationships with their studios.

Like Clint, some of them had trouble at first establishing their credentials with the knowing audience, and some still fail to attract the attention they deserve. How much more difficult it is today, when several generations have so thoroughly absorbed the romantic myths of moviedom, to establish one's seriousness through the exercise of simple professionalism. It might have helped Clint's reputation in some circles if he had, in this period, made one or two visibly unreasonable movies, might have helped it, too, if the most widely perceived pattern in his work—two or three clearly commercial works followed by something that seemed more "personal"—had seemed slightly less metronomic.

In interviews Clint has repeatedly denied conscious intent in this matter, always insisting that he never made a movie solely on the basis of box-office considerations, and most of the time one can discern, even in, say, a *Dirty Harry* sequel, its point of emotional contact with him. In the later eighties, however, he did not achieve the kind of consistency that he enjoyed between *Josey Wales* and *Bronco Billy.* One cannot entirely evade the feeling that his studio relationship was sometimes just a little too comfortable for his own good.

It's not that Clint failed to justify his rising cultural repute or that he did not make interesting and ambitious movies in the years between 1983 and 1990. Two or three of them rank among his best work. It's that he also made several of his weakest movies in that period. Some of these were projects the studio urged on him that he too readily acceded to. Some were films a sterner management might have counseled him to cast differently or have rewritten one more time, or just think about a little harder, so that an interesting idea could be converted into a truly arresting one. But Clint remained an impatient man, driven by his restless need to be up and doing, and sometimes one felt him working just to keep working, on pictures that detain his interest—and ours—only minimally. Naturally, incalculable chance being the largest determinant of a movie's fate, some of these turned out to be large hits, making it even harder to argue with his success, especially in Hollywood, where arguing with failure is the sport of choice.

★   ★   ★

Not that anyone in their right mind would have advised Clint to skip making a sequel to a $100 million grosser. *Any Which Way You Can* reunited him with all the principals except Manis from *Every Which Way but Loose.* Not to worry, though; the replacement Clyde was just fine, and so was the new screenwriter, Stanford Sherman. He came up with a nice running gag, which called for Clyde to solemnly stick his powerful fist out the pickup truck window whenever Philo said, "Right turn, Clyde." At a certain moment, when the Black Widows are once again menacing them, he gives the cue, and Clyde responds and smashes their leader, whose backward fall generates a domino effect, knocking the entire motorcycle gang off their hogs.

He came up with some other pretty good material—Clyde placidly dismantling a bad guy's car; Clyde and a "date" enjoying a motel room tryst, with the noise of their lovemaking engendering alarmed reactions from a frumpy middle-aged couple next door that are at least semi-precious—and a story line that is a little more coherent than the previous film's. After a fight Philo decides to retire from bare-knuckle boxing because, as he tells his pal Orville, he's beginning to like the pain. But mobsters want him to return for one last bout with an eastern champion, Jack Wilson (William Smith). When he refuses, they kidnap Locke's Lynne Halsey-Taylor (chastened and more agreeable now), telling Philo he must fight if he hopes to see her again. Naturally he sets forth to recapture her, and eventually the big fight takes place rather spectacularly; it wanders through what appears to be most of Jackson Hole, Wyoming, the crowd tagging along as Philo and Jack (who really rather like each other) slug it out.

The picture contains the only overt political statement Clint has ever made in a movie ("A handout is what you get from the government, a handup is what you get from a friend") and another sound-track duet, "Beers to You," with the star partnered this time by Ray Charles. Other than that, what is there to say? Only perhaps that it represented quite a decent directorial debut by Buddy Van Horn, Clint's longtime stunt coordinator. They had first worked together on *Coogan's Bluff* and *Two Mules for Sister Sara,* and, in their way, started to indicate mutual respect. "We kinda grunted at each other," is the way Van Horn puts it, "didn't say too much."

A soft-spoken, weather-beaten man of unshakable calm, Wayne Van Horn (to call him by his rightful name) was literally born into the business. His father was a veterinarian working and living on the Universal back lot, caring for the studio's menagerie, and Buddy grew up there, becoming a professional rider as soon as it was legal, then graduating to stunt work. He was, Clint judged, the ideal man to lead the troops through a film that was wall-to-wall "gags," as stuntpeople call even their unfunny work. If you like it you can direct it, Clint said when he called to say he was sending over the script. "I like it already," said Buddy.

The film profits from his uncondescending craftsmanship, and Buddy Van Horn profited from its success. He was not a man with a personal statement to make—one can only imagine the puzzled monosyllables that might greet a question on that topic—nor someone with a career to make; he was doing quite nicely with stunts, thank you. But he was, and is, a technically proficient moviemaker, the unabrasive spirit Clint had been looking for to guide low-key projects he didn't feel like directing himself. He would make two more films for Clint and continue to serve as his stunt coordinator and, since he is an expert player, Clint's location golfing partner.

In this instance, his entirely agreeable work made no new converts to the cause of low comedy, but among critics who dared to make fine distinctions in this realm it found a certain favor. *Any Which Way You Can* was, Janet Maslin (correctly) wrote, "better and funnier than its predecessor." Carrie Rickey, a self-confessed fan, didn't feel like going that far, but in a review that took the form of an open letter to Clint made a nice point: "A lot of my friends, armchair moralists that they are, complain that your movies are 'gratuitously violent.' Since they don't get to see your movies on principle (although they'll race out to see *Raging Bull* because it's 'art') they're unaware of the moralism that informs your screen persona."

But whether one liked it a little more or a little less than *Every Which Way but Loose* is beside the point. The film's salient defect was inherent; it could not surprise us as Philo Beddoe's first adventure had. It could only—well—ape it, which it very profitably did.

★   ★   ★

In the spring of 1982, some fifteen years into his movie stardom, someone finally, lengthily, attempted seriously to come to grips with the

Clint Eastwood phenomenon. The venue, *The New York Review of Books*, being no less remarkable than the effort, this was an event as portentous as the MoMA retrospective, a signal of arrival in intellectual territory no one had expected him to penetrate. The title of Robert Mazzocco's essay, "The Supply-Side Star," linked Clint's popularity to the new national spirit of the Reagan era, a thought that had, or would, occur to other, less nuanced observers. But this writer was after something more subtle. He saw the popularity of Clint's screen character as a reactionary phenomenon of a sort, but not a dangerous one. Noting that "the sixties was largely a decade of confrontation based on an egalitarian ethic, however falteringly understood, against the predatory and powerful, the seventies increasingly became an epoch of polarization, built on a jingoistic and retributive ethic," he observed that violence was common to both periods. He said it was turned inward in the earlier one, outward (as in Clint's movies) in the latter one. But he detected in Clint's screen persona none of that meanness of the conservative spirit on which it was Ronald Reagan's business to draw his happy faces. Rather, he saw an attempt to blend two traditional American modes, "the irreverence of the free spirit and the ruthlessness of the rugged individualist" and, certainly, an attempt to reanimate the Leatherstocking hero, "the saint with a gun."

But Mazzocco observed two more interesting aspects to Clint's work. "All the tropes of adversity, the primary male appetites—greed, honor, fraud, struggle, violence—are there, but significantly diluted of any real social, intellectual or even familial coloration." He also saw "how effectively" Clint "struggles against absorption into mere genre, mere style, even while appearing with his long-boned casualness and hypnotic presence to be nothing but style." What we seem to have here is an individualism that transcended its traditional representations onscreen and transcended, as well, its current cultural definitions, linking past and present in subtly suggestive ways.

By coincidence, this piece appeared less than three months before the movie that would, by indirection, prove its validity. *Firefox* is one of the most curious entries in the Eastwood filmography, for it is his only movie to rely heavily on special visual effects and the only one to deal directly with the Cold War. It is also one of his very few movies in which, to borrow Mazzocco's formulation, he is thoroughly "absorbed" in genre style, unable to assert his own.

Craig Thomas's novel, on which the film was based, was recommended to Clint by the pilot and the owner of the helicopter he used for aerial sequences. It told a very simple story: The Russians have developed in the eponymous jet fighter a plane so technologically advanced it could alter the balance of Cold War power. The United States must steal the prototype in order to learn its secrets and create a countervailing force. Mitch Gant, the character Clint would play, is the man for the job, since he speaks Russian and is a hot pilot.

Or is he? Haunted by his experiences in Vietnam, both as a man who killed innocent civilians and as a POW, Mitch is on extended leave from the service and sanity—"really kind of fragile goods," as Clint phrases it. Under pressure, the possibility of him freezing and cracking is large, and eventually we will find him disguised behind wimpish glasses and mustache quaking in a men's room during the course of a deadly chase through Moscow (for which Vienna was persuasively doubled). Since Firefox can be flown and fought by mental telepathy, a pilot prone to mental vapor lock may not be the ideal choice for this assignment, after all.

Clint naturally thought his weaknesses made Mitch all the more interesting to play. And he also liked the fact that when he got to Russia his underground allies were members of the Jewish underground, much put upon by Soviet anti-Semitism. Clint's contempt for windy Cold War rhetoric and vast geopolitical exertions was still very much intact; he has never wavered in his belief that it is, politically, *the* clear and present danger to individualism. But anti-Semitism is something he felt strongly about. It grounded the basic silliness afflicting all espionage stories in a reality he could comprehend.

As to special effects, *Star Wars, Star Trek, E.T.* and *Blade Runner* (the last two being among the movies *Firefox* would compete with in the summer of 1982) were creating a new "amphetamine aesthetic" in movies, as Andrew Sarris observed in his review of Clint's film. The trend, he said, was "away from realism in all categories, dramatic, psychological, sociological, even optical. The mania for location shooting in the sixties and seventies has given way to a return to glitzy studio sets, special effects, miniatures, and animation." Manifestly, Clint perceived this phenomenon too, so we have to see this film as a sort of experiment, an attempt to see how he would like working under the new dispensation.

Still, the effects the script called for were, literally, not too far out. Concentrated in the film's last third, after Mitch has filched the fighter, they are employed to visualize its pursuit by a second Firefox prototype and, eventually, their dogfight over Arctic seas and ice cap—"all in the atmosphere of this planet and all flying as we know it," as Clint puts it. Even so, he found this work frustrating. The first firm he tried to engage for the effects work drove him and Fritz Manes crazy with contractual wrangling (Bob Daley, perhaps because of his lack of enthusiasm for previous projects, perhaps because, as Clint somewhat unfairly grumbles, he seemed more interested now in collecting first editions than he was in producing movies, had departed). They turned, finally, to Apogee, John Dykstra's firm, which had worked on the first *Star Wars,* and eventually were entirely satisfied by its creations. But special effects are inevitably slow and costly, and at more than $20 million, this was far and away the most expensive budget, and the most expansive schedule (well over a year), Malpaso had ever indulged.

The film would later achieve substantial grosses. But in the final analysis, it was not worth the effort. There was many a draggy exposition scene in Russian and American situation rooms, and even though Bruce Surtees lit the passages dealing with underground activity "seriously"—at much lower light levels than we are used to in entertainments of this kind—they are not all that suspenseful. At the time Clint was evincing some real-life interest in freelance military operations, but skulking about is not something he knows or cares a lot about; it may seem to suit the cool side of his nature, but it is antithetical to his explosive side, and the film lacks the boyish élan the last two decades of spy movies had taught people to expect from the genre.

The film was poorly received. "A James Bond movie without the girls, a Superman movie without a sense of humor," said Vincent Canby. "Luke Skywalker trapped in Dirty Harry's soul," someone at *People* thought. David Denby in *New York* thought Mitch Gant might be meant to symbolize "America itself, traumatized by Nam," the movie intended possibly as "a shot in the arm for a country that (as the jargon goes) 'has lost its will' to fight Communism." In their various ways, they were trying to come to grips with the film's curiously detached manner. Sarris's analysis was the most persuasive: Clint, he wrote "is not the establishment figure his East Coast detractors imagine," but rather "a mysterious loner with few ties to civilization." Thus, the critic said, he "has always looked ill at ease in uniforms and organizations," and *Firefox* tended to "submerge the anarchic side of Eastwood." Thus the ecstatic flee-*and*-fight finale, by far the film's best passage, "serves . . . to express the liberation of a born and made loner from the constraints of a turgid cold war plot."

The film had two rather gratifying upscale premieres, which drew many of Sarris's dubious eastern swells, a society where Clint would more and more frequently find himself. The one in Washington, benefiting the USO, was chaired by Secretary of Defense Caspar Weinberger and his wife. The secretary found himself deserted the minute Clint made his entrance. In New York the beneficiaries were Clint's new best friends at MoMA, where an evening consisting of cocktails in

Blanchette Rockefeller's garden, a screening and a dinner dance at the Pierre raised $100,000 for the museum's film preservation fund.

But even as he hobnobbed with the elite, Clint found himself drawn into less elevated circles. Urged on by Fritz Manes, whose nostalgia for his Marine Corps service had transmuted into a romantic regard for paramilitary adventuring, he had in 1979 and 1980 been introduced to Bob Denard, who had mounted a successful mercenary invasion of the Comoros Islands, a former French possession off the east coast of Africa, and Mitchell Werbell III, one of the inventors of the silencer-equipped Ingraham Model II submachine gun and the proprietor of a counter-terrorist school. Both entered public, if dubious, claims that Clint was interested in developing screenplays about their adventures, but nothing came of these brief encounters.

Not so his connection with James G. (Bo) Gritz, a sometime Green Beret lieutenant colonel much decorated for his service in Vietnam. He approached Clint sometime in 1982 seeking financial support for an incursion into Laos from Thailand in search of American soldiers officially listed as missing in action, but according to Gritz (and to widespread fantasies of the time) actually being held in secret prison camps. His first idea, according to Clint, was to have him make, or pretend to make, a movie on the Thai border as a kind of diversion during which Gritz and friends would slip away on their mission. "Geez, that doesn't sound too smart," Clint replied, but still he kept listening. He was told that the Carter administration had deliberately hushed up evidence that the MIAs were still alive so that it would not have to take official action on their behalf. This sounded plausible to Clint, ever suspicious of government actions and inactions, and Gritz was "a really good salesman." At some point he found himself saying, "Boy, I'll tell you, I would not be able to sleep at night if I thought there was one person being held against his will and knowing that something could be done about it."

If Gritz was not exactly his kind of guy, he was certainly his kind of problem solver—impatient with talk, eager for direct action. So Clint offered him money—variously reported at thirty thousand dollars and fifty thousand dollars—and help rounding up other support as well. He did not approach William Shatner, who also gave the colonel ten thousand dollars in the form of an option on his life story, which he unsuccessfully tried to place with the TV networks, but Clint admits, "I did a lot of stuff for them, a lot of legwork"—mostly asking corporate CEOs to donate equipment to the would-be invaders. What he could not secure was the support of the Reagan administration, even though he called the president and got his pledge to look into the matter. The report Reagan got back from Robert McFarlane, chief deputy to the national security adviser, was that Gritz "was not somebody we ought to be involved with."

This word was evidently passed to Clint (though Gritz would later claim that he received back-channel intelligence support from the Pentagon). By this time, Clint was beginning to have his own doubts. He visited Gritz's training camp in northern California and was distinctly unimpressed by what he saw. When the local sheriff busted them for trespassing on somebody's back forty, he began to think, as he understates it, "These guys were maybe not all they were written up to be."

He did not feel, however, that he could back out honorably. So off Gritz and his little band flew to Thailand, which by this time was beginning to resemble a convention site for right-wing crazies, with about twenty groups poised there for expeditions into Laos. Gritz, accompanied by four Americans and fourteen Laotian guerrillas, pushed off on what he called Operation Lazarus in late November—"Like Laurel and Hardy or the Marx brothers go to Cambodia," as Clint ruefully puts it. They were ambushed three days later. One Laotian was killed, and one American was taken prisoner (he was later ransomed) in this fiasco, and much of their matériel was lost. Gritz retreated and regrouped and in February 1983 launched another, smaller foray. While he was gone Thai police arrested the radio operators he had left behind, and then Gritz himself was apprehended when he strolled out of the jungle empty-handed a couple of weeks later. He spent five days in jail, teaching the local police chief karate and making himself available to *Good Morning, America* for an interview. By this time, one of his compatriots had sold his story to *Soldier of Fortune* for five thousand dollars, generating much press attention and much paranoid irritation from the colonel.

Gritz has since spun completely out of control. He is the founder of a survivalist real estate development in Idaho, which he calls Almost Heaven, where he awaits the Apocalypse and rants against the New World Order, that conspiracy of the Rothschilds, the queen of England and the world bankers that he and his ilk imagine is planning to stamp every American citizen with a bar code, the better to control their lives.

Clint, who was making contributions to groups supporting the Equal Rights Amendment around the same time he was giving money to Gritz, obviously learned a lesson in caution from this incident. Aside from his two years as the nonpartisan mayor of Carmel, he has generally avoided public identification with causes and candidates, though he did admit casting a quixotic vote for Ross Perot (incidentally, another of Gritz's suckers) in the 1992 election. His response to rumors of larger political involvements—as late as 1995 there was hopeful talk in California Republican circles of a run for governor—is to cite his unwillingness to embrace the tedium of politics or to submit his private life to the kind of scrutiny the press now devotes to candidates for major office.

★   ★   ★

In the long line of this career, both *Firefox* and Colonel Gritz are aberrant; nothing like them had occurred before, and nothing has since. Indeed, even as Gritz was rounding up his troops, Clint was working on a movie that was in scale and tone as far from its immediate predecessor, in spirit as far from the lunatic Southeast Asian adventure, as it is possible to get.

Honkytonk Man is based on a novel by Clancy Carlile, who also adapted it for the screen. He was represented by William Morris, and Lenny Hirshan brought the book to Clint. It recounts the last weeks in the life of a country-and-western singer named Red Stovall, a drifter and alcoholic who is terminally ill with tuberculosis. The time is the 1930s, and he appears at his married sister's farm in Oklahoma as a dust storm wipes out her family's crop—their last hope for survival on this land. Reprobate though he is, Red is not without hope. After a lifetime singing his songs and passing the hat in road- and cathouses, he has an invitation to audition for the Grand Ole Opry in Nashville. His problem is getting there intact. He has a fine Lincoln convertible, but his energy and his driving skills are, at best, erratic. His relatives are about to abandon their farm and join the Okie migration to California, so it is decided that Red's young nephew, Whit, will be his driver and chaperone, and that they will give a lift to the boy's grandfather (John McIntire), who is going to join other kinfolk.

Clint took to the story because it offered him the opportunity to recreate the back roads of his boyhood, and, indeed, he doubled for Oklahoma one of the areas he knew from those days, the flat farmlands around Sacramento. It also gave him another opportunity to sing, which he did in a way that was right for the role, but, as it turned out, wrong for the reviewers. Finally, the part of Whit, Red's nephew, called for a fourteen-year-old boy, and he just happened to have one of those handy—his son, Kyle, who would bring something more than a persuasive genetic match to the role.

The project had some hidden attractions as well. One of these, curiously, had its roots in the weekend rodeoing of Clint's *Rawhide* days. He and his cohorts had often shared the bill with country-and-western groups, and these musicians, going nowhere in what was in those days a closed world, offering no hope of the crossovers some of its performers made later, fascinated him. So did the self-destructive ends of the legendary figures of this world, the likes of Hank Williams and Red Foley. "You wondered," he says, "why so many of them died on the highway."

Honkytonk Man did not propose a firm answer to that question, only a chance to explore it. In the self-made men of show business one often notices this intense interest in willed failure, perhaps because it is a trade in which the means of self-destruction come so readily to hand, perhaps because the luck that raised them up from lazy, hazy boyhood is so inexplicable, so easy to imagine never happening. In any case Clint's interest in this topic extends far beyond country pickers (*Bird,* for instance). Indeed, discussing this movie, Clint has more than once invoked the curious fate of Richard Nixon, painfully achieving his life's goal and then painfully trashing it.

Verna Bloom, who played Red's sister, puts it simply: "If Clint were a failure, he'd be Red." It's an interesting thought. If life had dealt differently with him, one can imagine Red's weary hardness and charm, a desperate effort not to explode—or more likely implode—in Clint.

Not that the movie openly adverts to such thoughts. We are pretty sure from the start that Red is a foredoomed figure, but the structure of the film is almost childishly linear, its tone, until the end, loose, light and unforced. The road Red, Whit and Grandpa share might be described as the road untaken—untaken by Red, that is, at any previous time precisely because it is a shared road.

If it is too late for Red to change his ways or his route, it is not too late for him to enjoy a few sunny days before the shadows close in around him. The ferociously inward man of the film's first passages, drunken and cynical, becomes almost boyish and unguarded in this company. Indeed, there is something prankish about the film's incidents. An angry bull is encountered and evaded; some chickens are stolen. Young Whit is introduced to sex in a bordello, and old Red is introduced to jail, from which his nephew cleverly springs him. Red does a little singing to help ends meet and, with some help from Whit, composes a new and rather good song ("Throw your arms around this honkytonk man / And we'll get through the night the best way we can"). Grandpa, who participated in the Oklahoma land rush, offers a lovely reminiscence about it, a reminder of the freshness of the American morning. In time, the old fellow departs and is replaced by Marlene (Alexa Kenin), who can't carry a tune, but can't abandon her dream of singing stardom. She sleeps once with Red, but without loss of her essential innocence.

The picture does not darken until Nashville is attained. Then with his audition going wonderfully—he's singing the song he and Whit composed—Red succumbs to a terrible coughing fit. The TB is now hard upon him, and the implication is that though he will probably die soon enough anyway, he will certainly die sooner if he goes on singing. But he has, at last, a recording offer—twenty dollars a song—and a last chance at a sliver of immortality. He comes to his final crisis in the studio (where, in tribute to Clint's youth, the backup band is supposed to be Bob Wills and His Texas Playboys). At the end of the film Whit and Marlene are seen walking away from Red's grave, and we hear a disc jockey introduce a new hit, "Honkytonk Man."

It is obviously a very simple film. And it was accomplished simply, too—on a five-week schedule for a budget of little more than $3 million, with the redemptive ending the studio urged on Clint carefully avoided. Clint treasures his memories of working with John McIntire, an actor much beloved in the business. He had offered this role first to James Stewart, but though he was only a year younger than the seventy-five-year-old McIntire, he told Clint he didn't want to play a grandfather just yet.

Verna Bloom, whose infant son was in the film, thought the work was hardest on Kyle: "It was a burden, that part—he had a lot to carry in the picture." Clint worried about that, too. But he "looks like a kid of the thirties," as he told a reporter at the time, and he was showing a real interest in his dad's line of work. Most important to Clint, he was not a professional. "I'm not crazy about kid actors," he said. "You can almost see their parents off camera, encouraging them to be cute." He asked Sondra Locke to handle the coaching, and working with his boy on camera he was, Bloom recalls, sterner than usual. He wanted a very straight performance, and he got it—that cautious alertness, that slight air of tension, that anyone might show if he was trying to please his dad was exactly right for a boy trying to take care of an explosive character like Red Stovall.

Critically, the film was radically undervalued. A number of reviewers made rather stupid *Camille* jokes at Clint's expense. "Well intentioned" and variants on the phrase were also much employed. There was, too, considerable criticism of Clint's singing, though simple resort to say "Barroom Buddies" would have demonstrated that he deliberately clouded his usually clear, light baritone in order to suggest the strangling effects of TB on Red's voice. The film's tone, its blend of muted humor and tragedy, its unmelodramatic way of insisting that life just kind of happens—which is its greatest success—seemed like a failure, a carelessness, to most observers. It got only one positive notice in a major publication. In *Time* this writer called it "a guileless tribute not only to plain values of plain people . . . but also to the sweet spirit of country-and-western music before it got all duded up for the urban cowboys."

In France, however, some critics compared *Honkytonk Man* to *The*

Grapes of Wrath. "My God," said Clint when a newspaperman reported this reaction to him. He must have had a similar reaction when he read Norman Mailer's profile the next year. The novelist saw in it "the steely compassion that is back of all the best country singing . . . and the harsh, yearning belly of rural America . . . making out with next to nothing but hard concerns and the spark of a dream that will never give up." In *Red* he saw "a subtle man . . . brought to life with minimal strokes, a complex protagonist full of memories of old cunning deeds and weary sham. It was one of the saddest movies seen in a long time, yet, on reflection, terrific. One felt a tenderness for America while looking at it."

★   ★   ★

And, perhaps, a certain tenderness for Clint Eastwood, who returned for his next two films to his most basic genre, the detective story. As someone once said, "A man's gotta know his limitations"—or anyway his audience's limitations. These *policiers* are, in different ways, among his most successful films. The first of them, *Sudden Impact,* was another *Dirty Harry* picture. But it grossed something over $70 million in the United States alone—his most substantial hit between *Any Which Way You Can* and *Unforgiven*—and got reviews that were more interested and engaged than *Honkytonk Man's* had been. In an unexpected way, it even did Clint's image some good.

It also gave him, of course, his signature moment, the line of dialogue with which he will forever be identified. One reason he says he kept returning to Dirty Harry is that he always got the good lines, and this one he recognized on the first reading of Joseph C. Stinson's script as "*the* punch line of the picture." Moreover, he liked the way it was contextualized. Preoccupied by yet another bawling out from his boss, Harry repairs to his favorite lunch counter for a cup of coffee and (unnoticed by most viewers) a study of a newspaper's help-wanted ads. Focusing on them, he doesn't notice that gunmen have the place under siege until his waitress, trying to send a silent signal, pours excessive amounts of sugar, which he doesn't take, into his cup. He finally gets the message, exits, returns through a back door, gets the drop on the criminals and starts referring to himself in the plural. We? Who's we? "Smith and Wesson and me," he replies tightly. Much shooting, screaming and property destruction ensue, with Harry finally holding a gun on the gang's leader while he, in turn, holds a gun to a hostage's head, threatening to pull the trigger if he is not allowed to escape. It is then that the great moment occurs: "Go ahead, make my day."

Strong as it was, Clint says, "I didn't realize it would ricochet around the world quite like it did." Neither did the reviewers. Only *Time's* Richard Corliss took significant notice of it. But it became a vernacular catch phrase in a matter of weeks, and then the president of the United States took it up. In March 1983, when Congress looked as if it might raise taxes, Ronald Reagan announced that he would happily veto the attempt and borrowed both the line and Clint's hissed delivery of it to suggest his resolve.

That was fine with Clint—the picture was still in release. What is not so fine is the way it goes on haunting him. Autograph hunters use it when they thrust pen and paper at him. Emcees use it to introduce him. When he takes questions from the floor after appearances even at august forums like the British Film Institute people ask him to repeat it. A woman interested in carnal knowledge of the star once hired an airplane to tow a banner displaying the phrase over a golf course where he was playing.

Clint was more than usually ambivalent about *Sudden Impact,* perhaps because its impetus was a marketing survey, about which he is habitually contemptuous. This one, however, was more than usually objective. Someone was testing the possibility of Sean Connery returning as James Bond and asked respondents how they would feel about other stars reprising their most famous roles. Clint coming back as Dirty Harry turned out to be their favorite idea. "So they [Warner Bros.] came to me and said I had to make another one," says Clint. "They were ready to start that Friday."

It took a few Fridays to come up with a story he liked—a story that, as it happened, had a very potent gimmick. But still . . . Dirty Harry again. Talking to Mailer on the set he said, "I thought I'd done all I can with it, and I might have. I don't know. But everybody kept asking about it." Years later he added, "It was a time in my life when I'd try the other things," he says, "and the public didn't flock to them."

"Some stiff's got himself a .38 caliber vasectomy," a cop informs Harry Callahan as he arrives at *Sudden Impact's* first crime scene, and, indeed, the corpse has two wounds—one in the genitals, the other in the brain. There will be others like him, but we soon understand that the killer is fragile, chilly Jennifer Spencer (Sondra Locke), painter of haunted pictures and victim along with her sister of a gang rape many years ago. The sister has been rendered catatonic by the experience; Jennifer, as we can see, psychopathic—a "Dirty Harriet" as many reviewers could not resist calling her. Such suspense as the film has to offer lies not in Harry's discovering the killer's identity, but in his determining whether or not to arrest her. Since he is in love with her, it is not hard to guess his decision.

This character—a woman bent on masculine-style vengeance, and accomplishing it—had a certain originality. There had been nothing quite like her on the screen before (and rarely enough since), and the novelty of the idea, as much as Clint's return to his signature role, accounts for *Sudden Impact*'s stunning popular success. Unfortunately, having determined to make this gesture, the film does not execute it as crisply as it might have. There is, as David Ansen wrote, "the makings of a fascinating multi-level melodrama" here, but it doesn't happen, perhaps, he speculated, because of mixed motives on Clint's part: "Eastwood doesn't want to let down his Dirty Harry fans, but at the same time he wants to take this character into deeper and murkier waters. The result is curious, a disquisition on the justice of revenge written with a spray can." In particular, one feels, the conventional jocularities of the series mix very uneasily with the intensity of Locke's character and the terrible nature of the wrong done her and her sister, which is quite unblinkingly recounted in flashbacks.

Yet because the film was rather interestingly shot—Clint's camera glides very coolly here, almost hypnotically—a certain tolerance for it was displayed in some critical quarters. David Denby in *New York* made the most salient point. Reviewing *Sudden Impact* in tandem with *Uncommon Valor* (a movie about a mission to rescue Vietnam MIAs that succeeds) he called both of them "surprisingly well-made" and identified the secret not just of their success (Ted Kotcheff's film was the unpredicted hit of the season), but of all such works: "They make contact with a stratum of pessimism that runs very deep in this country—a sort of lumpen despair that goes beyond, or beneath, politics. In these movies, America is a failure, a disgrace—a country run on the basis of expediency and profit, a country that has betrayed its ideals. The attack is directed not merely at liberals or 'permissiveness' but at something more fundamental—the modern bureaucratic state and capitalism itself."

Better late than never, this acute analysis of the new style in subversion. Better late than never the recognition that accrued to Clint as a "feminist filmmaker." It was a writer named Tom Stempel who advanced this idea at a moment when, seemingly, its time had come. His piece established a line that would be followed, especially by sympathetic feature writers, many of them women, to this day. Writing in the Los Angeles *Times,* Stempel was himself reacting to an article about strong heroines in recent films that had omitted mention of Locke and *Sudden Impact.* This oversight, he said, was the result of Clint's macho image; critics just didn't think to look in his movies for powerful female figures or were so preoccupied with him that they ignored them. He then proceeded to offer a list of such women, including, of course, Jessica Walter's mad stalker in *Misty* and Tyne Daly's female detective, but adding to it Locke's *Gauntlet* and *Bronco Billy* characters, Kay Lenz's Breezy and, more interestingly, the strong older women played by Ruth Gordon and Paula Trueman in, respectively, the *Which Way* films and *Josey Wales,* as well as the disparate Native American women in the latter picture and in *Bronco Billy*. It was an impressive, wide-ranging gathering.

Asked about the piece, Clint gave what would, with only small variants, become a practiced response: "It's very simple. I've always been interested in strong women. When I was growing up the female roles were equal to the men, and the actresses were just as strong as the actors. Now, in a lot of movies, you seem to have half a cast. The guy will be a big macho star. The woman will be a wimp. Women in the audience don't like that, and I believe men don't either."

He blamed this situation on his fellows. Men, he said, have the final decision in most movie casting and cast mainly for looks. "They cast an interesting man, and then for the woman they go for a model, a centerfold girl." He went the other way, he said in later reflections on this topic, out of simple self-interest. If he had a good actress in a strongly written part it made his job as a leading man that much easier; he had someone to share the burden with.

★   ★   ★

Something more than feminist sympathy was at work here; masculine ambivalence also contributed to his attitude. The joke among the guys in the Universal talent program, when they were asked to do certain kinds of scenes, was "Time to take my Man Pills," meaning time to go kick down a door and treat a woman rough. Clint always thought that was a stupid movie convention insisted upon by the sort of insecure, overcompensating males who, then as now, hold the front-office jobs in Hollywood. As we have long since observed, masculinity was a much more vexed topic for Clint. By the late eighties he was telling Carrie Rickey: "As far as the tormented male thing goes, maybe I'm interested in it because it's an obsolete thing—masculinity, I mean. There's very few things men are required for, except maybe siring. I guess I'm interested in the insecurities that keep outsiders outside."

In 1983 he bought a script by Richard Tuggle called *Tightrope,* which brought together the most visibly and darkly tormented male he had yet played and an extremely strong and hugely sympathetic feminist figure, a rape counselor named Beryl Thibodeaux (very well played by Geneviève Bujold). She is obliged to engage directly and tensely with

Clint's Wes Block, a New Orleans vice-squad detective, in an investigation of a series of sex crimes that becomes, as well, a metaphoric investigation of certain dark aspects of male sexuality.

There was originality in this concept. In movies, the flaws plaguing a hero are generally old-growth, the result of some long-ago wrong or trauma. But Wes Block is dealing with a live one, and a nasty one, a sexual issue that has arisen out of recent events in his life and is driving his nighttime behavior. Divorced and bitter about it, single-parenting his two daughters and happy about that, he is keeping his sex life rigidly separated from his home life, and rigidly separated from his moral sense as well. Not so his professional life. As a vice cop he knows where all the pretty bodies are cribbed, and he knows, too, which ones will submit to bondage, to the control he needs to reassert over women since his wife has slipped, as one might put it, the bonds of matrimony.

A psychopath is sadistically killing prostitutes, and seems to know, as well, that Wes shares his kinks, albeit acting on them in a much milder manner. There is even an attempt—not long or very persuasively pursued—to make us believe that Wes might just possibly be the killer, which in at least one draft Tuggle says he tried to stress more forcefully. (Changing his voice slightly, Clint did loop some of the lines spoken by the killer before we see his face, hoping to set up a few ambiguous resonances.) What emerged instead was a plot in which the murderer is identified as a former police officer Wes once arrested, with these new depredations designed first to frame Wes, ultimately to place his loved ones in deadly peril.

These are the elements, perhaps, of a slightly better than usual *policier*. Two factors transform them and the film into something more memorable. The first is Clint's willingness to play a character actually in the grips of an unsavory obsession, someone not just suspected or falsely accused of it, but actually acting on it. It is the same impulse (taken further) that permitted him to play the undone and nearly undone womanizers of *The Beguiled* and *Play Misty for Me*. It is, as well, a crucial, though generally unobserved, element setting Clint apart from his peers. As William Goldman once put it: "Here is one of the basic lessons a screenwriter must learn and live with: Stars will not play weak and they will not play blemished, and you better know that now."

Asked at the time how he dared break this most basic rule of above-the-title life, Clint was self-dismissive: "Just too dumb, I guess." Sure. But wouldn't the notion of "brutal frankness" cover the case more accurately? *Tightrope* may represent the largest, certainly the most obvious, payoff on that habit of mind.

Clint insisted on changing the story's locale from the scripted San

Francisco to New Orleans, in part to avoid confusion with the *Dirty Harry* films, in part because he liked the latter's funkiness. They shot in real New Orleans brothels, baths, sex shops and so on, in one of which, he recalls, the crew was afraid to touch the walls and furnishings for fear of contracting disease. The talk in this movie is as real as the settings, with a solid ring of quotidian truth about it. It is, for example, a film that acknowledges the propensity of children to ask astonishing, embarrassing questions. "Daddy, what's a hard-on?" one of Wes's kids pipes up, out of nowhere, as they are riding innocently along in a car one day. It is also a film in which, chided for turning down the offer of a male prostitute—"How do you know if you haven't tried it?"—the hero replies, "Maybe I have," and you don't entirely dismiss the possibility.

These contrasting exchanges mark the far ends of the psychological tightrope Wes teeters upon. It is Beryl's function to help him clamber down from this wire where he has strung himself out, and it is in their well-written and -acted exchanges, in the edginess with which they come closer to one another, that the movie finds much of its distinction. They meet professionally, and he uses the excuse of wanting to get her insights into the mind of the killer to pursue her. One day, he visits a self-defense class she conducts for women, watching quietly, unobserved by her, as she demonstrates against a dummy various karate moves they might apply to an assailant, climaxing with a sharp kick to the testicles. The manikin's eyes light up, its tongue lolls out of its mouth, and the tennis balls representing its genitals go bouncing across the floor toward Wes. He picks one up, holds it out to her and with his sweetest little-boy smile says, "Hi."

Soon enough they engage in a sharply testing exchange on a river steamer where one sunny, windy day they are sharing clams, beer and the beginnings of intimacy. He begins by wondering if she is unattached, which she says she is.

"What else were you wondering?" she asks.

"You really want to know?"

"Yeah."

"What it would be like to lick the sweat off your body."

Confused laughter. "Do you . . . do you always say exactly what's on your mind?"

"You don't like it?"

"Could be a little more subtle."

"What I said?"

"No, the way you said it."

"How would you like me to say it."

"As if you're not saying it to somebody every night."

"What else would you like?"

"I'd like to know what's underneath the front you put on."

"Maybe you wouldn't like what's there."

"Maybe you're afraid I would."

The scene is solidly on pitch—romantic comedy as it might be played by people who are neither as romantic nor as comedic as they might like to be.

In time they will talk about what his work has done to him. The first inspiration for Tuggle's screenplay was a manhunt for a serial rapist in the Bay Area who was never caught. In the course of his research he asked a vice cop how dealing constantly with the seamiest side of sex affected his private life. The man thought for a moment and replied, "It makes me treat my wife more tenderly in bed." He gave a variant on that line to Wes, and has Beryl ask, "How did she respond?" "She said she wasn't interested in tenderness," he replies.

Slowly his wariness dissipates. He introduces her to his daughters. They take a liking to her. He and Beryl begin to edge toward the bedroom. Once there, she picks up his handcuffs and asks him why the killer always uses them on his victims.

"Control," he says.

"Do you use them often?"

"Well, that depends."

"On what?"

"The situation."

"When you feel threatened?"

"Yeah, you could say that."

"With these, no one could get to you."

"They'll stop just about anyone."

At this point she snaps the cuffs on herself, and reaches out to touch his face. He flinches. But she is signaling trust; even though she knows the worst about him she is saying she does not fear submission to him. When he unlocks her handcuffs he also unlocks his emotions.

The film is in itself a kind of tightrope, dangerous if too slack, dangerous if too tightly strung, and the understated tension with which this scene is played is emblematic of the smart, believable middle way that it finds. As it happens, that was more difficult to achieve than anyone not present at its creation can possibly know.

Tuggle had sold his script on condition that he be allowed to direct. Clint, harking back to the passion with which Michael Cimino had animated his writerly vision, thought that was a good idea. But the two men are very different personalities. Cimino is a willful and decisive character. Tuggle, on the other hand, is a man who tends to see a dozen equally interesting alternatives in any situation and is not averse to exploring them all. Moreover, he did not have the experience that Cimino had gained making commercials, did not, therefore, know how to command a set. This last, perhaps, was his largest failing, for this was an Eastwood crew, used to moving quickly and ready to glance in his direction when a director faltered.

It seems Tuggle lasted no more than a day in full control of the location. One witness remembers him hesitating overlong on the placement of a picture in the background of a shot. Another recalls him choosing a camera placement that ensured a door that had to be opened in the scene would block the actors from view. And these were comparatively simple shots. "He didn't know how to function in a decision-making deal" is the way Clint puts it. He also suggests, and it is the only criticism of Tuggle that he offers, that the would-be director should have spent some time on other sets, observing how the job was done. It was too late now. There was much complicated work still to be done involving crowds, high-voltage action and sophisticated coverage, and Clint simply did not feel Tuggle would be able to handle it.

Here it was again, the near-endemic problem of trying to direct a star who was not only the film's de facto producer, but also his own best director (at least until someone proves otherwise to him)—vastly complicated in this case by the fact that Tuggle was manifestly "such a good guy," as Clint describes him. Even if the Directors Guild's Eastwood rule had not prevented Clint from taking over, he really didn't want to.

So a compromise was worked out. The writer would stay on, contribute what he could in a collaborative way and receive directorial credit, while Clint, literally, called most of the shots. Tuggle insists he made substantial contributions to his script's realization in this role, and Clint does not deny them. But our eyes tell us this is very much an Eastwood movie—his stylistic tracks are all over it—and the anecdotal evidence supports this reading.

The most unmistakable example of his imprimatur is the sequences involving the children. This was not troubling to Tuggle. He could see that Alison and Clint would be more comfortable working without third-party interference. Though they were playing roles close to real life—a father and daughter negotiating the shoals of divorce—Clint thought that was to their advantage. That "little parallel," he says, "made it easier for a ten-year-old to understand." Besides, when she had visited his sets she had always loved "being in front of the camera and hamming it up," and I said, 'You know, I should just get her in the right part and it will be all right.'"

So it was. She is excellent in a scene in which she is supposed to gently comfort her father when he comes home from work distraught and tipsy and falls woozily onto the living room couch. There his daughter finds him and wants to offer him some comfort. Clint had noticed Alison's fondness for the cat who lived in the house they had rented for use as the Block family home, quietly stroking and cuddling it between takes. When it came time to do this scene his instruction was simple: "Just think of your dad as this lost, stray cat. Just kind of relate to your dad like that."

What she did was remove his wedding picture from his hand, try to pat a comforter around him and then snuggle down on top of him, "warming with her tomgirl body the man her mother has rejected," as Kathleen Murphy nicely describes it. This proved to be a discomfiting moment to some reviewers, but it is also, in its straightforward behavioral honesty, a breathtaking one, not unlike the opening kiss in *The Beguiled,* one of those rare moments that breaks through the movieness of movies, transcending the conventions by which reality is generally represented in them, referring us to something less mediated, less calculated.

This movie is throughout touched with something of that spirit. For the "little parallel" Clint proposes is part of a larger parallel between his life and the life of the man he plays. As we have observed, Wes Block is a man trying to keep the compartments of his life sealed, desperately attempting to prevent the lives each contains to flow out into the others. Clint, obviously in less melodramatic circumstances, obviously with greater success, has always tried to do the same thing. Private man and public man, Carmel man and movie man, man's man, lady's man and family man—he keeps the overlap between them to a minimum. It has been his way of asserting control over a complicated life.

There is, of course, a significant difference between Wes Block and Clint Eastwood: There is an authentic monster invading Wes's professional life. And this monster will invade Wes's home, murder a babysitter and deposit his daughter, bound and gagged, in her father's bed, with the threat of further violation avoided by a hair's breadth. ("You motherfucker," the raging Wes cries; he is looking at his own image in a mirror when he does so.) Later, the killer invades Beryl's home—another, if newer, sacred place for Wes—and again catastrophe is narrowly avoided.

One does not want to make too much of these parallels between fiction and fact. But one does not want to make too little of them, either. For it is obvious that Clint's eagerness to involve his children in his work betokened self-awareness, his sense that compartmentalization cannot be carried to rigid extremes. It is equally clear that, in the age of the free-floating psychopath, public figures are subject to terrors of precisely the kind Wes Block confronts. Clint has been stalked (and for a time carried a licensed weapon for protection). His daughter would later be threatened in the same way. And that says nothing about the rapacious invasions of the gossip press on public lives (to which Clint's response has been a string of successful lawsuits). Simply put, *Tightrope* is, among other things, a dramatic projection of feelings (and situations) its star and unacknowledged director had known and imagined in reality.

It derives some of its power from that simple, unspoken fact. Unfortunately, Tuggle suffered for that. This was a project that engaged Clint passionately, one he could not surrender to someone whose lack of professional experience seemed certain to undermine its force. What Clint did, in effect, was make Tuggle the film's dramaturge, a role he handled gracefully and effectively. "We really did see eye to eye on the script," Tuggle says. "It was shot word for word almost. I think we both wanted to make the same movie, and I was real happy with the movie." Tuggle, though, cannot completely bury all of his resentments at being pushed aside. Assured that Clint still makes no large claims to the film's authorship, and that he speaks with great warmth about him, Tuggle replies, with quiet bitterness: "No, there's no reason to criticize me. You only criticize someone if you've lost a war or an argument. If you have won, you have no criticism."

It is too bad he can't content himself with an incontestable credit, that of writing one of the most interesting films to which Clint Eastwood ever applied his talents. Of his many explorations of maleness and its meanings, none came closer to the heart of the matter—what we might call "control anxiety" (especially as it is expressed in love relationships)—and none, excepting *Unforgiven,* more effectively used simple and powerful melodramatic devices to create ambiguous social and psychological resonances.

When it arrived in the theaters in the summer of 1984, Kael and her coterie—the "Paulettes" as they were coming to be known—deplored it. Most of the other notices were mixed. Some found it a true inheritor of the film noir manner, especially in that subgenre's insistence on the close psychological relationship between cop and criminal mentalities. Others felt this parallel not persuasively worked out. But whatever their judgment of the film, their approval of Clint's performance was nearly unanimous. J. Hoberman in the *Village Voice* called Clint "one of the most masterful under-actors in American movies," and Jack Kroll in *Newsweek* acutely noted the "forlorn lust" that Clint communicated in his pursuit of prostitutes and his "vulnerability" in his scenes with his children. "He gets better as he gets older; he seems to be creating new nuances beneath his stony exterior." David Denby agreed: "He's become a very troubled movie icon: That forehead, where all the energy appears pent up in the bulging veins, looks ready to explode. He gives a genuinely spooked performance."

Precisely because his characterization was located within a genre film of the kind with which he had been most closely (and most controversially) associated, he provided the reviewers a convenient basis for comparison. They could look upon it, consult their memories of *Dirty Harry* and see "growth" of a kind that had been harder to perceive in eccentricities like *Bronco Billy* or *Honkytonk Man*. To put it another way, the critics on the whole undervalued the film, but finally evaluated Clint's strengths as an actor correctly. As a result, Joe Hyams says, his job became easier than ever. He would not in the future have nearly as much trouble getting reviewers to at least approach an Eastwood movie seriously. He was so excited that he took out an ad for *Tightrope* in *The New York Review of Books*. The studio, gratefully counting excellent grosses, would mount its first "For Your Consideration" campaign for Clint during the next winter's Academy Award season.

FOURTEEN

THE MOTH SIDE

S tardom's hoariest rite was belatedly accorded Clint when he was promoting *Tightrope;* he was invited to place his hand and footprints in the concrete of Grauman's Chinese Theater's famous forecourt in Hollywood. Taking stylus in hand, and bowing to dull expectation, he scratched, "You've made my day," into the cement block. It had scarcely hardened before he had another picture in release.

This was *City Heat,* and before it was finished—before it was started—it became the playground for much trickier Hollywood rituals. Indeed, it developed into something like a paradigmatic conflict between someone trying to conduct business as usual, Hollywood style, and someone fully intending to do business as usual, Eastwood style. The script, under another title, had been submitted to Warners by its writer, Blake Edwards, who intended to direct it as well. It was a period piece, set in Kansas City in 1933, during the waning days of Prohibition, and it featured a bantering relationship between private eye Mike Murphy and police detective Lieutenant Speer, who had once been partners on the force but were now on the outs. The freelance investigator is a raffish sort, the cop more dour and often obliged to rescue his pal from the potentially deadly consequences of his insouciance. It had something of the air of those quick, tough little movies Warner Bros. used to make about once a month in the thirties, which Clint had always enjoyed.

When the studio passed it on to him, however, he passed on it—too talky. There the matter might have rested, except that "Blake was kind of a bad boy," says Clint. He sent the script to Sondra Locke, proposing that she again play the part of an heiress in difficulty. She—as Edwards surely expected she would—mentioned the offer to Clint and asked him why he hadn't liked the script. He replied that he hadn't entirely hated it and, rereading it, began to see self-satirizing possibilities in what he calls "the Pat O'Brien part," a sort of superego in a snap brim, imagining Burt Reynolds—then doing rather disheveled sequels to his *Smokey and the Bandit* and *Cannonball Run* successes—as the piece's Cagneyish id, the high-stepping Murphy, and giving Sondra a chance at a colorfully comedic part.

So it was done—handshakes all around—and then immediately undone. It turned out that Edwards had been using Locke to get to Clint. He announced that he had actually—well, er—promised the part to his daughter. This precipitated a small Eastwoodian explosion. There was also talk at some point of using Edwards's wife, Julie Andrews, in the role of Murphy's secretary. This brought outraged yelps from Reynolds. He had just worked with her, under Edwards's direction, in *The Man Who Loved Women,* and was not eager to repeat the experience. Clint, predictably dismayed by these shenanigans, threatened to withdraw.

A project-saving compromise was reached when all parties agreed not to employ any loved ones in the picture, but, needless to say, Clint remained wary. This was to be a back-lot picture—as thirties crime stories had always been—and now Edwards was insisting that a house be rented for him in Bel-Air so he did not have to make the long daily commute from his house in Malibu to the Warners and Universal lots where he would be working. The need for a car and driver was also mentioned. What was not being mentioned were certain rewrites that Edwards had promised Clint, who was aware, as well, that Reynolds was growing increasingly skittish with the situation. Of Edwards, Clint said to a studio executive, "This guy is just on a different planet."

Actually he was just on Planet Hollywood. Edwards had been around town since the forties, when he began his career as an actor, had gone on to large success in television (*Peter Gunn*) and features (*Breakfast at Tiffany's, The Pink Panther* and its sequels, *10*) and obviously knew all its ropes. Indeed, he had recently made a vicious, hilarious satire on Hollywood, *S.O.B.* He should have known better. Certainly he should have known his leading man's reputation better.

Clint had had enough. "I'll tell you what," he said, "why don't we do this some other time, on some other script down the line that we both like?"

Warner Bros., however, decided to persist. The studio liked this attractive star pairing in a picture they were confident could be a hot Christmas release. So they fired Edwards. And turned the project over to Clint, though both Malpaso and Reynolds's company, Deliverance, would eventually share production credit. That and Clint's billing ahead of him were all right with Reynolds—"He's taller than I am," he wisecracked.

The stars decided to talk to Richard Benjamin about taking over as director. Well known as an actor (*Goodbye, Columbus*), Benjamin had recently directed two period pieces, *My Favorite Year* and *Racing with the Moon,* doing particularly good work on the former. He was sent Edwards's script to read before his preliminary meeting with Clint and Reynolds and remembers thinking it was long, a little "diffuse," but with some interesting undertones. At the meeting, however, Clint told him he thought it contained too many "long, complicated psychological speeches which were not in his movie style," and that he had engaged his *Sudden Impact* writer, Joe Stinson, to do a rewrite. This—or some portion of it—he now pressed on Benjamin, telling him, however, that if there was anything that had been excised from Edwards's script that he particularly liked they would certainly consider reintroducing it.

In the event, Benjamin found Clint not particularly receptive to the few such changes he proposed. But since time had been wasted in the wrangling with Edwards, pressure to begin shooting was mounting, and the director thought Stinson's revision quite serviceable. So they forged ahead, using most of the actors Edwards had cast. The one new hire was Madeline Kahn, for the role that had briefly been Locke's.

Kahn was excellent. So was Jane Alexander as Murphy's plain, sensible secretary, not so hopelessly in love (as it turns out) with Speer. So were Rip Torn and Tony Lo Bianco as over-the-top gang bosses. The inherent problem with the movie was an incoherently complex plot, involving, of all things, underworld financial records that Murphy has stolen and . . .

Oh, forget it. No one was supposed to pay much attention to that. All eyes were supposed to be focused on the stars and their banter. They had some good moments. Clint, for example, got to use upscale words like "chagrin" and "ilk" in his dialogue, as if Speer were taking a night-school course to improve his vocabulary. He also got to send up his image with improbably cool competence in the killing arts. Reynolds had his fair share of impudent dialogue ("You're supposed to flush that, not smoke it," he says, eyeing a hood's El Ropo cigar). And there is a merry moment when both stars draw huge, wildly phallic pistols and competitively evaluate each other's equipment. But the heat promised by the movie's title rarely climbs higher than lukewarm, and that's mostly Reynolds's fault.

He's smooth and competent, not at all self-referential, and many reviewers would ultimately compliment him on a return to lost form. But in its making he threw the picture off stride. It was shot more or less in order, and the first—perhaps best—scene went wonderfully. It is set at a lunch counter, where the estranged Speer and Murphy meet by chance. They are seated at the farthest ends of the counter, snarling at one another, when some yeggs enter and proceed to beat up Murphy, while his sometime friend looks on blandly, refusing to help him until, in the course of the fracas, his coffee gets spilled.

Unfortunately, Reynolds's jaw was broken in the melee, and he developed temporomandibular joint disorder, a disease that disturbs one's sense of balance. As a result, he took a fall in his trailer and thereafter became "distracted" in Benjamin's word, nervous and cautious about subsequent action scenes. He found loud gunshots, of which there were many in this movie, particularly unsettling. As production wore on he seemed to become more and more withdrawn, and Clint suspected what Reynolds later admitted in his autobiography, that he had become temporarily addicted to the painkiller Percodan. In short, he made everybody anxious, and in a role that was supposed to energize the film, he often had the opposite effect.

Clint, according to Benjamin, did everything possible to compensate for his costar's derelictions. The director said he had never worked on a film where the star was so frugal, so selfless in relation to the camera or so helpful to a director confronting serious, unexpected problems. He describes, for example, going to Clint a few days before starting to see if he had attended to his wardrobe, and being informed that it was taken care of.

"When did you get it?" the director asked.

"I got it yesterday. I think it cost about four hundred dollars. Come and look at it. I got it at Brooks Brothers. They had it on sale." He grinned happily. "The clothes are the same. Those coats in the thirties and these coats are all the same—the hats are all the same."

In a world where tens of thousands can be spent on a star's wardrobe, which tends to go home with him or her after the production finishes, this was a revelation to Benjamin. Then when it was time to change a setup, he was startled to see Clint grab a cable and start dragging it to the next position before any of the crew members moved. Time being money, the star was not above setting an example for them.

On another occasion the only take Benjamin had made of a Clint close-up came back from the lab scratched and, rather shamefacedly, the director told him they'd have to do it over. Clint, however, looked at it in the projection room and told him not to worry. It was a short night shot that they would print dark anyway; nobody would ever see the scratch.

Clint's lack of selfishness, his predilection for throwing scenes to other actors—partly out of generosity, partly out of a serene confidence in the force of his own presence—had by this time been much commented upon by coworkers, as was his preference for seeing himself underlit, but it came as a surprise to Benjamin. One time he set up a shot in which the camera moved in a half circle around him, to which the star made no objection until the midpoint of the camera rehearsal when he muttered, "Oh, God." "What?" Benjamin inquired. "Well, you're gonna end up on the moth side of me." "The moth side?" "The light side," said Clint, where such illumination as the shot contained would be fully perceived by the lens, where, if there were any flying insects present, they would congregate. He had wanted—as he generally does, when it is at all feasible—backlight.

His genial spirit was put to its largest test by a gun battle in a warehouse between the two leads and the massed forces of gangsterdom. It was going to be noisy and complicated, and Benjamin had meticulously preplanned every shot for a schedule consuming four nights. Reynolds, however, went to Clint and told him he did not think he was physically up to the sequence. They were now on location in downtown Los Angeles, and Clint took an hour-long walk with his old friend through the deserted streets, trying to reassure him.

Afterward, Clint told Benjamin, "You've got one night. This guy's falling apart." Benjamin had perhaps a hundred setups in mind, with the eye lines of the actors' exchanging shots all carefully matched. Clint proposed radical simplification. First of all, he said, don't waste a lot of time lighting—just keep it low and simple. It used to drive Don Siegel crazy, he recalls, when people would start hanging extra scrims on the lights at the last moment: "Half the time they just fall off anyway." Next, concentrate on Burt; "We can do my shit later." Finally, in Clint's recounting, he told Benjamin, "All you have to do is get the general geography of the scene right, and then fire off a lot of rounds." He thinks he may also have quoted another Siegelism to the director: "You don't want to get paralysis from analysis."

It's very simple, really. Once the audience knows where everyone's starting point in the sequence is, knows where they stand in relationship to one another, they can thereafter move almost randomly without confusing the viewers. So Benjamin grabbed shots of all the actors ducking, loading, firing, looking and shooting left, right and straight ahead, then moving in various directions from their starting positions. Mixed and matched in the cutting room with cutaways to shattering glass, squibs exploding in the walls—all the familiar whatnots of a big gunfight—it was impossible for anyone to tell for certain if a shot and the reaction to it were perfectly matched or not. Indeed, Benjamin thinks the sequence has more energy than his original plan might have delivered.

Benjamin soon returned Clint's support in kind. Since Kansas City at the time in which the picture was set was a famous jazz center, Lennie

Niehaus was engaged to write a score in that idiom. One night when Benjamin was working late in his office at Malpaso, Clint happened by. "You want to hear something?" he asked, and took him into his office where he played a nice boogie-woogie riff of Niehaus's. "I don't know if he was asking me something or telling me something," Benjamin says, but he inquired if Clint wanted to play in the movie. "I don't know, I don't know if I'm good enough," he replied. "Well, it sounds great to me," the director said, and thus encouraged, Clint played on camera and later joined the professional musicians at their scoring session.

There, though, Clint had trouble with one or two passages and always mindful of cost, perhaps embarrassed to look amateurish in the presence of people like Joe Williams, the great jazz singer who was there to lay down the title song, was ready to quit: "We're wasting time here; I'll never get it." To which Benjamin replied, "Yes, you will. You'll get this." And he did, much to his pleasure. "That seemed so important to him, to play on the album," the director adds.

Clint had one last surprise for him. When the picture was finally pulled together, he and Benjamin ran it in a screening room. At the end, Clint asked the director, "Do you like it?"

"I like it" came the reply.

"I like it, too." Pause. "Let's ship it."

Benjamin could not believe his ears. In his experience, the director's cut was more a beginning than an end, the basis for many test screenings and arguments.

Of course, this is a perquisite available to Clint Eastwood and to very few others, though in this case discretion was distinctly the better part of valor. Both Clint and Benjamin implicitly understood that there was nothing more to be done with *City Heat,* no retakes, no stroke of postproduction brilliance, that might transform it into something more than it was, a largely agreeable, entirely forgettable movie that did not deliver the sizzle, buzz and blockbuster grosses the studio had expected from Clint and Burt. Audiences treated it as a sort of second-choice movie, something to see if the hit police comedy of the 1984 Christmas season, Eddie Murphy's *Beverly Hills Cop,* was sold out. "Disappointment"—studiospeak not for a failure to make money, but for a failure to live up to inflated expectations—was expressed by a Warners spokesman.

★   ★   ★

Clint kept his feelings about the film to himself. He went off and made another movie—*Pale Rider*—as *City Heat* was being prepared for release and later did little to publicize it. He was much more interested in "The

Clint Eastwood Magical Respectability and European Accolade and Adulation Tour" as John Vinocur dubbed it in the cover story—"Clint Eastwood, Seriously"—he wrote about it for *The New York Times Magazine*. With one of the Warner Gulf Streams at his disposal, with Terry Semel and Lenny Hirshan at his side some of the time, this consumed two weeks in January 1985, including a visit to Paris where the Cinémathèque had been running a retrospective of his work since mid-December and where he received his chevalier of arts and letters medal ("I'm sorry I don't speak French," he said at the ceremony, "but I have enough trouble with English"), a stop at the Film Museum in Munich for another retrospective and then the first of his *Guardian* lectures in London, where the sponsoring newspaper's coincident critical essay was headed "A Die-Hard Liberal behind the Magnum Image."

Vinocur made much of the contrast between the reception accorded Clint on his Royal Progress and the fact that "until a couple of years ago Eastwood, actor or director, had been consistently reviled as a cinematic caveman, a lowbrow and a lunkhead," and rather nicely caught the confusion of cultural officialdom, aware of how recently he had emerged from Stygian realms, unsure of whether he was fully worthy of the empyrean ones to which they were rather self-consciously conducting him.

Clint was cool about the whole complicated business. Asked why he had gone to all this trouble—the weather was terrible much of the time and some of the flights white-knucklers—he replied, "Well, it's like this. They're pretty nice people. And I hadn't been to Europe for a while." He resisted adding the obvious, that word (by Vinocur among others) of Europe's regard for him flashed back to that portion of the American audience that had most resisted him was alone worth the trouble.

In that respect, 1985 would turn out to be a very good year for him. In a Roper poll conducted for one of the newsmagazines, he was named the figure most admired by young Americans, finishing ahead of Mother Teresa, among others. In April of that year he would be at the White House, sitting at Nancy Reagan's table when her husband bestowed National Medals of Art on the likes of Louise Nevelson and Leontyne Price. The following fall he would be back in Washington for the official state reception for Prince Charles and Princess Diana, even taking a turn on the dance floor with the princess.

In between those two dates he premiered *Pale Rider* at the Cannes Film Festival, thus realizing an old ambition while bringing to one of its early peaks his new desire for the good opinion of the cinematically conscientious. Clint would decide his accommodations (a rented yacht snugged up to a quay) were too confining and too close to the action;

he would, in future years, discover the Hôtel du Cap. But otherwise things went well. It was he who spoke the official word declaring the festival open, and for the first time he knew the heady pleasure of mounting the broad staircase leading to the Palais des Festivals, its chief venue. It offers actors the kind of entrance that made them go into the business in the first place: processional music; thousands of eyes, not to mention the television cameras of the world, fixed on you and you alone; complete isolation on a glorious red-carpeted platform; the mass intake of breath when you appear; the cheers crescendoing when you turn to wave halfway up; the sighing exhale when, with a last wave, you disappear into the building. William Goldman, who has written brilliantly about Cannes, quotes Paul Newman on this moment: "Oh, I get it, I'm an emperor now, I can deal with that."

Mostly Clint dined well—he referred to his party as the American eating team—and, between meals, sat on his yacht, cracking open the odd bottle of beer, sipping occasionally on a glass of white wine, entertaining a parade of notebook-toting visitors with low-key comments on life, career, forthcoming films. Asked about Burt Reynolds, he called him "my other child." When someone mentioned the gray in his hair, he said, "It gives you a little respect." A reporter who had interviewed him earlier in his career remarked that words seemed to come more easily to him now, and he admitted to being less measured. "Then I thought everything should be the absolute truth. Now I'm willing to take my chances with life." At a press conference, someone asked him if, when he gunned down the villain at the end of *Pale Rider,* he was perhaps—how shall one say?—symbolically killing Sergio Leone, his cinematic father. He bemusedly observed that it was biologically improbable, since they were the same age (he still didn't know that they were not). Jean-Luc Godard dedicated *Detective,* his ill-received entrant in the competition, to Clint—half ironically—in the spirit of his dedication of *Breathless* to Monogram Pictures.

Pale Rider won no prizes—Clint hadn't expected it to—and he left a few days before the festival ended, stopping off for an evening in Paris on the way home. There he had dinner with his old friend and supporter Bertrand Tavernier and discovered that Warner Bros., which had previously shown interest in *Round Midnight,* Tavernier's story of a black jazzman living out his life in Paris, was now hesitating over his casting of a nonstar, Dexter Gordon, himself a legendary musician, in the lead role. Clint had always been enthusiastic about this project, and when he ran into Terry Semel the next night in London, he made a plea for it. At a cost of $4 million, he did not see how the studio could be hurt by the film (which was ultimately well received critically and won some Academy Award nominations). Semel agreed to restudy the proposition and shortly thereafter approved it. Subsequently Tavernier effusively credited Clint with rescuing his film.

It was an agreeable climax to a completely satisfying trip, for he had been the big story out of Cannes. Stars of his magnitude usually do not risk playing their pictures—especially if they are westerns—in competition, and the noncritical press could not get enough of the irony they perceived in Dirty Harry hobnobbing with the European swells. Their dispatches about him and his festival-worthy western helped dress *Pale Rider* for success.

★   ★   ★

The movie was the only one he had ever involved himself in before a word was placed on paper. It had begun some four years earlier in a meeting with Michael Butler and Dennis Shryack, of *The Gauntlet*. They had always wanted to do a western, and Clint invited them to come back and bounce some ideas around. The genre might be in general disfavor, but he thought that if they could find a middle course between dull archetype and the revisionism that he had himself pioneered they might have a viable project. Or as he put it in a prerelease interview: "Basically I wanted to have contemporary concerns expressed within . . . the classical tradition."

Out of their discussions came the notion of placing some independent gold miners—"tin pans," as they are called in the film—in mortal conflict with a land baron named LaHood (Richard Dysart), who is using hydraulic strip mining to flush the ore out of the land. Ecologically his operation is brutal, and so is the small army he employs to drive off the little community of miners whose place, on what all believe to be a potentially rich stream, he covets. These peaceful souls are presented in the film almost as a hippie commune, in obvious need of a protector, which the first-draft script provided them in the form of an itinerant preacher who also happens to be good with guns.

So far, so good: *Shane* with an ecological spin—cattle baron and homesteaders replaced by big miners and small ones—and an antiorganization one, too. "I think the bureaucratic workings of nations and corporations have encouraged people to form counter-societies," Clint said. "It seems like the growing complications of our lives have made us wonder if there isn't some way to cut out all of that."

With the classic references in place and updated, the problem now was to add some reflexiveness. Perhaps, Clint suggested, the stranger should have some unfinished business with someone in the enemy camp—like, say, Marshall Stockburn (John Russell), LaHood's chief en-forcer—to motivate him. Perhaps, he also thought, this stranger might be "a supernatural being or an emissary from a higher plane." He was, with these notions and his basic costume, a frock coat, admittedly hark-ing back to the *High Plains Drifter* theme—"I guess maybe I felt I hadn't explored it enough."

Explored what? The possibility that the retribution may, indeed, be divine on occasion? The hope of immortality that dares not speak its name to a secularist? Or the notion that a spook is the ultimate nihilist, a figure no man can collar or question? The last of these seems most likely.

There was another relationship between *Drifter* and *Rider.* The latter would also rather casually avail himself of a good woman, Sarah Wheeler (Carrie Snodgrass), and with less justification, since she is liv-ing with a decent and inoffensive man, Hull Barrett (Michael Moriarty), the stranger's most welcoming friend in this community. A trope from another Eastwood movie, *The Beguiled,* was also revived here. This was his character's relationship with a very young girl, fourteen-year-old Megan Wheeler (Sydney Penny). As in the earlier film, it is she who sees him first. As she completes reading the passage from the Bible that sug-gested the film's title—"and I looked and beheld a pale horse: and his name that sat on him was Death, and Hell followed with him"—Clint's preacher ("quite the drollest of Clint Eastwood's mythic disguises," as Richard Jameson wrote) appears outside her window. And like Amy in the older film, she openly adores him, even, unlike the younger child, discreetly offers herself to him. She is, of course, gently rebuffed.

Was realism of this kind intended as a kind of balance to the eeri-ness of the stranger's character? Was it, like the ecological and commu-nitarian themes, an attempt to give it a more modernist edge? Or was it just another quite innocent spin on *Shane,* with a smitten girl standing in for that film's hero-worshiping boy?

These passages discomfited several reviewers though not as much as the film's insufficiently disguised debt to the George Stevens film did. Critic after critic cited the 1953 movie as a source for this one. Others, like Richard Corliss, chastised Clint for playing God—or, anyway, a close associate—with too much relish and authority. On the other hand, some reviewers welcomed the picture very warmly, with Vincent Canby graciously acknowledging that it had taken him too many years to rec-ognize Clint's "very consistent grace and wit as a filmmaker." Michael Wilmington of the Los Angeles *Times* shined the most interesting light on *Pale Rider,* writing that the film's tableaux seemed both "contempo-rary and remembered, vivid and fervently elegiac." He concluded that "novelty isn't always a sign of talent. Sometimes it's the way the film-

maker brings new inflections . . . to old stories that reveal his highest
qualities. By remaking *Shane* . . . Eastwood takes a fond backward glance
at a slice of the past worth treasuring. And he proves that his own acting
and directing are among the treasures of the present.'"

His last point is his best one. Bearded, wearing a tall semistovepipe
hat with his tightly buttoned frock coat, Clint has at first glance a marvelously forbidding air and at second glance just a slight sense of humbug. As he settles in with the miners one begins to sense something just
slightly off-key in his pieties—"There's plain few problems can't be
solved with a little sweat and some hard work." They seem studied and
a little forced, something like the gaseous humanism of Ivy League
Episcopalians working slum parishes today. It's good, sly stuff, Eastwoodian humor at its driest. And it is extended to his physical confrontations with the forces of evil. There is, for example, some flashy
business with an ax handle and four bullies that is a very conscious, very
humorous homage to Kurosawa's magically adept samurai.

Clint's direction is as assured as his playing. He made the film on his
standard five-week schedule in the early fall of 1984, mainly on location
in the Sawtooth Range in Idaho (convenient to his Sun Valley home) in
a manner that consciously reversed *Shane*'s. The older picture was uncannily neat and tidy. Stevens wanted to leave no doubt that the Old
West was an American Eden. He also wanted to imply what *Pale Rider*
would say more literally, that his eponymous hero was touched by supernatural powers. Blond and pallid in his white buckskins, Alan Ladd
sometimes seems to give off a near-angelic glow. Clint, of course, went
the other way, toward autumnally lit scruffiness.

He also created two outstanding action pieces. One was the opening
raid on the miners' settlement by LaHood's hoods—shadowy riders in
the dappled woods, faster and faster cutting as they sweep down on victims, the harsh rhythms of panic and brutality when unfair combat is
joined. This is virtuoso action staging, stressing the casual pleasure evil
takes in its own depredations, the stunned disbelief of its victims. And it
all happens so quickly.

The concluding confrontation between the stranger, the marshal
and his deputies is still more remarkable. By this time we have seen the
stigmata Clint's character carries. We know he has been shot repeatedly
in the back by someone. We know from the marshal's puzzlement over
this distantly glimpsed figure—it must be, it can't be—that it is he who
victimized him. We do not know, and never find out, what the issue was
between them; the silence on this point is Leonesque. But the shoot-out
in the mean, muddy streets of a little western town, the lone avenger
against a half-dozen opponents, consciously cross-refer to the conclu-

sion of *High Noon*. One difference here is Clint's ability to appear and disappear at will; another is that he wants to make sure, in their final face-off, that the marshal has no doubt about whom he is confronting. So the distance that is usually maintained in these sequences is radically shortened. Instead of being a block apart when they draw, they are feet, then inches, apart. And by rubbing our noses into the squalor and chaos of violent death, the filmmaking here brilliantly reverses classicism's more abstract take on the subject.

There was more than the usual interest in *Pale Rider* during the run-up to its release, more than the customary concern in tracking its box-office returns in the period after it opened. So many westerns of the sixties and seventies had taken the closing of the frontier as their theme that people wondered if a movie could again live comfortably in an earlier western era. To many it seemed that Cimino's *Heaven's Gate,* offering more empty grandiosity than epic grandeur, had, perhaps, put a period to the genre; no significant westerns had been made since its release in 1980. But now Lawrence Kasdan was set to bring out his star-encrusted *Silverado* almost simultaneously with *Pale Rider,* and the press, ever eager to make a trend out of coincidence, wondered volubly if this represented a renaissance or a last gasp for the form. The decision was that it still had viability if Clint was the star. For *Pale Rider* was the nation's top-grossing film—about $9 million—during its first week of release and eventually took in close to $50 million at the domestic box office alone.

Still, *Pale Rider* remains the most problematic of the westerns Clint directed. It is an altogether smoother picture than *High Plains Drifter,* the work of a mature artisan in full and tasteful command of an inherently improbable tale. But one misses the rough outrageousness of the previous film. Nor can one quite make the kind of emotional connections with this visible shade that one made with Josey Wales, struggling with his less visible demons. Finally, the film lacks the realistic intensity—and the moral urgency—of *Unforgiven,* which turns on a kind of rebirth, too, but a much more riveting one.

★   ★   ★

As *Pale Rider* went into the theaters, Clint was completing the first (and only) film he ever directed for television and the last in which he would direct Sondra Locke. This was "Vanessa in the Garden," an episode for the *Amazing Stories* series Steven Spielberg was producing for NBC. A prestigious, heavily publicized effort to revive the spooky spirit of the old *Alfred Hitchcock Presents* and *Twilight Zone* anthologies, the network was financing these half-hour programs generously, and Spielberg was recruiting feature-film actors and directors to work on them (Martin Scorsese, Peter Weir and Brian De Palma were among the latter). According to Clint, Spielberg hailed him on the main street of the Warners lot one day, and told him he had a script that he had himself written for the series that he thought would be ideal for Clint to direct.

At first glance it is difficult to see why. It is a variant on the *Portrait of Jennie* theme and a period piece, set more or less in Edith Wharton—or maybe one should say Merchant Ivory—country. In it, Vanessa, the wife and principal model of a painter named Byron Sullivan (a miscast Harvey Keitel), is killed in a riding accident on the eve of his first important show. In his bereavement he destroys most of his work and turns to drink. When he tries to burn a picture called *Vanessa in the Garden,* however, a wind blows out his match, and when he awakes the next morning he hears Vanessa's voice, singing sweetly. Returning to the painting he finds her image vanished from it and then glimpses her wandering in the setting he had used for its background. Later he finds her sitting in a large wicker chair, posed as she was for another painting. He imagines that if he creates more such scenes she will return and inhabit them. He's right, and he becomes a man obsessed. Sullivan's gallery manager and best friend (Beau Bridges), in turn, makes him a rich and famous one—which means nothing to him in comparison to the happiness he has found in (quite literally) immortalizing his beloved.

Spielberg had the right man for this job. "Vanessa in the Garden" was yet another "exploration" of the possibilities of life after death, with Clint making a sunny, formal, gently romantic chamber piece out of it. With Locke more playful than ethereal in her work, there is an unexpectedly cheerful air about this little anecdote.

Off-screen, however, Clint's relationship with Sondra was drifting toward more uncomfortable territory. If their arrangement was in its more visible aspects unconventional, considering her continuing legal—and emotional—commitment to Gordon Anderson, it was in some respects quite traditional. She urged Clint to sell (to Fritz Manes, as it happens) the little house on the wrong side of Mulholland Drive that he and Maggie had shared so long ago, and that had remained his Los Angeles pied-à-terre. She helped him find something more suitable in Bel-Air, a dark but airy Spanish-style structure, the decorating of which, also Spanish accented, she supervised.

Locke has described herself as "very much the obliging girl-woman" in these years, "just head over heels in love with this incredibly dominant man. I thought he hung the moon." According to a lengthy article on their breakup by Rachel Abromowitz, he "took to calling himself

Daddy, as in 'Daddy is going to take care of this.'" He does not deny his paternalism. He always felt "protective" toward her.

"Indulgent" might be an equally good word. His constant use of her in his films is the most obvious evidence of that. Locke was, at best, a character lead, not a star, yet he employed her as such when few others had or would. More to the point, he bought her the house that she shared with Gordon when she was not with Clint.

This was, to say the least, a remarkably tolerant arrangement. When, in 1989, she brought her palimony action against Clint, lawyers commenting on the case observed that it is not uncommon for people to settle into new relationships, and maintain them for years, without finalizing their divorces. This is clearly true; it is what Clint had done earlier. But very few of them continue to live part-time with their legal mates.

Clint had, he says, understood the intricately woven nature of Sondra's relationship with Gordon at the outset and had not imagined that it would be quickly or easily untangled. He expected, however, that eventually that would happen. As the years wore on, though, Sondra and Gordon continued as before, and Clint's resentment of their arrangement grew. He says he kept waiting for something to happen—a "conversation," as he puts it, "that would go like this: 'Clint, I'm going to divorce Gordon Anderson and make myself available if you would like this to become a permanent kind of relationship.'"

This issue became more pressing for him in 1984, when his own divorce from Maggie was completed. (In April of the following year she married—not for long and not very happily, as it would turn out—Henry Wynberg, the onetime used-car salesman who had gained momentary fame as one of Elizabeth Taylor's boyfriends.) "Well, I'm divorced," he remembers saying to Sondra at the time. "Why don't you show your hand?" Her reply, he says, was "I have to stay married to him for tax purposes."

This was, to him, palpable nonsense. Who would not rather file joint returns with Clint Eastwood instead of with a not-very-successful sculptor, at the moment, according to Fritz Manes, preoccupied with manufacturing miniature guillotines? But, of course, Sondra's significant joint returns were of quite a different—emotional—kind.

Clint says that even when she was with him, Sondra continued to spend hours on the phone with Gordon, talking him through this or that crisis. One time, Clint recalls, a lover deserted him, and Gordon recruited her to accompany him as he drove around town, late at night, seeking this absent friend. "I, to tell you the truth, was extremely concerned about it," says Clint, "because she was out there in the middle of the night in an unpredictable situation." Gordon, she kept telling him, "was like a child to her, and that may be true." But he was also a man approaching forty, and there does come a time. . . .

It is reasonable to ask why Clint Eastwood, a man completely capable of asserting his needs in every other area of life, was so reluctant to press them in this matter. It is also fair to say that he has no coherent answer to that question, except to say that he enjoyed the freedom that lack of a full commitment from Sondra granted him. We may also note in his nature a profound reluctance to engage in emotional confrontations.

This he did, probably without quite acknowledging it to himself or to Sondra. She might as easily have been cast in *Pale Rider* (or in *Tightrope*) as she was in his other films, but she was not. She might have been included on some of his longer and more glamorous junkets, which she was not. In the summer of 1985 *Newsweek* published a cover-length story entitled "Clint: An American Icon," another acknowledgment of his new cultural status as well as *Pale Rider*'s hit status, and it quoted him thus about Sondra: "We're very close friends. She's very smart and good for me. She's somebody I feel has my best interests at heart."

It was spoken like a gentleman, but also rather dispassionately. And the story went on: "It's clearly a serious relationship, but his friends say it's an open one. . . . 'She gives him his space,' one says."

Perhaps more than she knew. For it was around this time that he entered into a relationship with Jacelyn Reeves, a former flight attendant, who was then living in the Carmel area. A warm and seemingly uncomplicated woman, with no desire to share his public life, she wanted children, and eventually bore him two—a boy and a girl. Clint supports them unstintingly, is attached to them emotionally while maintaining with their mother the same sort of agreeable connection that he did with Roxanne Tunis. He is, obviously, a man entirely unshirking about the consequences of *all* his acts.

All of this was, of course, handled discreetly—it was a long time before the tabloid press reported anything about this liaison—but, on the other hand, it was never a deep secret either: Many of Clint and Jacelyn's friends in Carmel knew of their relationship. If there is such a thing as a masterpiece of compartmentalization, this is surely one. More important, though, it signals, in a very obvious way, Clint's impatience with Locke and her failure to make a definitive choice between him and Gordon.

But still, he was as yet unwilling to break with her. Instead, he offered her extremely generous support in an attempt at professional renewal. Her acting career had stalled. In the time she spent with Clint her filmography reveals only two feature-film roles for other producers and an impersonation of Rosemary Clooney in a television biopic about the singer. She was now thirty-eight and beginning to worry—justifiably—about her future. Actresses of that age, far more popular than she was, have had for the last two decades trouble continuing to get work in the movies. It is one of the most discussed issues in modern Hollywood.

She thought directing might be an alternative for her, and Clint agreed. "You don't have to worry about the twenty-eight-year-old that's running up behind you," he said. He also felt she had good qualifications for the job. She had a strong historical background in movies and good critical sense about them. She had always taken a keen interest in the filmmaking process when they worked together. And as an actress she was naturally sympathetic to the needs of other performers.

So she began looking around for scripts and found a curious little fantasy called *Ratboy* by a writer named Rob Thompson, whose credits included *Hearts of the West,* an engaging portrait of Gower Gulch Hollywood in its early days. This newer script had been making the rounds for some time—Warner Bros. had once had it under option—and Clint thought it "kind of interesting," if a little "far out." But Sondra had a taste for fables, and this one, about a half-human, half-animal creature, discovered and exploited by a media-savvy woman who eventually learns something worthwhile about herself and the world from this innocent, seemed to suit her sensibilities.

He would make it, he said, as a Malpaso production, securing studio approval of an $8 million budget, and providing his entire A-Team, all people she had worked with before, to make her feel secure: Fritz Manes would be the line producer; Ed Carfagno would design it; Bruce Surtees would shoot it; Joel Cox would edit; Lennie Niehaus would score. David Valdes, who had been working his way up with Clint and was soon to be his executive producer, would be first AD. Buddy Van Horn would be the stunt gaffer. Rick Baker, legendary creator of features for imaginary creatures, was engaged to design the title character's makeup. It was further agreed that Clint would stay away, so Locke would not feel he was looking anxiously over her shoulder. It is safe to say that no first-time director ever started a film more safely cradled by strong, experienced, sympathetic arms.

No one, however, reckoned with Gordon Anderson. The onetime director of amateur theatricals began consulting with his wife on script rewrites. Mostly this was done without Clint's knowledge, although at one point Sondra came to him and asked if she might cast Gordon in the film. "Yeah," he remembers saying vaguely, "if there's some small part." But when, at last, he was permitted to see the revised script, it had become, he says, "a tribute to Gordon Anderson. All of a sudden he was like the major lead—besides the Ratboy. And I'm going, 'Wait a second here.' And besides that, forgetting all of that, the material sucked. It was just awful . . . very, very bizarre." Manes offers one example: Gordon's character sprawled shirtless on a bed, ladling mayonnaise into his navel, dipping carrot sticks into it and happily proclaiming that his new diet seemed to be working.

Clint felt betrayed. "You showed me a script," he told Sondra. "You said you liked it. I talked the studio into going on the line with it." And now, arbitrarily, without consultation, the agreement he had undertaken and guaranteed was being undermined. "Look," he said firmly, "I am not making this script."

She retreated. This draft, she insisted, was still a work in progress. It could be returned to something like its original form. All right, he said, "just don't try to back-door this whole deal." Her story is, of course, different: "I was acting in a take-charge capacity instead of being a little obedient girl. I didn't know what impact it would have."

But she might have guessed. Anyone who had ever worked with him might have. The issue here was not obedience or disobedience, but trust—and professionalism, minimally defined as self-discipline and honorable dealings with one's backers. She had not met those standards, and that is an issue he is always willing to confront.

In the end she shot a movie that, by all accounts, reasonably matched Thompson's original blueprint, though, according to Clint, the writer remained no more than a puzzled and distant onlooker. Gordon Anderson's sole contribution to it was the voice of the Ratboy, who was played on camera by a woman, Sharon Baird. Manes claims there were troubles on the set about which Clint knew nothing, displays of temper from the director, and days when she froze in panic.

Clint was true to his word, staying away from the shoot and largely absenting himself from the lengthy postproduction period, though it seems there were some disagreements then, too. Locke, however, turned an untroubled face to the world. In interviews, she very much wanted to be understood as an independent woman, admittedly advantaged by her relationship with Clint, but determined to succeed or fail on her own merits. With the press she played down Clint's involvement, pointing out that her relationship with Warner Bros. (which had produced *The Heart Is a Lonely Hunter*) antedated her relationship with him (neglecting to observe that its ownership had since changed), saying that though the contacts she had made through Clint had got her in the door, she had thereafter proceeded independently. She admitted she had heretofore been perceived as his "appendage"; now people would see what she could do on her own.

Not many of them, though. The studio clearly saw no commercial possibilities in *Ratboy*. It opened in one small New York theater in October 1986, and on a single multiplex screen in Los Angeles the following spring. In the interim it was shown at the Deauville Film Festival and played Paris, where it fared rather well with the critics. In the United States, however, it was largely ignored. For the newspaper of record, Janet Maslin called the film not "really funny, or fanciful or even very far out of the ordinary." She noted a certain physical resemblance between the Ratboy and Roman Polanski. Michael Wilmington, in Los Angeles, thought it "gentle, likeable, made with few pretensions."

They were being kind. Aside from an enlivening performance by Robert Townsend as a street hipster hired as a companion for the Ratboy, the film is almost unwatchable. This is largely because it has no firm point of view. Locke never determined whether she was doing social satire or a *Beauty and the Beast* variant, opting instead for a listless, charmless and distancing realism. She never addressed, let alone overcame, the film's obvious, central problem, which is that, however sympathetically he is treated, a rodent clone is unlikely ever to become anyone's favorite cuddle. Locke's own performance as Nikki Morrison, the window dresser who discovers the title creature, is as unfocused as the rest of the movie, skidding heedlessly from the cynical to the maternal.

Aesthetics aside, the picture did not accomplish what it was supposed to do. It did not free Locke from being seen as Clint's "appendage." Rather the opposite; *Ratboy* was perceived as his most embarrassing largesse. Thoughts of D. W. Griffith and Carol Dempster, Herbert Yates and Vera Hruba Ralston, flitted through the back of one's mind. After this disaster Clint Eastwood and Sondra Locke would never fully repair their relationship.

★　★　★

"It's all my fault he ran for mayor," Sondra "chuckled" to an interviewer in the spring of 1986, shortly after Clint was installed as Carmel-by-the-Sea's chief executive, meaning that with his staff preoccupied by her picture he had time on his hands. There may have been a grain of truth in the remark. He had always spent as much time as possible in this pretty place, and at the moment was certainly not averse to undertaking a job that would give him a convenient excuse for spending ever more time there.

But the key to Clint's decision to enter local politics was that he believed himself to have been disrespectfully treated by the little city's administration, and he was angry about it. The trouble started with the building behind which, down a walkway, his Hog's Breath restaurant was located. He had bought this structure, which was in disrepair, intending to tear it down and replace it with something more handsome and profitable. He delayed work on the project while work proceeded on another building down the block to minimize disruption on the street they shared. In the meantime, plans were drawn and approved by Carmel's planning commission, whose decision was then overturned by the city council.

Clint was outraged and went to the city administrator to find out what he needed to do to win approval. "Give me a pointer," he remembers saying, "tell me what you want. Do you want it white or brown. I'll do it whatever way you want." No, he was told, it doesn't work that way. He would have to start all over again, and he would have to keep guessing what might please the council.

Now he was nonplussed. He had proceeded as he did with all his enterprises, offering a sensible, low-key, entirely reasonable idea, one that he imagined would redound to everyone's benefit. Naturally he hoped eventually to make a profit on his investment, but in the meantime he would be replacing an eyesore with a handsomer structure that would be a useful addition to the tax rolls, too. What could be wrong with that?

Nothing, except that it challenged local custom and culture. Carmel had been settled by Spanish missionaries, but it had been discovered at the turn of the century by San Francisco bohemians looking for a secluded retreat in an area of stunning natural beauty. Over the years, the village and the area surrounding it grew steadily as wealthy people, many of them retirees, settled there and happily embraced the exclusionary values of its founders. But as the legend of Carmel's quaintness spread, a substantial tourist trade also developed. Inevitably, conflict occurred between preservationists, who felt that any attempt to accommodate the visitors would radically alter the character of their little community, and another bloc, most of them businesspeople, who thought it impossible to stem the tide, but quite feasible to channel it so that both reasonable civility and decent cash flows were maintained.

The protectionists held as their sacred scroll the 1929 city zoning ordinance, the preamble of which declared it to be "predominantly a residential city wherein business and commerce have in the past, are now and are proposed to be in the future subordinated to its residential character." There were no numbered addresses in the village, few streetlights, and a city forester watched over its many pines and cypresses, some of which grew unhampered in the middle of some streets. Their opponents had no desire to tamper with these traditions, but they did cite figures that showed something over two-thirds of the $6 million municipal budget deriving from taxes on businesses, most of which were dependent on tourism. These businessmen wanted at least some responsiveness to their needs.

Clint's building plans had been caught in this ongoing conflict. In a city where you could be busted for changing the landscaping in front of your house without permission—all shrubbery was registered with city hall—the preservationist-dominated town council automatically rejected most construction permits, even if the proposed building would actually improve the urban prospect. It is also possible that he was victimized by celebrity prejudice. The new edifice would, after all, be called the Eastwood Building. Maybe that alone would make it an attraction for the despised tourists. Maybe the council simply felt compelled to demonstrate that it could not be intimidated by the famous movie star.

And maybe it had not seen enough *Dirty Harry* movies. Clint promptly sued the city, eventually winning an out-of-court settlement that permitted him to proceed with his building. But the matter did not end there. Even now words like "punitive," "dictatorial," even "fascist," creep into his conversation when he thinks back on this issue. In any case, his fight with city hall brought Clint into closer contact with the business community and led to discussions about challenging the incumbent mayor, a woman named Charlotte Townsend, now approaching the end of her second term. Clint heard himself saying, "I'll help out. I'll campaign—anything anyone wants me to do." He then felt avid eyes turning to him. Bud Allen, a local innkeeper, finally said: "You run, Clint. We'll bust this town wide open."

He demurred, of course, but the dissident group kept working on him. Finally, Clint said, "OK, I'll run. But if I run I want to win. I don't want to do this halfway." So he attached a caveat to his acceptance. He would get an independent opinion on his candidacy before announcing it. A mutual friend put him in touch with Eileen Padberg, partner in a political consulting firm in Costa Mesa, California, that worked with Republicans and had enjoyed considerable success with local campaigns. At their first meeting in his Malpaso office, she suggested an exploratory telephone poll of the electorate. Clint thought that a good idea and proposed this agreement to Padberg in case he finally did run: "If you don't tell me how to make movies, I won't tell you how to run a campaign."

The poll results were ambiguous. Obviously, his name recognition was high, but there were problems. For one thing, most of the voters expressed satisfaction with Charlotte Townsend's administration. And many were, as Padberg puts it, "taken aback" at the thought of a movie star holding the mayoralty. Many felt his presence in office would create "a circus atmosphere" in town, while others wondered how seriously he would take the job; they thought he might be off making movies instead of attending to their political business.

Padberg phoned Clint at home one night to report these findings and to tell him that his campaign entailed a high risk of embarrassment for both of them. It would clearly attract national attention, and the media would install him as the automatic favorite. If he should then lose, which her poll showed was a real possibility, it would scarcely do his image any good. And it would harm hers as well; she would be the political consultant who couldn't get a movie star elected mayor of his hometown. He asked her for a little time to think this over. An hour later he rang back to say, "I'm in if you're in."

So on January 30, 1986, just hours before the deadline, he filed nominating papers and launched his campaign. Padberg's strategy was very basic: He must never attack Townsend directly, lest he look like "the gunslinger from Mexico"; he must give no interviews to the national press, thus allaying suspicions that this was some kind of publicity ploy; he must stay in town as much as possible, especially on the weekends, until the April 8 election; he must watch his sometimes-salty language and, oh, yes, it would be a good idea if he was not seen around town accompanied by a woman.

She selected a sixty-year-old woman named Sue Hutchinson, gray haired and low-key in manner, to be his on-site campaign manager and, aside from a single brochure, they did almost no paid advertising—just some buttons and bumper stickers; local ordinances naturally limited placarding and other unseemly political displays. With the help of volunteers they divided the city into five sections and went over the voter lists, trying to identify pros, cons and undecided. Then they chose sympathetic residents in each area to host social events Clint would attend. The ground rule was simple: The hosts were obliged to invite forty registered voters from their district, but could invite five friends from outside it to rub up against the star. There were, of course, some more formal forums, including a debate with Townsend and two other candidates who were never factors in the race.

"I never wrote a speech the whole time," Clint says. "I would just get up and start philosophizing." Informal as he was, he proved to be, Padberg says, an ideal candidate. Unlike most of the professional pols she had worked with, he took direction amiably; she was impressed by his self-possession, too. "Either you control your ego, or your ego controls you," Padberg says, and in her eyes he outshone more experienced candidates in this respect. He was, she says, awkward as he confronted rooms full of voter-gawkers, but that worked to his advantage. They took to his good-humored shyness, and liked his earnest answers to their questions.

It was, all in all, one of the most tasteful campaigns in the history of modern American politics. He politely refused to sign autographs when he was out on walking tours (though he occasionally obliged bedazzled matrons at a genteel tea or luncheon). All campaign contributions that were volunteered to him were turned over to the local boys' club. Though he occasionally criticized Mrs. Townsend and her supporting slate of city council candidates for their "negative attitude" and "killjoy mentality," he never personalized his remarks.

His slogan was simple, "Bringing the Community Together," and in his talks he stressed his desire to build bridges between the business community and the residential community. He intended, he said, "to be an officer of the whole community . . . to be for everybody," his highest priority being "to alleviate the fear . . . about how the business community is going to gobble up the residential community. It's just not true. It's not going to happen." He added: "I don't think it's a fair thing to do, to use [merchants] as villains in the drama. They're there; you can't just ignore them."

In short, he presented himself for what he is, a principled pragmatist. One has to believe, though, that he heard Clinton Eastwood Sr. whispering in his ear—Show them what you can do, show them why they need you. As for the media shouting in his ear, the din was louder and more persistent than either he or Padberg had imagined it would be. Had not Norman Mailer seen in Clint "a presidential face"? Was not Garry Trudeau doing a series of "Doonesbury" strips about the election? Was there not an irresistible analogy to be drawn between him and that other movie star presently occupying the White House? Both were Californians and conservatives, both were unpretentious actors and agreeably self-deprecating men, both had worked successfully in pictures with an adorable ape.

The press converged on Carmel from all over the world. Reporters were reduced to covering Clint's public appearances and to pursuing public opinion on the streets of Carmel. Not a photo op, not an exclusive interview, did he grant them, though in speeches he did what he could to still speculation about larger ambitions. "My interests are in Carmel," he said in a typical version of an often-repeated statement. "It's the city I've lived in for some time, it's the city I love. That's where my political interests start and stop." He always told Padberg that he was running for only one two-year term, unless he felt passionately at the end of that time that he had not accomplished what he set out to do.

He was far more realistic than the newspeople covering him. He knew, for example, that he could never quit making movies. His passion for his work, and his success with it, ensured that. He could also see already that he would soon become impatient with the pieties, politesse and picayune details of politics.

In this campaign, for example, Clint was obliged to take a stand on second kitchens. Through the years many older residents had installed them, so they could rent out part of their houses while continuing to live in them. Now the administration was proposing to regulate them strictly, even perhaps eliminate them. "If you've read that ordinance," Clint said hyperbolically, "it's like Adolf Hitler knocking on your door. A lot of people could be evicted from their homes." Then there was the great ice cream war. The previous year the council refused to grant a business license to a store that proposed selling ice cream cones that might—gasp!—be eaten on the streets, an activity strongly discouraged in an official tourist brochure. The story made the wires—"Scrooge City" someone dubbed Carmel—and when he was asked about it at an electoral forum, Clint deplored the action: "At first it was funny, then after a while you started thinking, Wait a second. Wasn't this a waste of official time? Weren't there more pressing matters to be dealt with?"

Of course, in the end, all these questions were subsumed by the only topic of real interest, which was, of course, Clint Eastwood himself. The media's descent on Carmel was, his opponents argued, a harbinger of unwanted attention to come. Mayor Eastwood would himself become the town's number one tourist attraction. The answer to this concern was, simply, good humor. He knew some people had come to town hoping to glimpse him, Clint told one gathering, but he guessed that a certain number of nonfans stayed away for the same reason. "Maybe it balances out," he said. By this time, though, his seriousness was clear to everyone, and it was beginning to seem unfair to deny him a job he was qualified for just because he was a celebrity.

Ms. Townsend's response was square and inept. Confronting one of the great ironists of the age, she came across as cranky and befuddled. Her slogan was negative—"If you want progress, don't vote for me"— and she had to confess that she had never heard of Dirty Harry—"I had a friend explain it to me." In the end, Clint was the overwhelming victor. Voter turnout was twice more than usual, and Clint received 2,166 votes, 72.5 percent of those cast. Maggie and their children joined him at campaign headquarters for the election-night celebration, as Townsend confessed herself "bewildered and astonished" by the margin of her rejection. She added bitterly, "I understand the bus tour companies are already getting ready to advertise tours to Carmel-by-the-Sea council meetings." Ronald Reagan called to congratulate Clint and make monkey jokes. At a brief, rain-spattered inaugural ceremony a week later, Clint presented Townsend and two of her council allies who were also turned out with some potted redwood seedlings as reconciliatory gifts.

Clint fulfilled to his own satisfaction all his major campaign promises. The first council meeting he presided over was, predictably, inundated by the press, which was given just six of the sixty seats available in the chambers, but was provided with closed-circuit TV coverage of it in a nearby tent. Thereafter, though, things settled down to the customary civic drone. A couple of months after taking office Clint and his council allies fired most of the do-nothing planning commission. He made the streets safe for ice cream. He made it somewhat easier to build or to renovate property. He got a tourist parking lot constructed—it was surfaced with granite chips he donated from a quarry that stood on land he owned—along with beach walks and public restrooms (Clint contributed stones for those, too). A library annex, talked about for years, was finally opened in a disused bank building, dedicated to use by children, and it is the accomplishment of which he is most proud.

His administration was exactly what one might have expected of him; he governed as he made movies—as a populist with an eye on the bottom line, as a realist without formal ideological biases but with a strong sense of what was right, wrong and, above all, practical. It may be that his most lasting and valuable contribution to his adopted community will turn out to be one that was quite unofficial—his purchase of Mission Ranch late in 1986. It was a sometime dairy farm that had long ago been converted into a tourist facility, the bar of which Clint fondly remembered from his days at Fort Ord. It had, however, fallen into disrepair and disrepute and in recent years had become a controversial issue in town. A real estate corporation had acquired the property, proposing to tear down its standing structures and replace them with eighty condominiums. Townsend's administration sued to block construction, and this had been a point of contention between her and Clint in the campaign. In office, he caused the lawsuit to be dropped, but the more he thought about them the less happy he became with the developer's plans. The ranch's buildings had historic value, the property offered a fine view of the bay that he didn't want privatized, and, most important, it bordered on extensive wetlands that would be threatened by commercial development.

He began to look around for someone to take over the property and refurbish it as it stood. "I thought I could come up with a dream philanthropist," he told a reporter. "The guy I talked into it was me." The cost was around $5 million, but that was only the beginning. He had thought a coat of paint and some new wiring and plumbing were all that was needed to bring the place back, but in the end a full overhaul was required, with the ranch being shut down while every room was redecorated and a new bar and restaurant added. The result is an upscale mini-resort of the kind that attracts the sort of prosperous visitors even Carmel finds desirable.

About a year into his term Clint was sure he was not going to run for reelection. He began to reach this conclusion one day when he was standing in a chilly garage, surrounded by staff and council members trying to decide if a prominent citizen, a doctor, would be permitted to change the slope of his garage roof. Life was too short for this sort of pettiness. Since council members were elected for four-year terms, he knew that his people would retain a majority in its deliberations after he left. Late in 1987 he announced that he would not stand for a second term.

In all, this experience had a larger effect on him than it did on Carmel. A decade later, the village remains physically attractive. Its much-argued-over business district is still shady and sedate, with rather more galleries selling indifferent scenic art than one might think the traffic would bear. The other shops sell the kind of mall merchandise available the world over. We are all now united under Benetton's colors, and Carmel, no more than the rest of us, has not been able to resist that trend—Ms. Townsend would not have prevailed against it any more than Clint or his successors did.

As for Clint himself, his longtime editor Joel Cox thinks he became a little looser, a little more open with strangers, as a result of having to deal with so many of them in his campaign and in his council chamber. Indeed, it could be argued that it transformed him—not in his own eyes, but in ours. For decades movie stars and politicians have been flattering one another by their attentions. We are used to reports of glamorous Beverly Hills fund-raisers on behalf of chic presidential candidates. We are used to reports of starry sleepovers in the Lincoln bedroom. We are by this time perhaps fed up with the passionate advocacy of exotic causes in inappropriate forums by inappropriate spokespeople. What we are not used to is celebrities engaging themselves in meaningful discussions about the issuance of sewer bonds.

That a man famous for the inarticulate impatience of his screen character was willing to do so struck people as remarkable. It suggested something interesting, unexpected, about his character. And when it became clear that Clint had no ulterior motives or larger ambitions, it rendered him admirable even to people who rarely see movies unequipped with subtitles.

FIFTEEN

FRINGED OUT

Clint permitted himself only two films while he was mayor—
Heartbreak Ridge early in his term, *Bird* very late in it—with *The
Dead Pool,* last and least of the *Dirty Harry* pictures, pushed out
quickly in the months immediately afterward. If his production schedule was slightly diminished by his political preoccupations, its basic
pattern was unaffected: a genre film with some amusingly disguised
aspirations, an essay in biography that was the most self-consciously aspiring film Clint ever undertook and a sequel with no aspirations beyond predictable entertainment.

These movies, which showed a career Marine Corps noncom coming confusedly to the end of his final hitch, a jazz genius's final burnout
and a famously outraged cop's anger cooling into curmudgeonliness,
had in common a somewhat autumnal air. Each of these protagonists is,
in his way, looking for a concluding unscientific postscript—and not
finding it.

Particularly after he finished *Bird,* a long-cherished expression of a
deep and formative passion, Clint now fifty-six, admitted to feeling
"fringed out" by his passage at politics. Instincts require some tutoring,
and for two years he was out of touch with industry trends, audience
moods, his own best impulses. He had time, amid his political preoccupations, to devote to the work immediately at hand, but he did not have
time to think ahead coherently. As a result, his career would lose mo-
mentum and direction in the period between 1988 and 1991, during
which time an ugly personal crisis would further distract and depress
him.

This turn of events would prove to be all the more shocking because
he was so entirely unprepared for it. His political venture, managed with
such discretion and dignity, had brought him to new heights of public
esteem, and the films he made in the period prior to his slump all turned

out to be, each in its way, successful. Nothing in his life predicted the unhappy passage soon to come.

Heartbreak Ridge, though not very well reviewed, was commercially successful and represented an off-line venture not entirely dissimilar from *Bronco Billy* or *Honkytonk Man* in that it took up, in genially entertaining—not to say comically outrageous—form issues that had long bemused him. "You ought to be sealed in a case," his new CO tells Gunnery Sergeant Tom Highway, USMC (Clint), when he reports for his last posting as a marine. The case, he adds, ought to be labeled "Break Open Only in Case of War." There's much to be said for this point of view. The sergeant has a Medal of Honor and a set of attitudes that even the Corps, officially striking the softer, gentler poses of a new age, regards as antediluvian. Clint saw this as material for satire. "*Heartbreak Ridge* is my ultimate statement about macho," he says. "He's supermacho, and he's full of shit—just completely ignorant."

But, of course, delicious to play. We hear Highway before we see him, a familiar voice essaying a soaring aria of obscenities, a parody of foulmouthed masculine assertion, far beyond the call of any movie's duty to realism. Eventually the camera conducts us to its source, and we find the sergeant—drunk and disorderly—in a holding pen; challenged by a yet more brutish type he reduces him to a quivering mass of protoplasm with some precisely executed violence. Clint had, of course, known men like Highway when he was in the service, and he flashed back, too, on Colonel Gritz and his soldiers of misfortune. There is something pathetic about war lovers when they are denied the object of their affections. "What does a warrior do when there is no war?" he muses.

Highway has nostalgically requested that his last tour of duty be on the base, where he served his first enlistment, knowing as well that his estranged wife, Aggie (Marsha Mason), still lives nearby and that they have unfinished emotional business to attend. His professional task is to whip a reconnaissance platoon, composed entirely of flakes and fuckups, into fighting form. But that cannot occupy him (or us) fully—topkicks have been doing that for decades in the movies. There's plenty of time left over for an unusual activity—brooding. Does it really make any difference, in the age of high-tech warfare, if these guys are battle ready or not? Has he made any difference—medals or not—with *his* dutiful and screwed-up life?

It is often painfully funny to watch disused wheels start to turn as Highway pours the oil of rueful memory into his brainpan, to see him scanning women's magazines (he's like an adolescent sneaking a peek at *Penthouse*) in order to learn a little new male lingo to try out on Aggie

("Did we mutually nurture one another?"), trying to relate to Private Stitch Jones (Mario Van Peebles), a street-smart black kid, something of an anarchist, who talks trash to a rap beat.

Stitch is, at heart, a good kid, but like the rest of Highway's troops, like the rest of America these days, he has lost touch with the military virtues. So besides confronting his own failures as a traditional family man Highway must now confront his surrogate family's failure to provide him the camaraderie, yes, the "nurture," he had always thought he could count on it to provide. No wonder the man drinks and swears and brawls.

And no wonder Clint Eastwood decided to do this movie on the basis of "about fifteen good pages" in James Carabatsos's first-draft screenplay (despite his sole credit, the result of a Writers Guild arbitration, most of the final version was, Clint says, by Joe Stinson). Highway is, if you will, Harry Callahan at the end of his tether, another individualist who has paradoxically sold his soul to an organization, and paid a price for it. The difference is that Highway's organization, being much more rigidly hierarchical, has caused him to repress more anger. And that means his head of steam has a lot more heat and pressure in it. Unlike Harry, this man is often parodically stupefied by outrage.

Clint loved the role. When he costarred in *Unforgiven* with Gene Hackman, the latter told him he thought Highway was his best work. Here and there were reviewers who agreed with him. "His most complex, fully dimensional character," Dave Kehr wrote in the Chicago *Tribune*. Vincent Canby called his performance "the richest he's ever given" and praised his "essential humor . . . now overt." He also said: "At 56, Mr. Eastwood doesn't look especially young, but neither does he look old. Nor does he look preserved, or perhaps surgically improved, like some of his contemporaries. He looks as if he's absorbed the years and turned them into guts and grit."

If Canby came late to a recognition of Clint's humor, he perceptively recognized the quality that would be the most important factor in perpetuating his career: the decision not to hide his age but to play it gracefully. His practical, director's judgment is that actors who resort to cosmetic surgery or diffusion filters just make the problem worse by calling attention to it in a way the camera, and thus the audience, can't help but notice.

After his electoral efforts it was a relief for Clint to be among people with whom he did not have to watch his language, among whom he was the tested professional. His on-screen antagonist Marsha Mason (giving one of her best performances) had worried about Clint's habit of not rehearsing much; she was an actress who liked to polish things in private. But on her first day he greeted her with the reassuring promise that they wouldn't shoot until she felt fully rehearsed and ready. Later, she had to dance with him in a party scene, when he was duded out in stiff dress blues and had to direct all the movement and act at the same time. Jack Green was using a steadicam and moving around them as they danced, and Mason couldn't figure out exactly how Clint knew where to lead her, since they had choreographed nothing. Oh, he said casually, "I was catching the light as it played across your face."

With Van Peebles, young enough to be his son, he was much more the mentor. Interviewed a few years later, when he was well along in his own directing career, Van Peebles quoted as his credo some advice he got from Clint on this picture: "Whip me, beat me, but don't bore me." All kinds of bonding took place on this picture—but not with military officialdom.

The title refers to the bloody Korean War engagement in which Highway is supposed to have won his Medal of Honor. It had been primarily an army battle, and Clint had originally sought its cooperation in filming. When the army objected to the script, he turned to the marines, who permitted the company to shoot first at Camp Pendleton, then at Vieques, a base in Puerto Rico, where they were able to join marine maneuvers, doubling them for the Grenada invasion that rather awkwardly brings the film to a climax.

But as the movie went into prerelease screenings objections arose on every hand. Army veterans insisted it would have been historically impossible for a marine to serve, let alone win a medal, at Heartbreak Ridge. Then the marines expressed pique with Fritz Manes, who had for some strange reason disported himself on location in a marine major's uniform, an affair that, along with some other curious incidents, led to his departure from Malpaso. Then marine officialdom, hearing the film's rough dialogue coming at them from the screen, beat a strategic retreat. They primly declared that it did not accurately represent current training procedures and compared it unfavorably to *Top Gun,* which had done wonders for navy recruiting. They demanded that acknowledgment of corps cooperation in filming be removed from the credits and that premieres scheduled to benefit marine relief organizations be canceled.

This controversy, as well as a televised "All Star Party for Clint Eastwood," a variety show-cum-tribute, assured a successful launch for the film, which grossed solidly. With the exceptions noted, however, it fared poorly with the critics, who expressed general dismay at its raucousness. One or two found some of the dialogue excessively homophobic, which is true; there are times when realism must yield to social realities.

Many objected to its triumphant conclusion, the tin-pot invasion of Grenada.

Clint does not entirely disagree. "It was a stupid invasion," Clint now says, "kind of a Mickey Mouse operation." He had not suddenly turned cold warrior, but he felt he had to, as he puts it, "tour the group," that is, put them in some life-and-death situation where their sergeant's hard work would pay off, and this was an available option. He would have been glad to ironize it—it might have completed Highway's cycle of disillusion very forcefully—but he was shooting with Marine Corps cooperation, and marines tend not to be ironic about such matters. Moreover, this was at heart a comedy requiring an upbeat ending—a band playing, flags flying, Marsha Mason misty-eyed as the troops come home. Clint notes dryly that at least he kept the welcoming crowd "sparse," and not exactly wild with patriotic fervor.

★   ★   ★

"I'd have done it even if the script was no good," Clint says of *Bird*. It had been out there for years, Joel Oliansky's screenplay about the short life, troubled times and soaring gifts of Charlie Parker. Clint had heard about it, and vaguely resented the fact that someone else was going to tell the life of his musical idol. Producer Ray Stark controlled the property, which had been developed with Richard Pryor in mind: one dangerous master of the improvisational riff, one famously self-destructive genius, one notorious addict of controlled substances, playing another.

But after the freebasing accident of 1980, in which Pryor suffered third-degree burns over half his body, both his spirit and his career had been sadly tamed. By the mideighties the project was languishing. So was another one, *Revenge,* an adaptation of a Jim Harrison novel that Clint had passed on, and Warner Bros. had on its shelf. Learning that Stark was sniffing around this tale of a husband seeking retribution against his wife and her lover who had tried to kill him, he proposed a simple swap for the Oliansky script, which by this time he had read (he swiped a copy from Lenny Hirshan's office) and liked.

This deal was completed shortly before Clint began his run for public office. But shooting did not begin until two years later, delayed by his political duties and his quest for absolute musical authenticity. "A jazz movie had never been made by someone who really liked jazz," Clint said later. He particularly recalled *Young Man with a Horn,* the movie based loosely on the life of Bix Beiderbecke, which he had seen in 1950: "The breathing was off, the dubbing was terrible, and the plot line—I thought, oh God, what have they done, and I went out of the theater dejected." He was determined that *Bird* would avoid such mistakes and somehow re-create the improvisational excitement of a live performance as no fictional film ever had.

As is always the case in films of this kind, the source of music for the many scenes of Parker working in jazz clubs or in studios had to be recorded before shooting, so that the mimed playing of the actors could be synchronized accurately with the sound track. Moreover, Clint did not want to hire a contemporary alto player to imitate Parker; he wanted to find a way to use Bird's original recordings in the film. But most of the music Parker recorded in studios, where the sound quality was passable, was very short—useless for the live-performance sequences, where Parker typically played longer pieces. Some of this material had been recorded, but on inferior equipment. It would be embarrassing emanating from a modern theatrical sound system.

The solution was to track down these fugitive tapes and reprocess them. Clint led the pursuit of material (some of which was found just a couple of miles from the studio); Lennie Niehaus, his old friend from Fort Ord, who was now virtually his composer in residence, supervised the reconstruction, which required many months of sixteen- and eighteen-hour days. He and his technical crew electronically eliminated from the old tapes the frequencies carrying the other instruments, leaving Parker's work standing alone. He then brought in the best available sidemen to reproduce the work of the other musicians, and when no other alternative was available, Charles McPherson, a San Diego–based sax man, to stand in for Bird. The resultant mix was recorded on state-of-the-art equipment. While this work was proceeding, Niehaus, who had begun his musical career as an alto saxophonist, had to teach the young actor engaged to impersonate Bird, Forest Whitaker, to play well enough to look plausible on the bandstand.

Fortunately, Whitaker required only minimum makeup to pass for Bird. More important, he had some musical training—he had studied voice in college—and was by nature a rather studious sort. He read up on Parker, played his records day and night, studied the scraps of film in which he appeared, flew to Paris to talk with Chan Parker, his fourth and last wife, on whose unpublished memoir, *Life in E-Flat,* Oliansky's script was largely based. At the same time, Clint consulted with many musicians who had worked with Parker, drawing particularly on the memories of Red Rodney, the white trumpet player whose role in the film is probably somewhat larger than it was in Parker's life, since writer and director wanted to provide white audiences with a surrogate to help draw them into this essentially black world.

The issue for everyone was the same: sustaining period authenticity while retaining dramatic values. Cinematographer Jack Green recalls an early meeting where Clint told him that he wanted the movie lit as if it were being shot in black and white. Green, who had also been a youthful jazz fan, flashed on "these beautiful black-and-white photographs, very hard, very contrasty," that had been a feature of *Downbeat* and the other jazz publications of the fifties, and shot some tests in this manner. Clint immediately recognized their inspiration, and according to the cameraman, the film became "easy and simple" for him precisely because "the whole lighting concept was just absolutely ironclad."

Despite an offer from Oliansky to do some rewrites on what he considered to be a first-draft screenplay, Clint went with what he had, though he cut about forty pages from a script that still required close to three hours to realize on-screen. He began shooting in October 1987, working with a kind of contented conviction, depicting "the music of the forties and fifties or the feeling of a club the way it was."

For this, he was able to draw on memory. The decor of each jazz joint might be unique, but the smoke and funk of these rooms was universal, he thought. In one important respect he could improve on memory. When he was a kid he could not afford a trip to New York's West Fifty-second Street, bebop's avatar. Now, on a budget near $10 million, he could afford to have Ed Carfagno, his art director, re-create it with meticulous historical accuracy.

He lingered over *Bird* longer than he did most of his films—it had a nine-week shooting schedule. Both Whitaker and Diane Venora, who gave a remarkable performance as Chan, spoke of his patience in letting them find their characters. "In one scene," she said, "I did three different things in three different takes and I knew it wasn't right. Clint said, 'Good, now play all three things at once.' I did, and that was it." She also remembers his interrupting the flow of an intense fight scene between Chan and Charlie in order to dismiss the two-year-old who was playing their son as soon as he had all the reaction shots from him he could possibly use. "I don't want to be responsible for him having to see a psychiatrist when he's fifteen or sixteen," she recalls him saying.

But for all the punctiliousness Clint brought to it, much of *Bird*'s distinction derives, paradoxically, from its very free structure. Covering Parker's last months, beginning with a suicide attempt, ending with death suddenly choking off his laughter at a television show, but illuminating this passage with a deliberately disorderly array of flashbacks, it is Clint's only radical break with linear narrative, and with what one might call linear morality, that is to say, the pistol point QED that brings most of his movies to an end. Finally, to risk stating the obvious, this film is the freest of the burden of self-reflection that the presence Clint Eastwood, actor, inevitably imposes on Clint Eastwood, director.

Bird was almost invariably described as a "personal" film by the press when it was released, since it was obvious that a powerful star had persuaded his studio to allow him to spend major money exploring an obsession shared by no more than a minor cult. What only a few observers saw was that something more than nostalgia was moving in *Bird*. Reflecting on the life of Charlie Parker, Clint was able to reflect on certain issues in his own life.

When he reviewed *Bird* for the Chicago *Tribune,* Dave Kehr drew an apt analogy between jazz and the kind of vernacular American moviemaking Clint practices. Both, he said, "operate in the gray areas between the popular and the personal, the bluntly commercial and the purely idealistic," therefore "as much as it is a movie about jazz, it is a movie about filmmaking as practiced by Clint Eastwood and the generations of self-effacing American moviemakers who have come before him." This was more than a matter of riffing on popular themes as most genre movies do. Kehr daringly analogized Charlie Parker's saxophone to Dirty Harry's .44 Magnum; both are "outsized tools used by the individual to confront society, to give expression to emotions and impulses that otherwise would remain bottled up," presenting their adepts with enormous issues of self-control, issues that Harry (narrowly) overcomes and Bird succumbs to. Finally, like the adolescent Clint, he observed that playing an instrument is "a way for the individual to hide his identity while channeling his emotions into a less personal, less threatening form."

One of the film's severest critics, Stanley Crouch, suggested, without knowing he was doing so, a more basic connection between director and subject. In reviewing *Bird* he compared Charlie Parker to "the gangster hero, the charming anarchist that Cagney introduced in *Public Enemy.*" To Crouch, the musician was, like Cagney, all "velocity," a man rubbing out musical clichés with the same joyous élan with which Cagney erased his thickheaded enemies in a film where, like Bird, he lived fast and died young.

Parker was, however, more awesome and, in a certain, narrow sense, more imitable to Clint than the actor was. Surprisingly, Clint told one reporter in a prerelease interview that he had, in adolescence, thought of himself as "really a black guy in a white body." Now he consciously understood what he had no more than instinctively grasped as a young man: that bebop, so spiky and challenging to traditionalists, was, as many jazz experts now claim, protest music—or at the very least a radical assertion of black singularity.

Clint also understood that Bird's racial experience, like the deepest sources of his genius, was impenetrable to an outsider (it is the film's great strength that it offers no simple dramatizations of either). He was, however, "the single most confident individual I've ever seen in my life when he was playing the saxophone," Clint says, yet when he was finished, "he would just drift into the woodwork." Clint would do his idol the honor of presenting him in a movie in the same way that he presented the characters he himself played—coolly, unsentimentally, enigmatically.

Still, he believes those possessed by genius have certain obligations to it, and he needed to make that point too. There is in *Bird* a central symbol, which is in fact a central cymbal. Legend has it that when Parker was a kid, playing out of his league in a Kansas City jam session, a drummer sailed one at him in disgust. This was a turning point. Bird took his horn into a retreat during which, for three or four years, he did nothing but play alone, eleven to fifteen hours a day, obsessively evolving the style by which he would create his musical revolution. The image of that cymbal, traveling through the air in slow motion, recurrently haunts *Bird,* signifying death and rebirth and, above all, the film's morality, which holds that redemption is achieved only through disciplined effort in whatever work we undertake.

About this, Clint was quite clear. "Everyone," he told jazz writer Gary Giddins, "is the product of some sort of setback or something, the thing where you snap and say, I don't give a crap what they say, I'm going to overcome this." Pressed to name such a moment in his own life Clint rather diffidently offered that matinee showing of *Ambush at Cimarron Pass,* when, after the embarrassment and despondency passed, "I mustered up the sand and said, I'm going to win this game."

What he could not understand was why, having made a similar, more consequential effort, Charlie Parker would not husband the grace it granted him and build on it, morally as well as musically. That mystery is set forth in a remarkable sequence that is scarcely mentioned in any of the critical writing on the movie, perhaps because it is not musical, perhaps because it is so austerely realized. We do not expect a movie's turning point to consist of insert shots of typewriter keys striking paper and platen and a monologic voice-over.

Bird is playing in California, shacked up with another woman, when a telegram from Chan arrives, informing him of their daughter's death. He then composes a series of telegrams attempting to justify his failure to return to his daughter's bedside (and now to her obsequies) and, more significantly, all his failures as husband, father, artist. It was, as Clint says, the point of no return in Bird's flight, so crucial to our understanding of him that he reshot the inserts when it was discovered that they had in minor ways misquoted the originals. "Reading them in sequence," Clint says, "you can just see the whole story unfolding, you can see the man collapsing, mentally just disintegrating in that period of an hour or two."

There is no more possibility of "understanding" a human failure of this kind than there is a possibility of "understanding" genius. One may respond to it with compassion, just as one may respond to sublime artistry with awe. But, finally, they are enigmas. What the movie does, in compensation, is posit an alternative Bird, a morally instructive double in the figure of Dizzy Gillespie (splendidly played by Samuel E. Wright).

He is the true hero of this film, a man whose contributions to the evolution of jazz were as significant as Parker's, but who was utterly responsible to his talent, his colleagues, his race. "They're going to talk about you when you're gone, Bird," he says, understanding it will be more romantic and intense than whatever may be said about himself. But he also insists, this wise and distinctly undizzy man, that especially for a black man in racist America, blowing your own horn is not enough, no matter how entrancingly you do so. It is necessary also to maintain your sharpness and stamina, to be, if you are gifted with talent and fame, "a leader of men," which Gillespie, who played on serenely into his seventies, surely was.

To put it another way, the purpose of *Bird* was to glorify its protagonist's music, but not to further romanticize yet another of art's youthfully fallen heroes, a man who, as Clint (who does rather tend to personalize this loss) once put it, "takes his genius away from us as fast as he came on the scene and gave it to us." His film, he acknowledges, "was actually a way, a left-handed way, of paying tribute to all the great geniuses—the Ellingtons, the Dizzy Gillespies, the Count Basies, the Fats Wallers—the people over the years who did live normal lives, and did have a normal existence."

This refusal of conventional sentiments and simplicities is the film's great strength. No moral judgment is passed on Bird's descent into drugs. Nor is any easy explanation—the childhood trauma, the shattering love affair—offered for it. But neither is blame shifted decisively to others, so that Bird can be read as society's victim. Bird is the sole author of his own misery—and quite unapologetic about it. He *likes* drugs, likes what they do for him. And the dark glamour with which Clint realizes the jazz world becomes their objective correlative—a moral (actually an immoral) force in the story. Bird is, in every way, an addict of half-lights, real and chemically induced. It is—to tell the truth of this movie—where he does his best work.

* * *

Clint completed principal photography on *Bird* toward the end of January 1988. He would finish postproduction and have it ready to enter in competition at Cannes three months later. It was not his only service to jazz in this period. When producer David Valdes and production assistant Tom Rooker were scouting possible locations for the film in Kansas City, they noticed in a musicians' union hall a poster for a jazz documentary called *The Last of the Blue Devils,* about a regional group of the late 1920s that included Count Basie and others who would later form the core of his legendary band.

They pulled it in, and everybody liked it so much that Clint got in touch with its producer, Bruce Ricker, and bought from him the French and Italian rights to it, releasing it in those territories under Clint's name, in part because Joe Hyams thought it would help establish his credentials as a jazz enthusiast prior to *Bird.* But there were larger consequences to this action. Ricker had for years been trying to put together a documentary on Thelonious Monk, drawing on some twenty hours of previously unseen cinema verité material that had been shot by a filmmaker named Christian Blackwood as well as rare performance footage. He had fought his way through problems involving rights and finance, but still needed $400,000 to complete the film. He mentioned this to Clint one day. In less than twenty-four hours Clint called back to say Warner Bros. would put up the finishing money. The resulting film, *Thelonious Monk: Straight No Chaser,* edited and directed by Charlotte Zwerin, is a hypnotizing portrait of a figure every bit as enigmatic and as significant to the history of modern jazz as Charlie Parker was. "We made money on it, too," Clint adds proudly.

As if this were not enough activity, Clint knocked out *The Dead Pool* while *Bird* was in postproduction. Morally, if not contractually, he felt he had to cross-collateralize the commercially chancy *Bird* with this surefire *Dirty Harry* sequel. As of a few months earlier, Detective Callahan "had been pretty much in my mind a closed chapter," he says. But his interest in diet and health had brought him into contact with Durk Pearson and Sandy Shaw, authors of a best-selling self-help book called *Life Extension,* in which a regimen they had tailored for Clint was discussed. Soon after publication they let it be known that they were developing some ideas for him, in which they were aided by a young writer named Steve Sharon. Among them was the story that became *The Dead Pool.*

One of the things Clint liked about it was the sequence that turned out to be the one (and only) thing most people remember about the finished film—a car chase in which Harry and his partner (this time an

Asian played by Evan C. Kim) are pursued by a toy vehicle, radio-controlled and loaded with explosives. It was, he thought, a nifty parody of the famous *Bullitt* car chase.

So . . . all right. He would run and jump, shoot and snarl, more or less as before—under Buddy Van Horn's amiable direction. Doing his best to keep Harry within the conventions of the series, he would show his age—many reviewers mentioned his graying and receding hair, the ever more visible throbbings in the prominent vein in his temple—but he would not allude to it as openly as his Tom Highway character had. He would let his anger show, but more often than not as a kind of senior-citizen grumble rather than as full-throated rage. And though he would now and then sneer contempt at departmental fumblings, his heart would not truly be in it. For what Sharon's script put at the forefront of Harry's mind was something that had not escaped Clint's attention—celebrity and the media's dance of attendance on it.

His testimony at a Mafia trial has made Harry locally famous, and now he can't do his job without someone thrusting a microphone or a TV camera in his face. Then confirming his new status, he discovers that his name is entered in the "dead pool" being run by Peter Swan, a grimly pretentious horror-picture director, played with appropriate grandiloquence by Liam Neeson. In this game entrants make up lists of well-known people they expect to die within the year, the person with the most correct guesses being the winner. Soon enough listees are being murdered with alarming regularity, among them a female movie critic (perhaps some wish fulfillment here) and a trashed rock idol—hilariously played by Jim Carrey, then billing himself as James, in his first telling movie role. The young actor—cheeky, bright and anarchic—was Clint's kind of kid, and a mutual admiration society formed. Clint would give Carrey a small role in *Pink Cadillac,* and when stardom came to him, Clint appeard with him at his Chinese Theater footprints ceremony. Carrey, in turn, cohosted Clint's AFI Life Achievement banquet.

The film's more serious business is tracking down the serial killer who cuts short Carrey's role. Harry must do so while a TV reporter named Samantha Walker (Patricia Clarkson, a Locke-alike in the eyes of several reviewers) tags along, doing a profile of him, with which his bosses have ordered him to cooperate. Their hostility is predictable; so perhaps are their debates about whether the media by so avidly covering crime does or does not encourage it; so, undoubtedly, is the fact that they eventually make love without exactly falling into it. In the end, she is abducted by the killer—a screenwriter rejected by Swan and trying to get even with him—and saved by Harry, who employs his most phallic weapon yet, a harpoon gun, to dispense with the villain.

If the film's criticisms of pack-traveling journalists and its satirical thrusts at the pomposities of Swan's auteurism were not notably original, they were at least unexpected, and not unintelligent. But there was no heat left in Harry. Reviewers treated him indulgently now. In a little over a decade and a half, he had made the journey from unconscious fascist to incipient fogey. Clint was tired of him too: "There's only so much you can do with a character, and Dirty Harry was pretty much at the end of his rope." Clint was also losing interest in the urban action genre, which was beginning to give itself over to careless raptures of violence, more detached from reality (and affect) than *Dirty Harry*'s original critics could ever have imagined. *The Dead Pool*'s grosses—smaller than any of the other *Dirty Harry* pictures, though still highly profitable—confirmed what Clint already knew: that it was time to bestow on Harry his grateful regards and ask him to take early retirement. It is a decision he has never regretted, though people still speak wistfully to him about Harry, wondering if, just possibly, he might someday return. As what? one wonders. A security guard?

*   *   *

Leaving Buddy Van Horn and the rest of his staff to complete *The Dead Pool,* Clint took off for Cannes and *Bird*'s world premiere in an optimistic mood. He felt it had a better chance for a prize than *Pale Rider* had. And, indeed, *Bird* was well received by the audience. He again enjoyed the "awesome" experience of the Palais steps, stayed in the theater just long enough to make sure the sound was all right, then sneaked away. He told William Goldman, who was a juror that year, and who has written with rare wit about the experience, "I just couldn't have sat there. I didn't have nerve enough. Too terrifying. To sit there and agonize over the choices you've already made after you've seen it so many times." A few minutes before the film ended he returned to face the music—the music of applause, as it happened. "That was a wonderful moment. Of course, it's always wonderful when they don't throw cabbages at you."

The problem was getting a similar response from the jury, and here the defects of *Bird*'s virtues surfaced for the first time. Goldman observed what we have also seen: "No apologizing, no excuses, self-pity's been banished. Warts and all, it says, here I am. Like me or not." He also observed: "It was by far the outstanding directorial work of the fortnight. The only stigma being Eastwood and our memories of all those action films. How dare he attempt a serious movie? And bring it off. I believe that if Francis Coppola had directed it, frame for frame, the critics would have put him back on top with Woody Allen. And if Allen had done it, they would have elevated him up alongside Welles."

The front-runners for the Palme d'Or were Bille August's *Pelle the Conqueror* and Chris Menges's *A World Apart,* each in its way the kind of film that festival juries and critics find easy to approve. The former, the story of a Swedish farmhand and his son looking for work in the midst of an agricultural depression in nineteenth-century Scandinavia, was handsomely made and quite unsentimental in its humanism. The latter was much more ordinary, a predictable antiapartheid drama. Still, Goldman believed Clint had a real shot as best director and did his best to sway the jury in that direction. But the debate over the two leading contenders was so intense that when *Pelle* won, they decided to give two consolation prizes to its leading competitor. *A World Apart* was given the customary runner-up award, the jury prize, and its three leading ladies were jointly presented the best actress award. Then Forest Whitaker was given the best actor nod. Politically, this sealed Clint's fate. The jury was not going to give two awards to yet another film, and, indeed, the Argentine, Fernando Solanas, won the directing award for *Le Sud,* a movie Goldman insists is largely about scrap paper blowing artfully through the empty streets of Buenos Aires.

Clint kept his disappointment to himself. *Bird* had at least been in serious contention, his leading actor had won a prize, and the generally good reports of it flowing out of Cannes heightened his hopes for the movie, which was given its American premiere at the New York Film Festival in September.

Bird's critical reception was the most interesting (because it was the most serious and engaged) so far accorded any Eastwood film. Partly, this was because some new voices, writers whose first allegiance was to jazz, not film, were added to the dialogue. They were not always appreciative, but the length and the passion of their arguments were stimulating. Some, like Giddins and Leonard Feather, were inclined to concede the film its musical and dramatic licenses, delighted at last to have a fictional jazz film that was both passionate and emotionally authentic. Others were determined to hold it to stricter historical accountability. Crouch, for example, deplored the rerecording of Parker's music, insisting that recent remasterings of his work would have served as well, not understanding that this material could not have been persuasively played on a modern theatrical sound system. He also made much of *Bird*'s failure to go more deeply into Parker's family history—he thinks Parker was overindulged by a mother who was, at the same time, emotionally withholding—its elimination of significant liaisons with women other than Chan, its failures of detailed musicological history. More interestingly, this would-be biographer of Parker insisted there was an intellectual arrogance and a competitive hardness in him that Whitaker and Clint did not capture. He quotes pianist Walter Davis Jr.: "You can't have a movie about Bird and not have him run over somebody. This was a very aggressive man. He took over and made things go his way. If you weren't strong, Charlie Parker would mow you down like grass."

A movie biography, however, unlike a literary one, has a need to compress and symbolize, and if every significant character in Bird's life is not present here, most of its significant issues are. Certainly Whitaker's soft-gliding performance, patiently accumulating sympathy for Bird until we are devastated by his demise, was a sensible strategy, especially since he conveys very well the man's infantile, premoral quality and the erratic willfulness that typically accompanies that condition.

The mainstream reviewers, eschewing biographical detail, responded to Bird more flatteringly. They had not previously paid much attention to Clint as a filmmaker, in part because his controversial stardom had so often preoccupied them, in part because his directorial manner had been so self-effacing. But because he was not distractingly present in Bird, and because its striking look and tragic subject matter were so obviously singular, they were encouraged to write up to his ambitions.

That drove Pauline Kael crazy, especially coming as it did not long after Wesleyan University and the Museum of Modern Art had established Clint Eastwood archives, his papers going to the former, his films to the latter, with a black-tie dinner at the Museum of Modern Art celebrating the occasion. She loathed Bird, calling it "a rat's nest of a movie" that looked as if Clint "hadn't paid his Con Ed bill." Then lecturing at the University of Pennsylvania, she charged the critics with praising this "perfectly atrocious" director "because they would like to be Clint Eastwood. It is basically as silly as that. I mean, he is tall and his stardom is very sexy, and a lot of people on magazines who lead lives that are not exciting imagine him to have a terrific time."

But she's the one drawing the dirty pictures, and advancing a curious critical theory as well. Hereafter, anyone praising any star must be suspect, since all stars do, indeed, lead lives that are "sexier" (using the word in its broadest sense, and probably its narrower one, too) than the typical journalist. Employing this principle, what is one to make of her career-long infatuation with Marlon Brando? Her shorter, more self-destructive crush on Warren Beatty, for whom she briefly abandoned reviewing to become his story editor?

More rationally, Kael joined a number of other critics—Janet Maslin, John Simon and Stanley Kauffmann—in finding Bird's structure confusing, and chastising its failure to find and sustain a conventional dramatic line conducting us smoothly to exemplary tragedy. They might be prepared to grant Bird his mystery. But in the end, they wanted it solved, wanted to see the crucial betrayal—by Mom or women or the unfeeling world, whomever or whatever. Alternatively, one feels, they might have settled for something more sentimental and hagiographic. Responding to such criticism, Helen Knode, writing in the *L.A. Weekly,* observed that "Parker didn't live his life as though he were the greatest musical innovator since Beethoven. He lived his life like we all do, as best he could. He lived inside the legend, not outside it." It would have been wrong, as she correctly suggests, to impose upon it the glib comforts of psychology and the grander consolations of tragedy.

Perhaps because of its refusal to romanticize or sentimentalize Charlie Parker's story, there was a dutiful quality to much of the critical regard for *Bird*. It made only a few ten-best lists, and it was no more than a minor contender in the award ballotings of the critical organizations. Showbiz reporters listed it, Clint, Whitaker and Venora as potential Oscar nominees, and the studio campaigned for them; films of this kind get made largely in hopes that heavy Academy attention will bring reluctant customers in, but it lacked the triumphal note Academy members respond to, and only Lennie Niehaus got a nomination (and, eventually, a statuette). Clint's only consolation prize was a Golden Globe as best director of a drama.

This reception hurt and puzzled Clint. Almost two years to the day after its ambiguous reception at Cannes predicted its ambiguous fate elsewhere, he would tell an interviewer, "We just didn't seem to have enough people in America who wanted to see the story of a black man who in the end betrays his genius. And we didn't get the support through black audiences that I'd hoped for. They really aren't into jazz now, you know. It's all this rap stuff. There aren't enough whites who are, either. . . ."

★   ★   ★

Preoccupied first by politics, then by this film, Clint had not been attending closely to his relationship with Sondra Locke. They were still seeing each other, and she had accompanied him to Cannes for the *Bird* premiere. But she had not participated in his mayoralty—not even attending his inaugural—and as he puts it, "The handwriting was slowly becoming murky on the wall, so I started withdrawing a little bit."

He dates the beginning of his final disaffection to a relatively trivial incident. When he was shooting *Heartbreak Ridge* he invited her, on the spur of the moment, to spend a weekend with him. She declined. She said she had promised to drive Gordon and a friend to Ojai, felt she couldn't renege at the last moment—and, oh, by the way, could she borrow Clint's car for the trip? It was something like the showerhead incident with Maggie, a moment that crystallized the anger that had been building up in him for years. As always, he felt Sondra's first allegiance was to Gordon, not to him.

The upshot was predictable. "All of a sudden, you start looking around"—looking around, that is, in his public and professional world. At first, he did not do so with any consequential results. Indeed, something over two years drifted by with Clint more or less content not having to explain himself or justify his movements to anyone. This condition began to change around six o'clock on the evening of October 2, 1988, when Frances Fisher made a spectacular entrance into the preproduction party for *Pink Cadillac,* which was held around the pool of a Holiday Inn in Reno, Nevada. Wearing shorts, she zipped in on roller skates, and she says she was smitten by her first glimpse of the star.

She had auditioned on tape for her small part in this somewhat shaggy comedy, and so had not met Clint previously. Nor had she seen more than a couple of his films. All she had to go on "was, you know, 'tough guy Clint Eastwood, blah-blah-blah.'" But her first thought was, Well, he doesn't seem so tough. He looked, in fact, extremely attractive, and eventually she made her way to him, hopping over a small Jacuzzi to introduce herself. "He looked right at me, the way he does every other woman in the world, but it got to me, too. I mean, when he turns it on, he can turn it on, and I just went, Oh my God, look at that. There was a human being there—I just saw such beauty in his presence. And I felt like a big piece of the puzzle had fallen into place."

In other words, it was love at first sight—on her part; almost certainly not on his. Fisher is an intense and willful woman, who wears her emotions very openly. Thirty-six years old at the time, and a New York actress in the fullest sense of the term—Actors Studio, Off Broadway, low-budget independent movies—she had recently moved to Los Angeles hoping to establish a more mainstream career. The product of a wandering childhood—her father had been a construction engineer, working all over the world—she had been married once, very briefly, but had been single for more than a decade and a half. Now with her biological clock beginning to tick loudly she quite frankly wanted a man, a child and a more settled life.

She proposed a date. She had never been to Reno before and asked Clint if he would show her the sights. He called for her at her room a couple of hours later. They had dinner. They danced. They made love. She had a week's work in the film, and they kept company during that period. Later in the shoot he called her in Los Angeles and asked her to rejoin him for another week, which she did.

He was, she says, both frank and not frank about his personal situation. He said he was seeing other women, but he did not specifically mention Sondra Locke. And Fisher—surprisingly—did not think to ask about her. She saw, or thought she saw, only "this lost, lonely, shut-down person," whom she was convinced she could "open up."

Having made the instant judgment that "this was the man I was going to spend the rest of my life with," she told Clint, in their first week together, "everything I wanted in my life. I said, 'I want you to know everything about me, and I want to know everything about you.'" This was not necessarily "the worst thing I could have said to him," but it was certainly risky.

It was also attractive to him. While they were together, people who did not know her kept insisting that Frances and Sondra were alike. But beyond a certain superficial physical resemblance—blond hair, fine features—they are in most respects entirely different. Frances is more sturdily built (one of Clint's nicknames for her was "Muscles"), and no one would ever describe her spirit as "ethereal." The contrast obviously interested Clint.

Still, he maintained a certain reserve. When the picture wrapped, he saw Frances when he was in Los Angeles, but never at his house, never exclusively and, it would seem, always on his timetable. She remained, she says, unaware of Locke's significance in his life until their breakup became public in the spring of 1989, which is hard to believe, though given Clint's capacity for selective silences—and his confusion of feelings at this time—not entirely implausible.

It is clear that, like most people who are not emotionally confrontational, Clint was hoping that time was on his side. Perhaps, sensing the growing chill between them, Sondra would look elsewhere for warmth, or beat a defensive retreat. His largest hope in this regard was professional preoccupation, for she was prepping her next directorial assignment, a picture called *Impulse,* which their mutual friend, Al Ruddy, was producing for Warner Bros. The film was to star Theresa Russell, playing an undercover cop who feels herself succumbing to the lures of the illicit life. Alas, at this early stage it did not fully command Locke's attention, and a series of incidents ensued that assured a bitter estrangement between her and Clint.

The first of these involved his relationship with Kyle. He was now twenty, attending USC and living in the Bel-Air house with Clint. This pleased him, for like all divorced dads he was always looking for ways to make up for lost time with his kids. It displeased Sondra, who began inquiring about apartments for Kyle with real estate agents. When Clint discovered this, he was furious. "Never come between blood and blood," he says grimly.

Around this time another unpleasant outburst occurred. The holidays tend to make Clint a little edgy, and he usually retreats to Sun Valley for a fresh-air cure. This time he invited both children as well as Sondra and assorted friends, including his old pal Jane Brolin, to join him. On New Year's Eve day she and Sondra squabbled. Clint hints that Locke may have heard of his involvement with another woman—not necessarily Frances—and that she may have been trying to enlist Brolin on her side. Their discussion grew heated, and Clint finally intervened: "Why don't you both get the hell out of here? I just want to be here with my kids. Leave me alone. Let me have a nice holiday."

New Year's Eve found Sondra alone and visibly distraught in the tiny Sun Valley airport, where she was observed by several people who knew her, a scene that was subsequently reported in the gossip press. In other circumstances, says Clint, this quarrel might have been patched up after a week or two of mutual sulking, except that "the relationship was long deteriorating at that point."

They scarcely saw each other in the months that followed; Clint was away much of the time in early 1989, in Carmel, and also, briefly, in Europe, where *Bird* was opening. In Rome, Sergio Leone called him, the first time in some years he had attempted to get in touch. He asked Clint to meet him for lunch, and he found the director in a mellow and nostalgic mood, the bitterness of his public comments about Clint now dissolved. They had such a good time that they agreed to meet again for dinner, to which Leone brought his friend Lina Wertmüller, the director. He was mortally ill, knew it, but said nothing. It was not until he died, a couple of months later, that Clint understood Leone had been making his final farewells.

Returning home, Clint resolved to make his final farewells to Sondra. Clint, who had long been threatened by celebrity stalkers, was at this point receiving particularly menacing death threats by phone. Seeking clues to their source he asked a friend of his, an electronics expert, to place a tap on his phone. He learned nothing about the stalker, but he did discover, to his amazement, that Sondra was making calls from his house to a divorce lawyer, discussing what charges she might or might not bring against him in a palimony action. She discussed the same matter with Gordon in other recorded conversations. Shortly thereafter, she was seen entering the lawyer's office (somebody's legal secretary spoke to someone else's legal secretary), and Clint was advised by his attorneys to ask Sondra to give up her keys to his house and remove her belongings from it. He summoned her to the house early on the morning of April 3 and broached the matter. ("I told him I couldn't believe that was all he had to say to me after thirteen years," she averred in a statement she filed in court later that month.) She had been night shooting the previous evening, had only had four hours of sleep and easily persuaded him to delay this discussion until her picture was in the can.

There, perhaps, the matter should have rested. But lawyers will lawyer, and so a week later, a legal letter, addressed to Mrs. Gordon Anderson, was delivered to Locke on the set. It read, in part: "Mr. Eastwood has asked you to vacate the premises. You have refused to do so. This is to let you know that in view of your intransigence, the locks on all the entrances to the house have been replaced. . . . Accordingly, your belongings will be placed in storage."

She said she fainted. But she awoke with the upper hand in the battle of the tabloids that was soon joined. He looked like the very gunslinger Eileen Padberg had warned him not to seem when he ran for mayor. She looked like the fragile victim of a rich and insensitive man. "They don't call him 'Dirty Harry' for nothing," read one fairly typical lead to a story about the case.

In her initial filing, leaked to the Los Angeles *Times,* Locke requested that Clint be barred from the house in Bel-Air (the house at which she, not he, was the visitor) "because I know him to have a terrible temper . . . and he has frequently been abusive to me." Contradictorily, she also stated that "from the start of our relationship Clint told me that he wanted us always to be together and that he would take care of me forever," adding that "Clint repeatedly assured me that regardless of whether we were married, everything he had was ours together. . . ." Most damagingly, she also alleged that over the years she had endured two abortions and submitted to a tubal ligation at his request.

By the standards of the game they were playing, her settlement proposal, reflecting the weakness of her position that her marriage imposed, was relatively modest: title to both the Bel-Air house and the one Clint had given her and Anderson, an immediate cash settlement of $250,000 and seven years of further support—$15,000 per month for five years, $10,000 in the sixth year, $7,500 in the final year.

Clint, nevertheless, was outraged. She had not fully shared his house or his life during their relationship, and he also felt that over the years he had given generously at the office. About this, however, he said nothing for publication. "I was not going to get down in the muck with her," he says. What he did respond to—forcefully—were her allegations about the abortions and the tubal ligation. "I adamantly deny and deeply resent the accusation that [they] were done at my demand, request or even suggestion," he said in his court filing. These decisions were, he insisted, "entirely hers." He issued his only public comment through a press agent: "I am deeply disappointed and saddened that she's taken this kind of action. It will soon come to light that these accusations are unfounded and without merit, however this matter will be dealt with in an appropriate legal arena."

He was not, however, as flinty in private as he was in public. In the spring of 1989 he was a man obsessed by this conflict. Sooner or later he would bring any conversation around to it, and to his sense of betrayal by this woman he had once loved. Months later he would tell a reporter what he said to friends at the time: "I felt so disappointed. And the disappointment was with myself. How could I have spent so many years with Sondra? How could I have been such a bad judge of character?"

At the time, however, he was unable to muster even that much reflective calm. His manner was like that of a kid falsely accused of cheating in school, but unable to prove that he had not. All he could do was keep reassuring friends and loved ones that there was another side to this story while maintaining his public silence.

He had been maneuvered into a position where a quick settlement, on her terms, was the only way to end the flow of calumny against him. The parties engaged a jurist to arbitrate the case privately and on May 31—his fifty-ninth birthday—gathered in a courtroom in Woodland Hills to try to reach an agreement. Nothing conclusive resulted. It was reported that the case would probably go to trial in the fall.

It did not. But neither was it settled. It would linger unresolved for almost two years. In the interim, Locke was diagnosed with breast cancer—she said stress contributed to her condition—and underwent a double mastectomy. It would appear, however, that her illness added impetus to the search for a resolution, and someone, probably Al Ruddy, who confessed to engaging in "shuttle diplomacy" between Clint and Sondra, suggested that a development deal with Warner Bros. might break the impasse.

It made sense. She had all along stressed her desire to achieve professional autonomy. The chance to make pictures of her own choosing, for a studio whose executives she knew well, and who appeared sympathetic, was more attractive to her than a settlement consisting solely of cash and property. She would later quote Terry Semel saying, "It makes us happy that this ugly scenario can end," and adding, optimistically, "You have top talent and promise as a filmmaker."

The contract they eventually signed was for a standard development deal, in which over the course of three years the studio agreed to underwrite her salary and expenses, at a cost of $1.5 million, while she worked up projects on which it would have first look. The studio could, as well, present her with ideas it thought suited her. The arrangement was unusual in two respects. One of them is obvious: Players of her modest standing generally do not get deals of this kind. The other is less so: Unknown to Locke it was being underwritten by Clint Eastwood.

Protective silence was maintained on this point. And why not? It was such a neat solution to such a vexing issue. For a while things went smoothly enough. In the spring of 1991 Clint and Sondra achieved a settlement. Though they agreed not to discuss its terms publicly, it was reported that she received title to the home she shared with Gordon Anderson, while surrendering claim to the Bel-Air house. Clint also paid her a lump sum of $450,000, which she claimed, and he denied, was due her for previous services to Malpaso. There was also, undoubtedly, an agreement for monthly support payments. That behind her, and now fully recuperated from her illness, Locke proceeded to try to fulfill her studio contract.

That is to say, she entered into "development hell." She had in hand over the next three years at least a couple of films that were ultimately produced—one as *Junior,* the Arnold Schwarzenegger comedy; the other as *The Specialist,* a Sylvester Stallone action film—but not, apparently, in the form she offered them. Clint says that he supported her cause, in particular recommending her to direct the American version of *La Femme Nikita,* which was not completely dissimilar in tone from *Impulse,* which within its limits she had handled quite adroitly. Locke remembers showing him a script called *Paperback Hero,* getting an enthusiastic response and a promise to recommend it to the bosses.

Nothing came of it. Nothing came of any of the thirty-odd projects she proposed to Warners. They were subsequently represented by studio spokesmen as gloomy and unsympathetic, without significant popular appeal. Locke said that her efforts to see material the studio owned that she might undertake were rebuffed. After her contract expired, she sued Warners, charging breach of contract and good faith as well as sexual discrimination and fraud.

This action was summarily dismissed in 1995, but Locke brought another suit against Clint, charging fraud, seeking some $2 million in damages and claiming she would not have agreed to their earlier settlement had she known he was standing behind her Warner Bros. contract. For, she contended, his underwriting virtually guaranteed that the studio would not move forward with any of her projects.

Her reasoning was that Clint was ultimately liable for all her development costs if she made no pictures, but that if she made one, those costs would be shifted to its budget and borne by Warner Bros. Ergo, it was in the studio's interest not to produce anything of hers and to let Clint cover the cost of her contract. At the very least, she came to believe that the production hurdle was higher for her, by however many feet or inches $1.5 million translated to, than it was for other producers.

Possibly so, possibly not. She reckoned without Clint's clear-cut economic interest in her success and Warner's close ties to him. Its executives would not have been eager to stick one of their most valuable assets with a $1.5 million tab. That's chump change in studio terms—many films carry much higher development charges—thus nothing that would greatly influence its decisions. It can also be said that it is not uncommon for very little to develop from development deals, and that Clint paid a steep price for this failed compromise; most, if not all, of the studio's expenses were ultimately deducted from his *Unforgiven* takings. Worse, he was forced to settle Locke's civil suit for an undisclosed sum in September 1996, when it became clear that a jury was going to find for her. In interviews with the press, jurors made it clear that Clint's angry appearance on the stand, where he made much of Locke's earlier campaign against him in the gossip press, combined with her well-projected air of victimization, weighed heavily with them. In her testimony she had referred to Clint as "the unfightable one" and in her comments to reporters later she called hers a victory for "the little person." Assuredly it was a loss for a powerful and manifestly aggravated man to whom it was easy to impute devious motives.

All of that was far in the future in the spring of 1989, when contentiousness between Clint and Sondra was at its height. His other preoccupations included performing his hostly duties for the *Gary Cooper: American Life, American Legend* documentary (one of his rare television appearances), preparing *White Hunter, Black Heart,* which was scheduled to begin shooting in Africa in June, and readying *Pink Cadillac* for release.

Neither the critical reception nor the box-office performance of the latter would do anything to lighten his mood. Directed by Buddy Van Horn, it is the story of a skip tracer named Tommy Nowak, who falls into unlikely love with Lou Ann McQuinn (Bernadette Peters), a woman he is assigned to apprehend. John Eskow's script was pressed on Clint by the studio, which thought, as he did when he read it, that it had something of the knockabout spirit of the orangutan films. Clint—as we know, a man not insusceptible to the joys of Groucho glasses—liked the fact that Tommy employed outlandish disguises in his work. At various points in the film he appears as a cowbell-wielding radio personality, a rodeo clown, a casino sharpster wearing a gold lamé jacket and a pencil mustache and a brain-dead bumpkin. He also thought Peters's character was an excellent foil for him. Fleeing with her baby from an abusive husband, who is also a right-wing crazy of the survivalist persuasion, not knowing that her eponymous vehicle contains $250,000 belonging to his organization's treasury, she may look like trailer-park trash, but she has a ferocious spirit—especially when the survivalists kidnap her baby. Finally, perhaps most important to Clint, the film had the kind of range—farce, romance, crazy action—that he likes in comedies.

Dave Kehr, virtually the film's only critical supporter, would eventually argue that Tommy constituted a statement no less personal than the ones Clint had made in weightier works, offering him a character through which he could pay tribute to the escapist and self-expressive pleasures he had found in performance. When Nowack dons false colors "he lights up with self-enjoyment; the straight bearing softens, the gestures expand, and he can't stop smiling," the critic observed.

Clint does not disagree with this reading. The problem was context. These sweet, goofy moments are contained in a movie of mercurial mood shifts. As Clint says, there were moments when Lou Ann, dealing with the loss of her baby, comes close to tragic bereavement. At other times the picture skirts country traversed by hundreds of pickup trucks in dozens of redneck road comedies. At the end, Buddy Van Horn and Clint deliver an assault on the survivalists' redoubt, full of high-impact car stunts and automatic weaponry; it belongs in a different movie.

In short, the film develops no firm point of view toward its varied elements. It is genial enough, but it has a definitely slapped-together quality. Tall tales need to be told confidently, and *Pink Cadillac* achieves that spirit only occasionally, generally when Clint is cutting up or Peters, belying the airhead voluptuousness of the first impression she creates, zings someone with a one-liner. (She has the movie's best line, a response to a flasher inquiring of her what she sees: "Looks just like a penis, only smaller," she says sweetly.)

Unaccountably, the studio decided to release *Pink Cadillac* on the Memorial Day weekend, the traditional opening of the summer movie season and, by more modern tradition, a period ceded to some high-decibel action movie—that year *Indiana Jones and the Last Crusade*. It may be that studio executives thought of Clint's film as counterprogramming to this surefire blockbuster, something a slightly older crowd might get a kick out of. Then again, they may not have been thinking at all.

The show-business press immediately made a contest out of this situation—Clint Eastwood versus Indiana Jones. It was, of course a mismatch—this shaky little comedy going against Steven Spielberg's handsomely mounted behemoth. The latter grossed $37.7 million; Clint's picture did $4.4 million, about half of what recent Eastwood movies had been doing on their first weekends. Much was made of this, all of it deleterious to Clint's standing as a box-office favorite.

Clint was not quite willing to admit that he had reached an age and a stage where he could no longer afford such seemingly regressive film-making. But he did derive some consolation from the higher standards to which he was now being held. He remembers thinking, People wanted me to go another step and maybe that's good—at least they're rooting for you to go somewhere.

★   ★   ★

Pink Cadillac opened on Friday, May 26. By the following Wednesday, all the bad news about its disastrous grosses was in as he confronted Locke in the unpleasant, unsuccessful attempt to reach a settlement. Almost immediately thereafter he left for the media-free zone of Lake Kariba in Zimbabwe, where he would shoot *White Hunter, Black Heart*.

We can judge the state of his spirit at this time by noting that Frances Fisher did not accompany him. He had, she says, previously hinted that he would like her to come along, but in the end he did not even call to say goodbye. Obviously he could not so soon undertake another serious relationship. He needed instead to immerse himself in the healing routines of a far-distant production.

On the way to Africa, Clint stopped off in Paris for its annual air show, where he completed arrangements to purchase the most expensive indulgence he has ever permitted himself, an Acurielle helicopter, known outside its country of origin as an A-Star. Fulfilling the promise he had made to himself when he first took the controls of one of those contraptions on the *Paint Your Wagon* location, he was now a fully qualified pilot, and though his machine was shipped home for him, he ferried himself and others from place to place in Africa, using choppers leased to the production.

Much as *White Hunter, Black Heart* meant to Clint, it meant even more to Peter Viertel, author of the book from which it derived, for this production represented the culmination of a dream deferred for well over three decades. The son of émigré movie people—his mother had been Greta Garbo's favorite screenwriter; his father had been a promising director in Weimar Germany (and latterly the model for the leading character in another roman à clef about the movies, Christopher Isherwood's *Prater Violet*)—he had been hired in 1951 by John Huston, who had once worked on a script for Viertel's father, to polish James Agee's screenplay for *The African Queen*. He had accompanied the director (and, of course, Bogart, Hepburn and the rest of the company) to the film's Congolese location, returning with material for a melodramatized account of a movie director clearly modeled on Huston, obsessed with shooting an elephant at the expense of shooting his picture. The novel became a best-seller in 1953, thanks in part to an ending suggested by Huston himself, in which his character is portrayed more monstrously than he was in real life. The book was sold to Columbia, and then entered upon what must be one of the longest preproduction odysseys in the history of the movies.

Viertel was engaged to make his own adaptation, which proved unacceptable to the studio. Over the course of the years, two writer-directors, James Bridges and Burt Kennedy, wrote new versions of the screenplay, with the property finally passing into the hands of Ray Stark. As it happened, Stanley Rubin, whom Clint had known since he produced *Francis in the Navy,* back in his Universal days, was working for Stark at the time, and he brought *White Hunter, Black Heart* to Clint's attention. He read one draft of the script, then another and another, then Viertel's novel, and found himself utterly absorbed.

The Huston character, called John Wilson in book and screenplay, is a figure any actor would relish playing. His macho swagger not untouched by self-destructive impulses, his romanticism darkened by selfishness, cynicism and a talent for manipulation, his rebellious posturings undermined by his taste for the good life; there is an inescapable grandeur about him—and, to modern eyes, an air of humbug as well. Here was a chance for Clint to meditate on the most "daunting" of all American ideas about manhood, that of Hemingway and his school (Viertel was also a friend of the novelist's and introduced Huston to him). For Wilson, his strutting (and rather literary) masculinity was no less "full of shit" than Tom Highway's, and with fewer excuses, since he is an intelligent man who, in full, mocking consciousness of both his intentions and their absurdity, sacrifices friendship, work and the good opinion of others to the glamour of grandiose folly. "You're about to blow this picture out of your nose," the Viertel character rages at him, as he expensively delays its start "to commit a crime, to kill one of the rarest, most noble creatures that walks this crummy earth." But that's just the point. "It's the only sin you can buy a license for and then go out and commit," Wilson replies, relishing his existential rebelliousness.

Clint would admit Wilson's redeeming aspects. He has, for example, a speech to the Viertel character (played in the film by Jeff Fahey) in which he tells him he will never be a great screenwriter "because you let eighty-five million popcorn eaters pull you this way and that." In the

years since, Clint has often quoted that dialogue to interviewers seeking
his own filmmaking credo. In a later passage Wilson deliberately picks a
fight with a white racist in an African hotel, knowing he will lose.
Sometimes, he says, as he staggers away from this encounter with his
younger, stronger opponent, you have to volunteer for lost causes or
"your guts will turn to pus." Clint could respond to that, too. Nevertheless, it was the man's monstrousness that compelled him. Here, truly,
was a character to test the limits of an audience's sympathy.

In the novel, Wilson finally bags his elephant, in the process setting
off a stampede in which his native guide is killed. In the movie, he does
not make his kill. At the moment of truth, confronting his prey, he
funks, but with the same deadly consequences to the guide. He returns
to the first day of work on his film visibly chastened, possibly even broken, slumping into his director's chair and almost inaudibly rasping out
"Action."

It is a much more clear-cut and devastating comment on the hol-
lowness of macho posturing. Indeed, the picture in general improves on
its source. For Viertel was very much a bedazzled hanger-on in the
Hemingway-Huston world, where people distracted themselves in far-
flung pursuits of dangerous and expensive pleasures. He could moralize
about them, but he could not entirely evade his enchantment by them.
Some of his novel's seductiveness when it first appeared derived from
the glimpse it offered to goggling provincial eyes of the enviably posh
path to self-loathing the privileged permitted themselves. Clint would
take his tone from Viertel's admirable title, so straightforward in the
ironies and moralities it hints at, not from the more ambiguous atmosphere that suffuses the work itself, refusing even to present Africa in a
handsome light. There are very few grand, glamorizing vistas captured
at sunrise or sunset here.

If Clint's directorial choices were admirable in this austerity, his
most basic choice as an actor was more debatable. Early on, he had to
decide whether or not to imitate Huston's well-known mannerisms—
the rich drawl of his voice, the kingly elegance of his gestures. There
were arguments on both sides. Knowledgeable people had for decades
understood that *White Hunter, Black Heart* was a roman à clef. They had,
indeed, made it part of the vast Huston legend, part of what they knew,
or thought they knew, about him. Even if one was unfamiliar with this
historic gossip, the film within Clint's film was rather obviously a version of *The African Queen,* the most widely beloved of all Huston's films,
and also central to his legend. It was hard in this context to pretend that
John Wilson was John Doe, and self-defeating as well. It would surely
help the commercial prospects of the project if one legend could be

clearly discerned portraying another. On the other hand, thanks to Huston's second career as an actor, his mannerisms were very well known. A close imitation of them would inevitably invite narrow comparisons between art and reality at the expense of the film's larger issues and pleasures.

Clint did not hesitate over this matter. Before leaving for Africa he gathered footage of Huston, studied it closely and, despite the disparity in the timbre of their voices, created a very passable impression of him. But since he directed the actors who played such easily recognizable figures as Hepburn, Bogart and Lauren Bacall away from detailed imitation, his decision in the last analysis is difficult to understand. His propensity for realism certainly went into it. So did his love of character acting. It is possible, however, that at this particular moment in his personal history Clint did not want to appear before the public in a persona closely resembling his own.

When he completed work on the Zimbabwe location, he had two weeks of work to do on *White Hunter, Black Heart* in and around London. There the tabloids observed him keeping company with Maggie, herself hurting from the ending of her second marriage. The papers incorrectly rumored reconciliation, especially when they took a short vacation together in the south of France. But as Clint has often said, his relationship with Maggie has turned out to be better in divorce than it was in marriage, and they turned to one another now for reliable, well-tested warmth and trust.

Once back in the United States, Clint was in no hurry to finish his picture, which would mean making himself available to the press, and in no mood to disport himself in public, for to him it seemed the stories about his breakup with Sondra would not die: "Everywhere I went, I couldn't get away from it. When a story was written by one person, everyone else picked it up. It was so parasitic. It made me so uncomfortable."

Other discomfiting matters surfaced as well. It was now that the press revealed Kimber's existence, and in the fall of 1989, Alison, then seventeen, and in a rebellious phase, was arrested for drunk driving in Beverly Hills. She was jailed overnight, fined and had her license suspended. She had suffered more from the Eastwoods' divorce than her brother had. And also, perhaps, from her father's stardom, having herself become the target of a celebrity stalker. Clint acknowledges now that at that time his communication with his daughter was strained. He says that one of the factors drawing him to *Absolute Power,* the film he shot in the summer of 1996, was that William Goldman's adaptation of the best-selling novel stressed a troubled father-daughter relationship. "I'd been there," he said. "I could relate to that."

At the time, he remained silent about these matters. If he was obliged to attend a public function he would take as his date Jane Brolin or Dani Crane, David Janssen's widow and his old friend from the Universal talent program. This remained true for some months, even though Frances Fisher had returned to his life.

No one outside his closest circle knew this. He was more than ever determined to keep his private life private. This reconciliation began in the late summer of 1989, when Frances had a late-afternoon audition on the Warners lot. Burying her pride, and convinced that she knew what was best for both of them, she dropped in at the Malpaso offices sometime after six, where she found Clint at work with Joel Cox in their editing room. She was, she says, greeted by a sheepish grin, but she encouraged him to call her, and over the next few months they drifted into what would soon become an exclusive relationship. She was living then in Manhattan Beach, a long drive from his house and from her working rounds. It made sense for her to stay over in Bel-Air, to begin leaving a few clothes there, and that seemed perfectly agreeable to him. Pretty soon, without their ever formally discussing it, they were living together, although Frances took an apartment in town—she says she spent a total of six nights there—so he would not feel she was trying to entrap him. Finally, early in 1990, he began introducing her to his friends, the first such occasion being an evening they spent with Arnold Schwarzenegger and Maria Shriver. A little later, he invited her to spend time with him at his Shasta County ranch, the retreat he shares only with true intimates. She remained, by her own account, more in love with him than he was with her. But if this was never a grand passion, he was grateful to her for restoring a sense of calm and normalcy to his life.

★ ★ ★

By the spring of 1990 he was ready to return to work, and to public life. It must be said that the latter was more gracefully managed than the former.

The Rookie, the picture he began working on in April, was another script Warner Bros. controlled and urged on him. It was a cop-buddy picture, with Clint cast as an old, low-life pro working grand theft auto (not exactly the most riveting of crimes), and Charlie Sheen as a rich kid assigned to be his partner but in serious need of maturing. The thinking was obvious: About to turn sixty, Clint was getting too old to carry an action picture single-handed; maybe by being paired with a young hotshot he could refresh his grip on this traditional franchise. His was virtually a supporting role, and he went along with it because he thought directorially he might be able to make something of it. "Also, I didn't have something else to do at that time."

Except carefully tend to the launch of *White Hunter, Black Heart.* He knew, of course, that it was not going to be a hugely popular film, and that, like *Bird,* it would require sober journalistic attention if it was going to make any impact on the public. He knew that was obtainable at Cannes, and so he entered the new picture in competition there, abandoning work on *The Rookie* to attend the festival.

This strategy contained a significant fringe benefit. After his long season in the tabloid sun, and a year of avoiding personal encounters with the press, he would be presenting himself to reporters as the direc-tor of a very serious film. They would not, in this context, dare to ask him the kind of gossipy questions they were dying to pose. Moreover, his careful reflections on this film would remind readers that he was in possession of a career and character that could not, should not, be re-duced to a sheaf of scandalous innuendoes.

He was indeed treated respectfully by the interviewers. His film, however, did not create the kind of buzz that pictures in serious con-tention for the jury's favor must stir. Some wondered if Anjelica Hus-ton's presence on the panel harmed its chances (Clint thinks not). Many saw it as an exercise in idle historicism, without much relevance to a contemporary audience. This was the unintended, if not entirely unpre-dictable, consequence of Clint's Huston imitation. It caused people to reflect on the director, who had died just two years earlier, not on John Wilson, and on the interesting questions about fame, power and mascu-line self-delusion that he embodied.

Clint finished principal photography on *The Rookie* in June and, as postproduction proceeded, returned to the high road on behalf of *White Hunter, Black Heart.* He took it to the Telluride festival in August, and it was the centerpiece of a retrospective of his directorial work at the Walker Art Center in Minneapolis. A couple of days later, he screened it at the Toronto Film Festival.

It opened in limited release—twenty-five screens—in mid-Septem-ber, and at first it seemed that Clint's work for the film would be re-warded. Grosses were good initially, and the major reviewers, on the whole, were not less enthusiastic than they had been for *Bird.* Several of them unequivocally called it his best work yet as a director. Doubts pre-dictably centered on his performance. Michael Wilmington in the Los Angeles *Times* spoke for many when he wrote, "Huston's persona be-comes Eastwood's own big tusker; the prey he can't quite shoot." He thought it might have been better to "soft-pedal" Huston's mannerisms, but the real issue was that Clint could not soft-pedal his disdain for this character, or forgive him his trespasses. Perhaps, to him, this man's art was insufficient compensation for his flaws. Perhaps his articulateness, implying a capacity for self-awareness that Tom Highway and Charlie Parker did not share, put him off. Perhaps the outworn theatricality of Huston's manner, so curiously mixed with the posturings of perpetual adolescence, so completely unlike his own, interfered with his empathy.

A sense of these ambiguities, this antiheroism, leaked through the critical enthusiasm for *White Hunter, Black Heart*. And the word of mouth didn't help; this was not the Clint his public loved. Grosses quickly dwindled, and the studio never appreciably widened the film's release. Its domestic takings were even less than *Bird*'s $2 million, and there was no consolation to be found in the overseas market either.

This is too bad. For one has to know John Wilson if one is to know Clint Eastwood, since this is the farthest he ever went in trying to imagine an alternative identity for himself, quite obviously as an actor, less obviously, but perhaps more significantly, as a filmmaker. For this anti-romantic director to make a movie about this darkly romantic figure was in itself a daring, even quixotic, gesture, the furthest he had ever ventured, both geographically and emotionally, from his main line.

Given Clint's sensibility, this effort was perhaps foredoomed. He lacked the joyousness with which Huston—not to mention the heroes of his pictures—pursued slightly dishonorable success; therefore, he had to settle for honorable failure. Yet no movie of Clint's—not even *Bird*—more forcefully foreshadowed the expansion of ambition that would preoccupy him in his sixties, our 1990s.

Similarly, no movie more clearly betokened the need to make that transition than *The Rookie* did. Not since *The Eiger Sanction* had Clint made a film so completely lacking in personal resonance, so nakedly, if ineptly, calculating of the marketplace. Given his aspiring recent work, given the honest weight he had always imparted to his action films, it puzzled and offended everyone. And since critics and public alike understood him to be the auteur of his own fate, he could not take the usual star's way out and place the blame for this disaster elsewhere.

It is not merely that the macho jiving between Clint and Charlie Sheen is so desperately lacking humorous élan. It is not just that the look of the film is so glum and flat, or that Raul Julia and Sonia Braga, Hispanic actors, are so weirdly miscast as Germanic villains; it is that the entire film is so actively, even assaultingly, distasteful. Never more so than in a scene where Braga, having captured Clint and trussed him to a chair, forces him to have sex with her at razor point. In the abstract it is an interesting turnaround—the hero obliged to endure a heroine's jeopardy—but it is protracted in an ugly way, and obviously uncomfortable to both performers. It is, like almost everything else in this thoroughly depressing movie, very clearly at odds with the cheeky spirit and the nonstop accumulation of stunts and special effects that films like *Lethal Weapon* and *Die Hard* had taught audiences to expect and *The Rookie* was supposed to imitate.

There are, to be sure, a couple of spectacular sequences in the film—a car containing Clint and Sheen escaping an explosion by hurtling out of a fifth-story window that was well managed by John Frazier, the mechanical-effects master (*Twister* owes much to him), a high-speed car chase, involving Clint with an auto transporter dumping its cargo in his way, which Buddy Van Horn thinks may be the most complicated gag he ever supervised—but compared to its models, *The Rookie* seemed impoverished even in this respect.

The reviewers were uniformly appalled. As with *Pink Cadillac* the studio threw the picture into a holiday rush—this time at the Christmas season—and again the grosses were dreadful, and widely noted by the press. Indeed, a new note crept into some of the commentary on this picture. In the last four years, as the press was well aware, Clint's hits had been smaller than they had previously been, and his failures had been embarrassingly large. One article referred to him as Warner's "fading house star." Here and there critics wondered aloud if he was about to follow Burt Reynolds and Charles Bronson to the commercial fringe. There was in some of these remarks an almost gleeful animus, as if the writers couldn't wait to see this Ur-celebrity drama, a version of Norman Maine's story in *A Star Is Born,* reenacted.

Clint was stoic in this adversity and is stoic in recalling it: "Sometimes these things work; sometimes they don't. It's just hard to come up with good material all the time." Some of this equanimity was based on personal history, on recollections of the several remarkable transformations that had marked and shaped this career, but he also knew something the outsiders did not, that he had in his possession a script that would return him triumphantly to his genre roots and yet speak in clear metaphors to certain pressing issues of the moment. He had held it quietly to himself not because he had any doubts about it, but because he knew that a day would come when he would need to draw on its redemptive power. Before he went off to shoot it in the fall of 1991, he made one, and only one, significant revision in David Webb Peoples's screenplay: When he originally purchased it, the script had been called *The Cut-Whore Killings.* That had been changed to *The William Munny Killings.* Now Clint ordered another title change. Henceforth, this film would be known as *Unforgiven.*

SIXTEEN

LUCKY IN THE ORDER

Clint had two metaphors to describe his feelings for *Unforgiven*. One was as a talisman: "It was something I could sit on and bank on and I kind of hung on to it like a nice little gold watch. It was a nice feeling to know that I had it back there." The other was as a treat: "It was kind of a little plum I was savoring. It's like you have something good on your plate, and you're saying, 'I'll eat this last.'"

Both were apt. David Webb Peoples had written this script on spec in 1976, as he would later put it, "sheltered by ignorance and anonymity," not yet a professional screenwriter, not yet knowing the tricks of the trade—which is one reason his work, full of novelistic digression and dialogue that rambles, as conversation does in life, is so good. Francis Ford Coppola at one time held an option on it, but he let it drop, and in 1983, when Clint was looking for a writer to work on another project, *The Cut-Whore Killings* was shown to him as a sample of Peoples's work, and he optioned it "in a minute."

Sonia Chernus heatedly objected. "We would have been far better off not to have accepted trash like this piece of inferior work," she wrote in a memo to Clint. She hated its rough language (toned down somewhat in production), hated the basic situation, hated the way it was developed. "I can't think of one good thing to say about it," she concluded. "Except maybe, get rid of it FAST." Obviously, he ignored his story editor's opinion—concluding a deal for the script in 1985—but he remains amused by its unwonted passion. He called Peoples, who by this time had earned a shared writing credit on *Blade Runner* and whom he would not meet in person until he had finished *Unforgiven*, and said: "I can't do what Francis Coppola would do, but I think I can bring something to it."

He denies saving the script for a rainy day or that his recent string of box-office failures constituted threatening weather. "I don't think I ever really thought about it as I've got to get out there and make a hit to keep up my Hooper Rating." The delay, he insists, was entirely a matter of aesthetics; he thought "age would be a benefit" when it came to playing Will Munny. Even though the script described Will as a man of thirty-five or forty, he was a hard-used and grizzled figure, psychologically far older than those years. Neither did Clint see the film as an atonement for his own wicked on-screen ways; he has never felt the slightest need to make such a gesture. Nor did he consciously plan this to be a farewell to westerns—though, as he would frequently say during and after production, "If there's going to be a last one this is a perfect one."

At its simplest level, he believed the film said something useful and intelligent about the cheapness with which life was held in America, especially in its popular culture. He also guessed that it might do all right commercially—perhaps grossing in the $50 to $60 million range, as *Pale Rider* had. That being so, he didn't think he had to cut corners as he had with some of his other heartfelt projects. He also imagined the film someday providing him the kind of retrospective satisfaction that *Josey Wales* had.

In preproduction it became clear that Clint felt the film had greater potential, but that he was disciplining himself against discussing it; he did not want to be disappointed again. But you could read these unvoiced ambitions elsewhere, for instance in a production schedule that was twice as long as *Pale Rider*'s, a film that was, if anything, slightly larger in scale. You could see them in his casting of the other major roles. In a typical Eastwood film they would have been played by good, solid, relatively anonymous character men; in *Unforgiven* they were played by Gene Hackman, Morgan Freeman and Richard Harris, stars in their own right. You could discern them, too, in the physical production. Henry Bumstead's set for Big Whiskey, the miserable little Wyoming county seat, circa 1880, where most of the action was staged, contained no false fronts. Its buildings were solidly, expensively rooted on this land; every structure was fully practical, and all of the film's interiors were made here, not on a soundstage.

Above all you could measure Clint's seriousness by the remoteness and discomfort of the location. He always likes to make his movies far up-country, isolating himself with his cast and crew well away from distractions, personal and professional, where they can create their own private world. But he had outdone himself this time. Sited deep within the vastness of the E.P. Ranch in Alberta, Canada, Big Whiskey was some sixty miles southwest of the nearest major city, Calgary. If you had placed a camera atop its highest point, its windmill, you could have panned it 360 degrees without revealing the slightest evidence of modern civilization, not a house or a highway, not a power line or a railroad track.

This isolation imposed substantial hardships on the company, numbering about 150 at full strength, as it worked six-day weeks, many of them given over to night shoots that did not end until two in the morning. No one had family with them, and most crew members were quartered in High River, an unprepossessing small town, where the motels and restaurants offered minimal creature comforts. From there it was about twenty-five miles to the ranch gate, after which they were confronted with a long ride along a jolting, ungraded, single-track road hastily scraped across a high plain. It deposited you at a base camp, erected at the foot of the hill where Big Whiskey had been constructed. This was a circle of mobile homes and trailer-drawn temporary buildings, where the company tethered its horses, stored its costumes, took its meals and did its paperwork.

In his pursuit of authenticity, the director had banned motorized traffic between set and base camp (the only exception was the rarely used camera crane, which was mounted on a truck). Everyone moved up and down the hill on foot, on horseback or by hitching rides on the horse-drawn wagons that plodded between the two points when they weren't being used to dress a sequence. There was a practical reason for this; Clint didn't want to waste time erasing anachronistic tire tracks from the set's main street, which was constantly watered to keep it looking authentically muddy. But there was a psychological reason for it, too: A few minutes on a bouncing buckboard is a form of time travel, quickly jolting you out of the present and into the past.

The director was serenely content out here. "That's part of the appeal of a western," Clint said one sparkling September day. "You get out on location, the air is fabulous, like it is right here"—he paused and sniffed appreciatively—"and if you sat out here, if you didn't go back into town in the evenings, you'd eventually think, Yeah, this is the world for me. For a brief moment, whatever the schedule is, you're in another era, another time."

And, in this instance, Clint Eastwood was in a moral universe different from any that he had previously inhabited. When *Unforgiven* was released the following summer it was almost invariably tagged "a revisionist western." But that's not quite the right word for it. The first revisionists—Leone, Peckinpah and the rest—had slashed a wide, bloody—absurdist, if you will—swath through the genre. Their basic message, as Clint said while he was shooting, was that "life was sometimes extremely cheap—you know, you see a lot of nameless bodies falling off buildings and so forth."

Unforgiven cuts a narrower, deeper path through the form's conventions. None of its bodies are nameless. All its deaths count for some-thing. In that sense, it might better be termed a "re-revisionist" western, carefully supplying everyone with reasonable, carefully explicated mo-tives for their behavior, but bringing them to bloody chaos anyway. On its way to that conclusion, it casually, almost incidentally, subverts our comfortable expectation of stock western types and situations. This is a movie in which whores turn out not to be golden-hearted, but angry and vengeful; a movie in which a seemingly reasonable lawman turns out to be an ugly sadist who, unlike the reassuring peacekeeper of west-ern lore, is not the source of his community's stability, but of its chaos; a movie in which the celebrity gunfighter, before whose reputation all are supposed to tremble, is revealed to be an empty blowhard, and the seemingly psychotic adolescent, who aspires to similar fame, turns to mush when he actually kills someone. It is finally a movie in which the presumptive hero, lured out of retirement to right a wrong, does not find moral satisfaction in the act, but despair, rage and something very close to madness.

That figure, of course, is Clint's Will Munny. Once a killer of terri-fying mien and repute, he believes, when we meet him, that he has been reformed by the love of a good woman, though as we will learn there is more of escapism in his piety than true regeneration. His wife, more-over, has died, and the widower, trying to raise two children alone, is eking out a precarious living as a hog farmer when the young would-be gunfighter, styling himself the Schofield Kid (Jaimz Woolvett), seeks him out. He tells him that two drunken cowboys have brutally slashed a whore in Big Whiskey when she laughed at the "teensy little pecker" displayed by one of them. The other prostitutes, feeling that the sheriff, Little Bill Daggett (Hackman), has not punished them sufficiently, are offering a bounty for their execution. Will at first rejects the venture, then begins to see it as his last hope of escaping poverty. He asks Ned Logan (Freeman), his old partner in crime, now also retired, to accom-pany him, and meeting the kid on the trail they all make for Big Whiskey and their complicated fates.

They are about to learn (or perhaps one should say demonstrate) the several stupid reasons men drift into violence—out of simple greed (to some degree moving almost everyone in this story), out of macho pos-turing (the Kid), out of misapprehended reality (Munny, since rumor has vastly exaggerated the wrong done the prostitute, providing a con-venient rationale for his venality), out of misplaced loyalty (Ned, who is the most innocent, therefore the most tragic, figure in the story), out of oversimplified morality reinforced by psychopathy (Daggett), out of egotism and moral laziness (Harris's English Bob, the professional killer).

These last two figures require further comment. The sheriff is a clever and even attractive lunatic, using his rigid attitude toward law enforcement to justify, and a genial and folksy manner to disguise, a deeply sadistic spirit. It would be easy to see him as a small-town hypocrite, familiar for decades in popular fiction. But his soul is more deeply riven than that, so that it is finally impossible to say whether he is a fundamentally evil man with a useful capacity for good or, alternatively, a good man with a perversion that must will out. Whichever he is, he is also a premature gun-control advocate. Signs at the edge of town order visitors to surrender their firearms to him; what they do not say is that if strangers fail to comply, he will cheerfully beat them senseless. This is what he does to English Bob, who is a sort of deadly con artist, lording it over the provincials with his foreign accent and grandiloquent ways, but in reality a self-deluded coward.

"I like it that the good guys aren't all good and the bad guys aren't all bad," Clint said one morning on location, getting to the heart of the matter. "Everyone has their flaws and everyone has their rationale and a justification for what they do," he added, unconsciously echoing the unforgettable tag line—"In this world, everyone has his reasons"—from Jean Renoir's great comedy of mixed motives, *The Rules of the Game.*

The brutal encounter between Little Bill and English Bob (which takes place on July Fourth, tying violence and American nationhood together) establishes the film's dialectic. A confident moralist and a confident immoralist, they represent, respectively, the attitudes between which the more ambiguous bounty hunters, everyone else in this movie, will be caught and tortured. If only they could be so certain. . . .

The most significant of these others is Bob's one-man entourage, his "biographer," W. W. Beauchamp (Saul Rubinek). He represents all those westering hacks whose nineteenth-century dime novels and penny dreadfuls would become the source of most of the western movies' classic tropes. The symbol of everyone's desire to convert the mean realities of the frontier experience into inspiring national myth, he is, quite literally, a man who will print the legend instead of the truth. He will also abandon English Bob for Little Bill when he bests Bob, and at the end, when Will Munny defeats Daggett, he will try to attach himself to the man who has proved to have, in the writer's eyes, the largest star quality, for, yes, *Unforgiven* is also a meditation on celebrity.

Will's dubious triumph will be hard and desperately earned. The idyllic world he and his companions ride through on their way to Big Whiskey—verdant fields and forests, sparkling streams—disappears when they arrive. A storm is brawling across the hilltop, and we will not see it in a fresh morning light again, for there is no virtue in this village; *pace*

John Wayne, it is as corrupt as Lago in *High Plains Drifter*. Moreover, Will arrives there shaking with ague. While his friends visit the whores on the second floor of Greely's saloon he settles down to nurse a drink and himself. There Daggett, showing off for Beauchamp—he grows more brutal and self-regarding under the writer's avid attention—identifies Will as the kind of saddle tramp he will have none of in his town, correctly accuses him of failing to abide by the firearms ordinance and beats him unmercifully. Will is obliged to crawl for the door, and the next we see of him is his being nursed back from near death by Ned.

We understand that he has been seized by something more terrible than a bad case of the flu and a beating's aftereffects. He has been hallucinating for days, confronting in his fevered dreams his past sins, visions of his dead wife rotting in her grave, the angel of death beckoning him. It is a soul sickness that is harrowing him.

Will Munny has been two quite distinct men in his past: first a drunken and near-psychotic killer, then the pig farmer piously mouthing the platitudes his wife taught him. The former parodied the western clichés of badness, the latter its clichés of goodness, with the man we have seen up to now caught between them and rendered defenseless by his confusion.

The fever burns away that confusion. He emerges from it, like the figures Clint played in his other major westerns, reborn. His killing skills are returned to him, and his piety is stripped away. He is possessed now with the knowledge of original sin—death in his dreams had serpent's eyes—and he accepts the fact that redemption is not found in a state of passive goodness, but is a lifelong struggle fallen man cannot escape. He is also reborn—and it is here the movie claims its greatest originality—as a modern man. That is to say, he is cursed with guilty self-consciousness, haunted by the knowledge that all actions carry with them the threat of terrible, unintended consequences.

Witness the events that follow his recuperation. We know, though the bounty hunters do not, that a distinction should be drawn between the two lads they seek to kill. Mike, who actually slashed Delilah, bears the largest guilt and is the least remorseful. Davey, his companion, tried to stop him and has tried to make amends for their act. Naturally, it is the latter that Will and his companions come upon first—in a box canyon where he is branding strays with some other ranch hands. It is Ned, expert with his long-range rifle, who must try to make the kill. But ambiguity renders his hand unsteady, and he manages only to wound Davey's horse, which falls on the boy, breaking his leg. Will takes the rifle from Ned and after several tries manages to wound Davey mortally. It is a pathetic sequence, with the boy crying for mercy and Will committing nothing less than cold-blooded murder—the only such crime a Clint Eastwood character has ever perpetrated. It ends with the dying Davey begging for water and Will shouting to the cowboys to give it to him while he holds his fire—compassion rendered feckless by its belatedness.

At the end of this terrible confrontation, a broken Ned deserts Will and the Kid. Riding away, he is apprehended by one of Daggett's posses, then flogged to death by the sheriff, trying to obtain information about his companion—another prolonged and undeserved death. The moral balances of this movie are closely calculated, but always very brutally achieved.

Now it is the Schofield Kid's turn for comeuppance. It has long since been established that he is not Billy the Kid, just a nearsighted wanna-be, looking for pulp-fiction immortality. But at last he must face the consequences of his desire. He kills ugly, catching Mike at his most vulnerable, when he is squatting in an outhouse, and at morally vivifying close range, where even his myopic eyes can take in the horror of violent death.

Later, we find him and Will on a hilltop, storm clouds gathering around them, the boy sucking on a liquor bottle, trying unsuccessfully to summon up his lost bravado. Finally, he breaks down: "It don't seem real. How he's dead. How he ain't gonna breathe no more. Never. Or the other one neither. On account of just pullin' a trigger." Will understands. Looking not at the boy but into the gray distance, he speaks the film's most obvious moral: "It's a hell of a thing, killing a man. You take away everything he's got and everything he's ever gonna have." The youth responds with a last desperate rationale: "Well, I guess they had it comin'." To which Will replies flatly, "We've all got it comin', Kid."

Got it coming stupidly in all likelihood. Not one death, not one act of cruelty, so far shown in this movie is justifiable, only rationalizable. And now it is time for Little Bill Daggett to learn this truth. Ned must be avenged. His body, lit by torchlights, is being displayed in an open coffin in front of Greely's saloon. Inside, Daggett and his deputies are planning to continue their search for the remaining killers. Out of the darkness the saddle tramp Daggett once so casually brutalized appears. He is carrying a shotgun. Unhesitatingly he kills Skinny, the saloon keeper, for making a spectacle of Ned's corpse. Now, at last, the lawman recognizes him: "You be William Munny out of Missouri, a killer of women and children." "I've killed everything that walks and crawls," comes the hoarse reply, "and now I'm here to kill you, Little Bill, for what you done to my friend." When Will's rifle misfires, Daggett shouts to his men to shoot. But for the first time in his life Will is armored in righteousness as well as with a backup pistol. Magically, he guns down all the deputies and wounds Daggett, the improbability of the achievement signifying that he is now a man possessed—if not by the devil, then by impulses darker than he has ever known. Will turns to the bar for a drink. Beauchamp jabbers journalistic questions at him, like how did he know whom to shoot first. "I was lucky in the order," Will says numbly, then adds, with ineffable sadness, "I've always been lucky when it comes to killin' folks."

During this conversation we become aware that Daggett is conscious, and trying to draw on Will. Now Will notes that and advances on the prone lawman, holding a shotgun within inches of his head. "I don't deserve this," Daggett says calmly, "I was building a house"—as if his end, domestic tranquillity, justified his violent means to it. That is what John Ford and John Wayne once believed, and so they helped teach us all to believe it. Will Munny, himself a man who has tried to build a peaceful haven, can no longer believe it: "Deserve's got nothing to do with it," he says. "I'll see you in Hell, William Munny," Daggett replies, conceding nothing, even in his last moment. "Yeah," says Will, not at all disagreeing. We don't actually see him blow Little Bill's head off. The camera averts its eye. We hear the blast in darkness.

Will turns to leave. There is a groan, a stir from one of the downed deputies. As he exits, Will, without looking, flips a shot in the direction of the sound (it's a trick Clint used long ago in the Leone films), and it ceases. Gaining the street he yells mad threats at Big Whiskey. If its citizens try to stop him he will kill them all. And their children. And their dogs. On the street, in the rain, the American flag, which snapped so jauntily during English Bob's calvary, now hangs soaked and limp behind Will.

His rage is not really directed at the town. It is directed at his own fate, and at the chaotic universe. One thinks that as he looked into Little Bill's eyes in their last moment of life, absurd compulsion read absurd compulsion, a shared recognition of an awful kinship. The moral edge granting Will Munny his victory is, both lives fully considered, paperthin. We've all got it coming, Kid, because we are all guilty of something. Is it possible that Clint is guilty of making the first western to carry Hitchcock's basic moral?

Or is it possibly Kafka's? In a symposium attempting to define what we mean when we so casually describe something as "kafkaesque," the literary critic George Steiner cited a passage from *Unforgiven* in which, after Little Bill has savaged Will, Strawberry Alice accuses him of beating an innocent man. "Innocent of what?" the sheriff replies. This, Steiner said, is "one of the most tremendous summaries of Kafka I have ever heard. Those three words . . . are almost a password to our condition."

Certainly they are a password to this movie. Whether one defines the human condition as guilt omnipresent or innocence unobtainable, it comes to the same thing. We have no trouble seeing Will M. as Josef K., seeing Little Bill Daggett as the keeper of a dark castle, or as the judge at an endless trial where no one knows exactly what he has done to deserve such hard punishment. And we have no difficulty seeing *Unforgiven* as the most complex statement of those modernist and nihilistic themes Clint Eastwood had been pursuing since he first picked up their trail on Sergio Leone's sets.

In the end he rejected a conclusion he had himself proposed, in which Delilah, the cut whore, and Will take up a life together. The most he would concede his character was a return to sunshine and fresh air, to hard-won and perhaps more realistically apprehended normalcy. We see him last as we saw him first, at his farm, on the hilltop by his wife's grave. Then he pops off the screen—disappears into thin air, in the patented Eastwood manner. An epigraph tells us no one knows what became of Will Munny, though it was rumored that he moved to San Francisco where, under an assumed name, he prospered in dry goods. And, we imagine, in that anonymity that is the last—and proper— refuge of a hero who knows that heroism is nearly always an accident, a lie, a media fantasy.

★   ★   ★

Unforgiven is obviously a delicately checked and balanced movie and, given its view of human nature, about as dark as a genre film can be. Yet it does not play glumly. In part that is due to the writing. Very few modern anachronisms mar the formalities of its nineteenth-century diction (or the antique quaintness of its slang), which fall freshly and often funnily on the contemporary ear. Partly it is due to the waywardness with which the story is developed. We can sometimes predict its broad movements, but rarely the quirky spin of its incidents. Partly it is due to the richness of the acting—Clint's slightly "creepy" (Vincent Canby's word) piety giving way in slow stages to equally creepy vengefulness; Harris's wickedly fraudulent airs and graces; Freeman's stoic quizzicality as the only fully sane presence in the narrative; Woolvett's volatile innocence; Rubinek's underlying romanticism, more dangerous than cynicism; above all, Hackman's beamish menace, the psychopath as good ole shit-kicker. Partly it was due to its visual style—"classicism at its most august," as Richard Jameson would later write. There was, as he said, "something more" in some of its shots "than any interpretation can account for. The kind of something more we associate with the more magisterial moments of Murnau, Mizoguchi, Ford."

This classicism disarmingly masked supreme duplicity. *Unforgiven* offers a soberly formal presentation of deadly waywardness, satisfying our yearning for moral seriousness while at the same time obliging our anarchic desire for crazy action in a movie that constantly implies importance without ever seeming self-important, as most aspiring American movies do.

In work, this production had, as well, a serendipitous air that contributed to its ultimate success in ways that are also not fully analyzable. For example, when Clint called Richard Harris to offer him his role, the actor was watching a tape of *High Plains Drifter,* and he found the coincidence—not to mention what he quickly saw was a short but showy part—irresistible. Similarly, Gene Hackman had at first rejected the film—he felt, he said, that he had been in too many mindlessly violent movies—but Clint urged him to reread and rethink, which he was doing around the time of the Rodney King incident. Hackman perceived (the obviously unintentional) analogy between Daggett's little police force and the LAPD and signed on to play Big Whiskey's version of its chief, Daryl Gates, an analogy underscored by the casting of a black actor in the role of his most brutally put-upon victim. Indeed, one morning Hackman excused himself from an interview saying he had to go and do "my Rodney King scene," the sequence in which he supervises the torture of Ned Logan. The script even offered a perfect role—right down to the hair coloring—for Frances Fisher, who played Strawberry Alice, the relentless prostitute who organizes the act of vengeance from which all else derives.

It was a sunny shoot—literally. It soon became clear that "Malpaso weather" is not a purely American phenomenon. The days stayed pleasant even in northwest Canada with winter approaching. The many Eastwood veterans on the set sensed a slight mood shift in their director, a willingness to rehearse a little longer than usual, make more takes, do more coverage of complex scenes, and wondered, some of them, if this might be a farewell of sorts—to westerns, to Clint's directing and acting in the same picture, they couldn't say quite what. This was largely because his day-to-day manner was unchanged from the past—soft-spoken, good-humored, unhurried. Whatever he was thinking about his future, whatever exhaustion he felt as the long weeks wore on—"you do get brain tired, especially answering questions, thousands upon thousands of questions, all day long, and having to make decisions"—he kept to himself.

He was still a man who refused to begin a scene with the traditional cry of "Action." He thinks it jolts the actors, interfering with their concentration. Instead, he'll whisper something like "Whenever you're ready" to start things off.

He was still a man who trusted the skills of his seasoned cast and crew and gave them room to deploy them. "It's better if people can anticipate; you don't have to sit there and explain every detail. You can say, 'I'd like a shot that dramatically gives me this effect,' and then the camera department will go 'What about this?' or 'What about that?' and all of a sudden they're making suggestions that are right in line with what you're thinking about. So it's not really an auteur thing, it's an ensemble."

He was still a decisive director. As he once said to an interviewer, "if it works immediately, you've got to have enough wherewithal to say, 'That's it. That's good. That's what I want.' Because you have to have the picture in your mind before you make it. . . . If you don't, you're not a director, you're just a guesser."

He was still a director who believes boredom is the enemy of quality, believes as his executive producer, David Valdes, put it, "that moving quickly on the set, breaking the angle, changing a lens, helps everybody keep moving a little faster and that translates onto celluloid."

Above all, he remained a director appalled by noisy hysteria. "You'll never find a bullhorn on an Eastwood set," Lloyd Nelson, who had been his script supervisor for two decades, said one day. Instead, you'll find that stillness about which a wondering and grateful Richard Harris never stopped talking: "Nobody has to shout, nobody says 'Quiet please' because everybody *is* quiet." He added, "I've made forty-something movies, and one of the things that compels me not to work anymore has been the general sense of chaos on these big Hollywood pictures." Here, by contrast, he found himself surrounded "by the comfort and security of an organization that is absolutely working like a clock. Nothing goes wrong. And if something goes wrong it's dealt with with absolute calmness and authority."

And, if possible, a joke. The scenes in Greely's saloon were hard on everyone. They were shot at night, on a set that was small and jammed with actors and technicians, with fog machines befouling the air as they pumped out what the camera would read as the haze created by cigar smoke and a wood-burning stove. Moreover, the staging—of Little Bill beating Will, of the final deadly confrontation between them—was intricate and time-consuming. The company was cramped in there for the better part of a week. A crucial shot, obviously, was of Daggett knocking Will to the floor and kicking the stuffings out of him, after which he turned to the bar and poured himself a drink. When he and Hackman had completed this action to Clint's satisfaction, the director, from his prone position, rasped "Pour me one of those," instead of calling "Cut."

A couple of nights later, the situation was more serious: In the climactic shoot-out, the blanks in Clint's pistol kept jamming. These mishaps spoiled several takes—and Clint's concentration as well; he blew up, cursing the quarter-load blank cartridges, which lacked the power to clear the weapon's chamber. As soon as Eddie Aionna, his longtime property master, replaced them with half loads, the gun worked properly, and Clint was restored to himself. "Take that!" he cried triumphantly once the close-up of him blasting three or four subsidiary bad guys into eternity was safely in the can—the B-movie cliché banishing the accumulated tension.

"When the day comes that I don't enjoy it, I've socked away just enough to maybe be able to coast it out," Clint said one day, comically understating the resources available for his sunset years, but confirming what an eyewitness to this production had begun to suspect, that Clint had not so much thought of this film as a farewell but more so as a kind of test. If with a script of this moral weight and actors of this professional weight he could not be happy in his work and its results, well, then, yes, it might be time to reexamine some premises.

Not even a desperate conclusion to this happy time would cause him to do so. Even Malpaso weather does not last forever, and with just two days left on the schedule the first blizzard of the winter was forecast: twelve inches of snow, with a week of freezing weather to follow. Crisis. Should they proceed as planned, hoping the weatherman was wrong or the storm would be delayed? Or should they—could they—devise a crash schedule that would cram two days' work into one? Valdes proposed a virtually nonstop shoot, with just one four-hour break for sleep, no meals included. It was a dangerous plan. If the storm did not materialize, he would be faced with a huge, unnecessary bill for golden time and meal penalties. On the other hand, if the snows came, the cost would be infinitely higher, for they would have to hold everyone on salary waiting for a break in the weather. He and Clint decided to plunge ahead.

The ground froze. The water in the rain machines froze (among other sequences, they were doing Clint's storm-tossed exit from Big Whiskey). The star's teeth were chattering so badly he had trouble saying his lines. In the wee hours of the final night a delegation from the crew demanded a pizza run, and the normally unflappable Valdes blew his stack. "We're in bumfuck, Alberta," he yelled, "and there's no Domino's around the corner." They got their last shot as dawn broke, and the first snowflakes of a blizzard, every bit as severe as predicted, began to fall. A few days later a small group moved on to Sonora, California, and its narrow-gauge railroad, for the sequences in which English Bob arrives in town. There, at last, the picture wrapped.

★ ★ ★

By mid-January, just two months after completion of principal photography, Clint and Joel Cox had a rough cut ready to screen. Even without music—Clint would contribute a theme to Lennie Niehaus's very spare score—the picture played powerfully. There was some talk, apparently, among Warners executives about asking him to trim it slightly, but no one had the nerve to broach the subject. Clint agreed to make an appearance at Sho-West, the annual Las Vegas convention of exhibitors, where all the studios present samples of their forthcoming wares at expensive, star-studded parties. *Unforgiven* was slightly misrepresented in the Warner Bros. product reel, which cannily combined violent moments from previous Eastwood westerns with similar shots from the new one to suggest a return to Clint's most profitable territory. It went over very well.

The film itself did the same when Clint invited David Webb Peoples to the studio to see it in finished form. It was their first meeting, and the writer, fearing the worst, sat well apart from Clint so his reactions could not be read. He noticed, but made nothing of, a few small changes in his script, principally because everything he really cared about was present. Peoples had the experience, uncanny for a screenwriter, of seeing his work come to the screen essentially as he had written it; only, he said, better. "I'd never seen or imagined anything so dark and relentless and powerful," he later wrote. "Without changing the words, Clint made the script . . . tougher, more uncompromising, without slickness, and the heart was still in it." Like Clint, who never takes them, Peoples is opposed to possessory credits, but graciously added: "If ever there was a picture that belonged to its director it is Clint Eastwood's *Unforgiven.*" In Clint's mind, though, it belonged to his mentors. He placed a dedication on the closing credits: "For Sergio and Don" (Siegel had died in 1991).

Peoples's response was heartening. But neither it, nor the enthusiasm of other early viewers, affected the prerelease campaign for the picture, which Clint insisted be low-key. He did not want to stir excessive expectations for the movie, or openly acknowledge his own. He also believed it was a picture that would profit by letting people come away from it with a sense of discovery.

In press previews of the summer's releases, *Unforgiven* was scarcely mentioned. In the spring all eyes were fixed on the supposedly erotic thriller *Basic Instinct;* in the summer the media were transfixed by high-risk sequels—*Lethal Weapon 3, Batman Returns, Patriot Games*—and low-rent comedies like *Sister Act* and *Wayne's World.* No one was paying much attention to an oater, all of whose stars were in their fifties and sixties.

But *Unforgiven* was lucky in the order. There comes a time in early August when reviewers are overdosed on mindlessness, and a portion of the public, too, finds itself yearning for the finer things—or, at least, for something structurally coherent and dramatically meaningful. It's not a large window of opportunity, but it exists, and *Unforgiven* slipped through it, emerging with ecstatic reviews.

Besides "revisionist" the word most frequently attached to the film by reviewers was "masterpiece." Precisely because the movie so openly questioned western conventions, it allowed critics a chance to parade their analytical skills and their historical knowledge. More important, Clint was challenging them in a way they thought appropriate to him. He was not stretching as he had with *White Hunter* or *Bird* or *Honkytonk Man* into territories they believed to be foreign to him. Rather, as with *Tightrope,* he was exploring the limits of a genre in which his authority was unquestionable.

As it turned out, he was shrewd in the order, too. Let us take him at his word: It was purely an actor's choice to wait until he had aged into this part. But let us also note that he had now attained an age when a leading player, if he is still vigorous and active (and lucky) may begin to achieve legendary status. This role, with its tragic overtones and its sum-marizing undertones, called out for such an acknowledgment. Richard Corliss caught this sense of things very well. He described *Unforgiven* as "Eastwood's meditation on age, repute, courage, heroism—on all those burdens he has been carrying with such grace for decades. On Clintessence." Possibly some of these preoccupations might seem—es-pecially to the young—old-fashioned. "But to anyone who appreciates what Clint Eastwood has meant to the movies, old-fashioned is just an-other way of saying classic."

Corliss noticed something else as well, that the movie took its time "letting you watch Clint turn into Clint"—that is, into the righteous avenger the popular audience always wants him to be. But when the transformation was finally achieved it was "not thrilling but scary," a de-scent into temporary insanity. In short, there was something for every-one here—irony for the enlightened, a measure of simple kick-ass bliss for the groundlings, who did not notice—or care—in exactly what spirit Will Munny achieved his rough justice.

And so they all came in their millions. The film grossed a solid $15 million on its first weekend, leading the competition and giving Clint his best opening in six years. Moreover, it had legs. The film stayed in profitable release for about nine months, while the press, which had so largely ignored the film prior to release, tumbled over itself with follow-ups, reactions, second thoughts. Clearly, *Unforgiven* was going to be a serious contender for critical awards, especially when the late fall and early winter produced less-than-daunting competition.

On the whole, the film did very well in the Oscar preliminaries, winning four major prizes from the National Society of Film Critics and five from the Los Angeles Film Critics. Golden Globes were also acquired. The only disappointment was the New York Film Critics Circle, where, Hackman aside, *Unforgiven* was narrowly defeated in all the major categories. The big winner was *The Crying Game,* in which an IRA hitman falls in love with a transvestite, whose surprise revelation of his sex was a gimmick so cleverly managed that it was widely mistaken for art. Clint, among others, wondered if this late starter was going to emerge as an Oscar spoiler. Early on the morning of February 17 (5:30 a.m., in order to maximize p.m. coverage in the eastern time zones), when the Academy nominations were announced, *Unforgiven* received eight, two more than the Irish film, one less than *Howard's End,* with the other best-picture nominations including *A Few Good Men* and *Scent of a Woman,* humanistically flavored dramas of the kind usually favored by the Academy.

Clint was, he said, asleep in Sun Valley when the nominations were announced, receiving word of the results from a message left on his answering machine. "When I heard, I thought, well that's nice," he told a reporter. Surpassing cool! Though there were some among his friends, who know that he is a late sleeper, but who also knew how keenly Clint wanted this recognition, who did not entirely credit it.

If he did snooze through the Oscar announcements, it was his last inattentive moment until the morning after the awards. Just as he had refused all along to admit how much this film meant to him, he now refused to admit how much he wanted this recognition for it. He would just quietly do everything possible to assure the right outcome. The strategy was to remain tastefully present in the minds of Oscar voters, without looking as if he was desperate for their favor. Something like a half-dozen major profiles appeared in important magazines during the first three months of 1993 when Academy members had their ballots in hand. He sat for television interviews with Barbara Walters and David

Frost and appeared in a retrospective documentary about his career. He accepted a Director of the Year Award from Sho-West, a career achievement award from the American Cinema Editors, something from the Publicists Guild and a California Governor's Award for the Arts—much meaningless metalwork, but reminders to the Academy that others were reckoning seriously with him.

This effort was complicated by a certain ambivalence about the Academy. He was a member, naturally, but a distant one, called upon to make contributions to various activities but never invited into its inner councils. Consequently he had come to think of it as a self-protective and exclusionary institution. "I'm popular with the public," he told a reporter when there was talk of an acting nomination for *Tightrope,* "but that doesn't make me popular at the country club." In the same interview, he said, "You've got the Golden Globe crowd who don't know a thing about acting and who don't even try to learn. And then you've got the Academy Awards group, which is more political and so often gives [Oscars] to actors who don't have popular appeal and therefore aren't threatening—people like F. Murray Abraham or Ben Kingsley." He wasn't putting them down, but what about Paul Newman, at that time a frequent nominee, but not a winner?

For that matter, what about Cary Grant and two of his best directors, Alfred Hitchcock and Howard Hawks, and all the other distinguished nonwinners of the past, men and women whose long and legendary careers far outshone many of those who had enjoyed Oscar's fleeting favor? And what about the fact that no pure western had ever won the best-picture prize? Among the sixty-four winners to date the genre was represented only by the decrepit *Cimarron* of 1930, which had men on horseback, but no classic western themes, and *Dances with Wolves,* which an English reviewer neatly dubbed "the first Perrier western."

So his inner conflict played out. If a friend tried to engage him in speculation about the balloting, he would always retreat, saying how crazy it made him, pondering imponderables. He focused, instead, on the small pleasantries of the award season, like starstruck Emma Thompson. The effervescent English actress, nominated (and eventually a winner) for her work in *Howard's End,* kept turning up at the same ceremonies he did, professing herself thrilled to be in his company. When she was growing up, her father, who was also an actor, kept taking her to see Clint Eastwood pictures and telling her that that was what acting was all about—not letting it show.

Then three weeks before the Academy Awards ceremony, he received concrete encouragement from the Directors Guild. Its award banquet is traditionally a long sit, especially for nominees, and Clint found himself growing particularly irritable with a nearby table of Warners executives, laughing and chatting easily, not in the least sharing his angst. It was not until later that he learned the Guild has a satellite banquet in New York, which takes place three hours earlier than the one in Los Angeles, and that a studio representative attending it had already informed management that Clint was the winner.

The Guild award is a nearly infallible Oscar predictor in the director category. But Clint was taking no chances. On March 29, the night of the Academy Awards, he showed up wearing a slightly geeky red leather bow tie. It had been fashioned by an extra on *Bird,* and Clint had sworn to wear it should he ever be nominated.

He ran into Jack Nicholson as they headed toward their seats. His occasional golfing partner, due to present the best-picture prize, said he was sure Clint would win—"You should have had it for *Bird,"* he said. Clint hoped he was right. Early in the evening Hackman and Joel Cox won statuettes. He hoped that was a good sign. Later, Neil Jordan beat out Peoples for the best original screenplay award. He hoped that was not a bad sign. He would remember glancing at his mother, wondering if he had brought her all this way, subjected her ailing heart to all this pressure, for nothing. Actually, of course, that loss was good news; the screenplay award is a customary consolation prize for nonwinners of the best-picture prize. But naturally his anxiety grew again when Al Pacino beat him out as best actor, though again this signaled nothing important about *Unforgiven.* It was the Academy belatedly rewarding an actor whom it had nominated five times for this prize, twice as a supporting actor—for his highly mannered performance in *Scent of a Woman.*

Now it was time for the director's award. And he says he could tell from Barbra Streisand's grin that he had won, even before she read out his name. He was barely back in his seat when Nicholson, mercifully cutting out his scripted jokes, was calling his name. He mimed a golf stroke as Clint stepped on-stage. Clint mimed one in return. He did something unprecedented; he thanked the critics for their support. And he remembered Steve Ross, who had "predicted this outcome" not long before he died the previous December.

Then he was backstage, fielding questions from the press. Somebody asked how it felt to win a prize so late in his career, and he said he thought there was a danger in winning too young: "You wear a monocle and leggings and walk around thinking you're a great genius."

He dropped by the Governor's Ball then headed for Nicky Blair's restaurant. He had meant this as a sentimental occasion. Blair had been a young actor with Clint, plying his out-of-work colleagues with homemade pasta, and Clint had never forgotten. When Blair opened his restaurant, Clint was one of the opening-night customers. Now he thought it would be nice to celebrate at his old pal's place. He invited a carefully chosen list of friends, family and *Unforgiven* coworkers. Alas, the studio got wind of it. This would not do. Where were the A-list names? Where was the press? Suddenly the crowd was three or four times the restaurant's capacity, and suddenly Clint was trapped with an endless succession of interviewers. Even when they let him go, he could scarcely make his way through the crush. By that time he was thoroughly befogged.

Asked how he felt the morning after, he simply said, "Tired." Asked to analyze his victory, "industry insiders" made much of the fact that it was Clint's turn, making the well-worn point that if you hang in long enough you are bound to achieve official recognition from haute Hollywood. Even Clint was not immune to that idea. "I think it helped me that I had a couple of years where nothing much was happening with me. They said, 'Hey, he's back.'"

These are basic realities. But they ignore the more interesting ones: that this was one of the rare occasions when the best American movie of the year actually won the best-picture Oscar; that for once that picture was neither slick escapism nor a fake-serious hymn to the human spirit, that it was, if anything, the opposite, a dirge to all that was dispiriting in human nature. Which is to say that somehow Clint achieved his largest triumph for his most dangerous and subversive work. A couple of weeks after the Academy Awards, *Unforgiven*'s cumulative domestic gross reached $100 million. That, too, was unprecedented for him.

SEVENTEEN

NATURAL EMINENCE

Will Munny was finally lost in the chaos of *Unforgiven,* blotted up, blotted out. No less than the men he left dead, it stripped from him all that he had and all that he would ever have. That figure evanescing before our eyes in its last shot took with him as well the hard, cold core of a screen character. That wearily vengeful redeemer of what little was left of the American Dream has not appeared again in a Clint Eastwood movie.

Will's last option—a new name, a new life—is not available to movie stars. They are lifers, without hope of parole from their celebrity, which finally includes their audience's unreasonable disappointment when, visibly, stars fail to resist the ravages of time. If they are wise and graceful—and very few are when the burden of the years begins to weigh on them—their best hope is to acknowledge, with what grace they can muster, the cost and limits that age places on heroism.

It requires a certain gumption to follow this course; you never can tell how people will respond when reality is imposed on their fantasies. Face-lifts (and doubles for the action scenes) have a certain cowardly appeal. Unless, of course, you have all along based your career on brutal frankness. Then you have no choice but to act your age.

There is, however, no law against acting it in the best possible light. In the three movies Clint has released since *Unforgiven,* wistfulness often replaces willfulness, vulnerability substitutes for vengefulness, and the play of memory preoccupies his characters at least as much as the drive for mastery. Two of these films leave him frustrated and disconsolate, not necessarily wiser than he was when he entered the narrative, but infinitely sadder, a condition not unknown to men and women who undertake daring or strenuous adventures late in life.

These movies also represent a change in Clint's approach to the filmmaking process. As we have seen, he learned from *Unforgiven* the value of money well spent—on a richer mise-en-scène than he had usually offered, on acting colleagues of significant stature. They commanded attention in ways that the pictures he had "made for a price," as the Hollywood saying goes, did not. Most important, he could see that this slightly more conventional approach to his craft relieved him of a burden. Despite his huge central role in the creation of *Unforgiven* he had not been obliged to carry it to success single-handed.

Take, for example, *In the Line of Fire*. Budgeted at close to $40 million, it was far and away the most expensive movie to which he had ever lent his talents—"lent" being the operative word. It was not a Malpaso production, and though a few of Clint's people worked on it, production responsibility was entirely vested with Castle Rock, with Columbia Pictures financing and distributing. Clint was unquestionably the star of the movie; if it failed, he would take much of the blame for it. But he was operating here within a well-calculated commercial package that placed beneath him the kind of wide, closely woven net other stars of his stature expected as a matter of course, but which he had rarely enjoyed.

In essence *In the Line of Fire,* which was released in the summer of 1993, is a deadly, darkly funny, two-handed game played by Clint's Frank Horrigan and John Malkovich's Mitch Leary. The former is a Secret Service agent haunted by his failure, thirty years earlier, to react in time to save John F. Kennedy's life. The latter is eventually identified as a one-time CIA operative twisted into psychosis by his grievances against the agency, against government in general, and therefore determined to kill the current occupant of the White House. Theirs is an intimate duel, its winner to be determined by which man best reads the other's mind. But it is played out against the background of an election campaign, all jostling crowds, primary colors and brassy music, which impart to the movie the kind of glossy production values that are in themselves an attraction.

Casting is of a piece with the film's careful mounting. Malkovich is every bit Hackman's peer, but far more obviously than that canny underplayer, he represents a style that critic Kenneth Turan called "instinctively adversarial" to Clint's. Having honed his chops in Chicago's Steppenwolf company, he was an actor known for his bold, black, utterly unpredictable comic effects, which make his essential menace all the more terrifying. Adopting an absurdly languid manner, issuing his taunts and threats in a whispery drawl, he turns the movie into an aesthetic contest as well as a conflict between good and evil.

Rene Russo as Lilly Raines, the much younger Secret Service agent drawn into a bantering, ultimately affecting love affair with Frank, also represents a new force in the Eastwood universe. He had occasionally traded quips with a woman on an equal opportunity basis before, but never in quite the same romantic spirit that he did here (some critics invoked Hepburn and Tracy for comparison's sake).

But it was not entirely, or even primarily, packaging that drew Clint to this project. It was Frank Horrigan, that complex mass of cross-references. The first and most basic of these is to Clint himself. Frank describes himself to Lilly as a "white, piano-playing, heterosexual male over the age of fifty" and at various points acknowledges that both his slang and his come-ons are slightly outmoded. (His first words to her are: "The secretaries are getting prettier and prettier," to which she replies with a line Russo says Clint invented, "And the field agents are getting older and older.") That thumbnail description obviously fits the real-life Clint, and we can certainly imagine him—any male of his age—making the kind of innocently sexist gaffe that initiates this relationship. Unquestionably the gentle jazz Frank plays on the piano in an attempt to seduce her—it works—is well within the actor's off-screen repertoire, too.

These self-referential passages are handled with disarming casualness; it is the principal device by which the film evades the more typical fate of the big-budget action movie, which is to turn into a runaway machine. But there is a larger fascination in the film's subversions of Clint's on-screen persona. Frank is, to be sure, another loner living in an apartment untouched by female hands, his long-gone experiment in family life lost to professional exigencies. But he is also the first law enforcement officer Clint ever played who is not in some way disaffected from his professional life. He is contentedly at home within the organization he serves. All his professional conflicts are with outsiders, most notably the president's political handlers, who think Frank's caution (and precautions) are harming the president's image and his reelection campaign.

More interesting still, Frank Horrigan's first obligation, unlike, say, Harry Callahan's, is to self-sacrifice, not self-assertion. For a Secret Service agent is sworn to violate the most basic of all human instincts—the survival instinct—to throw himself recklessly into harm's way if his president (or other distinguished charges) is assailed. His apotheosis is not firing the decisive bullet, but taking it. It captured Clint's imagination, this reversed definition of heroism: "If anybody told me I had to jump in front of somebody and be shot instead, I'd say, 'You've got me confused with somebody else.'" It challenged him as an actor: "That mentality, that you take the bullet for somebody you might not even respect, is very hard to understand, but at the same time admirable." And he sensed that it was a gift to him as a star, always on the lookout for variations on his basic themes: "You know, it's always appealing to play a character who has to overcome himself as well as an obstacle."

There is one final cross-reference, perhaps the most significant of all, to consider. As the critic Howard Hampton noted, "The operative mode . . . is playback: Leary pushing Horrigan's buttons the same way *Dirty Harry*'s Scorpio Killer pushed Harry's (and the audience's)—only with far more élan and psychological sophistication (Malkovich has much better buttons at his disposal, in terms of both script and acting technique, than poor drooling Andy Robinson did)."

This striking resemblance, however, contains a striking reversal. It is *In the Line of Fire*'s heavy, not its hero, who feels himself victimized by a bureaucracy. As Leary points out, it was the CIA that made him what he is today, a perfectly poised, perfectly heartless killer, then turned him out when the Cold War thawed and it had no further use for the talents it conspired to create. There are, he says, no causes worth fighting for anymore. "All that's left is the game," he tells Frank. "I'm on offense. You're on defense." And why does he initiate play? Well, as revenge of course. But also "to punctuate the dreariness."

Their connection, to be sure, is accidental. Working a counterfeiting case, Frank and his partner stumble on the assassin's lair, but Leary (who at first calls himself Booth, as in John Wilkes, because the man had "flair, panache") is delighted. He knows Frank by reputation and knows he will prove a worthy foe. "Fate has brought us together," he says. "I can't get over the irony."

He loves such high-flying palaver, our Mitch, and he has a nice line in weary intellectuality. He satirically quotes the famous "I have a rendezvous with death" line to Frank in one of their creepy phone conversations. When the latter identifies Alan Seeger as its author, Mitch sneers, "It's a bad poem, Frank." Which, as it happens, is true—like a lot of his cynicism. It is that, finally, which sets him apart from the ever-growing filmography of sniper-psychos; he's a sinuous stylist of evil.

Frank, too, is a much more worked-out figure than Harry is. He is cooler, wryer, much less clenched. His psychic wound—his failure in Dealey Plaza—is widely known, openly worn, unlike Harry's never-explained damage. He is, as he says to Lilly, "a living legend, the only active agent who ever lost a president." The line contains another slant rhyme to Clint's own status, but more important it signals healthy self-awareness beyond, say, Harry Callahan's reach. Mitch, however, is betting that, deep down, Frank is truly his double, a man whose loyalty to the system has also been ill rewarded, a man who may, therefore, have reason to throw its game. Or, conversely, overplay it and make mistakes out of an anxious need to redeem himself.

One does not want to press these notions of gaming and doubling too far. The movie doesn't. But they are there, just as they were in *Dirty Harry*. The older picture, though, played them out in a hotter, harsher climate, whereas there is a certain breezy slickness about *In the Line of Fire*. Whether or not this is an improvement is debatable. *Dirty Harry* ran on its rawness. That is what made it controversial; that is what has kept it lodged in people's minds all this time. *In the Line of Fire* does not make that kind of impact.

But then, how many movies do? For that matter, how many action films, these days, achieve its pleasurable lightness of being? How many of them play so knowingly and cleverly with a star persona? How many of them offer supporting performances as wily as Malkovich's? How many of them blend menace, romance, action, humor and impeccably gathering suspense so deftly?

It is not nothing, this kind of Hollywood professionalism, and it is derived, in part, from determined commitment to the project by its producer, Jeff Apple, and the writer of its final screenplay, Jeff Maguire. The former had nursed the idea since Lyndon Johnson's day, when he first witnessed a presidential motorcade and found himself fascinated by the men protecting Johnson. He commissioned his first script for the film something like a decade before it was produced. Maguire came aboard as a replacement writer and took the script through many drafts without much reward. On the day he heard that it was finally going to be produced, he also heard from the electric company—with a shut-off notice. At that time he told reporters he and his wife were packing for a retreat to New England and some less frustrating profession.

The problem Apple and Maguire kept encountering was, frankly, ageism. Studio readers wanted this to be a story about a younger man, so that they could cast a hot young stud in the lead (never mind that this would have eliminated the Kennedy back story that lends the film its poignancy).

Curiously, the last studio to consider it was Warner Bros., and that's when Lenny Hirshan first heard about it. He got a call from one of its executives saying he wasn't sure, but it might be for Clint, and asking if the agent would like to read it. From a brief description it sounded good to Hirshan, but this was a Friday, he was heading for Palm Springs, and he said he'd have a copy of the script picked up on Monday. That morning he learned from *Variety* that Warners had let the piece go to Castle Rock. Now he begged a copy from the script's agent, read it that evening and on Tuesday called two Castle Rock executives asking them not to make any casting decisions until Clint had read it.

They were less welcoming than they might have been. They said they were thinking about Robert Redford, Nick Nolte and some others. This was the spring of 1992, *Unforgiven* had not yet been released, and Clint was still in his cold spell. Finally, however, they agreed to let Hirshan submit the script to Clint. "But this is not an offer," they kept saying.

Clint read and took to *In the Line of Fire* immediately. "It's funny," he said to Hirshan. "It's almost as if it's written for me." It was odd that others missed that simple point, though not, seemingly, to Clint. Ever the realist, he had long imagined the day when he would not, as he says, "deliver" at the box office, and a dialogue something like this would ensue:

"Hey, Clint, how ya doing?"

"Fine."

"Yeah. How about stepping out of the way."

That was the way of things. He would, however, console himself in these gloomy moments with a thought he expresses this way: "There's always somebody who's going to want to take a flyer with you, figuring that lightning will strike like it did in the old days. We've seen that with Marlon Brando. They're always hoping."

He didn't think he had reached that point; he knew, if no one else did, what he had in *Unforgiven*. And, soon enough, Castle Rock came to its senses and struck a deal. Then there was even some talk of Clint directing, but he passed. There was not enough time for him to prepare the picture and attend to the opening of *Unforgiven*. He did have director approval, though, and suggested Wolfgang Petersen, whom he had never met. Clint knew his great international success, *Das Boot,* but it was a relative failure, *Shattered,* that interested him; he was talking about it on the *Unforgiven* set. It was a routine blend of overplotting, amnesia and bad behavior among the rich, at heart not much more than an upscale TV movie. But Clint thought Petersen brought something spirited and enlarging to it, and he filed his name away for future use.

The two men took to one another immediately. Petersen is energetic and confident, unpretentious in manner, well versed in his craft and, since his film-school days in Germany, an admirer of the Eastwood-Leone collaborations (he eventually engaged Ennio Morricone to write the score for *In the Line of Fire*). Moreover, they immediately agreed on what was needed to make the picture work. "Give it scope, a spectacular look," as Petersen later put it, "but at the same time focus totally on the intimate side of the story." In short, balance spectacle with the kind of believable human interest that has all but disappeared from the modern action film.

On the set Clint sometimes grew a little testy about extra takes ("Was I in focus? Then let's move on," he has been reported saying). And there were times, he told a visiting journalist, when he had to restrain himself from interfering; "I think to myself, 'Why is Wolfgang doing this?' And then I catch myself and say, 'This may not be the way I'd do it, but his way may be a better way.'" But warmed by Petersen's regard, trusting his manifest professionalism and observing that this was a director who did not feel his manhood threatened when the star posed a question or made a suggestion, he was an essentially happy collaborator. "I always felt good when the door opened in the morning and Clint came to the set," Petersen said. "Very often that is not the case with a director and a star."

There was real sparkle on the screen in Clint's relationship with Rene Russo, who became an after-hours pal of his and Frances's. As one critic put it, "When he smiles at her, twenty years fall away." What was to become the film's most discussed moment—when the camera detects tears in Clint's eyes as he summons up for Lilly that shattering, long-ago day in Dallas—happened in part because he had an acting partner to whom he could entrust his feelings. "I've never been against that," he commented dryly, when an interviewer mentioned his suddenly visible vulnerability. To another he recalled tearing up in *The Outlaw Josey Wales*. To yet a third he observed, "I've been knocking at the door of that kind of thing for a long time. But if anyone wants to think this is the time I'm breaking out, that's fine."

As with Russo, so with Malkovich, an actor who, like Clint, liked to "jump right into" a scene without much preparation and who from his perspective in deep left field caught the heart of Clint's nature and appeal as well as anyone ever has. "There are quite a lot of Americans who are capable of treating you justly and fairly," he said one time, "but if you don't respond in kind, they are capable of shooting you." There was a compliment implicit in this remark—one visibly volatile actor acknowledging the more restrained dangerousness of another. There was also some personal history in it. Clint, Malkovich said, reminded him of his father, an Eastwood fan, whom he described as a mass of contradictions—"very elegant, very handsome, very strange and self-contained; he was quite funny and had a bad temper." We are talking actor heaven here—the chance to project powerful, unresolved feelings onto a fellow player smart enough to encourage him.

Their crucial moment occurs in their first face-to-face confrontation. At the end of a rooftop chase they achieve a version of the famous fable of the scorpion and the frog crossing the river. All Frank has to do is shoot Mitch to bring their duel to an end. Unfortunately, if he does so, Mitch will loose his grip on him, and he will plunge to his death. It brings up the movie's central question: Is the Secret Service man who was unable to take a bullet for his president willing to take a fatal fall for him?

This time the question is posed not to unpredictable instinct, but to rational calculation. As things work out, Frank is permitted to elude the question for the moment. But not before the devilish Malkovich, without warning or rehearsal, took Clint's gun into his mouth. It's not the done thing—surprising a star that way. In his whole daring career, John Malkovich has probably never done anything more dangerous.

But the star laughed. He had encouraged Petersen and the producers to make adjustments in their schedule in order to accommodate Malkovich's needs, and here was patience's payoff—the challenges the actor posed to Clint.

Clint kept rising to these tests more enthusiastically than Petersen had dreamed possible. He, too, was lucky in the order. "*Unforgiven* got so much play right when we were shooting," says Petersen, "and I think he was then, psychologically, willing to take risks—be more accessible and give more layers to his performance." It was, he adds, "just wonderful to watch him grow in this great way," grow it seemed to Petersen without conscious effort—"I don't know what he did"—and without any specific goading or instruction on his own part.

Their harmony extended through postproduction. Clint had offered to supply a fresh eye, as Don Siegel sometimes had for him, should Petersen get lost in his own imagery in the cutting room, and the director showed his rough to Clint before letting anyone else see it. Clint's response was, "I just can't stop watching this." "That's a nice thing," adds Petersen. "A star normally just sees himself and how many close-ups he has."

All in all, it was a happy, effective collaboration, and an islet of tranquillity in a period that was about to turn confusing and harried for Clint.

★ ★ ★

"I ain't like that no more," Clint would say, quoting William Munny, when Frances Fisher taxed him about his capacity for faithfulness. This was for her, as it had not been for Sondra Locke, a pressing issue. She says she had always told Clint that if he proved incapable of a fully committed relationship she would leave, and now, four years into their relationship, she began to harbor suspicions.

These were confirmed, she says, on a Sunday morning in December 1992. Clint had gone to Carmel for a few days while she stayed behind in Bel-Air because she was working in a movie. Around nine a.m. she received a call from Courtney Ross, informing her that Steve Ross had died a few hours earlier, after a long struggle with prostate cancer. Frances tried to call Clint with the news, but there was no answer, and she assumed he had turned off the phone. A few minutes later, however, he walked in, wearing a business suit and looking surprised to see her—she had been scheduled to work that morning, and he did not know that her call had been put back. He told a not-entirely-persuasive story about an early meeting in Carmel and a quick flight to Los Angeles. Neither timing nor wardrobe supported his claim, and she would later learn that he had been at a party the night before in Los Angeles at Dani Janssen's, with his subsequent whereabouts unmentioned.

This, obviously, was not the moment to challenge him. She said something about needing to talk later and then informed him of Ross's passing, which, expected though it was, hit him hard. Processing it, Clint seemed to Frances even more withdrawn than usual during the holiday season in Sun Valley.

It was but the first in a rush of events that would distract them from the confrontation she believed they needed to have. But when Frances confirmed her suspicion in early 1993 that she was pregnant—they were stunned; all the customary precautions had been taken—she was ecstatic and he was . . . well . . . cheerful once he digested the news. He had never discouraged her when she mentioned children, though he had attached the classically masculine "someday" to their conversations. This time, he told friends, he meant to participate in the event as he had not been able to when Kyle and Alison were born. This he would do.

Meanwhile, he was preoccupied with an Academy Award campaign, and throwing himself into another project, *A Perfect World*. He had been shown the script as—once again—a sample of a screenwriter's work, in this case John Lee Hancock's, and found in it a part he would have loved to have played twenty years earlier, that of Butch Haynes, a hardened convict who softens under the influence of a seven-year-old boy he takes hostage after a jailbreak. He said he would be interested in directing it. Around the same time the film's producer, Mark Johnson, showed the script to Kevin Costner, who also liked the role and was the right age for it.

Meetings ensued. Clint wondered if Costner, whose best screen roles were as a sort of beleaguered rationalist, could summon the dangerous, near-psychotic edge this character required, but was reassured after talking to him. Costner, in turn, wondered if Clint might not like to take the small but engaging role of Red Garnett, the Texas Ranger in charge of the manhunt that largely preoccupies the movie. Eventually Clint agreed to do so; it was a comparatively easy role and could be shot separately from the scenes between Costner and the boy, which would be more taxing directorially. They agreed on a start date in February or March. At that point, they reasoned, Clint would be well rested from *In the Line of Fire,* and they would be able to finish well before Costner had to begin work on his epic western, *Wyatt Earp.*

They did not reckon on Clint's Oscar preoccupations, and so they pushed *A Perfect World* back to April. This increased the pressure on both of them, which climbed higher once they went to work on locations in and around Austin, Texas. Clint had cast an adorable child, T. J. Lowther, as the kidnapped boy, Phillip Perry, but had not remembered how short a seven-year-old's attention span is. Nor had he known what a carefully calculating actor Costner is, the kind of player who will spend many happy minutes debating the placement of props on a table, or the timing of a minuscule movement. It was the opposite of Clint's way: "I like to work with the foundation more and put the garnish on later. He'll garnish forever." Costner, who is not the most succinct of conversationalists, is, also, as he confesses, someone who comes to work with a lot of directorial ideas—maybe the kid should be in the backseat for this scene, maybe he should snuggle into me during this take. These notions had to be respected and talked out.

For once, a Malpaso production actually fell behind schedule. Clint, however, remained the picture of patience; he probably did his best acting in this film off camera. He would gently kid "Teege" when he wandered out of a shot—"Did you have a vodka and tonic for lunch?" With Costner he engaged in an endless seminar on the art of screen acting. Out of earshot, his crew waited for the inevitable explosion.

It came in a scene where the fugitives are supposed to sneak into a farmyard and steal some clothes off a washline. Their owner is to be seen on a tractor in a field, and Costner is supposed to disarm him with a friendly wave. Clint placed the camera behind the actor so he could hold him and the far-distant farmer in the same shot. But the day player, who was supposed to wave back, missed his cue, and the star snapped something unpleasant. They tried again, and again the man on the tractor fouled up. Now Costner threw down a bag he was carrying and stomped off the set. Clint looked around and spied his stand-in, dressed in the same costume, and gestured the man over. With his back to the camera, and with Clint using a couple of tighter close-ups—legs walking, an arm waving—the scene worked fine. He moved on to some shots of Butch running and a closer one of the puzzled farmer dismounting from his tractor.

By this time, Costner had simmered down and reappeared. Their dialogue, according to Clint, went like this:

"What's up?"

"Nothing. We shot everything."

"What do you mean?"

"It's all done. I used your double here."

"Whoa. Well, I mean, you shouldn't have. I mean, you didn't have to. . . ."

We are free to imagine a Dirty Harry squint along about here, accompanying the following statement of principle:

"Daly and Semel pay me to shoot film. If you walk off, I'll shoot close-ups of this double. Because I'm going to shoot film."

"You wouldn't do that, would you?"

"You watch. This guy'll play the whole movie. It may not match anything, but you know, that's what I'm here for. I'm not here to jerk off."

Pause. Half smile from Costner. "OK."

"Everything went pretty well after that," Clint sums up mildly, and bearing no grudge; the battle between stars and directors for dominance of the set never ends, and Clint, as we are well aware, has sometimes been on the other side of this conflict. He continues to believe, correctly, that Costner did the best work of his career in *A Perfect World*.

Clint was still hard at work in Texas—unable to contribute much to the launch of *In the Line of Fire* beyond a few print interviews—when the film opened to splendid reviews in early July. One night in Texas, reflecting on stardom in general, and Clint's in particular, Costner said, "You evolve, or you don't evolve, in front of millions of people. You evolve in front of the dads, and then in front of their children," and in the sense of being able to show now on-screen that "he's a man with a life" he thought Clint had come "tremendously far." That was the quality critics and the public picked up on in Clint's performance as Frank Horrigan. People hadn't actually realized it until they saw it, but this is the place where they had always wanted Clint—perhaps any popular star—to come to. Taking nothing away from Malkovich, Russo or Petersen's flawless balancing of the script's diverse elements, it was the sheer lovability of this performance that made *In the Line of Fire* his second $100 million grosser in a row.

It was not a triumph he was allowed to dwell on. For one thing, the studio decided that *A Perfect World* should be a Thanksgiving release, which required a relentless devotion to postproduction. For another, nature decided to move up the baby's release date. Clint and Frances had repaired to the Shasta County ranch, where Clint worked with Joel Cox and his assistant, Michael Cipriano, on the rough cut of the film as he wound down from the shoot. What with one thing and another Clint and Frances had been remiss in attending natural-childbirth classes, intending to do a crash course when they returned to Los Angeles a month or so before the baby's predicted arrival in mid-September. But early one morning the water broke. Frances's obstetrician was hastily consulted, and he told them there was no time to fly to Los Angeles. He would join them at the nearest hospital, which was in Redding, Clint's boyhood way station. Later, the idea of a circle being completed did occur to him.

He bundled Frances into the helicopter and in less than an hour they were checking into the hospital, worrying about their lack of preparation: "The actor's nightmare," as Frances puts it, "going on stage naked, not knowing what play you're doing." Frances was in labor for twenty-two hours, with Francesca Ruth Eastwood, who arrived at 5:38 on the morning of August 7. Clint, in Frances's retelling, played his part perfectly. He was with her, encouraging her as best he could, often, rather comically, in the language of bodybuilding, which was all that he could think of at the time—"OK, it's like doing one more rep, just tough it out."

When they had recovered from that long ordeal, they entered upon what she calls a "miraculous" time—five weeks devoted almost entirely to nurturing one another and the baby. "He became the person I always knew was in him" is how Frances puts it. "He was there. He cooked breakfast, lunch and dinner for me. I'd be nursing the baby, and he'd be feeding me so I could hold the baby." He'd excuse himself occasionally to work with the editors, with Francesca, often as not, accompanying him. A tone was established in those weeks that persisted for months. The three of them were constantly together, and on the rare occasions when they were apart Clint always stayed punctiliously in touch.

Their idyll in the wilderness ended in September when Clint traveled to London, where he was made a fellow of the British Film Institute and lent his presence to the London premiere of Warner Bros.'s *The Fugitive*. Prince Charles made the presentation at the BFI theater, and David Thomson, observing from the audience, wrote, "A visitor from another planet, advised on how to recognize modern royalty—its natural eminence, its grace and authority, its sense of divine right made agnostic in simple glamour—would have had no doubt which man was the prince." Charles, he said, "could not stand beside Clint without looking uneasy, a sad fidget, a tailor's dummy denied life or glory." The next night, in the receiving line after the premiere, which Princess Diana patronized for one of her charities, Clint exchanged little jokes with his sometime White House dancing partner about the *scandale* they might have caused had only he thought to ask her to be his date for the Film Institute function.

The following month he flew to New York for another MoMA gala, celebrating the addition of more Eastwood titles to its archive and benefiting its film preservation fund, but these brief trips aside, nothing intruded on the perfect world of Clint, Frances and Francesca but *A Perfect World*. It obliged him to long postproduction hours, crammed into a short span. And there were other problems, too. There was a ratings board squabble to attend to; Costner's agent, Michael Ovitz, kept pressing Clint for a premature peek at the film; trailers had to be cut and sent to Costner, who had a contractual right to approve them. "Wait a minute," Clint remembers saying at some point in this muddle, "this isn't the way it's supposed to be in my senior years."

Worse, this rush was in aid of a cause in which he did not believe— that November release date. *A Perfect World* was scarcely light holiday fare. Nor did it offer much in the way of that humanistic uplift that stirs Academy voters. Besides, given the attention lavished on *Unforgiven* earlier in the year, and the more recent success of *In the Line of Fire,* which was still playing widely, he thought he was for the moment overexposed. It would be better to take a hiatus and reappear in the spring, which is, anyway, a better season for quirky films like this one.

The studio, however, was thinking of *A Perfect World* primarily as a Costner vehicle. Studio executives felt he might have a shot at an Oscar nomination. And they did not want to hold it until spring, when its release would impinge on the early summer release of the much riskier *Wyatt Earp.* Finally, they had done extremely well in the late fall of 1992 with Costner's *The Bodyguard* and were convinced that similar lightning was going to strike. "They spend millions on research," Clint was heard to grumble, "and then they release it on superstition."

So he soldiered on—only to be proved right. The picture was a box-office failure, though, as we will see, with an asterisk. Opening opposite *Mrs. Doubtfire,* it did considerably less than half its rival's business, and, at about $11 million on its first weekend, also finished behind *Addams Family Values,* which was in its second week of release. It would attain a domestic box-office gross of a little more than $30 million.

This was particularly disappointing because the reviews were every bit as good as those for *Unforgiven;* there was no more dissent amid the general chorus of approval, and some critics actually preferred the new film. They endorsed both Costner's playing of a smart, guarded and dangerous sociopath slowly permitting himself to be disarmed by a hostage who becomes his surrogate son, and the representation of the boy, made miserable by his mother's repressive fundamentalism, learning to have roughneck fun with his lowlife mentor. They praised the patience with which the script revealed the source of Butch's crude, often comically expressed, tenderness, which is that he was a victim of child abuse. They liked the kiddishness of T. J. Lowther's kid, who projected, one has to think, some of the good, toughening things Clint had learned on his boyhood roads and was not a preternaturally wise or competent movie brat of the Macaulay Culkin type.

In particular, the critics observed the uninsistent fatalism of the movie. For example, we learn, somewhat to our surprise, that Butch and Clint's pursuing Rod Garnett were linked in the past. When Red was a young lawman, he was instrumental in taking Butch from his mother and placing him in a foster home, which he now regrets. We learn, to our horror, that the good nature we have seen emerging in Butch as his odyssey proceeds is much more delicately poised than we thought; when a seemingly gentle black farmer who has given him and Phillip shelter suddenly strikes his young grandchild, the convict cannot control the emotional firestorm, fueled by memories of his own tormented past, that overwhelms him. And then we see that a thrown-away moment early in the film, when Butch casually lets Phillip play with his gun, is, in fact, a foreshadowing. When the boy gets his hands on it again, in the raging confusion that ensues when Butch turns on the farmer it becomes the instrument that sends him reeling to his tragic end.

There was, as well, near unanimity on the quality of Clint's work as director. Critics liked his sense of period—*A Perfect World* is set in Texas in the autumn of 1963, on the eve of John F. Kennedy's fatal visit to Dallas—and they liked the way the pace of the narrative seemed to match the gently rolling quality of the countryside through which it moves. They enjoyed the contrast he struck between the rollicking spirit of Butch and the boy on their (petty) crime spree and the claustrophobia of Red, a criminologist who is a premature feminist (Laura Dern) and an FBI man exuding bureaucratic evil trapped in a jouncing, windowless trailer the governor has pressed on them as a mobile command center. Everyone thought, too, that the film's climax was brilliantly managed: Butch, gutshot and bleeding, sheltering under a lone tree in a field, the boy riotous with emotions too large for him to handle, helicopters whirring overhead, serried ranks of lawmen training their rifles on them from a distance, Red hopelessly trying to prevent a needless, pointless tragedy.

"The high point of Mr. Eastwood's directing career thus far," Janet Maslin wrote. She named several other recent films (including *Mrs. Doubtfire*) that had taken up the subject of "men's legacies to their children, and of their failures and frustrations in bringing up those children," but this film, she said, "gives that subject real meaning." David Denby saw in Clint "a newly born classical master" no less.

If the qualities of this movie, featuring two extraordinarily popular stars at the peak of their careers, were completely visible to a wide range of observers, why did it fail? One extremely curious answer was offered by Michael Medved and Richard Grenier, right-wing ideologues masquerading as movie reviewers, who accused Clint of selling out to political correctness. Talk about circles closing! The man formerly accused of fascist tendencies was now criticized for liberal excess. The film, Medved observed, "offers passing condemnations of shameful sexism in the workplace, joyless religion, authoritarian parents, sexual harassment, murderous FBI men, mistreatment of juvenile offenders, dehumanizing preoccupation with money, sexual abuse of children, and, above all, the devastating impact of corporal punishment on kids." Are we to assume that the reviewer favors all these things, since he makes no effort to disown them?

Grenier, who attacked *A Perfect World* in two articles, insisted it was Clint's stance on these matters that doomed his enterprise. He spoke as a disappointed lover, for writing in *Commentary* ten years earlier he had attributed Clint's popularity to his crystallization of gun-'em-down conservatism for a popular audience starving for such raw meat as they bent under the tyranny of liberalism's moral vegetarianism. The film's commercial failure, he explained, was because Clint had become "a startling example . . . of a public figure suddenly abandoning the moral values of the populace for those of the liberal elite." He guessed the public would forgive Clint his feminism and his attacks on the CIA, FBI and fundamentalist religion—as if there were, indeed, an unexamined reverence for these institutions everywhere in American life—"but going soft on the punishment of evildoers robs him of his very identity."

We are in a realm here every bit as loopy as the one Pauline Kael so long ago staked out. Indeed, they were making the same mistake she had, trying to comprehend Clint Eastwood in narrowly ideological terms. There was, however, a grain of (nonideological) truth in Grenier's last remark. Red Garnett is the first lawman Clint ever played who is unable to take command of a dangerous situation. Swigging Geritol and confessing to an antediluvian partiality to Tater Tots, he conveys a drawling, slightly out-of-it air, and, at the end, unable to prevent the bloodthirsty FBI man from slaughtering Butch, he is reduced to impotent rage. "I don't know nothing. I don't know a damn thing," he snarls, unable to explain to anyone, including himself, how these events got so tragically out of hand. This was not—let us make the point one last time—the way audiences wanted to see Clint.

Beyond that, some of the qualities that most pleased the critics may have disturbed the popular audience, perhaps most notably the movie's lifelike—as opposed to movielike—lurches from the comic to the menacing, its refusal of conventional sentiments. For all its pleasures and honesties, it does not finally provide us a fully satisfying emotional release. That "us," however, is not all-encompassing. *A Perfect World* was accepted much more widely and enthusiastically by audiences abroad, where rootlessness is often perceived as one of the more romantic aspects of the American experience, quirky outlawry as one of the more appealing aspects of the American character. Overseas, the film grossed well over $100 million, turning it—belatedly—into one of Clint Eastwood's more successful ventures.

★   ★   ★

One day on one of the *Perfect World* locations, Clint casually inquired of a visitor if he had read *The Bridges of Madison County,* then in its tenth month of its near-endless stay on the best-seller lists. Yes, the man said, and it had made him think of Clint. "It's one of the great American fantasies," he said. "The husband and kids are away, you're bored, you're lonesome, and one morning you look up and there's Clint Eastwood standing in your driveway." Clint lifted a quizzical eyebrow, not entirely appreciating the cynicism. He was inclined to take this thing seriously.

And why not? The part of Robert Kincaid, the rootless photographer who finds a few days of happiness and a lifetime of regrets in a three-day liaison with an Iowa farmwife, Francesca Johnson, was right for him. He had himself been a man in a pickup truck looking for something he could not quite explain, settling for such romance as chance put in his way; he was, indeed, still such a man at heart.

But all of that aside, *Bridges* offered him a chance at something he had never tried before as an actor—classic, flat-out, leading-man romanticism. That it was controlled by his friend Steven Spielberg, who was at that time thinking of directing it himself, added to its appeal, as did the fact that Spielberg could not get at it for a while. Clint was determined to take some time off, beginning in December 1993, when the release of *A Perfect World* was behind him.

His primary goal was to spend as much time as possible with his new daughter, and this he did. One of the more delightful cognitive dissonances available to his friends that winter was being greeted at his front door by Dirty Harry with a burbling baby cradled in his arms. He was not entirely idle, of course. There was his usual round of celebrity golf tournaments to play in, he was trying to develop a film script based on *Golf and the Kingdom,* a fable beloved by the game's devotees (he has yet to lick it), he was looking forward to Cannes again, this time returning as chairman of the festival's jury, and, as the spring came on, there were unsatisfying drafts of the *Bridges* script to study. The press was reporting interest in the project by Robert Redford, but given its auspices one had the impression that the role was Clint's to turn down.

This calm, however, was soon shattered by tragedy. On the first weekend in April Clint joined Frank Wells, who was now the chief operating officer of the Walt Disney Company, and some other friends for a weekend of high-altitude skiing in Nevada. It is a sport for true aficionados, involving helicopter flights into virgin snowfields high in the mountains, beyond the reach of ordinary ski lifts. They had "a great day" on Saturday, under cloudless skies. Sunday, however, the weather was more threatening, and after a few runs Clint decided to leave. He had flown his own helicopter to the resort where they were staying, was due in Sun Valley later in the day and feared he might not be able to take off if the weather continued to worsen.

It was a decision that almost certainly saved his life. When he reached Sun Valley he put in a call to Wells to see how the rest of the day had gone. He was answered by a hysterical receptionist telling him that his friend and the rest of his party—all except one man—were dead. The chopper that had been sent in to retrieve them at the end of the afternoon had crashed in a canyon. Heavily laden, it apparently lacked the power to overcome whatever winds it encountered as it tried to lift off.

This was a devastating loss to Clint. Wells, who had taken time off between his Warners and Disney jobs to try to climb the tallest peak on every continent (only Everest defeated him), was in his rhythms and sensibility probably as close to a soulmate as Clint had ever known. In his tribute to him at his memorial service Clint sang a few lines from "Hey, Jude," a song he had heard Wells singing as he schussed down his last mountain.

By now his relationship with Frances was reverting to its former troubled state. Clint's mother, Fisher says, "told me on a number of occasions that she thought I loved him too much." She is also, in her own words, "very demanding" and now, as the mother of their child, saw no reason to be shy about making her needs known. He, in his turn, was beginning to find some of her "new age" ideas—which included strong reformist impulses about traditional masculine modes as well as theories of feminism—puzzling, irritating and, as they applied to his own ways of thinking and being, impossible to adopt. He also says he found himself once again under pressure to find roles for an actress who had a large personal claim on him.

It does not appear that their bad feelings were often or very openly discussed at this time. They went off to Cannes *en famille,* took a villa in the hills above town and lost themselves happily in the pleasures of the occasion. Clint enjoyed his official duties enormously. He says he found his experiences as mayor useful in conducting the jury's business and stoutly denies the rumor that he had unduly influenced its choice of a controversial American film, *Pulp Fiction,* as winner of the Palme d'Or. With its bold mixture of violence and comedy it was undeniably his kind of movie. But his tastes are wildly eclectic—he voted for *Beauty and the Beast* in the Academy balloting of 1992, and the actress he is most frustrated about not working with is Maggie Smith—so he would have been open to almost anything. He says Quentin Tarantino's film won on the first ballot, with only one juror holding out against it.

After the festival they spent a night in Paris before flying on to Scotland and a week of golf before returning home. It was during that brief stopover that another of those seemingly minor incidents that seem to crystallize emotional issues for Clint occurred. They had carried several trunks with them, but it seemed foolish to tote them all on to Scotland, since their flight back to the United States was to leave from Paris. They decided to buy a couple of suitcases and leave the rest of their belongings behind. Frances said she would take care of that, but it was late, and their driver said the only nearby shop likely to be open was Louis Vuitton. She splurged, returning with something like ten thousand dollars' worth of luggage. Clint, who is not much of a comparison shopper— or for that matter any kind of shopper—said nothing.

Long dissolve. Frances goes off to Texas to appear in *The Stars Fell on Henrietta,* a little film about an oil boom that Clint executive-produced. Her costars were Robert Duvall, Aidan Quinn and Brian Dennehy. The director was James Keach, who is married to Jane Seymour, on whose television program, *Dr. Quinn, Medicine Woman,* Frances had appeared. She had flown in on a private plane, and Frances asked if she could borrow it for a night to fly to Los Angeles for the premiere of *Babyfever,* a Henry Jaglom film in which she had had an important role. She told the charter service to bill her directly for the cost, but it required a credit card as collateral, and she gave them one Clint had provided her.

Another dissolve. Somehow the bill for the plane—less than the Vuitton charges, by the way, but still substantial—does not go directly to Frances. It appears on the credit card statement along with the luggage bill. Since Clint lives as he produces movies—without ostentation—he flew into a rage, which abided.

Perhaps it persisted in part because he was also simmering over *The Bridges of Madison County*. It had to start shooting in Iowa by Labor Day or else wait until the next year. But the scripts he had seen were full of superfluous flashbacks and fantasies; one draft, he says, even proposed reuniting modern subliterature's most famously sundered lovers in Katmandu or some such exotic locale. Richard LaGravenese's excellent adaptation was, at least, in work, but had not yet reached its final form. And Spielberg, exhausted by *Jurassic Park* and *Schindler's List,* had begged off directing. Bruce Beresford, the Australian whose Academy Award–winning *Driving Miss Daisy* seemed to qualify him for handling small, tender stories, had been engaged to replace him.

Clint claimed to find him personally agreeable, but, unfortunately, Beresford fell into a casting dither. Certain substantial names were mentioned for Francesca—Anjelica Huston and Meryl Streep (always Clint's leading candidate) among them—but he decided to fly off to Europe to test other, younger actresses for the role. The material he returned with was, at best, inconclusive.

Beresford, as he should have known, had sailed into dangerous waters and was now caught in an angry riptide. Clint issued an ultimatum: Either this issue was quickly resolved, or they could add a leading man to their list of casting problems. Somehow, Beresford disappeared in the ensuing hubbub. Clint, despite his recent, oft-repeated resolve to "wean myself away" from double duty, took over as director. He got Streep's number from their mutual friend, Carrie Fisher ("I guess she hands out my number to anybody," Streep would say later), and called to ask if he could send her a script.

She was not immediately receptive. Jodie Foster had quit her role in the projected film version of Richard Preston's *Crisis in the Hot Zone,* and her *Out of Africa* costar, Robert Redford, was quite persuasively talking to her about joining him on the picture (which, ultimately, was canceled). Besides, Clint was just a man in a "boxy" jacket she had met once at a party. She knew little of him as either actor or director, but she knew she loathed Robert Waller's novel, especially the overripe prose of its love scenes. (Four or five people had given her the book, suggesting that she should play Francesca.) When her assistant asked to borrow one of her copies she tossed it in the wastebasket, saying "You can't read this—it's a crime to literature."

But because of its auspices, she read LaGravenese's script immediately, and saw that it solved the crime. The bad metaphors were gone, and a subtle rebalancing had taken place. The characters of the son and daughter, who discover their mother's diary and must come to terms with its revelations, were enlarged, with their responses adding a certain resonance to the shallow romanticism of the book. Streep went out and rented a couple of Eastwood movies. One was *Unforgiven,* which her husband and son recommended, and in which she found a directorial "wholeness" effortlessly achieved. The other was *In the Line of Fire,* where Clint's acting impressed her: "I'd never seen somebody of his age do that stuff, go out on a limb that way."

She signed on, thereby turning *Bridges* into a go project. By so doing—and quite unknowingly, of course—she was instrumental in bringing Clint and Frances's relationship to its final crisis. Given its precarious condition, Frances guessed that a couple of months' separation, while he was on location, would be fatal to it. She therefore proposed herself for the role of the daughter, and he rejected her. Personal issues aside, she had just finished another Malpaso picture, and he was more than ever determined not to repeat the Sondra Locke scenario. But still it hurt. According to her, he was not very encouraging when she proposed a visit, though eventually she and the baby did spend a few days in Iowa toward the end of the shoot.

It was centered in and around Winterset, Madison County's seat (and, another faintly described circle completed, John Wayne's birthplace). It may have been the happiest of all Eastwood locations. Logistically, this was a comparatively simple production—relatively few locations, a small cast, no taxing action to stage. At its center there were simply two actors acting. And loving it: "One of my favorite things I've ever done in my life" is the way Streep put it.

In the doing, it fulfilled her hope that this might turn into the kind of acting experience she had known in the theater, something "we'd be making up as we went along, exploring its evolution." It also banished her greatest fear. She had worked with two actor-directors, Woody Allen and Albert Brooks, and in her scenes with them she always felt a third, directorial eye staring objectively at her, disconcerting her. This happened only once on *Bridges*—in some shots where Clint was off camera, feeding her lines. She gently called him on it, and he stopped. There was another time, watching dailies of a scene where they were in bed together, half-naked, when she caught Clint making silent gestures behind her back to Jack Green. This time it made her laugh to see him doing his other job when he was supposed to be full concentrated on . . . well . . . sex, or, to be more accurate, its simulacrum. He responded with a mock complaint: "It's very fatiguing work."

What Streep liked best was his first-take spontaneity. She has a reputation as a "technical" actress, someone who seems to calculate her effects too closely, and is defensive about it. "I really always have loved that first encounter," she said one day in her trailer. "I almost always like the first reading better than anything we ever do subsequently." Therefore, she said, "this is heaven. Clint's very instinctual. If it feels good, he says, 'We're outta here.'" As a result, she said, the film's emotional moments "feel captured, as opposed to set up and driven into the ground."

Her feelings were reciprocated, and they moved well ahead of schedule. However, when a newsmagazine reported this, it irritated Clint. He thought it made it sound as if they were working carelessly. "We're not making *Plan Nine from Outer Space,*" he growled. They also were not enacting the cowboy-and-the-lady scenario that many journalists had imagined. They were generally affectionate, mutually respectful, often-joshing colleagues. One perfect autumn morning Clint ambled up to a little bridge where they were to shoot a silent scene in which Streep, in age makeup, reads her last communication from Robert Kincaid, a deathbed letter. The air was clear, the sky blue, a light breeze rippled leaves turning photogenically. Eyeing the scene, he sighed happily: "Great, I'll make the cover of *Cahiers du Cinéma.*"

Joking aside, the film's visual quality—pretty, but not overwhelmingly so—was emblematic of other, less obvious rebalancings of Waller's basic narrative. In a genially cynical review of one of his other books, Robert Plunket, himself a novelist, rather cleverly gave a name to the genre this author had virtually invented: "Old Adult" fiction, as opposed to the "Young Adult" books "aimed at the anxious adolescent, feeling alone in the world, who needs some validation and reassurance." Old Adult fiction, he said, provides the same service for the middle-aged reader trapped miserably in a Wal-Mart universe. It says: "You're a good person. Your suffering isn't depressing—it's romantic. And to prove it I'm going to reward you with some really good sex for once in your life."

Streep disagreed. She thought the film, at least, was not about belated rewards, sexual or otherwise, but about "regret. And lost chances. And how you come to things at the wrong time." She caught in these few words the difference in tone between source and adaptation. Waller in his klutzy way was striving for the ineffable. The movie, more gracefully, strives merely to be treasurable. It grants its lovers a resonant happiness, but not a transformative one.

Clint finished *Bridges* stirred up, on a high. He had never worked so intensely or with such intimacy over so many weeks with an actor or actress of Streep's caliber. Nor had he ever worked on any film even remotely comparable to this in its romantic force. It made a man think—especially a man approaching his sixty-fifth birthday, especially a man returning to a house alternately silent and quarrelsome, and rife now with suggestions that some sort of therapy might be in order.

Talk about cognitive dissonance. If he had ever felt "lost, lonely, shut-down" he surely did not now. He had just played a figure who embodied the first two qualities, and though Clint's grasp on the difference between reality and fantasy was as firm as ever, this character had found at least a momentary transfiguration. Why couldn't he?

There were good days and bad in the months ahead, as ambivalence tugged him this way and that. If Frances's fierce zeal to create a life antithetical to his nature, ever resistant to therapeutic pieties, it was yet the product of a loving and idealistic nature. Then, too, there were the interests of a much loved child to consider. And the ugliness of his breakup with Sondra Locke still weighed on his mind.

By the end of the Christmas holidays, though, it was clear to both of them that there was virtually no hope of salvaging their relationship. Now Frances discovered his "other family," as she called Jacelyn Reeves and the children. She could accept them, but not the fact that Clint had failed to tell her about them. Then in January his old friend Jane Brolin died in an auto accident. When the news came, he cried, the first and only time Frances saw him in tears, the first and only time some of his friends were aware of him reaching out—shyly, indirectly, but palpably—for consolation.

He had always said he was too busy living to think much about dying. But this death, following so closely that of Frank Wells, rendered thoughts of mortality, and questions about the quality of the years left to him, inescapable; he did not want to spend them trying to be someone else's idea of who he should be, and apologizing for his inevitable failures in that regard. One detected no anger or bitterness in him as he reached this conclusion, though there was some on Frances's part. But then he had, or thought he might have, someplace else to go.

He had met Dina Ruiz two years earlier in Carmel. She was twenty-eight years old, a news anchor on KSBW, a television station in Salinas, when she was assigned to do a sort of local-boy-makes-good interview with Clint after he won his *Unforgiven* Oscars. She was yet another woman who had not seen many of his films, but they got along very comfortably on camera, so much so that when Dina showed her footage to her boss, Maria Barrs, she—astonishingly—predicted a marriage someday. More immediately, she ordered Dina to expand her piece to a five-part series, and she supplemented her material by doing an interview with Clint's mother.

They did not see each other again for something like a year. Then they were seated next to each other at a civic function in Carmel, and once again conversation flowed easily between them. He signaled that, from a distance, he had been keeping up with her by asking knowledgeable questions about some of her recent broadcasts. Now, the more they talked, the more interested he became. She had been raised in Fremont, where his grandmother had lived, and they found that, despite their differences in age, they shared a sense of place, of comparable formative experiences. They came from similarly modest backgrounds; her father was a high-school teacher, her mother (whom Dina had brought along on that first interview) an appliance salesperson at Montgomery Ward. At the end of the banquet he asked if he could call her, and when she gave him her number he said its last four digits—1565—would be easy to remember: "Your age and mine."

Later on he would tell people that part of Dina's attraction is that she is not an actress. It is a shorthand way of saying that she is of his private world on the Monterey Peninsula, a world from which the movie business is firmly excluded, not of his public life. More than that, she is a lively, articulate and straightforward woman, and a born journalist, curious about everything and quirkily well informed. It is a sensibility that is novel and refreshing to him.

They continued to see each other—occasionally, chastely—over the next months. Before he went off to make *Bridges* there was a night when they stayed up until five in the morning "smooching and talking" as she puts it. In January a photographer caught them in a kiss at the Pebble Beach Golf Tournament. It interested the press and, of course, infuriated Frances—and Clint as well. "She's a friend," he insisted at the time. "I'm not saying I wouldn't be interested, if my circumstances were different. . . ." "We didn't become a couple," as Dina genteelly, but firmly, puts it, "until he was free."

This he was by early spring. Frances and Francesca moved temporarily into the guest house on his Bel-Air property, while she looked for other quarters. He happily continued his fatherly duties, which included baby-sitting when Frances was busy.

He did manage to compose a theme for *Bridges,* which he called "Doe Eyes," a rather obvious reference to Dina. A gossipy buzz occurred when he appeared without Frances at the Academy Awards ceremony in the spring of 1995 to accept his Irving Thalberg Award. There was no buzz at all when he appeared solo at the premiere of *Bridges,* which also inaugurated the handsome new Steven J. Ross Theater on the Warner Bros. lot on the eve of Clint's sixty-fifth birthday. By this time it was common knowledge that he and Frances were separated. It was far from common knowledge, however, that he was in love with Dina Ruiz. He was not at all eager to subject her, and their relationship, to a confusion of realms.

Bridges launched as gently as any picture he had ever made. Basically, the critics heaved a collective sigh of relief when they saw it. Many could not bring themselves to rave over a movie drawn from this contemptible source, but most could very warmly appreciate the way the sappiness of the novel had been blanched away, leaving, they had to admit, a surprisingly solid emotional core exposed. The film did not jerk tears; it gently encouraged, at most, a rueful tingle behind the eyes.

Almost a year later, in a long critical consideration of the movie, Richard Combs made explicit what was implicit in many of the early notices. The film's success, he argued, was based on its "spatial and temporal" framing, which the novel had only hastily attended. It grounds these characters in a realistically observed place and in a historical continuum, as Waller's fiction does not. Francesca is seen to be rooted in this countryside. And her sense of panic at a future in which she abandons all that it represents in the way of stability and sustaining duty is vividly reflected in Streep's eyes. Thus real space and imagined time become in the film what they never quite are in the novel—palpable, potent antagonists in a tale moved not by desperate prose but by the easy, natural rhythms of an honestly, and gently, felt reality.

As Combs says, the movie's erotic passages are "a matter of charged space, the way characters move around each other. What's kept apart is as important as what's brought together in this scheme. . . ." The long sequences—rather daringly extended by a director who simply will not be hurried—in which Robert and Francesca get to know one another, full of tentative approaches and withdrawals, are among the most painfully authentic and suspenseful seduction scenes ever recorded on film.

In this context Streep's Francesca ceases to be a ditsy romantic mooning in goofy animalistic metaphors over a superstud, but a woman caught in true and anguished conflict. And Clint's Robert ceases to be Waller's faux poetic "last cowboy" and becomes a man recognizing that his wandering ways are the expression of a flawed spirit. Indeed, in the playing, he becomes a rather pathetic figure, a man grasping desperately for a last chance at happiness. When he and Francesca see each other for the last time, he is the one out in the rain, looking like a stray cat; she is sheltered and at least minimally warmed by her husband's benign, if uncomprehending, presence.

The public responded very warmly to this conscientious, carefully unexploitative production. By Labor Day the film had grossed in the neighborhood of $70 million, enough to edge it into the top-ten summer releases. It did even better abroad, so that it came close to the $200 million mark in worldwide grosses.

Its release in Europe offered Clint an occasion to introduce Dina— gently, he hoped—to his celebrity existence. He asked her and two other couples, friends from Carmel, to join him on a promotional tour to England, France and Italy, which included stops at some of the better golf courses. None of them had ever been exposed to this side of his life, and seeing it from the inside left them dazed: the crowds, the demands, the frenzy.

It may have left Dina dazed in another way. For Clint granted an interview with *Paris-Match* in which he was more open about his private feelings than he had ever been before with a journalist. As he had once or twice in the past, he confessed to his fondness for women of a certain age; maturity made them more interesting, more attractive, to him than their younger sisters. Aha, said the alert reporter, What about Ms. Ruiz? (then just past thirty). "She's someone very rare, very special," came the astonishingly open reply. "She is beautiful, generous, full of life. . . ." Love, he said in answer to another question, "is much stronger when one meets in the second half of one's life. It hits you when you least expect it. If I have a message, it is simply to say, 'Don't let anything pass.'" Which is, of course, the lesson he had taken very much to heart from *The Bridges of Madison County*.

Here, it seemed, was a new Clint Eastwood, or at least a new *public* Clint Eastwood. He was then, and he has remained since, a visibly smitten man. With Dina he would become a cuddling, nuzzling, nibbling, almost-adolescent figure. "My silly son-in-law," Dina's mother would soon start calling him.

For in September, shortly after they returned from Europe, Clint presented Dina with a diamond-and-ruby engagement ring. On December 29, he lured her into the courthouse in Hailey, Idaho, near Sun Valley, on the pretext of showing her its architecture. He'd always wanted to use it in a movie, he said. It was odd, she thought, how he kept insisting she bring her purse with her. It was, she soon learned, so she could produce some ID for the county clerk when they applied for their marriage license. He swore everyone in the office to secrecy, which they managed to maintain for at least forty-eight hours.

On the last weekend in March, when Dina and a group of women she had known since her school days were scheduled to make their annual girls-only outing to Las Vegas, Clint showed an unusual interest in the affair, and on Friday, lounging at the pool of the Mirage Hotel, Dina heard herself being paged. The occasion had proved irresistible to him. All her old friends were gathered around her; his friend Steve Wynn, the casino magnate, had a perfect venue for a wedding, the patio of his home just off his Shadow Creek golf course; it would be easy to fly both their families in from northern California on short notice. What better moment for a marriage?

And so, in forty-eight hours, it was done—flowers ordered, menus set, music chosen. Just in case word leaked out, the control tower at nearby Nellis Air Force Base, which commands the air space over Wynn's property, was alerted to be on guard against low-flying paparazzi. With everything in hand, Clint decided to pass the afternoon on the golf course—"I played pretty well, too"—as did Dina's father. Clint spotted him strolling toward the eighteenth green just as the ceremony was about to begin, and it was delayed until he finished his round and changed into a suit so he could escort his daughter down the aisle. The band played "Doe Eyes." Kyle Eastwood was his father's best man. Everyone agreed that it was the prettiest wedding a man and a woman could hope for.

One is tempted to leave him there, dancing in the desert twilight with his bride while the band plays "Unforgettable." But this is not a life susceptible to fade-outs, freeze-frames, any of those convenient and arbitrary devices by which we bring stories to some kind of a conclusion—not yet, anyway.

A month before their wedding Dina had been next to him, with his mother on the other side, at the banquet when he received the American Film Institute Life Achievement Award. A month later, after a week's honeymoon in Maui, she would accompany him to New York when he received a similar prize from the Film Society of Lincoln Center for what he described on that occasion as "a blessed career." A month after that they would be separated for a few weeks while he did the location work for his next film, *Absolute Power,* in Baltimore and Washington. Sometime during *that* period they learned, for certain, that they were going to have a baby. After that he was set to direct another film, the adaptation of *Midnight in the Garden of Good and Evil.* There is, it would seem, no end in sight!

Somehow F. Scott Fitzgerald's phrase, which Clint used as the epigraph on *Bird*—"There are no second acts in American lives"—insinuates itself in the mind of someone observing this particular American life, doubtless because it so definitively disproves the novelist's dubious generalization. This is a life that has refused to confine itself to an act structure, or any other structure for that matter, and is, as we speak, redefining itself one more time.

EPILOGUE
THE BACK NINE

These things we now know about Clint Eastwood:

That his movie heroes have taken the American male deeper into the country of disaffection than he has ever ridden before on-screen, reversing the great theme of our adventure movies, which has been male bonding, and insisting upon the opposite, the difficulty men have in making connections—not just with other men, but with communities, with women, with conventional morality, with their own best selves. Clint's screen character represents an isolation more radically withdrawn than anyone has ever offered in movies intended for, and embraced by, a popular audience.

That in many of his best films he has explored the various ways that a man can fail to do what a man's got to do, showing how through sexual arrogance, self-absorption, self-destructiveness, pride, perversity and even stupidity, he can fail, or come perilously close to failing, this primary obligation of the screen hero.

That in the presentation of that figure he has brought a self-consciousness—not so much in the playing, but in the life that goes on behind his eyes—that is the very hallmark of what we now routinely refer to as "post-modernist," though almost never when we are thinking about moviemaking of the kind he practices.

That when he inserts this character into an action film he places it in a context radically changed from the one traditionally inhabited by the screen hero. Action movies, we have observed, resemble action painting in that their pleasures have always been found on their surfaces, in the tension arising from the arrangement of abstract elements (the good, the bad, the ugly, as it were). When, starting sometime in the sixties, movies began to acknowledge that fact openly, a cultural crisis—otherwise known as the sex-and-violence controversy—that persists to this day was initiated. It grew largely out of the dawning realization among filmmakers that the audience really doesn't care a rap about who shoots whom or why, so long as the matter is handled with—yes—a certain "panache."

That this revised context to some degree revises the nature of screen heroism, encouraging us to root for our guy on the basis of his superior style, not his heavier moral weight. In this new universe, Dirty Harry's wisecracks cease to be idle verbal decor and become something like the heart of the matter. Talk about "daunting ideas"! What could be more daunting than the notion that there are no reliable guides to masculine assertion, that we succeed or fail in this matter by the degree of wit we bring to the matter? What could be more subversive to our traditional codes of heroism than the idea that its largest imperative is to style, to cool improvisation in the heat of the deadly moment?

There is something else we know, too, not only about Clint Eastwood, but about all of us: that there comes a time in life when we need to take stock, of where we have been and where we may be going, of who we have been and who we might yet become, of what we have meant to others and how we might further clarify that relationship.

It is obvious that the movies Clint has made in his sixties, so different in tenor from most of those that he had previously done, are part of the process of reconciling his accounts. It is equally clear—to me, at least—that his patient involvement with this book, as well as his pleased participation in those celebrations of his life's achievements that have preoccupied so much of his public life since winning his Academy Awards, is also part of that process.

We may take pride, some of us, in the fact that we have improvised our way through the chance universe with a certain grace. But we need to know, too, that we have not arrived entirely by chance at our present condition, need to think, too, that some general principles, conceivably of value to others, may be gleaned from that experience. We may take pride, as well, in our independence, in our ability to function without the sanction of the social and cultural arbiters, but in some secret chamber of our hearts we covet their endorsements, if only as a sign that in quixotically choosing the more isolated path we did not preclude the summit.

My book and his apotheosis having coincided, I attended most of the large tributes that have been paid Clint in recent years. They stirred in me no desire to recant what I wrote in the prologue: I still think the desire to recast him as icon, legend, national treasure, is a way of evading his singularity, or at least to tame and domesticate it. Our desire to press celebratory hardware on figures like Clint does not reflect a desire to grapple honestly with the past, but a need to nostalgize it, and by so doing soften its conflicts, resolve its ambiguities. Our national disease, one sometimes thinks, is long-term memory loss, and though our standing ovations signal authentic affection for their recipients, they also testify that the human capacity for forgetfulness is as large as its capacity for remembrance.

I cannot say if, on these grand occasions, stray thoughts of the old criticism, criticism couched as calumny, crossed Clint's mind. But they surely crossed mine. For in researching this book, my largest astonishment was at the breadth, persistence and vitriolic misunderstanding of the early attacks on him. It is hard to credit now, informed opinion having shifted so decisively in his favor in recent years, but it is true nevertheless: No actor in the history of the medium has attained the kind of stature Clint now enjoys in the face of such large critical contempt exercised for so long a period. One time in the midst of his recent acclaim he asked me if I'd happened to see an interview in which Pauline Kael said that one of her regrets about retirement was that she no longer had a forum in which to criticize Clint Eastwood. "Can you imagine that kind of bigotry?" He sighed. The answer was that at that moment, with the chorus of past disapprovals ringing loud in my ears, I could—perhaps better than he, who has willfully deafened himself to it.

It was only in the slightly wondering air that he wore to these gala occasions that I thought I detected an awareness of the contrast between the checkered shade in which he once danced and the bright light of acclaim in which he is now caught. But that might well have been an illusion. If, as we have observed, he has a desire to convert heroism into antiheroism, he has a similar desire to convert formality into informality. Movies are, as Joseph Campbell once remarked, but "the genial imaging of enormous ideas," and Clint wanted all of us, himself included, to be aware of something like that usefully deflating thought.

So he addressed the thousand or two assembled in their stiff banquet finery as if they were a half dozen gathered comfortably in his living room for postprandial inconsequences, or as if they were his biographer. It is usually incongruity in the behavior of someone we know well that grasps our attention. What riveted mine at these tributes was the congruity I perceived between this honoree of theirs and this interviewee of mine. I had grown used to seeing him in quite a different light, a late-afternoon light, as a rule, but always a dim one. In life, as in his movies, Clint prefers to underlight—the famous squint is less a product of temperament than of an unusual sensitivity to glare—and there were times when the room would grow almost completely dark before he switched on a lamp.

Dress and manner were, naturally, different too. Clint on these occasions was dressed in his usual day wear—T-shirt, wash pants, sneakers. His long legs propped on a coffee table, a brew sometimes in hand, he spoke softly, sometimes too softly for the tape recorder to pick up, often pausing to grope for a memory or the right words to express it. If I fumbled the flip from the A side to the B side of the tape he would reach for the recorder and do it for me: "Like we used to say in aircraft maintenance, if all else fails, force it."

But we forced nothing else. These were actually more conversations than interviews, rambling and leisurely, full of asides and digressions, tending to encircle a point rather than to overwhelm it by frontal assault. If there was a significant difference between the man responding to questions in his living room and the man responding to adulation in public, it was one of forbearance. We often talked on after the tape ran out; he was always quick to make his escape from the panegyric podium. Other than that, however, the continuity between the man bending earnestly to the task of recollection, seeking the proper balance between disclosure and discretion, and the figure bowing awkwardly on stage, seeking the proper balance between pride and modesty, was seamless.

I have wondered, sometimes, if as they left the hall the celebrants of this life's achievement have felt deprived of closure by the inconclusive conclusions he supplied these evenings. Finally I have guessed not. The way he plays them suits their needs as well as the Man with No Name or Dirty Harry or Josey Wales suited them in earlier times; closure is exactly what they do not want from him.

By accepting their prizes and their accolades with a sort of genial fatalism he conveys an idea that they are part of the natural order of things, to be dealt with not as some grand culmination, but as a pleasant interruption in a life still unpredictably unfolding, something like, say, a round of golf: diverting, absorbing, a matter to be taken seriously for the moment, but not dwelt upon for very long.

Clint likes to refer to the passage he is now traversing as "the back nine of life," adding that he often finds it to be golf's better half, a time when one starts playing the shots rather than the score, begins to enjoy the day, the stroll, the company. Ambling toward the clubhouse, as it were, an ironic smile on his face, the double bogey on eight all but forgotten, the birdie on fourteen happily recalled, the possibility of closing out the round with a par or two still lively, he is most of the time now a man visibly content within his chosen metaphor.

And as we see him looking great and working well we happily accept from him the final gift it is within fame's power to confer, a hopeful, even inspiring, example of grace under the pressure of the years. He hints to us the possibility of edging slowly toward the exit unflustered, steady on our feet, all our buttons firmly attached.

Doubtless we are indulging another of the fantasies with which we habitually surround celebrity, ignoring the fact that stardom nearly always begins with a lucky genetic accident, and that the older we get the luck of the DNA draw more and more determines how we will be permitted to play life out. Still, it is a pretty thing to think otherwise, and, in my opinion, a useful thing.

There are those, made of sterner stuff, who disagree. David Thomson thinks slightly ill of Clint's late-life achievements. A more forthright acknowledgment of the growing shadow of death, he believes, would become Clint. "Gary Cooper had seen doom ahead some time in the mid-1940s, and it gave him grandeur. Eastwood wants to suffer in his recent films—but it's still a reach, just a little bit beyond his experience or imagination."

There is some truth in that. But some untruth also. There was much discomfiting pathos in Cooper's slo-mo decline, some unspoken plea for pity that is as we know antithetical to Clint's nature. Something Andrew Sarris said about Charles Chaplin, imagining his own demise in *Limelight,* also applies. To do so, especially if you are an actor with a singularly and sharply outlined screen persona, is to imagine, he wrote, the death of the world, "a conception of sublime egoism." Such conceptions, sublime or otherwise, are truly beyond the range of Clint's experience and imagination.

His need is the opposite—to render death an anticlimax. It is why he so often ends his films with a sudden disappearance, why, perhaps, he has so often toyed with the idea of reincarnation. Each implies that the end is, comparatively speaking, nothing; not, certainly, when the comparison is to life.

We have to agree that this thought lacks doomy grandeur. But it is not without a certain gallantry and, in this case, a certain honesty and instructive power. This is who Clint Eastwood is now, what he has come to be at this stage in his long career. The business of movie stars is not to impersonate others. It has never been interesting to say of them that they only play themselves. Of course they do. The only worthwhile question is, with what honesty and subtlety do they do so?

That is why we often come to our deepest affection for them—and our deepest alienation from them—later in life, when we see how they have played out the challenge of the years. Suppose, for the moment, that Clint Eastwood had played his Sergio Leone characters as the director originally wanted him to—with openness and articulateness that did not at that age suit the actor. Suppose, by contrast, he had gone on playing that silently disdainful figure decades later, when he had, in fact, become in life a man capable of expressing himself much more fully. In either case, we would have sensed the lie—or, worse, the arrested development—and likely turned away from him. Or suppose he had stopped his evolution at the next stage, with the more openly, but still brutally expressed, outrage of *Dirty Harry*. It was appropriate to that season of Clint's life, but not to its subsequent ones.

The point is that we like to see, need to see, in male movie stars—not in female ones, wherein lies their terrible problem—what we need to see, hope to see, in ourselves: the capacity not so much to grow, but to find and project the best of themselves in the context of the encroaching years. It is what the great ones—Tracy, Grant, even John Wayne in his blunter way—contrived to do. It is what Clint is now doing, as he plays characters searching for the kind of reconciliations we are all ideally obliged to seek in our seventh decade. In so doing he guarantees the truth of his previous incarnations. He has always done what he honorably could with what he had at the particular moment—no duplicity, very little in the way of artifice or artfulness.

Younger, smoldering with anger, but struggling to control it, he confronted the chaos attendant upon our culture's redefinitions of manhood with the willed application of a sometimes-violent irony. Confronting age—that universally redefining force—irony, slightly sadder in its expression, more gently wielded, remains his weapon of choice.

Sitting with Clint in the fading light of certain wintry afternoons, searching through his life for such meanings as could be extracted from it, I have thought: He is a different man now than he was then . . . and then . . . and then. At virtually the same moment I have seen that at his core he was then . . . and then . . . and then the same man. And I have asked: Aren't we all? And are we all? And I have thought that the power of his presence on our screens, in our minds, in the life of our times, derives from the elegant and enigmatic double helix he has spun from those questions.

FILMOGRAPHY

NOTES

BIBLIOGRAPHY

ACKNOWLEDGMENTS

INDEX

FILMOGRAPHY (1955–96)

REVENGE OF THE CREATURE (1955)
Universal-International
Producer: William Alland
Director: Jack Arnold
Screenplay: Martin Berkeley
Director of Photography: Charles S. Welbourne
Editor: Paul Weatherwax
Cast: John Agar, Lori Nelson, John Bromfield, Nestor Paiva, Grandon Rhodes, Dave Willock, Robert B. Williams, Charles Cane, Clint Eastwood as Jennings, a lab technician

FRANCIS IN THE NAVY (1955)
Universal-International
Producer: Stanley Rubin
Director: Arthur Lubin
Screenplay: Devery Freeman
Director of Photography: Carl Guthrie
Editors: Milton Carruth, Ray Snyder
Cast: Donald O'Connor, Martha Hyer, Richard Erdman, Jim Backus, Clint Eastwood as Jonesy, David Janssen, Leigh Snowden, Martin Milner

LADY GODIVA (1955)
Universal-International
Producer: Robert Arthur
Director: Arthur Lubin
Screenplay: Oscar Brodney, Harry Ruskin

Director of Photography: Carl Guthrie
Editor: Paul Weatherwax
Cast: Maureen O'Hara, George Nader, Victor McLaglen, Rex Reason, Clint Eastwood as First Saxon

TARANTULA (1955)
Universal-International
Producer: William Alland
Director: Jack Arnold
Screenplay: Robert Fresco, Martin Berkeley
Director of Photography: George Robinson
Editor: William M. Morgan
Cast: John Agar, Mara Corday, Leo G. Carroll, Clint Eastwood as First Pilot

NEVER SAY GOODBYE (1956)
Universal-International
Producer: Albert J. Cohen
Director: Jerry Hopper
Screenplay: Charles Hoffman
Director of Photography: Maury Gertsman
Editor: Paul Weatherwax
Music: Frank Skinner
Cast: Rock Hudson, Cornell Borchers, George Sanders, Ray Collins, David Janssen, Shelley Fabares, Clint Eastwood as Will, a lab assistant

STAR IN THE DUST (1956)

Universal-International
Producer: Albert Zugsmith
Director: Charles Haas
Screenplay: Oscar Brodney
Director of Photography: John D. Russell Jr.
Editor: Ray Snyder
Music: Frank Skinner
Cast: John Agar, Mamie Van Doren, Richard Boone, Leif Erickson, Coleen Gray, James Gleason, Randy Stuart, Terry Gilkyson, Paul Fix, Harry Morgan, Clint Eastwood as a ranch hand

AWAY ALL BOATS (1956)

Universal-International
Producer: Howard Christie
Director: Joseph Pevney
Screenplay: Ted Sherdeman
Director of Photography: William Daniels
Editor: Ted Kent
Music: Frank Skinner
Cast: Jeff Chandler, George Nader, Julie Adams, Lex Barker, Keith Andes, Richard Boone, William Reynolds, Charles McGraw, Jock Mahoney, John McIntire, Clint Eastwood as a sailor

THE FIRST TRAVELING SALESLADY (1956)

RKO
Producer/Director: Arthur Lubin
Screenplay: Devery Freeman, Stephen Longstreet
Director of Photography: William Snyder
Editor: Otto Ludwig
Music: Irving Gertz
Cast: Ginger Rogers, Barry Nelson, Carol Channing, David Brian, James Arness, Clint Eastwood as Jack Rice

ESCAPADE IN JAPAN (1957)

RKO/Universal-International
Producer/Director: Arthur Lubin
Screenplay: Winston Miller
Director of Photography: William Snyder
Editor: Otto Ludwig
Music: Max Steiner
Cast: Teresa Wright, Cameron Mitchell, Jon Provost, Roger Nakagawa, Clint Eastwood as Dumbo, a pilot

LAFAYETTE ESCADRILLE (1958)

Warner Bros.
Producer/Director: Willaim A. Wellman
Screenplay: A. S. Fleischman
Director of Photography: William Clothier
Editor: Owen Marks
Music: Leonard Rosenman
Cast: Tab Hunter; Etchika Choureau; Marcel Dalio; David Janssen; Paul Fix; Clint Eastwood as George Moseley, a fighter pilot; Bill Wellman Jr.

AMBUSH AT CIMARRON PASS (1958)

Regal/20th Century–Fox
Producer: Herbert E. Mendelson
Director: Jodie Copeland
Screenplay: Richard G. Taylor, John K. Butler
Director of Photography: John M. Nickolaus Jr.
Editor: Carl L. Pierson
Music: Paul Sawtell, Bert Shefter
Cast: Scott Brady, Margia Dean, Clint Eastwood as Keith Williams, Baynes Barron, William Vaughan, Ken Mayer, John Manier, Keith Richards, John Merrick, Frank Gerstle, Dirk London, Irving Bacon, Desmond Slattery

FISTFUL OF DOLLARS (1964; U.S. 1967)

Jolly Film/Constantin/Ocean/United
Artists
Producers: Arrighi Colombo, George
Papi
Director: Sergio Leone
Screenplay: Sergio Leone, Duccio
Tessari, Victor A. Cantena, G.
Schock
Director of Photography: Jack Dalmas
(Massimo Dallamano)
Editor: Roberto Cinquini
Music: Ennio Morricone
Cast: The Stranger (Joe), Clint
Eastwood; Ramon Rojo, Gian
Maria Volonté; Marisol, Marianne
Koch; Silvanito, Pepe Calvo; John
Baxter, Wolfgang Lukschy; and
Sieghardt Rupp, Antonio Prieto,
Margarita Lozano, Daniel Martin,
Bruno Carotentuto, Benito
Stefanelli, Richard Stuyvesant, Josef
Egger, Mario Brega

FOR A FEW DOLLARS MORE (1965; U.S. 1967)

Produzioni Europee Associates/
Constantin Arturo Gonzales
Producer: Alberto Grimaldi
Director: Sergio Leone
Screenplay: Luciano Vincenzoni,
Sergio Leone
Director of Photography: Massimo
Dallamano
Editors: Giorgio Ferralonga, Eugenio
Alabiso
Music: Ennio Morricone
Cast: The Stranger (Monco), Clint
Eastwood; Colonel Mortimer, Lee
Van Cleef; El Indio, Gian Maria
Volonté; and Klaus Kinski, Josef
Egger, Rosemary Dexter, Mara
Krup, Mario Brega, Aldo Sambrel,
Luigi Pistilli, Benito Stefanelli,
Panos Papadopoulos, Roberto
Camardiel

THE GOOD, THE BAD, AND THE UGLY (1966; U.S. 1968)

Produzioni Europee Associates/United
Artists
Producer: Alberto Grimaldi
Director: Sergio Leone
Screenplay: Luciano Vincenzoni,
Sergio Leone
Director of Photography: Tonino Delli
Colli
Editors: Nino Baragli, Eugenio Alabiso
Music: Ennio Morricone
Cast: Blondie, Clint Eastwood; Tuco,
Eli Wallach; Angel Eyes, Lee Van
Cleef; and Aldo Giuffre, Mario
Brega, Livio Lorenzon, Luigi
Pistilli, Rada Rassimov, Enzo
Petito, John Bartha

THE WITCHES (1965; U.S. 1979)

Dino De Laurentiis/Les Productions
Artistes Associes
Executive Producer: Alfredo De
Laurentiis
Producer: Dino De Laurentiis
Director (Part Five, "A Night Like
Any Other"): Vittorio De Sica
Screenplay: Cesare Zavattini, Fabio
Carpi, Enzio Muzii
Director of Photography: Giusseppe
Rotunno
Editor: Adriana Novelli
Music: Pierto Piccinoi
Cast: Giovanna, Silvana Mangano;
Husband, Clint Eastwood; and
Armando Bottin, Gianni Gori,
Paolo Gozlino, Angelo Santi, Piero
Torrisi

HANG 'EM HIGH (1968)

United Artists/Malpaso
Producer: Leonard Freeman
Director: Ted Post
Screenplay: Leonard Freeman, Mel
Goldberg
Directors of Photography: Richard
Kline, Lennie South
Editor: Gene Fowler Jr.

Music: Dominic Frontiere
Cast: Jed Cooper, Clint Eastwood;
  Rachel, Inger Stevens; Captain
  Wilson, Ed Begley; Judge Adam
  Fenton, Pat Hingle; Jennifer, Arlene
  Golonka; Preacher, James
  MacArthur; and Ben Johnson,
  Charles McGraw, L. Q. Jones,
  Bruce Dern, Ruth White, Alan
  Hale Jr., Dennis Hopper, Bob
  Steele

COOGAN'S BLUFF (1968)
Universal
Executive Producer: Richard E. Lyons
Producer/Director: Don Siegel
Screenplay: Herman Miller, Dean
  Reisner, Howard Rodman
Story: Herman Miller
Director of Photography: Bud
  Thackery
Editor: Sam E. Waxman
Music: Lalo Schifrin
Cast: Coogan, Clint Eastwood; Sheriff
  McElroy, Lee J. Cobb; Julie, Susan
  Clark; Linny Raven, Tisha Sterling;
  Ringerman, Don Stroud; Mrs.
  Ringerman, Betty Field; Sheriff
  McCrea, Tom Tully; and Melodie
  Johnson, James Edwards, Rudy
  Diaz, David F. Doyle, Louis Zorich,
  Meg Myles, Seymour Cassell, James
  Gavin

WHERE EAGLES DARE (1968)
Metro-Goldwyn-Mayer
Producer: Elliott Kastner
Director: Brian G. Hutton
Story and Screenplay: Alistair MacLean
Director of Photography: Arthur
  Ibbetson
Editor: John Jympson
Music: Ron Goodwin
Cast: John Smith, Richard Burton;
  Lieutenant Morris Schaffer, Clint
  Eastwood; Mary Ellison, Mary Ure;
  Vice-Admiral Rolland, Michael

Hordern; Colonel Wyatt Turner,
  Patrick Wymark; and Robert
  Beatty, Anton Diffring, Donald
  Houston, Ferdy Mayne, Neil
  McCarthy, Peter Barkworth,
  William Squire, Brook Williams,
  Ingrid Pitt

PAINT YOUR WAGON (1969)
Paramount
Producer: Alan Jay Lerner
Director: Joshua Logan
Screenplay and Lyrics: Alan Jay Lerner
Adaptation: Paddy Chayefsky
Director of Photography: William
  Fraker
Editor: Robert Jones
Music: Frederick Loewe, André Previn
Cast: Ben Rumson, Lee Marvin;
  Pardner, Clint Eastwood; Elizabeth,
  Jean Seberg; Rotten Luck Willie,
  Harve Presnell; Mad Jack Duncan,
  Ray Walston; and Tom Ligon,
  Alan Dexter, William O'Connell,
  Ben Baker, Alan Baxter, Paula
  Trueman, Robert Easton,
  Geoffrey Norman, H. B. Haggerty,
  Terry Jenkins, Karl Bruck,
  John Mitchum

KELLY'S HEROES (1970)
Metro-Goldwyn-Mayer
Producers: Gabriel Katzka, Sidney
  Beckerman
Director: Brian G. Hutton
Screenplay: Troy Kennedy Martin
Director of Photography: Gabriel
  Figueroa
Editor: John Jympson
Music: Lalo Schifrin
Cast: Kelly, Clint Eastwood; Big Joe,
  Telly Savalas; Crapgame, Don
  Rickles; General Colt, Carroll
  O'Connor; Oddball, Donald
  Sutherland; and Gavin MacLeod,
  George Savalas, Hal Buckley,
  David Hurst, John Heller

TWO MULES FOR SISTER SARA (1970)

Universal/Malpaso
Producer: Martin Rackin
Director: Don Siegel
Screenplay: Albert Maltz
Story: Budd Boetticher
Director of Photography: Gabriel Figueroa
Editor: Robert Shugrue
Music: Ennio Morricone
Cast: Hogan, Clint Eastwood; Sister Sara, Shirley MacLaine; Colonel Beltran, Manolo Fabregas; and Alberto Morin, Armando Silvestre

THE BEGUILED (1971)

Universal/Malpaso
Producer/Director: Don Siegel
Screenplay: John B. Sherry, Grimes Grice
Novel: Thomas Cullinan
Director of Photography: Bruce Surtees
Editor: Carl Pingitore
Music: Lalo Schifrin
Cast: John McBurney, Clint Eastwood; Martha Farnsworth, Geraldine Page; Edwina Dabney, Elizabeth Hartman; Carol, Jo Ann Harris; Doris, Darleen Carr; Nellie, Mae Mercer; Amy, Pamelyn Ferdin; Abigail, Melody Thomas; Lizzie, Peggy Drier; Janie, Pattye Mattick

PLAY MISTY FOR ME (1971)

Universal/Malpaso
Producer: Robert Daley
Director: Clint Eastwood
Screenplay: Jo Heims, Dean Reisner
Director of Photography: Bruce Surtees
Editor: Carl Pingitore
Music: Dee Barton
Cast: Dave Garland, Clint Eastwood; Evelyn Draper, Jessica Walter; Tobie Williams, Donna Mills; Sergeant McCallum, John Larch; and Clarice Taylor, Irene Hervey, Jack Ging, James McEachin, Don Siegel, Duke Everts

DIRTY HARRY (1971)

Warner Bros./Seven Arts/Malpaso
Executive Producer: Robert Daley
Producer/Director: Don Siegel
Screenplay: Harry Julian Fink, Rita M. Fink, Dean Reisner
Director of Photography: Bruce Surtees
Editor: Carl Pingitore
Music: Lalo Schifrin
Cast: Detective Harry Callahan, Clint Eastwood; Lieutenant Bressler, Harry Guardino; Chico, Reni Santoni; Mayor, John Vernon; Scorpio, Andy Robinson; Chief, John Larch; DiGeorgio, John Mitchum; and Mae Mercer, Lyn Edgington, Ruth Kobart, Woodrow Parfrey, Josef Sommer, William Paterson, James Nolan, Maurice S. Argent, Jo de Winter, Craig G. Kelly

JOE KIDD (1972)

Universal/Malpaso
Executive Producer: Robert Daley
Producer: Sidney Beckerman
Director: John Sturges
Screenplay: Elmore Leonard
Director of Photography: Bruce Surtees
Editor: Ferris Webster
Music: Lalo Schifrin
Cast: Joe Kidd, Clint Eastwood; Frank Harlan, Robert Duvall; Luis Chama, John Saxon; Lamarr, Don Stroud; Helen Sanchez, Stella Garcia; and James Wainwright, Paul Koslo, Gregory Walcott, Dick Van Patten, Lynne Marta

HIGH PLAINS DRIFTER (1973)

Universal/Malpaso
Executive Producer: Jennings Lang
Producer: Robert Daley
Director: Clint Eastwood
Screenplay: Ernest Tidyman
Director of Photography: Bruce Surtees
Editor: Ferris Webster
Music: Dee Barton

Cast: The Stranger, Clint Eastwood; Sarah Belding, Verna Bloom; Callie Travers, Marianna Hill; Dave Drake, Mitchell Ryan; Morgan Allen, Jack Ging; Mayor Jason Hobart, Stefan Gierasch; Lewis Belding, Ted Hartley; Mordecai, Billy Curtis; Stacey Bridges, Geoffrey Lewis; and Scott Walker, Walter Barnes

BREEZY (1973)

Universal/Malpaso
Executive Producer: Jennings Lang
Producer: Robert Daley
Director: Clint Eastwood
Screenplay: Jo Heims
Director of Photography: Frank Stanley
Editor: Ferris Webster
Music: Michel Legrand
Cast: Frank Harmon, William Holden; Breezy, Kay Lenz; and Roger C. Carmel, Marj Dusay, Joan Hotchkis, Jamie Smith Jackson, Norman Bartold, Lynn Borden, Shelley Morrison, Dennis Olivieri, Eugene Peterson

MAGNUM FORCE (1973)

Warner Bros./Malpaso
Producer: Robert Daley
Director: Ted Post
Screenplay: John Milius, Michael Cimino
Director of Photography: Frank Stanley
Editor: Ferris Webster
Music: Lalo Schifrin
Cast: Harry Callahan, Clint Eastwood; Lieutenant Briggs, Hal Holbrook; Charlie McCoy, Mitchell Ryan; and David Soul, Felton Perry, Robert Urich, Kip Niven, Tim Matheson, Christine White

THUNDERBOLT AND LIGHTFOOT (1974)

United Artists/Malpaso
Producer: Robert Daley
Director: Michael Cimino
Screenplay: Michael Cimino

Director of Photography: Frank Stanley
Editor: Ferris Webster
Music: Dee Barton
Cast: John "Thunderbolt" Doherty, Clint Eastwood; Lightfoot, Jeff Bridges; Red Leary, George Kennedy; Goody, Geoffrey Lewis; Melody, Catherine Bach; Curly, Gary Busey; and Jack Dodson, Gene Elman, Lila Teigh, Burton Gilliam, Roy Jenson, Claudia Lennear, Bill McKinney, Vic Tayback

THE EIGER SANCTION (1975)

Universal/Malpaso
Executive Producers: Richard D. Zanuck, David Brown
Producer: Robert Daley
Director: Clint Eastwood
Screenplay: Warren B. Murphy, Hal Dresner, Rod Whitaker
Novel: Trevenian
Director of Photography: Frank Stanley
Editor: Ferris Webster
Music: John Williams
Cast: Jonathan Hemlock, Clint Eastwood; Ben Bowman, George Kennedy; Jemima Brown, Vonetta McGee; Miles Mellough, Jack Cassidy; Anna Montaigne, Heidi Bruhl; Dragon, Thayer David; and Reiner Schoene, Michael Grimm, Jean-Pierre Bernard, Brenda Venus, Gregory Walcott

THE OUTLAW JOSEY WALES (1976)

Warner Bros./Malpaso
Producer: Robert Daley
Director: Clint Eastwood
Screenplay: Philip Kaufman, Sonia Chernus
Novel: Forrest Carter
Director of Photography: Bruce Surtees
Editor: Ferris Webster
Music: Jerry Fielding
Cast: Josey Wales, Clint Eastwood; Lone Watie, Chief Dan George;

Laura Lee, Sondra Locke; Terrill, Bill McKinney; Fletcher, John Vernon; Grandma Sarah, Paula Trueman; Jamie, Sam Bottoms; and Geraldine Keams, Woodrow Parfrey, Joyce Jameson, Sheb Wooley, Royal Dano, Matt Clark, John Verros, Will Sampson, William O'Connell, John Quade

THE ENFORCER (1976)

Warner Bros./Malpaso
Producer: Robert Daley
Director: James Fargo
Screenplay: Stirling Silliphant, Dean Reisner
Director of Photography: Charles W. Short
Editors: Ferris Webster, Joel Cox
Music: Jerry Fielding
Cast: Harry Callahan, Clint Eastwood; Kate Moore, Tyne Daly; Lieutenant Bressler, Harry Guardino; Captain McKay, Bradford Dillman; DiGeorgio, John Mitchum; Bobby Maxwell, DeVeren Brookwalter; Mayor, John Crawford; and Samantha Doane, Robert Hoy, Jocelyn Jones, M. G. Kelly, Nick Pellegrino, Albert Popwell

THE GAUNTLET (1977)

Warner Bros./Malpaso
Producer: Robert Daley
Director: Clint Eastwood
Screenplay: Michael Butler, Dennis Shryack
Director of Photography: Rexford Metz
Editors: Ferris Webster, Joel Cox
Music: Jerry Fielding
Cast: Ben Shockley, Clint Eastwood; Gus Mally, Sondra Locke; Josephson, Pat Hingle; Blakelock, William Prince; Constable, Bill McKinney, Feyderspiel, Michael Cavanaugh; and Carole Cook, Mara Corday, Douglas McGrath, Jeff Morris

EVERY WHICH WAY BUT LOOSE (1978)

Warner Bros./Malpaso
Producer: Robert Daley
Director: James Fargo
Screenplay: Jeremy Joe Kronsberg
Director of Photography: Rexford Metz
Editor: Ferris Webster
Cast: Philo Beddoe, Clint Eastwood; Lynne Halsey-Taylor, Sondra Locke; Orville Boggs, Geoffrey Lewis; Echo, Beverly D'Angelo; Ma Boggs, Ruth Gordon; and Walter Barnes, George Chandler, Roy Jenson, James McEachin, Bill McKinney, William O'Connell

ESCAPE FROM ALCATRAZ (1979)

Paramount/Malpaso
Producer/Director: Don Siegel
Screenplay: Richard Tuggle
Novel: J. Campbell Bruce
Director of Photography: Bruce Surtees
Editor: Ferris Webster
Music: Jerry Fielding
Cast: Frank Morris, Clint Eastwood; Warden, Patrick McGoohan; Doc, Roberts Blossom; Clarence Anglin, Jack Thibeau; John Anglin, Fred Ward; English, Paul Benjamin; Charley Butts, Larry Hankin; and Bruce M. Fischer, Frank Ronzio

BRONCO BILLY (1980)

Warner Bros./Malpaso
Executive Producer: Robert Daley
Producer: Dennis Hackin
Director: Clint Eastwood
Screenplay: Dennis Hackin
Director of Photography: David Worth
Editors: Ferris Webster, Joel Cox
Cast: Bronco Billy McCoy, Clint Eastwood; Antoinette Lily, Sondra Locke; John Arlington, Geoffrey Lewis; Doc Lynch, Scatman Crothers; Lefty LeBow, Bill McKinney; Leonard James, Sam Bottoms; Chief Big Eagle, Dan

Vadis; Lorraine Running Water,
Sierra Pecheur; and Walter Barnes,
Woodrow Parfrey, Beverlee
McKinsey, Douglas McGrath, Hank
Worden, William Prince

ANY WHICH WAY YOU CAN (1980)
Warner Bros./Malpaso
Executive Producer: Robert Daley
Producer: Fritz Manes
Director: Buddy Van Horn
Screenplay: Stanford Sherman
Director of Photography: David Worth
Editors: Ferris Webster, Ron Spang
Cast: Philo Beddoe, Clint Eastwood;
Lynne Halsey-Taylor, Sondra
Locke; Orville Boggs, Geoffrey
Lewis; Jack Wilson, William Smith;
James Beekman, Harry Guardino;
Ma Boggs, Ruth Gordon;
and Michael Cavanaugh,
Barry Corbin, Roy Jenson,
Bill McKinney, William O'Connell,
John Quade

FIREFOX (1982)
Warner Bros./Malpaso
Executive Producer: Fritz Manes
Producer/Director: Clint Eastwood
Screenplay: Alex Lasker, Wendell
Wellman
Novel: Craig Thomas
Director of Photography:
Bruce Surtees
Editors: Ferris Webster, Ron Spang
Music: Maurice Jarre
Cast: Mitchell Gant, Clint Eastwood;
Kenneth Aubrey, Freddie Jones;
Buckholz, David Huffman; Pavel
Upenskoy, Warren Clarke; and
Ronald Lacey, Kenneth Colley,
Klaus Lowitsch, Nigel Hawthorne

HONKYTONK MAN (1982)
Warner Bros./Malpaso
Executive Producer: Fritz Manes
Producer/Director: Clint Eastwood
Screenplay: Clancy Carlile
Novel: Clancy Carlile

Director of Photography: Bruce Surtees
Editors: Ferris Webster, Michael Kelly,
Joel Cox
Music: Steve Dorff
Cast: Red Stovall, Clint Eastwood;
Whit, Kyle Eastwood; Grandpa,
John McIntire; Marlene, Alexa
Kenin; Emmy, Verna Bloom; Virgil,
Matt Clark; and Barry Corbin,
Jerry Hardin

SUDDEN IMPACT (1983)
Warner Bros./Malpaso
Executive Producer: Fritz Manes
Producer/Director: Clint Eastwood
Screenplay: Joseph C. Stinson
Story: Earl Smith, Charles B. Pierce
Director of Photography: Bruce Surtees
Editor: Joel Cox
Music: Lalo Schifrin
Cast: Harry Callahan, Clint Eastwood;
Jennifer Spencer, Sondra Locke;
Chief Jannings, Pat Hingle; Captain
Briggs, Bradford Dillman; and Paul
Drake, Audrie J. Neenan, Jack
Thibeau, Michael Currie, Albert
Popwell

CITY HEAT (1984)
Warner Bros./Malpaso/Deliverance
Producer: Fritz Manes
Director: Richard Benjamin
Screenplay: Sam O. Brown (Blake
Edwards), Joseph C. Stinson
Director of Photography: Nick McLean
Editor: Jacqueline Cambas
Music: Lennie Niehaus
Cast: Lieutenant Speer, Clint
Eastwood; Mike Murphy, Burt
Reynolds; Addy, Jane Alexander;
Caroline Howley, Madeline Kahn;
Primo Pitt, Rip Torn; Ginny Lee,
Irene Cara; Dehl Swift, Richard
Roundtree; Leon Coll, Tony Lo
Bianco; and Nicholas Worth,
Robert Davi, Jude Forese, John
Hancock, Jeb Thacker, Gerald S.
O'Loughlin

TIGHTROPE (1984)
Warner Bros./Malpaso
Producers: Clint Eastwood, Fritz
  Manes
Director: Richard Tuggle
Screenplay: Richard Tuggle
Director of Photography: Bruce Surtees
Music: Lennie Niehaus
Cast: Wes Block, Clint Eastwood;
  Beryl Thibodeaux, Geneviève
  Bujold; Detective Molinari, Dan
  Hedaya; Amanda Block, Alison
  Eastwood; Penny Block, Jennifer
  Beck; and Marco St. John, Rebecca
  Perle, Regina Richardson, Randi
  Brooks,
  Jamie Rose

PALE RIDER (1985)
Warner Bros./Malpaso
Executive Producer: Fritz Manes
Producer/Director: Clint Eastwood
Screenplay: Michael Butler, Dennis
  Shryack
Director of Photography:
  Bruce Surtees
Editor: Joel Cox
Music: Lennie Niehaus
Cast: Preacher, Clint Eastwood; Hull
  Barrett, Michael Moriarty; Sarah
  Wheeler, Carrie Snodgrass; Josh
  LaHood, Christopher Penn; Coy
  LaHood, Richard Dysart; Megan
  Wheeler, Sydney Penny; Club,
  Richard Kiel; Spider Conway,
  Doug McGrath; Marshall
  Stockburn, John Russell

VANESSA IN THE GARDEN (1985)
Amblin Entertainment/NBC
Executive Producer: Steven Spielberg
Producer: David E. Vogel
Director: Clint Eastwood
Screenplay: Steven Spielberg
Director of Photography: Robert
  Stevens
Editor: Jo Ann Fogle
Music: Lennie Niehaus

Cast: Byron Sullivan, Harvey Keitel;
  Vanessa, Sondra Locke; Ted,
  Beau Bridges

HEARTBREAK RIDGE (1986)
Warner Bros./Malpaso
Executive Producer: Fritz Manes
Producer/Director: Clint Eastwood
Screenplay: James Carabatsos
Director of Photography: Jack N. Green
Editor: Joel Cox
Music: Lennie Niehaus
Cast: Sergeant Tom Highway, Clint
  Eastwood; Aggie, Marsha Mason;
  Major Powers, Everett McGill;
  Sergeant Webster, Moses Gunn;
  Little Mary, Eileen Heckart; Roy
  Jennings, Bo Svenson; Lieutenant
  Ring, Boyd Gaines; Stitch Jones,
  Mario Van Peebles; and Arlen Dean
  Snyder, Vincent Irizarry, Ramon
  Franco, Tom Villard, Mike Gomez,
  Rodney Hill, Peter Koch, Richard
  Venture

THELONIOUS MONK: STRAIGHT NO CHASER (1988)
Warner Bros.
Executive Producer: Clint Eastwood
Producers: Charlotte Zwerin, Bruce
  Ricker
Editor: Charlotte Zwerin

THE DEAD POOL (1988)
Warner Bros./Malpaso
Producer: David Valdes
Director: Buddy Van Horn
Screenplay: Steve Sharon
Director of Photography: Jack N. Green
Editor: Ron Spang
Music: Lalo Schifrin
Cast: Harry Callahan, Clint Eastwood;
  Samantha Walker, Patricia Clarkson;
  Peter Swan, Liam Neeson; Al
  Quan, Evan C. Kim; and David
  Hunt, Michael Currie, Michael
  Goodwin, Darwin Gillett, Anthony
  Charnota, Christopher Beale, John
  Allen Vick, Jeff Richmond, Patrick

Van Horn, Singrid Wurschmidt,
James Carrey

BIRD (1988)
Warner Bros./Malpaso
Executive Producer: David Valdes
Producer/Director: Clint Eastwood
Screenplay: Joel Oliansky
Director of Photography: Jack N. Green
Editor: Joel Cox
Music: Lennie Niehaus
Cast: Charlie Parker, Forest Whitaker;
   Chan Richardson, Diane Venora;
   Red Rodney, Michael Zelniker;
   Dizzy Gillespie, Samuel E. Wright;
   and Keith David, Michael McGuire,
   James Handy, Damon Whitaker,
   Morgan Nagler

PINK CADILLAC (1989)
Warner Bros./Malpaso
Executive Producer: Michael Gruskoff
Producer: David Valdes
Director: Buddy Van Horn
Screenplay: John Eskow
Director of Photography: Jack N. Green
Editor: Joel Cox
Music: Steve Dorff
Cast: Tommy Nowak, Clint Eastwood;
   Lou Ann McGuinn, Bernadette
   Peters; Roy, Timothy Carhart; and
   Michael Des Barres, John Dennis
   Johnston, Jimmy F. Skaggs, Bill
   Moseley, Tiffany Gail Robinson,
   Angela Louise Robinson, Geoffrey
   Lewis, William Hickey, Frances
   Fisher, James Carrey

**WHITE HUNTER, BLACK HEART
   (1990)**
Warner Bros./Malpaso
Executive Producer: David Valdes
Producer/Director: Clint Eastwood
Screenplay: Peter Viertel, James
   Bridges, Burt Kennedy
Director of Photography: Jack N. Green
Editor: Joel Cox
Music: Lennie Niehaus

Cast: John Wilson, Clint Eastwood;
   Pete Verrill, Jeff Fahey; Miss
   Winding, Charlotte Cornwell;
   Paul Landers, George Dzundza;
   Kiru, Boy Mathias Chuma; Kay
   Gibson, Marisa Berenson; and
   Edward Tudor Pole, Roddy
   Maude-Roxby, Richard Warwick,
   John Rapley, Catherine Neilson,
   Richard Vanstone, Norman
   Lumsden

THE ROOKIE (1990)
Warner Bros./Malpaso
Producer: Howard Kazanjian, Steven
   Siebert, David Valdes
Director: Clint Eastwood
Screenplay: Boaz Yakin, Scott Spiegel
Director of Photography: Jack N. Green
Editor: Joel Cox
Music: Lennie Niehaus
Cast: Nick Pulovski, Clint Eastwood;
   David Ackerman, Charlie Sheen;
   Strom, Raul Julia; Liesl, Sonia
   Braga; Eugene Ackerman, Tom
   Skerritt; Sarah, Lara Flynn Boyle;
   and Pepe Serna, Marco Rodriguez,
   Pete Randall

UNFORGIVEN (1992)
Warner Bros./Malpaso
Executive Producer: David Valdes
Producer/Director: Clint Eastwood
Screenplay: David Webb Peoples
Director of Photography:
   Jack N. Green
Editor: Joel Cox
Music: Lennie Niehaus
Cast: William Munny, Clint Eastwood;
   Little Bill Daggett, Gene Hackman;
   Ned Logan, Morgan Freeman;
   English Bob, Richard Harris; The
   Schofield Kid, Jaimz Woolvett;
   W. W. Beauchamp, Saul Rubinek;
   Strawberry Alice, Frances Fisher;
   Delilah Fitzgerald, Anna Thomson;
   and David Mucci, Rob Campbell,
   Anthony James

IN THE LINE OF FIRE (1993)
Castle Rock/Columbia
Executive Producers: Wolfgang
    Petersen, Gail Katz, David Valdes
Producer: Jeff Apple
Director: Wolfgang Petersen
Screenplay: Jeff Maguire
Director of Photography: John Bailey
Editor: Anne V. Coates
Music: Ennio Morricone
Cast: Frank Horrigan, Clint Eastwood;
    Mitch Leary, John Malkovich;
    Lilly Raines, Rene Russo;
    Al D'Andrea, Dylan McDermott;
    Bill Watts, Gary Cole; and Fred
    Dalton Thompson, John Mahoney,
    Jim Curley, Sally Hughes, Clyde
    Kusatsu, Steve Hytner, Tobin Bell,
    Patrika Darbo, Mary Van Arsdel,
    John Heard

A PERFECT WORLD (1993)
Warner Bros./Malpaso
Producers: Mark Johnson, David
    Valdes
Director: Clint Eastwood
Screenplay: John Lee Hancock
Director of Photography: Jack N.
    Green
Editor: Joel Cox
Music: Lennie Niehaus
Cast: Butch Haynes, Kevin Costner;
    Red Garnett, Clint Eastwood;
    Sally Gerber, Laura Dern; Phillip
    Perry, T. J. Lowther; and Leo

Burmester, Keith Szarabajka,
Wayne Dehart

THE BRIDGES OF MADISON COUNTY (1995)
Warner Bros./Malpaso
Producers: Clint Eastwood, Kathleen
    Kennedy
Director: Clint Eastwood
Screenplay: Richard LaGravenese
Novel: Robert James Waller
Director of Photography: Jack N.
    Green
Editor: Joel Cox
Music: Lennie Niehaus
Cast: Robert Kincaid, Clint Eastwood;
    Francesca Johnson, Meryl Streep;
    Caroline Johnson, Annie Corley;
    Michael Johnson, Victor Slezak;
    Richard Johnson, Jim Haynie

THE STARS FELL ON HENRIETTA (1995)
Warner Bros./Malpaso
Producers: Clint Eastwood, David
    Valdes
Director: James Keach
Screenplay: Philip Railsback
Director of Photography: Bruce Surtees
Editor: Joel Cox
Music: David Benoit
Cast: Mr. Cox, Robert Duvall; Don
    Day, Aidan Quinn; Cora Day,
    Frances Fisher; Big Dave, Brian
    Dennehy

NOTES

In order not to burden this book with excessive annotation these notes identify only those quotations from Clint Eastwood that are drawn from secondary sources—largely from books, magazines and newspapers to which, over the years, he has granted interviews. All unattributed Eastwood quotations in the text are taken from interviews the author conducted with him either in the fall of 1991, on the set of *Unforgiven,* or during the period 1993 to 1996, when this book was in active preparation.

I have not cited brief quotations from reviews where I have used only a phrase or two as a way of summarizing the general critical response to a particular film.

PROLOGUE

page 5 *an uncomplicatedly nice guy:* Richard Jameson, "Pale Rider," *The Weekly* (Seattle), February 12, 1986.

beasts of burden: John Updike, *In the Beauty of the Lillies,* p. 321.

6 *America's daunting ideas:* Janet Maslin, "Good and Evil in a More Innocent Age," *The New York Times,* September 14, 1994.

11 *He says very little to you:* Interview with Gene Hackman, September 18, 1991.

By and large: Interview with Morgan Freeman, October 21, 1991.

12 *Zen and the art of control:* Interview with Tom Stern, June 2, 1993.

12 *He's not an exclamation point:* Interview with Saul Rubinek, September 17, 1991.

someone's violated his world: Interview with Meryl Streep, October 19, 1994.

13 *Eastwood has an uncanny urge:* Thomson, "Forgiven," *The Independent* (London), August 22, 1993.

Oh, yeah, it's easy: Quoted in Norman Mailer, "All the Pirates and People," *Parade,* October 23, 1983.

16 *There's a rebel:* Quoted in Gerald Lubenow, "Rebel in My Soul," *Newsweek,* July 22, 1985.

CHAPTER ONE

19 *What an American:* Norman Mailer, "All the Pirates."
My dad was Scots-English: Ibid.
Did you once describe yourself: Quoted in John Vinocur, "Clint Eastwood, Seriously," *The New York Times Magazine,* February 24, 1985.

20 *the first one at a party:* Interview with Ruth Wood, November 26, 1995. All subsequent quotations from her are drawn from the same source.

24 *made out of Prince Albert cans:* Arthur Knight, "The Interview: Clint Eastwood," *Playboy,* February 1978.

25 *I come and go like The Whistler:* Ibid.

28 *I was terrific:* "The Barbara Walters Special," ABC Television, June 15, 1982.

34 *He went to the drive-in:* Interview with John Calley, May 4, 1994. All subsequent quotations from him are drawn from the same source.

36 *although I rebelled:* Wayne Warga, "Clint Eastwood: He Drifted into Stardom," Los Angeles *Times,* June 22, 1969.

37 *If a kid could ask:* Interview with Fritz Manes, August 11, 1994. All subsequent quotations from him are drawn from the same source.

39 *drew like crazy:* Bob Blumenthal, *Jazz Times,* September 1995.
the last bastion: Ted Gioia, *West Coast Jazz,* p. 60. I have drawn on this volume for much of my description of the jazz scene in California in the 1940s and 1950s.

40 *They never heard of him:* Quoted in Ralph Ellison, "On Bird, Bird-Watching, and Jazz," in *Shadow and Act,* p. 228.
Parker operated in the underworld: Ibid., p. 227.

41 *a grim comedy of racial manners:* Ibid., p. 225.

46 *There's a little guy right inside:* "Barbara Walters Special."

CHAPTER TWO

57 *enhanced their appreciation:* Milton Friedman, "Why Socialism Won't Work," *The New York Times,* August 13, 1994.
This man has had: Quoted in Lennie Niehaus, "The Measure of the Man," in *Clint Eastwood Tribute Book,* ed. Schneider, p. 14.

58 *We hit it off:* Quoted in Iain Johnstone, *Clint Eastwood: The Man with No Name,* p. 13.

61 *The dramatic art is a collective art:* Michael Chekhov, *To the Actor,* p. 41.
a way to help actors: Quoted in Foster Hirsch, *A Method to Their Madness,* p. 341.

63 *reaching out to your partner:* Quoted in Hirsch, p. 341.

CHAPTER THREE

66 *I just lacked the look:* Quoted in Lorenzo Caracaterra, "Dirty Harry Comes Clean," *Video,* May 1985.

starlets and studlets: Interview with Jack Kosslyn, August 29, 1994. All subsequent quotations from him are drawn from the same source.

68 *I thought I was an absolute clod:* Knight, "Interview."

I didn't know what I thought: Terri Lee Robbe, "Life without Clint," *Us,* February 16, 1982.

70 *very intense:* Interview with Brett Halsey, September 23, 1994. All subsequent quotations from him are drawn from the same source.

71 *authority:* This and subsequent evaluations of Clint's participation in the talent program are from internal Universal-International memoranda, June–October 1954, in Clint Eastwood's possession.

73 *That's the kind of control:* Interview with Robert Daley, August 1, 1994.

74 *He was always straight:* Quoted in Michael Neill, "Chatter," *People,* May 26, 1986.

75 *found myself becoming:* Clint Eastwood and Richard Schickel, "Director's Dialogue," presentation at Walker Arts Center, Minneapolis, September 5, 1990.

Its sole interest: See Bob Thomas, *Joan Crawford,* p. 162.

76 *it was hard:* DeWitt Bodeen, "Clint Eastwood . . . a Fistful of Fame," *Focus on Film,* Spring 1972.

77 *wouldn't make any impact:* Quoted in Lorenzo Caracaterra, "In Like Clint," *New York Daily News Sunday Magazine,* August 12, 1984.

78 *The first year of marriage:* Quoted in Minty Clinch, *Clint Eastwood,* p. 29.

80 Kardell's background is recounted in Joe Hyams, *James Dean: Little Boy Lost,* p. 150.

84 *a skinny-legged kid:* Interview with Wayne "Buddy" Van Horn, June 2, 1993.

87 *Please be advised:* Jack Baur to Joseph Dubin, Universal interoffice communication, September 22, 1955.

89 *Some of my friends:* Earl Leaf, "The Way They Were: Clint Eastwood," *Rona Barrett's Hollywood* [circa 1972].

91 *He had tried to get in:* See Clint Eastwood, "Directed By . . . ," in John Boorman and Walter Donohue, eds., *Projection 4½,* p. 56.

92 *Oh, I hated it:* Mailer, "All the Pirates."

You want to get rid of anger: Interview with Robert Donner, August 3, 1984. All subsequent quotations from him are drawn from the same source.

CHAPTER FOUR

100 *I haven't believed in anybody:* Burt A. Folkart, "Charles Marquis Warren, Western Writer," Los Angeles *Times,* August 13, 1990.

105 *No other type:* Richard Slotkin, *Gunfighter Nation,* p. 348.

108 *The scaling-down process:* Rita Parks, *The Western Hero in Film and Television,* p. 153.

111 *at once supremely powerful:* Slotkin, p. 383.

112 *heavy, ponderous, slow:* Interview with Ted Post, July 25, 1993. All subsequent quotations from him are drawn from the same source.

113 *I love him:* Arnold Hano, "How to Revive a Dead Horse," *TV Guide,* October 2, 1965.

116 *A Sunday supplement:* "TV Notes: At Home with Clint Eastwood," New York *Daily News Sunday Magazine,* May 22, 1960.
almost as badly: Knight, "Interview."

117 *He had this thing:* Robbe, "Life without Clint."
I'm not shooting orders: Knight, "Interview."
I was never very realistic: Robbe, "Life without Clint."

118 *What he wanted:* John Updike, "Baby's First Step," in *The Afterlife,* p. 251.
Sex is a small part of life: Quoted in Michael Munn, *Clint Eastwood: Hollywood's Loner,* p. 40.

119 *I kept thinking:* Bernard Weinraub, "Even Cowboys Get Their Due," *GQ,* April 1993.

120 *Having the security:* Knight, "Interview."

121 *You do 250 hours:* Ibid.
didn't direct much: Eastwood and Schickel, "Director's Dialogue."

122 *Like any other actor:* "This Cowboy Feels He's Got It Made," *TV Guide,* February 4, 1961.

123 *Calm on the outside:* Hank Grant, "On the Air," *The Hollywood Reporter,* July 7, 1961.

124 *the fifty-first of the 143 episodes:* Nancy Nalvin, *The Famous Mr. Ed,* p. 272. Other background information on this TV show is from the same source.

126 *It was thirteenth:* This and other ratings figures are from Hano, "How to Revive a Dead Horse."

130 *It was just about the worst:* Munn, p. 45.
I didn't know: Ibid.
It was not until Leone: See Johnstone, p. 35.

132 *But he also remembers:* Interview with Leonard Hirshan, November 9, 1993. All subsequent quotations from him are drawn from the same source.

CHAPTER FIVE

136 *I became decisively enchanted:* Quoted in Pete Hamill, "Leone: I'm a Hunter by Nature, Not a Prey," *American Film,* June 1984.
Publishing houses came out: Ibid.
In recent years: Pauline Kael, "Yojimbo," in *I Lost It at the Movies,* p. 242.

137 *the form had become:* See Pauline Kael, "Saddle Sore," in *Kiss Kiss Bang Bang,* pp. 38–46.
The western hero as a classical archetype: Andrew Sarris, "The

Spaghetti Westerns," in *Confessions of a Cultist,* p. 387.

137 *the western had been killed off:* Christopher Frayling, *Spaghetti Westerns,* p. 100.
The West was made by: Ibid.
They are only borrowing: Quoted in Michael Blowen, "Appreciation: Sergio Leone, Outsider's Insight," Boston *Globe,* May 2, 1989.
like a religion: Quoted in Frayling, *Spaghetti Westerns,* p. 15.

138 *The man of the West:* Quoted in Frayling, *Spaghetti Westerns,* p. 120.

139 *the strange look:* Quoted in Peter B. Flint, "Sergio Leone, 67, Italian Director Who Revitalized Westerns, Dies," *The New York Times,* May 1, 1989.

140 *are less transcendental heroes:* Sarris, "Spaghetti Westerns," p. 388.

the remnants of a code of behavior: Kael, *Kiss,* p. 240.

no great moral purpose: Donald Richie, *The Films of Akira Kurosawa,* p. 148.

the first great shaggy man movie: Kael, *Kiss,* p. 239.

142 *The Catholic dichotomy:* Robert C. Cumbow, *Once upon a Time: The Films of Sergio Leone,* pp. 220, 221.

irredeemably condemned: Quoted in Frayling, *Spaghetti Westerns,* p. 130.

very much the grizzled Christ: Richard Corliss, "Sergio Leone," in Richard Roud, *Cinema: A Critical Dictionary,* vol. 2, p. 618.

143 *not only a delirious descendant:* Ibid., p. 618.

148 *his unbridgeable distance:* Edward Gallafent, *Clint Eastwood: Actor and Director,* p. 17.

I take the real life actor: Johnstone, *Clint Eastwood,* p. 37.

149 *In real life, Clint is slow:* Quoted in Frayling, *Spaghetti Westerns,* p. 146.

In reality, if you think about it: Quoted in Hamill, "Leone."

151 *Fritz Manes remembers:* Manes interview.

was always there: "Clint's Kid," *People,* November 15, 1993.

I guess we never had: Quoted in Douglas Thompson, *Clint Eastwood: Sexual Cowboy,* p. 155.

I have tried to make an appointment: Quoted in Clinch, *Clint Eastwood,* p. 277.

152 *We looked at film:* Interview with Del Reisman, November 17, 1993. All subsequent quotations from him are drawn from the same source.

153 *Crackerjack western:* "Hawk," *"Per un Pugno di Dollari," Variety,* November 18, 1964.

155 *memories of the Monogram-Mascot:* Richard Jameson, "Something to Do with Death," *Film Comment,* March–April 1973.

156 *Leone has been tossed back:* David Thomson, "Leone, Sergio," in *A Biographical Dictionary of Film,* 3rd ed., p. 438.

seamless contradictions: Corliss, "Sergio Leone," p. 618.

158 *My story suddenly turned:* Quoted in Ashley Dunn, "Cowboy Villain Lee Van Cleef Dies," *Los Angeles Times,* December 17, 1989.

164 *utter shock:* Quoted in Hano, "Dead Horse." Unless otherwise noted, this and other quotations about *Rawhide* cast changes are drawn from this source.

In the first show: Hal Humphrey, "If Rawhide Fails, He's Big in Europe," *Los Angeles Times,* September 16, 1965.

It had been the network's only show: Bob Thomas, AP Newsfeature, February 11, 1966.

168 *a fine, sensitive actor:* "El Cigarello, Now Gary Cooper," *Los Angeles Herald-Examiner,* December 11, 1966.

173 *as an interruption:* Sarris, "Spaghetti Westerns," p. 388.

174 *That's like a Hawaiian pizza:* Interview with Eli Wallach, May 11, 1993. All subsequent quotations from him are drawn from the same source.

CHAPTER SIX

178 *Don't say you haven't been warned:*
Bosley Crowther, "Back in
the Saddle Again," *The New
York Times,* November 2,
1966.
Cowboy camp of an order: Bosley
Crowther, "Screen: 'A Fistful
of Dollars,'" *The New York
Times,* February 2, 1967.
deadpanned spoof: Bosley Crowther,
"A New Western Anti-Hero,"
The New York Times, February
5, 1967.

179 *the pleasures of the perfectly awful
movie:* Judith Crist, "Plain Murder All the Way," New York
World-Journal-Tribune, February
2, 1967.

181 *taking the western at its word:* Ethan
Mordden, *Medium Cool,* p.
199.
The fact that this film: Bosley
Crowther, "Screen: 'For a Few
Dollars More,'" *The New York
Times,* July 4, 1967.

183 *The Burn, The Gouge and The Man-
gle:* Renata Adler, "The Screen:
Zane Grey Meets the Marquis
de Sade," *The New York Times,*
January 25, 1968. Reprinted in
Renata Adler, *A Year in the
Dark,* pp. 23–24.
The temptation is hereby proved:
Charles Champlin, "'Good,
Bad, Ugly' Playing Citywide,"
Los Angeles *Times,* January 12,
1968.
Leone's skillful camera work: "Cin-
ema: The Good, the Bad and
the Ugly," *Time,* February 9,
1968.

188 *No, don't you do it:* Post interview.

189 *Is this the way:* Quoted in "Clint
Eastwood's Stock Hits New
High," United Artists press re-
lease, 1968.

190 *gentle and tender lover:* Joan Mellen,
*Big Bad Wolves: Masculinity in
the American Film,* p. 270.

191 *the year's grisliest movie:* "New
Movies: *Hang 'em High,*" *Time,*
August 23, 1968.
in these exacerbated times: Kevin
Thomas, "'Hang 'em High'
Playing Citywide," Los Angeles
Times, August 8, 1968.

193 *I want to be in the picture business:*
Interview with Leonard Hir-
shan, November 9, 1993. The
entire account of Hirshan's
early meetings with Lang is
drawn from this source, as are
all subsequent quotations from
Hirshan.

194 *you get into a rut:* Clint Eastwood, "The Padrón," *Film
Comment,* September–October
1991.
jocular fatalism: Andrew Sarris,
"The Pro," *Film Comment,* September–October 1991.
I didn't get a job offer: Quoted in
Sarris, "The Pro."

195 *surprisingly modest:* Don Siegel, *A
Siegel Film,* p. 297.
Sounds ominous: Ibid., p. 297.
I hate the script: Ibid.
I figured you didn't like it: Ibid.

196 *centered on the conflict:* Joel Doerfler,
Boston After Dark, July 14, 1970.

197 *Some of these guys:* Eastwood, "The
Padrón."
worked well under pressure: Ibid.
He always used to joke: Ibid.
He doesn't require: Quoted in
Christopher Frayling, *Clint
Eastwood,* p. 81.
You can't push Clint: Quoted in
David Ansen, "Clint: An
American Icon," *Newsweek,*
July 22, 1985.

198 *It's too obvious:* Quoted in Siegel, *Siegel,* p. 310.

201 *a joke told by someone:* Vincent Canby, "Screen: Sheriff Eastwood," *The New York Times,* October 3, 1968.

201 *Fast, tough and so well made:* "Cinema: Blood Sport," *Time,* November 5, 1968.

CHAPTER SEVEN

203 *We are like boxers:* Bridget Byrne, "Around L.A.: The Beguiled," Los Angeles *Herald-Examiner,* June 7, 1970.

205 *Where Doubles Dare:* Quoted in Melvyn Bragg, *Richard Burton: A Life,* p. 196.

206 *I'm just going through the motions:* This incident is recounted in Gene Siskel, "Clint Eastwood: Long Overdue Respect Makes His Year," Chicago *Tribune,* June 9, 1985.
   bunch-of-guys-on-a-mission: Quoted in Chris Willman, "Celluloid Heroes," *Los Angeles Times Calendar,* March 26, 1995.

207 *Eastwood would just stand:* Ibid.

210 *Why did you pick:* Quoted in Bernard Drew, "Brian G. Hutton: I've Made it, Baby," *The New York Times,* March 23, 1969.

212 *Elsewhere, other lunacies:* This incident was recounted in the author's interview with Tom Shaw, January 10, 1995.

216 *pieced together by:* Joshua Logan, *Movie Stars, Real People, and Me,* p. 211. All of Logan's other recollections of this production are drawn from this source, pp. 211–25

217 *Not since Attila the Hun:* Donald Zec, *Marvin: The Story of Lee Marvin,* p. 162.

221 *If I'm going to make mistakes:* Eastwood and Schickel, "Director's Dialogue."

222 *he hardly seems:* Pauline Kael, "Somebody Else's Success," *The New Yorker,* October 25, 1969. Reprinted in Pauline Kael, *Deeper into Movies,* pp. 32–39.

CHAPTER EIGHT

226 *one who you believe is a nun:* Quoted in Frayling, *Clint Eastwood,* p. 7.
   My men have become: Ibid., p. 9.
   seemed to be much more concerned: Ibid.

227 *an attempt to keep:* Stanley Kauffmann, "Stanley Kauffmann on Films," *The New Republic,* August 1, 1970.
   It's kind of The African Queen: Quoted in Warga, "Drifted into Stardom."

228 *It's hard to feel:* Quoted in Stuart M. Kaminsky, *Don Siegel: Director,* p. 229.
   she was a doll: Don Siegel, *Siegel,* p. 335.
   There are to be no changes: Ibid., p. 324.

229 *He can dream up:* Quoted in Wayne Warga, "Anything for Art in 'Mules for Sister Sara,'" Los Angeles *Times,* April 6, 1969.
   A movie lover's: Roger Greenspun, "Screen: 'Two Mules for Sister

Sara'," *The New York Times,* June 25, 1970.

230 *You'll find the conversation:* Meriel McCooey, "A Faceful of Dollars," *Sunday Times Magazine* (London), August 17, 1969.

Actors have their bag: Warga, "Drifted into Stardom."

his fussiness about his cars: Quoted in Aljean Harmetz, "The Man with No Name Is a Big Name Now," *The New York Times,* August 10, 1969.

as big as a bat: Quoted in Mc-Cooey, "Faceful of Dollars."

231 *Dr. Doolittle style:* Quoted in Harmetz, "Man with No Name."

As it turns out: Warga, "Drifted into Stardom."

Clint gives the feeling: Quoted in Harmetz, "Man with No Name."

In a matter of months: See Roberta Brandes Gratz, "Clint Hitches His Wagon to a Song," New York *Post,* October 26, 1969.

232 *encumbered by a wife:* Quoted in Harmetz, "Man with No Name."

tripped across the movie business: Ibid.

I'm an actor: Quoted in McCooey, "Faceful of Dollars."

234 *I didn't realize:* Quoted in "Don Rickles Is So Clean He Could Play the Vatican," *Parade* press release, December 16, 1993.

I can never think of anything: Quoted in Kathleen Carroll, "At War with a Movie—or 3 Days on Location," New York *Daily News,* August 17, 1969.

I'm always a little closed in: Quoted in Ben Reisfeld, "No One Got Hurt," Los Angeles *Times,* September 14, 1969.

We went twenty years: Quoted in Ann Guerin, "Clint Eastwood

as Mr. Warmth," *Show,* February 1970.

236 *in a fury:* Siegel, *Siegel.*

237 *the film has no resources:* Roger Greenspun, "The Screen: Hutton's 'Kelly's Heroes' Begins Run," *The New York Times,* June 24, 1970.

238 *a romantic love story:* Quoted in Siegel, *Siegel.* Siegel's other reminiscences, with the exception of all those noted below, are from the same source.

I said, 'If you'd written this script': Quoted in Charles Higham, "Suddenly, Don Siegel's High Camp-us," *The New York Times,* July 25, 1972.

240 *For the daylight scenes:* Quoted in Fuensanta Plaza, *Clint Eastwood/Malpaso,* p. 22.

It just hit me wrong: Interview with Carl Pingitore, October 7, 1994. All subsequent quotations from him are drawn from the same source.

241 *a nice ordinary young man:* Quoted in Gallafent, *Clint Eastwood,* p. 81.

244 *the social construction:* J. Haberman, "At War with Ourselves," *Village Voice,* October 23, 1986.

Women are capable of: Quoted in Kaminsky, *Siegel,* p. 238.

247 *I was still:* Quoted in Pat McGilligan, "Clint Eastwood," *Focus on Film,* Summer–Autumn 1976.

a big fish: Eastwood and Schickel, "Director's Dialogue."

248 *I know exactly:* McGilligan, "Clint Eastwood."

with the big red scar: Interview with Jessica Walter, July 27, 1993. All subsequent quotations from her are drawn from the same source.

250 *He said, 'You seem to have it':* Eastwood, "The Padrón."

250 *I didn't know:* Quoted in "That Self-Sufficient Thing," *Time,* December 12, 1971.

251 *Part of his sex appeal:* Ibid.

253 *very, very surprised:* Interview with Pierre Rissient, June 1, 1993.

254 *very fancy, outrageous fantasizing:* Vincent Canby, "Clint Eastwood Is Star of Siegel's 'The Beguiled,'" *The New York Times,* April 1, 1971.

255 *Let me add two words:* Quoted in Gene Siskel, "Hype Casting Cowan Knows How to Keep the Stars Shining," *Chicago Tribune,* June 4, 1989.

too many easy decisions: Roger Greenspun, "Eastwood as Director," *The New York Times,* November 14, 1971.

CHAPTER NINE

262 *a stunningly well-made:* Pauline Kael, "The Current Cinema: Saint Cop," *The New Yorker,* January 15, 1972. A somewhat-longer version of the review is included in Kael, *Deeper into Movies,* pp. 484–89.

264 *neither tarnished nor afraid:* Raymond Chandler, "The Simple Art of Murder," *The Atlantic Monthly,* December 1944. Quoted in Philip Durham, *Down These Mean Streets a Man Must Go,* pp. 95–96.

you always had the feeling: Quoted in Richard Schickel, *James Cagney: A Celebration,* p. 18.

267 *The studio allowed six nights:* Quoted in Judy Fayard, "Who Can Stand 32,580 Seconds of Clint Eastwood?" *Life,* July 23, 1971.

272 *a sad and perhaps inevitable step downward:* Roger Greenspun, "Screen: 'Dirty Harry' and His Devotion to Duty," *The New York Times,* December 23, 1971.

bound to upset: Jay Cocks, "Cinema: Outside Society," *Time,* January 3, 1972.

273 *we are gradually being conditioned:* Pauline Kael, "Stanley Strangelove," *The New Yorker,* January 1, 1972. Reprinted in Kael, *Deeper into Movies,* p. 475.

274 *The real target:* Eric Patterson, "Every Which Way but Lucid: The Critique of Authority in Clint Eastwood's Police Movies," *Journal of Popular Film and Television,* Fall 1982.

the basic contest: Kael, "Saint Cop."

crime is caused by deprivation: Ibid.

275 *on sensual and primitive levels:* Kael, "Author's Note," in *Deeper into Movies,* p. xv.

a pragmatic willingness to kill: Lawrence Alloway, *Violent America: The Movies, 1946–1964,* p. 11.

276 *to dig into the sexiness:* Pauline Kael, "Peckinpah's Obsession," *The New Yorker,* January 29, 1972. Reprinted in Kael, *Deeper into Movies,* pp. 494–99.

277 *which unites our lumpen proles:* Henry Louis Gates Jr., "Annals of Race: Thirteen Ways of Looking at a Black Man," *The New Yorker,* October 23, 1995.

Those saved by the social revolutions: Thomson, "Forgiven."

Somewhere along the line: Quoted in James Wolcott, "On Television: The Dennis Menace," *The New Yorker,* June 11, 1994.

279 *I don't make political movies:* Quoted in Paul Gardner, "Siegel at 59: Director, Rebel, Star," *The New York Times,* May 31, 1973.

279 *Not once throughout* Dirty Harry: Siegel, *Siegel*, p. 373.
in a world of bureaucratic corruption: Quoted in R. Allen Kider, "Dirty Clint," *Good Times*, December 1977.
Harry is a terribly honest character: Quoted in Guy Flatley, "At the Movies," *The New York Times*, December 17, 1976.
It's just the story: Quoted in Stuart M. Kaminsky, *Clint Eastwood*, pp. 125–26.

281 *Nietzschian superman:* Garrett Epps, "Does Popeye Doyle Teach Us How to Be Fascist?" *The New York Times*, May 21, 1972.
a virtually fascist endorsement: Mellen, *Big Bad Wolves*, p. 294.
282 *I'd hate to turn around:* Quoted in Charles Champlin, "A Mellow Eastwood Keeps His Edge," Los Angeles *Times*, June 30, 1984.

CHAPTER TEN

283 *Name all of:* Interview with Joe Hyams, June 30, 1994.
285 *I'd take the script:* Quoted in Patrick Goldstain, "Hey, Crime Does Pay," Los Angeles *Times* Calendar, October 18, 1995.
Clint doesn't like indecision: Interview with James Fargo, January 31, 1994. All subsequent quotations from him are drawn from the same source.
290 *I would have liked:* Interview with Verna Bloom, February 23, 1994. All subsequent quotes from her are drawn from the same source.
293 *part ghost story:* Vincent Canby, "'High Plains Drifter' Opens on Screen," *The New York Times*, April 20, 1973.
male sexual fantasy: Judith Crist, "Git 'Em Up, Move 'Em On," *New York*, April 30, 1973.
295 *I called him Bill:* Quoted in James Brady, "In Step With: Kay Lenz," *Parade*, May 23, 1993.
296 *I could have been wearing tinfoil:* Quoted in Mary Murphy, "Actress Who Grew into Role," Los Angeles *Times*, February 18, 1974.
298 *Where's Gregory Peck:* Quoted in Weinraub, "Even Cowboys."

298 *It's not good writing:* Ibid.
299 *I'll be so old:* Quoted in Peter Biskind, "Any Which Way He Can," *Premiere*, April 1993.
302 *Whichever way you want it:* Quoted in Bridget Byrne, "Eastwood's Round 'em Up, Move 'em Out Film Making Style," Los Angeles *Herald-Examiner*, June 24, 1973.
You have to learn: Quoted in Post interview.
303 *that silent containment:* Interview with Hal Holbrook, December 11, 1995.
304 *wooden impassivity:* Pauline Kael, "Killing Time," *The New Yorker*, January 14, 1974. Reprinted in Pauline Kael, *Reeling*, pp. 251–56.
308 *It is the essentially gentle:* Robin Wood, *Hollywood from Vietnam to Reagan*, p. 223.
309 *I've got to talk to you:* Quoted in interview with Michael Cimino, September 24, 1993. All subsequent quotations from him are drawn from this source.
You are that guy: Quoted in Stephen Farber, "Star without a Smash," *Movieline*, October 4–10, 1985.

312 *returned rentals of a solidly profitable level:* Stephen Bach, *Final Cut,* pp. 82–83.

314 *flamed out:* Mike Hoover, "Man against Mountain and Vice Versa during the Filming of 'The Eiger Sanction,'" *American Cinematographer,* August 1975.

315 *It sounds real close:* Ibid.

CHAPTER ELEVEN

322 *exposed by an Alabama newspaperman:* See "Is Forrest Carter Really Asa Carter?" *The New York Times,* July 26, 1976.

wrote a piece: See Dan T. Carter, "The Transformation of a Klansman," *The New York Times,* October 4, 1991.

If Forrest Carter was: Clint Eastwood, "Happy Transformation," *The New York Times,* October 16, 1991.

323 *Today we live:* Quoted in "Self-Made Man," *People,* September 6, 1976.

I suppose they see me: Quoted in "Portrait of a Mean B.O. Winner," *Variety,* September 15, 1976.

324 *the saga of it:* Clint Eastwood's remarks on the appeal of this project are drawn from Eastwood and Schickel, "Director's Dialogue."

326 *the original novel:* Quoted in Allen Barra, "Philip Kaufman: Right Stuff! Wrong Package," Washington *Post,* August 1, 1993.

Philip Kaufman asked for: Thomson, "Forgiven."

327 *He just had a great charisma:* Eastwood and Schickel, "Director's Dialogue."

328 *Oh, the stumps look fine:* Quoted in Anthea Disney, "Sondra Locke Enjoys Her Life as Clint Eastwood's Sidekick," Los Angeles *Herald-Examiner,* April 14, 1978.

329 *the weird two:* Quoted in Lois Armstrong, "Off the Screen: Sondra Locke's Stock Rises in Surviving Eastwood's Mayhem and Hollywood's Whispers," *People,* February 13, 1978.

would act, feel and think: Quoted in Peer J. Oppenheimer, "They Call Her 'The Beautiful Fake,'" *Family Weekly,* November 24, 1968.

331 *I do all the stuff:* Quoted in "Portrait of a Mean B.O. Winner," *Variety.*

336 *an oddly abashed form:* Jack Kroll, "Erb-Man," *Newsweek,* September 13, 1976.

He says Kael actually feels: Quoted in Mary Murphy, "Clint and Kael," Los Angeles *Times,* April 12, 1976.

337 *She was taken by Last Tango:* Quoted in Larry Cole, "Clint's Not Cute When He's Angry," *Village Voice,* May 24, 1976.

338 *That was a wonderful film:* "The Merv Griffin Show," no. 2725, taped July 1, 1982 (transcript).

CHAPTER TWELVE

340 *Their effort was better:* Associated Press, "Dirty Harry Script Is Right on Target," Los Angeles *Times,* September 3, 1976.

343 *I thought the woman:* Quoted in Todd Coleman, "Clint's Women," unpublished article, January 31, 1996.

343 *When my lawyer:* Quoted in "Tyne Daly Gets Her Gun," *People,* January 31, 1977.

344 *Harry has found:* Marjorie Rosen, "Dirty Harry Meets His Better Half," *Ms.,* March 1977.

346 *The girl's part is:* Richard Thompson and Tim Hunter, "Clint Eastwood, Auteur," *Film Comment,* January–February 1978.

349 *a single thought:* Vincent Canby, "Screen: Eastwood 'Gauntlet,'" *The New York Times,* December 22, 1977.

350 *sophisticated character interplay:* Tom Allen, "Dirty Harry Cleans Up His Act," *Village Voice,* December 26, 1977.

Everybody would love: Quoted in Armstrong, "Locke's Stock Rises."

351 *I have just finished:* Clint Eastwood, "Mail," *People,* March 6, 1978.

354 *had the notion:* Interview with Alain Silver, September 27, 1994.

355 *That picture's going:* Interview with Barry Reardon, September 23, 1993.

357 *Their relationship, in the beginning:* Interview with Richard Tuggle, July 26, 1994. All subsequent quotations from him are drawn from the same source.

an artist and director: Interview with Michael D. Eisner, December 11, 1995.

358 *If I lost my squint:* Quoted in William Bates, "Clint Eastwood: Is Less More?" *The New York Times,* June 17, 1979.

360 *this is not a great film:* Vincent Canby, "Screen: 'Alcatraz' Opens," *The New York Times,* June 22, 1979.

361 *With Francis Coppola's budget:* Quoted in Bates, "Clint Eastwood: Is Less More?"

364 *I wanted to say something:* Quoted in Vinocur, "Clint Eastwood, Seriously."

CHAPTER THIRTEEN

367 *sexy legend:* John Love, "Clint Eastwood: A Sexy Legend at 50," *Cosmopolitan,* July 1980.

368 *the intelligence and the financing:* Quoted in Connie Bruck, *Master of the Game,* p. 279.

369 *My father's dream:* Quoted in Vinocur, "Clint Eastwood, Seriously."

370 *Clint's greatest moment:* Interview with Frank Wells, October 12, 1993.

Clint takes the bullshit: Interview with Henry Bumstead, June 3, 1993.

371 *They don't do that for many:* Quoted in Jack Mathews, "Eastwood," *USA Today,* August 13–17, 1984.

372 *the truth is not:* James Wolcott, "Is That a Gun in Your Pocket?" *Vanity Fair,* July 1985.

376 *the sixties was largely:* Robert Mazzocco, "The Supply-Side Star," *The New York Review of Books,* April 1, 1982.

377 *amphetamine aesthetic:* Andrew Sarris, "Films in Focus: Cold Wars and Cold Futures," *Village Voice,* July 6, 1982.

378 *is not the establishment:* Ibid.

380 *was not somebody we ought:* Quoted in Michael J. Berlin, "POW Raid Leader Surrenders to Thais," New York *Post,* February 28, 1983.

383 *looks like a kid:* Quoted in Vernon Scott, "Scott's World: East-

wood and Son Co-Star," UPI dispatch, January 6, 1983.

384 *the steely compassion:* Mailer, "All the Pirates."

385 *So they came to me:* Quoted in Roger Ebert, "Clint Eastwood—America's Major Feminist Filmmaker," San Francisco *Examiner,* July 18, 1984.

386 *the makings of:* David Ansen, "Gunning Their Way to Glory," *Newsweek,* December 12, 1983.

They make contact with: David Denby, "Movies: The Last Angry Men," *New York,* January 16, 1984.

feminist filmmaker: Tom Stempel, "Let's Hear It for Eastwood's 'Strong' Women," Los Angeles *Times* Calendar, March 11, 1984.

387 *It's very simple:* Quoted in Ebert, "Feminist Filmmaker."

As far as the tormented: Quoted in Carrie Rickey, "In Like Clint," *Fame,* November 1988.

388 *Here is one of the basic lessons:* William Goldman, *Adventures in the Screenwriting Trade,* p. 37.

Just too dumb: Quoted in Ebert, "Feminist Filmmaker."

392 *warming with her tomgirl body:* Kathleen Murphy, "The Good, the Bad & the Ugly: Clint Eastwood as Romantic Hero," *Film Comment,* May–June 1996.

394 *He's become a very troubled:* David Denby, "Beyond Good and Evil," *New York,* August 27, 1984.

CHAPTER FOURTEEN

397 *diffuse:* Interview with Richard Benjamin, January 4, 1994. All subsequent quotations from him are drawn from the same source.

401 *The Clint Eastwood Magical Respectability:* Vinocur, "Clint Eastwood, Seriously."

402 *Oh, I get it:* Quoted in William Goldman, *Hype and Glory,* p. 117.

then I thought: Aljean Harmetz, "Eastwood Top Event at Cannes," *The New York Times,* May 13, 1985.

403 *Basically I wanted to have:* Quoted in Michael Henry, "Clint Eastwood, on 'Pale Rider.'" Interview included in Cannes Press Kit, April 1, 1995.

404 *I guess maybe I felt:* Ibid.

contemporary and remembered: Michael Wilmington, "Westerns Return on a 'Pale Rider,'" Los Angeles *Times,* June 28, 1985.

407 *very much the obliging:* Quoted in Rachel Abromowitz, "The Best Little Girl in Town," *Premiere,* July 1995.

409 *We're very close friends:* Quoted in Ansen, "American Icon," *Newsweek,* July 22, 1985.

411 *appendage:* Nancy Mills, "Locke Exercises Control over 'Ratboy,' Her Career," Los Angeles *Times,* August 19, 1986.

412 *It's all my fault:* Quoted in Mills, "Locke Exercises Control."

414 *If you don't tell me:* Quoted in interview with Eileen Padberg, March 15, 1996. All subsequent quotations from her are drawn from the same source.

416 *to be an officer:* Mark Stein, "Campaigning with Clint," *Los Angeles Times Magazine,* March 30, 1986.

416 *My interests are in Carmel:* Ibid.

417 *If you've read:* Paul A. Witteman, "Go Ahead, Voters, Make My Day," *Time,* April 7, 1986.

   At first it was funny: Stein, "Campaigning."

417 *I understand the bus tour:* Robert Lindsey, "Eastwood Marks Landslide Victory," *The New York Times,* April 10, 1986.

418 *I thought I could come up:* Paul A. Witteman, "No More Baby Kissing," *Time,* April 6, 1987.

CHAPTER FIFTEEN

422 *At 56, Mr. Eastwood:* Vincent Canby, "Charting Stars across the Decades," *The New York Times,* December 14, 1986.

423 *I was catching:* Marsha Mason, "Catching the Light," in *Clint Eastwood Tribute Book,* ed. Wolf Schneider, p. 10.

   Whip me, beat me: Quoted in Janet Maslin, "How the Black Panthers Came to Be, Sort Of," *The New York Times,* May 3, 1995.

424 *A jazz movie had never been made:* Quoted in Gary Giddins, "Clint Eastwood Shoots Us the Bird," *Esquire,* October 1988.

426 *these beautiful black-and-white:* Interview with Jack N. Green, June 2, 1993.

   In one scene: Quoted in Charles Champlin, "Bird's Venora Ever on Trail of a Dare," Los Angeles *Times,* January 12, 1989.

427 *operate in the gray areas:* Dave Kehr, "Eastwood's Skillful Creation 'Bird' Is Rare Indeed," Chicago *Tribune,* October 14, 1988.

   the gangster hero: Stanley Crouch, "Birdland: Charlie Parker, Clint Eastwood and America," *The New Republic,* February 27, 1989.

   really a black guy: Quoted in Jack Kroll, "Clint Makes Bird Sing," *Newsweek,* October 31, 1988.

428 *the single most confident:* Eastwood and Schickel, "Director's Dialogue."

428 *Everyone . . . is the product:* Giddins, "Clint Eastwood Shoots."

   Reading them in sequence: Eastwood and Schickel, "Director's Dialogue."

429 *takes his genius away:* Ibid.

432 *I just couldn't have sat there:* Quoted in Goldman, *Hype and Glory,* p. 174.

   No apologizing, no excuses: Ibid.

434 *You can't have a movie:* Quoted in Crouch, "Birdland."

   a rat's nest: Pauline Kael, "Bird Thou Never Went," *The New Yorker,* October 17, 1988 (reprinted in *Movieline*).

   perfectly atrocious: Quoted in Christopher Tricarico, "Outtakes: Go Ahead, Make My Lecture," *Los Angeles Times Calendar,* October 8, 1988.

435 *Parker didn't live:* Helen Knode, "This Is Your Life," *L.A. Weekly,* November 4, 1988.

   We just didn't seem to have: Quoted in Derek Malcolm, "Huston's Hexes," *The Guardian* (London), May 14, 1990.

436 *was, you know, 'tough guy':* Interview with Frances Fisher, May 30, 1995. All subsequent quotations from her are drawn from the same source.

439 *I told him I couldn't believe:* Quoted in Claudia Puig, "In the Matter of Locke vs. Eastwood," Los Angeles *Times,* May 8, 1989.

   Mr. Eastwood has asked: Quoted in Puig, "Locke vs. Eastwood."

439 *They don't call him:* Richard
Phillips, "Newsmakers: East-
wood Shoots Back," *Chicago
Tribune,* May 9, 1989.
because I know him: Quoted in
Puig, "Locke vs. Eastwood."

440 *I adamantly deny:* Ibid.
I felt so disappointed: Quoted in
Mary Murphy, "Is TV a Glint
in Clint's Eye," *TV Guide,* Jan-
uary 27, 1990.
It makes us happy: Quoted in
Abromowitz, "Little Girl."

442 *the unfightable one:* Quoted in Ann
W. O'Neill and Efrain Hernan-
dez Jr., "Eastwood, Locke, Settle Fraud Suit for Undisclosed
Sum," Los Angeles *Times,* September 25, 1996.

447 *Everywhere I went:* Quoted in
Murphy, "Clint."

449 *Huston's persona:* Michael Wil-
mington, "Clint Eastwood's
Acid Test," Los Angeles *Times,*
September 14, 1990.

CHAPTER SIXTEEN

452 *sheltered by ignorance:* David Webb
Peoples, "He's Going to Shoot
You If You Disappoint Him,"
in *Clint Eastwood Tribute Book,*
ed. Schneider, p. 12.
We would have been: Sonia Chernus
to Clint Eastwood, memoran-
dum, January 5, 1984.
I can't do what Francis: Peoples,
"He's Going to Shoot."

459 *one of the most tremendous:* Quoted
in D. J. Taylor, "Getting Inside
the Outsider," *The Sunday
Times* (London), June 20, 1993.

460 *classicism at its most august:* Richard
Jameson, "Deserve's Got
Nothin' to Do with It," *Film
Comment,* September–October
1992.

462 *if it works immediately:* Quoted in
Ric Gentry, "Clint Eastwood,"
Us, January 26, 1987.
that moving quickly: Interview with
David Valdes, September 17,
1991.

462 *You'll never find a bullhorn:* Interview
with Lloyd Nelson, October 9,
1991.
Nobody has to shout: Interview
with Richard Harris, September 17, 1991.

463 *We're in bumfuck, Alberta:* Quoted
in Biskind, "Any Which Way."

464 *I'd never seen or imagined:* Peoples,
"He's Going to Shoot."

465 *Eastwood's meditation:* Richard
Corliss, "The Last Roundup,"
Time, August 10, 1992.

466 *When I heard:* Quoted in Bernard
Weinraub, "3 Films Dominate
Nominations in Oscar Con-
test," *The New York Times,* February 18, 1993.

467 *I'm popular with the public:* Quoted
in Siskel, "Long Overdue."

468 *You wear a monocle:* Quoted in
Elaine Dutka and Robert
Welkos, "A Few Good Words
behind Scenes," Los Angeles
Times, March 30, 1993.

CHAPTER SEVENTEEN

472 *If anybody told me:* Quoted in Roger Ebert, "No Rest for Eastwood; He's Already on to Next Film,: Sacramento *Bee,* July 9, 1993.

That mentality: Quoted in Matt Spetalnick, "Clint for President," Toronto *Star,* July 9, 1993.

473 *You know, it's always appealing:* Quoted in Bernard Weinraub, "Clint Eastwood, Back on the Side of the Law," *The New York Times,* December 7, 1992.

The operative mode: Howard Hampton, "Sympathy for the Devil," *Film Comment,* November–December 1993.

475 *Give it scope:* Interview with Wolfgang Petersen, July 20, 1993. All subsequent quotations from him are drawn from the same source.

476 *Why is Wolfgang:* Quoted in Weinraub, "Side of the Law."

I've never been against that: Quoted in Matt Spetalnick, "Dirty Harry in Tears?" *The Reuters Library Report,* July 7, 1993.

I've been knocking: Janet Maslin, "Make His Day? Museum Does That for Eastwood," *The New York Times,* October 27, 1993.

There are quite a lot of Americans: Quoted in Spetalnick, "Clint for President."

very elegant, very handsome: Quoted in Bernard Weinraub, "An Actor Seeks Variety and Finds Success," *The New York Times,* September 7, 1993.

480 *You evolve, or you don't evolve:* Interview with Kevin Costner, June 3, 1993.

481 *A visitor from another planet:* Thomson, *Dictionary of Film,* p. 220.

484 *The high point:* Janet Maslin, "When Destiny Is Sad and the Scars Never Heal," *The New York Times,* November 24, 1993.

offers passing condemnations: Michael Medved, "It's a PC, PC 'World,'" New York *Post,* November 24, 1993.

a startling example: Richard Grenier, "Clint Eastwood Goes PC," *Commentary,* March 1994.

488 *I guess she hands out my number:* Streep interview. All subsequent quotations from her are drawn from the same source.

490 *aimed at the anxious adolescent:* Robert Plunket, "Zing Went the G-Strings of My Heart," *The New York Times Book Review,* February 5, 1995.

492 *Your age and mine:* Quoted in interview with Dina Ruiz, May 6, 1996. All subsequent quotations from her are drawn from the same source.

493 *spatial and temporal:* Richard Combs, "Old Ghosts: The Bridges of Madison County," *Film Comment,* May–June 1996.

494 *She's someone very rare:* Quoted in Dany Jucaud, "Clint Eastwood: L'amour, Ce N'Est Pas' une Question d'Age," trans. Robert Lloyd, *Paris-Match,* September 21, 1995.

EPILOGUE

500 *Gary Cooper had seen:* Thomson, "Forgiven."

BIBLIOGRAPHY

The amount of printed material generated by a career as long as Clint Eastwood's is almost literally staggering. Therefore, this bibliography is, of necessity, selective. In it I have listed items that I have quoted from extensively in the text or which otherwise contributed significantly to my understanding of his life and may help others to do the same. Shorter and more ephemeral journalistic items directly quoted in the text are cited in the Notes and are not included here. All publishers are located in New York unless otherwise indicated.

BOOKS AND PAMPHLETS

Adler, Renata. *A Year in the Dark*. Random House, 1969.

Agan, Patrick. *Clint Eastwood*. London: Coronet Books, 1975.

Agee, James. *A Death in the Family*. McDowell-Obolinsky, 1956.

Alloway, Lawrence. *Violent America: The Movies, 1946–1964*. The Museum of Modern Art, 1969.

Bach, Stephen. *Final Cut*. William Morrow, 1985.

Bernardoni, James. *The New Hollywood*. Jefferson, N.C.: McFarland & Company, 1991.

Bingham, Dennis. *Acting Male*. New Brunswick, N.J.: Rutgers University Press, 1994.

Boorman, John, and Walter Donohue, eds. *Projections 4½*. London and Boston: Faber and Faber, 1995.

Bragg, Melvyn. *Richard Burton: A Life*. Boston: Little, Brown, 1988.

Bruck, Connie. *Master of the Game*. Simon & Schuster, 1994.

Chekhov, Michael. *To the Actor*. Harper & Brothers, 1953.

Clinch, Minty. *Clint Eastwood*. London: Coronet Books, 1995.

Cole, Gerold and Peter Williams. *Clint Eastwood*. London: W. H. Allen, 1983.

Cumbow, Robert C. *Once upon a Time: The Films of Sergio Leone*. Metuchen, N.J.: Scarecrow Press, 1987.

Downing, David, and Gary Herman. *Clint Eastwood: All-American Anti-Hero*. London: Omnibus Press, 1977.

Durham, Philip. *Down These Mean Streets a Man Must Go*. Chapel Hill: University of North Carolina Press, 1963.

Ellison, Ralph. "On Bird, Bird-Watching, and Jazz." In *Shadow and Act*. Vintage Books, 1972. Reprinted from *Saturday Review*, July 28, 1962.

Farber, Manny. *Negative Space*. Praeger Publishers, 1971.

Frayling, Christopher. *Clint Eastwood*. London: Virgin Publishing, 1992.

Frayling, Christopher. *Spaghetti Westerns*. London: Routledge & Kegan Paul, 1981.

Gallafent, Edward. *Clint Eastwood: Actor and Director*. London: Studio Vista Books, 1994.

Gioia, Ted. *West Coast Jazz*. Oxford University Press, 1992.

Goldman, William. *Adventures in the Screenwriting Trade*. Warner Books, 1983.

———. *Hype and Glory*. Villard Books, 1990.

Hirsch, Foster. *A Method to Their Madness*. W. W. Norton, 1984.

Horner, William R. *Bad at the Bijou*. Jefferson, N.C.: McFarland & Company, 1982.

Hyams, Joe, with Jay Hyams. *James Dean: Little Boy Lost*. Warner Books, 1992.

Johnstone, Iain. *Clint Eastwood: The Man with No Name* 2nd ed. Quill/Morrow, 1988.

Kael, Pauline. *Deeper into Movies*. Bantam, 1974.

———. *Going Steady*. Boston: Atlantic–Little, Brown, 1970.

———. *I Lost It at the Movies*. Boston: Atlantic–Little, Brown, 1965.

———. *Kiss Kiss Bang Bang*. Boston: Atlantic–Little, Brown, 1968.

———. *Movie Love*. Plume, 1991.

———. *Reeling*. Boston: Atlantic–Little, Brown, 1976.

———. *State of the Art*. E. P. Dutton, 1985.

———. *Taking It All In*. Holt Rinehart Winston, 1980.

———. *When the Lights Go Down*. Holt, Rinehart & Winston, 1980.

Kaminsky, Stuart M. *Clint Eastwood*. New American Library, 1974.

———. *Don Siegel: Director*. Curtis, 1974.

Logan, Joshua. *Movie Stars, Real People, and Me*. Delacorte Press, 1978.

Lyon, Christopher, ed. *The International Dictionary of Film and Filmmakers*. Perigree, 1985.

Mellen, Joan. *Big Bad Wolves: Masculinity in the American Film*. Pantheon Books, 1974.

Mordden, Ethan. *Medium Cool*. Alfred A. Knopf, 1990.

Munn, Michael. *Clint Eastwood: Hollywood's Loner*. London: Robson Books, 1992.

Nalvin, Nancy. *The Famous Mr. Ed*. Warner Books, 1991.

Parks, Rita. *The Western Hero in Film and Television*. Ann Arbor, Mich., and London: UMI Research Press, 1982.

Plaza, Fuensanta. *Clint Eastwood/Malpaso*. Carmel Valley, Calif.: Ex Libris/Publisher, 1991.

Richie, Donald. *The Films of Akira Kurosawa*. Berkeley, Los Angeles, London: University of California Press, 1984.

Roud, Richard, ed. *Cinema: A Critical Dictionary*. 2 vols. Viking Press, 1980.

Sarris, Andrew. "The Spaghetti Westerns." In *Confessions of a Cultist*. Simon & Schuster, 1970.

Schickel, Richard. *Clint Eastwood Directs*. Minneapolis: Walker Art Center, 1990.

———. *James Cagney: A Celebration*. Boston: Little, Brown, 1985.

Schneider, Wolf, ed. *Clint Eastwood Tribute Book*. Los Angeles: American Film Institute, 1996.

Siegel, Don. *A Siegel Film*. London and Boston: Faber & Faber, 1993.

Slotkin, Richard. *Gunfighter Nation*. Atheneum, 1992.

Smith, Paul. *Clint Eastwood, a Cultural Production*. Minneapolis: University of Minnesota Press, 1993.

Steig, Laurence, and Tony Williams. *Italian Westerns*. London: Lorrimer, 1975.

Thomas, Bob. *Golden Boy, the Untold Story of William Holden*. St. Martin's Press, 1983.

———. *Joan Crawford*. Simon & Schuster, 1978.

Thompson, Douglas. *Clint Eastwood: Sexual Cowboy.* London: Smith Gryphon, 1992.

Thomson, David. *A Biographical Dictionary of Film.* 3rd ed. Alfred A. Knopf, 1994.

Updike, John. *The Afterlife.* Alfred A. Knopf, 1995.

———. *In the Beauty of the Lillies.* Alfred A. Knopf, 1996.

Wood, Robin. *Hollywood from Vietnam to Reagan.* Columbia University Press, 1986.

Zec, Donald. *Marvin: The Story of Lee Marvin.* St. Martin's Press, 1980.

Zmijewsky, Boris, and Lee Pfeiffer. *The Films of Clint Eastwood.* Citadel Press, 1993.

MAGAZINES AND NEWSPAPERS

Abromowitz, Rachel. "The Best Little Girl in Town." *Premiere,* July 1995.

Adler, Renata. "The Screen: Zane Grey Meets the Marquis de Sade." *The New York Times,* January 25, 1968.

Allen, Tom. "Clint: An American Icon." *Newsweek,* July 22, 1985.

Ansen, David. "Dirty Harry Cleans Up His Act." *Village Voice,* December 26, 1977.

Armstrong, Lois. "Off the Screen: Sondra Locke's Stock Rises in Surviving Eastwood's Mayhem and Hollywood's Whispers." *People,* February 13, 1978.

Associated Press. "Dirty Harry Script Is Right on Target." Los Angeles *Times,* September 3, 1976.

Barra, Allen. "Philip Kaufman: Right Stuff! Wrong Package." Washington *Post,* August 1, 1993.

Bates, William. "Clint Eastwood: Is Less More?" *The New York Times,* June 17, 1979.

Biskind, Peter. "Any Which Way He Can." *Premiere,* April 1993.

Blowen, Michael. "Appreciation: Sergio Leone, Outsider's Insight." Boston *Globe,* May 2, 1989.

Blumenthal, Bob. "Clint Eastwood." *Jazz Times,* September 1995.

Bodeen, DeWitt. "Clint Eastwood . . . a Fistful of Fame." *Focus on Film,* Spring 1972.

Bogdanovich, Peter. "Two Beeg Green Eyes." *New York,* November 1973.

Brady, James. "In Step With: Kay Lenz." *Parade,* May 23, 1993.

Breskin, David. "Clint Eastwood." *Rolling Stone,* September 17, 1992.

Byrne, Bridget. "Around L.A. the Beguiled." Los Angeles *Herald-Examiner,* June 7, 1970.

———. "Eastwood's Round 'em Up, Move 'em Out Film Making Style." Los Angeles *Herald-Examiner,* June 24, 1973.

———. "For Holden the '50s Never Died." Los Angeles *Herald-Examiner,* December 24, 1972.

———. "Outlaw's Shooting Star." Los Angeles *Herald-Examiner,* December 7, 1978.

Cahill, Tim. "Clint Eastwood: *The Rolling Stone* Interview." *Rolling Stone,* July 4, 1985.

Canby, Vincent. "Charting Stars across the Decades." *The New York Times,* December 14, 1986.

———. "Getting Beyond Myra and the Valley of the Junk." *The New York Times,* July 5, 1970.

Caracaterra, Lorenzo. "Dirty Harry Comes Clean." *Video,* May 1985.

———. "In Like Clint." *New York Daily News Sunday Magazine,* August 12, 1984.

Carroll, Kathleen. "At War with a Movie—or 3 Days on Location." New York *Daily News,* August 17, 1969.

Carter, Dan T. "The Transformation of

a Klansman." *The New York Times,* October 4, 1991.

Champlin, Charles. "A Mellow Eastwood Keeps His Edge." Los Angeles *Times,* June 30, 1984.

Chandler, Raymond. "The Simple Art of Murder." *The Atlantic Monthly,* December 1944.

"Clint's Kid." *People,* November 15, 1993.

Cole, Larry. "Clint's Not Cute When He's Angry." *Village Voice,* May 24, 1976.

Combs, Richard. "Old Ghosts: The Bridges of Madison County." *Film Comment,* May–June 1996.

Crist, Judith. "Plain Murder All the Way." *New York World Journal Tribune,* February 2, 1967.

Crouch, Stanley. "Birdland: Charlie Parker, Clint Eastwood and America." *The New Republic,* February 27, 1989.

Crowther, Bosley. "Back in the Saddle Again." *The New York Times,* November 2, 1966.

———. "A New Western Anti-Hero." *The New York Times,* February 5, 1967.

———. "Screen: 'A Fistful of Dollars.'" *The New York Times,* February 2, 1967.

———. "Screen: 'For a Few Dollars More.'" *The New York Times,* July 4, 1967.

Denby, David. "Movies: The Last Angry Men." *New York,* January 16, 1984.

———. "Beyond Good and Evil." *New York,* August 27, 1984.

DeVries, Hillary. "His Own Man . . . Always." Los Angeles *Times* Calendar, August 2, 1992.

Didion, Joan. "The Golden Land." *The New York Review of Books,* October 21, 1993.

Disney, Anthea. "Sondra Locke Enjoys Her Life as Clint Eastwood's Sidekick." Los Angeles *Herald-Examiner,* April 14, 1978.

"Don Rickles Is So Clean He Could Play the Vatican." *Parade* press release, December 16, 1993.

Drew, Bernard. "Brian G. Hutton: I've Made It, Baby." *The New York Times,* March 23, 1969.

Dunn, Ashley. "Cowboy Film Villain Lee Van Cleef Dies." Los Angeles *Times,* December 17, 1989.

Eastwood, Clint. "Happy Transformation." *The New York Times,* October 16, 1991.

———. "Mail." *People,* March 6, 1978.

———. "The Padrón." *Film Comment,* September–October 1991.

Ebert, Roger. "Clint Eastwood—America's Major Feminist Filmmaker." San Francisco *Examiner,* July 18, 1984.

———. "No Rest for Eastwood: He's Already on to Next Film." Sacramento *Bee,* July 9, 1993.

"El Cigarello, Now Gary Cooper." Los Angeles *Herald-Examiner,* December 11, 1966.

Epps, Garrett. "Does Popeye Doyle Teach Us How to Be Fascist?" *The New York Times,* May 21, 1972.

Faber, Monty. "Clint Eastwood Outgrew Pasta Westerns, But Is Still in the Big Dough." *People,* June 2, 1975.

Farber, Stephen. "Star without a Smash." *Movieline,* October 4–10, 1985.

Fayard, Judy. "Who Can Stand 32,580 Seconds of Clint Eastwood? Just About Everybody." *Life,* July 23, 1971.

Fischoff, Stuart. "Clint Eastwood & the American Psyche." *Psychology Today,* January–February 1993.

Flatley, Guy. "At the Movies." *The New York Times,* December 17, 1976.

Flint, Peter B. "Sergio Leone, 67, Italian Director Who Revitalized Westerns, Dies." *The New York Times,* May 1, 1989.

Folkart, Burt A. "Charles Marquis Warren, Western Writer." Los Angeles *Times,* August 13, 1990.

Friedman, Bruce Jay. "Could Dirty Harry Take Rooster Cogburn?" *Esquire,* September 1976.

Friedman, Milton. "Why Socialism Won't Work." *The New York Times,* August 13, 1994.

Fuller, Graham. "Liberal Harry." *Elle,* April 1990.

Gardner, Paul. "Siegel at 59: Director, Rebel, Star." *The New York Times,* May 31, 1973.

Gates, Henry Louis Jr. "Annals of Race: Thirteen Ways of Looking at a Black Man." *The New Yorker,* October 23, 1995.

Gentry, Ric. "Clint Eastwood." *Us,* January 26, 1987.

Giddins, Gary. "Clint Eastwood Shoots Us the Bird." *Esquire,* October 1988.

Goldstein, Patrick. "Hey, Crime Does Pay." Los Angeles *Times* Calendar, October 18, 1995.

Grant, Hank. "On the Air." *The Hollywood Reporter,* July 7, 1961.

Gratz, Roberta Brandes. "Clint Hitches His Wagon to a Song." New York *Post,* October 26, 1969.

Grenier, Richard. "Clint Eastwood Goes PC." *Commentary,* March 1994.

———. "The World's Favorite Movie Star." *Commentary,* April 1994.

Greenspun, Roger. "Screen: 'Two Mules for Sister Sara.'" *The New York Times,* June 25, 1970.

Guerin, Ann. "Clint Eastwood as Mr. Warmth." *Show,* February 1970.

Hamill, Pete. "Leone: I'm a Hunter by Nature, Not a Prey." *American Film,* June 1984.

Hampton, Howard. "Sympathy for the Devil." *Film Comment,* November–December 1993.

Hano, Arnold. "How to Revive a Dead Horse." *TV Guide,* October 2, 1965.

Harmetz, Aljean. "The Man with No Name Is a Big Name Now." *The New York Times,* August 10, 1969.

"Hawk," "Per un Pugno di Dollari." *Variety,* November 18, 1964.

Higham, Charles. "Suddenly, Don Siegel's High Camp-us." *The New York Times,* July 25, 1972.

Hobson, Dick. "Who Watches What." *TV Guide,* July 27, 1968.

Hoover, Mike. "Man against Mountain and Vice Versa during the Filming of 'The Eiger Sanction.'" *American Cinematographer,* August 1975.

Howell, Georgina. "Clint." *Vogue,* February 1993.

Humphrey, Hal. "If Rawhide Fails, He's Big in Europe." Los Angeles *Times,* September 16, 1965.

"Is Forrest Carter Really Asa Carter?" *The New York Times,* July 26, 1976.

Jameson, Richard. "Deserve's Got Nothin' to Do with It." *Film Comment,* September–October 1992.

———. "Pale Rider." *The Weekly* (Seattle), February 12, 1986.

———. "Something to Do with Death." *Film Comment,* March–April 1973.

Jucaud, Dany. "Clint Eastwood: L'amour, Ce N'Est Pas' une Question d'Age." Trans. Robert Lloyd. *Paris-Match,* September 21, 1995.

Kaufman, Ben. "UA Generating B.O. Excitement with Clint Eastwood Oaters." *Hollywood Reporter,* January 23, 1967.

Kehr, Dave. "Eastwood's Skillful Creation 'Bird' Is Rare Indeed." Chicago *Tribune,* October 14, 1988.

Kider, R. Allen. "Dirty Clint." *Good Times,* December 1977.

Knight, Arthur. "The Interview: Clint Eastwood." *Playboy,* February 1978.

Knode, Helen. "Clint Eastwood: Always Lighting Out for New Territories." *L.A. Weekly,* January 11, 1991.

———. "This Is Your Life." *L.A. Weekly,* November 4, 1988.

Kroll, Jack. "Clint Makes *Bird* Sing." *Newsweek,* October 31, 1985.

———. "Erb-Man." *Newsweek,* September 13, 1976.

Leaf, Earl. "The Way They Were: Clint

Eastwood." *Rona Barrett's Hollywood* [circa 1972].

Love, John. "Clint Eastwood: A Sexy Legend at 50." *Cosmopolitan,* July 1980.

Lubenow, Gerald. "Rebel in My Soul." *Newsweek,* July 22, 1985.

McCooey, Meriel. "A Faceful of Dollars." *Sunday Times Magazine* (London), August 17, 1969.

McGilligan, Pat. "Clint Eastwood." *Focus on Film,* Summer–Autumn 1976.

McWhorter, Diane. "Little Tree, Big Lies." *People,* October 28, 1991.

Mailer, Norman. "All the Pirates and People." *Parade,* October 23, 1983.

Malcolm, Derek. "Giving Good Clint." *The Guardian* (London), September 1, 1995.

————. "Huston's Hexes." *The Guardian* (London), May 14, 1990.

Maslin, Janet. "Film View: Three Big Stars Taking Big Chances." *The New York Times,* July 6, 1980.

————. "Good and Evil in a More Innocent Age." *The New York Times,* September 14, 1994.

————. "Make His Day? Museum Does That for Eastwood." *The New York Times,* October 27, 1993.

Mathews, Jack. "Eastwood." *USA Today,* August 13–17, 1984.

Mazzocco, Robert. "The Supply-Side Star." *The New York Review of Books,* April 1, 1982.

Medved, Michael. "It's a PC, PC 'World.'" New York *Post,* November 24, 1993.

Murphy, Kathleen. "The Good, the Bad & the Ugly: Clint Eastwood as Romantic Hero." *Film Comment,* May–June 1996.

Murphy, Mary. "Actress Who Grew into Role." Los Angeles *Times,* February 18, 1974.

Oppenheimer, Peer J. "They Call Her 'The Beautiful Fake.'" *Family Weekly,* November 24, 1968.

Patterson, Eric. "Every Which Way but Lucid: The Critique of Authority in Clint Eastwood's Police Movies." *Journal of Popular Film and Television,* Fall 1982.

Plunket, Robert. "Zing Went the G-Strings of My Heart." *The New York Times Book Review,* February 5, 1995.

"Portrait of a Mean B.O. Winner." *Variety,* September 15, 1976.

Puig, Claudia. "In the Matter of Locke vs. Eastwood." Los Angeles *Times,* May 8, 1989.

Reisfeld, Ben. "No One Got Hurt." Los Angeles *Times,* September 14, 1969.

Rickey, Carrie. "In Like Clint." *Fame,* November 1988.

Robbe, Terri Lee. "Life Without Clint." *Us,* February 16, 1982.

Rosen, Marjorie. "Dirty Harry Meets His Better Half." *Ms.,* March 1977.

Sarris, Andrew. "Films in Focus: Cold Wars and Cold Futures." *Village Voice,* July 6, 1982.

————. "The Pro." *Film Comment,* September–October 1991.

Schickel, Richard. "Clint on the Back Nine," *Film Comment,* May–June 1996.

————. "Good Ole Burt; Cool-Eyed Clint." *Time,* January 9, 1978.

"Self-Made Man." *People,* September 6, 1976.

Shales, Tom. "Eastwood Star: Risen." Washington *Post,* April 24, 1973.

Shechan, Harry. "Scraps of Hope: Clint Eastwood and the Western." *Film Comment,* September–October 1992.

Siskel, Gene. "Clint Eastwood: Long Overdue Respect Makes His Year." Chicago *Tribune,* June 9, 1985.

————. "Hype Casting Cowan Knows How to Keep the Stars Shining." Chicago *Tribune,* June 4, 1989.

Spetalnik, Matt. "Clint for President." Toronto *Star,* July 9, 1993.

————. "Dirty Harry in Tears?" *The Reuters Library Report,* July 7, 1993.

Stein, Mark. "Campaigning with Clint." *Los Angeles Times Magazine,* March 30, 1986.

Stempel, Tom. "Let's Hear It for Eastwood's 'Strong' Women." Los Angeles *Times* Calendar, March 11, 1984.

"That Self-Sufficient Thing." *Time,* December 12, 1971.

"This Cowboy Feels He's Got It Made." *TV Guide,* February 4, 1961.

Thomas, Bob. "Fleming Moseys along to Movies." Los Angeles *Times,* September 3, 1965.

Thompson, Anne. "Eastwood's World." *Entertainment Weekly,* December 10, 1993.

Thompson, Richard, and Tim Hunter. "Clint Eastwood, Auteur." *Film Comment,* January–February 1978.

Thomson, David. "Cop on a Hot 'Tightrope'." *Film Comment,* September–October 1984.

———. "Forgiven." *The Independent* (London), August 22, 1993.

"TV Notes: At Home with Clint Eastwood." *New York Daily News Sunday Magazine,* May 22, 1960.

"Tyne Daly Gets Her Gun. . . ." *People,* January 31, 1977.

Vallely, Jean. "Pumping Gold with Clint Eastwood, Hollywood's Richest Actor." *Esquire,* March 14, 1978.

Vinocur, John. "Clint Eastwood, Seriously." *The New York Times Magazine,* February 24, 1985.

Warga, Wayne. "Anything for Art in '*Mules for Sister Sara,*'" Los Angeles *Times,* April 6, 1969.

———. "Clint Eastwood: He Drifted into Stardom." Los Angeles *Times,* June 22, 1969.

———. "Eastwood a Pussycat behind the Camera." Los Angeles *Times,* January 2, 1973.

Weinraub, Bernard. "Clint Eastwood, Back on the Side of the Law." *The New York Times,* December 7, 1992.

———. "Even Cowboys Get Their Due." *GQ,* April 1993.

Willman, Chris. "Celluloid Heroes." *Los Angeles Times Calendar,* March 26, 1995.

Wilmington, Michael. "Westerns Return on a 'Pale Rider.'" Los Angeles *Times,* June 28, 1985.

Witteman, Paul. "No More Baby Kissing." *Time,* April 6, 1987.

Wolcott, James. "Is That a Gun in Your Pocket?" *Vanity Fair,* July 1985.

———. "On Television: The Dennis Menace." *The New Yorker,* June 11, 1994.

MISCELLANEOUS

"The Barbara Walters Special," ABC Television, June 15, 1982.

Chernus, Sonia, to Clint Eastwood. Memorandum, January 5, 1984.

Coleman, Todd. "Clint's Women." Unpublished article, January 31, 1996.

———. "Gradual Impact: A Hero's Journey." Unpublished article, January 31, 1996.

Eastwood, Clint, and Richard Schickel, "Director's Dialogue," presentation at Walker Arts Center, Minneapolis, September 5, 1990.

———. "*The Guardian* Lecture." British Film Institute, January 13, 1985.

Henry, Michael. "Clint Eastwood on 'Pale Rider.'" Interview included in Cannes Press Kit, April 1, 1995.

"The Merv Griffin Show." No. 2725, taped July 1, 1982.

Universal-International internal memoranda, June–October 1954, Clint Eastwood papers.

ACKNOWLEDGMENTS

Yes, writing is sometimes a lonely job. But writing the biography of a living subject is, perhaps, the most communal activity a writer can find, and I have been sustained in the making of this one by an extraordinarily supportive and responsive group of people who provided me with the information and insights on which it is based.

My first and most obvious debt of gratitude is to Clint Eastwood. For something over three years he has given unstintingly of his time and his memories and, often enough, helped me to gain access to others who could supplement his recollections. I thank him for that, of course. But I thank him more profoundly for the pleasure of his company, both when the tape recorder was on and when it was not. He is a man at once forthright and discreet, and I hope this book, over which he has exercised no control (except to check quotations), reflects those qualities as well as some of the others he has demonstrated to me—good humor, patience, quizzicality and a passion for the medium in which he most truly expresses himself. I am grateful that he trusted me with his "life" and hope that I have in no way betrayed that trust.

A second debt, at least as large, is less obvious. It is to my associate, Doug Freeman. In our television ventures his title is "coproducer," and that credit applies equally to this book. He is largely responsible for researching its printed sources, for assuring the accuracy of its annotations, bibliography and filmography, for transcribing my interviews and for undertaking, with unfailing energy and good cheer, dozens of other editorial tasks. More than that, he has been my reliable sounding board, trusted first reader and indispensable colleague on a journey far longer and in some ways more arduous than we imagined it would be. Without him, this book would be much the poorer—and much later in its delivery.

Which brings me—and it—to Jonathan Segal. The conventional wisdom these days is that editors no longer edit. Jon does—with grace, tact and passion. I'd rather argue with him than agree with anyone else in publishing and this book has been immeasurably improved by his deftness and devotion.

I must also thank a rather long list of individuals who have granted me interviews. Their contributions to this book go far beyond the direct quotations attributed to them in the text, for they enhanced my understanding of my subject in subtextual ways as well. They are Marco Barla, Richard Benjamin, Verna Bloom, Henry Bumstead, John Calley, Michael Cimino, Kevin Costner, Joel Cox, Robert Daley, Robert Daly, Robert Donner, Dina Ruiz Eastwood, Michael Eisner, James Fargo, Frances Fisher, Morgan Freeman, Jack Green, Gene Hackman, Brett Halsey, Richard Harris, Leonard Hirshan, Hal Holbrook, Joe Hyams, Don Kincade, Jack Kosslyn, the late Arthur Lubin, A. C. Lyles, Fritz Manes, Lloyd Nelson, Lennie Niehaus, Eileen Padberg, Wolfgang Petersen, Carl Pingitore, Ted Post, Barry Reardon, Del Reisman, Bruce Ricker, Pierre Rissient, Saul Rubinek, Terry Semel, Tom Shaw, Alain Silver, Tom Stern, Meryl Streep, Richard Tuggle, David Valdes, Buddy Van Horn, Eli Wallach, Jessica Walter, the late Frank Wells, Ruth Wood.

Joe Hyams, besides being the first person to suggest this book to me, has been helpful in more ways than I can count in easing the path to its completion. My old friend Eric Lax is the person who generously seconded Joe's motion, and by so doing got me going. Tom and Melissa Rooker of the Malpaso staff and Marco Barla, Clint's longtime unit publicist, have helped in more ways than they can possibly know, not least by their unfailing patience in the face of my endless requests for assistance. Harry Bernstein and others at Starwave, which produced a CD-ROM about Clint, to which I was a consultant, were extraordinarily generous in sharing material they gathered for that project. Bruce Jenkins, director of film and video at the Walker Art Center in Minneapolis, very kindly provided me with a transcript of the public dialogue Clint and I conducted at that most welcoming institution in September 1990. Jonathan Rosenthal of the Museum of Television and Radio provided me with an invaluable filmography of Clint's early TV work, Todd Coleman allowed me to see, and granted me permission to quote from, some excellent unpublished articles about Clint. As is so often the case, my friends Christopher Porterfield, Richard Jameson and Elliot Ravetz guided me to material I would not otherwise have found. Two executive assistants, Gail Alderete at Warner Bros. and Ida Giragossian at Knopf, were unfailingly kind, patient and helpful to an often harried author.

Finally, I wish to thank Barbara Isenberg, whose love, patience, understanding, good humor and common sense have sustained me through the many months when she was obliged to share my attentions with this book. My gratitude to her is unbounded and therefore inexpressible except in this most inadequate of ways.

Richard Schickel
June 25, 1996

INDEX